The Emerald Handbook of Fintech

The Emerald Handbook of Fintech: Reshaping Finance

EDITED BY

H. KENT BAKER
American University, USA

GREG FILBECK
Penn State Behrend, USA

AND

KEITH BLACK
University of Massachusetts, USA

emerald
PUBLISHING

United Kingdom – North America – Japan – India – Malaysia – China

Emerald Publishing Limited
Emerald Publishing, Floor 5, Northspring, 21-23 Wellington Street, Leeds LS1 4DL

First edition 2024

British Library Cataloguing in Publication Data
A catalogue record for this book is available from the British Library

ISBN: 978-1-83753-609-2 (Print)
ISBN: 978-1-83753-608-5 (Online)
ISBN: 978-1-83753-610-8 (Epub)

INVESTOR IN PEOPLE

We dedicate the book to Linda and Rory Baker, Judy, Janis, Aaron, Andrea, Kyle, and Grant Filbeck, and Melissa, Parker, and Patricia Black.

Contents

Section VI: Harnessing Data With Artificial Intelligence and Machine Learning

Section VII: Understanding Other Applications of Fintech

Section VIII: Shaping the Future of Fintech: What Lies Ahead?

List of Figures and Tables

Figures

Tables

About the Editors

H. Kent Baker, CFA, CMA, is a University Professor of Finance at the Kogod School of Business, American University. He is an award-winning author who has authored or edited 45 books, including several textbooks. Professor Baker coedited the Financial Markets and Investments Series (Oxford University Press) and is the editor and coauthor of The H. Kent Baker Investments Series (Emerald Publishing). As one of the most prolific finance academics, Professor Baker has published more than 215 peer-reviewed journal articles and 130 practitioner-oriented works. His articles appear in such journals as the *Journal of Finance, Journal of Financial and Quantitative Analysis, Review of Accounting Studies, Contemporary Accounting Research, Journal of Banking and Finance, Financial Management, European Financial Management, Journal of Corporate Finance, Financial Analysts Journal, Journal of Portfolio Management*, and *Harvard Business Review*. His publications have more than 16,400 Google Scholar citations. He serves on more than a dozen editorial/advisory boards. Professor Baker has consulting and training experience with more than 100 organizations and has conducted over 800 training programs in North America and Europe. He was the past President of the Southern Finance Association and its 2019 Distinguished Scholar. Professor Baker received a BSBA (management) from Georgetown University; an MBA (finance), MEd (educational administration), and DBA (finance) from the University of Maryland; and an MS (quantitative methods), MA (training and career development), PhD (educational administration and organizational development), and PhD (counseling and student development) from American University.

Greg Filbeck, CFA, FRM, CAIA, CIPM, FDP, PRM, holds the Samuel P. Black III Professor of Finance and Risk Management at Penn State Behrend and serves as Interim Vice Chancellor and Associate Dean of Academic Affairs. He previously served as the Director of the Black School of Business from 2016 to 2023 and Senior Vice President of Kaplan Schweser from 1999 to 2006. He also held academic appointments at Miami University (Ohio) and the University of Toledo, where he served as the Center for Family Business Associate Director. Professor Filbeck has authored or edited 16 books and published more than 110 refereed academic journal articles appearing in the *Financial Analysts Journal, Financial Review*, and *Journal of Business, Finance, and Accounting*, among others. He serves on the editorial board of the *Journal of Business and Economic Perspective*. Professor Filbeck is a Presidents Council Representative for the

Eastern Region United States for the CFA Institute. He also served as President of the CFA Society Pittsburgh from 2014 to 2018 and the Financial Analysts Society of Toledo from 1998 to 1999. Professor Filbeck was the President of the Southern Finance Association from 2015 to 2016. He received the Impact on Practice Award from the Black School of Business in 2015, the Outstanding Teaching Award among iMBA faculty in 2010 and 2012, the Penn State Behrend Regents Award for Outstanding Researcher in 2011, and the Penn State Behrend Outstanding Outreach Award in 2013. He has a BS (engineering physics) from Murray State University, an MS (applied statistics) from Penn State University, and a DBA (finance) from the University of Kentucky.

Keith Black, CFA, CAIA, FDP, CDAA, is an adjunct faculty member at the University of Massachusetts, Amherst, where he teaches cryptocurrency investments, alternative investments, and institutional investment consulting. Professor Black also serves as the Managing Director of education at RIA Channel, where he produced the Nasdaq Advisor Academy course on cryptocurrencies and the Apollo Academy course on alternative investments. He has written or contributed to over 30 books and refereed journal articles, including publications in the *Journal of Alternative Investments*, *Journal of Trading*, and *Journal of Investing*. Professor Black authored *Managing a Hedge Fund* (2004), *Investing in Cryptocurrencies and Digital Assets* (2024), and co-authored the second, third, and fourth editions of the CAIA Level I and II textbooks on alternative investments. He holds a BA from Whittier College, an MS from Carnegie Mellon University, and a PhD from the Illinois Institute of Technology.

About the Contributors

Sumit Agarwal is the Low Tuck Kwong Professor at the School of Business and Professor in the Departments of Economics, Finance, and Real Estate at the National University of Singapore. Previously, he held positions as a Professor of Finance at Georgetown University, a senior Financial Economist in the research department at the Federal Reserve Bank of Chicago, and a senior Vice President and credit risk management executive in the Small Business Risk Solutions Group of Bank of America. Professor Agarwal's research interests involve financial institutions, household finance, behavioral finance, international finance, real estate markets, urban economics, and capital markets. He has published in the *American Economic Review, Quarterly Journal of Economics, Journal of Political Economy, Journal of Finance, Journal of Financial Economics,* and *Review of Financial Studies.* Professor Agarwal received a PhD in economics from the University of Wisconsin-Milwaukee.

Ioannis Akkizidis is a Product Manager in analytical financial systems for Wolters Kluwer in Zürich, Switzerland. He has more than 20 years of experience in financial risk and profitability analysis and designing and implementing advanced solutions in the financial industry's risk management field, turning theory and market demands into practice. Dr Akkizidis has authored several financial books, book chapters, and articles. He is also a cofounder and board member of the Swiss Risk Association. He lectures at Universität Zürich on postgraduate courses in quantitative finance and holds a PhD in Applied Mathematics from the University of Wales, United Kingdom.

Tan Chek Ann, CFA, is a Principal Data Scientist at Phillip Securities Pte Ltd, a leading financial technology firm in Asia, delving into areas such as robo-advisory, portfolio management, and derivative trading. His academic research concerns machine learning, empirical asset pricing, and behavioral and household finance. He holds an MSc in Quantitative Finance from Singapore Management University under the SMU Impact on Asia scholarship and the Monetary Authority of Singapore Financial Scholarship Programme (Individual Track). He is a PhD candidate at the National University of Singapore.

Alessio Azzutti is a Lecturer in Law and Technology at the University of Glasgow's School of Law. He previously served as a Research Associate at the Centre for Banking and Finance Law at the National University of Singapore and as a Research Associate at the Institute of Law & Economics at the University of

Hamburg. He is a policy-oriented and interdisciplinary researcher at the intersection of the scientific fields of finance, law, and technology. He is affiliated with several international networks of researchers, including the European Banking Institute, the European Law Institute, the Hamburg Network of Artificial Intelligence and Law, and the Society for the Advancement of Socio-Economics. He received an MSc in Finance and Risk Management from the University of Florence and an LLM in Law and Economics from Utrecht University, and defended his doctorate juris dissertation at the University of Hamburg in June 2024.

John W. Bagby is a Professor Emeritus, Smeal College of Business and College of Information Sciences, Pennsylvania State University. He also held academic positions in business schools at the University of Kansas and the University of Cincinnati and visiting positions at McCombs School – University of Texas at Austin, California State University – Long Beach, and the Intelligent Transportation Society of America. Professor Bagby has conducted numerous sponsored research projects and is widely published in books, textbooks, monographs, collective research works, academic interdisciplinary and law journals, business journals, SSRN postings, and presentations. Topics include securities regulations, fintech, business organizations, product liability, modeling money damage computations, cybersecurity, privacy, transportation law and economics, intellectual property rights, electronic forensics, and regulatory policy/administrative law. He has a BA in Philosophy and Political Science from the University of Kansas and a JD from the University of Tulsa. Professor Bagby completed the MBA core at the Stern School, New York University, and received an MBA from the University of Kansas.

Hugo Benedetti is an Assistant Professor at ESE Business School, Universidad de Los Andes, Chile. His research focuses on entrepreneurial finance, venture capital, and fintech, particularly blockchain technology and blockchain-enabled assets. Professor Benedetti has published academic articles in the *Journal of Corporate Finance, Journal of Financial Research, Journal of Financial Crime* and *Economic Modeling*, coedited *The Emerald Handbook on Cryptoassets*, and coauthored chapters included in *The Emerald Handbook of Blockchain for Business*, *The Palgrave Handbook of Technological Finance,* and *Essential Concepts of Sustainable Finance: An A-Z Guide*. Professor Benedetti frequently delivers workshops on entrepreneurial finance, venture capital, and fintech to incubators, angel investor networks, and venture capital funds. He has advised and mentored several fintech and blockchain projects. Professor Benedetti is a Fulbright scholar and received a PhD in finance from Boston College.

David A. Burnie, CFA, CTP, is a Professor of Finance at Western Michigan University and Director of the Master of Science in Finance program. He is the current editor of the *American Journal of Business*. Professor Burnie has published in the *Journal of Business, Finance, and Accounting, International Journal of Finance and Economics, Global Finance Journal, The Financial Review, The European Journal of Finance, Applied Financial Economics, and the Journal of*

Corporate Accounting and Finance. His research interests are in short- and long-term corporate finance and investments. Professor Burnie has a BA from the University of Guelph, an MBA from the University of Windsor, and a PhD from Syracuse University.

Jeffrey M. Clark is a Senior Lecturer and the David Gaunt Faculty Fellow in Real Estate at the Finance Department, Isenberg School of Management, University of Massachusetts Amherst. Professor Clark is also the Faculty Director of the Master of Finance Program at the Isenberg School of Management. His teaching and research interests include real estate fintech, corporate real estate strategy, investment and development, capital markets, valuation, data and analytics, and project and process management. He is also a 35-year practitioner of real estate, including leading programs, teams, and organizations on six continents that have executed over 4,000 commercial real estate transactions and developed more than 40 million square feet of new office, industrial, manufacturing, critical data centers, retail and logistics sites, valued at over $5 billion. An active investor in US multifamily and residential properties, Professor Clark has created partnerships that have invested over $100 million. He holds a BA from the University of Massachusetts Amherst and an MBA from the University of Georgia.

Douglas J. Cumming, CFA, is the DeSantis Distinguished Professor of Finance and Entrepreneurship at the College of Business, Florida Atlantic University in Boca Raton, Florida. He is also a Visiting Professor of Finance at Birmingham Business School, University of Birmingham, United Kingdom. Professor Cumming has published over 230 articles in leading refereed academic journals, including 43 in the *Financial Times* top 50 journals. Examples include the *Journal of Financial Economics*, *Review of Financial Studies*, *Journal of Financial and Quantitative Analysis*, *Journal of International Business Studies*, and the *Journal of Empirical Legal Studies*. Clarivate listed him as one of the top 92 most cited researchers in the world in the business and economics category. According to Google Scholar, his work has been cited over 27,000 times. Professor Cumming's work has been reviewed in numerous media outlets, including *The Economist*, *The New York Times*, and *The Wall Street Journal*.

Adri de Ridder is an Associate Professor of Finance at Uppsala University, Campus Gotland, Sweden, and a Visiting Professor of Finance at the University of Groningen, the Netherlands. Previously, he worked for the Federation of Swedish Industries, Avesta Sheffield, and Skandia. His research focuses on payout policy and the relation between firm value and ownership structure. More recently, his research examines the pricing characteristics of Swedish art paintings. Besides several textbooks related to financial economics, he has published in finance and economic journals, including *the European Journal of Finance*, *Global Finance Journal*, *Journal of Multinational Financial Management*, and *the Quarterly Review of Economics and Finance*. He received a PhD from the University of Stockholm after his PhD studies at London Business School.

Zachary Glatzer is a doctoral student in finance at Florida Atlantic University in Boca Raton, Florida. Mr Glatzer has researched financial technology (fintech) throughout his coursework. He is developing papers on cryptocurrencies, mobile money and banking, high-frequency trading, fintech acquisitions, and initial coin offerings. He has presented and discussed papers on monetary systems, fintech, and cryptocurrency at finance conferences. Mr Glatzer also has experience in risk advisory consulting and teaching at secondary education institutions. He has a BS in Economics from the University of Florida and an MS in International Economics from Florida Atlantic University.

Halil Kiymaz, CFA, is the Bank of America Professor of Finance at Crummer Graduate School of Business, Rollins College. He has published six books and more than 90 articles in scholarly and practitioner journals. His research appears in such journals as the *Journal of Banking and Finance, Financial Review, Global Finance Journal, Journal of Applied Finance, Journal of Economics and Finance, Review of Financial Economics,* and *Quarterly Journal of Business and Economics.* He received several research awards, including the McGraw-Hill Irwin Best Paper Award and Outstanding Research Awards at the Global Conference on Business and Finance. He also serves on the editorial board of several journals. Professor Kiymaz is the former Academy of Financial Services president and finance editor of the *International Journal of Emerging Markets.* He has taught as a Visiting Professor at multiple international universities, including the East Chinese University of Science and Technology, the University of Paris, Kadir Has University, and Copenhagen Business School. He received an MBA, MA, and PhD from the University of New Orleans.

Fan Liu is an Assistant Professor in Economics at the International Business School Suzhou (IBSS), Xi'an Jiaotong-Liverpool University, China, an Honorary Lecturer at University of Liverpool, and a Fellow of the UK Higher Education Academy. She also serves as the Director of International for IBSS. Previously, she taught at the University of Iowa in the United States. Her teaching covers a broad range of topics in Economics and Finance. Professor Liu's research focuses on the areas of financial inclusion and resilience, financial intermediation, innovation and fintech, macroeconomics, entrepreneurship, and household finance. She has published in peer-reviewed journals such as the *Journal of Economic Behavior & Organization, Emerging Markets Review,* and *Empirical Economics.* She serves as an associate editor for a Social Sciences Citation Index (SSCI) journal. Professor Liu holds a PhD in economics from the University of Iowa.

Angela C. Lyons is a Full Professor in the Department of Agricultural and Consumer Economics and a Faculty Fellow at the National Center for Supercomputing Applications (NCSA) at the University of Illinois Urbana-Champaign. Her work focuses on emerging issues in development and behavioral economics, emphasizing economic and financial inclusion, financial and digital literacy, fintech, poverty and inequality, and the economic empowerment and protection of vulnerable populations. She has collaborated with over 40 countries in developing practical and sustainable models that improve the livelihoods, economic resiliency, and financial security of families and communities worldwide. Notably, Professor Lyons has served under five G20 Presidencies on the T20 (Think20), the research and policy advice network of the G20 countries, contributing to the global advancement of the future of work and education in the digital age. Her current work leverages the power of new frontier methods in data science, such as machine learning and geospatial analysis, to reduce global poverty and economic vulnerabilities and promote the achievement of the Sustainable Development Goals (SDGs). She has a PhD in Economics from the University of Texas at Austin.

Abdiel Martinez is an independent financial consultant with experience in foreign exchange and macro strategy. He received a BA in International Business from Rollins College, where he graduated summa cum laude.

Bora Ozkan is an Associate Professor of Finance at Temple University's Fox School of Business, where he also served as Academic Director of the school's online MBA and BBA programs. His research interests are fintech, ESG, corporate finance, and business education. He has published in the *International Journal of Economics and Finance*, *International Journal of Business and Society*, *Management Research Review*, and *Journal of Education for Business*. Professor Ozkan received a Master's degree in Financial Economics and Business Administration and a PhD in Financial Economics from the University of New Orleans.

Debidutta Pattnaik is an Assistant Professor at the International Management Institute, Bhubaneswar. He teaches corporate finance, financial markets, investment banking, and advanced research methods. Professor Pattnaik's research focuses on corporate finance, AI and ML applications, scientometrics, and text analytics. His work appears in the *Journal of Corporate Finance*, *Financial Review*, *Journal of Forecasting*, *Economics Modelling*, *Journal of Business Research*, *International Journal of Research in Marketing*, and *Journal of Service Research*. With a robust industrial background spanning over 14 years and prolific publications, Professor Pattnaik ranks among RePEc's top 25% of Indian economists. He received the '2021 Runner-up Outstanding JME Article of the Year Award', 'JMTP Article of the Year Award 2020', and multiple 'Top-cited Article of the Journal' awards. Professor Pattnaik has a PhD in Finance from the Malaviya National Institute of Technology, India, and holds a CFA charter from the Institute of Chartered Financial Analysts of India.

Dianna Preece, CFA, is a Professor of Finance at the College of Business, University of Louisville. She teaches undergraduates and MBA students, focusing primarily on financial markets and the banking system. Professor Preece has published over 30 academic articles and various book chapters on finance topics. Her research interests include banking, investments, and firm diversity. Professor Preece is a former board member of the Southern Finance Association. She often presents papers at the annual meeting and participates in panel discussions on topics ranging from hedge funds to debt markets. Professor Preece also teaches at the banking schools for the American Bankers Association, the Kentucky

Bankers Association, and the Iowa Bankers Association. She holds a BA, an MBA from Marshall University, and a DBA from the University of Kentucky.

Kerem Proulx is an independent financial consultant with experience involving operational risk, leveraged finance, and credit risk. He focuses on modeling tail risk using computational methods. Mr Proulx has a BBA in Finance from the Frank G. Zarb School of Business at Hofstra University. He received high honors for his research in applying machine learning methods to forecasting equity volatility.

Christian Rauch is an Associate Professor of Finance and Dean at Umm Al Quwain University in the UAE. His research focuses on financial intermediation and institutional asset management, especially alternative investments, focusing on fintech. Leading academic journals, like the *Journal of Financial Economics*, have published his work. Various newspapers, such as the *Financial Times* or *The Wall Street Journal*, have cited his work. Professor Rauch has been involved in pro bono advisory projects involving capital market regulation, such as the Venture Capital Scale-Up project for the UK government. He cofounded a business-to-business fintech start-up from Barclays Bank's RISE accelerator in London. Professor Rauch has been an active member of the London and UAE start-up communities by mentoring founders and advising investors. He obtained a PhD in Finance from Goethe University in Frankfurt, Germany, and degrees from the European Business School in Oestrich-Winkel, Germany, and the New York University School of Law.

Efthymios Rizopoulos is a RegTech/SupTech Associate at the Financial Conduct Authority. He has previously worked as a researcher at SOAS University of London and Alliance Manchester Business School, where he actively participated in launching the university's fintech center. His research experience focuses on market microstructure, financial economics, economic development, banking and fintech, and decentralized finance. His research interests span finance, economics, management, and information systems. His current work and publications comprise papers on high-frequency trading, stock markets, fintech, the banking and financial services industry, and nonfungible tokens. He holds a PhD in finance from the University of Manchester.

Dimitrios Salampasis is the Fintech Capability Lead and Senior Lecturer of Emerging Technologies and FinTech at the Swinburne School of Business, Law and Entrepreneurship in Melbourne, Australia. He holds international visiting professor positions and is a Financial Services Institute of Australasia Fellow. Professor Salampasis is an award-winning global thought leader, educator, researcher and sought-after keynote speaker, passionate about innovation and strategy, global affairs and geopolitics, digital economy, sustainability, and emerging technologies nexus. He specializes in the organizational, human, technological, geopolitical, regulatory and ESG sides of emerging technologies and FinTech. Professor Salampasis is a mentor and advisor for start-ups and scale-ups in Australia and overseas and is regularly involved in advisory work with international stakeholders. He holds a PhD in industrial engineering, business and management from the Lappeenranta University of Technology.

Georgios Samakovitis is a Professor of Fintech and Deputy Head of the School of Computing and Mathematical Sciences at the University of Greenwich, United Kingdom. He specializes in banking and payment systems technologies and artificial intelligence for fintech. His research focuses on governance technologies for anti-money laundering and financial crime and developing distributed ledger technology infrastructure for collective intelligence in fintech networks. Professor Samakovitis joined the Counter Fraud and Data Analytics Advisory Group of the HMG Cabinet Office and the FinCrime Working Group at the UK Payments Strategy Forum. He is a member of the Bank of England CBDC Technology Forum and the BSI UK Data Standards Expert Panel. His PhD focused on banking technology investment decisions from the University of Edinburgh.

Peter Scholz is a Full Professor of Digital Finance at the Baden-Wuerttemberg Cooperative State University (DHBW) in Mosbach, Germany, where he serves as the academic co-head of the banking department. Prior to joining DHBW, he was a Professor of Banking at the Hamburg School of Business Administration. Professor Scholz brings over than 10 years of practical experience from his tenure at Deka Investment and Deutsche Bank, where he worked in various financial market-related divisions, including asset management, global markets, risk management, and private and retail banking. His research interests focus on the financial sector's digital transformation, sustainable finance, and performance of active asset management and equity derivatives, with a particular emphasis on retail certificates and technical timing strategies. Professor Scholz has published in renowned journals such as the *Financial Analysts Journal* and the *Journal of Wealth Management*. He holds a PhD in business sciences from the Frankfurt School of Finance and Management.

Sean Stein Smith is an Assistant Professor of Business and Economics at Lehman College, City University of New York. He serves on the Advisory Board of the Wall Street Blockchain Alliance, where he chairs the Accounting Work Group. Professor Smith has published articles and books on the intersection of accounting and emerging technologies, including the Forbes Crypto & Blockchain vertical. He is an NJCPA Board of Trustees member and the NYSSCPA Manhattan-Bronx chapter president. Professor Smith was an AICPA Outstanding CPA of the Year (2022). He is on the Advisory Board of Gilded and is a Strategic Advisor to the Central Bank Digital Currency Think Tank. Professor Smith was a Visiting Research Fellow at the American Institute of Economic Research. He received a BS, MS, and MBA from Fairleigh Dickinson and a DBA from Capella University.

Iván Sosa Gómez is a distinguished professional with 14 years of experience exclusively focused on the insurance industry. As the Corporate Head Driver, he leads the definition of the vision, strategic objectives, and action plans that are driving InsurTech+. Besides this role, Dr Sosa serves as an InsurTech Advisory Board member, providing invaluable insights into business strategies for achieving growth objectives within the insurance sector. His contributions extend beyond his corporate responsibilities, as he actively engages in academic activities focused on the InsurTech ecosystem and its transformative impact on the industry. With his unwavering dedication to the insurance industry and hybrid expertise in business consulting and academic research, he is positioned as a key driver of change in the InsurTech landscape. He obtained a Master's degree in Marketing and Sales Management from IMF Business School and a Bachelor's degree in Business Administration from Rey Juan Carlos University.

Andrew C. Spieler, CFA, CAIA, FRM, is the Robert F. Dall Distinguished Professor of Finance in the Frank G. Zarb School of Business at Hofstra University. He has published in such journals as the *Journal of Financial Research, Real Estate Economics*, *Journal of Real Estate Finance and Economics*, *Journal of Real Estate Portfolio Management*, *Global Finance Journal*, and *Journal of Applied Finance*. He was the Chair of the Derivatives Committee at the New York Society of Securities Analysts. Professor Spieler is the Co-Director of the annual real estate conference sponsored by the Wilbur F. Breslin Center for Real Estate Studies. He received a BA in mathematics and a BS in economics from Binghamton University (SUNY), an MS in finance from Indiana University, and an MBA and PhD in Finance from Binghamton University (SUNY).

Manuel Stagars, CFA is an Economist and former senior researcher at Singapore-ETH Centre (SEC), with a research focus on the technological and institutional aspects of big data, open data, and data policy. He is also a serial tech entrepreneur with over a decade of global experience. Mr Stagars also directed several award-winning documentary films about fintech, blockchain technology, digital transformation, and deep tech. Mr Stagars holds a BSc degree in Economics from the London School of Economics and Political Science. He has published books on data quality, open data, entrepreneurship, and market place lending (with Ioannis Akkizidis) with publishers including Wiley, Springer and Palgrave Macmillan.

Ayan Tyagi, CRISC, is a seasoned professional serving as the Director of Technology Transformation at Citi Bank in the United States. With a rich and diverse background, he has contributed significantly to the architecture and development of high-performance trading systems, technology, and cybersecurity risk management. He has also spearheaded global digital transformations for prominent Wall Street banks. A published author with contributions to international journal articles, Dr Tyagi's expertise encompasses various domains, including blockchain technology, information governance, cloud computing, and enterprise risk management. He received a Bachelor of Engineering degree from MDU Rohtak, India, a Master's in Computer Science from Stony Brook University, and a PhD in Information Technology with a specialized focus on emerging technologies and information systems security from the University of the Cumberlands, Kentucky.

Omer Unsal is an Associate Professor of Finance at Merrimack College. His research focuses on corporate innovation, employee treatment, financial misconduct, and corporate governance. Professor Unsal has published in the *Journal of Corporate Finance*, *Financial Review*, *Journal of Financial Research*, and *Corporate Governance: An International Review*. He received an MBA from Western Michigan University and a PhD in Financial Economics from the University of New Orleans.

Carlos Humberto Munoz Valdez is an Assistant Professor of Finance at the IPADE Business School. He is a former executive from companies like Pfizer, Johnson & Johnson, 3M, and GE, with responsibilities as financial planning and analysis (FP&A) senior leader and project management office (PMO) leader. He is a DBA candidate at Crummer Graduate School of Business, Rollins College. His dissertation focuses on the relationship between adopting blockchain technology and its impact on cryptocurrency volatility. He is also a business advisor for family offices and real estate companies. Mr Valdez holds an MBA from the IPADE Business School.

Sebastian Vogel is an Assistant Professor of Finance at Erasmus University in Rotterdam. He is interested in market microstructure, market design, and asset pricing. His research includes work on using electronic trading platforms in OTC markets, the behavior of market participants in OTC markets, and topics related to corporate finance, like the advantages and disadvantages of auctions vs negotiations when selling a firm. Professor Vogel holds a Master's degree in finance from the Stockholm School of Economics, a Master's degree in mathematics from the University of Hagen, Germany, and a PhD in finance from EPFL and the Swiss Finance Institute.

Markos T. Zachariadis holds the Chair of Financial Technology and Information Systems at Alliance Manchester Business School, University of Manchester, where he is also the Founding Director of the Centre for Financial Technology Studies. Professor Zachariadis is also a member of the World Economic Forum's Global Future Council on the Future of Resilient Financial Systems, an Advisory Board member of the Abu Dhabi Global Market's Research Centre, and a FinTech Research Fellow at the Cambridge Centre for Digital Innovation, University of Cambridge among many other industry and academic appointments. His research sits at the cross-section of the economics of digital innovation, financial technology studies, and network economics and has studied the economic impact of ICT adoption on bank performance, the diffusion of payment networks, and the role of data and standards in payment infrastructures, financial markets, and digital banking extensively. He holds a PhD in Management and Economics of Digital Innovation in Finance: Information Technology and Strategy from the London School of Economics and Policy Science.

Acknowledgments

In 1968, Paul McCartney wrote 'The Long and Winding Road', which appeared in the Beatles' album *Let It Be*, in 1970. The lyrics of this reflective song talk about the journey of life and the memories created along the way. Thus, the long and winding road is a metaphor for a journey and the challenges encountered. Similarly, publishing this book has been a long and winding road with its twists and turns. This journey would not have been completed without the contributions of many people, each playing important but different roles. We want to recognize a few of these participants in this journey.

We relied on the chapter authors who took time from their busy schedules to share their knowledge and expertise on specific fintech topics. Being a chapter author requires much time, effort, and dedication. Without them, *The Emerald Handbook of Fintech: Reshaping Finance* would not have been possible. We are indebted to each chapter author. We are also grateful for all the highly talented professionals at Emerald Publishing who were involved with this book project. We especially thank Kirsty Woods (Books Commissioning Editor, Education), Lydia Cutmore (Content Development Editor), and Kousalya Thangarasu (Book Project Editor). Our respective institutions also provided support: Kogod School of Business at American University, the Black School of Business at Penn State Behrend, and the Isenberg School of Business at the University of Massachusetts, Amherst. Finally, our families also offered encouragement during the process.

Section I

Introducing Fintech

Chapter 1

Fintech: An Overview

H. Kent Baker[a], *Greg Filbeck*[b] *and Keith Black*[c]

[a]American University, USA
[b]Penn State Behrend, USA
[c]University of Massachusetts, USA

Abstract

Financial technology (fintech) refers to using new technology to improve and automate the delivery and use of financial services. This chapter provides a brief introduction to fintech. It also includes the book's purpose, distinguishing features, intended audience, and structure. A synopsis of Chapters 2 through 23 is offered. The chapter concludes that fintech is constantly evolving and is reshaping finance. Fintechs offer a new paradigm of growth.

Keywords: Financial technology; fintech; regulation; blockchain; cryptocurrencies; digital assets; artificial intelligence; machine learning; insurance; real estate; robo-advisors; online trading; big data; innovation; technology; payments; banking; lending

Introduction

Financial technology (fintech) is transforming finance. The two words – finance and technology – combined "symbolize the best of both worlds – simple financial management with the help of technology" (Paysera, 2023, p. 1). This catch-all term refers to the technology and innovation intended to simplify, improve, and automate financial transactions for consumers and businesses alike. Although fintech companies have already affected the daily lives of billions of people worldwide, this impact will increase as fintechs introduce an array of new products and services. As such, the financial services industry will see an expansion of revolutionary change in the next decade. According to a report by Boston Consulting Group and QED Investors (2023), fintech is projected to become a $1.5 trillion industry by 2030.

The Emerald Handbook of Fintech, 3–15

doi:10.1108/978-1-83753-608-520241001

As fintech companies have come of age, they have affected many segments of the economy. For example, technological advances have made artificial intelligence (AI) and machine learning (ML) accessible to practitioners without a programming background. New markets in cryptocurrencies and digital assets have made finance more global with lower transaction costs and faster transaction processing times. Robo-advisors and online trading have made financial markets more accessible to investors, even those younger or just making their first investments. Big data and alternative data are increasing the speed at which information is available on investments, allowing investors to predict corporate revenues before publicly traded companies disclose them. Regulation changes have provided new opportunities in crowdfunding and peer-to-peer (P2P) lending.

The future looks bright for fintech as it repositions for innovation. Simons (2023) points out that fintech is shifting from the competitive consumer markets into the enterprise or business-to-business services markets. AI is playing an increasingly important role in product capabilities and design. Fintechs are insulating themselves by partnering with more established financial institutions.

About This Book

This section discusses the book's purpose, distinguishing features, intended audience, and structure.

Purpose

The *Emerald Handbook on Fintech: Reshaping Finance* aims to provide insights into the rapidly changing world of fintech. It examines fintech's evolution, major segments and stakeholders, and obstacles and opportunities.

Distinguishing Features

The following characteristics help to distinguish this book from other books in this field.

- *The Emerald Handbook on Fintech: Reshaping Finance* offers a detailed examination of fintech from leading scholars and practitioners globally. Rather than purely technical or theoretical topics, it focuses on real-world challenges and opportunities.
- The handbook skillfully blends the contributions of experts into a practical handbook reviewing critical topics and issues about fintech. The contributors' varied backgrounds ensure different perspectives and a rich interplay of ideas. The book also reflects the latest trends and research.
- It has a clear and accessible style suitable for readers, with most chapters requiring little technological background.
- This work presents the results of empirical studies so a wide array of readers with different backgrounds can understand them.

- The end of each chapter contains four to six discussion questions reinforcing key concepts. The handbook provides guideline answers for each question at the end of the handbook. This feature should be helpful to faculty and students using the book in courses.
- The volume defines fintech and related terms and shows them in italics.

Intended Audience

This handbook should appeal to readers who want to understand fintech and its various applications. Academics may find the handbook helps in finding ideas for further research or topics to share with their students. Innovative companies can review the state of the industry in a way that may allow them to envision their role or niche in this fast-growing, ever-evolving industry. Most importantly, incumbent firms can view the pace of change and plan to keep pace with these innovations to profit from change. Regulators may also find this book useful in learning more about fintechs and assessing the trade-offs of future regulations and their potential impact on economic growth.

Other fintech books often focus on a specific area of the industry, such as cryptocurrencies or AI and ML. In providing a broad overview of the fintech industry, this handbook gives readers a comprehensive view of the technologies and products reshaping the industry, all in one volume. Given the interplay between rapidly evolving regulations, technologies, and products, readers should view fintech's risks and potential opportunities from this holistic view.

Book's Structure

The remainder of this book contains 22 chapters divided into 8 sections. Highlights of each section and chapter follow.

Section I Introducing Fintech

Besides the current chapter, this section contains three other chapters. Chapter 2 provides a bibliometric analysis of fintech. Chapter 3 provides specific situations in which a fintech product or service could be used. Chapter 4 deals with regulatory technology (regtech), which applies emerging technology to improve how businesses manage regulatory compliance.

Chapter 2 The Fintech Landscape: A Bibliometric Analysis **(Debidutta Pattnaik)**

This chapter uses data from the Scopus database to present a comprehensive bibliometric analysis of fintech research, focusing on publication trends, citation patterns, and thematic clusters within the field. The analysis reveals notable trends, including influential publications, prolific authors, and their affiliations. It identifies and explores publications categorized into 23 distinct themes, representing key areas of inquiry in fintech, such as technological advancements, financial inclusion, innovation, data analytics, sustainability, and regulatory compliance. The study also identifies research gaps, indicating areas within fintech that have received limited scholarly attention. These findings provide valuable insights for researchers, policymakers, and industry practitioners. Researchers can better understand the fintech landscape, identify research gaps, and guide future inquiries. Policymakers can develop effective regulations and policies based on identified trends and challenges. Industry practitioners can leverage fintech developments to enhance their strategies and operations.

Chapter 3 Use Cases in Fintech (Fan Liu and Angela C. Lyons)

This chapter examines three common fintech use cases transforming the financial industry. First, the chapter introduces fintech's role in enhancing financial services and promoting financial inclusion, especially through digital platforms. Second, it examines fintech applications that support financial institution management by harnessing the power of AI and ML. Finally, the chapter explores fintech use cases related to the regulatory environment, including regulatory technology (regtech), blockchain technology, and cryptocurrencies. The insights presented in this chapter cater to researchers and practitioners keen on exploring fintech's diverse applications in the ever-evolving financial industry landscape.

Chapter 4 Regtech Frontiers: Innovations, Trends, and Insights Redefining Compliance (Dimitrios Salampasis and Georgios Samakovitis)

This chapter discusses the contributions and challenges involving regulatory technology (regtech) in financial services. It explores the salient areas where regtech can and should focus, observing existing and forthcoming industry, technology, and legal developments. The chapter outlines regtech use cases to clarify the shaping of that industry sector. It draws on developments in industry and academia, where significant research sets the tone and direction of technological solutions and regulatory drivers. A brief critical account of the benefits and challenges in regtech is offered. The chapter presents potential future directions, focusing on the salient areas of environmental, social, and governance (ESG), cryptocurrency, and decentralized compliance.

Section II Reinventing the Banking and Payments Industry

This section contains two chapters focused on the evolution of banking and the payments industry. Chapter 5 discusses fintech's impact on the banking industry and financial services. Chapter 6 covers the evolution of alternative payment systems, including mobile payments and digital banking services.

***Chapter 5 Fintech's Impact on the Banking Industry and Financial Services* (Efthymios Rizopoulos and Markos T. Zachariadis)**

For over a decade, fintech has challenged traditional business models and processes in the financial services industry. The ongoing disruption has necessitated the digital transformation of financial institutions (FIs) to remain an integral part of the financial system. This paradigm shift is not merely a technological update. Still, it signifies a cultural and operational rebirth, compelling FIs to embrace innovation, adaptability, and a customer-centric approach in the digital era. Independent of the business model, FIs must become digitally ambidextrous, offer tailored and dynamic customer experiences, support financial inclusion, and promote an ESG agenda while leveraging data and remaining compliant. From digitalization to fintegration, the financial services industry's future is deemed to be an exciting and productive one.

***Chapter 6 Mobile Payments and Digital Banking Services* (Ardi de Ridder and David A. Burnie)**

This chapter examines mobile payments and digital banking services. The past decade has seen a rapid increase in the use of alternative payment systems, away from cash to electronic payments. The digitalization of payments includes business-to-business (B2B), customer-to-business (C2B), and government-to-business and consumers (G2B/C), whether the payments are by computer, wire transfers, and point of sale (POS) systems. POS systems have become a standard in many retail outlets. Mobile payments use a smart device for contactless pay. Consumers see the increasing prevalence of payment systems when they go to the retail checkout or service counter. Worldwide, mobile payments are approaching 50% of digital. Digitalized payment systems are becoming more secure, decreasing concerns over mistaken payments, fraud, and errors. Consumers' confidence in value and usage decreases with age. Most fraud is due to scams and not hacking. Greater access to improved infrastructure and affordable smart devices will expand the usage of digitalized payment systems worldwide.

Section III Raising Funds With Fintech: Digital Lending

The three chapters in this section discuss capital formation, including equity crowdfunding and marketplace lending, as well as risk management. Chapter 7 introduces marketplace lending, formerly known as peer-to-peer lending. Chapter 8 emphasizes the importance of risk management in the digital age, which includes special attention to cybersecurity risks. Chapter 9 discusses how fintech affects capital formation and capital markets regulation in areas including equity crowdfunding and Initial Coin Offerings.

***Chapter 7 Marketplace Lending Platforms for Borrowers and Investors* (Manuel Stagars and Ioannis Akkizidis)**

Marketplace lending has substantially changed since the first peer-to-peer lending platforms emerged in 2006. The industry is now an alternative to bank lending, predicted to total $70 billion for consumer and business loans worldwide by 2030. Marketplace lending is often deemed less safe than bank loans, mainly due to these portfolios' high degree of hidden information. These include needing more information on borrowers and potential correlations between them, which might lead to higher risk than is apparent at first glance. Deterministic processes cannot capture tail risk appropriately, so platforms and lenders should employ stochastic processes. This chapter introduces a Monte Carlo simulation and ML process to evaluate and monitor portfolios. For marketplace lending to become a viable and sustainable alternative to bank lending platforms, they must better evaluate, monitor, and manage tail risk in marketplace loans and develop tools to monitor and manage financial risk losses.

Chapter 8 Risk Management in Fintech (Ayan Tyagi)

This chapter examines the world of risk management within fintech. It initiates by emphasizing the crucial role of technology and risk assessment in shaping the fintech landscape. It discusses various risk categories prevalent in fintech operations, elucidating the nuances of technology, operational, compliance, strategic, and reputational risks. A comparative analysis across different fintech subsectors unveils their distinct risk profiles. The narrative extends to proactive risk management frameworks, contrasting prominent models like the COSO ERM, FAIR Risk Quantification, and NIST Cybersecurity Frameworks. Integral defense measures are scrutinized, encompassing data encryption, access controls, vulnerability assessments, and incident response plans. The chapter underscores the significance of building operational resilience through robust technology infrastructure, regular system updates, disaster recovery planning, and business continuity measures. Ultimately, the chapter culminates in a comprehensive summary, offering pragmatic recommendations to fortify technology risk management in fintech.

Chapter 9 Capital Formation and Crowdfunding (Keith Black)

Each company, large or small, starts with a dream and an idea for a new product or service. Companies can succeed or fail for a wide variety of reasons, including inexperienced managers, failure to build or sell the desired product, launching products into highly competitive environments, and a lack of capital. This chapter reviews the traditional methods of capital formation, including funding by angel investors and venture capital firms. These funding methods are only available to relatively large firms, leaving millions of small firms without reliable debt and equity funding sources to scale their business. The growth of the internet, blockchain technology, and fintech firms has introduced innovative funding methods, such as crowdfunding and Initial Coin Offerings (ICOs). While these structures have been successful in raising capital for smaller firms, changes in the regulatory environment, such as the JOBS Act, are needed for these new forms of capital formation to reach their full potential.

Section IV Transforming Personal Finance With Fintech: Digital Wealth Management

This section contains four chapters. Chapter 10 discusses robo-advisors, while Chapters 11 and 12 explain various aspects of online trading. Chapter 12 examines different personal finance applications of fintech.

Chapter 10 Demystifying Robo-Advisors: Benefits and Limitations (Peter Scholz)

In recent years, investing with robo-advisors has gained momentum and is seen as a simplifying approach for individual investors to participate in financial markets. This chapter contributes to a better understanding of the concept of a robo-advisory and its implications for private investors by discussing its past, present, and future. It explores key issues, like cost efficiency, historical performance, and automation levels, based on research and industry insights. Moreover, the chapter examines a robo-advisor's benefits, limitations, and challenges, like behavioral biases, regulation, and risk profiling. Finally, the importance of the ongoing megatrends of AI and green investing is examined concerning a robo-advisory.

Chapter 11 Online Trading: Part I (Sebastian Vogel)

This chapter discusses the evolution of online trading, its application in various market structures, and its benefits and potential concerns. Computers were first used in electronic communication networks among brokers and dealers to make trades and for informational purposes. Online brokers became popular with retail investors as the internet spread. Online trading comes with various trading protocols and order types. It enables traders to automate trading decisions and process data more easily using charting tools and customized programs connected to the broker's infrastructure. Electronic trading allows for greater centralization but can also be accompanied by market fragmentation. Market regulation has affected market structure and is still evolving. Centralization allows for more competitive prices and reduces search costs. Decentralized markets could cope better with asymmetric information.

Chapter 12 Online Trading: Part II (Abdiel Martinez, Kerem Proulx, and Andrew C. Spieler)

The history of online trading began in the 1960s with the emergence of electronic communication networks, which allowed the electronic execution of trades outside traditional exchanges. The internet revolution led to the development of online brokerage platforms such as E*Trade and Schwab, enabling noninstitutional investors to participate in the digital trading revolution. These platforms have evolved to serve the retail investor market, eventually adapting to mobile-first and commission-free models, significantly lowering the barriers to entry for financial markets. Platforms like Robinhood and other fintech firms have rapidly gained market share by offering services and products previously unavailable, such as commission-free trades, mobile trading, and novel products such as fractional shares and cryptocurrency investing. This chapter provides an overview of the history of online trading. It also introduces several new developments in fintech and the online trading industry and discusses various controversies and future implications of new technologies.

***Chapter 13 Personal Finance Applications of Fintech* (Sumit Agarwal and Tan Chek Ann)**

Fintech has revolutionized personal finance, introducing innovative tools that offer unprecedented access, efficiency, and security in managing finances. This chapter explains fintech's personal finance applications, from intuitive budgeting apps and advanced robo-advisors to peer-to-peer payment platforms. It articulates how these tools have shifted the control and management of finances into the hands of consumers, providing real-time financial data, customized investment strategies, improved credit scores, and streamlined transactions that eliminate the need for traditional intermediaries. Furthermore, the chapter features a select list of FinTech50 firms and highlights how individuals can leverage their services. This comprehensive guide is invaluable for individuals seeking to leverage fintech for personal finance optimization and for professionals keen on understanding and navigating the rapidly evolving fintech landscape.

Section V Emerging Innovations: Blockchain and Cryptocurrencies

This section contains two chapters: Chapter 14 focuses on how fintech can use blockchain, and Chapter 15 involves cryptocurrencies and fintech.

***Chapter 14 Blockchain in Fintech: A Catalyst for Disrupting the Financial World* (Halil Kiymaz and Carlos Humberto Munoz Valdez)**

Blockchain technology and its applications have recently received the attention of practitioners and academics. Visualizing the full impact these technologies will have on the world is challenging since their adoption is still in the early stages. This chapter explores how blockchain can disrupt the general business and financial world. Blockchain offers information transparency, live data synchronization, and immutable records that prevent fraud. Digital contracts and digital asset management may heavily depend on the development of blockchain and the adoption of smart contracts. Smart contracts can execute financial transactions automatically and enforce all parties' obligations without needing an intermediary and its cost. They can increase speed and simplify processes, reducing licensing ticketing costs and overhead charges. Blockchain also offers technology adoption solutions, like fair payment, cloud storage, smart contracts for financial assets, and international transactions with bilateral double taxation. It has further facilitated the creation of decentralized finance.

Chapter 15 Cryptoassets and Fintech (Hugo Benedetti and Sean Stein Smith)

Cryptoassets are a diverse category of digital assets that rely on blockchain technology. They encompass various categories, such as cryptocurrencies, utility tokens, security tokens, tokenized assets and securities, and stablecoins. Cryptocurrencies are decentralized digital units of value that enable secure and transparent transactions. Utility tokens provide access to specific services or products within a blockchain network. Security tokens offer rights and entitlements similar to traditional securities, representing ownership in real-world assets or participation in investment opportunities. Tokenized assets and securities are digital representations of tangible or intangible assets, allowing for fractional ownership and enhanced liquidity. Stablecoins are blockchain-based digital assets designed to maintain a stable value, often pegged to fiat currencies or physical assets. This chapter examines each category's characteristics, benefits, and risks, explores their implementations and current applications in the fintech ecosystem, and discusses relevant regulations and future development opportunities.

Section VI Harnessing Data With AI and ML

This section covers three chapters focused on the role AI and ML play in harnessing data. Chapter 16 discusses the role big data plays in fintech. Chapter 17 focuses on how the use of alternative data affects finance. Chapter 18 introduces concepts and illustrates the financial applications of AI and ML.

Chapter 16 Big Data's Role in Fintech (John W. Bagby)

Fintechs form the heart of considerable disruptive innovation. Fintech is the emerging financial infrastructure for modern business. Big data are the feedstock for AI that drives many fintech sectors – start-up finance, commodities and investment instrumentation, payment systems, currencies, exchange markets/trading platforms, market-failure response forensics, underwriting, syndication, risk assessment, advisory services, banking, financial intermediaries, transaction settlement, corporate disclosure, and decentralized finance. This chapter demonstrates how analyzing big data, largely processed through cloud computing, drives fintech innovations, scholarship, forensics, and public policy. Despite their apparent virtues, some fintech mechanisms can externalize various social costs: flawed designs, opacity/obscurity, cyber(in)security, and other malfunctions. Fintech suffers regulatory lag, the delay following the introduction of novel fintechs, and later assessment, development, and deployment of reliable regulatory mechanisms. Big data improve fintech practices by balancing three key influences: (1) fintech incentives, (2) market failure forensics, and (3) developing balanced public policy resolutions to fintech challenges.

***Chapter 17 How Alternative Data Are Changing Finance* (Douglas J. Cumming and Zachary Glatzer)**

This chapter focuses on how alternative data can change the nature of financial forecasting through improved short-term forecasting techniques and decreased informativeness from longer term sources. Increased use of social media data leads the charge in transforming this transition. Alternative data are data not from standard financial statements or formal reports. This chapter looks at alternative data from new sources (e.g., social media, Internet of Things, and digital footprints) and alternative data from new collection methods like web scraping for textual analysis, image analysis, and vocal analysis. It first discusses standard data in financial forecasting. Next, the chapter examines alternative data in financial forecasting. Finally, it discusses alternative data used in studying finance more broadly.

***Chapter 18 Artificial Intelligence and Machine Learning: Key Concepts, Applications, and Regulatory Considerations* (Alessio Azzutti)**

This chapter explores the role of AI, particularly its subfield of ML methods, as a core technology of the fintech revolution in the financial services industry. It simplifies some of the complex concepts related to AI by introducing the main ML paradigms and related techno-methodic aspects. This chapter uses real-world examples to illustrate how next-generation AI powered by ML is transforming the financial services industry. Next, in illustrating the risks associated with AI adoption, this chapter discusses the need for regulation to address the essential facets of AI governance, including transparency, accountability, ethics, and responsible use. Lastly, it looks at emerging regulatory approaches across leading global jurisdictions. The primary goal is to give readers an initial understanding of AI's profound impact on the financial sector.

Section VII Understanding Other Applications of Fintech

This section has three chapters focused on industries being disrupted by fintech. Chapter 19 discusses innovations in the insurance industry with apps providing insurance discounts and even tracking driver behavior. Chapter 20 focuses on real estate, including how services such as Zillow are breaking the monopoly that realtors have on property sale information. Chapter 21 discusses the broad impact of fintech on capital markets, including innovations such as AI and blockchain technology.

***Chapter 19 InsurTech: Disrupting the Insurance Industry* (Iván Sosa Gómez)**

The insurance industry has been slow to adopt digital technologies due to high barriers to entry, product complexity, capital reserves, solvency requirements, and regulatory constraints. This chapter focuses on how InsurTech is disrupting the insurance industry, resulting in a transformation from a traditional structure to a dynamic user-centric ecosystem. Next, it highlights the InsurTech ecosystem by providing an in-depth analysis of the new paradigm on how InsurTech is transitioning from the linear value chain to a more dynamic and interconnected value network. Finally, the chapter defines a perspective of InsurTech's impact by identifying three waves of transformation within the insurance industry and understanding the evolution and chronology of InsurTech's influence. Thus, this chapter provides insights into the opportunities and challenges of this technological breakthrough, offering a comprehensive view of InsurTech's transformative journey within the insurance landscape.

***Chapter 20 Revolutionizing the Real Estate Industry With Fintech* (Jeffrey M. Clark)**

The real estate industry has rapidly changed due to technological advances across residential and commercial real estate from the perspective of occupiers, investors, and service providers. Owners and buyers of properties have access to increasing information in the marketplace, including access to residential real estate platforms such as Zillow. Automated appraisals and AI in the mortgage application process speed up home buying. Commercial real estate uses fintech to source deals, perform due diligence, and execute property management requests. The chapter includes a practitioner's view of the current and future information data needs, processes, and point solutions in the evolving technology landscape, including how tools such as ChatGPT apply. It concludes that the real estate fintech revolution has only begun, as data gaps in the real estate market require resolution before yielding better process automation and as the business model of real estate service providers shifts to strategic advisory roles.

***Chapter 21 Fintech in Capital Markets* (Christian Rauch)**

In recent years, new and technologically innovative financial products and services, generally subsumed under the fintech umbrella, have permeated all areas of capital markets at an exponential rate. Primarily driven by developments in Web3 and advancements in AI, fintech solutions offer valuable benefits to all existing markets and participants and are the basis for introducing wholly new segments to classic capital market ecosystems. However, this increasing fintech adaptation does not come without challenges. Due to the technologies' nascent nature and often unregulated status, many products are susceptible to manipulation and fraud. The result can be sizable investor losses and excessive regulatory and public scrutiny. This chapter highlights the most essential and prominent fintech solutions used in capital markets today, along with their features, value-additiveness, and degree of adaptation.

Section VIII Shaping the Future of Fintech: What Lies Ahead?

This section consists of two chapters focusing on the future of fintech and the key developments that will impact it most. Chapter 22 looks at technologies and emerging trends impacting fintech's future. Chapter 23 investigates both the challenges and opportunities that exist going forward.

***Chapter 22 Technologies and Emerging Trends Shaping Fintech* (Omer Unsal and Bora Ozkan)**

This chapter examines the patterns influencing the trajectory of fintech enterprises. With the looming challenge of climate change, the financial realm's responsibility in mitigating climate risks has surged into focus. The chapter investigates fintech enterprises' response to climate-related corporate social responsibility in six main domains: (1) climate risk assessment tools, (2) green bonds and sustainable investment tools, (3) ESG integration, (4) carbon trading and carbon credits, (5) sustainable banking, and (6) DeFi and climate initiatives. It also investigates how fintech firms recognize the impact of climate change within their official declarations and efforts to amplify consciousness about climate-related concerns. The chapter assesses climate-linked terminology and expressions using quantitative and qualitative approaches, illuminating these firms' dedication to assimilating climate risk within their operational blueprints.

***Chapter 23 The Future of Fintech: Challenges and Opportunities* (Dianna Preece)**

This chapter explores the vast array of fintech opportunities. The industry commanded approximately $250 billion in revenue in 2022, which is predicted to grow to $1.5 trillion by 2030. Fintech firms are involved in everything from digital currencies to payment systems, lending platforms, and embedded finance. Firms use AI and ML to create personalized financial products. One of the most important benefits to society is that fintech makes finance more inclusive to the traditionally underserved. However, fintech has its challenges. Regulations evolve, making compliance a challenge. Also, the industry is vulnerable to cyberattacks and money laundering. Companies hold large amounts of sensitive data, making them obvious targets for bad actors. As with many industries, governance, compliance, and transparency are essential for fintechs as they transform the financial services landscape.

Summary and Conclusions

Fintech is constantly evolving and is reshaping finance. Fintech refers to the "... innovation and technology aimed at challenging traditional methods used in the financial services industry" (Howat, 2020, p. 1). This broad term can apply to any innovation in how people transact business. This handbook discusses financial services that are changing in the new digital era. These innovations and applications involve mobile payments, digital lending, crowdfunding, robo-advisors, online trading, blockchain, cryptocurrency, insurance, and real estate. This list continues to expand as fintech's horizon continues to grow. Although the next innovations in the financial services industry are often difficult to predict, what is clear is that fintech will continue to challenge traditional methods used in the financial services industry and affect people's lives worldwide. AI and ML will play increasingly critical roles. Additionally, regulation is a major concern among governments as fintech companies evolve. The future of fintech promises opportunities for compelling product stories, product differentiation from competitors, market segment identification, and opportunities for profitability. This book provides academics, practitioners, students, and others with a broad understanding of fintech and its growing applications and challenges.

References

Boston Consulting Group and QED Investors. (2023, May 3). *Global fintech 2023: Reimagining the future of finance*. https://www.bcg.com/publications/2023/future-of-fintech-and-banking

Howat, E. (2020, May 16). What is fintech? *Fintech Magazine*. https://fintechmagazine.com/venture-capital/what-is-fintech

Paysera. (2023, November). *The ultimate fintech Jargon dictionary*. https://www.paysera.com/v2/en/blog/fintech-terms#:~:text=Fintech%20is%20a%20combination%20of,with%20the%20help%20of%20technoSilogy

Simons, T. (2023, October 30). *A brighter future for fintechs in 2024*. Thomson Reuters. https://www.thomsonreuters.com/en-us/posts/corporates/fintechs-future-2024/

Chapter 2

The Fintech Landscape: A Bibliometric Analysis

Debidutta Pattnaik

International Management Institute, Bhubaneswar, India

Abstract

This chapter uses data from the Scopus database to present a comprehensive bibliometric analysis of fintech research, focusing on publication trends, citation patterns, and thematic clusters within the field. The analysis reveals notable trends, including influential publications, prolific authors, and their affiliations. It identifies and explores publications categorized into 23 distinct themes, representing key areas of inquiry in fintech, such as technological advancements, financial inclusion, innovation, data analytics, sustainability, and regulatory compliance. The study also identifies research gaps, indicating areas within fintech that have received limited scholarly attention. These findings provide valuable insights for researchers, policymakers, and industry practitioners. Researchers can better understand the fintech landscape, identify research gaps, and guide future inquiries. Policymakers can develop effective regulations and policies based on identified trends and challenges. Industry practitioners can leverage fintech developments to enhance their strategies and operations.

Keywords: Financial technology; fintech; bibliometric analysis; publication trends; citation patterns; research gaps

Introduction

Financial technology, commonly called fintech, has undergone a remarkable transformation in recent years, revolutionizing the financial industry through technological advancements (Fuster et al., 2019; Schueffel, 2016). This chapter presents a comprehensive overview of existing fintech research by leveraging bibliometric analysis to uncover this rapidly evolving domain's dynamics, trends, and prospects.

The Emerald Handbook of Fintech, 17–42

doi:10.1108/978-1-83753-608-520241003

Academic interest in fintech has surged due to its rapid evolution and transformative impact on financial services. Previous reviews have shed light on various aspects of fintech, such as the intersection between demonetization and fintech (Jain et al., 2021) and the need for practical application frameworks in blockchain technology (Boakye et al., 2022). For reviews on artificial intelligence (AI) and machine language (ML) applications in finance, the focus on fintech remains limited (Ahmed et al., 2022; Goodell et al., 2021). García-Corral et al. (2022) and Pattnaik et al. (2023) identified research streams related to cryptocurrency, blockchain, and fintech. Ellili (2023) explored the relationship between fintech and sustainability. However, these studies have provided only fragmented insights into fintech's evolving research domain.

This chapter provides a bibliometric review to assess the fintech research landscape, offering a systematic and quantitative analysis of scholarly publications, citations, and themes (Baker et al., 2022; Pattnaik et al., 2022). By building upon the findings of previous works, the following research questions (RQs) provide a holistic understanding of the literature on fintech, contributing to the advancement of research in this field.

RQ1. What are the publication trends and citation patterns within the fintech literature?
RQ2. Who are the most influential authors and their affiliations in fintech?
RQ3. What constitutes the knowledge base of fintech research?
RQ4. How is research output distributed across various themes in fintech?
RQ5. What are the emerging trends and research gaps in the fintech research landscape?

This chapter identifies influential publications, prolific authors, and research institutions within the fintech domain, shedding light on the prominence and emerging trends in this field. It also highlights the distribution of research output across various themes, offering valuable insights into areas that have received limited scholarly attention. These research gaps present opportunities for future endeavors and emphasize the importance of interdisciplinary collaborations and methodological advancements in comprehensively understanding fintech's multifaceted nature. This chapter's findings can guide researchers in directing their inquiries, policymakers in formulating effective regulations and policies, and industry practitioners in understanding and harnessing the latest fintech developments.

The remainder of this chapter has the following organization. The Methodology section discusses the study's research methodology. The following section explores the evolution of fintech themes and enumerates future research directions. Finally, this chapter provides a summary and conclusions.

Methodology

This section provides the results of a systematic literature search using Scopus, a common database for bibliometric studies (Baker et al., 2022; Pattnaik et al., 2021,

2022). It aims to understand the fintech literature, including its corpus, key articles, top authors, author-affiliated countries, co-cited references, thematic clusters, and the evolution of fintech themes. Table 2.1 presents the systematic process adopted to determine the corpus, which comprises 1,736 articles.

The analysis determined the total number of publications (TP) in the fintech domain and examined publication trends across different years. An analysis of citations received by individual articles identified influential works, recording the total number of citations (TC) for each article. An analysis of authorship patterns identified the top authors in fintech research. The number of publications attributed to each author highlighted the contributions and expertise in the field. Analysis of authors' affiliations revealed the geographical distribution of fintech research. Further, a co-citation analysis identified fintech literature's most frequently co-cited references. Each reference's total co-citations (TC) indicated significance and influence within the field.

The collected publications were subjected to thematic analysis to identify key themes within the fintech literature. The author developed a comprehensive set of 23 themes to categorize and classify the research topics and areas of interest. Recording the number of publications associated with each theme (TP), total citations (TC), average citations (AC), and the average publication year (APY) provided insights into the prominence and evolution of each theme. The methodology for classifying the 23 themes within the fintech literature involved a multistep process, primarily using author-specified keywords and co-word analysis. This approach aimed to capture the underlying research topics and areas of inquiry in fintech.

Table 2.1. Selection Criteria.

	Accept	**Reject**
Search date: 03–05–2023		
Search engine: Scopus		
Search string: "fintech" OR "financial technology"		
Filter		
Initial data	5,019	
Subject filters: Finance, Economics, Econometrics, Business Management, Accounting, Social Science, Arts and Humanities	2,943	2,076
Article type: Articles, Reviews, and Book Chapter only	2,497	446
Valid author information:	2,482	15
Language (only English):	2,402	80
Content filter: Screening title and abstract	1,987	415
Publications until 2022	1,736	251

Note: This table shows the systematic process adopted to determine the final number of articles used in this study.

Initially, a comprehensive set of author-specified keywords related to fintech was compiled. The author obtained these keywords from the literature, including article titles, abstracts, and author-defined keywords. The author then manually reviewed and refined the keywords to ensure relevance and specificity to the fintech domain. The author identified recurring patterns and commonalities among the keywords to derive potential themes. This process involved examining semantic relationships, concept associations, and contextual relevance between the keywords. The derived themes underwent an iterative refinement process to ensure clarity and representativeness. The author then assigned the identified themes to the corresponding publications in the fintech literature. Next, the author manually reviewed and matched each article with the most relevant theme based on its content and research focus. The author carefully considered and judged articles encompassing multiple themes to determine the primary theme.

The author performed a co-word analysis on the revised themes to further validate and strengthen the thematic classification. Co-word analysis involves analyzing the co-occurrence patterns of the themes within the articles. By leveraging author-specified keywords, performing co-word analysis, and engaging in iterative validation, this methodology facilitated the classification of the 23 distinct themes within the fintech literature. The resulting thematic framework provides a comprehensive representation of the research topics and areas of focus in the dynamic field of fintech.

Findings

The following section presents the noteworthy findings of the analysis, which shed light on influential fintech publications, prolific authors, and their affiliations. The examination thoroughly explores publications, categorized into 23 distinct themes representing vital areas of investigation in fintech. The findings also highlight research gaps, drawing attention to underexplored aspects within fintech.

Research Trends

The *RQ1* centers around the fintech literature's publication trends and citation patterns. Table 2.2 and Fig. 2.1 provide an overview of the literature corpus on fintech between 1980 and 2022. Table 2.2 presents descriptive statistics and coauthorship information that allows for drawing meaningful insights. Fig. 2.1 reveals research trends by mapping the dynamics of the total publications and total citations. The graph indicates an exponential surge since 2016, signifying a turning point in scholarly explorations on fintech.

Table 2.2 shows that the total number of publications (TP) increased from 57 in 1980–2016 to 1,679 in 2017–2022. This change indicates a substantial surge in research activity and interest in fintech. The total citations (TC) received by the publications increased from 1,760 in 1980–2016 to 19,950 in 2017–2022. This substantial citation growth signifies the increasing influence and recognition of fintech research within the scholarly community. The average citations per

Table 2.2. Overview of Fintech's Corpus.

	1980–2022	1980–2016	2017–2022
Panel A. Descriptive Statistics			
Total publications (TP)	1,736	57	1,679
Number of cited publications (NCP)	1,298	47	1,251
Total citations (TC)	21,710	1,760	19,950
Average citations (TC/TP)	13	31	12
h-index	66	20	63
g-index	105	41	101
i-10	462	27	435
i-100	35	5	30
i-250	6	1	5
Number of active years (NAY)	27	21	6
Productivity per active year (PAY)	64	3	280
Panel B. Coauthorship Information			
Number of contributing authors (NCA)	4,323	91	4,232
Number of affiliated authors (excludes repetitions) (NAA)	3,734	88	3,652
Authors of single-authored documents (ASA)	417	31	387
Authors of coauthored documents (ACA)	3,362	57	3,308
Single-authored documents (SA)	486	34	452
Coauthored documents (CA)	1,250	23	1,227
Collaboration index (CI)	1.49	0.60	1.52
Collaboration coefficient (CC)	0.60	0.37	0.60
Average authors per coauthored article	3	2	3

Note: This table shows an overview of the descriptive statistics and coauthorship information related to fintech's corpus between 1980 and 2022.

publication (TC/TP) was 31 in 1980–2016 and 12 in 2017–2022. This decrease in TC/TP likely resulted from the shorter period available for citations.

The h-index, g-index, i-10 index, and i-100 index reflect the scholarly influence of the fintech literature. The *h-index* quantifies the impact of a researcher's publications. It is defined as the highest "h" publications, each receiving at least "h" citations. The *g-index* measures the cumulative impact of a researcher's publication quality and quantity. It signifies the "g" number of highly cited papers collectively cited at least "g^2" times. The i-10 and i-100 indices reveal a researcher's publications that have received at least 10 and 100 citations, respectively (Pattnaik et al., 2022).

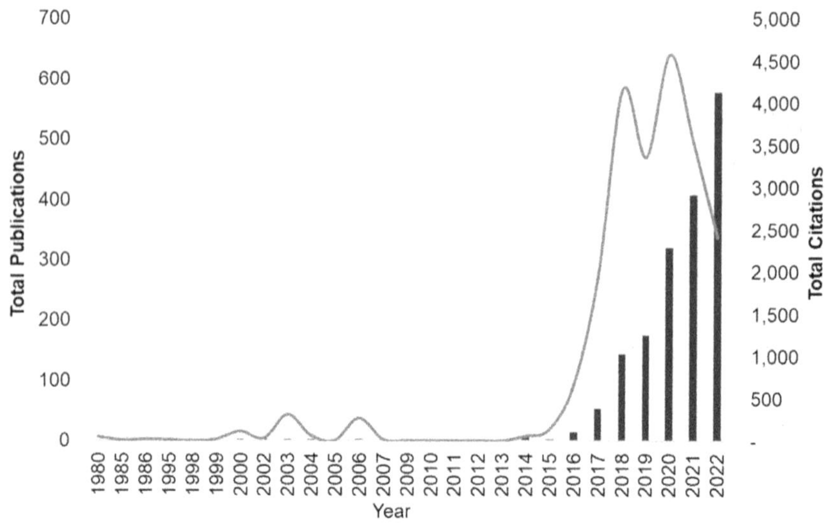

Fig. 2.1. Research Trends. *Note:* This figure maps fintech's research trends between 1980 and 2022. The bars represent total publications, and the line indicates total citations.

The h-index increased from 20 in 1980–2016 to 63 in 2017–2022, indicating higher scholarly impact and recognition. Similarly, the g-index increased from 41 to 101, indicating a broader and more influential set of highly cited articles.

The coauthorship information reveals collaborative trends among researchers in fintech. The average number of authors per coauthored article increased from two in 1980–2016 to three in 2017–2022, suggesting increased collaboration.

The literature corpus spans 27 active years between 1980 and 2022. The productivity per active year varied markedly, with productivity per active year (PAY) rising from three in 1980–2016 to 280 in 2017–2022. This change indicates a substantial increase in output on fintech per active year in recent years.

These findings from Table 2.2 highlight the fintech literature's growth, impact, and collaborative nature. The increasing number of publications and citations demonstrates the rising interest in and recognition of fintech research. The coauthorship patterns indicate a more collaborative research environment, while the productivity per active year increases interest on fintech topics. These insights contribute to understanding the trends and dynamics within fintech research.

Top Fintech Articles

Table 2.3 shows the top-cited articles in fintech literature and provides valuable insights into the influential works, prevalent research topics, interdisciplinary nature, and future research directions within the domain. The top-cited fintech

Table 2.3. Top Fintech Articles.

TC	Author(s)	Title
469	Gomber et al. (2018)	"On the Fintech Revolution: Interpreting the Forces of Innovation, Disruption, and Transformation in Financial Services"
462	Lee and Shin (2018)	"Fintech: Ecosystem, Business Models, Investment Decisions, and Challenges"
410	Gomber et al. (2017)	"Digital Finance and FinTech: Current Research and Future Research Directions"
313	Buchak et al. (2018)	"Fintech, Regulatory Arbitrage, and the Rise of Shadow Banks"
279	Berger (2003)	"The Economic Effects of Technological Progress: Evidence from the Banking Industry"
272	Gabor and Brooks (2017)	"The Digital Revolution in Financial Inclusion: International Development in the Fintech Era"
217	Thakor (2020)	"Fintech and Banking: What Do We Know?"
213	Haddad and Hornuf (2019)	"The Emergence of the Global Fintech Market: Economic and Technological Determinants"
189	Schueffel (2016)	"Taming the Beast: A Scientific Definition of Fintech"
186	Fuster et al. (2019)	"The Role of Technology in Mortgage Lending"
181	Xu et al. (2019)	"A Systematic Review of Blockchain"
177	Chen and Bellavitis (2020)	"Blockchain Disruption and Decentralized Finance: The Rise of Decentralized Business Models"
175	Chen et al. (2019)	"How Valuable Is FinTech Innovation?"
171	Belanche et al. (2019)	"Artificial Intelligence in FinTech: Understanding Robo-advisors Adoption Among Customers"
164	Anagnostopoulos (2018)	"Fintech and Regtech: Impact on Regulators and Banks"
162	Leong et al. (2017)	"Nurturing a FinTech Ecosystem: The Case of a Youth Microloan Startup in China"
158	Chang et al. (2020)	"How Blockchain Can Impact Financial Services – The Overview, Challenges and Recommendations from Expert Interviewees"
158	Fosso Wamba et al. (2020)	"Bitcoin, Blockchain and Fintech: A Systematic Review and Case Studies in the Supply Chain"
158	Milian et al. (2019)	"Fintechs: A Literature Review and Research Agenda"
157	Arner et al. (2017)	"FinTech, RegTech, and the Reconceptualization of Financial Regulation"

(Continued)

Table 2.3. *(Continued)*

TC	Author(s)	Title
143	Goldstein et al. (2019)	"To FinTech and Beyond"
136	Kou et al. (2021)	"Fintech Investments in European Banks: A Hybrid IT2 Fuzzy Multidimensional Decision-Making Approach"
136	Preda (2006)	"Socio-Technical Agency in Financial Markets: The Case of the Stock Ticker"
134	Shim and Shin (2016)	"Analyzing China's Fintech Industry from the Perspective of Actor-Network Theory"
132	Du et al. (2019)	"Affordances, Experimentation and Actualization of Fintech: A Blockchain Implementation Study"
129	Ryu (2018)	"What Makes Users Willing or Hesitant to Use Fintech?: The Moderating Effect of User Type"
127	Neu et al. (2006)	"Informing Technologies and The World Bank"
119	Cai (2018)	"Disruption of Financial Intermediation by Fintech: A Review on Crowdfunding and Blockchain"
119	Gimpel et al. (2018)	"Understanding FinTech Start-Ups – A Taxonomy of Consumer-Oriented Service Offerings"
118	Jagtiani and Lemieux (2018)	"Do Fintech Lenders Penetrate Areas That Are Underserved by Traditional Banks?"
116	Le et al. (2021)	"Time and Frequency Domain Connectedness and Spill-Over among Fintech, Green Bonds and Cryptocurrencies in the Age of the Fourth Industrial Revolution"
108	Marsal-Llacuna (2018)	"Future Living Framework: Is Blockchain the Next Enabling Network?"
103	Gozman et al. (2018)	"The Innovation Mechanisms of Fintech Start-Ups: Insights from SWIFT's Innotribe Competition"
103	Shiau et al. (2020)	"Understanding Fintech Continuance: Perspectives from Self-efficacy and ECT-IS Theories"
100	Albayati et al. (2020)	"Accepting Financial Transactions Using Blockchain Technology and Cryptocurrency: A Customer Perspective Approach"

Note: This table ranks the top fintech articles cited at least 100 times between 1980 and 2022 in Scopus on the search date. Here, TC = total citations.

articles have at least 100 citations between 1980 and 2022. The most cited article by Gomber et al. (2018) received about 469 citations on the search date, suggesting its substantial impact, followed closely by Lee and Shin (2018), with 642 citations, and Gomber et al. (2017), with 410. Interestingly, the three most highly cited articles occurred recently. The top articles cover diverse topics within fintech, like fintech ecosystems, business models, regulatory arbitrage, digital finance, robo-advisors, blockchain, and AI. This finding indicates the multidimensional nature of fintech research and scholars' wide range of interests.

Some articles featured in Table 2.3 address emerging trends in fintech, including decentralized finance (DeFi) (Chen & Bellavitis, 2020), regtech (Anagnostopoulos, 2018; Arner et al., 2017), cryptocurrency (Albayati et al., 2020), and green bonds (Le et al., 2021). These topics reflect the evolving landscape of fintech and the growing interest in exploring innovative and sustainable solutions. The articles represent a blend of disciplines, combining insights from finance, economics, technology, regulation, and the social sciences. This interdisciplinary approach highlights fintech's complex and interconnected nature, requiring a comprehensive understanding of various academic fields.

Some top-cited works present literature reviews and research agendas, indicating the need to synthesize existing knowledge and outline future research directions in specific areas of fintech. This finding suggests an ongoing effort to bridge research gaps and expand the understanding of key concepts and phenomena in the field.

Top Fintech Authors

The first part of *RQ2* investigates the authors who have influenced fintech most significantly. Table 2.4 shows the top fintech authors based on their publication records between 1980 and 2022. Pável Reyes-Mercado is the most prolific author with 11 publications, all sole-authored. Douglas W. Arner and Mustafa Raza Rabbani follow closely with 10 publications each, comprising a combination of sole-authored and coauthored articles.

Although some authors predominantly publish sole-authored articles, others tend to collaborate. Authors such as Douglas W. Arner, Mustafa Raza Rabbani, Ross P. Buckley, and Dariusz Wójcik have many coauthored articles, indicating their inclination toward collaboration. The collaboration index (CI) and collaboration coefficient (CC) provide further insights into the collaboration level among authors. CI is a metric that quantifies a researcher's extent of collaboration. CC assesses the collaborative nature quantified between 0 and 1 (Pattnaik et al., 2022).

Table 2.4 also presents the total citations (TC) received by each author and other citation-related metrics. Douglas W. Arner leads in total citations with 343, followed by Ross P. Buckley with 336 and Julapa Jagtiani with 238. These high citation counts suggest that these authors' works have been influential and widely referenced in the fintech literature. The table includes various productivity and impact indicators, such as the h-index, g-index, i-10 index, number of active years

Table 2.4. Top Fintech Authors.

Author	TP	SA	CA	NCA	AACA	CI	CC	TCP	TC	C/CP	*h*	*g*	*i-10*	NAY	PAY
Reyes-Mercado P.	11	11	0	11	–	–	–	2	2	1	1	1	0	2	5.50
Arner D.W.	10	0	10	32	3	2	0.69	7	343	49	6	7	5	6	1.67
Rabbani M.R.	10	1	9	37	4	3	0.73	10	225	23	7	10	7	3	3.33
Buckley R.P.	8	0	8	27	3	2	0.70	6	336	56	5	6	5	5	1.60
Wójcik D.	8	2	6	19	3	1	0.58	8	224	28	8	8	7	4	2.00
Rupeika-Apoga R.	7	0	7	23	3	2	0.70	7	101	14	5	7	4	4	1.75
Zetzsche D.A.	7	0	7	22	3	2	0.68	5	186	37	4	5	3	5	1.40
Baber H.	6	5	1	7	2	0	0.14	6	51	9	3	6	3	4	1.50
Koroleva E.	6	2	4	17	4	2	0.65	3	25	8	2	3	1	2	3.00
Okoli T.T.	6	1	5	11	2	1	0.45	6	10	2	2	2	0	2	3.00
Wonglimpiyarat J.	6	5	1	7	2	0	0.14	6	105	18	5	6	2	4	1.50
Ashta A.	5	2	3	9	2	1	0.44	5	95	19	4	5	2	2	2.50
Fenwick M.	5	0	5	13	3	2	0.62	3	32	11	3	3	2	2	2.50
Gozman D.	5	0	5	16	3	2	0.69	5	189	38	5	5	5	4	1.25
Hassan M.K.	5	0	5	18	4	3	0.72	5	94	19	4	5	3	3	1.67
Huang Y.	5	0	5	13	3	2	0.62	5	96	19	5	5	4	3	1.67
Jagtiani J.	5	0	5	14	3	2	0.64	5	238	48	4	5	4	4	1.25
Khan S.	5	0	5	17	3	2	0.71	5	120	24	5	5	4	2	2.50
Mohammed M.O.	5	0	5	14	3	2	0.64	3	6	2	2	2	0	4	1.25
Schwienbacher A.	5	0	5	13	3	2	0.62	5	188	38	4	5	4	2	2.50
Tewari D.D.	5	0	5	10	2	1	0.50	5	7	1	2	2	0	2	2.50

Note: This table shows the top fintech authors publishing at least five articles between 1980 and 2022. Here, TP = total publications, SA = sole-authored articles, CA = coauthored articles, NCA = the number of contributing authors, AACA = average authors per coauthored article, CI = collaboration index, CC = collaboration co-efficient, TCP = total cited publications, TC = total citations, C/CP = citations per cited publication, h = h-index, g = g-index, i-10 = i-10 index, NAY = the number of active years, and PAY = productivity per active year.

(NAY), and productivity per active year (PAY). These metrics provide insights into the longevity of an author's research career, the breadth of their impact, and their productivity over time. Thus, analyzing the top fintech authors provides valuable insights into their publication records, citation impact, and productivity measures. These findings contribute to understanding the key contributors in the field, their research output, and their influence on the broader fintech literature.

Fintech Research Hotspots

The second part of *RQ2* examines the affiliations of authors denoting the hotspots of fintech research. Table 2.5 provides insights into the top countries affiliated with fintech authors between 1980 and 2022. The table reveals that the United States, China, and the United Kingdom are the top three countries in total publications (TP). The United States leads with 250 publications, followed closely by China with 211 and the United Kingdom with 206. These countries demonstrate a strong research output in fintech. The collaboration index (CI) and collaboration coefficient (CC) shed light on the collaborative tendencies among authors affiliated with different countries. Notably, authors affiliated with the United States, China, and the United Kingdom exhibit moderate collaboration indices, suggesting that researchers from these countries tend to publish more independently or with fewer collaborators.

The United States exhibits the highest total citations (TC) with 5,136, followed by China with 3,663 and the United Kingdom with 3,543. These citation counts highlight the significant impact and influence of research from these countries within the fintech domain. Further, authors affiliated with countries such as the United States, China, and the United Kingdom demonstrate high productivity per active year (PAY), indicating consistent and substantial research output over time. Additionally, these countries exhibit notable h-index, g-index, and i-10 index values, suggesting their research's strong impact and influence within the fintech community.

Table 2.5 shows a diverse range of countries contributing to fintech research. Besides the leading countries mentioned earlier, authors affiliated with other countries such as Indonesia, India, Malaysia, Australia, Germany, Italy, Korea, Spain, and France also have a substantial presence in publication output. Each country exhibits its research profile, with varying proportions of sole-authored and coauthored articles. The citation metrics and productivity measures differ across countries, highlighting their unique contributions to the fintech literature.

Examining the top author-affiliated countries in fintech research identifies the leading contributors, their research output, collaboration patterns, citation impact, and productivity measures. These findings provide valuable insights into the global landscape of fintech research and the countries driving advancements in this field.

Knowledge Foundation of Fintech Research

RQ3 delves into the knowledge foundation of fintech research, exploring its underlying research base. Table 2.6 highlights the top co-cited references that

Table 2.5. Fintech Research Hotspots.

Country	TP	SA	CA	NCA	AACA	CI	CC	TCP	TC	C/CP	*h*	*g*	*i-10*	NAY	PAY
The United States	250	74	176	627	3	2	0.60	206	5,136	25	35	67	79	20	13
China	211	23	188	663	3	2	0.68	180	3,663	20	33	54	85	7	30
The United Kingdom	206	62	144	513	3	1	0.60	170	3,543	21	32	53	83	11	19
Indonesia	115	16	99	343	3	2	0.66	85	724	9	14	22	20	5	23
India	104	16	88	299	3	2	0.65	75	688	9	12	23	13	8	13
Malaysia	99	7	92	335	4	2	0.70	72	537	7	13	18	18	5	20
Australia	87	13	74	270	3	2	0.68	72	1,900	26	24	42	42	8	11
Germany	69	12	57	164	3	1	0.58	56	2,263	40	20	47	27	9	8
Italy	64	15	49	162	3	2	0.60	50	480	10	12	19	15	6	11
Korea	54	16	38	117	3	1	0.54	42	1,424	34	16	37	24	8	7
Spain	46	8	38	119	3	2	0.61	33	645	20	12	25	13	6	8
France	45	6	39	118	3	2	0.62	39	1,123	29	16	33	19	6	8
Singapore	39	14	25	89	3	1	0.56	32	799	25	12	28	13	6	7
Canada	35	10	25	90	3	2	0.61	26	442	17	10	20	10	8	4
Taiwan	32	8	24	85	3	2	0.62	26	357	14	9	18	9	5	6
Bahrain	31	6	25	93	3	2	0.67	25	325	13	10	17	10	4	8
Japan	31	15	16	59	3	1	0.47	18	162	9	9	12	7	6	5
The Netherlands	31	7	24	72	3	1	0.57	24	429	18	10	20	13	9	3
South Africa	31	8	23	63	2	1	0.51	25	223	9	7	14	5	5	6
United Arab Emirates	31	5	26	88	3	2	0.65	27	298	11	9	16	8	6	5

Pakistan	30	1	29	114	4	3	0.74	24	314	13	9	17	9	4	8
Switzerland	30	8	22	72	3	1	0.58	21	842	40	13	21	14	9	3
Turkey	29	7	22	80	3	2	0.64	19	264	14	6	16	5	5	6
Saudi Arabia	28	5	23	93	4	2	0.70	20	118	6	6	10	1	5	6
Poland	27	5	22	74	3	2	0.64	19	206	11	9	14	9	6	5
Viet Nam	27	4	23	81	3	2	0.67	19	303	16	10	17	10	3	9
Ukraine	23	3	20	94	5	3	0.76	19	175	9	7	12	7	5	5
Jordan	20	4	16	69	4	2	0.71	16	150	9	6	12	4	4	5

Note: This table shows the top fintech authors' affiliating countries publishing at least 20 articles between 1980 and 2022. Here, TP = total publications, SA = sole-authored articles, CA = coauthored articles, NCA = the number of contributing authors, AACA = average authors per coauthored article, CI = collaboration index, CC = collaboration co-efficient, TCP = total cited publications, TC = total citations, C/CP = citations per cited publication, h = h-index, g = g-index, i-10 = i-10 index, NAY = the number of active years, and PAY = productivity per active year.

Table 2.6. Top Co-cited References.

TC	Author	Title	TLS
79	Lee and Shin (2018)	"Fintech: Ecosystem, Business Models, Investment Decisions, and Challenges"	124
57	Buchak et al. (2018)	"Fintech, Regulatory Arbitrage, and the Rise of Shadow Banks"	136
43	Gomber et al. (2018)	"On the Fintech Revolution: Interpreting the Forces of Innovation, Disruption, and Transformation in Financial Services"	126
41	Anagnostopoulos (2018)	"Fintech and Regtech: Impact on Regulators and Banks"	113
41	Gabor and Brooks (2017)	"The Digital Revolution in Financial Inclusion: International Development in the Fintech Era"	115
37	Gomber et al. (2017)	"Digital Finance and Fintech: Current Research and Future Research Directions"	127
37	Schueffel (2016)	"Taming the Beast: A Scientific Definition of Fintech"	91
35	Haddad and Hornuf (2019)	"The Emergence of the Global Fintech Market: Economic and Technological Determinants"	114
31	Gai et al. (2018)	"A Survey on Fintech"	111
30	Fuster et al. (2019)	"The Role of Technology in Mortgage Lending"	57
29	Jagtiani and Lemieux (2018)	"Do Fintech Lenders Penetrate Areas That Are Underserved by Traditional Banks?"	104
29	Puschmann (2017)	"Fintech"	93
27	Suri and Jack (2016)	"The Long-Run Poverty and Gender Impacts of Mobile Money"	43
24	Ajzen (1991)	"The Theory of Planned Behavior"	48
24	Fornell and Larcker (1981)	"Evaluating Structural Equation Models with Unobservable Variables and Measurement Error"	49
24	Lin et al. (2013)	"Judging Borrowers by the Company They Keep: Friendship Networks and Information Asymmetry in Online Peer-to-Peer Lending"	52
24	Tang (2019)	"Peer-to-Peer Lenders Versus Banks: Substitutes or Complements?"	50
23	Davis (1989)	"Perceived Usefulness, Perceived Ease of Use, and User Acceptance of Information Technology"	68

Table 2.6. *(Continued)*

TC	Author	Title	TLS
22	Davis et al. (1989)	"User Acceptance of Computer Technology: A Comparison of Two Theoretical Models"	48
22	Mollick (2014)	"The Dynamics of Crowdfunding: An Exploratory Study"	36
20	Chen (2016)	"From Fintech to Finlife: The Case of Fintech Development in China"	65
20	Venkatesh et al. (2003)	"User Acceptance of Information Technology: Toward a Unified View"	59
19	Leong et al. (2017)	"Nurturing a Fintech Ecosystem: The Case of a Youth Microloan Startup in China"	90
19	Ozili (2018)	"Impact of Digital Finance on Financial Inclusion and Stability"	74
17	Belleflamme et al. (2014)	"Crowdfunding: Tapping the Right Crowd"	25
17	Thakor (2020)	"Fintech and Banking: What Do We Know?"	70
16	Henseler et al. (2015)	"A New Criterion for Assessing Discriminant Validity in Variance-Based Structural Equation Modeling"	28
15	Stewart and Jurjens (2018)	"Data Security and Consumer Trust in Fintech Innovation in Germany"	63
14	Chen et al. (2016)	"How Valuable Is Fintech Innovation?"	61
13	Belanche et al. (2019)	"Artificial Intelligence in Fintech: Understanding Robo-Advisors Adoption Among Customers"	26
13	Zalan and Toufaily (2017)	"The Promise of Fintech in Emerging Markets: Not as Disruptive"	41
12	Hair et al. (2011)	"PLS-SEM: Indeed a Silver Bullet"	32
12	Hu et al. (2019)	"Adoption Intention of Fintech Services for Bank Users: An Empirical Examination with an Extended Technology Acceptance Model"	38
12	Leong and Sung (2018)	"Fintech (Financial Technology): What Is It and How to Use Technologies to Create Business Value in Fintech Way?"	15
12	Mackenzie (2015)	"The Fintech Revolution"	20
12	Wonglimpiyarat (2017)	"Fintech Banking Industry: A Systemic Approach"	55

(Continued)

Table 2.6. *(Continued)*

TC	Author	Title	TLS
11	Goldstein et al. (2019)	"To Fintech and Beyond"	24
11	Mader (2018)	"Contesting Financial Inclusion"	18
11	Venkatesh and Davis (2000)	"A Theoretical Extension of the Technology Acceptance Model: Four Longitudinal Field Studies"	32
10	Anshari et al. (2019)	"Digital Marketplace and Fintech to Support Agriculture Sustainability"	20
10	Bernards (2019)	"The Poverty of Fintech? Psychometrics, Credit Infrastructures, and the Limits of Financialization"	18
10	Boot et al. (2021)	"Fintech: What's Old, What's New?"	40
10	Deng et al. (2019)	"Fintech and Sustainable Development: Evidence from China Based on P2P Data"	9
10	Drasch et al. (2018)	"Integrating the 'Troublemakers': A Taxonomy for Cooperation Between Banks and Fintechs"	53
10	Eisenhardt (1989)	"Building Theories from Case Study Research"	14
10	Emekter et al. (2015)	"Evaluating Credit Risk and Loan Performance in Online Peer-To-Peer (P2P) Lending"	18
10	Frost et al. (2019)	"Bigtech and the Changing Structure of Financial Intermediation"	15
10	Guo and Liang (2016)	"Blockchain Application and Outlook in the Banking Industry"	42
10	Kim et al. (2010)	"An Empirical Examination of Factors Influencing the Intention to Use Mobile Payment"	34
10	Langley and Leyshon (2021)	"The Platform Political Economy of Fintech: Reintermediation, Consolidation and Capitalisation"	10
10	Lee and Lee (2012)	"Herding Behavior in Online P2P Lending: An Empirical Investigation"	33
10	Shaikh and Karjaluoto (2015)	"Mobile Banking Adoption: A Literature Review"	20

Table 2.6. *(Continued)*

TC	Author	Title	TLS
10	Vives (2017)	"The Impact of Fintech on Banking"	32
10	Zhou (2013)	"An Empirical Examination of Continuance Intention of Mobile Payment Services"	35

Note: This table shows the top-cited references contributing to the knowledge foundation of fintech. Here, TC = total co-citations, and TLS = total link strength.

contribute substantially to the knowledge framework of fintech research. The table includes the authors, titles of the papers, total co-citations (TC), and total link strength (TLS) for each reference. The *TLS* measures prominence and interconnectedness quantitatively, highlighting a reference's significance and influence within the network. Co-citation network analysis identifies the semantic association of closely related references within the fintech literature. Fig. 2.2 shows the network's cohesiveness and interconnections among influential references. Their higher nodal size reflects Lee and Shin's (2018) prominence within the network. The thicker lines emanating from Buchak et al. (2018) indicate the strong semantic interconnection among Buchak et al. (2018), Jagtiani and Lemieux (2018), Fuster et al. (2019), and Tang (2019).

An inferential summary in Table 2.6 reveals key findings. First, Lee and Shin (2018) are widely recognized and cited, indicating their significant contribution to the knowledge foundation of fintech research. Buchak et al. (2018) have also significantly influenced the understanding of the relationship involving fintech, regulatory dynamics, and the emergence of shadow banks. Gomber et al. (2018) play a notable role in interpreting the factors driving innovation, disruption, and transformation within the fintech revolution. Another highly co-cited reference, Anagnostopoulos (2018), explores the effects of fintech and regulatory technology on the financial industry and the role of regulators and banks in this context. Gabor and Brooks (2017) have contributed to understanding fintech's impact on regulatory frameworks, banking systems, and global financial inclusion efforts.

Other articles in Table 2.6 have also received notable citations, indicating their contributions to the knowledge foundation of fintech research. These include works on assorted topics such as digital finance, peer-to-peer (P2P) lending, user acceptance of technology, AI in fintech, crowdfunding, and the role of technology in mortgage lending. These top-cited references have shaped the understanding of fintech research by addressing key aspects such as ecosystem dynamics, regulatory implications, innovation forces, financial inclusion, and technological advancements. Other researchers have cited them widely, demonstrating their influence and importance in advancing fintech's knowledge foundation.

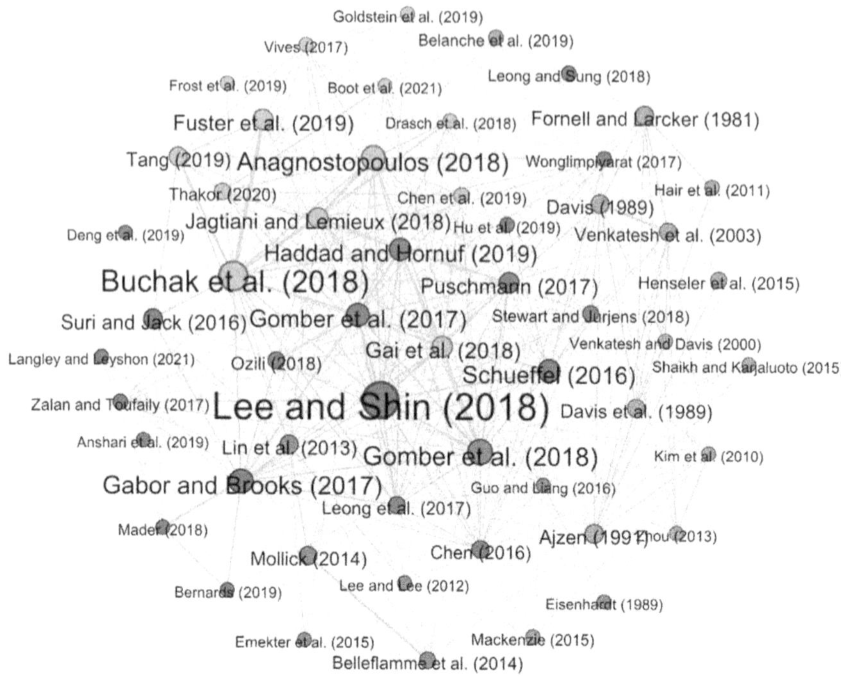

Fig. 2.2. Top Co-Cited References: The Knowledge Foundation of Fintech Research. *Note:* This figure reveals the top co-cited references in the corpus of fintech research. Each node refers to a top co-cited reference, the shading of the nodes reveals the intellectual cluster, and the node's size depicts an article's relevance. The strength of the links joining the nodes reflects the number of co-citations.

Fintech Themes

Fintech has emerged as a disruptive force in the financial industry, revolutionizing the delivery and consumption of financial services. Over the years, extensive research has been conducted to explore various aspects of fintech and its impact on different domains within finance. *RQ4* explores the distribution of research output across different themes in fintech. Table 2.7 and Fig. 2.3 analyze fintech's knowledge landscape by investigating the literature across 23 unique themes, providing valuable insights from the existing body of knowledge.

Table 2.7 highlights the total publications (TP), total citations (TC), average citations (AC), and the APY for each theme. Fig. 2.3 reveals their co-occurrence network. Themes such as "infrastructure and technology" and "innovation and startups" emerge as prominent areas with many publications, citations, and co-occurrences, indicating their significance and extensive scholarly attention.

Table 2.7. Evolution of Fintech Themes.

	1980–2016	2017–2022	TP	TC	AC	APY
Technological advancements	19	697	716	8,885	12	2020.3
Financial inclusion and access	21	611	632	7,499	12	2020.3
Performance and returns	2	31	33	226	7	2019.3
Regulatory and compliance	7	336	343	4,688	14	2020.1
Innovation and start-ups	17	1,178	1,195	17,056	14	2020.5
Services and offerings	2	103	105	2,357	22	2020.0
Data and analytics	4	134	138	1,571	11	2020.5
Alternative finance	3	106	109	1,610	15	2020.3
Sustainable finance	0	83	83	1,303	16	2021.1
Economic and global factors	11	360	371	4,990	13	2020.5
Business operations and strategies	12	506	518	6,506	13	2020.2
Infrastructure and technology	29	1,363	1,392	18,132	13	2020.4
Governance and policy	14	433	447	5,622	13	2020.1
Complexity and network theory	3	154	157	2,175	14	2020.4
Consumer behavior and preferences	7	445	452	5,998	13	2020.4
Health and pandemics	1	94	95	1,009	11	2021.3
Cultural and behavioral factors	1	27	28	198	7	2020.8
Regulation and legislation	2	88	90	1,278	14	2020.4
Risk and security	1	51	52	310	6	2020.8
International finance and trade	1	136	137	1,221	9	2020.6
Financial centers and hubs	0	36	36	482	13	2020.0
Financial efficiency and productivity	0	33	33	251	8	2020.8
Decentralized finance	1	40	41	845	21	2020.1

Note: This table shows the evolution of various themes covered in the fintech literature published between 1980 and 2022. Here, TP = total publications, TC = total citations, AC = average citations, and APY = average publication year.

Fig. 2.3. Thematic Structure of Fintech Research. *Note:* This figure reveals the themes detected in the corpus of fintech research. Each node refers to a fintech theme, the node's shading reveals the thematic cluster, and the node's size depicts the theme's relevance. Figures within parenthesis depict the average publication year of fintech themes while the strength of the links joining the nodes reflects the number of co-occurrences.

Conversely, themes like "performance and returns" and "cultural and behavioral factors" exhibit comparatively lower publication and citation numbers, suggesting their status as emerging or specialized areas in fintech research. Additionally, the APY across most themes aligns closely with 2020, indicating fintech research's recent and up-to-date nature. The subsequent section offers a concise overview of each fintech theme, highlighting each category's key aspects and focus areas.

- *Technological advancements* explore the evolving landscape of technological innovations in the fintech space. This theme delves into topics such as blockchain technology, AI, ML, and cybersecurity, highlighting the transformative potential of these advancements in shaping the fintech's future.
- *Financial inclusion and access* examine research investigating how fintech has facilitated greater financial inclusivity and improved access to financial services for traditionally underserved populations. This theme explores initiatives such as mobile banking, digital wallets, and microfinance platforms that have bridged the gap between individuals and formal financial systems.

- *Performance and returns* delve into the empirical analysis of fintech's impact on financial performance and investment returns. Researchers in this area have examined the effects of robo-advisors, algorithmic trading, and automated investment platforms on portfolio management, risk-adjusted returns, and overall market efficiency.
- *Regulatory and compliance* explore fintech's complex regulatory landscape, including regulatory sandboxes, digital identity verification, and anti-money laundering measures. This theme analyzes the evolving regulatory frameworks and their implications for fintech start-ups, incumbents, and consumer protection.
- *Innovation and start-ups* investigate the dynamic start-up ecosystem within fintech, highlighting research on entrepreneurial activities, disruptive business models, and innovation diffusion. This theme identifies the factors driving fintech entrepreneurship, start-ups' challenges, and the impact of venture capital funding.
- *Services and offerings* focus on the evolution of financial services and products in the fintech era. This theme covers digital banking, P2P lending, crowdfunding, and insurtech, examining the transformative effects of these innovations on traditional financial service providers.
- *Data and analytics* explore the growing importance of data-driven decision-making and advanced analytics techniques in fintech. This theme encompasses research on big data analytics, credit scoring models, fraud detection, and predictive analytics, providing insights into the potential of data analytics in enhancing financial services and risk management.
- *Alternative finance* examines the emergence of alternative funding models such as crowdfunding, P2P lending, and digital currencies. This theme explores the democratization of finance and the potential implications for traditional banking systems.
- *Sustainable finance* focuses on integrating environmental, social, and governance (ESG) factors within fintech and the growing importance of sustainable investing. This theme investigates the role of fintech in promoting responsible investing, green finance, and the achievement of the United Nations Sustainable Development Goals.
- *Economic and global factors* explore fintech's macroeconomic and global implications, including cross-border payments, international remittances, and the impact of fintech on emerging economies. This theme analyzes how fintech has reshaped financial systems and global economic landscapes.
- *Business operations and strategies* investigate fintech's strategic implications for traditional financial institutions. This theme encompasses research on digital transformation, business models, strategic partnerships, and customer engagement strategies in the fintech era.
- *Infrastructure and technology* focus on the underlying technological infrastructure supporting fintech ecosystems. This theme explores cloud computing, application programming interfaces (APIs), open banking, and distributed ledger technologies, shedding light on the enabling technologies and infrastructure critical to fintech innovation.

- *Governance and policy* explore the regulatory, legal, and ethical considerations surrounding fintech. This theme investigates topics such as data privacy, consumer protection, regulatory sandboxes, and the role of governments and regulatory bodies in fostering fintech innovation while ensuring market stability and security.
- *Complexity and network theory* delves into the application of complexity science and network theory in understanding the dynamics of fintech ecosystems. This theme explores network effects, systemic risk, financial contagion, and the interplay between stakeholders in the fintech landscape.
- *Consumer behavior and preferences* investigate the factors influencing consumer adoption and usage of fintech services. This theme encompasses research on consumer trust, perceived value, user experience, and behavioral biases in fintech decision-making.
- *Health and pandemics* explore the intersection of fintech and healthcare, particularly in the context of the COVID-19 pandemic. This theme examines how fintech solutions have facilitated contactless payments, telehealth services, and financial resilience during challenging times.
- *Cultural and behavioral factors* investigate the influence of cultural and behavioral factors on fintech adoption and usage. This theme explores cultural differences, social norms, trust, and user perceptions across different demographic segments.
- *Regulation and legislation* focus on the evolving regulatory landscape governing fintech. This theme examines the regulatory challenges, compliance requirements, and policy implications for fintech firms and their stakeholders.
- *Risk and security* explore the evolving landscape of fintech-related risks, including cybersecurity, data breaches, fraud, and operational risks. This theme investigates risk management practices, regulatory frameworks, and technological solutions to ensure fintech systems' security and resilience.
- *International finance and trade* investigate fintech's impact on international finance, cross-border transactions, and global trade. This theme explores digital currencies, blockchain-based trade finance, and fintech's potential to promote financial inclusion in developing economies.
- *Financial centers and hubs* concentrate on how financial centers and hubs foster fintech innovation and entrepreneurship. This theme examines the strategies adopted by financial centers to attract fintech start-ups, the development of fintech ecosystems, and the competitive landscape among global financial hubs.
- Financial efficiency and productivity center on fintech's impact on financial efficiency, productivity, and cost reduction. This theme investigates automation, process optimization, and financial institutions' adoption of fintech solutions to improve operational efficiency.
- *Decentralized finance* investigates the emergence of DeFi and its potential to reshape traditional financial systems. This theme explores decentralized exchanges, smart contracts, tokenization, and the implications of blockchain technology for financial intermediaries.

Temporal Evolution of Fintech Themes and Future Research Directions

RQ5 examines the emerging trends and identifies gaps within the fintech research landscape. Table 2.7 presents the thematic evolution in fintech literature from 1980 to 2016 and 2017 to 2022. Analyzing the different themes alongside their corresponding metrics provides valuable insights for future research directions.

Technological advancements, financial inclusion, and access have emerged as influential themes, indicating their ongoing relevance. Future research can explore how technological advancements, such as AI, blockchain, and biometrics, can further enhance financial inclusion and expand access to underserved populations.

The surge in publications and citations within innovation and start-ups reflects the growing interest in disruptive innovations and entrepreneurial activities within the fintech space. Future research can delve into the challenges and opportunities faced by fintech start-ups, their impact on traditional financial institutions, and the implications for regulatory frameworks.

The enduring prominence of infrastructure and technology underscores their critical role in supporting fintech development. Future research can explore emerging technologies, such as quantum computing and the Internet of Things (IoT), and their potential impact on fintech infrastructure, security, and scalability.

Regulatory and compliance, business operations and strategies, and governance and policy have consistently attracted attention, highlighting their significance in shaping the fintech ecosystem. Future research can delve into the evolving regulatory landscape, including consumer protection, data privacy, and risk management issues, and examine effective strategies for fintech firms to navigate regulatory challenges.

Themes such as data and analytics, alternative finance, economic and global factors, research and analysis, and consumer behavior and preferences offer promising avenues for future research. Areas of exploration can include the ethical implications of data usage in fintech, the impact of alternative financing models on traditional banking systems, the influence of economic and geopolitical factors on fintech adoption, the development of robust research methodologies, and the understanding of consumer preferences and decision-making in the context of fintech services.

Emerging themes like sustainable finance, health and pandemics, and decentralized finance present exciting opportunities for future research. Studies can focus on integrating ESG considerations into fintech practices, fintech's role in healthcare and pandemic response, and DeFi's potential to reshape traditional financial systems.

By considering these themes' evolution and future research directions, scholars can contribute to advancing knowledge in the fintech domain, addressing emerging challenges, and exploring innovative solutions to drive the industry forward.

Summary and Conclusions

By offering a panoramic view of the fintech research landscape, this chapter has presented an overview of the existing research on fintech using a bibliometric approach. Fintech's rapid evolution has sparked an immense academic interest. Understanding the dynamics and trends within the fintech literature is crucial for gaining insights into this rapidly changing domain's advancements, challenges, and prospects.

RQ1 identifies the publication trends and citation patterns in the fintech literature. The findings indicate a dramatic increase in fintech research since 2016. *RQ2* examines the leading fintech authors and their affiliations. Pável Reyes-Mercado emerges as the most prolific author, followed closely by Douglas W. Arner and Mustafa Raza Rabbani. The United States, China, and the United Kingdom are the top three research hotspots contributing to fintech knowledge. *RQ3* investigates the knowledge foundation of fintech research. The findings indicate that the top-cited references have significantly influenced the understanding of fintech research by addressing crucial aspects, including ecosystem dynamics, regulatory implications, innovation forces, financial inclusion, and technological advancements, among others. *RQ4* explores the distribution of research output across different fintech themes. This chapter has categorized the extensive body of fintech literature into 23 distinct themes. *RQ5* identifies important research gaps for future scholarship.

The chapter discussions have revealed important insights, including identifying influential publications, prolific authors, and their affiliations. Additionally, the distribution of research output across different themes has provided valuable insights into the prominence and emerging trends in fintech research. More importantly, research gaps highlighted within the fintech literature present opportunities for future study, interdisciplinary collaborations, and exploring emerging trends in fintech.

This chapter can guide researchers in identifying research gaps and directing future inquiries, policymakers in formulating effective regulations and policies, and industry practitioners in understanding and leveraging fintech developments. However, despite providing valuable insights and contributions, this analysis has limitations. For example, the data collected are from Scopus. Expanding the databases used could enhance the analysis.

Discussion Questions

- Explain the contribution of bibliometrics in understanding the fintech research landscape.
- Discuss how integrating diverse disciplines contributes to an understanding of fintech.
- Explain the prominent themes and trends within fintech identified through the bibliometric analysis.
- Provide examples of how this study's findings can be leveraged to drive innovation and advancements in the financial industry.
- Identify potential research directions and areas for further exploration within fintech.

References

Ahmed, S., Alshater, M. M., El Ammari, A., & Hammami, H. (2022). Artificial intelligence and machine learning in finance: A bibliometric review. *Research in International Business and Finance*, *61*(October), 101646.

Albayati, H., Kim, S. K., & Rho, J. J. (2020). Accepting financial transactions using blockchain technology and cryptocurrency: A customer perspective approach. *Technology in Society*, *62*(August), 101320.

Anagnostopoulos, I. (2018). Fintech and regtech: Impact on regulators and banks. *Journal of Economics and Business*, *100*(November–December), 7–25.

Arner, D. W., Barberis, J., & Buckley, R. P. (2017). FinTech, RegTech, and the reconceptualization of financial regulation. *Northwestern Journal of International Law & Business*, *37*(3), 371–413.

Baker, H. K., Kumar, S., Pattnaik, D., & Pandey, N. (2022). The journal of accounting and public policy at 40: A bibliometric analysis. *Journal of Accounting and Public Policy*, *21*(July), 107003.

Boakye, E. A., Zhao, H., & Ahia, B. N. K. (2022). Emerging research on blockchain technology in finance; a conveyed evidence of bibliometric-based evaluations. *The Journal of High Technology Management Research*, *33*(2), 100437.

Buchak, G., Matvos, G., Piskorski, T., & Seru, A. (2018). Fintech, regulatory arbitrage, and the rise of shadow banks. *Journal of Financial Economics*, *130*(3), 453–483.

Chen, Y., & Bellavitis, C. (2020). Blockchain disruption and decentralized finance: The rise of decentralized business models. *Journal of Business Venturing Insights*, *13*(June), e00151.

Ellili, N. O. D. (2023). Correction to: Is there any association between FinTech and sustainability? Evidence from bibliometric review and content analysis. *Journal of Financial Services Marketing*. https://doi.org/10.1057/s41264-022-00200-w

Fuster, A., Plosser, M., Schnabl, P., & Vickery, J. (2019). The role of technology in mortgage lending. *Review of Financial Studies*, *32*(5), 1854–1899.

Gabor, D., & Brooks, S. (2017). The digital revolution in financial inclusion: International development in the fintech era. *New Political Economy*, *22*(4), 423–436.

García-Corral, F. J., Cordero-García, J. A., de Pablo-Valenciano, J., & Uribe-Toril, J. (2022). A bibliometric review of cryptocurrencies: How have they grown? *Financial Innovation*, *8*(1), 1–31.

Gomber, P., Kauffman, R. J., Parker, C., & Weber, B. W. (2018). On the fintech revolution: Interpreting the forces of innovation, disruption, and transformation in financial services. *Journal of Management Information Systems*, *35*(1), 220–265.

Gomber, P., Koch, J.-A., & Siering, M. (2017). Digital finance and FinTech: Current research and future research directions. *Journal of Business*, *87*(5), 537–580.

Goodell, J. W., Kumar, S., Lim, W. M., & Pattnaik, D. (2021). Artificial intelligence and machine learning in finance: Identifying foundations, themes, and research clusters from bibliometric analysis. *Journal of Behavioral and Experimental Finance*, *32*(C), 100577.

Jagtiani, J., & Lemieux, C. (2018). Do fintech lenders penetrate areas that are underserved by traditional banks? *Journal of Economics and Business*, *100*(November–December), 43–54.

Jain, D., Dash, M. K., & Thakur, K. S. (2021). Development of research agenda on demonetization based on bibliometric visualization. *International Journal of Emerging Markets*, *17*(10), 2584–2604.

Le, T. N.-L., Abakah, E. J. A., & Tiwari, A. K. (2021). Time and frequency domain connectedness and spill-over among fintech, green bonds and cryptocurrencies in the age of the fourth industrial revolution. *Technological Forecasting and Social Change*, *162*(January), 120382.

Lee, I., & Shin, Y. J. (2018). Fintech: Ecosystem, business models, investment decisions, and challenges. *Business Horizons*, *61*(1), 35–46.

Pattnaik, D., Kabir Hassan, M., Dsouza, A., Tiwari, A., & Devji, S. (2023). Ex-post facto analysis of cryptocurrency literature over a decade using bibliometric technique. *Technological Forecasting and Social Change*, *189*(C), 122339.

Pattnaik, D., Kumar, S. & Burton, B. (2021). Thirty years of the Australian Accounting Review: A bibliometric analysis. *Australian Accounting Review*, *31*(2), 150–164.

Pattnaik, D., Kumar, S., Burton, B., & Lim, W. M. (2022). Economic modelling at thirty-five: A retrospective bibliometric survey. *Economic Modelling*, *107*, 105712.

Schueffel, P. (2016). Taming the beast: A scientific definition of fintech. *Journal of Innovation Management*, *4*(4), 32–54.

Tang, H. (2019). Peer-to-peer lenders versus banks: Substitutes or complements? *The Review of Financial Studies*, *32*(5), 1900–1938.

Chapter 3

Use Cases in Fintech[1]

Fan Liu[a] *and Angela C. Lyons*[b]

[a]Xi'an Jiaotong-Liverpool University, China
[b]University of Illinois Urbana-Champaign, USA

Abstract

This chapter examines three common fintech use cases transforming the financial industry. First, the chapter introduces fintech's role in enhancing financial services and promoting financial inclusion, especially through digital platforms. Second, it investigates various fintech applications that support financial institution management by harnessing the power of artificial intelligence (AI) and machine learning (ML). Finally, the chapter explores fintech use cases related to the regulatory environment, including regulatory technology (regtech), blockchain technology, and cryptocurrencies. The insights presented in this chapter cater to researchers and practitioners keen on better understanding fintech's diverse applications in the ever-evolving financial industry landscape.

Keywords: Fintech; financial services; financial inclusion; financial institution management; regtech

Introduction

Technology innovation and its subsequent adoption have historically been pivotal drivers of economic growth (Romer, 1990; You et al., 2019). In this context, fintech plays a central role in shaping the future landscape of the financial industry (Lee & Shin, 2018; Murinde et al., 2022). It increasingly garners attention from consumers, merchants, regulatory bodies, and policymakers (Geranio, 2017; Kanga et al., 2022). Data from the International Monetary Fund (IMF) reveal a remarkable fourfold increase in the market values of fintech companies since the

[1]This chapter was supported by the Research Development Fund (Grant No. RDF-22-02-044) from Xi'an Jiaotong-Liverpool University. The authors thank Ruijia Tian and Yiyu Feng for excellent research assistance in the early stages of this work.

The Emerald Handbook of Fintech, 43–64

doi:10.1108/978-1-83753-608-520241005

global financial crisis (GFC) of 2007–2009, with fintechs outperforming companies in many other sectors (He et al., 2017). Fintech's investment landscape has also remained strong over the past decade, reaching a record-high in 2021 of $247.2 billion invested across 7,843 deals (KPMG, 2023). This steadfast growth underscores the enduring significance and resilience of the fintech sector in the modern economy (Kanga et al., 2022).

By combining financial services with automated technology, fintech has been a transformative force, delivering cost-saving solutions to financial institutions while also reducing information asymmetries (Ahamed & Mallick, 2019; Banna et al., 2022; Liu & Villamil, 2021) and enhancing operational efficiencies (Cheng et al., 2022). In financial management, using fintech, such as robo-advisors, has allowed the financial sector to streamline its investment processes and offer more affordable and transparent investment options to clients, especially those with modest wealth. From a customer service perspective, fintech initiatives have substantially reduced labor costs and provided more real-time support to enhance customers' experiences. A prime example of fintech's ability to reduce institutional costs, particularly labor-related expenses, is Bank of America's introduction of Erica, a chatbot designed to address fundamental customer inquiries (Belanche et al., 2019; Crosman, 2018).

By introducing innovative and more user-friendly financial tools, fintech ensures that an individual's economic status does not hinder access to and usage of basic financial services. These avant-garde financial solutions broaden the range of accessible financial products and services, eliminating economic impediments to accessing and using financial services. Moreover, fintech's integration enhances the overall efficacy of financial service delivery. This situation is evident in the seamless execution of digital transactions, rapid computation of financial data, and the implementation of advanced automated billing mechanisms, all of which have collectively contributed to a more streamlined and efficient financial infrastructure.

This chapter discusses three common use cases in fintech transforming the financial industry. First, it introduces fintech's role in augmenting financial services through digital innovation, especially digital platforms – including digital payments and transfers, lending, wealth management and insurance. Second, fintech applications that support the management of financial institutions are highlighted. Specifically, examples are showcased where artificial intelligence (AI) and machine learning (ML) have been leveraged to assist in risk assessment and management, "Know Your Customer" (KYC) processes, the fortification of brand and reputation management, and the detection of fraudulent activities. Finally, the chapter presents use cases related to the regulatory environment in fintech, including the emergence of regulatory technology (regtech), blockchain technology, and cryptocurrencies. The insights from this chapter provide a useful starting point for researchers and practitioners interested in exploring fintech's myriad of use cases and applications in more detail. It illuminates fintech's dynamic landscape, offering a compass to navigate the financial industry's ever-evolving ecosystem. Table 3.1 provides an overview and summary of the chapter.

Table 3.1. Common Uses of Fintech That Are Transforming the Financial Industry.

1. Fintech applications that augment financial services and advance financial inclusion through digital innovation, especially digital platforms
• Digital payments and transfers
• Digital lending
• Digital wealth management
• Digital insurance
2. Fintech applications that support firm management
• Risk assessment and management
• Know Your Customer (KYC) and identity authentication
• Brand and reputation management
• Fraud detection
3. Fintech applications that bolster the regulatory environment
• Regtech
• Blockchain and cryptocurrencies

Note: This table presents an overview of this chapter, highlighting three prevalent use cases in fintech that are reshaping the financial industry.

Fintech Use Cases That Advance Financial Services

In 2011, only about half of the world's adult population reported having access to formal financial services. Recent reports indicate that 76.2% now can access a formal financial account (Demirgüç-Kunt et al., 2022). This transformative shift embodies the concept of *financial inclusion* (FI), the availability of equal opportunities for accessing and using financial services. FI's overarching goal is to provide affordable and sustainable financial solutions to underrepresented populations such as unbanked and underbanked individuals (Liu & Walheer, 2022; Lyons et al., 2022; Nanda & Kaur, 2016). Notably, FI initiatives have brought billions of people into the financial system since 2010 (Klapper, 2018), with fintech playing a crucial role by catering to the financial needs and demands of previously untapped populations (Bollaert et al., 2021; Dos Santos & Kvangraven, 2017; Guild, 2017; Kanga et al., 2022; Klapper, 2018; Liu & Walheer, 2022; Lyons et al., 2022; Lyons & Kass-Hanna, 2022).

However, the challenge of limited financial access extends beyond individuals. It also affects micro-, small-, and medium-sized enterprises (MSMEs), particularly in developing economies (World Bank, 2013). MSMEs have been widely recognized as critical economic development and poverty alleviation catalysts in these countries. According to UNCTAD (2021), MSMEs account for 90% of businesses, 60–70% of employment, and 50% of gross domestic product (GDP) worldwide.

In this sense, fintech has emerged as FI's enabler for individuals and MSMEs, ushering in a new era of financial instruments, such as digital payments and transfers, digital lending, digital wealth management, and insurtech, which will be briefly introduced in the following subsections. By alleviating the financial burdens individuals and MSMEs face, fintech provides a gateway to expanded financial products and services, allowing more people to access basic and advanced financial solutions. The following examples of digital financial services have radically changed the financial landscape in recent years. Bollaert et al. (2021) and Lyons and Kass-Hanna (2022) provide more detailed analyses.

Digital Payments and Transfers

Not surprisingly, Demirgüç-Kunt et al. (2022) report a global surge in the adoption of digital financial services. Currently, 64.1% of adults worldwide have embraced digital payments. Perhaps, most notably, the utilization of digital payments in developing economies has surged from 35% in 2014 to 57% in 2021. From the smallest merchants in rural areas to smallholder farmers, digital payments via mobile phones have become commonplace. Even among those still unbanked, one billion possess a mobile phone, and 480 million have internet access. These statistics reveal the potential for furthering financial inclusion via fintech and other digital solutions (Demirgüç-Kunt et al., 2018; Kass-Hanna et al., 2022).

Fintech also has ushered in major conveniences within and across many markets outside the financial sector. For example, digital payments have enabled healthcare facilities, even those in remote areas, to receive funds at minimal transaction costs, allowing them to expand their services to a broader population (World Health Organization, 2021). Similarly, in the retail sector, the convenience of online shopping during the COVID-19 pandemic led to substantial growth, with consumers spending $347 billion online with US retailers in the first half of 2020 (McKinsey & Company, 2020).

The efficiency of digital payments is particularly evident in China, where most businesses now accept digital payments. With two major competitors, Alipay and WeChat Pay, jointly holding a 92% market share in the digital payment industry, customers can seamlessly purchase a wide range of goods and services daily (Hsu & Li, 2020). In mature markets like Sweden, cash accounted for only 9% of total transactions by volume in 2020 (McKinsey & Company, 2020). This finding still underscores the widespread adoption of digital payments, even in mature markets that may not need to rely on digital payment methods.

Furthermore, digital transaction methods have revolutionized the financial landscape by expediting transactions and substantially reducing associated costs. Traditional payment mechanisms often entail a myriad of handling and intermediary transaction fees (Klein, 2022). However, the advent of advanced payment infrastructures and data science algorithms has led to substantial reductions in these expenses by financial institutions (Allen et al., 2021). Consequently, clients and financial entities can now retain a larger portion of their funds, enabling the reallocation of these resources to more pressing needs.

According to GSMA (2021), more than $2 billion is transacted digitally daily, with over $1 billion sent and received monthly for international remittances via mobile phones. In Africa, M-Pesa (M for mobile and pesa for money in Swahili) has become one of the world's most successful mobile money providers (Lyons & Kass-Hanna, 2022). It offers comprehensive branchless banking services that include deposits, withdrawals, money transfers, payments for goods and services, and access to savings and credit through mobile devices (Ndung'u, 2018).

Digital Lending

A particularly pervasive challenge experienced worldwide lies in the accessibility of viable lending solutions. Traditional financial institutions often exclude borrowers with limited or no credit history and individuals seeking smaller loan amounts to avoid default risk and the high costs associated with screening and monitoring. In recent years, fintech has provided financial institutions with cost-effective lending alternatives that reduce the costs and risks associated with information asymmetries (Ahamed & Mallick, 2019; Banna et al., 2022; Liu & Villamil, 2021). Notably, Fuster et al. (2019) reveal that fintech lenders in the United States saw their market share quadruple between 2010 and 2016, primarily because they could harness fintech's power to process mortgage loan applications faster than traditional banks, which allowed borrowers to refinance more quickly.

Fintech companies have also successfully offered lending opportunities to meet the borrowing needs of small- and medium-sized enterprises (SMEs), a segment that remains underserved by traditional banks (Bollaert et al., 2021; Lu, 2018). Jagtiani and Lemieux (2018) show that fintech lenders have successfully catered to geographical locations that traditional banks cannot reach. For instance, in China, Ant Group, formerly known as Ant Financial, owns the world's largest digital payment platform, Alipay, which extends substantial lines of credit in rural areas of China where traditional banking services have been limited (Hau et al., 2019). Another notable example is peer-to-peer (P2P) lending. Via crowdsourcing financing, P2P platforms connect investors and borrowers online, allowing them to set up lending agreements without involving a traditional financial institution (Lyons & Kass-Hanna, 2022).

Erel and Liebersohn (2022) provide a novel example of digital lending, the Paycheck Protection Program (PPP), that the US Small Business Administration (SBA) established and implemented with the support of the U.S. Department of the Treasury. The program provided SBA-backed loans to small businesses to assist them in meeting payroll obligations and keep their workforces employed during the COVID-19 pandemic. The program permitted several nontraditional lenders specializing in fintech to distribute PPP funds during this challenging time.

The banking sector has not remained passive in response to the rise of fintech innovations. Traditional banks have also undergone major transformations in recent years. They have proactively increased their investments in fintech and have been reshaping how they deliver financial services by leveraging fintech solutions (Lee et al., 2021). These transformations include establishing direct sales banks and shifting toward more streamlined digital transaction processes. Moreover, many banks have formed collaborative partnerships with fintech companies, striving to develop more successful hybrid business models (PwC, 2017).

Digital Wealth Management

Besides providing digital payments and lending, fintech is an important driver of innovation in wealth management, with robo-advisors playing a pivotal role (Lyons & Kass-Hanna, 2022). *Robo-advisors*, or intelligent investment advisors, are automated investment services designed to digitally interact with clients to gather financial information and choose suitable portfolio management products. The recommendations are determined via quantitative modeling and complex algorithms based on clients' personalized criteria, such as risk profile and investment objectives (Jung et al., 2018).

Traditionally, investors have sought advice from human financial advisors. However, human advisors sometimes face conflicts of interest, which can erode investor trust (Burke & Hung, 2019). Fisch et al. (2018) find that human financial advisors are often tempted by incentive-based compensation. They note that robo-advisors, driven by computer algorithms, can offer investment advice without potential conflicts while reaching more clients. Robo-advisors also typically favor passive portfolio management strategies that reduce transaction costs. This preference is relative to active portfolio management, which human advisors prefer.

Compared to human advisors, robo-advisors also offer other distinct advantages related to cost savings and increased transparency. For example, human financial advisors in the United States often charge advisory fees ranging from 1% to 2% of assets under management (AUM). In contrast, robo-advisors charge no more than 0.5%, and in some cases, nothing for smaller investors (Fisch et al., 2018). In addition, robo-advisors can continuously monitor their clients' portfolios in volatile markets and provide 24/7 access to financial services for every investor, a feat that is challenging for human advisors. They also can automatically rebalance portfolios based on data science algorithms, ensuring investment allocations align with clients' goals and adapt swiftly to market conditions and changes in demand (Fisch et al., 2018).

Besides cost savings and improved transparency, robo-advisors have made substantial strides in targeting the niche market of small investors who may not meet the minimum investment requirements established by traditional wealth management firms (Ludden et al., 2015; Jung et al., 2018). Human financial advisors often limit their services to clients with a minimum investment of at least $100,000, leaving many small investors unable to participate actively in the financial markets (Reiss, 2017). However, robo-advisor companies are willing to assist investors with minimum investable assets as low as $500 (e.g., Wealthfront) or even with no minimum balance requirement (e.g., Betterment), thus democratizing access to wealth management for small and lower-income investors (Bianchi & Brière, 2021; Fisch et al., 2018; Leonhardt, 2018; Lyons & Kass-Hanna, 2022; Oehler et al., 2022).

The success of independent robo-advisor companies has attracted diverse market players, including traditional asset management firms, banks, and high-tech companies worldwide, such as Vanguard, BlackRock, and Merrill Lynch (Fisch et al., 2018). The total assets managed by robo-advisors globally are projected to reach $2.76 trillion in 2023 (Statista, 2023).

The shift from traditional wealth management approaches toward fintech-based solutions like robo-advisors is expected to continue accelerating (Callaway, 2019). According to the EY Global e-Wealth Management Research Report (2023), over 40% of clients currently favor the virtual advisor interaction channel for financial planning and advice, a dramatic increase compared to the reported 12% in 2021. Since Betterment introduced its first major service in 2010, the robo-advisor market has amassed nearly $45 billion in AUM and continues to experience substantial growth (Allen et al., 2021).

Digital Insurance: Insurtech

Insurance companies have also observed a considerable shift in adopting fintech among their "most economically valuable customers" (Gulamhuseinwala et al., 2015). This heightened interest is reflected by the success of these firms in securing capital, as well as the recent and significant global increase in investments in insurtech (Lyons & Kass-Hanna, 2022). Notable examples include Lemonade, a well-known insurtech start-up that secured $300 million in funding in 2019, and ZhongAn Insurance, an online-only insurer in China that has amassed 460 million users since its inception in 2013 (Lin & Chen, 2020).

Insurers often face adverse selection and moral hazard problems. *Adverse selection* problems arise due to asymmetrical information, where a policyholder is priced in a specific risk group despite having a riskier profile. *Moral hazard* problems refer to policyholders exhibiting different attitudes or behaviors once covered by the insurance (Cortis et al., 2019). With the help of insurtech, including ML and AI techniques to analyze big data, the insurance industry is improving its pricing models to reduce these two problems and achieve better efficiency (Lin & Chen, 2020).

Today's technology generates vast amounts of data from various sources, including wearables like the Apple Watch. These data can be used for risk assessment, expanding beyond traditionally gathered data such as age, gender, location, car model, and claims experience to include biometric information like the number of steps, miles cycled, heart rate, blood pressure, and sleep data (Cortis et al., 2019). For instance, Lapetus Solutions, a US-based insurtech start-up, can determine a client's health status, disease susceptibility, and longevity directly from a 30-second video (Lapetus Solutions, 2023). This strategy appeals to customers and helps insurance providers mitigate unforeseen losses. The convergence of these advancements in digital financial services with precise health data metrics enhances financial service efficiency. It enables financial institutions to offer and deliver customers more personalized and accurate financial solutions.

Fintech Use Cases That Support Firm Management

Effective firm management can result in important benefits for financial institutions in terms of survival and development. In contrast, poor management can lead to diminished performance, financial insolvency, and even the onset of severe systematic risks. For example, operational risk events, including fraudulent activities, can result in substantial losses for the firm. In 2012, Bank of America and Citigroup incurred losses of $175.5 million and $22 million, respectively, due to operational risks. In 2013, Rabobank and Fondiaria-SAI experienced losses of $1 billion and 252 million Euros (Pakhchanyan, 2016). The 2008 Global Financial Crisis (GFC) which began with the collapse of Lehman Brothers (Wang et al., 2018), had a significant and negative impact on the global economy.

Unsurprisingly, the importance of quality firm management has garnered considerable attention from researchers and practitioners, especially within operations management. Quality firm management encompasses various aspects, including but not limited to product design and management, process management, and customer-centric approaches. All contribute to different dimensions of firm performance, such as financial performance, operational efficiency, product quality, and customer service (Nair, 2006). This section discusses four examples where fintech has supported firms' management and overall performance, with particular focus on financial institutions.

(1) *Risk assessment and management.* Fintech can play a crucial role in effectively assessing and managing a firm's risks.
(2) *KYC.* Fintech tools can enhance the KYC process, facilitating better understanding and management of customer relationships.
(3) *Brand and reputation management.* Fintech offers solutions to monitor and maintain a positive brand image and reputation and can assist when that image may be compromised.
(4) *Fraud detection.* Fintech can contribute to detecting and preventing fraudulent activities.

Risk Assessment and Management

Although integrating underrepresented populations into the financial system can expand financial institutions' market share and potentially boost profits (Ahamed et al., 2021; Sajid et al., 2023), providing financial services to unbanked and underbanked individuals can be costly. Liu and Villamil (2021) reveal that screening and monitoring costs associated with managing multiple small loans without collateral are considerably higher than those associated with managing a single large loan with collateral. Moreover, expanding branches to remote, unbanked areas also presents challenges in cost-effectively monitoring these distant locations (Brickley et al., 2003).

As discussed in the previous section, fintech provides innovative solutions to address these challenging management problems by reducing screening and monitoring costs, which are essential to financial institutions' functions, especially lending. Additionally, fintech has streamlined operations and cut costs by introducing branchless and mobile banking services to the market (Lyons & Kass-Hanna, 2022; Sajid et al., 2023; Zeidy, 2022).

Fintech also has played a pivotal role in driving cost reductions within financial institutions. Traditional payment methods, such as cash and checks, are time-consuming, particularly for large or interbank transactions (Hartatik & Aziz, 2021). This extended timeline primarily results from the regulatory diligence required to validate the authenticity and legitimacy of cash and checks. Consequently, customers often experience longer-than-average transaction clearance times. However, the emergence of digital payment methods has substantially increased the speed and efficiency of transactions. Digital payments eliminate the need to verify the authenticity of cash or worry about the security of cash or checks. Such financial innovation has substantially improved the operational efficiency of financial institutions.

Besides cost savings, fintech has made important contributions to transaction security. In the early days of digital payments, legitimate concerns arose about the security of these transactions. However, these concerns have been mitigated as technology advances, especially in incorporating biometric information (Zeidy, 2022). Financial institutions have adopted various advanced security measures to safeguard transaction data, including encryption, multifactor authentication, and real-time transaction monitoring. Available data indicate that financial institutions have reduced the risk of transaction data breaches to as low as 2% (Maurer & Hinck, 2020).

KYC and Identity Authentication

KYC processes necessitate documenting a client's identity, income, sources of funds, and other pertinent details. KYC aids financial institutions in managing risks, preventing fraud and illegal activities, and tailoring financial services to individual customer profiles. Regulations also mandate KYC to gather comprehensive customer information. Such identifications and KYC requirements can pose barriers for individuals and small businesses seeking access to financial services (Allen et al., 2021).

Fortunately, with the development of digital identity and electronic KYC (e-KYC) infrastructures, technology can mitigate such barriers and enhance financial inclusion (Arner et al., 2019). For example, India Stack (2024) provides a paperless e-KYC service to identify banking customers in India. Traditionally, KYC processes involved verifying proof of identity and address using photocopies of these documents, which required self-attested photocopies each time a customer opened a bank account or purchased insurance, among other financial transactions. The e-KYC service has eliminated the need for physical photocopies. Instead, customers can securely authenticate and share their electronic information in the Aadhaar system, operated by the Unique Identification Authority of India (2016). Allen et al. (2021) report an estimate from the Ministry of Finance of India, indicating that transitioning from traditional KYC to e-KYC in India reduced the cost of verifying customers from $15.00 to $0.50 and reduced the time spent on verifying customers from 5 days to seconds. India Post Payments Bank, expected to become the largest network promoting financial inclusion in the country, offers digital financial services and has simplified account opening using e-KYC (Arner et al., 2019).

Cloud services have also transformed the KYC process, substantially reducing personal data management costs and expediting loan application decision-making. ML algorithms are further employed to group customers based on their financial behavior and preferences using data collected through KYC. ML techniques allow financial institutions to improve their product offerings and customer engagement (Jain et al., 2023). Through cloud services, ML, and e-KYC, financial institutions can offer customers a more secure, efficient, and convenient method of identity verification, thereby enhancing the quality and effectiveness of their services.

Brand and Reputation Management

Brand and reputation are invaluable intangible corporate assets (Dowling, 1993). *Corporate reputation* refers to stakeholders' beliefs and attitudes about an organization (Money et al., 2017; Money & Hillenbrand, 2006; Nguyen et al., 2022), and financial institutions are not exempt from the need for brand and reputation management. Effective brand and reputation management can establish a positive image for financial institutions among the public and their clients (Davies & Miles, 1998).

Reputation carries financial and nonfinancial implications for financial institutions. Financially, reputation affects financial firms' profits, market share, and growth. Nonfinancially, it influences intentions to use services, customer retention, and loyalty (Nguyen et al., 2022). Moreover, brand and reputation management is particularly critical for financial institutions compared to other industries because it is closely tied to financial system stability and macroeconomic balance (Dell'Atti & Trotta, 2016). Therefore, effective brand and reputation management is imperative for financial institutions.

In the digital age, using sensitive financial data in technology introduces major risks that can damage a reputation and customer trust (Jain et al., 2023). Verizon (2019) reports that the financial industry has the highest number of incidences involving data losses. Notable cyberattacks include the theft of $81 million from the Central Bank of Bangladesh in February 2016 via transfer fraud and the 2019 Amazon Alexa and Capital One data breach that exposed credit card application data. These incidents resulted in direct costs, such as customer notification and post-breach customer protection, and indirect costs, including damage to reputation, loss of customer trust, and harm to the brand (Allen et al., 2021).

To this end, cybersecurity is one financial technology solution that can bolster brand and reputation management. *Cybersecurity* encompasses measures to safeguard data from unauthorized access, use, disclosure, disruption, modification, or destruction. Developing robust cybersecurity systems in financial institutions to protect sensitive information and reduce the risk of cyberattacks is crucial. This proactive step helps to prevent direct costs from such attacks and supports effective brand and reputation management (Jain et al., 2023).

Fraud Detection

Fraud detection is a critical concern in the financial industry, with common types of fraud including unauthorized transactions, phishing scams, and identity theft. Unauthorized transactions occur when an account holder does not initiate or approve banking or credit card transactions, resulting in financial losses. Research shows eight out of 10 mobile banking users are concerned about credit card fraud (Shevlin, 2021). In particular, customers can fall victim to phishing scams, leading to account takeovers, unauthorized transactions, or identity theft (TELUS International, 2022).

Fraud prevention is a top priority for financial institutions as it results in financial losses for banks, damages user experiences, and negatively impacts customer retention (TELUS International, 2022). Fortunately, several technologies can be employed for effective fraud detection in fintech. Cybersecurity is essential for identifying and preventing fraudulent activities such as phishing attacks and unauthorized access to financial information. ML is another valuable tool for training algorithms on extensive historical transaction data to recognize behavior patterns and detect fraudulent financial transactions (Allen et al., 2021; Grable & Lyons, 2018; Jain et al., 2023). ML and other types of big data analytics have become popular and useful tools for managing financial risk as they pertain to detecting existing fraud and predicting future financial crimes (HaratiNik et al., 2012).

Additionally, biometrics, frequently used to streamline the login and authentication process for financial services, play a crucial role in enhancing the security of online financial transactions and reducing fraud risk (Hizam et al., 2021). Biometrics can be used to detect and prevent fraudulent activities, including identity theft and account takeovers, while improving transaction security. Along this same line, the Internet of Things (IoT), which consists of interconnected devices capable of collecting and exchanging data, can be employed to detect and prevent fraudulent activities like unauthorized transactions and identity theft.

Finally, Natural Language Processing (NLP), a technology enabling computers to understand, interpret, and generate human language, is also being used to detect and prevent financial crimes such as money laundering (Jain et al., 2023; Kurum, 2023). Jain et al. (2023) provide additional comparisons of emerging technologies in fintech based on their purposes, use cases, and advantages for supporting firm management.

Fintech Use Cases That Support the Regulatory Environment

Regulators are responsible for overseeing the health of financial institutions, driven by two primary purposes: (1) safeguarding consumer interests and (2) upholding financial stability. Compared to regulatory oversight in other sectors, the supervision of the financial industry is notably more comprehensive. It encompasses off-site analysis of financial institutions' performance and extensive on-site inspections (Quintyn & Taylor, 2004). The effective and efficient execution of financial regulations remains an ongoing challenge. Governments continually evaluate and refine the policy and regulatory framework for the financial system, striving to maintain public trust in the system's safety and stability while preserving its flexibility and innovative potential (Organisation for Economic Co-operation and Development, 2010).

By contrast, financial institutions must also adhere to regulatory requirements apart from providing improved financial services and achieving high-quality management. Increasing efficiency to meet complex regulations is a persistent concern for the financial industry. Mishra and Reshef (2019) examine the professional experiences of central bank governors in the financial sector and provide considerable insights into the complexities of regulatory compliance. They use work experience as an indicator of preferences toward deregulation. Their findings reveal that governors with experience in the financial sector are associated with three times more deregulatory measures compared to those lacking financial experience. Fortunately, with the evolution of fintech, particularly involving regtech, financial institutions and consumers can benefit from innovative technology.

Another important concept in macroeconomics that is intricately linked to the regulatory environment and financial activities is the notion of money. Conventional textbooks define *money* as "the stock of assets that can be readily used to facilitate transactions." Money serves three fundamental functions: it acts as a store of value, a unit of account, and a medium of exchange (Mankiw, 2022). In 2009, a novel form of digital currency was introduced – bitcoin. Since then, amid the volatility in bitcoin's value, ongoing debates have persisted on whether bitcoin qualifies as a real currency (Mankiw, 2022; Yermack, 2015).

Bitcoin's introduction also brought to the forefront the technology that underpins it – blockchain, which has garnered substantial global acceptance. This technology's unique features, described later in this section, have resulted in its rapid development, diffusion, and adoption by the financial sector and other industries.

Regtech

Regtech encompasses the technical solutions designed to assist financial service providers in managing regulatory issues and the companies and organizations in developing and delivering such solutions (Bolton & Mintrom, 2023). Central to regtech is exploring how technology can achieve more effective regulatory outcomes (AFI, 2018). Regtech enhances risk management for regulatory compliance and streamlines adherence to government regulations (Bolton & Mintrom, 2023; Kurum, 2023). It involves automation and data-driven analysis of internal control systems, including compliance, risk management, audit functions, and internal and external reporting. Additionally, regtech can combat financial crime (Sumkovski, 2023).

A notable example of regtech's progressive implementation is the Electronic Data Gathering, Analysis, and Retrieval (EDGAR) system that the US Securities and Exchange Commission (SEC) introduced in the 1990s. This regulatory system mandated that firms electronically submit their financial statements via EDGAR, replacing the traditional practice of mailing paper copies to the SEC (Lai et al., 2023). The EDGAR public database now contains millions of public company and individual filings, substantially reducing investor information acquisition costs. This transformation has greatly increased the securities markets' efficiency, transparency, and fairness. The EDGAR system processes approximately 3,000 filings per day, annually serving up 3,000 terabytes of data to the public and accommodating an average of 40,000 new filers yearly (U.S. Securities and Exchange Commission, 2023). Fund managers have harnessed the capabilities of the EDGAR system to identify companies exhibiting abnormal stock returns and trading volumes (Chen et al., 2020).

Buckley et al. (2020) discuss the development of regtech in Europe, emphasizing its role in supporting extensive reporting requirements introduced after the GFC. During and after the crisis, regtech enhanced data protection, facilitated open banking to increase payment competition, and established a legislative framework for digital identification.

Although regtech originally focused on digitalizing manual reporting and compliance processes, its potential extends far beyond (Arner et al., 2017). Regtech innovations reduce firms' capital costs (Lai et al., 2023) and stimulate corporate mergers and acquisitions, particularly among growth firms, solo-bidder deals, and stock-based acquisitions (Gu et al., 2022). Regtech has recently been using AI and ML to reshape financial markets and improve institutional and market efficiencies (Adrian, 2021; Allen et al., 2021; Boukherouaa et al., 2021). Allen et al. (2021) and Bollaert et al. (2021) discuss fintech regulatory challenges.

Blockchain and Cryptocurrencies

Blockchain technology was initially developed as the underlying technology behind cryptocurrencies such as bitcoin. Blockchain technology has five distinctive features (Tapscott & Tapscott, 2017).

(1) *Decentralization.* Blockchain operates without intermediaries, granting all parties access to the entire database and transaction history. No single entity controls the data.

(2) *Peer-to-peer communication.* Communications occur directly between peers on the network, eliminating the need for a central node.
(3) *Transparency.* All transaction information is visible to all system users, each with a unique blockchain address.
(4) *Security.* Various computational algorithms ensure all transaction records are permanent, chronologically ordered, and available to all users on the network.
(5) *Automation.* Users can create algorithms and rules for automatic transaction execution between nodes.

Blockchain technology's first generation primarily provided cryptocurrencies with the function of a store of value. Subsequent generations have introduced more complex blockchain systems that allow cryptocurrencies to function as in-system currencies or tokens for user identification and verification (Howell et al., 2020). These decentralized fundraising mechanisms raise funds using cryptocurrencies and provide purchasing power within the blockchain-based system (Bogusz et al., 2020).

Blockchain's unique attributes apply to various areas beyond cryptocurrencies, including smart contracts and other financial services (Alam et al., 2021; Allen et al., 2021). According to He et al. (2017), based on blockchain technology, smart contracts offer increased speed, efficiency, and trust in contract execution, addressing issues like moral hazard and strategic default. Blockchain technology makes smart contracts self-executing and self-enforcing without intermediaries, reducing verification and enforcement costs.

Based on the diffusion of innovations theory, Allidina (2016) estimated that 2016 blockchain adoption within financial services had reached a rate of 13.5%. Research and Markets (2023) reports that the global blockchain market in the banking and financial services sector surged to an estimated value of nearly $2,034.1 million in 2021, representing a remarkable compound annual growth rate (CAGR) of 62.7% since 2016. Within the financial sector, financial institutions have harnessed blockchain to monitor transactions, reduce transaction costs, and improve client affordability (Alam et al., 2021; Allen et al., 2018), as well as ensure security and transparency while also streamlining international transactions (Javaid et al., 2022). Furthermore, blockchain has played a key role in evaluating credit, reducing dishonesty, addressing inconsistencies in compliance, and fostering openness, inclusivity, and security in credit services (Bogusz et al., 2020; Owen et al., 2019; Zhao, 2020). Blockchain technology's influence extends into other domains, including supply chain management, with notable applications in e-commerce and global trade and financing (Li et al., 2021).

Summary and Conclusion

This chapter introduced various fintech use cases. The key domains covered in this chapter included:

- *Augmentation of financial services.* Fintech is pivotal in enhancing financial services through digital platforms and applications. It has enabled financial inclusion, especially through digital financial inclusion, by providing convenient and efficient methods for digital payments, transfers, and access to basic financial and public services. Digital lending has improved efficiency and accessibility for SMEs and underserved populations. Digital wealth management offers advanced options for portfolio management, while insurtech is reshaping the insurance sector.
- *Support for financial institutions' management.* Fintech aids financial institutions in managing their operations more effectively. Advancements in AI and ML techniques have bolstered security measures, especially in risk assessment and management. AI and biometric verification help financial institutions "know their customers" better. Cybersecurity assists in brand and reputation management. Techniques like AI, ML, biometrics, cybersecurity, NLP, and the IoT are commonly used to detect fraud.
- *Bolstering of the regulatory environment.* Regtech has emerged as a valuable tool for achieving better regulatory outcomes, streamlining compliance, and offering cost-effective solutions for government legal supervision and industry regulatory compliance management. Initially developed as the technology behind cryptocurrencies, blockchain has applications in the financial sector and various other markets.

In conclusion, fintech represents a major technological innovation that has brought substantial benefits by expanding financial services cost-effectively and assisting financial institutions in different operational aspects. It provides individuals and businesses with a wider range of options for financial activities. Although challenges exist, ongoing technological development and regulatory adaptations are expected to address these challenges and continue reshaping the financial industry into a more advanced and inclusive ecosystem.

Discussion Questions

- List fintech's main use cases that enhance financial services and promote financial inclusion.
- List the areas where fintech applications can support and bolster financial institutions' management.
- Discuss fintech's role in supporting financial inclusion and sustainable growth.
- Describe how regtech can benefit legal supervision.
- Explain the relationship between blockchain technology and cryptocurrencies.

References

Adrian, T. (2021, October 29). *AI and regtech.* International Monetary Fund Virtual Workshop on AI & Finance. https://www.imf.org/en/News/Articles/2021/10/29/sp102921-ai-and-regtech

AFI. (2018). *Fintech for financial inclusion: A framework for digital financial transformation*. Alliance for Financial Inclusion. https://www.afi-global.org/wp-content/uploads/publications/2018-09/AFI_FinTech_Special%20Report_AW_digital.pdf

Ahamed, M. M., Ho, S. J., Mallick, S. K., & Roman, M. (2021). Inclusive banking, financial regulation and bank performance: Cross-country evidence. *Journal of Banking & Finance*, *124*(March), 1–20.

Ahamed, M. M., & Mallick, S. K. (2019). Is financial inclusion good for bank stability? International evidence. *Journal of Economic Behavior & Organization*, *157*(C), 403–427.

Alam, S., Shuaib, M., Khan, W. Z., Garg, S., Kaddoum, G., Shamim Hossain, M., & Zikria, Y. B. (2021). Blockchain-based initiatives: Current state and challenges. *Computer Networks*, *198*, 108395.

Allen, D. W. E., Berg, C., & Novak, M. (2018). Blockchain: An entangled political economy approach. *Journal of Public Finance and Public Choice*, *33*(2), 105–125.

Allen, F., Gu, X., & Jagtiani, J. (2021). A survey of fintech research and policy discussion. *Review of Corporate Finance*, *1*(3−4), 259–339.

Allidina, S. (2016, June 27). The future of blockchain in 8 charts. *Raconteur*. https://www.raconteur.net/latest/the-future-of-blockchain-in-8-charts

Arner, D. W., Barberis, J., & Buckey, R. P. (2017). FinTech, RegTech, and the reconceptualization of financial regulation. *Northwestern Journal of International Law & Business*, *37*(3), 371–414.

Arner, D. W., Zetzsche, D. A., Buckley, R. P., & Barberis, J. N. (2019). The identity challenge in finance: From analogue identity to digitized identification to digital KYC utilities. *European Business Organization Law Review*, *20*(1), 55–80.

Banna, H., Mia, M. A., Nourani, M., & Yarovay, L. (2022). Fintech-based financial inclusion and risk-taking of microfinance institutions (MFIs): Evidence from Sub-Saharan Africa. *Finance Research Letters*, *45*, 102149.

Belanche, D., Casaló, L. V., & Flavián, C. (2019). Artificial intelligence in FinTech: Understanding robo-advisors adoption among customers. *Industrial Management & Data Systems*, *119*(7), 1411–1430.

Bianchi, M., & Brière, M. (2021). *Robo-advising for small investors: Evidence from employee savings plans*. Working Paper 112-2021. Amundi Asset Management Research Center. https://research-center.amundi.com/article/robo-advising-small-investors-evidence-employee-savings-plans

Bogusz, C. I., Laurell, C., & Sandström, C. (2020). Tracking the digital evolution of entrepreneurial finance: The interplay between crowdfunding, blockchain technologies, cryptocurrencies, and initial coin offerings. *IEEE Transactions on Engineering Management*, *67*(4), 1099–1108.

Bollaert, H., Lopez-de-Silanes, F., & Schwienbacher, A. (2021). Fintech and access to finance. *Journal of Corporate Finance*, *68*, 101941.

Bolton, M., & Mintrom, M. (2023). RegTech and creating public value: Opportunities and challenges. *Policy Design and Practice*, *6*(3), 266–282.

Boukherouaa, E. B., Shabsigh, G., AlAjmi, K., Deodoro, J., Farias, A., Iskender, E. S., Mirestean, A. T., & Ravikumar, R. (2021). *Powering the digital economy: Opportunities and risks of artificial intelligence in finance*. Departmental Paper No 2021/024. International Monetary Fund.

Brickley, J. A., Linck, J. S., & Smith, C. W., Jr. (2003). Boundaries of the firm: Evidence from the banking industry. *Journal of Financial Economics*, *70*(3), 351–383.

Buckley, R. P., Arner, D. W., Zetzsche, D. A., & Weber, R. H. (2020). The road to regtech: The (astonishing) example of the European union. *Journal of Banking Regulation*, *21*(1), 26–36.

Burke, J., & Hung, A. A. (2019). Trust and financial advice. *Journal of Pension Economics and Finance*, *20*(1), 9–26.

Callaway, J. (2019). FinTech disruption: Opportunities to encourage financial responsibility. In J. Agnew & O. S. Mitchell (Eds.), *The disruptive impact of FinTech on retirement systems* (pp. 61–74). Wharton Pension Research Council: Oxford University Press. https://repository.upenn.edu/server/api/core/bitstreams/b3f3635e-54e7-4a79-97ab-41e26ad433d9/content

Chen, H., Cohen, L., Gurun, U., Lou, D., & Malloy, C. (2020). Iq from Ip: Simplifying search in portfolio choice. *Journal of Financial Economics*, *138*(1), 118–137.

Cheng, M., Qu, Y., Jiang, C., & Zhao, C. (2022). Is cloud computing the digital solution to the future of banking? *Journal of Financial Stability*, *63*, 101073.

Cortis, D., Debattista, J., Debono, J., & Farrell, M. (2019). InsurTech. In T. Lynn, J. G. Mooney, P. Rosati, & M. Cummins (Eds.), *Disrupting finance: FinTech and strategy in the 21st century*. Palgrave Studies in Digital Business & Enabling Technologies (pp. 71–84). Palgrave Macmillan. https://library.oapen.org/bitstream/handle/20.500.12657/23126/1/1007030.pdf#page=92

Crosman, P. (2018, June 13). Mad about Erica: Why a million people use Bank of America's chatbot. *American Banker*. https://www.americanbanker.com/news/mad-about-erica-why-a-million-people-use-bank-of-americas-chatbot

Davies, G., & Miles, L. (1998). Reputation management: Theory versus practice. *Corporate Reputation Review*, *2*(1), 16–27. https://doi.org/10.1057/palgrave.crr.1540064

Dell'Atti, S., & Trotta, A. (2016). *Managing reputation in the banking industry: Theory and practice*. Springer International Publishing. https://link.springer.com/content/pdf/10.1007/978-3-319-28256-5.pdf

Demirgüç-Kunt, A., Klapper, L., Singer, D., & Ansar, S. (2022). *The global findex database 2021: Financial inclusion, digital payments and resilience in the age of COVID-19*. The World Bank. https://elibrary.worldbank.org/doi/epdf/10.1596/978-1-4648-1897-4

Demirgüç-Kunt, A., Klapper, L., Singer, D., Ansar, S., & Hess, J. (2018). *The global findex database 2017: Measuring financial inclusion and the fintech revolution*. The World Bank. https://elibrary.worldbank.org/doi/abs/10.1596/978-1-4648-1259-0

Dos Santos, P. L., & Kvangraven, I. H. (2017). Better than cash, but beware the costs: Electronic payments systems and financial inclusion in developing economies. *Development and Change*, *48*(2), 205–227.

Dowling, G. R. (1993). Developing your company image into a corporate asset. *Long Range Planning*, *26*(2), 101–109.

Erel, I., & Liebersohn, J. (2022). Can FinTech reduce disparities in access to finance? Evidence from the Paycheck protection program. *Journal of Financial Economics*, *146*(1), 90–118.

EY Global e-Wealth Management Research Report. (2023). *When volatility causes complexity, how can wealth managers create opportunity*. EY. https://assets.ey.com/content/dam/ey-sites/ey-com/en_gl/noindex/ey-2023-global-wealth-research-report-final.pdf

Fisch, J. E., Labouré, M., & Turner, J. A. (2018). The emergence of the robo-advisor. In J. Agnew & O. S. Mitchell (Eds.), *The disruptive impact of FinTech on retirement systems* (pp. 13–37). Pension Research Council, The Wharton School of the University of Pennsylvania, Oxford University Press. https://repository.upenn.edu/prc_papers/10

Fuster, A., Plosser, M., Schnabl, P., & Vickery, J. (2019). The role of technology in mortgage lending. *Review of Financial Studies*, *32*(5), 1854–1899.

Geranio, M. (2017). Fintech in the exchange industry: Potential for disruption? *Masaryk University Journal of Law and Technology*, *11*(2), 245–266.

Grable, J. E., & Lyons, A. C. (2018). An introduction to big data. *Journal of Financial Service Professionals*, *72*(5), 17–20.

GSMA. (2021). *State of the industry report on mobile money 2021*. GSMA. https://www.gsma.com/mobilefordevelopment/wp-content/uploads/2021/03/GSMA_State-of-the-Industry-Report-on-Mobile-Money-2021_Full-report.pdf

Gu, M., Li, D., & Ni, X. (2022). Too much to learn? The (Un)intended consequences of RegTech development on mergers and acquisitions. *Journal of Corporate Finance*, *76*, 102276.

Guild, J. (2017). Fintech and the future of finance. *Asian Journal of Public Affairs*, *10*(1), 52–65.

Gulamhuseinwala, I., Bull, T., & Lewis, S. (2015). FinTech is gaining traction and young, high-income users are the early adopters. *Journal of Financial Perspectives*, *3*(3), 16–23.

HaratiNik, M. R., Akrami, M., Khadivi, S., & Shajar, M. (2012). Fuzzgy: A hybrid model for credit card fraud detection. In *6th international symposium on telecommunications (IST)* (pp. 1088–1093). IEEE. https://ieeexplore.ieee.org/abstract/document/6483148

Hartatik, N. F., & Aziz, A. (2021). Go-Payment: Towards cashless payment system for smart village application in Indonesia. In *2021, the 3rd international conference on cybernetics and intelligent systems (ICORIS)* (pp. 1–6). IEEE. https://ieeexplore.ieee.org/document/9649644

Hau, H., Huang, Y., Shan, H., & Sheng, Z. (2019). How FinTech enters China's credit market. *AEA Papers and Proceedings*, *109*, 60–64.

He, D., Leckow, R., Haksar, V., Mancini Griffoli, T., Jenkinson, N., Kashima, M., Khiaonarong, T., Rochon, C., & Tourpe, H. (2017). Fintech and financial services: Initial considerations. *International Monetary Fund Staff Discussion Note 17/05*, 1–49.

Hizam, S. M., Ahmed, W., Fahad, M., Akter, H., Sentosa, I., & Ali, J. (2021). User behavior assessment towards biometric facial recognition system: A SEM-neural network approach. In K. Arai (Ed.), *Advances in information and communication: Proceedings of the 2021 future of information and communication conference (FICC)* (Vol. 2, pp. 1037–1050). Springer International Publishing.

Howell, S. T., Niessner, M., & Yermack, D. (2020). Initial coin offerings: Financing growth with cryptocurrency token sales. *Review of Financial Studies*, *33*(9), 3925–3974.

Hsu, S., & Li, J. (2020). *China's fintech explosion: Disruption, innovation, and survival*. Columbia University Press. https://doi.org/10.7312/hsu-19656l

India Stack. (2024). *Identity*. https://indiastack.org/identity.html

Jagtiani, J., & Lemieux, C. (2018). Do fintech lenders penetrate areas that are underserved by traditional banks? *Journal of Economics and Business*, *100*, 43–54.

Jain, R., Prajapati, D., & Dangi, A. (2023). Transforming the financial sector: A review of recent advancements in FinTech. *International Journal for Research Trends and Innovation*, *8*(2), 250–266.

Javaid, M., Haleem, A., Singh, R. P., Suman, R., & Khan, S. (2022). A review of blockchain technology applications for financial services. *BenchCouncil Transactions on Benchmarks, Standards and Evaluations*, *2*(3), 100073.

Jung, D., Dorner, V., Glaser, F., & Morana, S. (2018). Robo-advisory: Digitalization and automation of financial advisory. *Business & Information Systems Engineering*, *60*(1), 81–86.

Kanga, D., Oughton, C., Harris, L., & Murinde, V. (2022). The diffusion of fintech, financial inclusion and income per capita. *The European Journal of Finance*, *28*(1), 108–136.

Kass-Hanna, J., Lyons, A. C., & Liu, F. (2022). Building financial resilience through financial and digital literacy in South Asia and Sub-Saharan Africa. *Emerging Markets Review*, *51*(Part A), 100846.

Klapper, L. (2018, August 8). How this one change can help people fight poverty? *World Economic Forum*. https://www.weforum.org/agenda/2018/08/reduce-poverty-give-poor-people-bank-accounts-leora-klapper/

Klein, A. (2022). China's payment reform and its implications for other countries. In D. Dollar & Y. Huang (Eds.), *The digital financial revolution in China* (pp. 45–82). Brookings Institution Press.

KPMG. (2023, July). *Pulse of fintech H1'23: Biannual analysis of global fintech investments*. KPMG. https://kpmg.com/xx/en/home/industries/financial-services/pulse-of-fintech.html

Kurum, E. (2023). RegTech solutions and AML compliance: What future for financial crime? *Journal of Financial Crime*, *30*(3), 776–794.

Lai, S., Lin, C., & Ma, X. (2023). Regtech adoption and the cost of capital. *Management Science*. Forthcoming. https://doi.org/10.1287/mnsc.2022.4660

Lapetus Solutions. (2023). *Facial analytics*. Lapetus Solutions Inc. https://lapetussolutions.com/facial-analytics/

Lee, C.-C., Li, X., Yu, C.-H., & Zhao, J. (2021). Does fintech innovation improve bank efficiency? Evidence from China's banking industry. *International Review of Economics & Finance*, *74*, 468–483.

Lee, In, & Shin, Y. J. (2018). Fintech: Ecosystem, business models, investment decisions, and challenges. *Business Horizons*, *61*(1), 35–46.

Leonhardt, M. (2018, July 9). This is the best robo-advisor for every investor, from beginner to advanced. *Money*. https://money.com/best-robo-advisors-beginner-advanced-2018/

Li, Z., Zhong, R. Y., Tian, Z. G., Dai, H.-N., Barenji, A. V., & Huang, G. Q. (2021). Industrial blockchain: A state-of-the-art survey. *Robotics and Computer-Integrated Manufacturing*, *70*(August), 102124.

Lin, L., & Chen, C. (2020, March). The promise and perils of InsurTech. *Singapore Journal of Legal Studies*, 115–142.

Liu, F., & Villamil, A. (2021). *Microfinance in the U.S.* SSRN Working Paper. https://papers.ssrn.com/sol3/papers.cfm?abstract_id=4219367

Liu, F., & Walheer, B. (2022). Financial inclusion, financial technology, and economic development: A composite index approach. *Empirical Economics*, *63*(3), 1457–1487.

Lu, L. (2018). Promoting SME finance in the context of fintech revolution: A case study of the UK's practice and regulation. *Banking & Finance Law Review*, *33*(3), 317–343.

Ludden, C., Thompson, K., & Mohsin, I. (2015). *The rise of robo-advice: Changing the concept of wealth management*. Accenture Research. https://vdocuments.mx/the-rise-of-robo-advice-changing-the-concept-of-wealth-management-a-t20160509t220506zw.html?page=12

Lyons, A. C., & Kass-Hanna, J. (2022). The evolution of financial services in the digital age. In J. E. Grable & S. Chatterjee (Eds.), *De Gruyter handbook of personal finance* (pp. 405–430). De Gruyter.

Lyons, A. C., Kass-Hanna, J., & Ana, F. (2022). Fintech development and savings, borrowing, and remittances: A comparative study of emerging economies. *Emerging Markets Review*, *51*, 100842.

Mankiw, N. G. (2022). *Macroeconomics* (11th ed.). Worth Publishers Macmillan Learning.

Maurer, T., & Hinck, G. (2020). *Cloud 3: Cloud security*. Carnegie Endowment for International Peace. https://www.jstor.org/stable/resrep25787.9

McKinsey and Company. (2020). *Global banking practice – The 2020 McKinsey global payments report*. https://www.mckinsey.com/~/media/mckinsey/industries/financial%20services/our%20insights/accelerating%20winds%20of%20change%20in%20global%20payments/2020-mckinsey-global-payments-report-vf.pdf

Mishra, P., & Reshef, A. (2019). How do Central Bank governors matter? Regulation and the financial sector. *Journal of Money, Credit, and Banking*, *51*(2–3), 369–402.

Money, K., & Hillenbrand, C. (2006). Using reputation measurement to create value: An analysis and integration of existing measures. *Journal of General Management*, *32*(1), 1–12.

Money, K., Saraeva, A., Garnelo-Gomez, I., Pain, S., & Hillenbrand, C. (2017). Corporate reputation past and future: A review and integration of existing literature and a framework for future research. *Corporate Reputation Review*, *20*(3–4), 193–211.

Murinde, V., Rizopoulos, E., & Zachariadis, M. (2022). The impact of the FinTech revolution on the future of banking: Opportunities and risks. *International Review of Financial Analysis*, *81*, 102103.

Nair, A. (2006). Meta-analysis of the relationship between quality management practices and firm performance – Implications for quality management theory development. *Journal of Operations Management*, *24*(6), 948–975.

Nanda, K., & Kaur, M. (2016). Financial inclusion and human development: A cross-country evidence. *Management and Labour Studies*, *41*(2), 127–153. https://doi.org/10.1177/0258042X16658734

Ndung'u, N. (2018). The M-pesa technological revolution for financial services in Kenya: A platform for financial inclusion. In D. L. K. Chuen & R. Deng (Eds.), *Handbook of blockchain, digital finance, and inclusion* (Vol. 1, pp. 37–56). Academic Press.

Nguyen, Y. T. H., Tapanainen, T., & Nguyen, H. T. T. (2022). Reputation and its consequences in fintech services: The case of mobile banking. *International Journal of Bank Marketing*, *40*(7), 1364–1397.

Oehler, A., Horn, M., & Wendt, S. (2022). Investor characteristics and their impact on the decision to use a robo-advisor. *Journal of Financial Services Research*, *62*(1), 91–125.

Organisation for Economic Co-operation and Development. (2010). *Policy framework for effective and efficient financial regulation: General guidance and high-level checklist*. https://www.oecd.org/finance/financial-markets/44362818.pdf

Owen, R., Mac an Bhaird, C., Hussain, J., & Botelho, T. (2019). Blockchain and other innovations in entrepreneurial finance: Implications for future policy. *Strategic Change*, *28*(1), 5–8.

Pakhchanyan, S. (2016). Operational risk management in financial institutions: A literature review. *International Journal of Financial Studies*, *4*(4), 1–21. https://doi.org/10.3390/ijfs4040020

PwC. (2017). Summary of the 2017 global FinTech survey in China. https://www.pwccn.com/zh/financial-services/fintech/global-fintech-survey-chinasummary-2017.pdf

Quintyn, M., & Taylor, M. W. (2004). *Should financial sector regulators be independent?* Economic Issues. No. 32. International Monetary Fund. https://www.imf.org/external/pubs/ft/issues/issues32/index.htm

Reiss, D. (2017, October 5). Getting financial advice when you have less than $100,000 to invest. *U.S. News*. https://money.usnews.com/investing/investing-101/articles/2017-10-05/getting-financial-advice-when-you-have-less-than-100-000-to-invest

Research and Markets. (2023, January 11). *Blockchain in banking and financial services global market report 2023: Increasing demand for real-time fund transfers bolsters growth*. Research and Markets. https://www.globenewswire.com/en/news-release/2023/01/11/2586769/28124/en/Blockchain-In-Banking-And-Financial-Services-Global-Market-Report-2023-Increasing-Demand-for-Real-Time-Fund-Transfers-Bolsters-Growth.html

Romer, P. M. (1990). Endogenous technological change. *Journal of Political Economy*, *98*(5, Part 2), S71–S102.

Sajid, R., Ayub, H., Malik, B. F., & Ellahi, A. (2023). The role of fintech on bank risk-taking: Mediating role of bank's operating efficiency. *Human Behavior and Emerging Technologies*, *2023*, 1–11. https://doi.org/10.1155/2023/7059307

Shevlin, R. (2021, July 29). Mobile banking adoption in the United States has skyrocketed (but so have fraud concerns). *Forbes*. https://www.forbes.com/sites/ronshevlin/2021/07/29/mobile-banking-adoption-has-skyrocketed-but-so-have-fraud-concerns-what-can-banks-do/?sh=9a19355dc61d

Statista. (2023). *Robo-advisors worldwide*. https://www.statista.com/outlook/dmo/fintech/digital-investment/robo-advisors/worldwide

Sumkovski, I. (2023). The use of RegTech in fighting financial crime. *Journal of Financial Compliance*, *6*(2), 138–147.

Tapscott, A., & Tapscott, D. (2017). How blockchain is changing finance. *Harvard Business Review*, *1*(9), 2–5. https://capital.report/Resources/Whitepapers/40fc8a6a-cdbd-47e6-83f6-74e2a9d36ccc_finance_topic2_source2.pdf

TELUS International. (2022, September 23). How is AI transforming fraud detection in banks? *TELUS International*. https://www.telusinternational.com/insights/trust-and-safety/article/ai-fraud-detection-in-banks

UNCTAD. (2021). MSMEs: Key to an inclusive and sustainable recovery. Micro-, Small and Medium-sized Enterprises Day 2021. https://unctad.org/system/files/information-document/diaeed_2021_06_28_en_concept_note_0.pdf

Unique Identification Authority of India. (2016, May). Aadhaar e-KYC: API specification-version 2.0. https://uidai.gov.in/images/aadhaar_ekyc_api_2_0.pdf

U.S. Securities and Exchange Commission. (2023). *About EDGAR*. https://www.sec.gov/edgar/about

Verizon. (2019). 2019 data breach investigations report (DBIR): Results and analysis. *Verizon*. https://www.verizon.com/business/resources/reports/dbir/2019/results-and-analysis/

Wang, G.-J., Jiang, Z.-Q., Lin, M., Xie, C., & Eugene Stanley, H. (2018). Interconnectedness and systemic risk of China's financial institutions. *Emerging Markets Review*, *35*, 1–18.

World Bank. (2013). *Doing business 2014: Understanding regulations for small and medium-size enterprises*. The World Bank Group. https://archive.doingbusiness.org/content/dam/doingBusiness/media/Annual-Reports/English/DB14-Full-Report.pdf

World Health Organization. (2021). *Digital technologies for health financing: What are the benefits and risks for UHC? Some initial reflections*. Health Financing Working Paper No. 19. World Health Organization. https://iris.who.int/handle/10665/343505

Yermack, D. (2015). Is bitcoin a real currency? In D. K. C. Lee (Ed.), *The handbook of digital currency* (pp. 31–44). Elsevier.

You, K., Bianco, S. D., Lin, Z., & Amankwah-Amoah, J. (2019). Bridging technology divide to improve business environment: Insights from African Nations. *Journal of Business Research*, *97*(C), 268–280.

Zeidy, I. A. (2022). *The role of financial technology (FINTECH) in changing financial industry and increasing efficiency in the economy*. COMESA Monetary Institute. https://www.comesa.int/wp-content/uploads/2022/05/The-Role-of-Financial-Technology.pdf

Zhao, Y. (2020). Research on personal credit evaluation of internet finance based on blockchain and decision tree algorithm. *EURASIP Journal on Wireless Communications and Networking*, *2020*(213), 1–12.

Chapter 4

Regtech Frontiers: Innovations, Trends, and Insights Redefining Compliance

Dimitrios Salampasis[a] *and Georgios Samakovitis*[b]

[a]Swinburne University of Technology, Australia
[b]University of Greenwich, UK

Abstract

This chapter discusses the contributions and challenges involving regulatory technology (regtech) in financial services. It explores the salient areas where regtech can and should focus, observing existing and forthcoming industry, technology, and legal developments. This chapter outlines regtech use cases to clarify the shaping of that industry sector. It draws on developments in industry and academia, where significant research sets the tone and direction of technological solutions and regulatory drivers. A brief critical account of the benefits and challenges in regtech is offered. This chapter presents potential future directions, focusing on the salient areas of environmental, social, and governance (ESG), cryptocurrency, and decentralized compliance.

Keywords: Fintech; regtech; compliance; financial regulation; emerging technologies

Introduction

Developments emerging from technological advancements have elevated competitive dynamics within the financial services sector to a new level. The emergence of technology-driven business models and disruptive ecosystem changes aiming at inherently transforming the industry has put substantial pressure on incumbents to examine their strategies, organizational capabilities, and cultures, ultimately redefining the purpose of their existence and role within the broader financial system.

The Emerald Handbook of Fintech, 65–87

doi:10.1108/978-1-83753-608-520241008

The global financial crisis (GFC) of 2007–2009 resulted in a massive erosion of public trust in financial institutions (Baxter, 2016). The crisis also led to major increases in the volume and complexity of financial regulation, signaling a new era of regulatory oversight (Eggert, 2014; O'Brien, 2017). The more recent events of the global COVID-19 pandemic and Russia's invasion of Ukraine, including the associated sanctions on individuals and organizations, have contributed to increased global instability, igniting a spiral of developments in effective risk management practices. Financial institutions globally have faced considerable pressure due to the ever-perplexing, evolving, changing, and costly supervisory, regulatory, and compliance requirements imposed by regulatory and supervisory authorities, resulting in substantial difficulties in diligently monitoring and reporting to ensure compliance.

At the same time, the international financial system has experienced turbulence due to the rise of a new digital finance ecosystem characterized by the high speed, transformation, and systemic risk inherent to digital innovations and emerging digital finance business models. Digital finance has three pillars: (1) new players (stakeholders), (2) new assets, and (3) new infrastructures. Each pillar contributes to developing a suite of financial activities in the form of technical services or various financial products and services. Entities usually develop such services in-house or under strategic partnerships among fintechs, incumbents, and big techs, often in a fragmented and unregulated manner (Beau, 2023).

All these conditions set the stage and foundations for the materialization of fintech. They also seeded the need for substantial regulatory transformation and the potential for financial technologies to be applied within regulation and compliance, inspiring developments and effective mechanisms for novel regtech deployment.

The remainder of this chapter is structured as follows. The first section discusses the main pressure points and transitions associated with regtech's emergence and the need to incorporate digital technologies in regulatory solutions. Next, it brings together insights from the extant literature trying to codify the definition, value proposition, and various discourses revolving around regtech. The following section provides an overview of the benefits and challenges that financial institutions, regulators, and supervisors need to consider when adopting and integrating regtech solutions. A typology of the most prominent use cases of regtech is then offered, aiming to set clearer boundaries across different implementation motivations and to inform a better understanding of technological trajectories in future regtech applications. This chapter closes by discussing new dimensions and regtech's future and providing concluding remarks.

Pressure Points and Transitions

Regulation in financial services traditionally sits between (1) consumer protection, (2) support of a healthy and secure environment conducive to business growth and innovation, and (3) compliance monitoring and sanctioning. Legal compliance largely drives regulation. Its role is *reactive* (i.e., responding to events and occurrences in the financial transactions ecosystem) and *proactive* (i.e., scaffolding the relevant legal compliance frameworks to support present and forthcoming market and technological developments). This is the contextual perimeter where regtech, the technological tooling for facilitating regulatory tasks and overcoming related challenges, becomes critical.

The financial services industry and the associated financial regulations have experienced a series of major transitions that have encouraged and further pivoted initiatives around incorporating digital technologies in shaping regulatory and supervisory schemes. These unfolding transitions and pressure points originated within an international environment driven by complexity, uncertainty, and risk. Economic and geopolitical tensions and the exponential growth of digital technologies have opened pathways for new market entrants, business models, security levels, cybersecurity, and privacy risks, encouraging collaboration between regulators and financial services institutions.

The increasing volume of risk management, reporting, and compliance requirements imposed by regulatory and supervisory authorities worldwide put pressure on financial institutions and fintech stakeholders to explore novel and more effective ways of delivering on regulatory monitoring, compliance, and risk management (Becker & Buchkremer, 2018). Simultaneously, this pressure increases compliance costs that affect budgets, especially during global recession and slow economic development. Moreover, the increasing imposition of fines due to noncompliance, misconduct, and poor behavior is pushing stakeholders and policymakers to look for low-cost but high-quality solutions to cater to regulatory, compliance, and supervisory obligations attempting to put derisking strategies in place while battling with existing poor compliance practices and corrosive cultures. According to SteelEye's inaugural Fine Tracker, five key regulators imposed financial penalties during 2022 exceeding $7 billion (Chmiel, 2023). Fenergo's research shows a 52% increase in global anti-money laundering (AML)-related fines in 2022 ($4.15 billion), with a total of $56.1 billion for AML from Markets in Financial Instruments Directive (MiFID), environmental, social, and governance (ESG), and data privacy compliance breaches since the GFC (Fenergo, 2023). The increased attention to financial regulation and the intensified endeavors by regulators to scrutinize and penalize financial institutions for compliance breaches, malpractices, and violations require high-quality and efficient reporting accuracy, along with digital capabilities to navigate across the complexities, heterogeneities, and volumes of data received from the market.

Given these observations, classifying the pressure points (themes) in the regtech industry can help navigate the landscape. This kind of classification is primarily informed at three dimensions: (1) market developments in the wider fintech space, (2) opportunities for innovative financial products and services, and (3) new threat vectors that surface as side effects of (2) above or even as new criminal business models. These dimensions are briefly outlined below, with the above three dimensions cutting across themes.

- *Data sharing.* Driven primarily by anti-FinCrime requirements, the need for data sharing among financial institutions and between industry and regulators is ubiquitous. The persistent problem, especially money laundering, inadvertently raises questions about the efficacy of existing technological solutions and resident regulatory frameworks' suitability for data protection and privacy. At the intersection of the two, technological developments in areas such as confidential data pooling (ACPR, 2022; FATF, 2021) and federated learning (Ludwig & Baracaldo, 2022) seek ways to deliver shared ecosystems of actionable intelligence.

- *The volume of available data.* The data collected, stored, and processed, together with the abundance of Open-Source INTelligence (OSINT), substantially raise the importance of advanced data privacy, anonymization, and cybersecurity. An urgent need exists for data sharing between fintechs and regulators for anti-financial crime. Additionally, strong motivation exists for privacy-preserving technologies (PPTs) to be implemented across the entire fintech value chain, from transactions to entity resolution and onboarding. A large body of literature in computer science (Carvalho et al., 2022; Ferradi et al., 2022) seeks to leverage data-driven intelligence without compromising identity or other sensitive data features.
- *Diversity and complexity.* The increased diversity and complexity of fintech offerings alter the compliance risk profile of the financial product space and call for commensurate complexity in regulating these products. Since most new products concern cross-border interaction, regulatory complexity is further increased. Competition in the fintech space also presents consumers and businesses with opportunities for real-time onboarding, presenting regulators with an acute problem in real-time monitoring and intervention despite being highly desirable to the end user.
- *New threat vectors.* Directly emanating diversity and complexity, novel affordances of such new products and services often introduce new vulnerabilities and, in so doing, inform new threat vectors. The decentralized finance (DeFi) space is acutely manifesting this situation, hosting new industry players that remain largely unregulated. A notable example is cryptocurrencies, which are associated with money laundering activities and purchases through the dark web. Fenergo's research shows a 92% rise in fines issued to crypto-related financial institutions and employees, approaching about $193 million (Fenergo, 2023). Money laundering, terrorism financing, and proliferation financing remain at the forefront of compliance requirements and are among the highest risks for financial institutions. According to the United Nations Office on Drugs and Crime estimates, the money laundered globally in 1 year ranges between 2% and 5% of global gross domestic product (GDP) or between $800 billion and $2 trillion.
- *Cost, implementation, and monitoring.* The wide spectrum of established regulatory requirements is costly and suffers in implementation and monitoring speed, which damages customer experience and product attractiveness (Kshetri & Voas, 2022). Such requirements mainly relate to reporting, transactional monitoring, client identity management, data protection, and risk management. These requirements necessitate advanced technological solutions in the

regulatory space, especially given the volume and complexity of available data, as outlined in (2) above.

- *Cross-jurisdictional compliance.* The cross-border nature of most new fintech offerings necessitates more precise cross-jurisdictional compliance for products and services. This situation highlights the critical need for modern regulatory frameworks and onboarding mechanisms to accommodate far more complex and interwoven rules to support compliant operations across jurisdictions. This task requires a heavier technological contribution.

The above taxonomy of pressure themes is nonexhaustive, as other external conditions contribute to the apparent complexities in regtech. It was compiled to accommodate a commercially minded viewpoint, especially since regulatory technologies seek to support regulation's aim of consumer protection, a healthy and secure environment for business, and compliance monitoring. A discussion of other pressure themes follows.

Debanking and Other Social and Geopolitical Drivers

Geopolitical and macroeconomic conditions are associated with regtech's growth. Global sanctions disrupted supply chains. High inflation and the rising cost of living have accelerated the growth of fraud and criminal activities beyond money laundering. These phenomena come at times of increased digital onboarding requirements within the financial services sector, seeking more efficient, effective, and secure ways to facilitate proper customer onboarding while reducing risk. In this context, the importance of risk is elevated. One view is that customers performing financial activities outside a financial institution's risk tolerance and appetite perimeter are liabilities, resulting in debanking.

Debanking or *denial of banking services* refers to the behavior adopted by a financial institution that can refuse service, restrict, or even shut down a customer's account and relationship, resulting in loss of access to the regulated global financial system. This behavior is "informed" by the discretionary and calculated risk perceived by financial institutions to avoid breaching national and international compliance requirements, especially anti-money laundering/counter-terrorism financing (AML/CTF) rules imposed by national and international regulators. Moreover, such behavior can also be driven by the fact that an individual or organization may be associated with or located in a high-risk jurisdiction on a "blacklist" due to high risk for money laundering, financing terrorism, or inability to comply with international standards. Additional drivers of debanking can include increased capital requirements, profitability, prudential requirements, reputational risk, and geopolitical situations. Financial institutions aim to minimize the risk of being penalized with large regulatory fines due to potential violations, "ensuring that there is rigorous adherence to all written policies and procedures" (The Clearing House, 2017, p. 4). Money laundering poses a general societal risk since it is conceptualized and contextualized as an externality problem supporting illegal channels of the economy with direct negative effects on the legitimacy of the financial sector and society (Masciandaro, 1996; Rose, 2019a). The emergence of globalization and the technologically enabled ways of transactional and trading relationships have given rise to complex and difficult-to-unlock money-laundering schemes (Rose, 2019b).

Some contend that ideological or political controversies may also fuel the perceived reputational risk for financial institutions rather than a case-by-case determination of the risk associated with each customer. Others maintain that debanking also stems from the unwillingness of financial institutions to conduct proper and in-depth customer due diligence (CDD) because it is not worth the risk, or they lack the right infrastructural capacity and internal means of support. This situation creates a dichotomy between perceived and assessed risk and how certain industries, customer segments, and jurisdictions are deemed risky without solid foundations and grounds. Similarly, several factors drive debanking, like compliance requirements, business and operational costs, and regulatory burdens.

Based on the abovementioned analysis, the following key characteristics relate to debanking (Haley, 2018):

- Closure of bank accounts or even refusal to open related to certain individuals or firms, limiting at the same time financial integration.
- Withdrawal or even restriction of banking services from money transfer organizations, including other types of remittance facilities affecting primarily poorer countries that depend heavily on such capital flows while affecting endeavors toward poverty reduction and sustainable development and
- Severance of correspondent banking relationships that can result in systemic effects and inefficiencies within the international payments system.

Debanking is directly associated with humanitarian issues, increased financial exclusion, and the inability of relevant stakeholders to access the provision of financial services equally (Durner & Shetret, 2015). Debanking can result in the inability of individuals, businesses, in principle charities and humanitarian organizations, or even countries, especially underdeveloped, emerging, and developing economies, to have access to financial services provisions, considering them as liabilities for financial institutions (Cohen & Yim, 1996). Attributes like geographical and location peculiarities, citizenship, international sanctions, and refugee status usually fuel this inability. Incidents of debanking have also been associated with reasons of ethnicity, racism, and censorship, grounded on the monopolistic behaviors of financial institutions. Such perceived linkages can cause substantial reputational damage and deficit to financial institutions. The decision to debank an entity is usually arbitrary, and the entity cannot dispute it (Durner & Shetret, 2015).

The sophisticated nature behind fintech business models, in conjunction with legacy systems, processes, and the overall transformation of the financial services industry, has been encouraging the rethinking of regulatory perimeters, the norms, and discourses around the shaping and materialization of new regulation, the regulation and supervision practices associated with both traditional and emerging digital finance, along with, the necessity to use data for real-time information collection, decision-making, and optimization.

The Global Regtech Industry

According to KPMG's Pulse in FinTech H2 '22 report (KPMG, 2023), global regtech attracted investments of $18.6 billion in 2022, rising from $12.1 billion in 2021, experiencing a growth of 53.7%. Despite the headwinds within the global fintech industry, regtech has shown strong signs of resilience and potential for future growth, especially in the areas of crypto regulation, cross-border payments, gaming, nonfungible tokens (NFTs), AML and Markets in Financial Instruments Directive II (MiFID II) regulations and mandatory ESG reporting, requiring the deployment of technology-enabled regulatory solutions to optimize, streamline, enhance, and manage compliance and reporting activities in light of the complex and evolving regulation. Juniper Research foresees that global spending in regtech could exceed $204 billion by 2026 (Businesswire, 2022).

Literature Insights

Fintech is "a new financial industry that applies technology to improve financial activities" (Schueffel, 2016, p. 45). Its foundation rests on a distributed model allowing for the convergence of emerging technologies and new service development while incentivizing new discourses of value cocreation and customer-centricity. Conceptually, fintech enables the emergence of structural and purposeful change, highlighting a lack of readiness for incumbents to understand, manage, and face (Nicoletti, 2017). Fintech aims to leverage new ways to meet and address constantly changing customer needs by generating new offerings based on understanding customers' behavioral traits, patterns, and expectations.

Financial innovation and regulation are not usually synchronized (Grueter, 2017). Over the years, fintech innovation has experienced exponential growth driven by technological breakthroughs and innovative business models to provide differentiated and diversified offerings while opening new pathways for entrepreneurial ventures and business opportunities (Lee, 2017). Compared to regulatory developments, technological developments tend to be faster, with regulation showing an inability to maintain momentum and proactively keep up with new and emerging fintech offerings (di Castri & Plaitakis, 2018; Fenwick et al., 2017). Regulators and policymakers have begun to realize and understand that existing regulatory frameworks and approaches to developing regulation are no longer compatible with the sentiment created around fintech-enabled business models (He et al., 2017). In this frame of reference, the new fintech paradigm challenges fundamental principles within the core DNA of financial regulation.

Regtech is a new but rapidly evolving umbrella term that has recently gained momentum. It is a concept driven by complexity, continuous evolution, multidisciplinary, data centrality, and higher digitalization (Grassi & Lanfranchi, 2022).

Although no universally accepted definition of regtech exists (Waye, 2019), the term refers to a wide range of data-led technological solutions aimed at helping financial institutions and companies with ad hoc regulatory requirements. Regtech is the nexus of data, technology, and regulation (Grassi & Lanfranchi, 2022). The technological underpinnings associated with regtech cover a wide spectrum of emerging and exponential technologies, such as artificial intelligence (AI) and machine learning (ML), biometrics, cloud computing, computer vision applications, blockchain, natural language processing (NLP), and robotic process automation. A major challenge is that their deployment does not usually occur within compliance departments.

Regtech's new breed of regulation and technology aims to provide a new suite of regulatory services, signaling a dynamic shift from manual to digital and smart compliance (Butler & Brooks, 2018). Moreover, these emerging technologies disrupt specific legal doctrines and practices, gradually impacting the engagement between regulators and the regulated (Anagnostopoulos, 2018; Michaels & Homer, 2018; Waye, 2019). Table 4.1 highlights the leading digital technologies associated with regulation.

Table 4.1. Digital Technologies Associated With Regtech

Technology	**Applications/Uses**
Cloud computing	• Regtech-as-a-service. • Affordable data storage. • Disaster recovery and safe data backup.
Machine learning and big data	• Analyzing patterns leveraging diverse datasets to identify anomalies. • Detecting fraud and improving risk management. • Analyzing tax reports to warn on tax issues. • Providing country localization complexity rankings for international businesses. • Leveraging large datasets.
Blockchain	• Secure and immutable processing and finalizing financial transactions. • Data integrity and safety. • Transaction automation. • Validation of records using digital signatures.
Biometrics	• Enhanced identity management processes. • Additional layers of identification using alternative sources and data types (e.g., fingerprint, retina scanning, and voice recognition). • Enhanced customer onboarding experience.

Source: Developed by the authors.

Note: This table shows the most prominent digital technologies associated with regtech, presenting key applications and uses.

The definition of regtech is threefold. It refers to using technological underpinnings concerning regulatory monitoring, reporting, and compliance, aiming at bringing digitization in existing manual processes while ultimately incentivizing a paradigm shift toward reconceptualizing financial regulation (Arner et al., 2017). Moreover, regtech's definition encapsulates the suite of ventures or organizations that have developed a specialization in this business domain (Becker et al., 2020). Furthermore, regtech is associated with governmental efforts to harness technical solutions to support and institutionalize more efficient targeting and conduct of regulatory monitoring and enforcement (Bolton & Mintrom, 2023). Regtech's emergence has given rise to other similar terms, including algorithmic regulation (Ulbricht, 2018; Yeung, 2018), dynamic/adaptive regulation (Baxter, 2016), and smart regulation (Zetzsche et al., 2017).

Some view regtech as a subdivision of fintech, especially due to the technological lens involving regulatory requirements delivery (Anagnostopoulos, 2018; Butler & Brien, 2019). Moreover, digital financial regulation can substantially improve financial development outcomes (Muganyi et al., 2022). However, the perceived efficiency and effectiveness of digital regulatory compliance can extend beyond financial services. These use cases and applications should be considered independent and sector-agnostic since doing so allows additional and alternative stakeholders to be integrated. Moreover, regtech's evolution is observable via the emergence of various sectors, including policing, food and hospitality, healthcare, international trade, forestry management, and supply chain management (Waye, 2019).

Anagnostopoulos (2018) considers regulation to be a source of disruption, positioning it among the key enablers of fintech change and growth. Johansson et al. (2019) consider regtech vital for keeping up with compliance and regulatory changes. Integrating regtech solutions can assist a bank's regulatory management process, supporting strategic management activities and enhancing regulatory processes (Von Solms, 2021). As previously mentioned, regtech has been associated with an emerging system called algorithmic regulation, allowing for the use of computational algorithms to set standards, monitor, and modify the behavior of different datasets (Hildebrandt, 2018; Teichmann et al., 2023; Ulbricht, 2018; Yeung, 2018). Campbell-Verduyn and Lenglet (2022) challenge the solutionist vision behind regtech, highlighting static visions of regulation and the narrow, individual finance-driven problems being the two major failures of regtech. The authors conclude that regtech "reflects continuities with a pre-crisis era and fails to tackle key market and regulatory changes occurring since then" (Campbell-Verduyn & Lenglet, 2022, p. 1).

Regtech's Benefits and Challenges

Like any new technological advancement aiming to bring transformative change and potentially disrupt existing practices and processes, the developments and integration of regtech have benefits and challenges worth considering. Table 4.2 presents some of these benefits and challenges.

Table 4.2. Regtech's Benefits and Challenges.

Benefits	**Description**
Automation and efficiency	• Automation of repetitive and manual tasks. • Improvements and efficiency of the regulatory process. • Time and cost savings due to reduced operational costs associated with compliance. • Reduction of paperwork and manual work. • Increased accuracy of "true positives" and reduction of "false positives."
Enhanced compliance	• Organizations can navigate across complex regulatory requirements, ensuring compliance. • Provision of real-time monitoring and alerts to regulatory changes and developments. • Timely identification and flagging of potential compliance issues. • Penalties and regulatory breaches minimization. • Adaptability and adjustment of organizational compliance strategies.
Risk assessment accuracy	• Risk accuracy enabled by advanced analytics and ML algorithms. • Analysis of vast amounts of data for informed decision-making. • Effective identification of potential risks, anomalies, and patterns.
Improved data security	• Protecting sensitive data. • Minimizing the risk of data breaches. • Reducing unauthorized access to regulatory data and information.
Enhanced reporting transparency	• Accurate and comprehensive reporting on organizational and regulatory compliance. • Improved transparency. • Easy access to relevant information for stakeholders, auditors, and regulators.

Table 4.2. *(Continued)*

Benefits	Description
Challenges	*Description*
Implementation and data quality	• Integration to legacy systems. • Resource-intensive: expertise, time, resources, and cost. • The quality of regulatory data might be questionable or fragmented.
Data privacy	• Data privacy and security concerns. • Need for robust data governance practices ensuring organizational compliance with data protection regulations.
Regulatory complexity	• The magnitude of regulatory frameworks and perimeters. • Frequent changes and updates require monitoring of evolving requirements.
Customization	• Potentially limited and costly capacity for tailored-made solutions to specific organizational needs, risk indicators, or typologies. • The potential need for internal process adaptation to ensure regtech is "fit-for-purpose."
Technology dependency and vendor "lock-in"	• Over-reliance on technology. • Risk for technological disruptions resulting in risk exposure and regulatory noncompliance. • Dependency on regtech-as-a-service vendors. • Outsourcing prudential risk and compliance to a service provider. • Transferring regtech implementation to a service provider.
Regulatory lag	• Technological advancements outpace regulatory frameworks. • Challenging the value logic behind regtech.
Workforce displacements and skills gap	• Digital regulatory technologies can put jobs in jeopardy. • Reskilling and upskilling employees: time-consuming, challenging, and costly. • Potential lack of specialized technical skills: talent deficiencies.

Source: Developed by the authors.

Note: This table summarizes regtech's most important benefits and challenges that businesses must consider.

Understanding its benefits and challenges is important for financial institutions planning to integrate regtech solutions in their systems, operations, compliance, and risk management processes. Undergoing adoption and integration exercises is critical to understand how regtech changes current practices while maintaining the highest compliance standards. Balancing automation and human involvement in the regulatory, compliance, and reporting processes is crucial.

Regtech's Use Cases

Regtech use cases consist of four main categories: (1) compliance management, monitoring, and reporting; (2) regulatory intelligence, reporting, and documentation; (3) risk management and assessment; and (4) identity and fraud management. Table 4.3 summarizes the most prominent regtech use cases.

Table 4.3. Regtech Use Cases.

Use Case	Description	Examples
Compliance management, monitoring, and reporting	• Monitoring and reporting regulatory compliance. • Staying current with regulatory and compliance requirements, including new laws and guidelines. • Providing real-time insights as a competitive advantage. • Enhancing transparency. • Reporting process automation.	• Preventing financial crime by detecting illicit activities. • Using AI and ML, data analytics, and big data. • Automating customer onboarding and due diligence. • Derisking the ANL and KYC process.
Risk management and assessment	• Engaging in risk assessment and management. • Using data analytics, predictive modeling, AI, and ML. • Using market surveillance and compliance mechanisms.	• Managing cybersecurity risks. • Engaging in real-time threat intelligence. • Complying with various regulatory schemes and perimeters.

Table 4.3. *(Continued)*

Use Case	Description	Examples
Regulatory, intelligence, reporting, and documentation	• Offering automation, streamlining, and optimization. • Providing accuracy, consistency, and time efficiency. • Ensuring compliance with reporting obligations.	• Automating data collection. • Standardizing reporting formats. • Streamlining ESG reporting, assisting organizations toward meeting ESG disclosure requirements.
Identity and fraud management	• Digital onboarding transition. • Digital identity and identity verification. • Identity management via APIs. • Reduction of onboarding and compliance costs. • Enhanced customer experience and meeting client expectations.	• Using AI-based automation and biometrics. • Engaging in real-time progress reporting and automation. • Increasing approval rates. • Engaging in enhanced customer credit scoring. • Eliminating fraud. • Using transaction and trade data tracking.

Source: Developed by the authors.

Note: This table summarizes the major use cases of regtech that businesses must consider.

Compliance management, monitoring, and reporting solutions aim at supporting financial institutions to comply with regulatory requirements by providing monitoring, reporting, and auditing tools. Regulatory intelligence, reporting, and documentation solutions help financial institutions automate submitting regulatory reports to regulatory authorities. Risk management and assessment solutions allow financial institutions to identify, manage, and assess various risks associated with regulatory compliance provisions. Finally, identity and fraud management solutions provide financial institutions with tools to diligently verify the identity of customers, employees, and other relevant stakeholders and associate and triangulate the identity with potentially fraudulent transactions and illicit activities.

Although these use cases are presented within the context of financial institutions, they can also be leveraged and used within other industries and sectors of the economy. Moreover, financial institutions and regulatory and supervisory authorities can use regtech to support ad hoc processes in a bidirectional manner.

New Dimensions and the Future of Regtech

Financial institutions and regulators face complex and diverse regulatory challenges. Addressing these challenges requires operational, structural, and legal adjustments. In this context, financial institutions and regulators leverage digital regulatory solutions to address evolving and demanding regulatory frameworks at national, international, supranational, and cross-jurisdictional levels. Regtech has emerged via different technology ecosystems, which financial institutions can tap into to enhance the efficiency, effectiveness, scalability, and robustness of their compliance programs and activities. The common denominator across these changes is data. Risk, compliance, and oversight (supervision) are increasingly data driven.

Adopting regtech solutions is primarily observed in several functional areas: AML and transaction reporting, Know Your Customer (KYC) and identity management, and regulatory reporting. Cryptocurrencies, DeFi, and ESG reporting may accelerate regtech solutions and regulatory innovations.

Generative AI

Regtech's future depends on emerging, interconnected, and complex dimensions. The accelerated developments in generative AI, particularly related to Open AI's app ChatGPT, at the time of writing, the leading GenAI framework, raise questions about compliance transformation by combining human judgment and machine intelligence. AI and automation play a pivotal role in the reshaping of compliance. Generative AI will further unlock regtech's power using ML to help financial institutions comply with regulations. Google Cloud recently announced the launch of a customizable application programming interface-enabled AML tool for banking institutions. It leverages AI's power, discontinues rules-based inputs, and reduces human input in money-laundering risks screening processes (Tokar, 2023). Financial institutions must identify, explain, and validate the effectiveness of AI tools in conjunction with their ad hoc compliance needs and the calibration of their AML tools. These actions become critical in showing proactive preparedness and capability building toward the evolving AI-driven regulatory landscape while understanding the inherent opportunities, risks, and implementation challenges associated with generative AI.

Digital and Cryptographic Assets

Digital and cryptographic assets, including global Web 3.0 developments and the metaverse, are other critical dimensions for regulatory technologies, regulation, and regulators. Numerous authorities globally are working on regulatory perimeters and frameworks for cryptographic assets, exploring new ways to position and integrate digital and cryptographic assets decentralized and disintermediated nature within legal frameworks. The global nature of these assets requires proper regulatory tools for navigating and exploring the risks and opportunities. A broader consensus exists that these emerging business models using cryptographic assets or other digital assets, including currencies, do not fit within existing regulatory schemes, putting pressure on regulators and policymakers to modernize prudential architectures to ensure and protect financial stability. The accelerated growth, industry trends, and scams associated with cryptocurrencies put forward new thinking into emerging risks, regulatory implications, and new forms of finance that require new tools for compliance, audit, reporting, and risk management.

Financial institutions must ensure compliance concerning capital, liquidity, and other requirements in the broader spectrum of tokenization, which allows for the creation and emergence of other forms of digital assets. Cryptographic assets have attracted polarized views and divergent approaches relating to technological neutrality versus technology-specific requirements, applying existing regulations like other financial assets and launching competitive offerings such as central bank digital currency (CBDC).

Detection of Fraud, AML/CTF, and Sanctions Compliance

A critical dimension of regtech within a continuously evolving digital world is the increasing rise of different, sophisticated forms of financial crime threatening financial institutions. Enhanced fraud detection and investigation processes are among the measures financial institutions take. Similarly, the processing of large volumes of data to assist financial institutions in identifying patterns, anomalies, or associations indicative of financial crime phenomena (e.g., fraud, money laundering, and CTF) requires deploying advanced data analytics, computational and processing power, and innovative algorithms for financial crime prevention. In this context, regtech encourages collaboration among financial institutions, technology companies, and the public sector (e.g., regulators, supervisors, and policymakers) to develop new capabilities.

Decentralized Compliance

Blockchain and distributed ledger technologies (DLTs), the foundation underlying cryptoasset developments, also offer affordances to power regtech solutions for monitoring and compliance across centralized and decentralized value exchange environments. There are three main developments in decentralized compliance. One involves use cases of tokenization capabilities to support new types of AML and transaction monitoring models that mirror entire transaction networks on DLT overlays and to share exchange information and entity relationships without divulging personal data or other sensitive information. Other concerns use cases of distributed KYC, where decentralized agents operate as third-party secure onboarding vehicles, hence outsourcing CDD and identity verification. A third development involves use cases where smart contract capabilities are tools for what may appear under the banner of embedded compliance. *Embedded compliance* is implementing programmable assets where complex compliance rulesets can often be encoded on-asset, transforming compliance from process to feature. Such affordances may form part of a promise to revolutionize compliance in all electronic asset exchange transactions.

Quantum Computing

Another major dimension of regtech that is gradually materializing within the finance industry is the advancements in quantum computing, an emerging technology based on quantum theory. The behavior of energy and matter could have profound effects and implications on society and computational systems (Butler, 2020). Quantum computing aims to outperform classical computers in computational speed for finance algorithms and applications. Financial institutions in strategic partnerships with technology companies are exploring potential use cases (e.g., Monte Carlo algorithms, simulations, and complex financial computations) while building an in-house "quantum culture" (JP Morgan Chase) or advanced "learning efforts" capabilities (Wells Fargo). A key focus is developing post-quantum resistant or agile cryptographic techniques (PQC) since quantum computing could make all existing data encryption systems redundant.

An interesting example is the rising cybersecurity threat of "Harvest Now, Decrypt Later" that allows hackers/attackers to steal/collect encrypted data today and decrypt them in the future when quantum computers become more advanced and accessible. Such phenomena create issues and have profound compliance implications. Financial institutions need to develop and deploy proper mitigation plans to protect themselves from further liabilities and losses, ensuring, at the same time, financial data security, value, and integrity in the future. With Project Leap (2023), the Bank for International Settlements, in partnership with the Banque de France and the Deutsche Bundesbank, recently announced the successful establishment of a secure communication channel using a quantum-resistant VPN tunnel between various servers aiming at protecting financial data from future quantum computing-enabled threats.

ESG Sustainability and Humanitarian Regulation

Regtech's last foundational dimension is the emergence and proliferation of ESG regulation, especially considering mandatory reporting and disclosure requirements. Financial institutions consider ESG an emerging governance risk that integrates risk management, internal audit, and reporting processes under ESG performance and resilience metrics. ESG factors are a multidisciplinary, multi-dimensional, and sophisticated amalgamation of corporate sustainability factors, metrics, and requirements financial institutions must consider, integrate, and follow. This complexity becomes more critical due to the overwhelming volume and variations of ESG rules and requirements across different areas (Murray, 2023) and the global misalignment due to the substantial divergence of ESG standards (Ross, 2023). Integrating ESG considerations is at the heart of how organizations do business. Current discourses show a major shift in ESG from preferability to enforceability since ESG is gradually becoming a key priority for regulators and corporate governance professionals. Continuously evolving and regularly introduced regulations and standards revolving around ESG reporting (e.g., the EU Sustainability Action Plan and the International Sustainability Standards Board) require new reporting procedures, risk-based policies, compliance provisions, and mechanisms.

Additionally, comprehensive data and information are needed on sustainability-related risks, opportunities, and challenges for informed decision-making relating to sustainability. Due to the nature of ESG issues and the complexity behind the acquisition, analysis, and governance of ESG data, a need exists for proper triangulation to ensure transparency, accountability, and assurance. Thus, financial institutions must focus on renewing, realigning, and developing targeted and distinctive sustainability-oriented capabilities (Demirel & Kesidou, 2019). Regtech solutions can support financial institutions and diligently integrate ESG considerations within broader, interconnected, and interrelated risk management approaches strategically and organizationally aligned to ad hoc business models and value creation mechanisms.

Considering regtech's evolution and the emerging trends and developments within the financial industry and beyond, Fig. 4.1 provides an updated typology of the main regulatory application areas integrating existing and evolving regtech application areas to be considered by financial institutions.

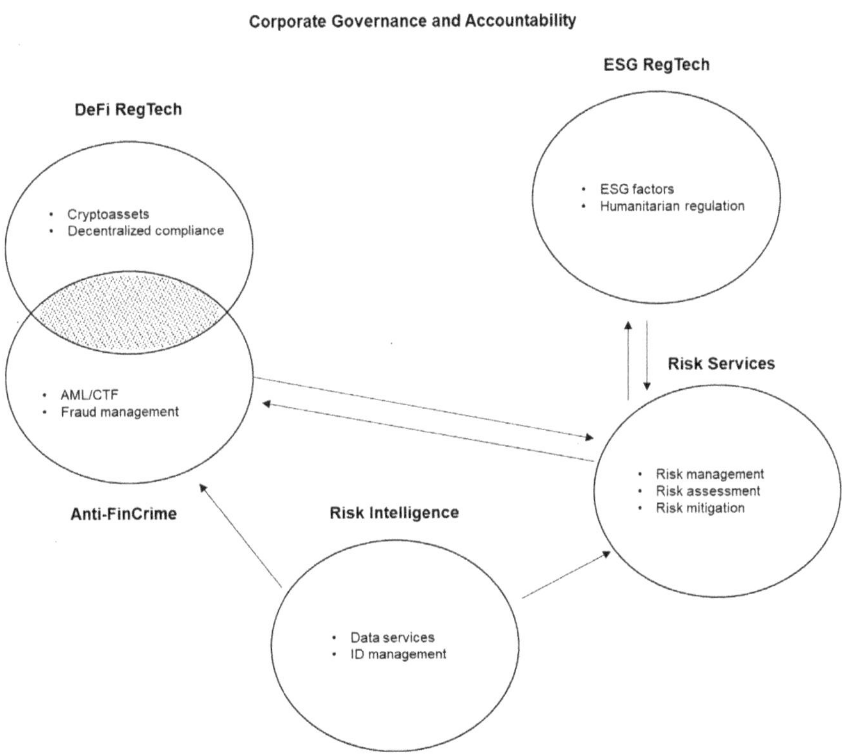

Fig. 4.1. Typology of Regtech Application Areas. *Note:* This figure illustrates a typology of the main regtech application areas integrating existing and evolving regtech applications by financial institutions. *Source:* Developed by the authors.

Summary and Conclusions

Regtech's value proposition revolves around enhancing regulatory compliance and reducing compliance costs while leading a new regulatory innovation and compliance culture. Regtech provides financial institutions and regulators with novel digital tools for supervising, monitoring, and enforcing compliance while reducing the heavy burden of in-house regulatory compliance. Regtech has also opened new pathways to regulatory innovation, enabling openness, flexibility, and adaptability of regulatory frameworks to technological advancements. Finally, regtech can facilitate new strategic partnerships and revenue streams regarding innovative technology development.

Fig. 4.2 shows that regtech occurs in the nexus of three areas defining/representing the three dimensions – (1) societal/security, (2) business, and (3) law and tech. The latter is called the "normative framework." The double arrows demonstrate the circular/bidirectional relation between the three dimensions of the use cases: (1) data

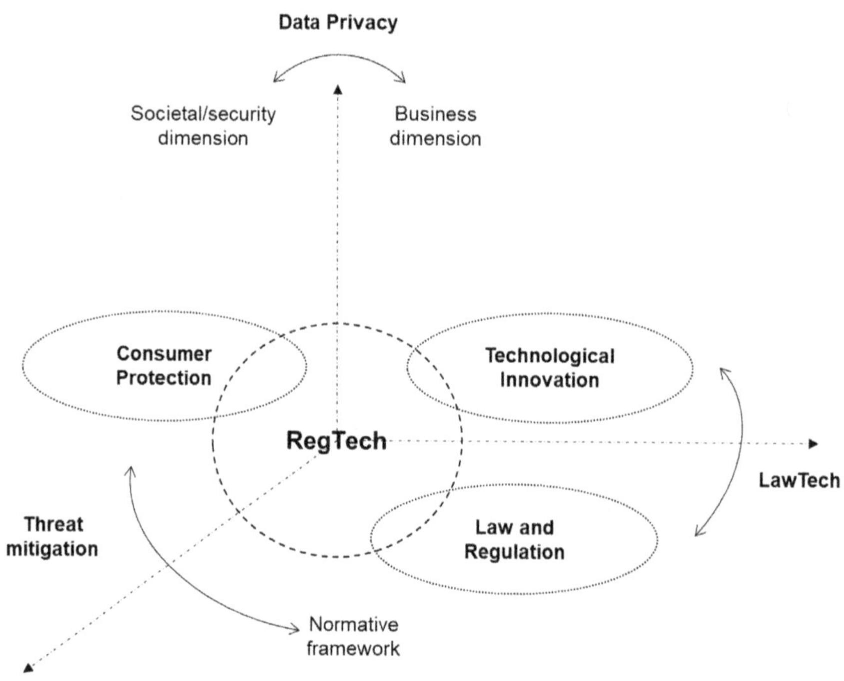

Fig. 4.2. Regtech Nexus. *Note:* This figure shows that regtech is positioned in the nexus of three areas: (1) societal/security, (2) business, and (3) law and tech. The double arrows demonstrate the circular/bidirectional relation between the three dimensions with use cases involving data privacy, threat mitigation, and lawtech. *Source:* Developed by the authors.

privacy – connecting business with consumer protection, (2) threat mitigation – connecting law with consumer protection, and (3) lawtech – connecting law with business.

Financial institutions and the delivery of financial services are experiencing a data-driven paradigm shift. The blend of technological underpinnings and regulation aims at supporting financial institutions, but also other businesses, to (1) automate and simplify processes, (2) optimize cost, (3) manage fraud and risk, (4) infuse digital regulatory compliance, and (5) leverage compliance data harnessing the scalability potentialities of emerging technologies. Regtech can transform regulation by leveraging real-time information and data and incorporating analytics and algorithms. In this context, regtech applications and use cases allow for facilitating regulatory reporting schemes and assembling ethical compliance management structures.

Questions remain around regulatory inertia and adopting regtech solutions by financial services organizations: bureaucracy, lack of compliance data, ensuring the development of algorithms in compliance with regulatory policies, and good business cases for financial services organizations. Collaboration among stakeholders, better communication with regulatory and supervisory authorities, optimized processes and standards regarding compliance data consistency, structure, and interoperability, new legal requirements around paper documentation, and the ability of computers to read released regulations can facilitate the broader adoption of regtech solutions within financial institutions and beyond.

The bundle of regulatory requirements is not always as agile and flexible or even able to follow these transformational shifts, often creating hurdles for innovation. Regtech and suptech (supervisory technology) can transform regulatory compliance and supervision by enabling regulators to monitor compliance in real time and improving the regulation's effectiveness. Regtech and suptech play a key role in regulatory digitization by enabling the development of machine-readable regulations to facilitate compliance systems and requirements (Eyers, 2022). Regtech opens doors for innovation in addressing various regulatory hurdles. It automates even the most routine compliance duties while leveraging advanced data analytics to enhance financial institutions' understanding of risks and regulatory concerns. Adopting regtech's capabilities translates into new and enhanced diagnostic abilities for financial institutions.

Although regtech can enhance regulatory outcomes and decrease expenses, it does not replace regulatory reform. As regtech solutions aim at simplifying regulatory processes, technological advancements place a greater responsibility on regulators and policymakers to ensure that regulations are well-founded in terms of necessity and design.

A critical question moving forward is striking the delicate balance among effective digital, regulatory, and supervisory transformation. This balance requires maintaining an overarching culture of innovation and compliance that emphasizes the importance and value of human judgment. Such an approach could ease the resistance expressed by financial institutions to embrace regtech solutions for compliance and broader business purposes.

Discussion Questions

- Define regtech in the context of financial services.
- Identify regtech's benefits and challenges.
- List regtech's applications (use cases) in the financial industry and the broader business world.
- Identify the most promising dimensions that will determine regtech's future.

References

ACPR. (2022). *ACPR techsprint on confidential data pooling: Summary report*. https://acpr.banque-france.fr/sites/default/files/media/2023/01/12/20230112_tech_sprint_2022_summary_report_en.pdf

Anagnostopoulos, I. (2018). FinTech and RegTech: Impact on regulators and banks. *Journal of Economics and Business*, *100*(C), 7–25.

Arner, D. W., Barberis, J., & Buckey, R. P. (2017). FinTech, RegTech, and the reconceptualization of financial regulation. *Northwestern Journal of International Law & Business*, *37*(3), 371–414.

Baxter, L. G. (2016). Adaptive financial regulation and RegTech: A concept article on realistic protection for victims of bank failures. *Duke Law Journal*, *66*(3), 567–604.

Beau, D. (2023). Digital transformation and financial systems turbulence: What lessons for regulators and supervisors? *Banque de France*. https://www.bis.org/review/r230606a.pdf

Becker, M., & Buchkremer, R. (2018). Ranking of current information technologies by risk and regulatory compliance officers at financial institutions –A German perspective. *The Review of Finance and Banking*, *10*(1), 7–26.

Becker, M., Merz, K., & Buchkremer, R. (2020). RegTech – The application of modern information technology in regulatory affairs: Areas of interest in research and practice. *Intelligent Systems in Accounting, Finance and Management*, *27*(4), 161–167.

Bolton, M., & Mintrom, M. (2023). RegTech and creating public value: Opportunities and challenges. *Policy Design and Practice*, 1–17.

Businesswire. (2022). Juniper research: RegTech to account for over 50% of regulatory compliance spend globally by 2026, as AI reshapes digital onboarding. https://www.businesswire.com/news/home/20220418005042/en/Juniper-Research-Regtech-to-Account-for-Over-50-of-Regulatory-Compliance-Spend-Globally-by-2026-as-AI-Reshapes-Digital-Onboarding

Butler, T. (2020). What's next in the digital transformation of financial industry? *IT Professional*, *22*(1), 29–33.

Butler, T., & Brien, L. O. (2019). Understanding RegTech for digital regulatory compliance. In T. Lynn, J. G. Mooney, P. Rosati, & M. Cummins (Eds.), *Disrupting finance: FinTech and strategy in the 21st century* (pp. 85–102). Palgrave Macmillan.

Butler, T., & Brooks, R. (2018). On the role of ontology-based RegTech for managing risk and compliance reporting in the age of regulation. *Journal of Risk Management in Financial Institutions*, *11*(1), 19–33.

Campbell-Verduyn, M., & Lenglet, M. (2022). Imaginary failure: RegTech in finance. *New Political Economy*, 1–15.

Carvalho, T., Moniz, N., Faria, P., & Antunes, L. (2022). *Survey on privacy-preserving techniques for data publishing*. https://doi.org/10.48550/arXiv.2201.08120

Chmiel, D. (2023, January 31). Regulators slapped industry with record fines in 2022, SEC in the Lead. *Finance Magnates*. https://www.financemagnates.com/institutional-forex/regulators-slapped-industry-with-record-fines-in-2022-sec-in-the-lead/

Cohen, M., & Yim, S. (1996). Debanking: A strategic option for foreign banks in the US. *International Financial Law Review*, *15*(5), 13–15.

Demirel, P., & Kesidou, E. (2019). Sustainability-oriented capabilities for eco-innovation: Meeting the regulatory, technology, and market demands. *Business Strategy and the Environment*, *28*(5), 847–857.

di Castri, S., & Plaitakis, A. (2018). *Going beyond regulatory sandboxes to enable FinTech innovation in emerging markets*. https://ssrn.com/abstract=3059309

Durner, T., & Shetret, L. (2015). Understanding bank derisking and its effects on financial inclusion: An exploratory study. In *Global centre on cooperative security*. Oxfam International. https://oxfamilibrary.openrepository.com/handle/10546/582310

Eggert, M. (2014). *Compliance management in financial industries: A model-based business process and reporting perspective*. Springer Science & Business Media. Springer.

Eyers, J. (2022, February 2). APRA says crypto will force changes to the 'regulatory architecture'. *Australian Financial Review*. https://www.afr.com/companies/financial-services/apra-says-crypto-will-force-changes-to-the-regulatory-architecture-20220202-p59t77

FATF. (2021). *Stocktake on data pooling, collaborative analytics and data protection*. FATF. https://www.fatf-gafi.org/publications/digitaltransformation/documents/data-pooling-collaborative-analytics-data-protection.html

Ferradi, H., Cao, J., Jiang, S., Cao, Y., & Saxena, D. (2022). *Security and privacy in big data sharing: State-of-the-art and research directions*. https://doi.org/10.48550/arXiv.2210.09230

Fenergo. (2023). Reading between the fines: A deep dive into financial institutions penalties in 2022. *Fenergo*. https://resources.fenergo.com/aml-fines/reading-between-the-fines-2022#main-content

Fenwick, M., Kaal, W. A., & Vermeulen, E. P. M. (2017). Regulation tomorrow: What happens when technology is faster than the law. *American University Business Law Review*, *6*(3), 561–594.

Grassi, L., & Lanfranchi, D. (2022). RegTech in public and private sectors: The nexus between data, technology and regulation. *Journal of Industrial and Business Economics*, *49*(3), 441–479.

Grueter, G. (2017, March 14). FinTechs have advantages over established banks, but regulation is a major challenge. *LSE Business Review*. https://eprints.lse.ac.uk/79943/1/blogs.lse.ac.uk-Fintechs%20have%20advantages%20over%20established%20banks%20but%20regulation%20is%20a%20major%20challenge.pdf

Haley, J. A. (2018). *Derisking of correspondent banking relationships: Threats, challenges and opportunities* (pp. 1–27). Wilson Center Canada Institute. https://www.wilsoncenter.org/sites/default/files/media/documents/article/2018_haley_report-edits-2-2018-final.pdf

He, D., Leckow, R. B., Haksar, V., Mancini Griffoli, T., Jenkinson, N., Kashima, M., Khiaonarong, T., Rochon, C., & Tourpe, H. (2017). FinTech and financial services: Initial considerations. *International Monetary Fund Staff Discussion Note, 17*(05).

Hildebrandt, M. (2018). Algorithmic regulation and the rule of law. *Philosophical Transactions of the Royal Society A: Mathematical, Physical & Engineering Sciences, 376*, 1–11.

Johansson, E., Sutinen, K., Lassila, J., Lang, V., Martikainen, M., & Lehner, O. M. (2019). RegTech – A necessary tool to keep up with compliance and regulatory changes. *ACRN Journal of Finance and Risk Perspectives, 8*, 71–85.

KPMG. (2023). *Pulse of FinTech H2 2022: Biannual analysis of global FinTech investments*. https://kpmg.com/xx/en/home/industries/financial-services/pulse-of-fintech.html

Kshetri, N., & Voas, J. (2022). RegTech's rise. *Computer, 55*(12), 24–26.

Lee, E. (2017). Financial inclusion: A challenge to the new paradigm of financial technology, regulatory technology and anti-money laundering law. *Journal of Business Law, 6*, 473–498.

Ludwig, H., & Baracaldo, N. (2022). *Federated learning: A comprehensive overview of methods and applications*. Springer.

Masciandaro, D. (1996). Money laundering: The economics of regulation. *European Journal of Law and Economics, 7*(3), 225–240.

Michaels, L., & Homer, M. (2018). Regulation and supervision in a digital and inclusive world. In D. L. K. Chuen & R. H. Deng (Eds.), *Handbook of blockchain, digital finance, and inclusion, volume 1: Cryptocurrency, FinTech, InsurTech and regulation* (pp. 329–346). Academic Press.

Muganyi, T., Yan, L., Yin, Y., Sun, H., Gong, X., & Taghizadeh-Hesary, F. (2022). FinTech, RegTech, and financial development: Evidence from China. *Financial Innovation, 8*(1), 1–20.

Murray, S. (2023, June 21). In-house lawyers grapple with ESG demands. *Financial Times*. https://www.ft.com/content/6e094e6d-b97d-45dd-941f-39f5b5fa1f14?desktop=true&segmentId=d8d3e364-5197-20eb-17cf-2437841d178a#myft:notification:instant-email:content

Nicoletti, B. (2017). Financial services and FinTech. In H. Arslanian & F. Fischer (Eds.), *The future of FinTech: Integrating finance and technology in financial services* (pp. 3–29). Palgrave Macmillan.

O'Brien, J. (2017). A question of trust: Post-truth paradigms and the challenge to financial regulation. *Law and Financial Markets Review, 11*(1), 20–32.

Project Leap. (2023). Quantum proofing the financial system. *Bank for International Settlements*, 1–50. https://www.bis.org/publ/othp67.pdf

Rose, K. J. (2019a). Regulating the externality of money laundering-halfway there. In *Copenhagen business school, CBS LAW research paper* (pp. 12–19). https://papers.ssrn.com/sol3/papers.cfm?abstract_id=3344469

Rose, K. J. (2019b). Derisking or re-contracting the way around money laundering risks. In *Copenhagen business school, CBS LAW research paper* (pp. 19–37). https://papers.ssrn.com/sol3/papers.cfm?abstract_id=3474298#

Ross, A. (2023, June 22). ESG investors play the long game. *Financial Times*. https://www.ft.com/content/959dfa93-e6de-441e-9328-9a99c11bd54d?segmentId=6faa8072-922c-4fbf-5b33-45a1342b0cc3

Schueffel, P. (2016). Taming the beast: A scientific definition of FinTech. *Journal of Innovation Management*, *4*(4), 32–54.

Teichmann, F., Boticiu, S., & Sergi, B. S. (2023). RegTech-potential benefits and challenges for businesses. *Technology in Society*, *72*(C), 102150. https://EconPapers.repec.org/RePEc:eee:teinso:v:72:y:2023:i:c:s0160791x22002913

The Clearing House. (2017, February). A new paradigm: Redesigning the U.S. AML/CFT framework to protect national security and aid law enforcement. *The Clearing House*. https://bpi.com/wp-content/uploads/2018/07/20170216_tch_report_aml_cft_framework_redesign.pdf

Tokar, D. (2023, June 21). Google cloud launches anti-money-laundering tool for banks, betting on the power of AI. *The Wall Street Journal*. https://www.wsj.com/articles/google-cloud-launches-anti-money-laundering-tool-for-banks-betting-on-the-power-of-ai-2512ccce?mod=djem_WealthJournal

Ulbricht, L. (2018). When big data meet securitization: Algorithmic regulation with passenger name records. *European Journal of Scientific Research*, *3*(2), 139–161.

Von Solms, J. (2021). Integrating regulatory technology (RegTech) into the digital transformation of a bank treasury. *Journal of Banking Regulation*, *22*, 152–168. https://doi.org/10.1057/s41261-020-00134-0

Waye, V. (2019). RegTech: A new frontier in legal scholarship. *Adelaide Law Review*, *40*(1), 363–386.

Yeung, K. (2018). Algorithmic regulation: A critical interrogation. *Regulation and Governance*, *12*(4), 505–523.

Zetzsche, D. A., Buckley, R. P., Barberis, J. N., & Arner, D. W. (2017). Regulating a revolution: From regulatory sandboxes to smart regulation. *Fordham Journal of Corporate and Financial Law*, *23*(1), 31–103.

Section II

Reinventing the Banking and Payments Industry

Chapter 5

Fintech's Impact on the Banking Industry and Financial Services[1]

Efthymios Rizopoulos[a] *and Markos T. Zachariadis*[b]

[a]Financial Conduct Authority, UK
[b]University of Manchester, UK

Abstract

For over a decade, fintech has challenged traditional business models and processes in the financial services industry. The ongoing disruption has necessitated the digital transformation of financial institutions (FIs) to remain an integral part of the financial system. This paradigm shift is not merely a technological update. Still, it signifies a cultural and operational rebirth, compelling FIs to embrace innovation, adaptability, and a customer-centric approach in the digital era. Independent of the business model, FIs must become digitally ambidextrous, offer tailored and dynamic customer experiences, support financial inclusion, and promote an environmental, social, and governance (ESG) agenda while leveraging data and remaining compliant. From digitalization to fintegration, the financial services industry's future is deemed to be an exciting and productive one.

Keywords: Fintech; fintegration; disruption; transformation; digitally ambidextrous; financial inclusion

Introduction

The world of finance is undergoing a revolution. At the heart of this transformative journey lies financial technology (fintech). Fintech has challenged traditional business models of financial intermediaries and enhanced financial services by acting as the research and development (R&D) function of financial

[1]The views expressed in this chapter are the author's alone and do not reflect the views of their employers.

The Emerald Handbook of Fintech, 91–108

doi:10.1108/978-1-83753-608-520241010

services in the digital world and making them simpler, more accessible, transparent, efficient, and cost-effective. Peer-to-peer (P2P) lending platforms, mobile payment applications, blockchain technologies, and robo-advisory services are just a few examples of how fintech has disrupted the industry. These innovations have created a user-centric financial ecosystem, with more democratized access to financial services and inclusivity as a cornerstone of financial globalization. Consumers now expect financial services that are seamless, convenient, and tailored to their unique needs. Traditional financial intermediaries must adapt and evolve in this new environment or risk becoming obsolete. However, this transformative journey raises important questions regarding data privacy and cybersecurity, for which regulators must find an answer while balancing market stability and consumer protection with competition and innovation.

Given the importance of financial intermediaries (FIs) in the economy, understanding fintech's impact on the banking and financial services industry is crucial. This process becomes even more imperative considering that the industry has already experienced extensive technological and regulatory transformations, fueled in part by factors such as deregulation, liberalization, advancements in information and communication technologies, innovative transaction and savings methods, shifts in cybersecurity practices, and the process of digitization. Incumbent FIs should determine how they will interact with fintech firms in this environment. Similarly, governments and regulators must decide whether they will support an ecosystem where fintech firms complement existing market players, promoting fintegration in that way, or they will place certain restrictions.

This chapter contributes to this ongoing discussion about fintech and provides insights that reinforce comprehension of its effect on banking, financial services, and the industry's future. This chapter first attempts to unravel the DNA of financial intermediation and provide useful insights into how financial institutions (FIs) operate, manage risks, and their vital role in economic growth and stability. Then, it focuses on technology and its presence in the financial services industry over the past decades, the legacy challenges of traditional financial intermediaries, and the birth of financial technology. It also discusses the domains that fintech has disrupted and how regulation has been addressing the challenges that it brings. This chapter analyzes how traditional FIs respond to the evolving environment. It concludes by elaborating on the fintegration, the path of digital transformation, and the future characteristics of financial intermediaries that will help them stay relevant, survive, and compete.

Deciphering the "Genetic Code" of Financial Intermediation

Understanding the DNA of financial intermediation is the first essential step to grasp the intricate web of activities and mechanisms that underpin the functioning of the global financial system. This journey into the core elements of financial intermediation will provide essential information about the role of FIs in the economy and their operations and risk management functions. At the same time, it will lay the foundation for comprehending finance's broader landscape and its pivotal role in the interconnected world. More importantly, it will assist in drawing inferences concerning fintech's potential impact on the banking and financial services industry. After briefly discussing different theories, this section presents a basic framework of financial intermediation that assists in interpreting the impact of technology on FIs and explains why financial intermediation can be seen as an information business.

What Is Financial Intermediation?

Financial intermediation has undergone considerable transformation over time, as has the view among economists and finance theorists of its rationale and importance. Consider, for example, an Arrow-Debreu economy (i.e., complete market or complete system of markets), where information is perfect, transaction costs insignificant, and goods are state-contingent (Arrow & Debreu, 1954; McKenzie, 1954). Here, interactions between households and companies occur through the market, resource allocation is Pareto efficient, and financial intermediation plays no role (Allen & Santomero, 1997). Similarly, in a market with frictionless reallocations of resources, the Modigliani–Miller theorem on the irrelevance of pure financing decisions would suggest that financial intermediation cannot create any value (Fama, 1980).

However, this approach to financial intermediation, albeit an intriguing theoretical exercise, sharply contrasts with what is observed in practice. Financial intermediation, at least as a basic idea, has been a fundamental feature of human societies since ancient times (Murinde et al., 2022). From Mesopotamia to Ancient Greece, Rome, and India, focal points, such as temples, treasuries, and affluent individuals, serve as the epochal financial intermediaries. In many instances, this form of financial activity signifies the economic superiority of the city, region, or civilization and its social and cultural advancement. In the centuries to follow, banks, credit unions, insurance companies, and other FIs play a central role in the economy.

The quest to explain this role naturally leads to the emergence of various models that constitute the field known as intermediation theory. At its core, the theory traces the origins of financial intermediation in the presence of frictions, such as transaction costs (Gurley & Shaw, 1960) and asymmetric information (Campbell & Kracaw, 1980; Leland & Pyle, 1977). In this framework, both market imperfections are crucial factors in explaining the creation, need, and importance of FIs in the economy (Bhattacharya & Thakor, 1993; Dewatripont & Tirole, 1994; Freixas & Rochet, 1997; Santomero, 1984). However, this traditional view of financial intermediation fails to explain why gradual improvements in market imperfections over the years are not matched with a subsequent decrease in financial intermediation. Although different explanations exist for this paradox (e.g., participation costs as proposed by Allen & Santomero, 1997), one important argument is certain: financial intermediation has always been evolving.

A Framework of Financial Intermediation

A succinct framework is required to understand contemporary technological development's impact on the "genetic code" of financial intermediation. Based on this framework, independently of how someone wants to approach and interpret financial intermediation, everything sums up two fundamental functions: asset transformation and brokerage services (Murinde et al., 2022). These functions can be distinct types of financial intermediation, but for the most part, they are intertwined and performed by the same FIs. The first function is customarily defined as the financial process through which FIs transmute funds obtained by savers or investors into a different array of assets to satisfy the requirements of borrowers, spenders, or other market participants that play the role of the counterparty. In essence, this process involves the non-mutually exclusive transformation of asset attributes, the most common of which are duration or term-to-maturity, liquidity, credit risk, divisibility or unit size, and currency identity (Greenbaum et al., 2019).

Changing the duration of assets is an important economic function, mainly undertaken by banks and a limited number of nonbank financial institutions (NBFIs). Typically, FIs will use short-term funds acquired through deposits or short-term debt to originate long-term assets, such as loans, mortgages, or bonds (Bryant, 1980; Diamond & Dybvig, 1983, 1986). By maintaining assets with longer duration than their current liabilities, FIs effectively shorten the duration of their customers' claims. FIs may also improve the liquidity of such claims, as they can offer more liquid assets than those they hold or lower credit risk by offering assets less likely to default than those they maintain (Greenbaum et al., 2019). FIs perform similar transformations on claims' unit size or currency identity characteristics.

Nevertheless, any asset transformation by default implies a mismatch concerning the respective characteristics on the FI's balance sheet. This process may expose the FI to risks, such as interest rate, inventory, credit, liquidity, or any other relevant risk. FI's conscious acceptance of such exposure fundamentally makes risk an integral part of asset transformation (Greenbaum et al., 2019).

According to Merton (1989), risk-pooling and risk-sharing are key elements of FIs, and their management becomes crucial to their operation and role in the economy. This risk management can take one of the following forms: (1) risk elimination/diversification, (2) risk transfer, and (3) risk absorption (Allen & Santomero, 1997). In general, FIs decide the form of risk management they will implement considering the nature and characteristics of the claim, the nature of risk, the characteristics of the claimants, and other potential risk-related factors. When risk management takes the form of risk transfers using suitable financial instruments, such as swaps, futures, forwards, and options, it effectively gives the asset transformation function the features of the brokerage function, which is the second key activity of FIs.

The brokerage of match-making or transactional function of FIs usually comprises fee-based activities that convene market participants with complementary needs, such as individuals or firms that need capital and those that have spare capital or companies that need intermediation for payment services (Murinde et al., 2022). Through this function, FIs act as fundamental liquidity providers in the financial system. The financial literature on FI's liquidity provision has been comprehensive, with typical examples including Diamond and Dybvig (1983, 1986), Gatev and Strahan (2006), Gorton and Pennacchi (1990), Holmström and Tirole (1998), and Kashyap et al. (2002). The provision of liquidity, specifically by banks, and their risk management is also interconnected with their ability to offer payment services (Navaretti et al., 2017). Without the following examples being exhaustive, brokerage services may involve transactional-based services, financial advice, screening and certification, origination, issuance, and funding (Greenbaum et al., 2019).

Financial Intermediation as Information Business

FIs are compensated, normally with fees, for asset transformation and brokerage functions. They create value by leveraging their distinctive position, enabling them to analyze (hard and soft) information and assess risks effectively. This ability is particularly important for banks. It constitutes the principal reason why banking and, to a certain extent, many interconnected services are primarily information businesses (Murinde et al., 2022). Either functioning as brokers or performing asset transformation, banks capitalize on their central role in the financial system to observe and interpret not readily accessible signals and then reuse the acquired cross-sectional (across customers) and intertemporal (through time) information to create value for their customers (Greenbaum et al., 2019). For example, consider the case of a loan. A bank collects and analyzes information at the application and initiation stage but also continues to gather relevant information during the loan's duration.

Access to such reusable information empowers banks to harness economies of scale and scope while simultaneously mitigating pre- and postcontract information problems, such as adverse selection, duplicated screening, and moral hazard, through comprehensive credit analysis and risk management (Greenbaum et al., 2019; Murinde et al., 2022). This situation becomes even more valuable, given that technological developments have changed how information is stored, analyzed, transferred, and accessed. The above functionalities for intermediation are part of the DNA of banks and FIs in general and have kept them going for centuries. More importantly, it is one of the reasons many people would rather transact with a bank than a less-known entity. In other words, banking institutions are in the business of creating trust between unequally informed agents to facilitate economic activity.

The Fintech Narrative and the Accompanying Digital Disruption

The financial services industry has historically been one of the major investors in technology. Therefore, it comes as no surprise that technology has been a force or a catalyst of these forces that shaped this industry and its role in the economy, albeit taking distinctive forms and having different impacts on the status quo over the years. Fintech is an apt example of such influence. Over the past decade or so, it has been disrupting the entire financial services value chain, championing the reevaluation and change of contemporary business models, and necessitating the transformation of existing regulation. This section focuses on the technology in the financial services industry, the birth of fintech, and the industry domains it has been disrupting. It briefly discusses the available approaches in regulators' arsenal and their response to fintech disruption.

The Tech in Fin and the Legacy Hurdle

Technology has been present in the financial services industry for over 160 years, as Fig. 5.1 shows. The journey started with the telegraph, which emerged in the mid-19th century, revolutionizing communication in the financial world. This technology facilitated faster transmission of stock prices, market news, and trading orders, greatly enhancing the efficiency of early financial markets. Advancements in the mid- and late-1800s, such as the invention of telegraphy and ticker tape, facilitated signature verification in banking transactions and

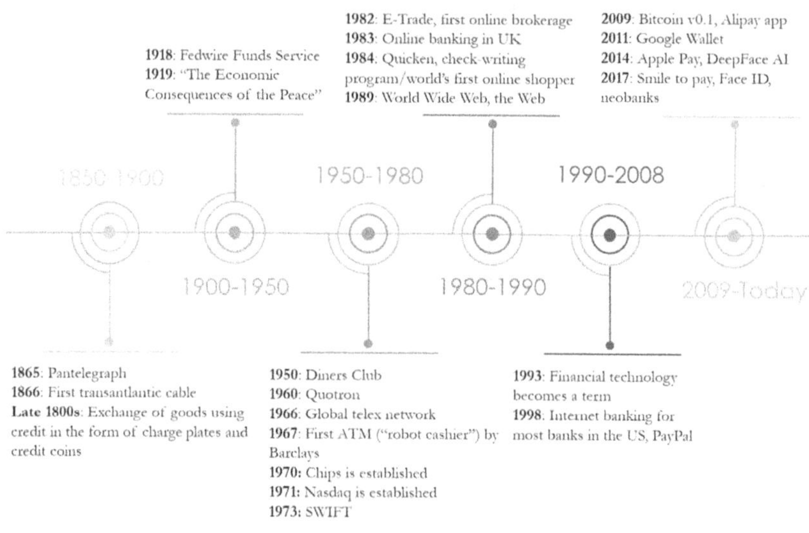

Fig. 5.1. 160 Years of Technology in Finance.
Note: This figure shows the evolution of technology within the financial services industry since 1850. It highlights important technological and technology-related milestones ushered in six distinct periods of evolution in the banking and financial services industry. Along with other technological developments, these milestones contributed to the shaping of financial services and set the stage for the emergence of FinTech.

streamlined dissemination of financial information, respectively. In the 1950s, the emergence of mainframe computers was instrumental in automating various financial processes and greatly improving the speed and accuracy of financial operations. In the 1950s and 1960s, electronic trading platforms began to replace the traditional open outcry trading systems on stock exchanges. The advent of the automated teller machine (ATM) in 1967 signified a new wave of technological innovations in financial services, while the Quotron system provided real-time stock quotes and financial news to traders and investors (Bátiz-Lazo & Carlos Maixe-Alté, 2011; Hernández de Cos, 2019).

In the following years, electronic communication networks (ECNs) allowed traders to access financial markets directly. The 1980s marked a major shift toward fully electronic trading on stock exchanges. For example, the New York Stock Exchange (NYSE) introduced its Designated Order Turnaround (DOT) system in 1984, allowing for electronic order entry. This innovation laid the foundation for the fully automated electronic trading systems that are now commonplace in today's markets. The 1990s marked the era of online trading with the rise of internet-based brokerage firms like E-Trade, Charles Schwab, and Ameritrade, empowering individual investors to trade stocks and manage their portfolios from the comfort of their homes and democratizing access to financial markets. High-frequency trading (HFT) algorithms emerged in the early 2000s, using technology to execute thousands of trades per second, revolutionizing market dynamics. These developments laid the groundwork for the digital transformation of financial markets in the subsequent decades (Arner et al., 2016).

During these decades, FIs expanded their product and service portfolios to satisfy the increasing demand of corporate and retail customers and attempted to tailor offerings to align with their preferences. With concurrent technology, they mainly aim to improve the efficiency of their operations and reduce costs. Effectively, this situation leads to an organizational and technological architecture that centers around products, creating in the process silos of information that cannot readily be used for a comprehensive understanding of customers, their profiles, and their evolving preferences. Until recently, FIs and especially incumbent banks have been initiating projects aimed at complete digitization of their records and further automation of their operations, resulting in quicker and more cost-effective services for their clients. Although these investments fit the story of a tech-engaging industry, they fundamentally do not lead to a re-evaluation of value chains across different services, the development of new products, or the transformation of existing ones to align with the digital age. Indeed, one of the biggest issues for FIs is their legacy systems. Still, the attempt to create a digitized version of the current structure, which fosters fragmentation of information, will have limited effectiveness in maintaining the competitiveness of FIs, especially incumbent banks. This situation is particularly true when facing competition from technology companies and major players in telecommunications and other industries, so-called big techs, which are looking to exploit opportunities and enter various segments of the financial industry (Murinde et al., 2022).

The Fintech Birth

Undeniably, the period after the global financial crisis (GFC) of 2007–2009 has witnessed an unparalleled surge in innovation and a rapid ascent of digital technologies, which led to what can be aptly described as the "digitization of nearly every aspect of life" (McAfee & Brynjolfsson, 2016, p. 65). From cloud computing to sensor systems, the availability of data related to economic transactions and human interactions over the internet and online platforms has been expanded. Machines that can gather and analyze vast quantities of data characterize a new era of algorithmic processing, machine learning (ML), and neural networks, bringing the realization of potentially autonomous intelligent agents and artificial intelligence (AI) closer. All these advancements leave a profound mark on numerous industries and set the stage for disrupting obsolete value chains and redefining current markets. The banking and financial services industry has not been immune to this technological disruption, leading to the emergence of the fintech movement.

The term *fintech*, a portmanteau of financial technology, first appeared in the 1990s and quickly became a word that typically refers to technological advancements with the potential to revolutionize the delivery of financial services, leading to the emergence of innovative business models, applications, procedures, and products (Arner et al., 2015; Sironi, 2016). Since then, it has been used interchangeably to describe start-ups and other new firms that enter banking and financial services, leveraging existing technology to provide innovative solutions to individuals and incumbent firms. Fintech is distinct from previous technological breakthroughs because it profoundly influences the entire array of financial services, with solutions that aim to bridge existing gaps more efficiently and inclusively. In addition, several academics, practitioners, and industry commentators discuss different versions of fintech, with the period after the GFC defined as a fintech 3.0 period (Arner et al., 2016). Although such a distinction has its merit, it obscures a fundamental difference. While the fintech versions of the past focused on cost and operational efficiencies through automation, the current fintech version is focused more on re-evaluating existing business processes in their entirety and promoting new business models (Zachariadis, 2020).

Where Is Fintech Disruption Happening?

Of the two main functions of financial intermediation, fintech mainly disrupts the brokerage function. Several factors have seconded this disruption, including the stricter regulatory requirements for traditional FIs and the exploitation of regulatory arbitrage opportunities, the lack or scarcity of traditional financial infrastructure in some areas, the cost reductions driven by proprietary technologies, and the access to data from adjacent business activities. All these reasons have also fostered fierce competition and a trend toward disintermediation, with fintech and big tech firms directly connecting borrowers and lenders through online platforms, bypassing traditional FIs. Peer-to-peer (P2P) lending platforms, such as LendingClub and Prosper, and Amazon and Alibaba, with their loans to small businesses, are good examples of this trend. Big techs can take advantage of the detailed information they gather through trading records or payment data and evaluate their clients' creditworthiness, partly accomplishing the brokerage function of traditional FIs (Murinde et al., 2022).

Despite this level of disintermediation, some suggest that fintech firms cannot entirely replace FIs in the lending space but can coexist (Navaretti et al., 2017; Tang, 2019). A potential reason is that the provision of liquidity is now limited to all but traditional FIs, as the former neither have access to central bank liquidity nor can engage in asset transformation at the level of traditional FIs, especially depository FIs. In fact, with maturity transformation, instances exist where online platforms have allowed or have not detected maturity mismatches, with borrowers repaying loans slower than lenders earning back their money (Dermine, 2017). Any potential substitution of banks in the space will also depend on the costs related to regulation and financing, customers' opinions on incumbent FIs, safety and insurance measures, and the presence of collateral (Thakor, 2020).

Apart from the lending space, "payments" is another industry domain that has attracted much attention from fintech and big tech firms. Companies like Google, Apple, Alibaba, and PayPal have already established their presence in the space and offer solutions that cut across the entire value chain of payments, leveraging their tech infrastructure or unique expertise. A crucial advantage of these firms over incumbent FIs is their ability to become the chosen interface by customers enjoying the offered experience through online platforms and mobile applications. This process facilitates bundling existing platform services with others, normally provided by traditional FIs. It promotes a supermarket-type model, a "one-stop-shop" solution for customers to buy different products and services from competing vendors. This "envelopment" strategy further strengthens the market position of such firms, allowing them to gather an enormous amount of data related to customers (Eisenmann et al., 2011). They can then leverage to provide personalized products in payments and across the financial services value chain. An example of this "super-platform" approach is Tencent's messaging engine, WeChat, which provides various financial services, from business-to-consumer (B2C) and customer-to-customer (C2C) payments to wealth management (Tanda & Schena, 2019). WeChat is also an example of a phenomenon known as the "chatification" of money, in which external services use the basic infrastructure of a messaging platform as a channel to reach out and communicate with customers (Brunton, 2018).

Traditional FIs have been at the core of the infrastructure for payments and transactions, controlling the clearing and settlement functions, which are crucial for the smooth operation and security of the entire system. However, the emergence of decentralized finance (DeFi) will reinforce further disintermediation. First, DeFi platforms, such as Compound and Uniswap, offer services directly to users through blockchain technology and smart contracts, including lending, borrowing, trading, and asset management. This disintermediation reduces the need for traditional banks and intermediaries, potentially leading to cost savings for users and greater financial inclusion. As DeFi adoption grows, traditional intermediaries may face increased competition and pressure to adapt to this evolving landscape. Second, DeFi introduces the concept of programmable money, where smart contracts execute financial transactions automatically based on predefined rules. This automation can reduce the need for intermediaries in the execution and settlement of financial transactions, potentially speeding up processes and reducing the risk of human error. Traditional FIs that rely on manual processes for tasks like clearing and settlement may need to adopt blockchain technology and automation to stay competitive.

Open banking initiatives are another facet of fintech's disruption of the banking and financial services industry. One competitive advantage of incumbent FIs, especially banks, has been the access to credit information for many customers. This process has facilitated better risk assessment and assessment of creditworthiness, as well as better comprehension of customers' needs (Navaretti et al., 2017). As previously discussed, big tech firms can also leverage information about their customers. However, this is more behavioral, which is not as suitable as credit history data for making lending decisions. Open banking legislations, like PSD2 in the European Union (EU) or Open Banking in the United Kingdom (UK), mandate existing FIs to share customer data securely with third parties upon customers' permission (Zachariadis, 2020). This fosters competition by enabling fintech companies to access financial data and develop new services (Dinckol et al., 2023). There are also ongoing consultations to allow access to a consumer's entire financial footprint and thus move from Open Banking to Open Finance era. How many fintech and big tech firms will obtain the required license for this information is still unclear. However, sharing customer data with third parties, although potentially beneficial for social welfare, can be a considerable hit for banks.

Fintech has also disrupted wealth management with robo-advisors offering automated investment advice and portfolio management. These platforms use algorithms to create diversified investment portfolios tailored to users' risk tolerance and financial goals. Robo-advisors typically charge lower fees than traditional financial advisors, making wealth management services more accessible to a broader demographic. Research also suggests that robo-advisers significantly impact under-diversified investors, whereas they mitigate well-known behavioral biases for all investors (Alsabah et al., 2020; D'Acunto et al., 2019).

The insurance sector has also witnessed much innovation. Start-ups leverage data analytics and AI to underwrite policies, detect fraud, and enhance the customer experience. Usage-based insurance models, driven by telematics and Internet of Things (IoT) devices, allow insurers to offer personalized premiums based on individual behavior and risk factors.

Before moving to the impact of fintech on financial regulation, discussing the extent to which fintech has disrupted asset transformation, the first function of financial intermediation, is important. As stated in the first section, this function is mainly undertaken by banks and a very limited number of NBFIs. The emergence of fintech has led to the advent of challenger banks and neobanks, with authors and commentators often using the terms reciprocally. However, the main difference between these two terms is that the former describes digital banks with a banking license and sometimes physical presence through a limited branch system, whereas the latter does not. By trade, challenger banks, such as Monzo, Tandem, Starling in the UK, N26 in Germany, and Revolut in the EU, can compete against and disrupt traditional FIs in the asset transformation function by leveraging their banking license. By contrast, neobanks act as brokers and generally need to partner with a traditional FI (Murinde et al., 2022). Nevertheless, both types of institutions focus on technology, emphasize in-person customer relationships, and are characterized by agility, which allows them to offer competitive rates, lower fees, and streamlined services.

What About Regulation?

Banking and financial services are heavily regulated industries worldwide. Decades of interventions by regulation, endeavors by supervision, and government guarantees have undoubtedly left their unfading imprint on the industry. These regulatory frameworks, implemented to instill trust in FIs and ensure the financial system's stability, form a "legacy infrastructure" that establishes them as a constituent part of the economy. However, stringent regulation, especially on banks, can also act as a constraint, restricting their capacity to innovate and remain profitable in an environment characterized by fierce competition. Although consumer protection, stability, and integrity of the financial system are crucial, competition and innovation are equally important. Establishing the right balance in the regulatory scale of financial services has been a challenging but indispensable task for regulators worldwide (Murinde et al., 2022).

Undoubtedly, the regulatory environment in the financial sector is undergoing a profound transformation in response to the rapid growth of fintech. Regulators worldwide have recognized the need to adapt to the changing financial landscape. This task becomes increasingly stringent due to challenges such as capacity constraints, speed of technological innovation, lack of transparency and traceability, lack of knowledge and understanding of novel technologies, fragmentation, and decentralization in the fintech space (Appaya & Gradstein, 2020; Ehrentraud et al., 2020).

In response to these challenges, regulators worldwide have followed different approaches to provide an appropriate legal, regulatory, and supervisory framework.

- *Wait-and-see approach.* This approach is based mainly on regulators' observation and monitoring of fintech when the respective technology is at its initial stages.
- *Test-and-learn approach.* This approach is characterized by agility in implementing the existing regulation on a case-by-case basis while maintaining the existing regulatory standards.
- *Innovation facilitator approach.* In this approach, regulators drive initiatives instead of simply observing fintech developments. This approach takes one of the following forms: innovation hubs (physical space promoting

industry-changing products), regulatory sandboxes (testing grounds for new models not currently protected or supervised by regulatory bodies), regulatory accelerators (for companies that are looking to scale their businesses rapidly), and tech sprints (who use technology to solve a specific problem statement).

- *Transformation of regulation and reforms approach.* This approach occurs when existing policies are unsuitable for fintech (Appaya & Gradstein, 2020).
- Besides sandboxes, regulators are exploring innovative approaches to adapt to the challenges posed by fintech, including regulatory technology (regtech) and digital identity solutions, like electronic Know Your Customer (e-KYC), to enhance security and streamline customer onboarding and authentication processes. These efforts aim to reduce the risk of identity theft and financial fraud while ensuring customer privacy and data protection.

The Path to Digital Transformation and the Future of Banking

Throughout their existence, FIs have been able to evolve and adapt accordingly in response to changing environments. In the current dynamic ecosystem of financial services, dominated by rapid technological developments and competition by actors not native to the industry, FIs harness digital solutions to improve their capabilities, survive, and compete. This digital transformation signifies an era in their evolution, fundamentally reshaping their operations, engagement with customers, and delivery of products and services. However, the approach to digital transformation and the choice of interaction with fintech and big tech firms may vary from one FI to another, depending on various internal and external factors. In that respect, this section reviews the current response of traditional FIs, explains the need for digital transformation and the concept of "fintegration," and considers key characteristics of FIs that will help them prevail in this new environment.

The Response of Traditional FIs in a Changing Ecosystem

Until now, traditional FIs have taken diverse approaches to address fintech disruption as they seek to balance preserving their existing strengths with pursuing new opportunities in the digital era. In this regard, Hernández de Cos (2019) summarizes potential scenarios and choices of interaction between incumbent FIs, fintech, and big tech firms. However, some universal recognition of the need to embrace technology and innovation to remain competitive exists. Therefore, many traditional FIs have actively engaged with fintech firms, improved their digital services, and explored new business models to adapt to the changing financial landscape.

Some traditional FIs have chosen to collaborate with or invest in fintech start-ups. These partnerships, which cut across the entire financial services value chain, aim to leverage the innovation and agility of fintech firms while benefiting from the established customer base and regulatory compliance of traditional banks. For example, in the United Kingdom, the six largest banks have mainly invested in fintech firms that engage in payments, banking, and financial management solutions, with the specific spaces accounting for 42% of the total funds from these banks (Murinde et al., 2022). Others have established innovation labs where internal teams develop proprietary technology solutions, enhance digital services, and explore blockchain and AI applications. This approach allows FIs to control and tailor their technology to meet their needs. Several FIs have expanded their online and mobile service offerings to compete with fintech firms. These offerings include features like robo-advisors for automated investment management, digital payment wallets, and P2P lending platforms. In addition, some incumbent banks are shifting toward more customer-centric approaches, emphasizing personalization, offering financial advice, and improving customer service, as they gradually recognize the importance of a positive customer experience in retaining and attracting clients.

Independently of which approach incumbent FIs will choose to interact with the fintech ecosystem, their digital transformation is necessary to equip them with the right tools to deal with competition and reach the next stage in their evolution by leveraging new business models and digital strategies. Digital transformation is a "process that aims to improve an entity by triggering significant changes to its properties through combinations of information, computing, communication, and connectivity technologies" (Vial, 2019, p. 121). In that respect, incumbent FIs have already begun to use digital technologies aiming at amending the value-generating channels of the past. For instance, a clear downward trend exists in the number of branches in certain countries between 2003 and 2020, such as a decrease of 40% in the Netherlands, Lithuania, and the United Kingdom, indicating a gradual disentanglement from the traditional brick-and-mortar business model to a digital one (Murinde et al., 2022). However, for traditional FIs to achieve sustainable results, digital transformation should be treated as an ongoing process in their trajectory (Vial, 2019). Fintech has the potential to help them succeed in this undertaking.

A core proceeding of the discussion for digital transformation is that the financial services ecosystem and the existing FIs within are bound to evolve. A key feature of the fintech era from the perspective of incumbent FIs is that to prevail, they must now compete with other firms that have not been part of their traditional competition. Fintech and big tech firms, neobanks and challenger banks, telecommunications companies, retail companies, and firms from other sectors compete for market share in different domains within the financial services industry (Murinde et al., 2022).

So, what should traditional financial companies do about it? A good starting point for incumbent FIs is understanding their new competitors' business models and processes. Then, leveraging their centrality in the financial system, they should experiment with the business model that suits their strategy better. Apart from the centrality, FIs, especially incumbent banks, have an additional strategic competitive advantage and should capitalize on it to evolve. They are the focal point for customers' identification and reference data, verifying and protecting their identity in online transactions. The confluence of identity and money intensified in the digital age (Birch, 2014), further underlining the importance of wielding this power. This advantage can become a solid base for future business model changes, leveraging novel authentication protocols and communication standards.

Fintegration and the Road Ahead

A potential way the digital transformation of traditional FIs may occur is by implementing platform-based business models. With the introduction of open banking and, eventually, open finance, under such models, FIs as platform providers will connect sellers and buyers by leveraging digital technologies such as open application programming interfaces (APIs), greatly expanding their current broker capabilities. In this setting, they could bring to the table features such as identification and verification of customers, provision of accounts, and processing of payments. At the same time, they could also guarantee the smooth and exceptional integration of fintech firms into a mutually beneficial ecosystem (Zachariadis et al., 2018). This "fintegration" can serve as a role model for incumbent banks to enter other industries, connect with other applications and platforms, access new data, and realize the banking concept everywhere and anytime (King, 2018; Zachariadis & Ozcan, 2017). Such platform-based business models could promote increased modularity, collaborations with developers, the creation of innovative services and products, cultivation of network externalities, better onboarding experience for stakeholders, healthier competition among ecosystem participants, and accelerated growth.

In this journey, FIs may be transformed from money brokers to services brokers, with data being a central asset. By analyzing various data sources beyond credit history data, FIs will improve customer service by predicting their needs more accurately and addressing legacy challenges (Murinde et al., 2022). In addition, the existing capabilities in big data and predictive analytics, and potentially in AI, will assist in data decoding and automating customer journeys. Incorporating digital technologies can also help traditional FIs adapt and be agile in a rapidly evolving industry (Fitzgerald, 2016; Kohli & Johnson, 2011). This agility involves not only technological capabilities and flexible organizational structures but also leadership and strategic decisiveness, which may require FIs to sacrifice established revenue streams in a process of "creative destruction" to embrace innovation.

FIs must become "digitally ambidextrous" to succeed as they balance maintaining core capabilities and exploring new opportunities while experimenting and remaining ambitious, leveraging innovation and data-driven learning to stay competitive (Gupta et al., 2021). Although many FIs have started investing in digital transformation strategies, some remain tied to product-oriented cultures and inherited organizational structures.

In the future, FIs are expected to shift away from fixed product and service propositions to more tailored and dynamic ones based on customer needs and leveraging data and analytical technologies. The provision of financial services will evolve toward investing in experiences rather than products, becoming "appified" through "in-app infrastructures" or platforms as the primary access points for financial interactions, fundamentally altering the user experience

(Brunton, 2019). Within this framework, banking may happen automatically in the background ("invisible banking"), physical branches will be transformed into "phygital" stations mixing physical branches and digital interfaces like chatbots, holograms, and augmented reality, all enhancing and personalizing customer service and convenience.

At the same time, AI is set to play a pivotal role in the future of banking. FIs with the best access to well-structured and relevant data will have a competitive advantage. At the same time, privacy and trust will be paramount, with FIs playing a potential role as trustworthy allies in safeguarding customer data. Emerging technologies such as quantum computing will also play an important role in speeding up processes and boosting data-driven models (Murinde et al., 2022). Several countries are also exploring the concept of central bank digital currencies (CBDCs). A *CBDC* is the digital form of a country's fiat currency. It offers the potential for faster and more secure payments, increased financial inclusion, and improved monetary policy implementation.

Finally, the future of banking aligns with the growing focus on sustainability and ethical banking practices. It is expected that FIs will also be more socially responsible regarding environmental, social, and governance (ESG) issues. For example, they can increasingly support environmental issues such as recycling and waste management and encourage sustainable behavior by customers. This process can be done via their digital communication channels with the customers and even by embedding some practices in their products. For example, they can incorporate recommendations for green investing and rank opportunities based on carbon emissions data.

Summary and Conclusions

Technology has been a part of the banking and financial services industry, if not as a direct force of change, certainly as a catalyst of these forces that have been shaping it. The character of this impact on the industry has been evolving along with changes in the identity of FIs, the introduction of new players and competition, business needs and priorities, and changes in demographics, among other factors. However, fintech has altered this status quo by challenging existing processes, systems, and practices and proposing new solutions, particularly in transactions, lending, payments, wealth management, and insurance. Doing so has effectively challenged traditional FIs and their business models in their core functions, reinforcing the need for digital transformation and promoting efficiency, transparency, and cost-effectiveness. At the same time, fintech has highlighted the importance of changes in cybersecurity and the necessity for global collaboration and forward-looking regulation.

This synergy between fintech and traditional FIs, so-called fintegration, will likely continue. The future of banking and financial services is a dynamic and evolving landscape driven by emerging technologies such as AI, ML, and quantum computing, new types of currencies such as CBDCs, and changing customer expectations. Traditional FIs must address legacy challenges, transform from "rich in data, poor in insight" institutions to those that leverage data and even identity for enhanced operations, and adapt to the evolving landscape where customer mobility increases as data sharing frameworks lower switching costs. By adopting novel business models, focusing on their digital transformation, and harnessing data resources, they can create new value and foster ecosystems across industries. The banking and financial services industry is at a pivotal moment, with the potential to enhance financial inclusion, improve customer experiences, and drive economic growth through the continued evolution of fintech and integration with traditional banking. As incumbent FIs continue to navigate this shifting terrain, one thing is clear: those who are agile, innovative, and customer-centric will be well-positioned.

Discussion Questions

- Define financial intermediation and its core functions and explain what makes it an information business.
- Discuss how technology has shaped the financial services industry.
- Identify the domains that fintech has affected, and discuss this impact.
- Explain how traditional FIs are responding to the fintech challenge.
- Discuss the future of the banking and financial services industry.

References

Allen, F., & Santomero, A. M. (1997). The theory of financial intermediation. *Journal of Banking & Finance*, *21*(11−12), 1461–1485.

Alsabah, H., Capponi, A., Ruiz Lacedelli, O., & Stern, M. (2020). Robo-advising: Learning investors' risk preferences via portfolio choices. *Journal of Financial Econometrics*, *19*(2), 369–392.

Appaya, S. M., & Gradstein, H. K. (2020). *How regulators respond to fintech: Evaluating the different approaches – Sandboxes and beyond.* FinTech Note. No. 4. The World Bank. https://openknowledge.worldbank.org/handle/10986/33698

Arner, D. W., Barberis, J. N., & Buckley, R. P. (2015). The evolution of fintech: A new post-crisis paradigm. *Georgetown Journal of International Law*, *47*, 1271.

Arner, D. W., Barberis, J., & Buckley, R. P. (2016). 150 years of fintech: An evolutionary analysis. *JASSA − The Finsia Journal of Applied Finance*, *3*, 22–29.

Arrow, K. J., & Debreu, G. (1954). Existence of an equilibrium for a competitive economy. *Econometrica*, *22*(3), 265–290.

Bátiz-Lazo, B., & Carlos Maixe-Alté, J. (2011). Managing technological change by committee: Adoption of computers in Spanish and British savings banks (circa 1960−1988). *Revista de Historia Industrial*, 117–150.

Bhattacharya, S., & Thakor, A. V. (1993). Contemporary banking theory. *Journal of Financial Intermediation*, *3*(1), 2–50.

Birch, D. (2014). *Identity is the new money*. London Publishing Partnership.

Brunton, F. (2018). Messaging apps and new social currency transaction tools. In J. Wade & S. Murray (Eds.), *Appified: Culture in the age of apps* (pp. 179–187). University of Michigan Press.

Brunton, F. (2019). *Digital cash: The unknown history of the anarchists, utopians, and technologists who created cryptocurrency*. Princeton University Press.

Bryant, J. (1980). A model of reserves, bank runs, and deposit insurance. *Journal of Banking & Finance*, *4*(4), 335–344.

Campbell, T. S., & Kracaw, W. A. (1980). Information production, market signaling, and the theory of financial intermediation. *The Journal of Finance*, *35*(4), 863–882.

D'Acunto, F., Prabhala, N., & Rossi, A. G. (2019). The promises and pitfalls of robo-advising. *Review of Financial Studies*, *32*(5), 1983–2020.

Dermine, J. (2017). Digital disruption and bank lending. *European Economy – Banks, Regulation and the Real Sector*, *2*, 63–76.

Dewatripont, M., & Tirole, J. (1994). *The prudential regulation of banks*. MIT Press.

Diamond, D. W., & Dybvig, P. H. (1983). Bank runs, deposit insurance, and liquidity. *Journal of Political Economy*, *91*(3), 401–419.

Diamond, D. W., & Dybvig, P. H. (1986). Banking theory, deposit insurance, and bank regulation. *Journal of Business*, *59*(1), 55–68.

Dinckol, D., Ozcan, P., & Zachariadis, M. (2023). Regulatory standards and consequences for industry architecture: The case of UK open banking. *Research Policy*, *52*(6), 104760.

Ehrentraud, J., Ocampo, D. G., Garzoni, L., & Piccolo, M., (2020). *Policy responses to Fintech: A cross-country overview. FSI Insights on policy implementation*. No. 23. Bank of International Settlements. https://www.bis.org/fsi/publ/insights23.htm

Eisenmann, T., Parker, G., & Van Alstyne, M. (2011). Platform envelopment. *Strategic Management Journal*, *32*(12), 1270–1285.

Fama, E. F. (1980). Banking in the theory of finance. *Journal of Monetary Economics*, *6*(1), 39–57.

Fitzgerald, M. (2016). General motors relies on IoT to Anticipate customers' needs. *MIT Sloan Management Review*, *57*(4), 1–9.

Freixas, X., & Rochet, J.-C. (1997). *Microeconomics of banking*. MIT Press.

Gatev, E., & Strahan, P. E. (2006). Banks' advantage in hedging liquidity risk: Theory and evidence from the commercial paper market. *The Journal of Finance*, *61*(2), 867–892.

Gorton, G., & Pennacchi, G. (1990). Financial intermediaries and liquidity creation. *The Journal of Finance*, *45*(1), 49–71.

Greenbaum, S. I., Thakor, A. V., & Boot, A. W. A. (2019). *Contemporary financial intermediation*. Academic Press.

Gupta, R., Mejia, C., Gianchandani, Y. B., & Kajikawa, Y. (2021). Ambidextrous firm strategy: Insights from internet of things linked interfirm deals. *IEEE Transactions on Engineering Management*, *70*(1), 1–16.

Gurley, J. G., & Shaw, E. S. (1960). *Money in a theory of finance*. Brookings Institution.

Hernández de Cos, P. (2019). Financial technology: The 150-year revolution. Basel Committee on Banking Supervision Speech. https://www.bis.org/speeches/sp191119.htm

Holmström, B., & Tirole, J. (1998). Private and public supply of liquidity. *Journal of Political Economy*, *106*(1), 1–40.

Kashyap, A. K., Rajan, R., & Stein, J. C. (2002). Banks as liquidity providers: An explanation for the coexistence of lending and deposit-taking. *The Journal of Finance*, *57*(1), 33–73.

King, B. (2018). *Bank 4.0: Banking everywhere, never at a bank*. John Wiley & Sons.

Kohli, R., & Johnson, S. (2011). Digital transformation in latecomer industries: CIO and CEO leadership lessons from Encana Oil & Gas (USA) Inc. *MIS Quarterly Executive*, *10*(4), 141–156.

Leland, H. E., & Pyle, D. H. (1977). Informational asymmetries, financial structure, and financial intermediation. *The Journal of Finance*, *32*(2), 371–387.

McAfee, A., & Brynjolfsson, E. (2016). Human work in the robotic future: Policy for the age of automation. *Foreign Affairs*, *95*(4), 139–150.

McKenzie, L. W. (1954). On equilibrium in Graham's model of world trade and other competitive systems. *Econometrica*, *22*(2), 147–161.

Merton, R. C. (1989). On the application of the continuous time theory of finance to financial intermediation and insurance. *The Geneva Papers on Risk and Insurance – Issues and Practice*, *14*(52), 225–261.

Murinde, V., Rizopoulos, E., & Zachariadis, M. (2022). The impact of the FinTech revolution on the future of banking: Opportunities and risks. *International Review of Financial Analysis*, *81*(C), 102103.

Navaretti, G. B., Calzolari, G., Mansilla-Fernandez, J. M., & Pozzolo, A. F. (2017). Fintech and banking: Friends or foes? *European Economy-Banks, Regulation, and the Real Sector*. https://european-economy.eu/2017-2/fintech-and-banks-friends-or-foes/

Santomero, A. M. (1984). Modeling the banking firm: A survey. *Journal of Money, Credit, and Banking*, *16*(4), 576–602.

Sironi, P. (2016). *FinTech innovation: From robo-advisors to goal-based investing and gamification*. John Wiley & Sons.

Tanda, A., & Schena, C.-M. (2019). BigTech strategic approaches: Worrying competition? In *FinTech, BigTech and banks, chapter 3* (pp. 37–50). Palgrave Macmillan.

Tang, H. (2019). Peer-to-peer lenders versus banks: Substitutes or complements? *Review of Financial Studies*, *32*(5), 1900–1938.

Thakor, A. V. (2020). Fintech and banking: What do we Know? *Journal of Financial Intermediation*, *41*(C), 100833.

Vial, G. (2019). Understanding digital transformation: A review and a research agenda. *The Journal of Strategic Information Systems*, *28*(2), 118–144.

Zachariadis, M. (2020). How open is the future of banking? Data sharing and open data frameworks in financial services. In M. R. King & R. Nesbitt (Eds.), *The technological revolution in financial services: How banks, FinTechs, and customers win together* (pp. 129–157). University of Toronto Press.

Zachariadis, M., & Ozcan, P. (2017). *The API economy and digital transformation in financial services: The case of open banking*. SWIFT Institute Working Paper, No. 2016−001. http://dx.doi.org/10.2139/ssrn.2975199

Zachariadis, M., Ozcan, P., & Dinckol, D. (2018). The Economics and Strategy of platforms: Competing in the era of open banking. In E. Maslaveckas (Ed.), *The book on open banking: A series of essays on the next evolution of money* (pp. 59–70). Bud Financial Limited.

Chapter 6

Mobile Payments and Digital Banking Services

Adri de Ridder[a] *and David A. Burnie*[b]

[a]Uppsala University, Sweden
[b]Western Michigan University, USA

Abstract

This chapter examines mobile payments and digital banking services. The past decade has seen a rapid increase in the use of alternative payment systems, away from cash to electronic payments. The digitalization of payments includes business-to-business (B2B), customer-to-business (C2B), and government-to-business and consumers (G2B/C), whether the payments are by computer, wire transfers, and point of sale (POS) systems. POS systems have become a standard in many retail outlets. Mobile payments use a smart device for contactless pay. Consumers see the increasing prevalence of payment systems when they go to the retail checkout or service counter. Worldwide, mobile payments are approaching 50% of digital. Digitalized payment systems are becoming more secure, decreasing concerns over mistaken payments, fraud, and errors. Consumers' confidence in value and usage decreases with age. Most fraud is due to scams and not hacking. Greater access to improved infrastructure and affordable smart devices will expand the usage of digitalized payment systems worldwide.

Keywords: Fintech; mobile payments; digital banking; smart devices; fraud

Introduction

Payments by a business, consumer, or for person-to-person purposes are frequent and have been since the beginning of trade. Beyond barter, transactions were completed using cash payments for several centuries. In the early 20th century, Western Union offered a charge card to customers (Rampton, 2016), followed by other retailers. In 1950, the Diners Club card began the path to credit cards like Visa.

The Emerald Handbook of Fintech, 109–131

doi:10.1108/978-1-83753-608-520241011

Online banking and bill payment began in 1994, followed by mobile web payments in 1997 and cellphone-based mobile payments. Rampton (2016) offers further detail on developing the electronic to mobile payments world.

Almost all consumers use mobile digital payments, whether they realize it or not. These payments include transactions at checkout via a mobile point of sale (POS) device from a wireless device, a debit card, or even a check, which converts the information into an electronic payment for processing. Mobile wallets may be used, including online payment systems, mobile person-to-person (P2P) transfers, or other systems based on Bluetooth Low Energy (BLE) or Near Field Communication (NFC). The number of systems continues to expand, with start-ups offering various specialty systems for a targeted clientele. Some have come and gone, but new offerings continue to appear. Major players in digital mobile payments include early entrants such as PayPal, Zelle (clearXchange), Apple Pay, Cash App (Square), Android Pay, Samsung Pay, and Google Wallet. In 1999, mobile phone companies and operators Ericsson and Telenor Mobil allowed patrons to buy movie tickets. Large retailers such as Walmart also introduced their mobile payment products to consumers. These types of products enabled companies like Walmart to target customer phones with directed coupons and special deals and use their account to make payments at the point of sale. Interac, primarily associated with card payment systems in Canada, offers mobile payments, as do Elavon and Moneris (owned by two large banks) and the WIX payments processor.

Many buy now, pay later (BNPL) suppliers are in the marketplace (de Best, 2023). Many use digital platforms and payments. This segment will not cover these services.

Rise of Smart Payments

The number of users of contactless pay via mobile phone in the United States through Apple Pay, Starbucks, Google Pay, and Samsung Pay in 2022 was 45.4, 32.8, 24.5, and 14.1 million, respectively. Such transactions are expected to increase to 56.7 million for Apple Pay, 40.8 million for Starbucks, 31.1 million for Google Pay, and 14.6 million for Samsung Pay (Insider Intelligence, 2022). Using mobile pay is expected to expand over time. For example, the three US providers above are forecasted to grow at a 5.8% compound annual rate, and including Samsung, the overall growth rate is forecast to fall to 5.2%, based on the authors' calculation from data in Insider Intelligence (2022).

The rise of service providers and digital payments has been accomplished with the increasing adoption of internet and wireless services. Table 6.1 shows that fixed-broadband subscriptions on a percent per capita basis doubled from 2010 through 2022 and are expected to grow modestly through 2040. Although period-by-period growth of internet users is highly variable, overall, it is expected to increase by about 74%, from about 4.6 billion in 2020 to 8 billion in 2040. Smartphone devices are a tool of convenience; there were about 0.5 billion smartphone users in 2010, with 7.6% of the population using them. The number

Table 6.1. Worldwide Telecommunication Service Usage and Forecast.

	2010	2015	2020	2022	2030	2035	2040
Percent fixed-broadband subscriptions per capita	7.90	11.70	16.10	15.90	18.00	19.10	19.80
Smartphone penetration (% of the population)	7.60	31.30	59.10	65.80	78.90	82.10	83.80
Smartphone users in billion #	0.50	2.20	4.40	5.00	6.40	6.90	7.30
Internet users in billions #	1.90	3.00	4.60	5.40	7.30	7.70	8.00
Percent growth in internet users period by period		57.90	53.30	17.40	35.20	5.50	3.90

Source: Recast and added calculations based on Statista Market Insights, 2/2023 data from the International Monetary Fund, World Bank, United Nations, and Eurostat.

Note: This table shows broadband, smartphone, and internet usage and projected usage through 2040.

of smartphone users grew to 5 billion by 2022, covering 65.8% of the population. The forecast is that the vast majority of the population will be smartphone users by 2040 at 83.8%, and that will cover some 7.3 billion of the users (Statista, 2023a).

Users of smart payment systems have met much success. A survey of US consumers aged 18 and older (CivicScience, 2021) finds a large market to capture regarding the six platforms: Paypal, Venmo, Zelle, Apple Pay, Google Pay, and Cash App. The five categorical response choices were (1) Used it and liked it, (2) Used it but did not like it, (3) Plan to use it, (4) Not Interested, and (5) Never heard of it. In Category 1, the responses were 38%, 16%, 14%, 10%, 7%, and 6% across the six platforms, respectively, and averaged only 15.17% with a favorable response. Category five responses were 21%, 41%, 48%, 39%, 39%, and 50% across the six platforms, respectively, and averaged 39.67%. In 2021, many individuals have not heard of many of these apps. On average, the category with the next largest choice percent was "Not Interested." In 2021, the survey results show that although digital and smart payment systems have a large user base, a huge untapped segment for these services still exists.

The number of providers of digital payment services is immense. New providers appear regularly, while many fail for various reasons. Statista (2023a, 2023b) collects data on online processed payments, mobile POS payments, digital consumer commerce transactions, online cross-border payments, and remittance sending. Table 6.2 shows the largest market share by providers in the United States and China. Major US players accounted for 27% of the world-market share, while major Chinese players accounted for 42% in 2022. Others with recordable percent share comprised 27%; the remaining 4% is widely disbursed. The largest single identified player was Alipay with 17%, followed by WeChat Pay with 16% and Apple Pay with 11% market share. Paypal is fourth with 6% of

Table 6.2. Worldwide Digital Payment Market Share by Brand in 2022.

Players	Age (%)
Alipay	17
Apple Pay	11
Cash App	4
Google Pay	5
Other	27
PayPal	7
Tenpay	3
UnionPay	6
WeChat Pay	16
Total US majors market share	27
Total China majors market share	42
Other plus residual market share	31

Source: Statista Market Insights and the authors' calculations.

Note: This table shows the major players in digital payments and residual market share of the remaining providers.

the worldwide market, and another four companies and market shares were identified. The block of smaller world-market share players is labeled as other (27%). This group may include players such as Wise in the United Kingdom and Swish in Sweden, which hold a large percentage of their market but are small on a global basis. Other players, such as Zelle, are popular for payments between individuals. Stripe is a payment service processor and provider popular with small businesses that lets merchants process credit and debit cards and other types of payments.

Worldwide Digital Activity

Digital transactions worldwide are divided into three categories in Table 6.3: Digital Commerce, Digital Remittances, and Mobile POS payments. Digital Commerce was $2.98 trillion in 2017, grew by $1.10 trillion to $3.99 trillion in 2020, and another $1.43 trillion to $5.42 trillion in 2022. By 2027, digital commerce is expected to reach $9.04 trillion in 2027. In Table 6.4, the year-over-year growth rates are mostly in the 10%–11% range, except for the large jump in 2021 of 21.8% during the height of COVID-19. Digital commerce has made strong and steady growth in business over the past several years.

Digital Remittances worldwide were $0.06 trillion in 2017, growing by $0.01 trillion annually through 2020 before increasing by $0.03 trillion in 2021. The forecast is for remittances to increase to $0.17 trillion by 2027. Although these changes appear small, Table 6.4 shows the yearly growth rates averaging just

Table 6.3. Worldwide Transaction Value by Segment in Trillion USD (US$).

	2017	**2018**	**2019**	**2020**	**2021**	**2022**	**2023**	**2024**	**2025**	**2026**	**2027**
Digital commerce	2.98	3.27	3.53	3.99	4.86	5.42	6.03	6.68	7.40	8.25	9.04
Digital remittances	0.06	0.07	0.08	0.09	0.12	0.12	0.14	0.15	0.16	0.17	0.17
Mobile POS Payments	0.33	0.76	1.19	1.98	2.51	2.82	3.30	3.82	4.39	4.98	5.58
Total	3.36	4.10	4.80	6.06	7.48	8.35	9.46	10.65	11.95	13.40	14.78

Source: Statista (2023a).

Note: This table shows historical values of digital transactions and mobile payments with forecasts through 2027.

Table 6.4. Percent Transaction Value Change by Segment.

	2018	2019	2020	2021	2022	2023	2024	2025	2026	2027
Digital commerce	9.90	8.10	12.80	21.80	11.60	11.20	10.80	10.90	11.40	9.60
Digital remittances	23.9	20.00	13.90	21.60	3.90	12.90	9.80	7.10	4.80	4.70
Mobile POS Payments	131.60	55.60	66.80	26.60	12.40	17.20	15.80	14.80	13.60	11.90
Total	22.00	17.10	26.10	23.40	11.70	13.30	12.50	12.20	12.10	10.30

Source: Statista (2023a).

Note: This table shows the historical and forecast growth rates of digital transactions and mobile payments through 2027.

under 20%. Digital remittances are also a convenient tool for sending funds to families in other parts of the world. The growth rates of higher single digits are expected to be mid-single digits by 2027 (Statista, 2023a).

Mobile POS payments have changed dramatically over the past 6 years. Table 6.3 shows that mobile POS payments were $0.33 trillion in 2017. These payments increased to $2.82 trillion in 2022 and are expected to increase to $5.58 trillion in 2027. In Table 6.4, the initial year-over-year growth rates are high (given the low starting base) but grew at 12.4% in 2022 and are expected to grow to mid-teen rates through 2027. In comparison, Mobile POS payments averaged about 52% of digital commerce in 2021 and 2022 but are expected to equal about 57% in 2024 and increase a few points each year to be about 62% by 2027. The change in payment behavior is moving toward mobile POS payments as the growth rate in digital commerce is slowing more than in mobile. In all years, 2022 through 2027, the percentage change in mobile POS payments is greater than digital commerce and digital remittances growth, as shown in Table 6.4.

Select Country Trends in Digital Payments

The worldwide transactions in digital payments are available (Statista, 2023a), and Table 6.5 provides a sample of countries.

- *The United States.* The United States tops the list with a total transaction value of $740 billion of activity reported in 2017, which increased to $1,765 billion in 2022. The forecast is for total US digital payment transactions to reach $3,528 billion by 2027. The compound growth rate in digital payments between 2017 and 2022 was 19%. The forecast is for a further 15% compound growth through 2027.
- *China.* China is the leader in digital payment volume by value, starting with $1,362 billion in 2017. By 2022, the Chinese transaction value in digital payments was $3,337 billion, exhibiting a 19.6% compound growth rate. The transaction value by 2027 is forecast to be $4,908 billion at a slower compound growth rate of 8%. In Table 6.5, the United Kingdom is the next highest transaction value, with $373 billion at a 16.4% growth rate over the past 5 years (2017–2022). It is projected to grow 14.7% (author calculation from Table 6.4 data) over the next 5 years through 2027 to $741.3 billion in transaction value. With a large and growing population, India had a modest $42.77 billion in transactions in 2017 but grew to $153.3 billion by 2022 at a compound rate of 29.1%. India is forecast to grow to $321.7 billion by 2027 at a compound rate of 16%.
- *France.* France grew at a 19.6% compound rate between 2017 and 2022 from $169.7 billion and is forecast to grow by 14.2% through 2027.
- *Germany.* Germany started from a higher base of $116 billion but grew to $227.2 billion at a 14.4% growth rate. An 11.3% increase is forecasted over the next 5 years.

Table 6.5. Digital Payments Activity of Select Countries Between 2017 and 2027.

	2017	**2018**	**2019**	**2020**	**2021**	**2022**	**2023**	**2024**	**2025**	**2026**	**2027**
The United States	740.10	867.50	1019.00	1252.00	1527.00	1765.00	2041.00	2362.00	2724.00	3128.00	3528.00
China	1362.00	1738.00	2014.00	2599.00	3048.00	3337.00	3639.00	3924.00	4237.00	4589.00	4908.00
Canada	46.47	52.77	61.23	74.23	99.65	117.30	137.00	157.60	180.20	204.90	229.40
France	69.34	79.39	89.54	119.50	152.30	169.70	199.00	228.00	259.90	294.80	329.60
Germany	116.00	132.90	144.00	152.50	207.00	227.20	257.60	289.50	322.50	357.30	387.60
India	42.77	54.29	71.21	96.41	130.50	153.30	180.40	210.20	243.80	283.40	321.70
Mexico	18.35	25.81	35.82	44.96	63.94	76.97	90.01	103.40	118.40	135.90	151.70
Sweden	16.82	19.48	22.52	28.83	36.87	39.00	46.26	53.07	60.64	69.07	77.36
The United Kingdom	174.60	196.80	217.30	272.30	340.70	372.70	439.30	510.90	582.60	661.40	741.30

Source: Statista (2023a).

Note: This table shows the historical payment activity of the various countries and the forecast of digital payments through 2027. The transaction value comparison is in billions of US dollars.

- *Sweden.* Sweden had $16.82 billion in transactions in 2017, growing at an 18.3% compound rate to $39 billion in 2022. The forecast is to grow at a 14.7% rate to $77.36 billion in transaction value by 2027.

The North American partners, Mexico and Canada, experienced quick growth in transaction value from 2017 to 2022.

- *Mexico.* Mexico had $18.35 billion in transaction value in 2017 and grew to $76.97 billion in 2022 at a compound rate of 33.2%. Mexico is forecast to grow to $151.70 billion in US dollar equivalent transaction value by 2027 at a rate of 14.5%.
- *Canada.* In 2017, Canada's transaction value was $46.7 billion, which grew to $117.3 billion in 2022 at an annual compound rate of 20.3%. The transaction value is expected to grow by 14.4% to $229.4 billion by 2027.

Across this select set from the worldwide list in Statista, almost every country has experienced a high growth rate in the teens to 20% or more between 2017 and 2022. The countries are all forecast to have continued growth in 2023 for the next 5 years at a greater than 10% compounded rate. The steady to rapid advances in financial technology tools coupled with the increased access to telecommunication services shown in Table 6.1 will likely continue the increase in usage and transaction value.

Select Country Trends in Mobile Payments

Tables 6.3 and 6.4 show that mobile payments will likely dominate the digital payments world. Table 6.6 provides an overview of the transaction value worldwide for mobile POS payments in trillions of US dollar equivalents. Total mobile POS payments were $0.33 trillion in 2017 and grew to $2.82 trillion in 2022. Estimates are $3.82 trillion for 2024, $4.98 trillion in 2026, and $5.58 trillion in 2027. The second line of the table gives the percentage change of the total mobile POS payments year by year; the first reported change in the table shows a 131.6% jump in activity, dropping to 55.6% the next year and then dropping over the next 2 years to 12.4% in 2022 with forecast ranging from 17.2% increase in 2023 down to an 11.9% growth for 2027. The number of mobile POS system users was $0.3 trillion in 2017, which grew at a 38% compound rate through 2022 and is expected to grow at 5.3% through 2027. The reported penetration rate for mobile POS payment system users was 4.1% in 2017, growing to 19.7% in 2022 and expected to grow to 24.4% by 2027. The low penetration rate still indicates that Mobile POS payments can grow considerably as infrastructure and economic capabilities expand in countries worldwide.

The growth in all forms of digital payments will continue as more shopping is done online and in convenience-style purchase arrangements from corner stores to major retailers. The growth of mobile POS payments by transaction value (US $-based equivalent) for the same select countries in Table 6.5 is reported in Table 6.7.

Table 6.6. Mobile POS Payments Worldwide.

	2017	2018	2019	2020	2021	2022	2023	2024	2025	2026	2027
Total	0.33	0.76	1.19	1.98	2.51	2.82	3.30	3.82	4.39	4.98	5.58
Total % change		131.6	55.60	66.80	26.60	12.40	17.20	15.80	14.80	13.60	11.90
Users (in billions)	0.30	0.63	0.90	1.33	1.49	1.50	1.59	1.68	1.77	1.86	1.94
Percent penetration	4.10	8.60	12.20	17.80	19.70	19.70	20.70	21.70	22.70	23.60	24.40

Source: Statista (2023b).

Note: This table shows total historical mobile POS payment activity, percent growth, number of users, and penetration with forecasts through 2027. The transaction value is in trillions of US Dollars.

Table 6.7. Worldwide Digital and Mobile POS Payments – Select Countries Between 2017 and 2027.

	2017	2018	2019	2020	2021	2022	2023	2024	2025	2026	2027
The United States	97.70	160.20	237.70	376.30	468.20	542.00	651.30	787.60	945.00	1115.00	1284.00
China	197.30	493.40	717.30	1132.00	1351.00	1482.00	1649.00	1829.00	2014.00	2206.00	2393.00
Canada	1.25	3.74	8.13	15.36	23.09	29.19	36.39	43.85	52.48	61.82	71.17
France	0.31	2.13	7.33	20.25	33.44	43.62	60.45	74.1	89.08	105.00	121.00
Germany	0.15	1.13	3.50	9.31	19.30	25.04	34.24	41.55	49.48	57.84	66.21
India	1.48	4.31	8.01	14.98	21.07	25.42	30.79	36.41	42.40	49.06	55.48
Mexico	0.30	2.05	4.70	7.73	12.02	15.69	19.48	22.46	25.61	29.11	32.54
Sweden	0.90	2.66	5.11	9.85	14.03	14.61	18.90	22.50	26.40	30.60	34.71
The United Kingdom	6.43	17.93	33.33	68.18	100.90	110.10	143.70	175.00	207.2	242.00	277.30

Source: Statista (2023b).

Note: This table shows historical digital and mobile POS payment usage for select countries between 2017 and 2027. The transaction value comparison is in billions of US dollars.

- *The United States.* Mobile POS payments in the United States were \$97.7 billion in 2017, jumping to \$540 billion in 2022, and are forecast to reach \$1,284 billion by 2027.
- *China.* China's mobile payments were \$197.3 billion in 2017, grew to \$1,482 billion in 2022, and were estimated to be \$2,393 billion by 2027.
- *India.* India's mobile payments stood at \$1.48 billion in 2017, reached \$25.42 billion in 2022, and are forecasted to more than double to \$55.48 billion by 2027.
- *The United Kingdom.* The United Kingdom started with \$6.43 billion in transaction value in 2017, climbed to \$110.10 billion in 2022, and is expected to almost triple to \$277.3 billion by 2027.
- *Sweden.* Sweden started at a \$0.9 billion transaction value in 2017, grew rapidly to \$14.61 in 2022, and is expected to achieve \$34.71 billion in transaction value by 2027. The other four countries also had rapid growth in the use of mobile POS payments. These payment structures are expected to continue as an important part of the payment landscape.

Mobile Growth Trends

How have the different payment systems changed over time? Are there any trends of interest? What should businesses and individuals expect to experience with these systems? The trend in the usage rate of mobile POS payments versus the total digital payments for the selected countries in Tables 6.5 and 6.7 are compared in Table 6.8. The percentage of mobile POS payments relative to total digital payments is provided.

- *The United States.* Mobile POS payments in the United States were 13.2% of total digital payments in 2017 and grew to 30.71% in 2022. Based on the forecasts, this trend percentage is expected to be 36.39% in 2027; over one-third of all US digital payments are expected to be mobile.
- *China.* China had a 14.49% mobile POS rate versus total digital payments in 2017 and 44.41% in 2022. This rate is forecast to reach 48.76% by 2027, or almost half of all digital payments will be mobile. India had a modest 2017 rate of 3.45% of mobile POS payments versus total digital payments, which increased to 16.58% by 2017 and is expected to reach 17.25% by 2027.
- *France.* France had a low 0.45% mobile POS payment as a percentage of total digital payments in 2017, which has increased rapidly to 25.70% as of 2022 and is expected to reach 36.71% by 2027.
- *Sweden.* In 2017, Sweden had 5.37% of total digital payments via mobile POS, and by 2022, the POS payment percentage had increased to 37.46%. Sweden is expected to top 44.87% in mobile POS payments relative to total digital payments by 2027. The increasing fractions of mobile POS payments as a percentage of total digital payments support the view that businesses and customers are becoming more comfortable with the use and convenience of these payment methods.

Table 6.8. Transaction Value Percent Comparison Mobile POS Payments Versus Digital Payments by Country.

	2017	2018	2019	2020	2021	2022	2023	2024	2025	2026	2027
The United States	13.20	18.47	23.33	30.06	30.66	30.71	31.91	33.34	34.69	35.65	36.39
China	14.49	28.39	35.62	43.56	44.32	44.41	45.31	46.61	47.53	48.07	48.76
Canada	2.69	7.09	13.27	20.69	23.17	24.88	26.56	27.82	29.12	30.17	31.02
France	0.45	2.68	8.19	16.95	21.96	25.70	30.38	32.50	34.27	35.62	36.71
Germany	0.13	0.85	2.43	6.11	9.32	11.02	13.29	14.35	15.34	16.19	17.08
India	3.45	7.93	11.25	15.54	16.15	16.58	17.07	17.32	17.39	17.31	17.25
Mexico	1.64	7.94	13.11	17.20	18.80	20.38	21.64	21.72	21.63	21.42	21.45
Sweden	5.37	13.68	22.70	34.15	38.05	37.46	40.86	42.40	43.54	44.30	44.87
The United Kingdom	3.68	9.11	15.34	25.04	29.62	29.54	32.71	34.25	35.56	36.59	37.41

Source: Calculated from Table 6.7 divided by 6.5.

Note: This table shows how much mobile POS payments constitute a percentage of all reported digital payments in the country.

If China and Sweden are evidence of the long-term trend, then expectations are that about half of digital payments will be mobile.

Differences across countries can exist for many reasons. In some cases, access to development and availability of systems has put some in the lead, and others must play catch up. Culture and government policy have pushed digital systems into the forefront in some countries. The cost of putting systems in place and customers having the money to acquire the mobile device are important to others.

Digital Service Providers in the United States

Digital service providers have changed due to the need for robust hardware, user-friendly software, and the ability to attract enough business to survive. The largest two US providers of digital services are Apple Pay and Google Pay. Apple Pay was estimated to have 631 million active users in 2021, with a total transaction volume of $650 billion, up from $6.6 billion in 2017 (Curry, 2023b). Google Pay was estimated to have $3.5 billion in transaction volume in India in 2019, about 1% of total US volume (Johnson, 2022). As these data are not broken out in the Alphabet financials, a no-growth estimate based on volume to revenues for 2022 would be $617 billion (Google Annual Report, 2020, 2022). Apple and Google are ubiquitous through their other services and devices, such as smartphones, computers, watches, and email.

The three more successful US survivors to be discussed next are PayPal (and Venmo), Block (Square, Square Cash, now CashApp), and Zelle.

PayPal and Venmo

PayPal started in 1998 as Confinity in security software. In 1999, electronic payments started. In 2000, a merger with X.com culminated with a focus on payments. The X.com name became PayPal in 2001. PayPal went through a going public transaction, then a subsidiary transaction, before being spun out as a separate entity (Wikipedia Contributors, 2023a). It has acquired many related services to make the company safer, minimize potential fraud, and offer more services. PayPal is available in many countries worldwide. It launched a peer-to-peer payment platform in 2015. Several online selling platforms use PayPal as a primary payment tool.

Venmo is the mobile payment service offered by PayPal. Venmo allows money transfers between two parties. A Venmo account is linked to a bank account or credit card. The process is quick and convenient for parties on the Venmo system. The app is a popular tool for sharing or splitting costs among social contacts. Venmo's payment volume in 2022 was $200 billion (Curry, 2023a; Horsey, 2023), second in activity of the four.

Block (Square and CashApp)

Block changed its corporate name from Square to Block in December 2021 to reflect the wider business, including Square and CashApp (Wikipedia Contributors, 2023b). Cash App allows users to send, spend, and invest in stocks or Bitcoin.

Square is still a mobile payments provider, but its business app set allows mobile transactions at POS, among other business services. Dizon (2023) reports that Square had over 33 million downloads and over 2 million active users. Businesses can also accept payment via CashApp for a transaction charge. Users primarily would have a bank account attached to their CashApp account. CashApp earns a fee for transfers. If a user does not have a direct deposit account, funds can be withdrawn from ATMs for a fee. Square was third in payment volume at $186.4 billion in 2022 (Curry, 2023a).

Zelle

Zelle started as clearXchange in 2011 by Bank of America, JPMorgan Chase, and Wells Fargo. The service was to offer person-to-person, business-to-consumer, and government-to-consumer payments. In 2016, clearXchange was sold to a new entity, Early Warning Service, LLC, owned by the bank group Bank of America, Truist, Capital One, JPMorgan Chase, PNC Bank, US Bank, and Wells Fargo (Wikipedia Contributors, 2023c). Many financial institutions are affiliated with the system. The Zelle payment system was released in 2017. Zelle's users have their Zelle account linked to their bank account. Thus, no separate account is needed. Funds are transferred between registered accountholders in the system. Users can also request payment from other users on the system. A shortcoming is that payments in Zelle cannot be canceled, and as in all systems, some have occurred. Zelle had the highest payment volume of these services listed in 2022 at $629 billion.

Business Use of Digital Payments

The consumer-to-business activity in digital payments is well documented in the data previously discussed. Business-to-business (B2B) activity in digital payments has occurred for many years. Payments by cash or check have been declining as a payment method as ACH debits/credits have been applied across the banking system. The Digital Payments Survey (Association for Financial Professionals, 2022) reports that B2B payments via checks have fallen nine percentage points to 33% since 2019 in North America (the United States and Canada), with a world average of 31%. Receipts average 30% in North America by checks and 29% worldwide. In North America, ACH credits have increased to 39%, ACH debits are 7%, various wires are 13%, and eWallets are 1%.

Respondents, on the likelihood of converting the majority of B2B payments to digital payments within 3 years, show that 27% are already digital; of these 24% of North American respondents were already digital, and 38% of international respondents were already digital. The top benefit of sending digital payments is the speed of settlement, chosen by 53% overall. This result rose to 68% for receipt of payment. The top two major barriers to digital payments were (1) difficulty in convincing customers to pay digitally (30%) and (2) shortage of information technology (IT) resources for implementation (34%). Many payments from business customers are made via a card, with 74% of respondents accepting online card payments and 52% POS payments, among others.

Digital payments provide faster payments and settlement, which recipients desire. Concerns about faster payments raise other issues. Some 38% of survey respondents agreed that faster payments could mean faster fraud and potentially increased business costs, as 36% were concerned that monitoring payments would be necessary outside of business hours.

Digital and Mobile Payments in North America

Many consumers and businesses have positively received digital payment transactions. Benefits for consumers seem to outweigh any costs, given the rapid rise in usage. Businesses have added costs of paying for the systems, potential fraud, and monitoring expenses. A potential advantage is that these systems do not all need to be based on bank accounts.

The estimated unbanked is 4.5% of US households and about 5.9% of households globally in 2021 (FDIC, 2023). Consumers may be unbanked due to insufficient funds to maintain minimum balances, insufficient trust in the system, or other reasons. The advent of digital payment systems allows the unbanked to complete desired transactions. Some digital systems have their holding account and allow withdrawal via ATMs, including others not listed previously. These methods expand opportunities for the unbanked. All consumers, banked or unbanked, can still face challenges and frustrations with the payment systems. Canadian consumers, 57%, reported payment friction over the first 6 months of 2021. Some 29% stated security in executing payments as the greatest frustration. Issues of paying bills, sending or receiving international payments, tax payments, and P2P transfers were other concerns, with many tied to not having the specific payment method the business used to accept payment (Payments.ca, 2021). The expected growth of digital payments will move banked and unbanked consumers and businesses further into using them.

Fintech and the Market for Payments – Some Observations From Sweden

The technological development and digitalization of primary payments have accelerated in the last decade. These developments have reduced the traditional payment for goods or services in cash – a payment transfers purchasing power from one (the payer) to another (the payee). However, besides the single payment with a digital transaction, other information has also been added: (1) who the payer is, (2) to which account the payment is to be made, and (3) when the payment is executed.

Comprehensive machinery that guarantees correct, timely, and inexpensive payment is required to achieve an efficient digital payment structure. This market also needs a well-functioning infrastructure among traditional banks, financial institutions, and regulatory entities. This infrastructure aims to provide a market with reliable data, excellent functional coordination between the providers, and a system that clears all payments. Therefore, the ability to undertake digital payments should be based on a system characterized as efficient with low transaction costs.

Sweden, Norway, Denmark, and Finland are at the forefront of digital payments. Sweden's retail payment market is one of the most digitalized markets globally. Specifically, cash, checks, and paper-based credit transfer payments have practically disappeared in Sweden, and card payments dominate. Riksbank (2019a) reports that 57.6% of all transactions were by card, 23.1% were electronic, direct debit accounted for 5.83% of payments, 6.39% were Swish, 6.43% were cash-based, and 0.66% were other paper-based forms of payments. Seven of 10 Swedes used Swish for payment (Riksbank, 2019b). In 2021, card payments made up 59.7% of all payment transactions (Riksbank, 2023).

The payment infrastructure in Sweden is undergoing major changes. Of interest is that more payments are carried out instantly, 24 hours a day, all year round. However, some restrictions still exist in the system related to cross-border payments. Increased cooperation exists among the Nordic and European market participants to reduce large infrastructure investments, such as IT support and automatic compliance phases.

Obstacles

Although many people use digital payments, the system has excluded large groups of people, including older adults, people with disabilities, and those who have directed legal representation. How to overcome this issue is not obvious. For instance, shortcomings in cooperation among market participants, central government, and civil society existed after the COVID-19 pandemic. Many shops in Sweden were closed or limited the number of customers, resulting in waiting time. To handle these problems, several food stores introduced and speeded up the option to buy online, where the goods could be delivered to the residence or picked up in specific "boxes" in the shop. This option requires an e-ID (an electronic identification tool) and an electronic payment. As previously mentioned, using cash for payments has declined over time. However, the demand for cash has remained virtually unchanged between 2020 and 2022 at 8%–9% (Riksbank, 2022). Hence, one interpretation is simple: people want to hold cash for various reasons.

Perhaps the most important obstacle to digitalization is that the digital payment market excludes some people. In Sweden, most people can access a payment account or an e-ID (electronic identity card). To obtain an e-ID, the providers require that the individual have a unique social security number. Some people, even if residing in Sweden, cannot access an e-ID because the social security number is not in the appropriate format. In addition, the Swedish system, with the unique social security number, is used by most market participants and governed institutions, like police, hospitals, and schools, but they are excluded without it.

Financial literacy refers to insights into the tools used in financial markets. Examples are an individual's familiarity with specific terms and attributes, like investment risk. A second obstacle is "digital exclusion," indicating that even if someone has access to digital systems, that person faces technological challenges. For instance, an elderly individual can have difficulty using a smartphone and all its application tools. Moreover, the rapid development of technology linked to smartphones implies new applications requiring the latest version. For instance, the payment service Swish used to have a code that enabled direct payment. Today, the system is based on the Quick Response (QR) system, which requires a user to scan the code to enable a payment. The development of different and reliable systems to avoid financial fraud implies that users must adopt new tools and technology.

Access to an Account

Two important challenges related to digital payments must be solved: (1) money laundering and (2) terrorist financing. A well-designed payment system must be protected from these activities. From a legal perspective, the compliance function of market participants, like banks and financial institutions, must completely control the individuals and their accounts, even if data shortage is a problem. One aspect of these potential payment problems is restricting the frequency and the value of payments for a user. For example, general rules limit the number of transactions and value unless a specific contract exists between the bank and the customer.

One feature of a reliable payment system is that payments should work even if the infrastructure is under great strain. Thus, individuals should be able to make payments even if the payment system is "down" due to disruptions in the electricity supply or electronic communication. Alternative payment methods must be available for firms that supply essential goods such as food, medicines, and fuel.

The Individual and the Digital Payment Market

A digital payment is easier and faster than a traditional payment with cash. At the same time, simplicity can result in overconsumption and, at worst, over-indebtedness. Another risk linked to the electronic payment market is fraud. From a legal perspective and also from the providers of different payment systems, crime linked to payments will result in less confidence in the digital payment market. In 2019, card fraud was only nine cases per 1,000 transactions in Sweden compared to 21 in Denmark, 35 in the United Kingdom, and 43 in France (Riksbank, 2019c). In 2021, card fraud was reported to have declined by 27% in Sweden based on police reports (Riksbank, 2021). Also, as was the case following COVID-19, the expansion of e-commerce has helped to blur the distinction between a payment and a credit. Thus, one important task that should be on the regulatory body's agenda is promoting financial literacy for individuals and young people.

What About Integrity?

With access to detailed information on individual's purchasing patterns, the digitalization of the payment market raises questions about privacy, secure identification and processing of personal data, and the effects of failure in these respects will have on the financial system. Today, the e-ID in Sweden is maintained by a private firm owned by Swedish and Scandinavian banks. As the information gathered by this entity has commercial value, whether a national-e-ID should be introduced is valid.

Competition

New market participants have challenged traditional Swedish banks and financial institutions in recent years. For instance, at the Stockholm Stock Exchange, the number of "traditional banks" is four, although a limited number of "new fintech" banks have been floated. A feature of these banks is that they are heavily digitalized, focusing on retail investors and platforms for trading stocks.

Competitive pressure is also put closest to the user by introducing new services and applications. In contrast, less competition occurs in the clearing and settlement system as it benefits from economies of scale.

Swish – The Major Payment Provider in Sweden

Six of the largest Swedish banks launched Swish's payment service on December 12, 2012. Swish is operated by Getswish AB (Swish, 2023). Since its launch, Swish has become one of the major payment tools. In June 2023, 8 million individuals, representing 77% of the population, had access to a Swish account. The application and electronic identification of Bank-ID enabled payments within 24 hours. Statistics show that 95% of individuals aged 15–65 use the system. Roughly 300,000 firms, ranging from supermarkets to dentists, are linked to the system and thus accept payments through the Swish application. In 2021, about 770 million Swish payments occurred across the three groups: private, company, and merchants. In 2022, approximately 902 million payment transactions occurred across the three groups. Private transactions were about 420 million in 2021 and 460 million in 2022 (Swish Stats, 2023). For individuals, the mean value of monthly payments is still low, about SEK 600 (roughly $60), where the average number of monthly transactions is around five.

Table 6.9 illustrates an increase in the frequency of individuals and firms using Swish. The number of individuals using the system was 8.6 million; in June 2023, the number of transactions was 43.2 million (Swish Stats, 2023).

Fig. 6.1 shows the monthly Swish transactions between June 2022 and June 2023 (Swish Stats, 2023). A seasonal effect can be observed in December, representing 41.4 million transactions, attributed to the Christmas and New Year holidays. Swish activity has continued to grow since its inception in 2012.

Table 6.9. Financial Activity Data for the Payment Platform Swish, June 2023.

	Number of Accounts	Year-Over-Year Growth	Number of Transactions	Year-Over-Year Growth	Mean Value of Transactions
Individuals	8,618,142	3%	43,178,694	4%	653
Firms	303,848	0%	10,420,727	8%	361
Shops	22,662	22,662	22,662	17%	357

Source: Swish Stats (2023).

Note: This table shows digital activity on the Swish platform in Sweden and the mean value of transactions in Swedish Krona.

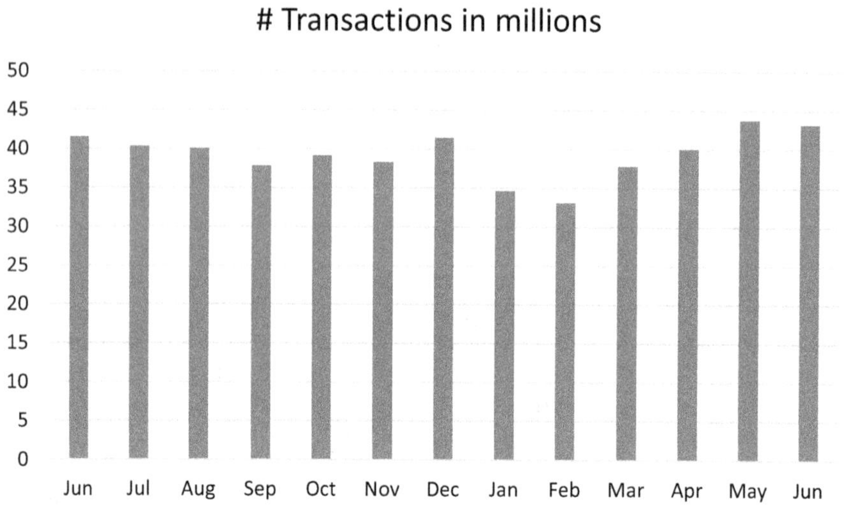

Fig. 6.1. Number of Swish Transactions by Individuals Between June 2022 and June 2023. *Note:* This figure shows the digital payment activity among individuals in Sweden. *Source:* Swish Stats (2023).

Summary and Conclusion

The digitalization of the payment system has grown markedly since 2017. Businesses offer more payment mechanisms, and customers accept them readily. Mobile POS payments are rising, potentially growing from about 52% of digital commerce transactions in 2022 to 57% by 2024 and up to 62% by 2027. As more than 60% of transactions are completed via mobile, all parties must be prepared, particularly businesses with multiple systems access. Payment behavior is moving toward mobile POS payments.

The move to digitalization has benefits and drawbacks. The benefits are increased convenience, reduced costs, and a lower need to make cash transactions. In Sweden, using cash is almost obsolete, with less than 7% of transactions completed in cash. Several mobile and electronic payment systems offer services without being tied to a bank account. The problem of being unbanked can be reduced through these mechanisms. The drawbacks are security concerns, giving up control of individual information, and fraud. Internal controls have improved, and issues such as hacking, while still occurring, are lower; business fraud concerns still exist, resulting in increased monitoring costs and the greater threat of fraud existing via nefarious schemes.

Digitalization is here and is topping 50% of payments across most of the world. The lower usage areas need added infrastructure and low-cost, affordable smart devices to provide these services to a greater share of the population.

Discussion Questions

- Describe the digitalization of the payments system.
- Identify the two countries with the most market share of digital consumer commerce transactions and discuss the future growth outlook.
- Define mobile payment and identify the leaders in mobile payments in the United States.
- Discuss the long-term growth trend in mobile payments and how it relates to all digital payments.
- Explain the recent impact of cash and check usage and discuss the most predominant methods.
- Discuss how Swish changed the payment landscape in Sweden.

References

Association for Financial Professionals. (2022). *Digital payments survey, comprehensive report.* https://www.afponline.org/publications-data-tools/reports/survey-research-economic-data/Details/epayments-survey

CivicScience. (2021, May–June). *Use of and interest in PayPal, Venmo, Cash App, Apple Pay, Google Pay, and Zelle among consumers in the United States in 2021.* https://www.statista.com/statistics/1203971/mobile-payment-app-experiences-usa/

Curry, D. (2023a, March 28). *Cash app revenue and usage statistics.* https://www.businessofapps.com/data/cash-app-statistics/

Curry, D. (2023b, May 2). *Apple statistics.* https://www.businessofapps.com/data/apple-statistics/

de Best, R. (2023, March). *Digital payments landscape in the United States – Statistics and facts.* https://www.statista.com/topics/4586/cashless-payments-in-the-united-states/#topicOverview

Dizon, A. L. (2023, March). What is square? How it works & why small businesses love it. *Fit Small Business.* https://fitsmallbusiness.com/what-is-square/

FDIC. (2023, May–June). *National survey of unbanked and underbanked households.* https://www.fdic.gov/analysis/household-survey/index.html

Google Annual Report. (2020). https://abc.xyz/assets/41/9c/0d82af85a0c1d73c5c6ded09557b/33c8c2856bcb5d1fba62328b1bcef3b4.pdf

Google Annual Report. (2022). https://abc.xyz/assets/d4/4f/a48b94d548d0b2fdc029a95e8c63/2022-alphabet-annual-report.pdf

Horsey, J. (2023, May–June). How does Venmo work when making and receiving payments. *Geeky Gadgets.* https://www.geeky-gadgets.com/how-does-venmo-work/

Insider Intelligence. (2022, March). Estimates on the number of users of selected contactless/tap to pay platforms in the United States from 2019 and 2021, with forecasts from 2022 to 2026 (in millions). https://www.statista.com/statistics/1337557/number-of-us-proximity-mobile-payment-users-by-platform/

Johnson, C. (2022, July 4). 23 interesting facts, trends + statistics. *Talk Radio News.* https://talkradionews.com/google-pay-statistics-23-interesting-facts-trends-statistics/#r

Payments.ca. (2021, August 18). Payments challenges and opportunities. Person to person payments in Canada – Interac. https://payments.ca/payments-challenges-and-opportunities-0

Rampton, J. (2016, July 17). The evolution of the mobile payment. *TechCrunch.* https://techcrunch.com/2016/06/17/the-evolution-of-the-mobile-payment/

Riksbank. (2019a, November 7). Payments in Sweden, the payment market is being digitalized. Card payments still dominate. https://www.riksbank.se/en-gb/payments–cash/payments-in-sweden/payments-in-sweden-2019/the-payment-market-is-being-digitalised/card-payments-still-dominate/

Riksbank. (2019b, November 7). Payments in Sweden 2019, more common to pay by mobile phone app (Swish). https://www.riksbank.se/en-gb/payments–cash/payments-in-sweden/payments-in-sweden-2019/the-payment-market-is-being-digitalised/more-common-to-pay-by-mobile-phone-app-swish/seven-out-of-ten-swedes-use-swish/

Riksbank. (2019c, November 7). Payments in Sweden 2019, Swedish payments are secure and efficient. Security in Sweden is high from an international perspective. https://www.riksbank.se/en-gb/payments–cash/payments-in-sweden/payments-in-sweden-2019/swedish-payments-are-secure-and-efficient/

Riksbank. (2021, November 3). Payments report 2021, are payments in Sweden safe? Downturn in number of card frauds. https://www.riksbank.se/en-gb/payments–cash/payments-in-sweden/payments-report-2021/2.-safety-and-efficiency/are-payments-in-sweden-safe/downturn-in-number-of-card-frauds/

Riksbank. (2022, December). The payment behaviour of the Swedish population. https://www.riksbank.se/en-gb/statistics/statistics-on-payments-banknotes-and-coins/payment-patterns/

Riksbank. (2023, July). Statistics on payments, card payments most common. https://www.riksbank.se/en-gb/statistics/statistics-on-payments-banknotes-and-coins/statistics-on-payments/

Statista. (2023a). *Digital payments worldwide.* https://www.statista.com/outlook/dmo/fintech/digital-payments/worldwide

Statista. (2023b). *Mobile POS payments.* https://www.statista.com/outlook/dmo/fintech/digital-payments/mobile-pos-payments/worldwide

Swish. (2023). *About Swish.* https://www.swish.nu/about-swish

Swish Stats. (2023, June). *Statistics regarding users and payments.* https://assets.ctfassets.net/zrqoyh8r449h/6W1yyPZxbFLJ4gGDxgnslP/70e136c0380130c7dfcf0b4d3630db7d/Swish_nu_engelska_juni_2023.pdf

Wikipedia Contributors. (2023a, June). CashApp. Wikipedia, The Free Encyclopedia. https://en.wikipedia.org/wiki/Cash_App

Wikipedia Contributors. (2023b, June). Paypal. Wikipedia, The Free Encyclopedia. https://en.wikipedia.org/wiki/Paypal

Wikipedia Contributors. (2023c, June). Zelle. Wikipedia, The Free Encyclopedia. https://en.wikipedia.org/wiki/Zelle

Section III

Raising Funds With Fintech: Digital Lending

Chapter 7

Marketplace Lending Platforms for Borrowers and Investors

Manuel Stagars[a] *and Ioannis Akkizidis*[b]

[a]Swiss Federal Institute of Technology (ETH), Switzerland
[b]University of Zürich, Switzerland

Abstract

Marketplace lending has substantially changed since the first peer-to-peer lending platforms emerged in 2006. The industry is now an alternative to bank lending, predicted to total $70 billion for consumer and business loans worldwide by 2030. Marketplace lending is often deemed less safe than bank loans, mainly due to these portfolios' high degree of hidden information. These include needing more information on borrowers and potential correlations between them, which might lead to higher risk than is apparent at first glance. Deterministic processes cannot capture tail risk appropriately, so platforms and lenders should employ stochastic processes. This chapter introduces a Monte Carlo simulation and machine learning (ML) process to evaluate and monitor portfolios. For marketplace lending to become a viable and sustainable alternative to bank lending platforms, they must better evaluate, monitor, and manage tail risk in marketplace loans and develop tools to monitor and manage financial risk losses.

Keywords: Marketplace lending; sensitivity analysis; credit rating; counterparty and credit risk; Chebyshev tensors

Introduction

Marketplace lending (MPL) matches borrowers and lenders through an online platform without using a traditional bank as an intermediary. Although the model started with the promise for individuals to borrow from often unsophisticated peer-to-peer (P2P) lenders, more institutional investors now fund MPL.

The Emerald Handbook of Fintech, 135–155

doi:10.1108/978-1-83753-608-520241012

The more descriptive term "marketplace lending" has supplanted "peer-to-peer lending" or "crowdlending" (Herrboldt, 2015).

This chapter aims to summarize the brief history of MPL and explain how loans originate on MPL platforms. It suggests a technical risk management approach for MPL portfolios based on machine learning (ML) that replaces stochastic processes to save time and CPU demands.

How does MPL work? A prospective borrower submits a loan application online in a loan transaction on an MPL platform. The MPL company then assigns a credit grade and interest rate to the loan with a proprietary credit scoring tool, which considers a borrower's self-disclosed information, like income. The loan request becomes available on the platform for retail investors to review and pledge funds based on their investment criteria. Institutional investors may also fund loans through whole loan purchases or securitizations.

MPL emerged from the rubble of the global financial crisis (GFC) of 2007–2009, when banks tightened credit markets, locking out borrowers without the highest credit ratings. Overnight, many private individuals and small and medium-sized enterprises (SMEs) found themselves without a credit line despite a satisfactory financial history and collateral. In 2005, Prosper launched the first P2P lending website in the United States, allowing consumers to receive online loans. In 2006, LendingClub followed suit, quickly becoming one of the biggest lenders in the MPL space. These platforms were uniquely positioned after the GFC. They filled this gap and offered borrowers a chance to raise P2P loans without using a bank as an intermediary.

Business Model and Risks

The MPL business model is simple. Borrowers post their requests for loans, to which platforms assign risk profiles with self-disclosure questionnaires, public data, such as credit ratings, and other data, such as borrowers' social media activity. Investors can then search these requests and fund the loans they like in exchange for yield. This alternative fundraising model gave borrowers direct and fast access to affordable credit. It offered investors the returns they sought in the low-interest rate environment after the GFC and persisted until 2022.

However, MPL has risks. Chava et al. (2021) document that consumers who borrow from MPL platforms have lower credit scores and higher default rates in the long run compared to applicants with similar profiles for bank loans. Platforms have little or no means of knowing how borrowers use the funds they raise on the platform. The self-disclosure of the financial situation of borrowers may be incorrect. A certain adverse selection risk exists, as lower quality borrowers may self-select MPL as their funding option of last resort.

In 2015, Akkizidis and Stagars (2016) conducted a stress test and analysis of LendingClub's MPL platform loan book. Although this study stressed portfolios with loans across the entire rating spectrum, the evidence shows almost no diversification and severe concentration risk in portfolios of marketplace loans regardless of diversification in the platforms' risk profiles. This evidence suggests that marketplace loans harbor hidden risks not disclosed in the platforms.

In 2016, LendingClub suffered from accusations of fraud and a lack of transparency that led to the ousting of its founder and chief executive officer (CEO) (Popper, 2018). LendingClub has since purchased a bank charter and retired the issuance of new notes (Lending Club, 2020). Despite concerns in the industry after the LendingClub case, new entrants grew the transaction value of MPL steadily, with a projected worldwide market size for alternative loans to consumers and businesses by 2027 of $34.7 billion and $37.42 billion, respectively (Statista, 2023). Fig. 7.1 shows that lending is stable between 2017 and 2022, ranging from $24.9 billion to $28.1 billion annually for consumers and between $7.6 billion and $8.2 billion for businesses, expected to remain within this range until 2027. As Fig. 7.2 shows, most of the growth in MPL is expected to occur in the business sector outside of the United States.

MPL and High Interest Rates

After the GFC and the fallout of the COVID-19 pandemic from 2020 to 2022, interest rates were at historic lows (Board of Governors of the Federal Reserve System (US), 2023). Fig. 7.3 shows the rate at which consumers and businesses borrow money is higher than the federal funds' effective rate. On top of regular lending rates, MPL loans incur several premiums to account for borrower risk ratings.

In a low-interest rate environment, fintech companies offer investors the yield they no longer find in the markets and their savings accounts. Low market interest rates validate the narrative that returns come with higher risk, some of which are hard to measure and even harder to diversify away and therefore favor MPL.

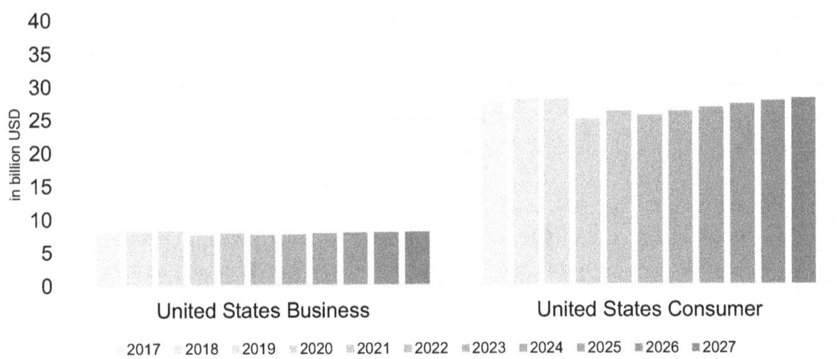

Fig. 7.1. Crowdlending Transaction Value in the United States. *Source:* Statista (2023). *Note:* This figure shows the growth of crowdlending transaction value in the United States.

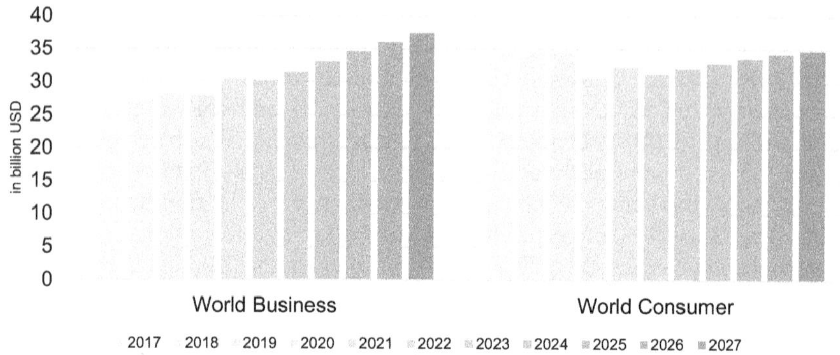

Fig. 7.2. Crowdlending Transaction Value Worldwide. *Source:* Statista (2023). *Note:* This figure shows the growth of the value of crowdlending transactions around the world.

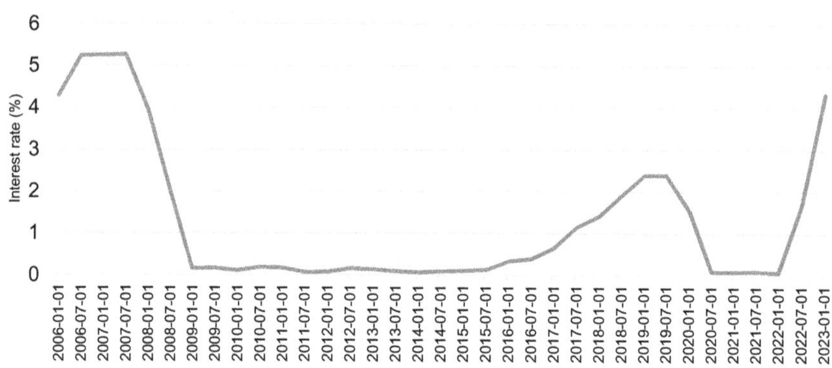

Fig. 7.3. US Federal Funds Effective Rate. *Source:* St. Louis Fed. *Note:* This figure shows that the GFC of 2007–2009 affected changes in the FED funds rate.

With rising interest rates, alternatives emerge for yield-seeking investors. Therefore, a rising interest rate might suppress the demand for investments in MPL loans. At the same time, as high interest rates imply slowing economic growth, some loan applicants might have no other option than borrowing at inflated rates to meet short-term obligations, increasing the demand for loans at high rates. Fintech companies might also offer new loan products, such as adjustable-rate loans, to entice riskier borrowers and more risk-seeking lenders. This situation, in turn, might persuade some investors to gamble on high returns with high risk, and it will also increase with a higher rate of default on lending platforms. In any event, MPL has too short a history in environments with higher interest rates to conclude ex ante.

MPL and High Inflation

High inflation is a new environment for MPL, and its impact on borrowing from online lenders is unclear. Fig. 7.4 shows that inflation never surpassed 4% since the GFC but has, in early 2023, been at multiyear highs (OECD, 2023). The coming years will provide insight into how higher expected prices might impact borrowing online.

Basic economic theory suggests that high inflation rates favor borrowers, as the purchasing power of their debt repayments gradually decreases over time. Borrowers repay their loans with money that is worth less and less over time. They would also rather spend now, when their money still has purchasing power, than later, when it might be worth less. However, higher expected price changes adversely impact consumers' reported readiness to spend (Bachmann et al., 2015). If corporate borrowing indicates the demand for business MPL loans during high inflation, Ropele et al. (2022) offer casual evidence. Using survey data from Italian firms, they find that firms with higher inflation expectations pay higher interest rates on average without changing the demand for loans but rebalance from longer term loans with lower rates to shorter term loans with higher rates. Financially savvy firms pay down existing loans with new long-term loans to lock in interest rate savings if they expect higher future interest rates and inflation in marketplace lending. Changing market risk factors depend on each borrower's idiosyncratic characteristics that are not indicated and included by systemic risk. A high idiosyncratic factor means that a borrower is largely independent of market risk factors. These idiosyncratic factors can be defined as inputs for a model that stresses portfolios of marketplace lending contracts and generates possible outcomes of losses. When modeling risk in marketplace lending, the assumption is a low idiosyncratic risk factor and a high correlation between borrowers.

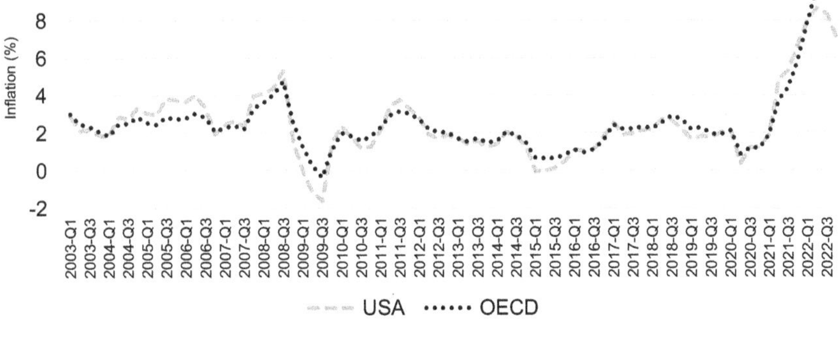

Fig. 7.4. Inflation and Consumer Prices. *Source:* OECD (2023). *Note:* This figure shows the pick-up in inflation of consumer prices starting in 2020.

The Risks of Bank Credit Portfolios

MPL is often deemed less safe than bank loans, mainly due to the high degree of fuzzy and hidden information in these portfolios. These include a lack of information on borrowers and potential correlations between them, which might lead to higher risk than is apparent at first glance. At the same time, bank credit loan portfolios come with risks, as they contain mainly fixed long-term loans, which may generate lower returns than the cost of their short-term liabilities when market conditions change quickly. With rising interest rates and high inflation, the maturity mismatch in Silicon Valley Bank's (SVB) portfolio led to its collapse in Q1 2023.

SVB faced a severe downfall due to its vulnerability to interest rate fluctuations and collapsed primarily because of its exposure to interest rate-sensitive assets and liabilities. When interest rates rose, the bank struggled to manage its interest rate risk effectively due to the absence of hedge instruments. The bank had a substantial portfolio of assets, including loans, deposits, and fixed-income securities sensitive to interest rate movements. On the liability side, the bank was exposed to very short-term deposit accounts, including savings and current accounts, against long-term assets. Unfortunately, the bank's risk management strategies and hedging techniques were insufficient to mitigate the adverse impact of interest rate changes.

Valuing MPL Credit Portfolios

The main issue in valuing, monitoring, and managing MPL portfolios is the simulation of tail risk. Borrowers' ratings will change with changing market conditions, such as rising interest rates and high inflation. Because contracts may contain fuzzy and hidden information, such as missing data on borrowers or the lack of potential correlations between them, deterministic processes, such as scenario analysis, fail to model rating migration and capture tail risk appropriately. Stochastic processes, like Monte Carlo analysis, can simulate all possible scenarios despite fuzzy and missing information. However, such processes may introduce a major computation bottleneck. Assume a simulation of 10,000 possible outcomes where each simulation takes one millisecond. Evaluating a portfolio with 1,000 loan contracts will, in this case, take 10,000,000 milliseconds, 10,000 seconds, 166 minutes, or almost three hours. This bottleneck can be overcome with a large server farm, but the approach is uneconomical and impractical, most certainly for the retail investor. Better alternatives provide, in this case, ML approaches, such as Chebyshev Tensors (CTs) or Deep Neural Networks (DNNs). They create proxies for tail risk cases that come very close to those in Monte Carlo analysis with a fraction of the CPU power necessary.

The following paragraphs will introduce the general process of stochastic techniques that can be useful in valuing MPL portfolios. Professional investors such as hedge funds know how to evaluate, monitor, and manage risks available, but retail investors may have to rely on platforms providing them with such tools.

When analyzing a portfolio of marketplace loans, the following assumptions are made about how a borrower takes out a loan and amortizes it:

- Option 1. The borrower pays interest (coupons) within a time interval (e.g., monthly) and the principal (capital) at the maturity date.
- Option 2. The borrower amortizes the interest (coupons) and principal amount within a time interval (e.g., monthly) to base the interest on the remaining principal.

Since the loans have exposure to market and credit risk factors, at t_0, the following rate spreads are set:

- The nominal interest rate (IR), e.g., 3%, is applied from t_0 to T (maturity).
- The credit spread (CS), e.g., 7%, indicates the borrower's – the counterparty's (CP) – credit rating. Since credit spreads contain a premium against counterparty credit default, counterparty risk is higher in marketplace loans than in conventional retail banking.
- The profit spread (PS), e.g., 3%, indicates the income of the lender.

The overall gross income rate is, therefore, $IR + CS + PS$. In the example above, it amounts to 13%.

In the case that at $t_1, t_2, \ldots, T$ the actual interest rates increase, let's say to $6\%, 6.5\%, \ldots, 7\%$, the following applies:

(1) For fixed-rate loans, given the fixed rate of 13% in the previous example:

- Assuming that the PS is steady, it implies that the spread curve adjusts to 4%, 3.5%, ... and 3%, respectively, indicating that the rating of the CP has been improved.
- Assuming that the credit rate is steady, i.e., 7%, this reduces the profit spread to $0\%, -0.5\%, \ldots -1\%$ to negative income.

(2) For floating-rate loans, if the forward interest rates increase in the same way as the actual rates, in the example above:

- The overall gross income adjusts to $16\%, 16.5\%, \ldots 17\%$ and
- CS and PS are set steady, but the new higher rate increases the default probability of the borrower, indicating higher expected credit losses.

Credit Portfolio Analysis Applicable to MPL

In a portfolio of loans, identifying if borrowers correlate with each other and to what degree they impact each other is essential. Defaults and, more generally, credit migrations are dependent across borrowers, and that positive correlation tends to increase the losses at the portfolio level. Borrowers have correlations for the following reasons:

- Common underlying macro and market risk factors impact them. For instance, inflation, economic growth, and interest rates affect borrowers in the same market.
- Since identifying the exact degree of correlation between borrowers and their risk factors is difficult, linking the borrowers to the segments they belong to is easier. Those segments stem from common characteristics like the same region, business sector, or other proxies.

A set of k sectors at time t and the sensitivity to the associated market risk factors or microeconomic factors must be defined. The idea is that the current and evolute macroeconomic factors and market risk factors, e.g., indexes, drive the correlation among borrowers belonging to k sector(s).

A sector, for instance, energy and tourism, relates to corresponding sector indices, inflation rates, and commodity prices. However, there are two types of sensitivity profiles θ_{ik} between segments k and risk factors i.

Given the different possibilities for allocating borrowers to different sectors, their structure and weights must be defined. The assumption in sector analysis is that the sectors have a strong influence on the participating obligors' performance in the sector. It also drives the correlation of defaults between the obligors. Sectors are associated with macroeconomic and market risk factors. Thus, the correlation and volatility of the risk factors define the corresponding correlation and volatility of the sectors and, consequently, the borrowers with links to them. Macroeconomic and market conditions hold significance for a couple of reasons. First, they determine the state of the sector, which subsequently impacts the likelihood of a borrower's rating change. Second, these conditions are crucial in establishing the loan's replacement value. This replacement value represents the fair value according to the rating status at any given future moment.

The following section outlines the main steps to determine the correlation among borrowers and to compute the progression of rating states via the Gaussian Copula Model.

Implementing the Future Correlated Rating States of Borrowers

The approach to model the credit migration correlation structure is the Gaussian Copula Model used in the CreditMetrics approach (J. P. Morgan, 1997). The initial proposal has evolved and branched out in multiple directions. The core component of CreditMetrics is the migration (or transition) matrix. This matrix captures the likelihood of transitions over a set period, often 1 year, during which an initial credit rating can either shift to a different rating or stay unchanged.

In the proposed model, rating change derived by indicator variable expressed as a suitable linear combination of a set of normalized systemic risk shocks $\epsilon S_{i,k}$, where $S_{i,k}$, $i = 0, \ldots, m$, are the macroeconomic or other market risk factors m, linked to k sectors, plus a component $\epsilon_{i,0}$ specific to the idiosyncratic characteristic of each borrower that is not indicated and included by systemic risk.

Given that the market and macroeconomic risk factors S_i model the systemic risk component, the Monte Carlo analysis stochastic process can be applied. A normalized shock, $\epsilon S_{i,k} = \Delta s_{i,k} = \frac{S_{i,k} - S_{i,k-1}}{\sigma_i \sqrt{T_{k+1} - T_k}}$, is applied where σ_i is the volatility of $S_{i,k}$, the normalized vector $\Delta s_{i,k}$ is distributed as $N(0, P)$ where P is the matrix of the correlations $\rho_{i,j}$ across S_i.

The states for the borrower, CP, is introduced based on Eq. (7.1):

$$\xi_{\mathrm{CP},j,\mathrm{TB}} = w_{\mathrm{CP},0}\epsilon_{\mathrm{CP},0,\mathrm{TB}} + \sum_{i=1}^{n} w_{\mathrm{CP},i}\epsilon S_{i,j,\mathrm{TB}} \tag{7.1}$$

where $w_{\mathrm{CP},i}$ defines the degree of sensitivity of the counterparty CP to the changes ϵ of the ith macroeconomic factor S_i. This coefficient of the model is an input factor that must be estimated and set. $w_{\mathrm{CP},0}$ defines the idiosyncratic factor specific to CP and is given by $w_{\mathrm{CP},0} = \sqrt{1 - w_{\mathrm{CP}}^{T} P w_{\mathrm{CP}}}$ with P representing the correlation matrix. Given the factor $w_{\mathrm{CP},0}$, the indicator variable $\xi_{\mathrm{CP},j,\mathrm{TB}} \sim \mathrm{N}(0, 1)$ is still standard normal distributed and fully systemic.

Note that with a yearly covariance matrix $\tau(T_{\mathrm{TB}}, T_{\mathrm{TB}} + 1)P$, the shocks $\epsilon S_{i,k,\mathrm{TB}}$ of the ith macroeconomic factor in the jth scenario and $\mathrm{TB}^{\mathrm{th}}$ time buckets are normally distributed. Furthermore, $\epsilon_{\mathrm{CP},0}$ represents the generated idiosyncratic risk independent of random Gaussian drawing numbers.

Assuming $\xi_i \sim N(0, 1)$ and defining Φ as the cumulative distribution function of ξ_i, then at t_{i+1} for the i th borrower, the $\Phi(\xi)$ results in the expected rating state $R_{i,t_{i+1}}$. As illustrated in Fig. 7.5, assuming that the initial rating stage of the borrower is B, if Φ returns a value smaller than α, then the borrower changes the rating stage from B to A. The borrower stays at rating B if the number is between

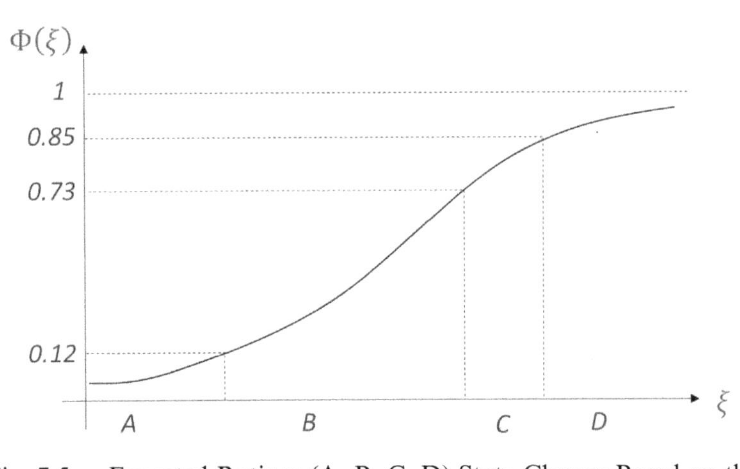

Fig. 7.5. Expected Ratings (A, B, C, D) State Change Based on the Cumulative Distribution Function Φ(ξ) of the Variable ξ_i. *Note:* This figure shows how the rating may change for the indicator variable ξ_i as defined in Eq. (7.1). Given the ξ_i, the cumulative distribution function Φ(ξ) defines the rating's change.

alpha and beta. In the case of $\beta < \Phi < \gamma$, the borrower moves from B to C; in other cases, the borrower defaults.

Allocation of Borrowers and Their Correlations

Each borrower may be independent or depend on more than one segment or sector, and relative systemic factor S_i, defined by sensitivity profile(s). Such a link is allocated based on a sensitivity profile, and the coefficient defines the dependency is denoted as w_{CP}. The next sections look at some possible ways of allocation.

Apportioning Borrowers Across Several Risk Factors

In such a case, a single borrower, CP, is allocated to a sector, k, linked to correlated risk factors S.

The correlation coefficient ρ_{S_i,S_j} between the macroeconomic or other market risk factors, S_i, S_j, is given by $\rho_{S_i,S_j} = \frac{\text{cov}(S_i,S_j)}{\sigma_{S_i}\sigma_{S_j}}$. Where $\text{cov}(S_i, S_j)$ is the covariance between S_i and S_j, whereas σ_{S_i} and σ_{S_j} are the standard deviation of S_i and S_j, respectively.

The systematic factors may affect each borrower CP, belonging to a sector k, leading to the uncertainty of the borrower's default rate.

It is necessary to attribute the systemic risk across various factors to model the systematic dependencies. Take, for instance, a borrower known as CP that belongs to a sector that is sensitive to fluctuations in two economic sectors, labeled S_i and S_j. The correlation between the sector and the systemic risk factors S demoted as $\theta_{k,S}$.

Common assumptions for such modeling might include:

- The definition of the proportion for systemic risk compared to risk that is idiosyncratic to the borrower: for instance, assuming a case where $\theta_{CP} = 30\%$ associated with idiosyncratic credit risk specific to the borrower itself, while the residual portion, which amounts to $1 - \theta_{CP} = 70\%$, is attributable to systemic factors.
- The allocation of the systemic risks across a sector k is determined by using the coefficient $\theta_{k,S}$. For instance, suppose θ_{k,S_i} accounts for 45% of the systemic risk, which is influenced by sector S_i, and θ_{k,S_j} represents 55% of the systemic risk which is linked to sector S_j.

This situation will result in systemic risk sensitivity coefficients $w_{\text{CP},kS_i} = (1 - \theta_{\text{CP}})\theta_{k,S_i} = 31.5\%$ and $w_{\text{CP},kS_j} = (1 - \theta_{\text{CP}})\theta_{k,S_j} = 38.5\%$.

Assuming a correlation between the risk factors, $\rho_{S_i,S_j} = 30\%$ it results in the determination of the specific coefficient as follows:

$$w_{\text{CP},0} = \sqrt{1 - \left(w^2_{\text{CP},kS_i} + 2\bullet\rho_{S_i,S_j}\bullet w_{\text{CP},kS_i}\bullet w_{\text{CP},kS_j} + w^2_{\text{CP},kS_j}\right)} = 82.4\%$$

Fig. 7.6 illustrates an example of allocating a borrower to a single sector k, which is linked to correlated risk factors i and j.

Apportioning Borrowers Across Several Sectors

Given that borrowers may correlate with several segments, the systemic risk must be allocated to a set of systemic factors S_i. Both idiosyncratic and systemic risk sensitivity coefficients $w_{\mathrm{CP},0}$ and w_{CP,kS_i} are calculated in a similar form as described in the above section. It's crucial to note that even if a borrower operates across multiple sectors, these sectors may be correlated because their systemic factors are interconnected.

Fig. 7.7 illustrates an example of allocating a borrower to two sectors k, which are linked to correlated risk factors, S_i.

Allocating Several Borrowers to a Common Single Sector

In this case, a borrower is allocated to a single sector k. The sector is linked to multiple market and microeconomic risk factors with sensitivities $\theta_{k,S}$. Assume that a single systematic factor affects the individual default rate volatility of each borrower. The following is true for such a model:

- It captures all concentration risk within the portfolio and excludes the diversification benefit of the fortunes of individual borrowers being subject to several independent systematic factors and
- It generates a prudent estimate of extreme losses.

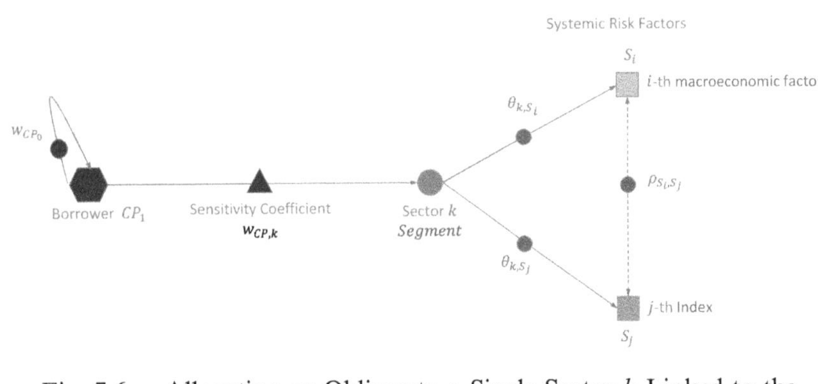

Fig. 7.6. Allocating an Obligor to a Single Sector k Linked to the Correlated Risk Factors i and j. *Note:* This figure shows how a single borrower CP_1 is linked to systemic macro and market risk factors S_i via sector or segment k.

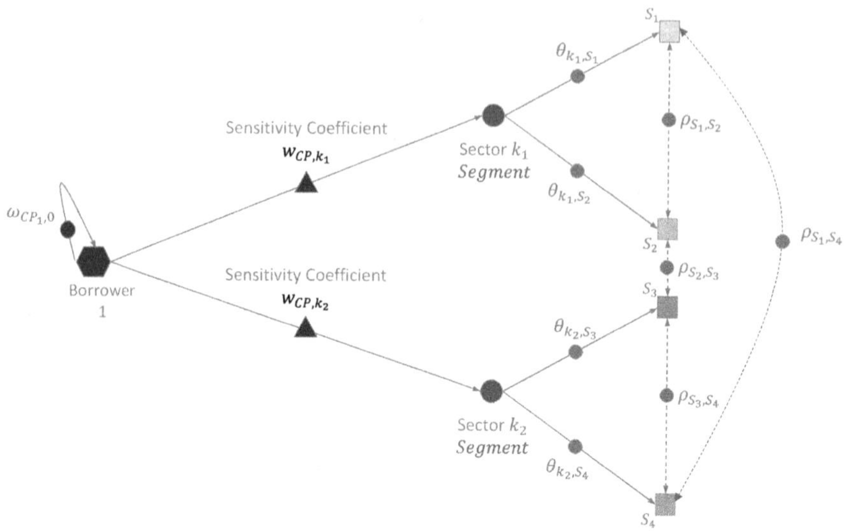

Fig. 7.7. Allocating a Borrower to Several Sectors k. *Note:* This figure shows the sensitivities of a single borrower CP_1 to systemic macro and market risk factors S_i via multiple (two) sectors or segments k. Note that the two sectors or segments can also be correlated via risk factors' correlation factor ρ_i.

Fig. 7.8 illustrates the allocation of three borrowers to a single sector with a link to a single risk factor. In this case, a sector can be considered a collection of borrowers with common properties.

Allocating Each Borrower to Independent Segments

In such a case, each borrower is allocated and linked with weights, $w_{CP,k}$, to a single independent sector k that also links to independent market and micro-economic risk factors with a sensitivity $\theta_{k,S}$. The assumption is that each borrower is subject to only one systematic factor responsible for the uncertainty of the borrower's default rate. Fig. 7.9 illustrates an example of allocating two borrowers to a single independent sector, k_1 and k_i, that are linked to uncorrelated risk factors S_1 and S_j. In this model, the following applies:

- It provides a diversification benefit for borrowers whose fortunes are affected by several independent systematic factors
- Once allocated to a sector, the borrower's default rate and default rate volatility are set individually.

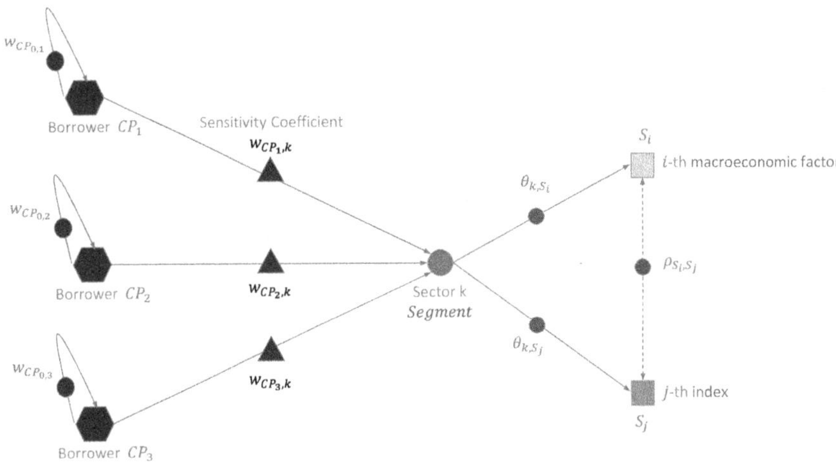

Fig. 7.8. Allocating Three Borrowers to a Single Sector k Linked to Risk Factors i. *Note:* This figure shows how several borrowers, e.g., $\text{CP}_1, \text{CP}_2, \text{CP}_3$ may be correlated via different degrees of sensitivities, such as $\lambda_1, \lambda_2, \lambda_3$ to a single sector or segment k.

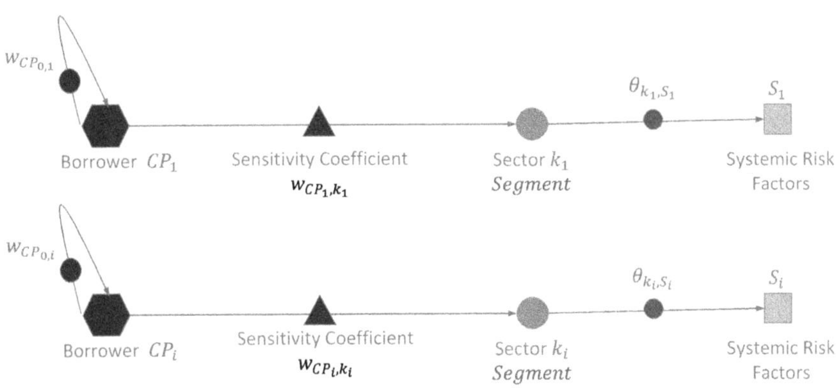

Fig. 7.9. Allocating Two Borrowers to a Single Independent Sector k_1 and k_i Linked to Uncorrelated Risk Factors. *Note:* This figure shows that borrowers, like CP_1, CP_2, may be uncorrelated due to sensitivities, like λ_1, λ_2, with independent sectors or segments k.

In this case, a diversification benefit exists. The fortunes of individual borrowers subject to several independent systematic factors are diversified away to a degree.

Borrower Correlation via Sector Correlation

In this case, several individual borrowers are allocated to sectors linked to correlated risk factors. The borrower's correlation is defined by considering the correlation between the sectors' underlying market risk factors. The correlation of the default probabilities of borrowers is therefore identified in the following manner:

- Weights $\theta_{k,S}$, where sectors are allocated to one of several risk factors and
- Correlations ρ_{S_i,S_j}, where the risk factors within and across sectors correlate.

The correlation between indicator variables of two different obligors CP_1 and CP_2 defined as:

$$\rho[\xi_{CP_1}, \xi_{CP_2}] = \mathrm{Cov}[\xi_{CP_1}, \xi_{CP_2}] = \omega_{CP_1}^T P \omega_{CP_2}$$

Fig. 7.10 illustrates a case where the allocation of three borrowers to a single sector is linked to two correlated risk factors.

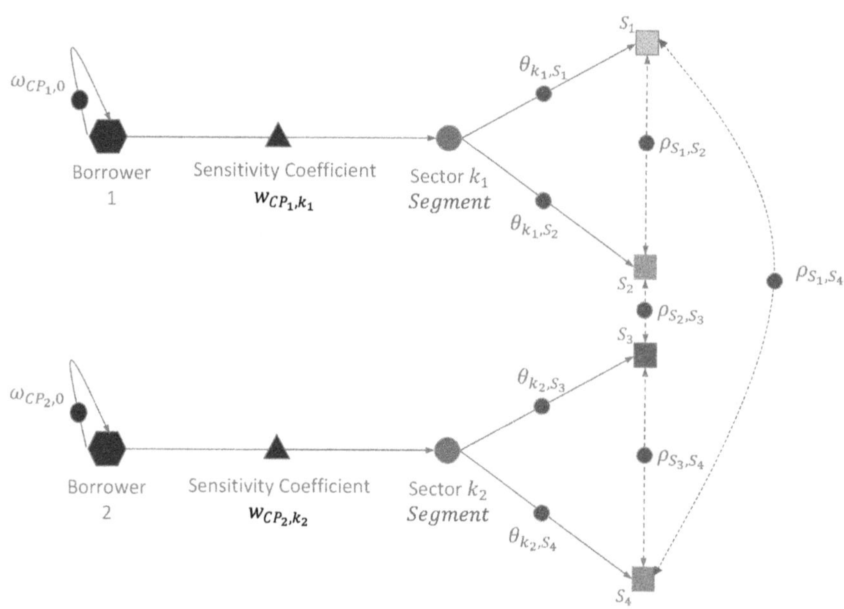

Fig. 7.10. Allocating Two Borrowers to a Single Sector k Linked to Risk Factors S_i. *Note:* This figure shows the case where borrowers, such as CP_1, CP_2, may be correlated due to sensitivities, such as $\lambda_1, \lambda_2 m$ with sectors or segments k that are correlated via the degree of correlation ρ_i between their systematic risk factors.

Market Conditions

At time t_{i+1}, the market conditions expressed as indices or macroeconomic risk factors play a significant role in defining the following:

- The status of the sectors is linked to the market conditions, where borrowers are associated with sectors that impact their migration probabilities.
- The transactions' replacement value is the fair value under the rating state at t_{i+1}, determined by market conditions.

Simulation and Analysis Elements

The market conditions and the sensitivities, $w_{i,o}$ and $w_{i,k}$, define the weights, $w_{i,0}$ and $w_{i,k}$, the main parameters under consideration in the Monte Carlo stochastic process. For a single time step from t_i to t_{i+1}, where the difference between the two times is the time horizon of the migration matrix, the following iteration of the steps takes place (as illustrated in Fig. 7.11):

- Step 1. Throw the dice for the market conditions at t_i.
- Step 2. Throw the dice for the sector conditions at t_{i+1} $\epsilon_{0,t+1}, \epsilon_{1,t+1}, \ldots, \epsilon_{k,t+1}$.
- Step 3. Considering the sector sensitivities $w_{i,k}$, calculate the ξ_i and derive for all scenarios the new (updating) rating distribution.
- Step 4. Calculate the exposure at default (EAD) of borrower i at t_{i+1}.
- Step 5. Calculate the expected cash flows from the gross exposure, collaterals, and recoveries.

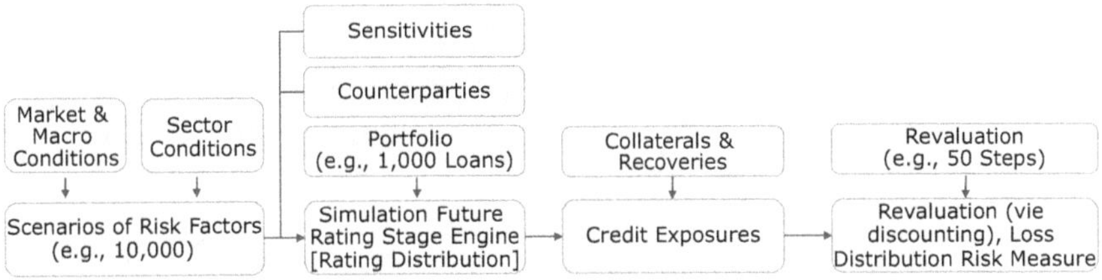

Fig. 7.11. Simulation Process of Rating Evolution and Revaluation of Credit Loans. *Note:* This chart outlines the process for updating loan ratings and their values. Initially, we use a Monte Carlo simulation – a random sampling technique – to reflect current economic and market conditions. Then, considering the borrower's starting credit rating and vulnerability to different risks, we predict how their rating might change. Next, we factor in any collateral to assess the likelihood of default and project future cash flows. Finally, after repeating these steps for each loan, we reassess the entire credit portfolio's value and estimate potential losses.

- Step 6. Discount the cash flows using the appropriate discounting spread for borrower i.
- Step 7. Repeat steps 3 to 6 for all borrowers.
- Step 8. Repeat steps 1 to 7 n times.
- Step 9: Revaluate the credit portfolio and calculate the losses and risks.

At time t, only the existing portfolio (current positions) and borrowers are under consideration. The evolution of market conditions is defined at t. This step is Step 1 in the simulation. Given the stochastic process applied to both market and sector conditions, the possible credit risk rating may change from t to $t + 1$. It is derived from the process described in steps 1 to 7. Fig. 7.12 shows an example.

Typically, around 10,000 paths of macro and market risk factors are generated in such a simulation process to project the evaluation of the future new rating stages. Given the new rating, the credit portfolio must be re-evaluated within various time-bucket points, often around 50. Based on these assumptions, approximately 500,000 nodes are created for rating and revaluation calculations. When dealing with a portfolio containing 1,000 loans, performing these calculations using a single CPU can take thousands of seconds. However, this needs access to a farm with thousands of CPUs.

Due to computational power limitations, practitioners often restrict the number of paths generated to a few thousand and the number of time points to a few dozen. Unfortunately, these limitations inevitably reduce the accuracy and quality of the risk calculation metrics.

One approach to address this suboptimal solution is to approximate the rating and valuation function that needs to be called multiple times within the stochastic process. In this case, the primary objective is to construct and utilize proxies for the ratings to evaluate the risk scenarios. To generate such proxies (as shown in Fig. 7.13), a set of grid points (sampling points) is identified within the population

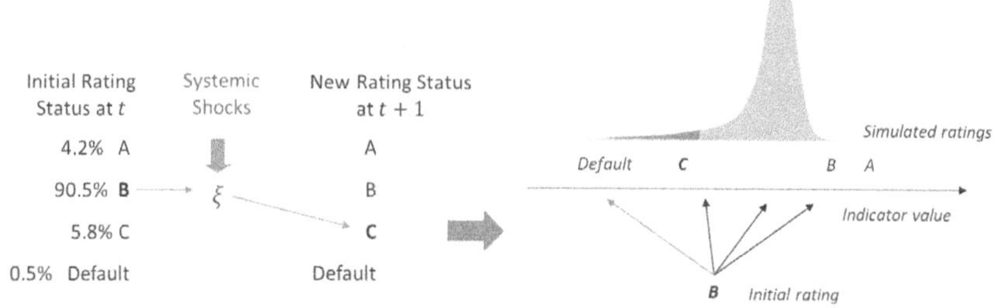

Fig. 7.12. Credit Risk Rating Migration Probabilities From t to $t + 1$ Under Static Analysis. *Note:* This figure shows the evolution of the credit risk rating migration probabilities, given the systemic shocks and their distribution at the initial and simulated future multiperiod under new market conditions.

Note: This figure shows the steps to apply the Chebyshev polynomial interpolation technique to stochastic analysis for credit rating analysis.

Training:

- Get x_i points, e.g., 1,000, of the sample scenarios.
- Given the x_i, get the 1,000-resulting, y_i, points of the rating points.
- Define the initial Chebyshev nodes (roots of a polynomial).
- Get from the "trained sample scenario data" the Chebyshev polynomial interpolated function. Evaluate the Chebyshev polynomial, approximating the remaining 9,000 scenarios.
- Get the interpolated rates (i.e., based on 1,000 sample scenarios), y_j.
- Since initial Chebyshev nodes are used to interpolate the results (e.g., ratings), they are the inputs $\boldsymbol{x}_j$ to evaluate the Chebyshev polynomial.
- The remaining scenarios are the specific Chebyshev nodes (roots of polynomial) (n_j) where interpolation applies.
- Calculate the error between the expected and proxy values and calibrate the input values.

Several advantages in terms of efficiency and accuracy are realized by integrating smart sampling approximation techniques such as CT or DNN into the rating distribution and revaluation process. These techniques enable faster and more reliable analysis of risk scenarios.

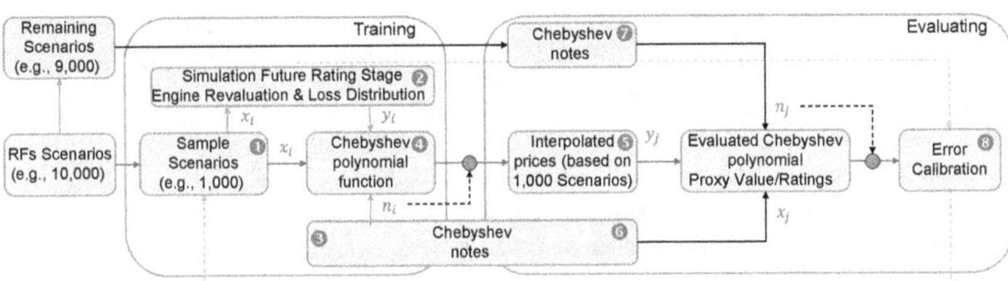

Fig. 7.13. Chebyshev Polynomial Interpolation Technique.

by the risk factor scenarios. These points represent the locations where the rating evolution is assessed to generate the proxy function. DNN systems that rely on training data and leverage CTs that employ polynomials can be implemented to accomplish this objective. By using these techniques, more accurate approximations for the rating function can be obtained, enabling the evaluation of the entire set of risk scenarios.

In the case of a DNN, the grid points can be selected randomly, although efficient methods are available for choosing them. Random selection ensures a diverse sampling of the risk factor scenarios. Conversely, when utilizing CTs, the grid points are specific nonrandom Chebyshev sample points. Chebyshev points are known for their optimal distribution properties, allowing for a more accurate and efficient approximation of the rating and valuation functions.

Both approaches, whether using DNNS or CTs, offer different strategies for selecting the grid points to build proxies for the ratings and perform evaluations within the stochastic process.

Fig. 7.13 assumes 1,000 grid points. These grid points are used within the exposure engine to calculate the resulting values, which are then used to construct the proxy function representing the rating distribution. For CTs, the proxy function can be generated using polynomials to approximate the rating distribution accurately. In the case of a DNN, its weights or parameters need to be tuned through training. This training process involves adjusting the parameters of the DNN using a training dataset to optimize its performance and accuracy in approximating the rating distribution. Once the proxy function is successfully constructed, its accuracy is such that the resulting rating distribution closely matches the rating distribution shown in Fig. 7.11. The proxy function effectively captures the rating behavior, allowing for reliable evaluation and analysis of the risk scenarios.

In conclusion, certain steps in the process are modified when using a smart sampling approximation technique like CT or DNN to approximate the rating distribution and revaluation process. Here are the typical five steps involved that Fig. 7.13 illustrates:

(1) *Data generation or collection.* The first step, which involves generating or collecting relevant data on risk factors, trade portfolios, and associated ratings, remains the same.
(2) *Grid point selection.* In the case of DNN, the grid points can be randomly selected or chosen using efficient methods to cover the space of risk factor scenarios. The grid points are chosen for CT as Chebyshev sample points due to their optimal distribution properties.
(3) *Simulation future rating stage engine.* The chosen grid points are forwarded to the rating stage engine, which executes the simulation of future rating values, revaluation, and loss distribution, as depicted in Fig. 7.11. In the case of DNN, the weights and parameters are tuned through training using the collected data. For CT, polynomials generate the proxy function for pricing or exposure values.
(4) *Proxy function construction.* The resulting rating engine values construct the proxy function representing the rating distribution. In the case of DNN, the trained DNN model provides the proxy function. For CT, the polynomial-based approximation generates the proxy function.
(5) *Revaluation process.* The revaluation process involves evaluating the risk scenarios using the proxy function. Instead of directly calculating each scenario's rating distribution or revaluation, the proxy function estimates the values. Compared to traditional methods, this approach is more efficient and scalable.

By incorporating smart sampling approximation techniques like DNN or CT, the rating distribution and revaluation process benefits from improved efficiency and accuracy, allowing for faster analysis of risk scenarios.

Valuation and Cash Flows on Defaulted and Nondefaulted Exposures

Single and multistep simulations should consider two possible scenarios for borrowers – default or no default.

(1) *Default within the period from t_i to $t_i + 1$ or within multiple periods.* In such a case, only the cash flows resulting from credit enhancements (e.g., collaterals, guarantees, recovery rates, and recovery patterns) will occur. These cash flows are discounted with the appropriate spread.
(2) *No default before $t_i + 1$ or before the end of each multiple period.* In this case, the expected cash flows are calculated using the corresponding ratings and the default probabilities for exposure and financial collaterals. Expected losses depend on the probability of default, while expected value depends on expected discounting spreads.

Input Data and Migration Matrix (MM)

The MM is the central mechanism of this approach. The MM is a transition matrix identifying the transition probabilities between ratings of borrowers. During a given time interval – typically 1 year – the initial rating status will remain the same or migrate to another rating. Using MM defines the distribution of all possible rating states whose probabilities must add up to 100%.

With the distribution of all possible rating states defined in the MM, a stochastic process, such as Monte Carlo simulation, can be efficiently applied. With the initial actual rating stages, rolling the dice for every counterparty can start. The correlations between borrowers are introduced via sector sensitivity analysis.

Asset Recovery in Case of Default

MPL platforms typically issue uncollateralized loans between individual lenders and borrowers. They bypass traditional financial intermediaries like banks because they fail to guarantee losses from borrower defaults. The main risk for lenders lies in the recovery process when a borrower fails to pay the lender's higher returns and the loan. In the event of a default, lenders may be unable to recover their funds unless they are securitized by the MPL platform or a financial company that purchased the loan portfolios and securitized the loans.

Since MPL platforms operate online under various regulatory frameworks, the legal recourse available to lenders may be unclear. Depending on each platform's jurisdiction and terms and conditions, lenders may have limited options for pursuing legal action to recover their funds. Even if legal action is well defined and the investor has rights to recovery, compensation in the case of defaults may be tricky because borrowers may lack the financial resources to repay the loan fully, legal action against borrowers may be too expensive, the collection process may be too complex depending on the type of the loan and counterparty class, or platforms lack operations to assist lenders in the recovery process.

Platforms often implement risk management strategies to mitigate the recovery problem in MPL. Such strategies involve borrower screening and credit assessment processes, diversification of loan portfolios, and collection efforts through third-party agencies. Additionally, lenders can consider spreading their investments across multiple loans to diversify risk and carefully evaluate the creditworthiness of borrowers before lending. However, loans may be concentrated in counterparty class, business, and region segments linked to common underlying macro and financial risk factors.

Summary and Conclusions

MPL has changed substantially since the first P2P lending platforms emerged in 2006. The industry is now an alternative to bank lending, predicted to total roughly $70 billion by 2030 for consumer and business loans worldwide. MPL is often deemed less safe than bank loans, mainly due to the high degree of fuzzy and hidden information in these portfolios. These include a lack of information on borrowers and potential correlations between them, which might lead to higher risk than is initially apparent. As a result, platforms and lenders should employ stochastic processes, such as the ones this chapter presents, to simulate tail risk.

Bank credit loan portfolios have risks, as they contain mainly fixed long-term loans, which may generate lower returns than the cost of their short-term liabilities when market conditions change quickly. This situation led to the collapse of SVB in Q1 2023. Marketplace loans typically have a shorter duration, so portfolios containing them can be rebalanced quicker to react to changing market conditions. MPL can be a sustainable alternative to bank lending, but only if investors understand the risks involved. Since marketplace loans often contain fuzzy and hidden information and the ratings of counterparties change in changing market conditions, modeling the risks of marketplace loans is complex and requires specific knowledge and techniques.

This chapter introduces stochastic processes like Monte Carlo simulation and ML techniques like CTs and DNNs that manage to simulate tail risk. By integrating these smart sampling approximation techniques into the rating distribution and revaluation process, several advantages regarding efficiency and accuracy are realized. Using a set of selected grid points or Chebyshev points provides a more streamlined and optimized approach for approximating the rating distribution and conducting revaluations. This approach leads to faster computations and reduces the computational burden, enabling faster analysis of numerous risk scenarios. Professional investors such as hedge funds know how to evaluate, monitor, and manage available risks, but retail investors may have to rely on platforms providing such tools. With these techniques, MPL platforms and investors can evaluate, monitor, and manage the risks of marketplace lending portfolios, consider the potential recovery challenges, and diversify their lending portfolios to mitigate the impact of possible defaults.

Discussion Questions

- Define the term marketplace lending.
- Discuss how market risk factors affect borrowers in MPL.
- Explain why risk assessment is difficult in portfolios of marketplace loans.
- Identify which techniques can efficiently simulate risk in MPL portfolios.
- Discuss how MPL can improve sustainability and become a viable alternative to bank lending.

References

Akkizidis, I., & Stagars, M. (2016). *Marketplace lending, financial analysis, and the future of credit: Integration, profitability, and risk management*. John Wiley & Sons.

Bachmann, R., Berg, T. O., & Sims, E. R. (2015). Inflation expectations and readiness to spend: Cross-sectional evidence. *American Economic Journal: Economic Policy*, *7*(1), 1–35.

Board of Governors of the Federal Reserve System (US). (2023, April 9). *Federal funds effective rate*. https://fred.stlouisfed.org/series/FEDFUNDS

Chava, S., Ganduri, R., Paradkar, N., & Zhang, Y. (2021). Impact of marketplace lending on consumers' future borrowing capacities and borrowing outcomes. *Journal of Financial Economics*, *142*(3), 1186–1208. http://www.sciencedirect.com/science/article/pii/S0304405X21002713

Herrboldt, A. M. (2015). Marketplace lending. *Supervisory Insights*, *12*(2), 13–19. https://www.fdic.gov/regulations/examinations/supervisory/insights/siwin15/siwinter15-article2.pdf

Lending Club. (2020, December 27). Does lending Club still issue new notes? https://help.lendingclub.com/hc/en-us/articles/360050574891-Important-Updates-to-the-LendingClub-Notes-Platform

Morgan, J. P. (1997). Introduction to CreditMetrics™. https://www.researchgate.net/publication/301776007_CreditMetrics_-_Technical_Document

OECD. (2023). Inflation (CPI). https://data.oecd.org/price/inflation-cpi.htm

Popper, N. (2018, September 28). LendingClub founder, ousted in 2016, settles fraud charges. *The New York Times*. https://www.nytimes.com/2018/09/28/technology/lendingclub-renaud-laplanche-fraud.html

Ropele, T., Gorodnichenko, Y., & Coidion, O. (2022). Inflation expectation and corporate borrowing decisions: New casual evidence. In *IZA discussion papers 15614* (pp. 1−39). Institute of Labor Economics (IZA).

Statista. (2023). Crowdlending (business) – Worldwide. https://www.statista.com/outlook/dmo/fintech/digital-capital-raising/crowdlending-business/worldwide#transaction-value

Chapter 8

Risk Management in Fintech

Ayan Tyagi

Citibank, USA

Abstract

This chapter examines the world of risk management within fintech. It initiates by emphasizing the crucial role of technology and risk assessment in shaping the fintech landscape. It discusses various risk categories prevalent in fintech operations, elucidating the nuances of technology, operational, compliance, strategic, and reputational risks. A comparative analysis across different fintech sub-sectors unveils their distinct risk profiles. The narrative extends to proactive risk management frameworks, contrasting prominent models like the COSO ERM, FAIR Risk Quantification, and NIST Cybersecurity Frameworks. Integral defense measures are scrutinized, encompassing data encryption, access controls, vulnerability assessments, and incident response plans. This chapter underscores the significance of building operational resilience through robust technology infrastructure, regular system updates, disaster recovery planning, and business continuity measures. Ultimately, this chapter culminates in a comprehensive summary, offering pragmatic recommendations to fortify technology risk management in fintech.

Keywords: Fintech; risk management; technology risks; risk assessment; cybersecurity

Introduction

The financial landscape is experiencing a seismic shift driven by the burgeoning field of financial technology (fintech). Fintech encompasses diverse, innovative technologies and business models that fundamentally reshape how individuals and businesses manage their finances (Gomber et al., 2018). From robo-advisors offering personalized investment solutions to blockchain-powered platforms enabling seamless cross-border transactions, fintech's transformative potential is

The Emerald Handbook of Fintech, 157–175

Published under exclusive licence by Emerald Publishing Limited
doi:10.1108/978-1-83753-608-520241015

undeniable, fostering financial inclusivity, streamlining services, and ushering in unprecedented convenience and accessibility (Lau & Leimer, 2021).

This revolution stems from the inherent advantages of technology applied to finance. Digitization facilitates real-time transactions, empowers data-driven decision-making, and allows for developing of personalized financial solutions tailored to individual needs (Rosário & Dias, 2023). Artificial intelligence (AI) algorithms can analyze vast datasets to optimize credit scoring, combat fraud with unparalleled accuracy, and predict market trends more precisely (Schmitt, 2020). With its distributed ledger and robust security, blockchain technology promises to revolutionize areas like trade finance and asset management, enhancing transparency and trust within financial systems (Laroiya et al., 2020). However, recognizing the inherent vulnerabilities associated with technology is crucial amid this wave of innovation. Data breaches, cyberattacks, and operational disruptions threaten fintech ventures' stability and security. Furthermore, algorithmic biases within AI models can perpetuate financial exclusion for underserved communities, necessitating ethical considerations and proactive mitigation strategies (Nikolinakos, 2023). Therefore, navigating the digital frontier requires a comprehensive understanding of technology risks and the implementation of robust risk management frameworks.

This chapter examines fintech's multifaceted landscape of technology risks, exploring established risk assessment frameworks and proposing mitigation strategies. Beyond revolutionizing services, fintech holds promise in fostering financial inclusivity, yet challenges persist in bridging the digital divide and building trust with underserved communities. Collaboration among fintech companies, regulators, and policymakers is critical for a responsible and inclusive digital financial future.

Embracing robust technology risk management is not just a precaution but fundamental for confidently navigating this dynamic landscape. Mitigating risks safeguards viability, protects customer data, and fosters trust, enabling fintechs to drive impactful innovations while democratizing financial access. Conversely, overlooking technology risks can lead to dire consequences, from cyberattacks to reputational damage, jeopardizing financial security and progress. Thus, investing in proactive risk management is imperative for fintechs to navigate the digital frontier responsibly and resiliently.

Thus, this chapter delves deeply into the multifaceted landscape of technology risks in fintech, explores established risk assessment frameworks, and proposes mitigation strategies to equip fintech companies with the tools necessary to navigate digital finance's exciting yet challenging landscape. By prioritizing technology risk management, fintechs can ensure their viability, safeguard customer data, and contribute to a sustainable and responsible financial future for all.

Financial Inclusion Through Technology

Fintech's transformative potential extends beyond revolutionizing existing financial services. It holds immense promise for fostering financial inclusion, particularly for underserved communities traditionally excluded from mainstream financial systems. For instance, mobile money platforms in developing countries allow the unbanked population to access essential financial services like savings, transfers, and payments using only their mobile phones (Tengeh & Gahapa Talom, 2020). Additionally, AI-powered credit scoring algorithms can assess creditworthiness beyond traditional parameters, enabling access to loans for individuals with limited credit history (Seth & Gandhi, 2023). However, addressing the digital divide and building trust with underserved communities remain critical challenges in achieving financial inclusion (Schuetz & Venkatesh, 2020). Addressing language barriers, ensuring digital literacy, and prioritizing data privacy are crucial considerations for fintech ventures seeking to bridge the gap and empower all individuals with access to essential financial services.

The Road Ahead: Navigating the Evolving Landscape

Opportunities and challenges lie ahead as the fintech landscape evolves at breakneck speed. Emerging technologies like blockchain, AI, and quantum computing hold immense potential for further innovation and disruption yet necessitate proactive risk management strategies and robust regulatory frameworks to mitigate potential threats (Girasa & Scalabrini, 2022). Collaboration between fintech companies, regulators, and policymakers is crucial for fostering a responsible and inclusive digital financial future. Promoting open dialogue, sharing best practices, and investing in research and development are essential steps toward navigating the evolving landscape and unlocking fintech's full potential for a more equitable and efficient financial system.

Embracing Robust Technology Risk Management for Sustainable Fintech Success

Amid the exhilarating wave of fintech disrupting the traditional landscape, a crucial counterpoint emerges of the paramount importance of robust technology risk management in ensuring fintech ventures' sustainable success and responsible growth. Although innovative platforms and algorithms lead to a future of personalized finance and seamless transactions, the inherent vulnerabilities of technology pose potentially crippling threats. Effective risk management becomes a prudent measure and the cornerstone of responsible fintech success within this delicate equilibrium of boundless opportunity and unforeseen challenges. Imagine a future where a data breach at a leading robo-advisor platform erodes client trust and crumbles its financial stability. Alternatively, consider the scenario where an algorithmic bias within a loan-approval system perpetuates financial exclusion for underserved communities. These are not dystopian nightmares but potential realities without a robust framework for managing the technological risks interwoven with the fabric of fintech.

By prioritizing technology risk management, fintechs can confidently navigate this dynamic landscape, safeguarding their viability while promoting responsible, inclusive, and sustainable financial progress. This proactive approach mitigates financial losses, protects customer data, and fosters trust – the lifeblood of any financial institution. It translates to long-term stability, enabling fintechs to refine their offerings, attract investments, and drive impactful innovations that democratize access to financial services. Failure to adequately address technology risks, however, poses dire consequences. Cyberattacks, operational disruptions, and compliance failures can negatively impact even the most promising fintech venture, shattering investor confidence and jeopardizing financial security.

Moreover, reputational damage from data breaches or unethical algorithms can harm customer trust, hindering further growth and innovation (Chatterjee, 2021). Therefore, investing in robust technology risk management is not simply a matter of caution but a strategic imperative for navigating the digital frontier with resilience and responsibility. Embracing established risk assessment frameworks, tailoring mitigation strategies to specific needs, and continuously adapting to the evolving threat landscape are crucial steps toward ensuring sustainable success in the dynamic arena of fintech.

Technology Risks in Fintech

As fintech ventures forge ahead in the digital frontier, they face technological pitfalls. Data security and privacy risks are among the most formidable challenges, posing potential threats to financial stability and customer trust. The following discussion delves into this complex domain, identifying and dissecting these critical threats.

- *Data breaches.* Akin to a digital heist, a *data breach* involves unauthorized access and exfiltration of sensitive financial information like account numbers, passwords, and transaction data. These breaches can occur through various means, from brute-force attacks to sophisticated phishing scams, leaving fintech companies and their customers vulnerable to financial losses and identity theft (Ahmed et al., 2021).
- *Cyberattacks.* A *cyberattack* is an orchestrated assault launched by malicious actors. Cyberattacks are a broader category encompassing data breaches and attempts to disrupt operations, manipulate systems, or extort ransom from fintech companies. From distributed denial-of-service (DDoS) attacks flooding servers with requests to malware compromising critical infrastructure, the sheer variety and unpredictable nature of cyberattacks underscore the ever-evolving threat landscape (Javaheri et al., 2024).
- *Unauthorized access.* Exploiting security vulnerabilities within systems or manipulating user behavior, unauthorized access grants individuals or entities without proper authorization entry into sensitive data or systems. This access can be used for financial gain, data manipulation, or sabotage operations, highlighting the importance of robust authentication and access control measures (Omotunde & Ahmed, 2023).

- *Data privacy violations.* Data privacy encompasses the ethical collection, storage, and utilization of customer data. Violations occur when such data are mishandled, used for unintended purposes, or inadequately protected from unauthorized access. In today's hyper-connected world, data privacy violations can erode trust, trigger regulatory sanctions, and damage brand reputation, demanding responsible data governance practices (Dupont, 2019).

These core threats represent merely the tip of the iceberg. The intricate interplay between technology and finance spawns ever-evolving risks, necessitating constant vigilance and proactive mitigation strategies. Addressing these challenges head-on through robust data security practices, rigorous access controls, ethical data governance, and continuous adaptation to the evolving threat landscape is paramount for fintech ventures to navigate the digital frontier with resilience and thrive in a landscape teeming with opportunity and peril.

Operational Risks in Fintech

Although data security and privacy risks stand as formidable sentinels guarding the digital frontier of fintech, another realm of potential pitfalls lurks in the shadows: operational risks. These seemingly mundane threats, woven into the fabric of technology, can trigger disruptions, inefficiencies, and even financial losses, demanding equal attention and proactive mitigation strategies. Consider a scenario where a simple software bug in a lending platform leads to inaccurate credit assessments, jeopardizing financial stability and eroding trust. Alternatively, consider the scenario where a system failure halts payments during peak hours, leaving customers frustrated and businesses paralyzed. Failure to address operational risks is not a hypothetical threat but a recipe for immediate and real-world consequences. Within this spectrum of operating vulnerabilities, several critical threats emerge (Dupont, 2019):

- *System failures.* System failures, from hardware malfunctions to network outages, can bring operations to a grinding halt. These failures can range from minor inconveniences to disastrous financial consequences, highlighting the critical need for robust infrastructure, redundancy measures, and disaster recovery plans.
- *Technology breakdowns.* The engines driving fintech innovation are susceptible to unexpected breakdowns. Outdated technologies, poorly maintained systems, and vulnerabilities in dependencies can create operational glitches, hinder performance, and expose the enterprise to cyberattacks.
- *Software bugs.* Even the most meticulously crafted software can harbor hidden bugs waiting to unleash unexpected consequences. These bugs can distort calculations, compromise data integrity, and lead to operational errors, demanding rigorous testing, bug-fixing protocols, and continuous software updates.

- *Human error.* Human error is the most overlooked yet potentially disruptive threat, which can introduce vulnerabilities across the entire operational spectrum. Accidental data entry mistakes, flawed configuration changes, and even employee fraud can trigger significant losses and reputational damage, necessitating training, stringent protocols, and robust internal controls.

Navigating this multifaceted terrain of operational risks requires a proactive approach. Implementing comprehensive risk assessment frameworks, investing in reliable infrastructure, fostering a culture of cybersecurity awareness, and prioritizing employee training are crucial steps toward building operational resilience and minimizing disruptions. By acknowledging the inherent vulnerabilities within technology and implementing robust mitigation strategies, fintech ventures can chart a course toward sustainable success, ensuring that unexpected operational pitfalls do not hinder innovation.

Compliance Risks in Fintech

Compliance risks stem from the delicate dance between cutting-edge technology and existing regulatory frameworks. Failure to comply with evolving regulations and data privacy laws can expose fintech ventures to financial penalties, reputational damage, and even operational paralysis, demanding meticulous attention and proactive navigation. Imagine a scenario where a pioneering peer-to-peer lending platform, oblivious to emerging Know Your Customer (KYC) regulations, unwittingly facilitates money laundering activities, triggering regulatory sanctions and eroding customer trust. Or consider the potential ramifications of a robo-advisor inadvertently violating data privacy laws, exposing sensitive financial information, and jeopardizing its operating license. Failure to navigate the evolving regulatory landscape exposes fintech organizations to immediate and potentially crippling compliance concerns. Within this realm of potential pitfalls, several key compliance risks warrant consideration (Anagnostopoulos, 2018):

- *Evolving regulations.* The regulatory landscape for fintech is a moving target, with new rules and amendments constantly emerging. Failing to stay abreast of these changes and adapt business practices accordingly can lead to non-compliance, hindering operations, and inviting regulatory scrutiny.
- *Data privacy laws.* Protecting customer data is paramount in today's digital age. Fintech ventures are subject to complex data privacy laws, such as the General Data Protection Regulation (GDPR) and the California Consumer Privacy Act (CCPA). Failure to comply with these regulations can result in fines, legal action, and irreparably damaged customer trust.
- *Anti-money laundering (AML) and counter-terrorist financing (CTF) requirements.* Fintech platforms are increasingly susceptible to exploitation for illicit activities like money laundering and terrorist financing. Non-compliance with stringent AML/CTF regulations can lead to hefty fines, reputational damage, and even operational shutdowns.

- *Regulatory uncertainty.* As fintech continues to evolve at breakneck speed, regulators often struggle to keep pace, creating a climate of uncertainty. This ambiguity can hinder innovation, discourage investment, and expose ventures to unforeseen compliance risks.

Building robust compliance monitoring and testing in legal expertise, adopting cutting-edge technology for regulatory monitoring, and fostering ongoing employee training are crucial to ensuring adherence to existing and evolving regulations. By recognizing the inherent challenges and implementing effective mitigation strategies, fintech can unlock its true potential as a driver of financial inclusivity and sustainable growth, all within the boundaries of responsible and ethical conduct.

Strategic Risks in Fintech

As fintech ventures navigate the churning seas of innovation, they face treacherous technical shoals, choppy regulatory currents, and vast, dynamic horizons teeming with strategic risks. These unseen waves, driven by unrelenting technological advancements, shifting market landscapes, and fierce competition, can capsize even the most seaworthy fintech ships, threatening their long-term voyage toward sustainable growth. This final leg of exploration unfurls the sails of foresight and navigates these strategic hurdles, charting a course toward a future of resilience and adaptability.

Consider a static robo-advisor blindsided by the meteoric rise of AI-powered competitors or a niche peer-to-peer (P2P) lender drowned out by platforms offering comprehensive services and frictionless experiences. These are not futuristic hypotheticals but imminent threats for fintech organizations that fail to adapt to the evolving strategic landscape (Ashta, 2021). Within this fluid domain, key strategic risks demand immediate attention.

- *Technological evolution.* Technological evolution renders static solutions obsolete at breakneck speed. Fintechs ignoring AI, blockchain, and advancements in quantum computing risk becoming stranded relics, unable to compete with agile rivals riding the tech tide (Mosteanu & Faccia, 2021).
- *Shifting market tides.* Customer needs and market dynamics are not constant but ebb and flow like unpredictable currents. Fintech ventures clinging to outdated business models or failing to identify new market opportunities risk being swept away by the changing tides of consumer preferences, leaving them stranded in stagnant pools of declining relevance (Ashta, 2021).
- *Competitive gale force.* Neglecting differentiation, strategic alliances, and adaptation within the dynamic fintech landscape exposes ventures to competitive dilution, customer churn, and stunted growth trajectories.
- *Regulatory squalls.* As regulatory frameworks adapt to fintech's rapid evolution, uncertainty can create unpredictable situations for long-term planning and investment. Failing to anticipate and proactively navigate changing regulations can impede growth and limit market access, leaving fintech ventures vulnerable to unexpected regulatory headwinds.

Fintech ventures must cultivate a culture of agility, foresight, and adaptability to conquer these strategic challenges. Building robust data analytics capabilities, fostering a culture of continuous innovation, and embracing strategic partnerships are vital anchors to help fintech ventures weather the storms and navigate the market's dynamic currents. By recognizing the inherent volatility of the digital financial future and implementing proactive strategies to stay ahead of the curve, fintech can chart a course not just of technological disruption but also of sustainable success and responsible financial inclusion (Ashta, 2021).

Reputational Risks in Fintech

The success of fintech ventures hinges on navigating not only technical and regulatory hurdles but also the intangible landscapes of reputational risk. Adverse publicity, data breaches, and customer dissatisfaction erode trust, the cornerstone of the industry. Even groundbreaking technologies lose their footing on shaky reputational ground.

Imagine a pioneering robo-advisor, lauded for its financial prowess, facing a headline-grabbing data breach exposing sensitive customer information. Alternatively, consider a P2P lending platform built on the promise of financial inclusion, facing widespread criticism for predatory lending practices. These scenarios are not derived from grim visions of a dystopian future; instead, they signify plausible results for fintech enterprises that overlook or fail to address the ongoing threat of reputational damage. Within this realm, several key reputational risks demand meticulous attention.

- *Negative publicity.* The digital age amplifies the echoes of every misstep, magnifying negative publicity into a racket that can drown out even the most positive achievements. A single disgruntled customer's viral tweet or a damning exposé in a leading financial publication can trigger a reputational tsunami, eroding trust and driving away potential users (Alwi et al., 2019).
- *Data breaches and privacy violations.* In a world where financial data are the lifeblood of fintech, data breaches, and privacy violations represent a particularly potent threat. Exposing sensitive financial information, mishandling customer data, or failing to comply with data privacy regulations can trigger hefty fines and legal consequences and irreparably damage trust and brand image (Hussain et al., 2021).
- *Customer dissatisfaction.* Dissatisfied customers are not merely lost business opportunities but potential public relations nightmares. A failure to deliver on promises provide adequate customer support, or address user concerns swiftly and effectively can lead to negative online reviews, social media backlash, and a decline in brand loyalty, ultimately eroding trust and undermining the foundation of fintech success (Alwi et al., 2019).

Fintech ventures need to foster an environment centered on transparency, accountability, and prioritizing customer needs to maneuver through these challenging circumstances. Robust data security protocols, preemptive communication plans, and a dedication to swiftly and efficiently addressing customer issues are vital defenses against damaging impacts on their reputation. Acknowledging the delicate nature of trust and proactively instituting measures to safeguard it enables fintech firms to navigate the intricate landscape of the digital era confidently. This approach ensures that innovation thrives in technological advancements and the cultivation and preservation of an outstanding reputation.

A Comparative Analysis of Risk Profiles in Fintech Sub-Sectors

Fintech's dynamic landscape comprises distinct sectors, each a mosaic of innovation and inherent risks. From the dynamic P2P lending market to the controlled environment of robo-advisors, every sector faces its blend of technical complexities, regulatory demands, and market intricacies, molding their risk landscapes into complex patterns. The following discussion embarks on a comparative exploration, delving into the diverse risk profiles among significant fintech sectors and the technologies driving their potential while posing potential hazards.

- *Lending.* The world of fintech lending, with its promise of democratized financing, pulsates with both opportunity and risk. Platforms facilitating P2P loans, for instance, face the twin challenges of credit risk (assuring borrower repayment) and operational risk (managing fraud and platform vulnerabilities). Meanwhile, alternative lending platforms focused on underserved markets grapple with regulatory uncertainty and the delicate balance between inclusivity and financial stability.
- *Payments.* The lightning-fast world of fintech payments, where transactions dance across digital arteries, presents unique risks. Security vulnerabilities in payment gateways and data breaches exposing sensitive financial information can be catastrophic, eroding trust and triggering regulatory scrutiny (Hussain et al., 2021). Additionally, fraudulent activities and the rapid evolution of regulatory frameworks pose constant challenges for fintech payment platforms navigating the ever-shifting landscape of digital transactions.
- *Wealth management.* In fintech wealth management, where algorithms and robo-advisors work with human expertise, the risks are as much about trust as they are about technology. Algorithmic biases and the potential for misleading investment advice can erode investor confidence and trigger legal repercussions (Alwi et al., 2019). Data security and the ethical implications of automated financial decision-making pose significant challenges for fintech wealth management platforms seeking to build sustainable trust with their clients.

Risk Assessment Frameworks for Proactive Management

In the evolving innovation landscape, fintech ventures encounter complex technical challenges, intricate regulatory landscapes, and concealed technological risks. Navigating these unseen hazards requires a robust tool: the risk assessment framework, functioning as the compass guiding fintech endeavors toward secure destinations of resilience and enduring growth. Consider a scenario where a robo-advisor operates without awareness of potential biases ingrained within its investment algorithms. Alternatively, envision a P2P lending platform unaware of vulnerabilities lurking in its data encryption protocols. Here, the risk assessment framework becomes crucial, equipped with a potent spotlight to reveal technological blind spots. It offers a structured method to identify, analyze, and prioritize the risks inherent in fintech endeavors. By systematically evaluating vulnerabilities across realms such as cybersecurity, data privacy, algorithmic bias, and operational resilience, this framework empowers fintech ventures to make informed choices and proactively implement mitigation strategies. Technology, while a driving force behind innovation, presents inherent risks in the fintech landscape. Embracing risk assessment frameworks is not a sign of apprehension but a testament to foresight and readiness (Girling, 2022). By leveraging this invaluable tool, fintech ventures can navigate a technological revolution and responsible innovation path, fostering trust and shaping a sustainable future in financial domains.

Comparative Analysis of Risk Management Frameworks in Fintech

As fintech ventures embark on their transformative paths, they encounter technical challenges, regulatory complexities, and a convoluted network of technological risks. Navigating this intricate network demands arming themselves with effective risk management frameworks as their map and compass. This exploration examines three recognized frameworks — the COSO Enterprise Risk Management (ERM), FAIR Risk Quantification, and NIST Cybersecurity — assessing their merits and constraints within fintech applications.

COSO ERM Framework

The COSO ERM Framework provides a comprehensive roadmap for identifying, assessing, and managing all types of risks, including technological ones. Its strength lies in its holistic approach, encompassing eight core components that guide the entire risk management process, from setting objectives to monitoring and reporting (Lanz, 2018). This comprehensive approach ensures that technological risks are not addressed in isolation but are integrated into the broader organizational risk landscape. However, the COSO ERM Framework's quantitative focus can be less relevant for certain fintech risks, particularly those with inherent uncertainty or qualitative dimensions. Additionally, its generic nature might require customization to address the specific nuances of fintech operations and technologies.

FAIR Risk Quantification Framework

The FAIR Risk Quantification Framework offers a data-driven approach to quantifying and prioritizing technological risks. By converting risks into financial terms, FAIR provides a clear and concise way to communicate risk to stakeholders and prioritize mitigation efforts (FAIR Institute, 2023). This data-driven approach is particularly valuable in fintech, where financial losses can be significant and quantifiable. However, the FAIR Framework's reliance on data and analytics can be challenging for smaller fintech ventures with limited resources or historical data. Additionally, its focus on financial impact may not fully capture the broader implications of technological risks, such as reputational damage or regulatory compliance issues.

NIST Cybersecurity Framework

The NIST Cybersecurity Framework provides a voluntary, flexible, and adaptable framework for managing cybersecurity risks. Its strength lies in its modular structure, allowing organizations to tailor the framework to their needs and risk profiles (Ross et al., 2019). This flexibility is particularly relevant for fintech, where cybersecurity threats constantly evolve and require adaptable responses. However, the NIST Cybersecurity Framework's non-prescriptive nature may need additional guidance and customization for effective implementation in fintech. Additionally, its primary focus on cybersecurity may not encompass fintech ventures' broader spectrum of technological risks.

Choosing the Right Framework

The choice of the most suitable framework for a fintech venture depends on various factors, including its size, maturity, risk profile, and specific technological challenges. Although no single framework is perfect, each offers valuable tools and insights for navigating the complex landscape of technological risks.

Holistic Integration: The Key to Success

Ultimately, the key to effective risk management in fintech lies not in choosing a single framework but in integrating the strengths of different frameworks to create a customized approach. By combining the holistic perspective of COSO with the quantitative precision of FAIR and the sector-specific guidance of NIST, fintech ventures can build a robust and adaptable risk management system that guides them toward a successful and resilient future. Although established risk assessment frameworks like COSO, FAIR, and NIST offer invaluable navigational tools, their true power lies in customization. Fintech navigates toward a future of resilience and sustainable growth by tailoring these frameworks to individual ventures' specific needs and risk profiles.

The beauty of tailoring risk assessment frameworks is that no two fintech ventures are born under the same constellation of risks. The intricate interplay of technology, business models, market dynamics, and customer base creates a unique risk profile for each voyage. A P2P lending platform navigating the shoals of credit risk needs a different risk map than a robo-advisor grappling with algorithmic biases. A digital bank facing the regulatory squalls of open banking requires a more nuanced approach than a blockchain-powered remittance service navigating cross-border compliance challenges. Therefore, adopting a "tailor-made" approach offers several distinct advantages (Anagnostopoulos, 2018).

- *Precision targeting.* By pinpointing the specific vulnerabilities and opportunities inherent in their unique DNA, fintech ventures can prioritize resources and mitigation efforts toward the most critical risks, avoiding the inefficiencies of a scattergun approach.
- *Agility and adaptability.* As the risk landscape shifts with technological advancements and evolving regulatory frameworks, customized frameworks allow for nimble adjustments, ensuring continuous preparedness and resilience.
- *Building trust and confidence.* Demonstrating a proactive and nuanced understanding of a fintech's risk profile fosters trust with customers, investors, and regulators, solidifying the foundations of sustainable growth and market differentiation.

Tailoring a risk assessment framework is not simply an exercise in technical adjustments; it is a dance between data and intuition, expertise and foresight. Leveraging industry best practices, collaborating with technology and risk management specialists, and continuously monitoring and refining the framework are critical steps in this vital endeavor.

Essential Defense Measures in Fintech

Fintech encounters the looming specter of cyber threats. These virtual adversaries, adept at extracting sensitive information, disrupting functionalities, and undermining confidence, necessitate the establishment of a resilient cyber defense. Within this digital stronghold, four pivotal pillars emerge: (1) robust data encryption, (2) stringent access controls, (3) diligent vulnerability evaluations, and (4) meticulously prepared incident response strategies.

Data Encryption

Picture a wealth of customer data, the vital essence of a fintech enterprise, exposed and defenseless within the digital sphere. This chilling prospect manifests in the absence of robust data encryption. Encryption is an impregnable barrier, transforming sensitive data into an incomprehensible code and rendering it futile for even the most astute cyber assailants (Mandel, 2017). Whether through the adoption of widely accepted algorithms such as AES-256 or sophisticated key management techniques, robust data encryption constitutes the fundamental cornerstone of cybersecurity within the fintech domain.

Access Controls

Beyond a robust gatehouse, every fortress necessitates vigilant guards. In the digital realm, these sentinels manifest as access controls, intricately regulating the entry points for sensitive data and systems. Through the adoption of least-privilege access models, multi-factor authentication, and resilient identity and access management (IAM) platforms, fintech enterprises guarantee that only authorized individuals possess the means to unlock the digital strongholds. Diligence at these virtual gates is pivotal in foiling unauthorized access attempts and averting internal breaches.

Vulnerability Assessments

No citadel is truly flawless. Cracks and vulnerabilities, if left undetected, can become entry points for even the most skilled thieves. This situation is where vulnerability assessments come into play. Regular, thorough assessments by skilled security professionals help identify weak spots in systems, networks, and applications, allowing fintech ventures to patch these vulnerabilities before they can be exploited (Mandel, 2017). Proactive vulnerability assessment is akin to a vigilant scout scouring the perimeter of the citadel, identifying and patching breaches before they become battlegrounds.

Incident Response Plans

Despite the best defenses, cyberattacks can occur. It is not a question of "if" but "when." Therefore, having a well-rehearsed incident response plan is akin to a well-coordinated fire drill. This plan outlines the steps to be taken in a cyberattack, ensuring a swift, efficient, and coordinated response that minimizes damage and restores operations as quickly as possible. Imagine a team of expertly trained and equipped digital firefighters ready to extinguish the flames of a cyberattack before they engulf the entire citadel.

Building Operational Resilience in the Fintech Frontier

Operational resilience is not a fixed goal but an ongoing process. Fintech firms can sail through the ever-evolving landscape of innovation by investing in dependable technology infrastructure, fostering a culture of continuous improvement, carefully strategizing for disaster recovery, and instituting strong business continuity practices. However, this pursuit is not a solo expedition. Sharing best practices, collaborating with technology providers, and actively engaging regulators cultivates a collective resilience safeguarding individual ventures and the entire fintech ecosystem. This collective effort steers toward a future marked by shared success and sustainable growth. Four fundamental principles serve as guiding beacons to fortify against operation disruptions: a dependable technology infrastructure, regular system updates, meticulous disaster recovery plans, and robust business continuity strategies.

Reliable Technology Infrastructure

Imagine a sophisticated fintech platform constructed upon unstable code and aging hardware. A single instance of technological turbulence could lead to catastrophic consequences. This situation underscores the significance of investing in a dependable technology foundation, which forms the fundamental pillar of operational resilience. Constructing atop robust cloud platforms, utilizing redundant systems, and implementing cutting-edge network security measures establish a resilient structure that fortifies the fintech journey against unforeseen disruptions.

Regular System Updates

Just as a ship's sails need ongoing care, the complex systems driving fintech operations require continual maintenance and fine-tuning. Regular system updates mend weaknesses, enhance performance, and counter new threats. Embracing automation, implementing continuous integration/continuous delivery (CI/CD) pipelines, and fostering a culture of proactive software updates ensure the fintech platform navigates the ever-changing technological terrain with flexibility and responsiveness.

Disaster Recovery Planning

Even the most experienced captain cannot anticipate every potential challenge. Hence, a meticulously designed disaster recovery plan acts as a safety measure in the face of unforeseen operational disruptions. Whether triggered by a natural disaster, a cyberattack, or a system outage, having a pre-established plan of action encompassing data backups, alternative operational sites, and clear communication protocols ensures a swift and decisive response, minimizing downtime and safeguarding critical operations.

Business Continuity Measures

Beyond immediate recovery from disasters, robust business continuity measures are an additional propulsion for the fintech platform, allowing it to advance despite disruptions. Diversification of revenue streams, forging resilient partnerships, and maintaining flexible operational models guarantee the continuity of financial operations, nurturing trust and confidence among customers and stakeholders, even in challenging scenarios.

Summary and Conclusions

Exploring the dynamic fintech landscape has revealed a treasure trove of opportunities powered by a dazzling constellation of technological advancements. This examination has shown the following:

- *Strategic agility.* Embracing a culture of innovation, continuous learning, and rapid adaptation to ensure the tides of market and technological change do not sweep away fintech ventures.
- *AI-Powered solutions.* From risk assessment and fraud detection to personalized financial products, AI promises to unlock a future of financial inclusivity and tailored solutions.
- *Fortress blockchain.* Secure, transparent, and compliant, blockchain offers a harbor for safeguarding data and streamlining regulatory compliance.
- *Cloud symphony.* Soaring on the wings of scalability and efficiency, cloud computing empowers fintech ventures to orchestrate agile and cost-effective operations.
- *Quantum conundrum.* While holding the potential for revolutionary advances in financial modeling, quantum computing casts a shadow of cryptographic vulnerability that demands proactive risk mitigation.

Amid the abundance of technology, a critical truth surfaces: Technology risk management is the navigational guide for fintech ventures amid these unknown territories. Without meticulous navigation, even the most impressive technologies can transform into hazardous obstacles, endangering financial stability, regulatory adherence, and fundamentally, the prosperity and endurance of fintech enterprises.

Therefore, prioritizing is imperative to rank,

- *Robust security protocols.* From data encryption to penetration testing, ensuring customer data's integrity and confidentiality is paramount.
- *Proactive risk management.* Identifying potential threats, assessing their impact, and implementing mitigation strategies are essential to weathering future storms.
- *Regulatory compliance.* Navigating the evolving regulatory landscape with transparency and accountability is crucial for building trust and maintaining a legitimate operation.
- *Collaboration and open innovation.* Working with regulatory bodies, academic institutions, and other industry players is critical to developing responsible and sustainable solutions.

By prioritizing technology risk management and approaching these transformative technologies with prudence and foresight, fintech ventures can harness their potential to revolutionize the financial landscape, fostering a future of financial security, inclusivity, and prosperity for all. Remember, the fintech odyssey is not a solo race but a collective voyage toward a brighter financial horizon, navigated by the steady hand of responsible technology risk management.

Practical Recommendations for Enhanced Technology Risk Management in Fintech

The fintech revolution has created a new era of financial innovation, promising convenience, accessibility, and efficiency. However, with this exhilarating growth comes the ever-present shadow of technology risks. Robust technology risk management practices are crucial for fintech companies, regulators, and policymakers to ensure the ecosystem's stability and long-term prosperity. The following are some practical recommendations for each stakeholder group.

Fintech Companies

- *Embrace a "security-first" mindset.* Ditch the reactive approach and ingrain security considerations into every facet of a company's operations. Implement a secure-by-design philosophy (Loruenser et al., 2018) from the initial development stages of products and services. Think encryption, secure coding practices, and rigorous vulnerability assessments.
- *Build a robust cybersecurity wall.* Invest in state-of-the-art cybersecurity measures like multi-factor authentication, data encryption, and intrusion detection systems. Conduct regular vulnerability assessments and penetration testing (Dey, 2023).
- *Foster a culture of cybersecurity awareness.* Knowledge is power, and empowering employees is critical regarding cybersecurity. Engage in training a team to identify and report suspicious activity, fostering a vigilant and proactive security culture (Parbhunath, 2021).
- *Prepare for the inevitable.* Develop a comprehensive incident response plan outlining proposed action in case of cyberattacks or other technology disruptions. This plan should address communication protocols, data recovery procedures, and business continuity measures (Johansen, 2020).
- *Embrace continuous improvement.* Technology is constantly evolving, as should a company's risk management practices. Regularly review and update the framework, incorporating learnings from past incidents and adapting to emerging threats.

Regulators

- *Strike a balance between innovation and safety.* Create clear and consistent regulatory frameworks that proportionately address the risks associated with different fintech activities. Such frameworks foster innovation while ensuring financial stability (Khan & Malaika, 2021).
- *Embrace regulatory sandboxes.* Provide safe spaces for fintech companies to test and refine their products and services under controlled conditions. This approach allows experimentation and innovation while mitigating potential risks for consumers and the broader financial system.
- *Promote collaboration.* Foster open communication channels between regulators, Fintech companies, and other stakeholders. This action facilitates knowledge sharing, enables swift responses to emerging risks, and builds trust within the ecosystem.
- *Invest in regulatory capacity.* Equip a company's team with the expertise and resources needed to oversee the rapidly evolving fintech landscape. This step includes staying abreast of technological advancements and developing specialized cybersecurity and data privacy skillsets.

Policymakers

- *Fuel innovation through research.* Invest in research initiatives on emerging technologies and their potential risks. This knowledge informs the development of effective regulatory frameworks and best practices for the fintech industry.
- *Bridge the digital divide.* Promote the development of accessible and affordable fintech solutions that cater to the needs of underserved populations. This action fosters financial inclusion and unlocks economic opportunities for all.
- *Think globally, act locally.* Collaborate with international counterparts on developing harmonized regulatory frameworks and cybersecurity measures. Such collaboration mitigates systemic risks and fosters a more stable global fintech ecosystem (Girling, 2022).
- *Make consumer protection paramount.* Striking the right balance between promoting innovation and safeguarding consumers' interests is critical. This step ensures data privacy, transparency, and robust complaint resolution mechanisms.

These practical recommendations can collectively build a more resilient and sustainable fintech ecosystem. Embracing a collaborative approach, prioritizing security, and fostering innovation can ensure that technology continues to be a force for good in the financial world.

Discussion Questions

- Identify the primary technological innovations reshaping the fintech landscape.
- Discuss how technology risks impact the sustainability of fintech ventures.
- Explain how fintech contributes to financial inclusion and identify the challenges that could hinder this progress.
- Discuss how collaboration among fintech companies, regulators, and policymakers can responsibly shape the future of digital finance.
- Explain why robust technology risk management is imperative for the long-term success of fintech ventures.

References

Ahmed, W., Rasool, A., Javed, A. R., Kumar, N., Reddy Gadekallu, T., Jail, Z., & Kryvinska, N. (2021). Security in next generation mobile payment systems: A comprehensive survey. *IEEE Access*, *9*, 115932–115950.

Alwi, S., Alpandi, R. M., Salleh, M. N. M., & Najihah, I. (2019). An empirical study on the customers' satisfaction on fintech mobile payment services in Malaysia. *International Journal of Advanced Science and Technology*, *28*(16), 390–400.

Anagnostopoulos, I. (2018). Fintech and regtech: Impact on regulators and banks. *FinTech – Impact on Consumers, Banking and Regulatory Policy*, *100*, 7–25. https://www.sciencedirect.com/science/article/pii/S014861951730142X

Ashta, A. (2021). Fintech–technology in finance: Strategic risks and challenges. In *Innovation economics, engineering and management handbook 2: Special themes* (pp. 137–143). Wiley.

Chatterjee, D. (2021). *Cybersecurity readiness: A holistic and high-performance approach*. SAGE Publications, Inc.

Dey, R. (2023). *An analysis of cybersecurity threats and countermeasures in the era of advanced technologies*. No. 10059. EasyChair. https://easychair.org/publications/preprint/P7Jw

Dupont, B. (2019). The cyber-resilience of financial institutions: Significance and applicability. *Journal of Cybersecurity*, *5*(1), 1–17.

FAIR Institute. (2023). From a compliance-based approach to a risk-based approach to cybersecurity and operational management. https://www.fairinstitute.org/what-is-fair

Girasa, R., & Scalabrini, G. J. (2022). *Regulation of innovative technologies: Blockchain, artificial intelligence and quantum computing*. Springer Nature.

Girling, P. X. (2022). *Operational risk management: A complete guide for banking and fintech*. John Wiley & Sons.

Gomber, P., Kauffman, R. J., Parker, C., & Weber, B. W. (2018). On the fintech revolution: Interpreting the forces of innovation, disruption, and transformation in financial services. *Journal of Management Information Systems*, *35*(1), 220–265. https://doi.org/10.1080/07421222.2018.1440766

Hussain, M., Nadeem, M. W., Iqbal, S., Mehrban, S., Nisar Fatima, S., Hakeem, O., & Mustafa, G. (2021). Security and privacy in FinTech: A policy enforcement framework. In *Research anthology on concepts, applications, and challenges of FinTech* (pp. 372–384). IGI Global.

Javaheri, D., Fahmideh, M., Chizari, H., Lalbakhsh, P., & Hur, J. (2024). Cybersecurity threats in FinTech: A systematic review. *Expert Systems With Applications*, 122697. https://www.sciencedirect.com/science/article/pii/S0957417423031998

Johansen, G. (2020). *Digital forensics and incident response: Incident response techniques and procedures to respond to modern cyber threats*. Packt Publishing Ltd.

Khan, A., & Malaika, M. (2021). *Central Bank risk management, fintech, and cybersecurity*. International Monetary Fund.

Lanz, J. (2018). Enterprise technology risk in a new COSO ERM world: Eight challenges facing management: Certified public accountant. *The CPA Journal*, *88*(6), 6–10. https://search.proquest.com/docview/2185468171?accountid=10378

Laroiya, C., Saxena, D., & Komalavalli, C. (2020). Chapter 9 – Applications of blockchain technology. In S. Krishnan, V. E. Balas, J. Golden, Y. Robinson, S. Balaji, & R. Kumar (Eds.), *Handbook of research on blockchain technology* (pp. 213–243). Jagan Institute of Management Studies, Rohini, Academic Press. https://www.sciencedirect.com/science/article/pii/B9780128198162000095

Lau, T., & Leimer, B. (2021). *Beyond good: How technology is leading a purpose-driven business revolution*. Kogan Page Publishers.

Loruenser, T., Pöhls, H. C., Sell, L., & Laenger, T. (2018). CryptSDLC: Embedding cryptographic engineering into secure software development lifecycle. In *Proceedings of the 13th international conference on availability, reliability and security* (pp. 1–9).

Mandel, R. (2017). *Optimizing cyberdeterrence: A comprehensive strategy for preventing foreign cyberattacks*. Georgetown University Press.

Mosteanu, N. R., & Faccia, A. (2021). Fintech frontiers in quantum computing, fractals, and blockchain distributed ledger: Paradigm shifts and open innovation. *Journal of Open Innovation: Technology, Market, and Complexity*, *7*(1), 19. https://www.mdpi.com/2199-8531/7/1/19

Nikolinakos, N. T. (2023). The proposed artificial intelligence act and subsequent 'compromise' proposals: Commission, council, parliament. In *EU policy and legal framework for artificial intelligence, robotics and related technologies – The AI act* (pp. 327–341). Springer International Publishing. https://doi.org/10.1007/978-3-031-27953-9_8

Omotunde, H., & Ahmed, M. (2023). A comprehensive review of security measures in database systems: Assessing authentication access control and beyond. *Mesopotamian Journal of Cybersecurity 2023*, 115–133.

Parbhunath, A. (2021). *An analysis of cybersecurity culture in an organisation managing critical infrastructure*. Master Thesis, Department of Computer Science. University of Cape Town.

Rosário, A. T., & Dias, J. C. (2023). How has data-driven marketing evolved: Challenges and opportunities with emerging technologies. *International Journal of Information Management Data Insights*, *3*(2), 100203.

Ross, R., Pillitteri, V., Graubart, R., Bodeau, D., & McQuaid, R. (2019). *Developing cyber-resilient systems: A systems security engineering approach*. National Institute of Standards and Technology. https://csrc.nist.gov/pubs/sp/800/160/v2/r1/final

Schmitt, M. (2020). *Artificial intelligence in business analytics, capturing value with machine learning applications in financial services*.

Schuetz, S., & Venkatesh, V. (2020). Blockchain, adoption, and financial inclusion in India: Research opportunities. *International Journal of Information Management*, *52*, 101936. https://www.sciencedirect.com/science/article/pii/S0268401219301872

Seth, S., & Gandhi, B. (2023). 15 revolutionizing risk assessment and lending decisions: The impact of digitalization and data analytics in Indian banks. *Commerce, Economics & Management*, *2023*, 111.

Tengeh, R. K., & Gahapa Talom, F. S. (2020). Mobile money as a sustainable alternative for SMEs in less developed financial markets. *Journal of Open Innovation: Technology, Market, and Complexity*, *6*(4), 163.

Chapter 9

Capital Formation and Crowdfunding

Keith Black

University of Massachusetts, USA

Abstract

Each company, large or small, starts with a dream and an idea for a new product or service. Companies can succeed or fail for a wide variety of reasons, including inexperienced managers, failure to build or sell the desired product, launching products into highly competitive environments, and a lack of capital. This chapter reviews the traditional methods of capital formation, including funding by angel investors and venture capital firms. These funding methods are only available to relatively large firms, leaving millions of small firms without reliable debt and equity funding sources to scale their business. The growth of the internet, blockchain technology, and fintech firms has introduced innovative funding methods, such as crowdfunding and Initial Coin Offerings (ICOs). While these structures have been successful in raising capital for smaller firms, changes in the regulatory environment, such as the JOBS Act, are needed for these new forms of capital formation to reach their full potential.

Keywords: Crowdfunding; initial coin offering (ICO); JOBS Act; regulation crowdfunding; venture capital; angel investors

Introduction

Historically, start-ups have found it challenging to introduce new products, scale revenue, raise capital, and survive beyond 5 years. The founders, their friends, and family fund nearly all small businesses. Access to capital from angel investors, venture capital (VC), and private equity (PE) funds is only available to firms with proven valuations in the millions of dollars.

This chapter reviews traditional forms of financing, including angels, VC, and PE funds, and newer forms of financing, including crowdfunding and initial coin offerings (ICOs). These newer financing methods make capital available to much

The Emerald Handbook of Fintech, 177–188

Published under exclusive licence by Emerald Publishing Limited
doi:10.1108/978-1-83753-608-520241016

younger businesses and make raising smaller amounts of capital more feasible. Although US financial market regulations have evolved to approve crowdfunding, regulations have not yet been established for ICOs and blockchain-based fundraising.

The US Small Business Administration (SBA) (US Small Business Administration Office of Advocacy, 2021) defines small businesses as those with less than 500 employees. The SBA counts over 6 million US companies with employees on the payroll and only 20,516 large businesses with over 500 employees. Small businesses, including over 26 million companies without employees, produce 43.5% of the US gross domestic product (GDP) and employ 46.8% of the private sector. From 1995 to 2020, small businesses created 12.7 million jobs in the United States (US). In contrast, large businesses created 7.9 million jobs. From 1994 to 2019, 48.9% of small businesses with employees survived at least 5 years after formation, while only 33.6% made it beyond 10 years. At any given time, start-ups may comprise 13% of small businesses, with young companies averaging 3.3 employees and established small businesses averaging 15.3 employees.

Traditional Methods of Capital Formation

The financing methods available to entrepreneurs vary by firm size, as measured by revenue or potential revenue, and the size of the desired fundraising. Although the smallest businesses have difficulty raising capital and must rely on their resources and those of their friends and family, larger businesses can raise capital from angel investors, VC, and PE firms.

Friends and Family

The SBA notes that 77% of small businesses funded operations from friends, family, personal savings, and business earnings (US Small Business Administration Office of Advocacy, 2021). A small minority of businesses received external financing through bank loans or equity investors. Godlewski (2023) notes that only 2% of non-employer businesses reach $1 million in revenue, while businesses with one to four employees average $387,000 in annual revenue. Annual revenues exceed $1 million for firms with 5–9 employees and $2 million for those with 10–19 employees. Of businesses that fail, 82% state that a lack of cash flow was a key factor in the demise of the venture. With over 86% of small business owners profiting less than $100,000 annually, most businesses will never require or receive external equity funding.

Angels

Angels are individual investors who make personal or club investments in private companies. A single angel is often an entrepreneur seeking to make investments for two reasons. The most obvious reason is to profit from the growth of companies in which they invest. A less obvious reason is that the angel is seeking a role as a mentor, hoping to pass personal entrepreneurial success along to a smaller and younger firm. Although some angels invest independently, others will join an angel club, with many investors periodically pooling resources to invest in small companies. The mentorship role of an angel club may be divided across industry lines, with angels mentoring companies in the industry where they have the most relevant personal experience. The Angel Capital Association (ACA) (2019) notes that angel groups invest in a median of 10 companies with a median investment of $100,000, while the average is 16 companies with investments of $215,000 per firm.

MacDonald Ventures (2022) defines pre-seed and seed angel and VC funding rounds. In the *pre-seed stage* of a company, the entrepreneur's idea is not fully developed, as their start-up is typically still building a prototype and seeking their initial customers. Given the extreme risk at this stage as a pre-revenue company, most funding comes from entrepreneurs, family, and friends. The *seed round* is typically the first time a start-up raises external capital, as capital is now necessary to scale the product and customer base established in the pre-seed stage. Pre-seed companies often require funding of $50,000–$250,000, which values the firm at $1–$3 million, while companies in the seed stage can raise $500,000–$2 million with valuations of $5 million–$15 million.

Few companies receive investments from VC or PE fund managers. Although some VC firms invest in seed-stage companies, most venture capitalists start investing in a company's A, B, and C rounds of funding, which come after a successful seed-stage investment. Most VC firms typically invest after the product is designed, the revenue is growing, and the company's valuation exceeds $15 million.

The Angel Capital Association (2019) notes that 60% of angel investments are made in the seed round, 3% in the pre-seed round, and 38% in the A, B, C, and later rounds VC firms commonly fund. Some angel investments are relatively small, with 40% of investments between $10,000 and $1 million, while others are larger, including 37% between $1 million and $3 million and 23% above $3 million. Over 63% of companies funded by angels had valuations of between $2.5 million and $8 million before the angel investment. Angels can invest in relatively small companies, with 74% of companies funded by angels having 10 or fewer employees at the time of the angel investment, 27% of companies having zero revenue, and 45% of companies funded earning from minimal revenue up to $1 million annually.

Martin (2022) reports that angels invest up to $24 billion annually in over 60,000 start-ups, a small portion of the 6 million US companies with employees. Although angels perform due diligence to understand the potential success of the entrepreneurs they are funding and mentoring, less than 10% of angel investments are profitable. However, the companies that succeed often do so in a big way, making most angels profitable after investing in at least 12 companies.

Although angels may have the reputation of investing in small companies, the ACA notes that just 6% of seed round investments are in companies with a pre-money valuation of less than $2.5 million. This statement means that most companies need substantial revenue or potential before reaching the angel funding stage. Most companies are never considered for investments by angels, let alone VC or PE funds.

Private Equity and Venture Capital

PitchBook (2023a) notes that private capital funds raised over $15.2 trillion from 2008 to the third quarter of 2023. This fundraising was dominated by $5.6 trillion in PE (37.0%), $2.5 trillion in VC (16.5%), and $2.2 trillion in private debt (14.7%). The final $4.8 trillion in funds raised for private capital (31.7%) were invested in real estate, real assets, funds of funds, and secondaries. The $4.4 trillion raised for buyout funds dominated PE fundraising.

Precisely allocating a specific investment amount into PE and VC can be difficult, as *dry powder*, the amount of committed and uninvested capital, recently totaled $1.5 trillion for PE and $650 billion in VC. For example, 46% of the assets committed by investors to PE funds in the 2020 vintage remained with the investors without being called by PE general partners (GPs) by the third quarter of 2023.

PE and VC funds tend to have a 10-year life. In the investment period, typically the fund's first three years, the GP identifies the portfolio companies and consummates the investments. Over the next 5 years, the fund manager seeks to reduce the debt on companies held in buyout funds and grow the companies held in VC funds. By the end of the fund's 10th year, the manager seeks to have exited as many companies as possible by selling their stake to an acquirer or the public markets through an initial public offering (IPO). PitchBook (2023b) calculates that approximately 25% of PE funds' assets under management (AUM) are exited in the average year, ranging from 11% to 41% in any given year. Of the $5.6 trillion raised since 2008 for PE funds, $5.1 trillion was distributed to investors and fund managers from the proceeds of exits. Companies have remained in PE funds for longer periods, with the median exit time rising from 3.7 years in 2007–2009 to 5.1–6.4 years in 2012–2023.

Although many investors believe that most exits from VC funds are through IPOs, PitchBook (2023c) explains that is untrue. From 2013 to the third quarter of 2023, only 9.7% of exits from VC funds were through IPOs, while 90.3% were through acquisition or buyout. However, 68% of the exit proceeds were through IPOs, as the companies going public were often *unicorns*, with average exit values exceeding $1 billion. In contrast, the average proceeds from an acquisition were $59 million, while the average buyout proceeds were $38 million.

The Regulatory Framework of Capital Formation

Best and Neiss (2014) provide a historical overview of securities regulation in the United States. The story started in the 1920s when states regulated securities offerings, but numerous unregistered securities were sold across state lines. Many of these securities were fraudulent, and market participants used substantial leverage to purchase these speculative stocks. After the stock market crash of 1929, half of these offerings were worthless, with investors realizing billions in losses.

In response to these interstate fraud issues and the deepening depression after the crash of 1929, the Federal government implemented securities regulations. The *Securities Act of 1933* regulates primary markets and the issuance of securities, requiring Federal registration of securities offerings and that each offering disclose all material information about the business and its risk profile. The Act also outlawed misrepresentation and fraud in the securities markets. The *Securities and Exchange Act of 1934* regulates the secondary trading of securities and established the Securities and Exchange Commission (SEC), which has regulatory and enforcement powers over brokerage firms. The 1934 Act regulates publicly traded companies, which must provide regular disclosures to investors.

Little changed in US securities regulation until 1982, when Regulation D was added to the 1933 Act to provide exemptions from registration requirements for some newly issued securities. Revised in 2016, *Regulation D* allows issuers to raise $10 million in any 12 months without registration.

According to Regulation D, *accredited investors* are (a) individuals with $200,000 in annual income or $300,000 in annual income as a married couple, (b) individuals or married couples with a net worth exceeding $1 million, excluding the value of their primary residence, or (c) those qualified as a financial professional or knowledgeable fund employee. *Qualified purchasers* have a net worth exceeding $5 million. Investments offered exclusively to accredited investors or qualified purchasers can qualify for a *private placement exemption* that relieves the obligation to register the offering and provide the transparency and disclosures required under the 1933 and 1934 Acts. Most PE, VC, and hedge funds are designed to qualify for this private placement exemption by marketing the offering exclusively to accredited investors or qualified purchasers. Offerings qualifying for the private placement exemption are not exempt from regulations prohibiting fraud and misrepresentation.

The SEC protects retail investors who do not qualify as accredited or qualified purchasers. The assumption may be that high-net-worth investors have the financial assets to afford losses and are sophisticated enough to evaluate investment risks or hire advisors who can advise them. The converse of that assumption is that investors without substantial wealth are less sophisticated and must be protected by regulations.

Securities Regulations in the Fintech Era: Crowdfunding

As evidenced by the history of US securities regulation, raising small amounts of capital or gaining access to unregistered securities offerings has been difficult for retail investors. The rise of the internet, the ready availability of investment information, and the growth of social media have changed the investing landscape. Fintech innovations such as crowdfunding and ICOs did not initially comply with US securities laws.

Dresner (2014) notes that *crowdfunding* is the intersection of social networking and collective investing to fund a new venture. Since crowdfunding would typically raise capital from accredited and retail investors, offerings would likely be regulated as securities requiring registration, including a prospectus and ongoing transparency.

The US passed the Jumpstart Our Business Startups Act (JOBS Act) to modernize securities regulations to accommodate crowdfunding. US Securities and Exchange Commission (2015) describes how Title III of the JOBS Act, *Regulation Crowdfunding*, exempted securities registration requirements to facilitate capital formation for small businesses, including sourcing investments from retail investors. Companies can raise capital through crowdfunding on the internet up to a limit of $5 million in any 12-month period. Investors with a net worth below $100,000 are limited to annual investments of $2,000 in crowdfunding offerings or 5% of their income or net worth. Investors are limited to $100,000 in annual investments across all crowdfunding offerings. After investing in a crowdfunding offering, investors are prohibited from selling these securities for 1 year. Although exempt from registration, some issuers of securities through Regulation Crowdfunding must provide transparency regarding the offering, the status and risks of the business, and financial statements.

Regulation Crowdfunding also requires that all fundraising occurs within the regulated environment of a broker-dealer or a funding portal. Funding portals must become a Financial Industry Regulatory Authority (FINRA) member. Portals must also provide educational information to investors, transparency from issuers, and track investor qualifications and the total amount invested. Portals are responsible for performing due diligence on crowdfunding issuers to protect investors from fraudulent issuers.

According to the US Securities and Exchange Commission (2024), offerings under Regulation A allow for much larger fundraising amounts than Regulation Crowdfunding. Under *Tier 1 of Regulation A*, issuers can raise $20 million in any 12-month period from accredited investors or retail investors, and issuers under *Tier 2* can raise $50 million annually. Tier 1 and 2 issuers must file an offering statement with the SEC. Tier 2 issuers must provide regular financial statements, while Tier 1 issuers are exempt from regular disclosures. Similar to Regulation Crowdfunding, retail investors are limited to the amount of Reg A securities that can be purchased each year.

Securities Regulations in the Fintech Era: ICOs

Investments made through crowdfunding offerings, VC funds, or as angels are highly illiquid. Although securities purchased through crowdfunding must be held for at least 12 months before being sold, the median time to the exit of portfolio companies in VC funds now exceeds 6 years. As previously noted, the SEC regulates these capital-raising methods explicitly through the JOBS Act or investor qualifications through private placement exemptions.

An ICO raises capital for start-up firms and projects with equity represented as tokens or coins with ownership tracked and traded on various blockchains. The projects are largely blockchains or distributed applications designed to run on blockchain platforms. Most ICOs are pre-seed investments, as most start-ups raise funds before completing a viable project. The developers detail their plans in a business plan termed a *white paper*, which describes the team, the project, and how the project will benefit users of the platform.

Chirag (2022) and CB Insights (2020) describe the fundraising environment of ICOs, calculating that ICOs raised $3.9 billion in 2017 and $7.8 billion in 2018. According to Chirag, ICOs can quickly raise funds, with 85% of 2017 ICOs completing their fundraising in 10–70 days. Sakovich (2018) notes that 46% of ICOs attempting to raise funds in 2017 and 2018 failed to do so, while 40% raised over $1 million each. Kalomeni (2018) states that 3,685 ICOs proposed between 2016 and 2019 received no funding, while 1,785 closed ICOs raised $26.5 billion. ICOs raised these funds from global investors without regard for the investors' sophistication or wealth and standardized disclosures of the risks of each ICO. Some large ICOs completing fundraising included Telegram, Ethereum, Polkadot, Tezos, EOS, Wax, TaTaTu, Huobi, Bancor, and Filecoin. Many of these projects were among the most valuable in the cryptocurrency universe at the end of 2023.

Although many of today's most valuable cryptocurrencies were funded as ICOs between 2016 and 2019, hundreds of other ICOs that successfully raised capital failed to deliver on the project outlined in the white paper. The line between fraud and simply investing in a failed business plan may be determined by the amount of effort invested by the team and the portion of the project completed. Teams with a substantial code base and an attempt to launch a blockchain-based project may be mourned as failed businesses. However, other teams that did not even begin to build the projects described in the white paper may be accused of fraud, as no evidence exists that the capital raised was used in an attempt to build the stated project. These frauds have hurt the cryptocurrency industry, as losses by retail investors and the inaction of the US Congress to build clear regulations for digital asset fundraising have led the SEC to regulate digital assets by enforcement without building clear and modernized guidelines for the new industry.

Although the JOBS Act, passed by the US Congress, legitimized crowdfunding, increased the capital available to small companies, and broadened the investment universe of retail investors, no such regulations have been established in the United States to legitimize or regulate ICOs. ICOs can be highly liquid but are often sold to retail investors without standardized and required disclosures. The US Securities and Exchange Commission (2023) believes many ICOs have been unregistered securities. Fundraising through ICOs fell to less than $400 million in 2019 after the SEC noted that ICOs of 2017 and 2018 were largely unregistered securities offerings and often fraudulent.

Although the cryptocurrency and digital assets industry wants crypto-specific regulations and definitions of which offerings are securities, the SEC points to the 1946 Howey Test and the fact that the definition of a security is independent of its form. The innovative ICO and digital asset industry is no different than any other type or form of security or fundraising project.

The Howey Test resulted from a 1946 lawsuit by the SEC against the WJ Howey Company, which sold acreage in its citrus groves to investors and sought to lease the groves back from the investors. The US Supreme Court upheld the assertion by the SEC that these land sales contracts were unregistered securities. The US Securities and Exchange Commission (2023) notes that "The US Supreme Court's Howey case and subsequent case law have found that an 'investment contract' exists when there is the investment of money in a common enterprise with a reasonable expectation of profits to be derived from the efforts of others." According to Howey, when determining whether fundraising requires registration as a security, the test has three parts: (1) an investment of money, (2) in a common enterprise, and (3) a reasonable expectation of profits to be derived from the efforts of others.

Crowdfunding

Crowdfunding transactions predated the JOBS Act, which became effective in tranches between 2012 and 2016. Best and Neiss (2014) provide a historical perspective on crowdfunding. Kickstarter, one of today's leading crowdfunding platforms, started in 2009 as a platform leveraging social media to raise funds.

Rewards-based crowdfunding was the initial application, where contributors to a project were rewarded with the investment's tangible output. The creative community often used this inception phase of crowdfunding for fundraising, with funders receiving access to CDs or concerts of musicians, DVDs of filmmakers, or early copies of video games from upstart tech companies. Rather than being securities offerings, rewards-based crowdfunding effectively functioned as pre-orders of products, with customers providing funding months or even years before receiving their product or service.

Donation-based crowdfunding brings the power of social media to engage a community in donating to a charitable cause in pursuit of emotional returns rather than financial returns. Such crowdfunding, as implemented on GoFundMe, often comes into play when a person or community experiences an accident or natural disaster and others seek to help the cause through charitable donations. The internet's viral nature can raise substantial sums for the most compelling stories, with communities responding with over $10 million after tragedies such as school shootings, pandemics, or social protests (Kelly, 2021).

Although donation-based and rewards-based crowdfunding are not regulated financial transactions, using crowdfunding to raise debt or equity capital may be subject to securities laws, such as Regulation Crowdfunding. *Debt-based crowdfunding* raises debt capital for individuals or businesses that must be paid back with principal and interest. Chapter 7 describes debt-based crowdfunding, peer-to-peer (P2P) lending, or marketplace lending on platforms such as LendingClub, Kiv, and Prosper in detail.

Equity-based crowdfunding allows retail investors to make small investments in growing companies, requiring all investments to be held for at least 12 months before being sold. The JOBS Act requires that equity-based crowdfunding occurs on regulated platforms like Republic or FundersClub. Similar platforms in the United Kingdom include Crowdcube and Seedrs.

Taylor (2022) describes the crowdfunding campaign of the Star Citizen video game. Starting with a 2012 Kickstarter campaign, Star Citizen is still raising funds and pre-selling video game access and in-game items. Despite raising over $500 million from more than 4 million funders, the game is still in alpha testing and has not yet been fully released. U-Haul's Investors Club has raised over $211 million since 2011, selling U-Notes backed by specific assets, such as trucks and trailers. Investors can purchase interest-bearing notes with 2–30-year maturities for as little as $100 (U-Haul, 2024).

Dix and Luzar (2014) describe the mechanics of crowdfunding platforms and provide a long list of global platforms segmented by industry. Crowdfunding campaigns are successful when at least 30% of the capital is pledged to the project before the campaign's official launch and a time limit, such as 60 days, is imposed to complete the fundraising. Although Kickstarter requires the stated capital raise to be completed before funds are released to entrepreneurs, Indiegogo can also have flexible campaigns and the all-or-nothing approach that Kickstarter applies. Industry-specific platforms listed by Dix and Luzar include Realty Mogul, Fundrise, and Prodigy Network for real estate; Windcentrale, SunFunder, and Mosaic for alternative energy; WeDemand for concerts and events; and Pubslush for books. Crowdfund Capital Advisors (2023a) notes that over 6,400 companies raised $2 billion before the third quarter of 2023.

As Crowdspace (2022) notes, Europe's most popular niche platforms for raising capital are dedicated to the real estate and clean energy sectors. It took until November 2021 for a pan-European crowdfunding regulation to be implemented (Crowdestate, 2023), replacing varying regulations across the European Union (EU) member states. Once a crowdfunding platform is appropriately licensed in its home jurisdiction, that registration can be used to raise funds across the European Union through a regulatory passport.

Equity or debt crowdfunding can lead to success in a young business (Kerrigan, 2014). The funding allows the business to provide their product or service first to their funders, an enthusiastic audience. The success of fundraising and providing a product to a thankful customer base can be a positive signal for angels and venture capitalists. Entrepreneurs who successfully engage with their crowdfunding backers may be building skills that will allow them to impress venture capitalists when the time comes to grow the business. According to the SBA, Crowdfund Capital Advisors (2023b) calculates that the 5-year business failure rate of businesses organized under Regulation Crowdfunding is less than 18% relative to the over 50% failure rate of all small businesses. Longevity is positively correlated to the amount of capital raised through crowdfunding platforms. Companies established by women and minority owners may have greater success and longevity when using crowdfunding platforms.

Summary and Conclusions

Historically, start-ups were largely funded through an entrepreneur's assets and funds from friends and family. Angel investors may be interested in funding businesses with valuations of $1–$10 million, while VC firms fund businesses with valuations above $10 million. Businesses valued below $1 million typically had no access to external financing. Only high-net-worth investors could invest in private companies.

The JOBS Act and Regulation Crowdfunding, implemented in stages between 2012 and 2016, accessed the power of the crowd, the internet, and social media to fund smaller businesses. The regulation, which allowed ordinary investors to invest in private companies, led to over $2 billion in fundraising through 2023. The JOBS Act, passed by the US Congress, was a positive regulatory development that facilitated capital formation and broadened investment opportunities for retail investors.

ICOs raised $26.5 billion globally for blockchain-related start-ups between 2016 and 2019. Although this innovation in tokenized, liquid VC promised to revolutionize fundraising, the SEC has prevented the growth of this market. Rather than modernize regulations and provide guardrails to investors, the SEC has accused ICOs of being unregistered securities offerings, which predictably led to over a 90% decline in funds raised through ICOs since the SEC's enforcement actions started in 2019. The cryptocurrency industry believes that a clear regulatory framework from the SEC regarding digital assets will draw more capital and allow the United States to retain its strong global standing in the finance and technology industries.

Discussion Questions

- Discuss a company's developmental stage and valuation level before it is eligible for funding by an angel or a VC firm.
- Describe the qualifications for accredited investors and the exemptions from regulation that status provides.
- Explain Regulation Crowdfunding and how the regulation facilitated capital formation by small businesses.
- Name the three parts of the Howey Test to determine when the SEC requires that a fundraising offering be registered as a security.
- Name and explain four different types of crowdfunding.

References

Angel Capital Association. (2019). *ACA angel funders report.*

Best, J., & Neiss, S. (2014). Crowdfunding: A historical perspective. In S. Dresner (Ed.), *Crowdfunding: A guide to raising capital on the Internet* (pp. 3–14). Bloomberg.

CB Insights. (2020, March 19). *The 2020 blockchain report.* CB Insights. https://www.cbinsights.com/research/report/blockchain-report-2020/

Chirag. (2022, November 17). *Why do ICOs fail? Are they still worth investing in 2019–2020?* Appinventiv.com. https://appinventiv.com/blog/why-icos-fail-and-their-worth-in-2019/

Crowdestate. (2023, July 20). *Crowdfunding regulation in the European union*. https://crowdestate.eu/article/crowdfunding-regulation-in-the-european-union

Capital Advisors. (2023a). *Celebrating a milestone: Crowdfunding soars beyond $2 billion*. https://crowdfundcapitaladvisors.com/celebrating-a-milestone-investment-crowdfunding-soars-beyond-2-billion-2/

Capital Advisors. (2023b). *Defying expectations: Regulation crowdfunding issuers prove more resilient than traditional companies*. https://crowdfundcapitaladvisors.com/defying-expectations-regulation-crowdfunding-issuers-prove-more-resilient-than-traditional-companies/

Crowdspace. (2022). *Crowdfunding industry report: Major regulatory, marketing, and tech challenges 2022*. https://thecrowdspace.com/whitepapers/crowdfunding-industry-report-2022/#wpcf7-f14547-o1

Dresner, S. (2014). *Crowdfunding: A guide to raising capital on the Internet*. Bloomberg Press/Wiley.

Dix, A., & Luzar, C. (2014). Current market dynamics. In S. Dresner (Ed.), *Crowdfunding: A guide to raising capital on the Internet* (pp. 47–80). Bloomberg Press/Wiley.

Godlewski, N. (2023, January 23). *Small business revenue statistics: Annual sales and earnings*. Fundera.com. https://www.fundera.com/resources/small-business-revenue-statistics

Kalomeni, M. (2018, September 27). *The ICO market isn't collapsing. It's Maturing*. Elementus. https://www.elementus.io/blog-post/ico-market-august-2018

Kelly, E. (2021, October 13). The 11 biggest GoFundMe fundraisers ever. *Newsweek*. https://www.newsweek.com/biggest-gofundme-fundraisers-ever-1637765

Kerrigan, K. (2014). Understanding the 'crowd'. In S. Dresner (Ed.), *Crowdfunding: A guide to raising capital on the Internet* (pp. 15–30). Bloomberg Press/Wiley.

MacDonald Ventures. (2022, December 22). *Pre-seed vs. Seed funding: What's the difference*. https://macdonald.ventures/insights/pre-seed-vs-seed-funding-what-is-the-difference/

Martin, K. (2022, July 22). Angel investor statistics – 15 pieces of data. *Wealthpursuits*. https://wealthpursuits.com/angel-investor-statistics/

PitchBook. (2023a). *Q3 2023 global private market fundraising report*. https://pitchbook.com/news/reports/q3-2023-global-private-market-fundraising-report

PitchBook. (2023b, December 18). *The 2024 venture capital outlook*. https://pitchbook.com/news/reports/2024-us-venture-capital-outlook

PitchBook. (2023c, December 19). *The 2024 private equity outlook*. https://pitchbook.com/news/reports/2024-us-private-equity-outlook

Sakovich, J. (2018, September 11). *Nearly 50% of ICOs failed, report claims*. Coin-speaker.com. https://www.coinspeaker.com/nearly-50-of-icos-failed-report-claims/

Taylor, M. (2022, September). *Star citizen now has over half a billion dollars in crowdfunding*. PCGamer.com. https://www.pcgamer.com/star-citizen-now-has-over-half-a-billion-dollars-in-crowdfunding/

U-Haul. (2024). *U-Haul Investors club*. https://www.uhaulinvestorsclub.com/HowItWorks

U.S. Securities and Exchange Commission. (2015). *SEC adopts rules to permit crowdfunding*. https://www.sec.gov/news/press-release/2015-249

U.S. Securities and Exchange Commission. (2023). *Framework for "investment contract" analysis of digital assets*. https://www.sec.gov/corpfin/framework-investment-contract-analysis-digital-assets

U.S. Securities and Exchange Commission. (2024). *Regulation A*. https://www.investor.gov/introduction-investing/investing-basics/glossary/regulation

U.S. Small Business Administration Office of Advocacy. (2021). *Frequently asked questions*. https://advocacy.sba.gov/wp-content/uploads/2021/12/Small-Business-FAQ-Revised-December-2021.pdf

Section IV

Transforming Personal Finance With Fintech: Digital Wealth Management

Chapter 10

Demystifying Robo-Advisors: Benefits and Limitations

Peter Scholz

DHBW Baden-Wuerttemberg Cooperative State University, Germany

Abstract

In recent years, investing with robo-advisors has gained momentum and is seen as a simplifying approach for individual investors to participate in financial markets. This chapter contributes to a better understanding of the concept of a robo-advisory and its implications for private investors by discussing its past, present, and future. It explores key issues, like cost-efficiency, historical performance, and automation levels, based on research and industry insights. Moreover, this chapter examines a robo-advisor's benefits, limitations, and challenges, like behavioral biases, regulation, and risk profiling. Finally, the importance of the ongoing megatrends of AI and green investing is examined concerning a robo-advisory.

Keywords: Robo-advisor; behavioral bias; regulation; risk profiling; artificial intelligence

Introduction

The famous quote "Banking is necessary, banks are not" emphasizes the importance of banking services while stressing the threat of being overrun by technological disruption. The quote traces back to a *Fortune* magazine interview with Dick Kovacevich, former CEO of Wells Fargo (Nocera, 1998). For other sectors of the economy, the rise of the internet has truly been a game-changer. Many stationary services have transformed into online services over the last three decades. Mobile devices like smartphones and tablets accelerated the development since customers can access offers and services anytime, influencing their behavior and expectations toward other business fields. Due to the tight financial regulation in many countries and regions like the United States and Europe, a

The Emerald Handbook of Fintech, 191–206

doi:10.1108/978-1-83753-608-520241020

regulatory shield mitigated, but did not prevent, the threat to the traditional financial industry by setting relatively high hurdles for start-ups to enter the banking sector. Still, over the past decade, robo-advisors have established themselves as an important innovation in the investment landscape. A few start-ups initiated the trend for automated investment advice and were followed by traditional asset managers.

Investing in financial markets can be daunting for investors, especially if they are novices, have little interest in finance, or lead busy lives. Robo-advisors are marketed as cost-efficient, reliable, low-effort alternatives to human financial advisors or self-investing. However, many are skeptical about the reliability of algorithms, the level of individualization in recommendations, and the potential lack of empathy exhibited by robo-advisors. This ambivalence results in the question: To what degree does a robo-advisory simplify investing for individual investors?

What Is a Robo-Advisor?

The term *robo-advisor* combines robot and advisor to define an automated investment service. Still, the level of automation may vary substantially. At a minimum, a wealth management process typically comprises the following elements: onboarding, risk profiling, investment recommendation, market analysis, sample portfolios, restructuring, rebalancing, monitoring, and tax reporting (Evensky et al., 2011; Scholz & Tertilt, 2021). At first glance, an investor might expect a robo-advisor to automate all these steps. In practice, considerable human impact is part of a robo's wealth management process. Whereas onboarding, risk profiling, monitoring, and rebalancing are typically automated, portfolio construction is frequently left to human investment committees.

Robo-advisors are not homogenous. Although some vendors combine automated investment advice with the option to contact human advisors in so-called hybrid models, others strictly rely on digital channels. Investment strategies are also a factor of discrimination. Some robo-advisors focus on passive investing with exchange-traded funds (ETFs) and basic asset classes like equity, fixed income, and cash. In contrast, others follow active investing and allow many other asset classes like commodities, real estate, and hedge funds. Regarding investment vehicles, some robo-advisors rely on proprietary funds while others consider third-party funds. Naturally, these differences lead to variances in cost, performance, and the client's perceptions.

The remainder of this chapter is organized into four sections. First, robo-advisory's past is examined by starting with a brief overview of the evolution of robo-advisors; then, the historical performance of robo-advisory is analyzed. The second section focuses on the present and displays the current market volume, clients, and players in the robo-advisory market. Further, an extensive discussion occurs regarding the most important benefits and limitations of robo-advisors. The third section provides an outlook on the future of robo-advisory, especially considering the two megatrends – artificial intelligence (AI) and sustainable investing. The final section offers a summary and conclusion.

Robo-Advisors: The Past

Trust is essential in financial markets, but the global financial crisis of 2007–2009 (GFC) shattered it. Robo-pioneers aimed to democratize wealth management and provide cost-efficient solutions for everyone. This section illustrates the history of robo-advisory and describes its past performance.

The Evolution of Robo-Advisory

Historically, until the 1990s, investment advisory was an individualized process. The client and advisor typically conversed over the phone or met in person to discuss the current investment needs. Advisors often acted like portfolio managers and included their market views in the portfolio recommendations. For institutions, this investment process comprised several issues. For example, liability issues focus on who is responsible for bad advice and financial losses. Quality issues concern how clients can be ensured of getting the same level of advice.

During the burst of the dot-com bubble, advisory companies strengthened institution-wide recommendations: If clients have similar risk profiles, they should get comparable portfolio allocations. At that time, institutions started systematically using the information from risk profiling questionnaires to generate portfolio recommendations based on predetermined rules. Nevertheless, the asset allocation rested on chief investment officers (CIOs) and investment committees. At the dawn of the GFC, trust in financial advisors was diminishing. The sales strategy was then product-centric rather than customer-centric: Financial advisors often had sales targets for certain investment products, and their recommendations did not always benefit clients. In extreme cases, advisors churned clients' portfolios (i.e., rebalanced assets only to generate fees).

The flaws of the existing financial system were important in establishing Betterment, an American financial advisory company providing digital investment, retirement, and cash management services. As Jonathan Stein, one of Betterment's founders, states, "Just because the financial system is designed a certain way, doesn't mean it's right. It's not necessarily the best it could be, or doing what anyone intended it to do – it's just evolved this way" (Stein, 2016). Dan Carroll, the co-founder of Wealthfront, reports similar experiences (Wealthfront, 2023e). His parents had suffered greatly from the GFC. While evaluating the extent of the losses, Carroll felt that too many investors did not get the quality of advisory given the cost. This view was his motivation to found Wealthfront, an automated investment service firm based in Palo Alto, California. Many consider Betterment and Wealthfront, which launched their retail operations in 2010, the first robo-advisors on the market. The robo-innovation quickly spilled over into Europe, where Nutmeg, an online investment management company based in London, was established in early 2011 (HM Government,

2023). One of the first robo-advisors in Germany was Quirion, which started operations in 2013 (Quirion, 2023), followed in 2014 by Scalable, now one of the largest non-US robo-advisors (Scalable, 2023c).

Whereas the first robo-advisors were mostly start-ups, traditional asset managers launched their robo-advisors later (Fisch et al., 2019). For instance, Vanguard and Charles Schwab started their robo-advisory in 2015. For existing asset management companies, automated investment advice is an opportunity to reallocate portions of their less profitable clients' capital to digital services (Becchi et al., 2018). The early robo-advisors typically provided portfolio recommendations based on passive ETF asset allocations since ETFs are rather cost-efficient. Now, many robo-advisors propose actively managed investment funds or even single stocks. Furthermore, some robo-advisors offer additional investment products like 401(k) plans or insurance. Another important trend was combining human and robo-advisors in hybrid models, mostly launched by traditional asset managers (Fisch et al., 2019).

The Performance of Robo-Advisory

A portfolio's expected performance is an important factor in investment decisions. Benchmarking without proper data is tricky since portfolios need similar levels of risk to be comparable. However, robo-advisors usually do not disclose detailed historical performance data.

Condor Capital Wealth Management (Condor) publishes a secondary source for performance analysis every quarter. It opened several accounts with an approximate 60/40 allocation at the most relevant US robo-advisors for tracking purposes. Currently, Condor has data for up to 5 years of investments. The exact methodology seems to be a black hole. Condor only publishes aggregated data, so users should carefully view the results. Based on Condor's recent report, Schapiro et al. (2023) find that Wealthfront, Zacks Advantage, and Fidelity Go portfolios show the best 5-year performance with around 6% annually. The worst performance in its 5-year sample is around 4% annually. Compared to their normalized benchmark, from a total of 19 robo-advisory portfolios, 12 underperformed, six outperformed, and one equaled the given reference portfolio with a range of −1.06% to +0.81% annually. The best portfolio, managed by Wealthfront, took an active allocation in the energy sector, a key driver for the outperformance. Hence whether this outperformance continues remains unclear.

Fisch et al. (2019) find that the robo-advisors from Betterment, Vanguard, Charles Schwab, and Personal Capital outperformed a 60/40 benchmark due to much higher equity quotas (i.e., above 87%), making a risk-adjusted comparison difficult. Scholz and Tertilt (2021) describe similar findings for the United States, the United Kingdom, and Germany: low granular data, returns that are hard to compare because of potential risk level biases, and performances that vary from above to below the benchmark in seemingly acceptable intervals. The authors question how robo-advisors will perform in bearish market environments, which Grealish and Kolm (2021) observed. For the "Corona-Crash," they reported using Backend Benchmarking data by Condor that robo-advisors could buffer the losses from the stock markets. But again, diversification in the fixed-income asset class largely drove this effect, which may not be risk-adjusted.

Robo-Advisors: The Present

Meanwhile, robo-advisors have become established in financial markets but still have much growth potential. This section examines the current status of robo-advisory and discusses key factors to consider when selecting a robo-platform.

Status Quo: Market Volume, Clients, and Players

The global market for robo-advisors has experienced substantial growth in recent years. Using assets under management (AUM) as a measure, it has multiplied from about $0.2 trillion in 2017 to an estimated $2.8 trillion in 2023 (Statista, 2023a). The United States, as the origin of robo-advisors, dominates the market with a share of around 40%, which corresponds to about $1.2 trillion in AUM; Europe follows with 30% and Asia with a 16% market share (Statista, 2023a, 2023b).

Initially perceived, these figures may seem impressive. Yet, comparing the global AUM from robo-advisory to the volume managed by the top three investment companies BlackRock ($9.5 trillion), Vanguard ($7.6 trillion), and Fidelity ($4.3 trillion) reveals that the market share of robo-advisors is still comparatively small (BlackRock, 2023; Fidelity, 2023; Vanguard, 2023a). Nevertheless, the growth is stable and in line with previous forecasts. In their 2017 dossier, Statista expected the global robo-advisory market to grow to around $2.5 trillion in 2023 compared to the $2.8 trillion currently estimated as mentioned above (Statista, 2017, 2023a).

Analyses from different market segments indicate that the average client of robo-advisory services is male, between 30 and 49 years old, and a middle-to high-income individual (Baulkaran & Jain, 2022; Fisch et al., 2019; Kaya, 2020; Statista, 2018). Based on an Italian study, financial literacy is another essential factor that seems to determine the use of robo-advisory as an investment service (Isaia & Oggero, 2022). Although younger people do not seem reluctant to adopt robo-advisory services, they supposedly do not broadly have the financial means to use them. Younger investors use social media to get information from Instagram or TikTok. They choose ETFs independently or invest in more speculative single stocks and cryptocurrencies.

In the most recent top-five rankings of global robo-advisors, only US robo-advisors appear. The question of which robo-advisors are the largest depends on a robo-advisory's definition. Using a broader definition and allowing hybrid services, Vanguard remains the largest provider of robo-advisory services. It operates two advice options: Personal Advisor and Digital Advisor (Vanguard,

2023b, 2023c). Both robo-advisors combined have almost $300 billion AUM as of March 31, 2023 (Adviserinfo, 2023a).

In public perception and, therefore, in more rankings, Edelman Financial Engines (Edelman) is now considered a robo-advisor (Woolley, 2021). With $242 billion in AUM as of April 20, 2023 (Adviserinfo, 2023), it is the second largest robo in the market with a focus on managing 401(k) accounts. Edelman evolved from the merger of Edelman Financial Services and the robo-advisor Financial Engines in 2018 (Tergesen & Gottfried, 2018). Edelman views itself as a financial planner using robo-support in the financial advising process rather than a robo-advisor company (Edelman Financial Engines, 2022a).

The next competitors have considerably less AUM. In third place, Schwab Intelligent Portfolios have about $66 billion AUM as of March 30, 2023 (Adviserinfo, 2023b). Next follows Betterment, probably the oldest robo-advisor, which reports $36 billion as of May 1, 2023 (Adviserinfo, 2023d). Wealthfront's AUM is ambiguous because it reports $35+ billion on its website (Wealthfront, 2023a). In contrast, the Investment Adviser Public Disclosure website states only $23 billion as of March 9, 2023 (Adviserinfo, 2023c). The German company Scalable is the largest robo-advisor outside the United States, surpassing the €10 billion AUM threshold in August 2022 (Scalable, 2022).

Discussion: Are Robo-Advisors Disrupting Human Advisors?

What are the benefits and limitations of automated investment advice? This section delves into this field and raises some important questions.

Is Robo-Advice More Cost-Efficient?

A typical assumption is that robo-advisors offer investment advice at low costs. Based on a market analysis of the most prominent robo-advisory services, non-hybrid advisory fees range from no fees (Charles Schwab, 2023) to 0.89% annually (Empower Advisors, 2023). Looking at the largest robo-advisors, Vanguard charges about 0.15% annually as an advisory fee for their Digital Advisor, which is half the cost for their hybrid Personal Advisor service (Vanguard, 2023f). Vanguard also demands a maximum of 0.3% annually for its other advisory services. Edelman Financial Engines' cost structure resembles that of a human advisor since it imposes relatively high fees, especially for lower investments. For example, Edelman charges 1.75% for investments up to $400k (Edelman Financial Engines, 2023). Betterment and Wealthfront collect 0.25% annually (Betterment, 2023a; Wealthfront, 2023c). Charles Schwab waives advisory fees but relies on earnings from Schwab ETFs, liquidity management, and order flow (Charles Schwab, 2023), which lacks transparency. By comparison, the largest German robo-advisor, Scalable, charges 0.75% annually (Scalable, 2023a). The investment products' total expense ratio (TER) must be added.

As Fein (2015) points out, the affirmation that robo-services are "free" or "low cost" may not be entirely accurate. The disclosure from Charles Schwab shows it can earn fees through kick-back payments by in-house investment vehicles and affiliated partners like brokers, custodians, and clearinghouses. In summary, robo-advisors are not as expensive as human financial advisors, but they still involve costs that may sometimes be difficult to determine.

How Automated Is Robo-Advisory?

Vanguard Personal Advisor, the robo-advisor with the largest market share for a long time, was originally a hybrid service. Starting in May 2015, it allowed clients access to a human advisor (Vanguard, 2023d). Meanwhile, the Personal Advisor has an accompanying service, the Digital Advisor, launched in 2019. The main differences are that the Digital Advisor does not allow contact with human advisors (Vanguard, 2023e) and has a lower minimum investment limit. The investment process seems the same: "Our hybrid discretionary offers include the same features as our robo discretionary offers, with the opportunity to consult with a financial advisor to refine your investment plan and goal(s)" (Vanguard, 2023e, p. 2).

Vanguard's *Advisor Client Relationship Summary* suggests human managers curate the sample portfolios for both robo-services: "We may propose the addition, removal, or adjustment of sub-asset class exposures based on continuing portfolio construction research performed by Vanguard Investment Strategy Group [...]" (Vanguard, 2023d, p. 13). "[In] our robo discretionary offers we provide online financial planning tools designed to help you create a goal-based financial plan, and the service will create an investment strategy aligned with your personal inputs. We'll monitor your enrolled accounts frequently using an algorithm" (Vanguard, 2023d, p. 1).

The second largest robo-advisor, Edelman Financial Engines, also has a hybrid structure. Hence, large parts of the investment markets do not rely on pure robo-advisory services but prefer at least some human interaction. The disclosure documents from Charles Schwab (2020) reveal the firm also offers hybrid services as a premium package and uses algorithms for rebalancing and monitoring but not primarily for managing the sample portfolios.

Although traditional wealth managers often use investment committees to construct portfolios, the picture differs with fintech advisors. Betterment and Wealthfront use more rule-based approaches for portfolio management. Betterment applies a strategy based on the capital asset pricing model (CAPM) and the Fama-French model. Wealthfront uses mean-variance optimization (Betterment, 2022b; Wealthfront, 2023b). Seemingly, fintech robo-advisors rely more on algorithms, and traditional wealth managers primarily use robo-technology as a cost-efficiency measure.

Do Robo-Advisors Mitigate Behavioral Biases?

A common perception, especially in media and promotions, is that robo-advisors are rational investors who avoid emotions in their investment process. An ongoing discussion exists about whether this situation is even a favorable feature. For example, investors might need empathy in bear markets (Allentuck, 2017).

Are robo-advisors devoid of behavioral biases? Scholz et al. (2021) reveal that robo-advisors exhibit certain unexpected attributes. One such bias is *home bias*, where investors prefer domestic stocks and underweight international stocks (French & Poterba, 1991; Tesar & Werner, 1995). Although international diversification benefits investment performance, home bias is difficult to measure. Still, Scholz et al. (2021) find that at the time of their study, large US robo-advisors, Vanguard, Charles Schwab, Betterment, Wealthfront, and Personal Capital, had domestic equity quotas from about 47% to 67%. Measured against the relative gross domestic product (GDP), the United States versus global, about 26%, all the previously mentioned US robo-advisors displayed a distinctive home bias. If the equity quotas are compared to the respective US quota of around 57% in the MSCI World index, the home bias would mostly be not evident. However, the US equity share in the MSCI World Index is high.

The two largest UK robo-advisors, Nutmeg and Moneyfarm, allocated about 25% and 12% in UK equity compared to a less than 6% share of GDP and around 3% share in the MSCI World index, indicating a more distinct home bias. For German robo-advisors, Scholz et al. (2021) cannot identify a clear home bias.

Overconfidence bias has positives and negatives. Most popular robo-advisors rely on diversification and index funds, like ETFs, and largely avoid actively managed funds. Hence, they do not use stock picking or market timing, which would be useless in efficient markets and a possible indicator of overconfidence. Conversely, many robo-advisors employ an investment committee rather than a purely rule-based approach for their recommended asset allocation, potentially leading to behavioral biases, like home bias. Due to higher profits, some robo-advisors, like Vanguard, offer actively managed funds (Vanguard, 2023f).

In their literature review, Darskuviene and Lisauskiene (2021) cite studies showing that robo-advisors might positively influence investors' emotional biases. Their review indicates that robo-advisors may help investors reduce behavioral biases, especially the disposition effect, home bias, and overconfidence associated with market timing. The following three articles are highlighted in their study. For an Indian robo-advisor, for example, D'Acunto et al. (2019) find that a robo-advisor helps private investors mitigate the disposition, trend-chasing, and rank effects. Since the examined robo-advisor is a rule-based tool using Markowitz mean-variance optimization to construct optimal portfolio weights, the automated investment process could reduce over-trading stocks, carrying the potential for emotional decision-making and improve diversification.

In contrast, D'Hondt et al. (2020) use a sample of Belgian retail investors but did not choose specific robo-advisors for their analysis. Instead, they explored robo-investing strategies commonly used in the industry, mainly mean-variance approaches and AI strategies. The authors show that robo-advisory reduces diversification bias and low-education investors benefit from the automated tools.

Loos et al. (2020) use a specific German robo-advisor to analyze if retail clients improve their investment behavior. They find that by applying automated investment advice, investors reduce behavioral biases like home bias, trend-chasing, and trading frequency. Moreover, the portfolios are less prone to diversification bias when clients use the automated tool.

How Reliable Is the Risk Profiling of Robo-Advisors?

A critical feature of robo-advisory is the risk profiling of investors. Typically, investors must answer a questionnaire to determine their risk budget and tolerance. In contrast to human financial advisors, these questionnaires are the only means for robo-advisors to "know your customer." Mueller et al. (2021) describe how valid and reliable tests of an investor's risk preferences must be designed, defining a minimum of questions that need to be employed. Tertilt and Scholz (2018) find that robo-advisors typically do not use enough questions to generate statistically reliable results for an investor's risk tolerance. More surprisingly, only about 60% of the employed questions in their sample affected the portfolio recommendation. Hence, robo-advisors fail to use the full potential of their risk profiling questionnaires for their portfolio recommendations. In extreme cases, only one question was decisive in determining the proposed equity quota for clients, thereby defining a large portion of the portfolio's risk. Some robo-advisors aim to create many different portfolios, measured in an equity quota, based on a little information. In another extreme case, one robo-advisor used only three questions on risk tolerance to choose between 23 different risk levels in its recommendation. This approach naturally raises doubts about the quality of the link between risk profiling and customized portfolio recommendations.

Is a Robo-Advisor More Trustworthy Than a Human Financial Advisor?

From a US regulatory perspective, a robo-advisor has to fulfill the same regulatory requirements as a human financial advisor (Fein, 2021). The Investment Advisers Act of 1940 (Advisers Act) is the primary federal law that regulates investment advisors in the United States. Robo-advisors are classified as investment advisors under this legislation, which falls under the authority of the Securities and Exchange Commission (SEC). Nonetheless, the SEC has identified several regulatory concerns caused by robo-advisory services, such as disclosures, suitability of recommendations, and compliance. The SEC also offers guidance on how existing regulations must be interpreted to match the robo-advisor's processes. Ji (2017, p. 1583) concludes that "robo-advisors are structurally capable of meeting the Advisers Act's duty of care standards."

In Germany, an example of European regulation, robo-advisors must have a license to operate, whether the service is a fintech or not (Hammer, 2021). The urge for regulation results from the recommendation of specific investment products. Suggesting an asset allocation alone would not require a license or regulation. European robo-advisors also challenge the current regulations. Online onboarding, hotlines and chats as communication channels, as well as cloud services present new hurdles in the framework, especially given the General Data Protection Regulation (GDPR). Hammer (2021) sees the need for regulation to evolve with technological innovation in the investment advisory sector and that the advisory services from humans and robots will converge. Still, the current regulation seems to mitigate most ramifications of robo-advisory (Maume, 2019).

Robo-Advisors: The Future

During the past decade, the market for robo-advisory has had stable growth, and this trend will probably continue: Statista (2023c) estimates the 2023–2027 global AUM growth at 14% annually, further increasing the robo-advisor relevance. This section highlights two current megatrends that may greatly impact the development of robo-advisory: AI and ESG investing.

Artificial Intelligence (AI) in Robo-Advisory

The public release of ChatGPT on November 30, 2022, marked an important milestone in AI's development. This chatbot's capabilities are impressive. Still, it refuses direct answers to select stocks for a portfolio. Based on a prompt entered into ChatGPT, it replied "... It's recommended to consult with a financial advisor or conduct your own research to identify stocks that are suitable for your specific investment needs and objectives." Lopez-Lira and Tang (2023) build a model in which they let ChatGPT analyze the probable impact of news headlines on a company's stock price. They found that ChatGPT-3 and ChatGPT-4 can predict stock prices in a quality that "outperforms traditional sentiment analysis methods from a leading vendor" (Lopez-Lira & Tang, 2023, p. 13).

In a similar experiment, finder.com let ChatGPT pick 38 stocks and equally weighted them in a portfolio. Based on the admittedly short track record of 73 days, the ChatGPT portfolio outperformed the average of the United Kingdom's top 10 most popular funds by 6.28% (Finder, 2023). Although such comparisons require caution, they suggest stock selection possibilities, especially with quantitative models. Fintech robo-advisors are likely to adopt AI to improve their portfolio selection efficiency.

Until 2022, AI was not widely prevalent in robo-advisory. As Thier and dos Santos Monteiro (2022, p. 1) report, in their sample, "only a minority actually uses AI." Based on interviews with robo-advisory executives, they find that before ChatGPT's release, executives focused more on the potential in sales than on portfolio management. Beck (2021) confirms this view stating that AI models may offer compelling opportunities for robo-advisory but will most likely significantly impact customer management. Their influence on portfolio management will be less pronounced. Regarding AI's empathy, Ayers et al. (2023, p. 590) find that chatbots may provide responses that "were preferred over physician responses and rated significantly higher for both quality and empathy" in the context of health care, which is a comparable sensitive topic to investing. This finding could help resolve the "lack-of-empathy" argument against robo-advisors if AI is implemented in the communication channels.

Robo-Advisory and ESG Investing

Although in some countries, like Belgium or France, environmental, social, and governance (ESG) investing has been an important factor for over a decade, it has globally gained momentum with the recent climate movement. Avoiding carbon emissions drives the so-called *green investments*, which finance environmentally sustainable projects and businesses. The growth in such investments was faster but is now slowing down from quarter to quarter. From Q4 2020 to Q4 2021, the global net inflows in sustainable funds were around $160 billion per quarter (Bioy, 2023). In the following quarters (Q1 2022 to Q1 2023), the net inflow dropped to around $30 billion to $60 billion per quarter.

Grealish and Kolm (2021) detect two major impediments for robo-advisors regarding sustainable investments. One impediment is identifying ETFs that provide enough liquidity and satisfy the requirements for sustainable investing. The other impediment is due to the diverse range of socially responsible investment (SRI) and ESG preferences among investors. Hence, robo-advisory may find developing a customized recommendation challenging.

Since ESG investing has become a factor in asset management, most large robo-advisors already offer an ESG solution for their clients. For example, Vanguard allows clients to choose an ESG option in their portfolio recommendations (Vanguard, 2023f). Edelman Financial Engines (2022b) also provides ESG models for their portfolio creation. By contrast, Charles Schwab does not appear to offer ESG options for their robo-advisors. Betterment's Broad Impact portfolio focuses on reduced carbon emissions, ethical labor, and diversity (Betterment, 2023b). It also comprehensively reports the portfolio's ESG construction (Betterment, 2022a). Wealthfront also offers an ESG portfolio for its clients (Wealthfront, 2023d). Scalable, a large non-US robo-advisor, offers three sustainable models: ESG Screened, ESG Enhanced, and SRI (Scalable, 2023b).

Summary and Conclusion

Are robo-advisors disrupting the financial advisory industry? The market for robo-advisory grew dramatically in the past and will likely continue to grow. Much growth stems from traditional asset managers with hybrid models. With the strategy of automated investment advice, they aim to reach previously low or uninvested investor groups. Robo-advisors also try to increase their cost-efficiency in lower wealth categories. Hence, the retail segment will probably be cannibalized or disrupted over time by robo-advisory, at least by hybrid models.

Several factors drive client acceptance of algorithms, including performance, cost, quality of advice and service, and empathy during crises. Regarding performance, robo-advisors deliver reasonable yet generally not superior risk-adjusted returns. Unsurprisingly, robo-advisory portfolios provide a wide range of returns and risks. Investors are well advised to learn about the investment philosophy of different robo-services and their past performance.

Robo-advisors are typically more cost-efficient than human financial advisors, especially the non-hybrid models, although the true costs are not always transparently displayed. On average, US robo-advisors seem more competitively priced than in countries like Germany or the United Kingdom. If clients want personal contact at certain times, this feature typically comes at extra cost, if available.

In terms of regulation, robo-advisors in the United States and Europe generally have rules similar to those of human financial advisors, making them comparably safe for investments. Yet, robo-advisors may have potential conflicts of interest through kickbacks, in-house financial products, and cooperation partners. Moreover, robo-advisors might need and store more data from investors, which could be an issue concerning data protection laws.

Regarding the quality of advice, robo-advisors face a dilemma involving risk profiling. On the one hand, they want to save users time to prevent them from not completing the questionnaire. On the other hand, they need a minimum number of questions to collect sufficient information. Robo-advisors do not use all the information gathered. Thus, improvements are needed in risk profiling and providing customized recommendations. Investment committees, not quantitative models, also manage most of the robo-advisory market volume. Yet, fintech robo-advisors rely more on quantitative rules in the portfolio creation process.

Concerning behavioral biases, more highly automated robo-advisory may be more favorable. Robo-advisors can help to mitigate but not eliminate behavioral biases. For example, they can reduce home bias in investors' portfolios.

In summary, robo-advisors are not perfectly rational investors. Flaws exist in their wealth management process, such as not providing customized recommendations. However, they may help build more diversified portfolios and simplify investing for users, especially private investors with low financial literacy or little interest in financial markets.

Discussion Questions

- List the main benefits of robo-advisors compared to human financial advisors.
- List the potential limitations of automated investment advice.
- Discuss if robo-advisory is a long-term disruptive force or a short-term fad.
- Explain whether investing with robo-advisors involves ethical dilemmas.
- Identify the essential factors that individual investors should know when choosing a robo-advisory vendor.

References

Adviserinfo. (2023). *Financial engines advisors form adv*. https://reports.adviserinfo.sec.gov/reports/ADV/104510/PDF/104510.pdf

Adviserinfo. (2023a). *Vanguard form adv*. https://reports.adviserinfo.sec.gov/reports/ADV/106715/PDF/106715.pdf

Adviserinfo. (2023b). *Charles Schwab intelligent portfolios form adv*. https://reports.adviserinfo.sec.gov/reports/ADV/151739/PDF/151739.pdf

Adviserinfo. (2023c). *Wealthfront advisers form adv.* https://reports.adviserinfo.sec.gov/reports/ADV/148456/PDF/148456.pdf

Adviserinfo. (2023d). *Betterment form adv.* https://reports.adviserinfo.sec.gov/reports/ADV/149117/PDF/149117.pdf

Allentuck, A. (2017, May 29). Robo advisors are taking the emotion out of wealth management – But not everyone thinks that's a good thing. *Financial Post.* https://financialpost.com/personal-finance/managing-wealth/robo-advisors-are-taking-the-emotion-out-of-wealth-management-but-not-everyone-thinks-thats-a-good-thing

Ayers, J. W., Poliak, A., Dredze, M., Leas, E. C., Zhu, Z., Kelley, J. B., Faix, D. J., Goodman, A. M., Longhurst, C. A., Hogarth, M., & Smith, D. M. (2023). Comparing physician and artificial intelligence chatbot responses to patient questions posted to a public social media forum. *JAMA Internal Medicine*, *183*(6), 589–596. https://doi.org/10.1001/jamainternmed.2023.1838

Baulkaran, V., & Jain, P. (2022). Who uses robo-advising and how? *Financial Review*, *58*(1), 65–89. https://doi.org/10.1111/fire.12324

Becchi, S. M., Hamaloglu, U., Aggarwal, T., & Panchal, S. (2018). *The evolution of robo-advisors and advisor 2.0 model: The future of investment management and financial advisory.* EY White Paper.

Beck, A. D. (2021). The role of artificial intelligence in robo-advisory. In P. Scholz (Ed.), *Robo-advisory – Investing in the digital age* (pp. 227–243). Palgrave Macmillan.

Betterment. (2022a). *Socially responsible investing portfolios disclosure.* https://www.betterment.com/legal/socially-responsible-investing-portfolio-strategy

Betterment. (2022b, October 19). *The betterment portfolio strategy.* https://www.betterment.com/resources/betterment-portfolio-strategy

Betterment. (2023a). *Pricing at betterment.* https://www.betterment.com/pricing

Betterment. (2023b). *Broad impact.* https://www.betterment.com/socially-responsible-broad-impact-portfolio

Bioy, H. (2023, April 25). *Global sustainable fund flows – Q1 2023 in review.* Morningstar.

BlackRock. (2023). *Report first quarter 2023.* https://s24.q4cdn.com/856567660/files/doc_financials/2023/Q1/BLK-1Q23-Earnings-Release.pdf

Charles Schwab. (2020). *Disclosure documents.* https://www.schwab.com/resource/schwab-intelligent-portfolios-and-schwab-intelligent-portfolios-premium

Charles Schwab. (2023). Costs and fees. https://intelligent.schwab.com/page/faq/payno-advisory-fees

D'Acunto, F., Prabhala, N., & Rossi, A. G. (2019). The promises and pitfalls of robo-advising. *Review of Financial Studies*, *32*(5), 1983–2020. https://doi.org/10.1093/rfs/hhz014

Darskuviene, V., & Lisauskiene, N. (2021). Linking the robo-advisors phenomenon and behavioural biases in investment management: An interdisciplinary literature review and research agenda. *Organizations and Markets in Emerging Economies*, *12*(2), 459–477. https://doi.org/10.15388/omee.2021.12.65

D'Hondt, C., De Winne, R., Ghysels, E., & Raymond, S. (2020). Artificial intelligence alter egos: Who might benefit from robo-investing? *Journal of Empirical Finance*, *59*(December), 278–299.

Edelman Financial Engines. (2022a, September 9). *Understanding robo-advisors.* https://www.edelmanfinancialengines.com/education/planning-investing/understanding-robo-advisors/

Edelman Financial Engines. (2022b). *ESG investing: Off the sidelines and into the mainstream*. https://www.edelmanfinancialengines.com/education/planning-investing/esg-investing/

Edelman Financial Engines. (2023, March 31). *Wrap Fee Brochure*. https://www.edelmanfinancialengines.com/wrap-fee-brochure/

Empower Advisors. (2023). *Management fee*. https://docs.empower.com/PDF/p/misc/management_fee.pdf?utm_source=pcap&utm_medium=referral

Evensky, H., Horan, S. M., & Robinson, T. R. (2011). *The new wealth management: The financial advisor's guide to managing and investing client assets. CFA institute investment series*. John Wiley & Sons, Inc.

Fein, M. (2015). *Robo-advisors: A closer look*. https://doi.org/10.2139/ssrn.2658701

Fein, M. (2021). Regulation of robo-advisers in the United States. In P. Scholz (Ed.), *Robo-advisory – Investing in the digital age* (pp. 105–131). Palgrave Macmillan.

Fidelity. (2023). *Fidelity by the numbers: Asset management*. https://www.fidelity.com/about-fidelity/our-company/asset-management

Finder. (2023). *Can ChatGPT be used for stock trading?* https://www.finder.com/uk/ai-investing

Fisch, J. E., Labouré, M., & Turner, J. A. (2019). The emergence of the robo-advisor. In J. Agnew & O. S. Mitchell (Eds.), *The disruptive impact of FinTech on retirement systems* (pp. 13–37). Oxford University Press.

French, K. R., & Poterba, J. M. (1991). Investor diversification and international equity markets. *The American Economic Review*, *81*(2), 222–226.

Grealish, A., & Kolm, P. N. (2021). Robo-advisors today and tomorrow: Investment advice is just an app away. *Journal of Wealth Management*, *24*(3), 144–155.

Hammer, C. (2021). Regulation of robo-advisory in Europe and Germany. In P. Scholz (Ed.), *Robo-advisory – Investing in the digital age* (pp. 133–160). Palgrave Macmillan.

HM Government. (2023). *Nutmeg saving and investment limited*. http://data.companieshouse.gov.uk/doc/company/07503666

Isaia, E., & Oggero, N. (2022). The potential use of robo-advisors among the young generation: Evidence from Italy. *Finance Research Letters*, *48*(August), 103046. https://doi.org/10.1016/j.frl.2022.103046

Ji, M. (2017). Are robots good fiduciaries: Regulating robo-advisors under the investment Advisers Act of 1940. *Columbia Law Review*, *117*(6), 1543–1583. https://columbialawreview.org/content/are-robots-good-fiduciaries-regulating-robo-advisors-under-the-investment-advisers-act-of-1940-2/

Kaya, O. (2020). *German robo-advisors: March of the machines driving passive investments*. Deutsche Bank Research. https://www.dbresearch.de/PROD/RPS_DE-PROD/PROD0000000000505172/German_robo-advisors%3A_March_of_the_machines_drivin.pdf

Loos, B., Previtero, A., Scheurle, S., & Hackethal, A. (2020). *Robo-advisers and investor behavior*. Working Paper. https://webarchiv.typo3.tum.de/MGT/FA/ls-df/fileadmin/w00chf/digitalfinance/pdf/RoboAdvisers.pdf

Lopez-Lira, A., & Tang, Y. (2023). Can ChatGPT forecast stock price movements? Return predictability and large language models. https://papers.ssrn.com/sol3/papers.cfm?abstract_id=4412788

Maume, P. (2019). Regulating robo-advisory. *Texas Journal of International Law*, *55*(1), 49–87. https://papers.ssrn.com/sol3/papers.cfm?abstract_id=3167137

Mueller, M., Resnik, P., & Craig, S. (2021). Risk preferences of investors. In P. Scholz (Ed.), *Robo-advisory – Investing in the digital age* (pp. 35–51). Palgrave Macmillan.

Nocera, J. (1998, May 11). Banking is necessary – Banks are not' why has banking become less and less important to America? Let us count the ways. *Fortune*. https://money.cnn.com/magazines/fortune/fortune_archive/1998/05/11/242040/

Quirion. (2023). Über uns. https://www.quirion.de/ueber-uns

Scalable. (2022). *Scalable capital surpasses €10 billion in client assets*. https://de.scalable.capital/newsroom/en-10-billion-in-client-assets

Scalable. (2023a). *World portfolio classic*. https://de.scalable.capital/en/world-portfolio-classic

Scalable. (2023b). *Nachhaltig investieren mit ESG und SRI ETFs*. https://de.scalable.capital/esg-sri-etfs

Scalable. (2023c). *About us*. https://de.scalable.capital/en/about-us

Schapiro, K., Goldstone, D., Leahy, T., & Jones, K. (2023). The robo report. *Condor capital wealth management* (Edition 27). 1Q 2023. https://www.theroboreport.com/data/total-portfolio-returns/?utm_source=Robo_Report&utm_medium=1Q23_PDF&utm_campaign=1Q23_Robo_Report_PDF

Scholz, P., Großmann, D., & Goldberg, J. (2021). Robo economicus? 2 The impact of behavioral biases on robo-advisory. In P. Scholz (Ed.), Robo-advisory – Investing in the digital age (pp. 53–69). Palgrave Macmillan.

Scholz, P., & Tertilt, M. (2021). Robo-advisory: The rise of the investment machines. In P. Scholz (Ed.), *Robo-advisory – Investing in the digital age* (pp. 3–19). Palgrave Macmillan.

Statista. (2017). *Robo-advice: Dossier*. https://de.statista.com/statistik/studie/id/48179/dokument/robo-advice/

Statista. (2018). *Robo-advisors in the US 2018 report*. https://www.statista.com/study/54930/robo-advisors/#professional

Statista. (2023a). *Global robo-advisors*. https://de.statista.com/outlook/dmo/fintech/digital-investment/robo-advisors/weltweit#anlagevolumen

Statista. (2023b). *Assets under management of robo-advisors in the United States from 2017 to 2027*. https://www.statista.com/forecasts/1259591/robo-advisors-managing-assets-united-states

Statista. (2023c). *Digital investment report 2023*. https://de.statista.com/statistik/studie/id/41704/dokument/fintech-report-digital-investment/

Stein, J. (2016). The history of betterment: How we started a company that is changing an industry. *LinkedIn*. https://www.linkedin.com/pulse/history-betterment-how-we-started-company-changing-industry-stein

Tergesen, A., & Gottfried, M. (2018, May 1). Robo adviser financial engines sold to private-equity firm. *The Wall Street Journal*. https://www.wsj.com/articles/robo-adviser-financial-engines-sold-to-private-equity-firm-1525189090

Tertilt, M., & Scholz, P. (2018). To advise, or not to advise – How robo-advisors evaluate the risk preferences of private investors. *Journal of Wealth Management*, *21*(2), 70–84. https://doi.org/10.3905/jwm.2018.21.2.070

Tesar, L. L., & Werner, I. M. (1995). Home bias and high turnover. *Journal of International Money and Finance*, *14*(4), 467–492. https://doi.org/10.1016/0261-5606(95)00023-8

Thier, C., & Monteiro, D. dos S. (2022, September 27). How much artificial intelligence do robo-advisors really use? *SSRN*. https://papers.ssrn.com/sol3/papers.cfm?abstract_id=4218181

Vanguard. (2023a). Vanguard facts and figures. https://www.nl.vanguard/professional/about-vanguard

Vanguard. (2023b). *Personal advisor*. https://investor.vanguard.com/advice/personal-hybrid-robo-advisor

Vanguard. (2023c). *Digital advisor*. https://investor.vanguard.com/advice/robo-advisor

Vanguard. (2023d, January). *Advisor client relationship summary*. https://personal.vanguard.com/pdf/vpabroc.pdf

Vanguard. (2023e, January). *Vanguard digital advisor and vanguard personal advisor important information*. https://personal.vanguard.com/pdf/vanguard-digital-advice-brochure.pdf

Vanguard. (2023f). *Compare advice options*. https://investor.vanguard.com/advice/compare-investment-advice

Wealthfront. (2023a). *Review*. https://www.wealthfront.com/reviews

Wealthfront. (2023b). *Wealthfront automated investing methodology*. White Paper. https://research.wealthfront.com/whitepapers/investment-methodology/

Wealthfront. (2023c). *Pricing*. https://www.wealthfront.com/pricing

Wealthfront. (2023d). *Socially responsible investing*. https://www.wealthfront.com/socially-responsible-investing

Wealthfront. (2023e). What is Wealthfront? https://www.wealthfront.com/origin

Woolley, S. (2021, September 24). *Roboadvisers target the new universe of retail traders*. Bloomberg. https://www.bloomberg.com/news/storythreads/2021-09-24/robo-advisors-like-schwab-vanguard-and-betterment-are-changing-tactics

Chapter 11

Online Trading: Part I

Sebastian Vogel

Erasmus University Rotterdam, Netherlands

Abstract

This chapter discusses the evolution of online trading, its application in various market structures, and its benefits and potential concerns. Computers were first used in electronic communication networks among brokers and dealers to make trades and for informational purposes. Online brokers became popular with retail investors as the internet spread. Online trading comes with various trading protocols and order types. It enables traders to automate trading decisions and process data more easily using charting tools and customized programs connected to the broker's infrastructure. Electronic trading allows for greater centralization but can also be accompanied by market fragmentation. Market regulation has affected market structure and is still evolving. Centralization allows for more competitive prices and reduces search costs. Decentralized markets could cope better with asymmetric information.

Keywords: Fintech; online trading; trading protocols; regulation; centralization

Introduction

This chapter introduces the historical development of online trading, discussing exchange and off-exchange markets in which traders have to interact with dealers. Computers have been used early in the latter, such as in the NASDAQ system or bond trading platforms. Online trading in exchange markets became popular when the internet spread to the masses at the end of the 20th century. This chapter also discusses various trading protocols, order types, and features of online trading platforms like application programming interfaces (APIs) and charting tools. Other topics include the advantages and disadvantages of the electronification of financial markets. Besides lower costs and easier market access,

The Emerald Handbook of Fintech, 207–220

doi:10.1108/978-1-83753-608-520241023

excessive trading could lead to market fragility. An evolution in market regulation accompanied the technological evolution. This chapter concludes by discussing the benefits of centralization versus decentralization.

History of Online Trading

Computers are responsible for the tremendous transformations of the largest financial markets over the last decades. On the customer side, electronic trading platforms have revolutionized over-the-counter (OTC) and exchange markets. Many innovations have occurred due to electronic trading by brokers and dealers. The latter even started to incorporate computers into their trading.

Financial institutions started to trade electronically through the Electronic Communication Network (ECN) Instinet. In 1971, the National Association of Securities Dealers Association Automated Quotations (NASDAQ) Stock Market began operating. Although trading was not done online, it allowed pulling together the bids and offers from around 500 dealers in the United States for over 2,500 securities. In 1984, NASDAQ introduced the Advanced Computerized Execution System, allowing orders to be passed electronically to other registered dealers. Ingebretsen (2002) provides additional information about NASDAQ's history.

Other examples of early ECNs for equities were Island and Archipelago, both started operating in 1997. In other asset classes, dealers operating as intermediaries in OTC markets established more centralized markets. In the foreign exchange (FX) market, the Reuters D2000-1 system emerged in 1989 (MTS, 2023) and received competition from the Electronic Brokering Services (EBS) trading platform in 1990. Also, in the FX market, platforms first started to offer quotes only (Reuters D2000), then allowed for bilateral trades (Reuters D2000-2), and then offered limit order books (e.g., Reuters D2000-2 or EBS). Most bonds are also traded in OTC markets, and markets between dealers feature many trading platforms operated by firms like MarketAxess, MTS, or Tradeweb. MTS launched the first electronic bond market in 1988 (MTS, 2023). Market participants have a vast choice of potential trading venues, especially in the bond market (Marsh & Detrixhe, 2016).

The fact that dealers and market makers can trade electronically among themselves does not mean that their customers receive the benefits of more efficient trading. Stoll (2006) contends that in NASDAQ, dealers artificially raised their prices by using given prices in fractions of even eighths and a practice called "preferencing," where brokers routed their orders to specific dealers. In this way, dealers and market makers could use electronic trading to manage their books and offset shocks to their inventories among themselves. Their clients, however, were still mostly getting a quote from one dealer or could hardly put dealers and market makers into competition.

However, following the innovations in the market among brokers and dealers, their clients could soon use electronic trading. In 1991, Etrade's online trading firm began, enabling customers to submit orders directly to stock exchanges like the New York Stock Exchange (NYSE) from their computers. Shortly afterward, firms like TD Ameritrade and Charles Schwab followed. Using online trading brought numerous benefits to retail investors wanting to trade exchange-traded contracts like stocks, futures, or options.

Even more obscure markets, like the market for bonds, credit default swaps, or currency forwards, have been transformed by electronic trading platforms. For example, MTS launched its BondVision platform to trade bonds in 2001 (MTS, 2023).

Online Trading in Different Market Structures

Today, financial markets are classified as exchange or OTC markets. An *OTC market* is any market not organized as a central exchange. An exchange is characterized by crossing supply and demand at one place, usually through a central limit order book (CLOB).

In a standard OTC market, traders contact their dealers to obtain quotes to trade an asset like a bond, forward, or swap. Usually, each trader gets a customized quote from a dealer. Although quotes vary by market conditions and the dealers' inventory, dealers also have incentives to take advantage of their bargaining power, as the early days of the NASDAQ market illustrate. Modern electronic OTC markets are characterized by a more complicated structure in which traders can contact their dealers individually and use electronic trading platforms to put dealers under competition. However, even in those more complicated structures, empirical evidence suggests that dealers use their bargaining power, and more connected traders can obtain better prices (Hau et al., 2021).

Trading platforms can offer various trading protocols. A common trading protocol in the so-called dealer-to-customer (D2C) market is the *request-for-quote* (RFQ) protocol. Through this protocol, a trader can contract multiple dealers at once and ask for a quote to buy or sell a given quantity of a specific asset, indicating the direction of the trade. For example, the trader may submit a request for a quote to buy a forward contract to exchange a million EUR into USD at a specific date. The contacted dealers may or may not respond. If at least one dealer responds, the trader can take the offered quote and trade. With the so-called *request-for-market* (RFM) protocol, the trader does not specify the trade's direction and asks for two quotes: one to buy a given quantity of a specific asset and one to sell a given quantity of the same asset. From the trader's viewpoint, the advantage of the RFM protocol over the RFQ protocol is that the trader does not reveal whether positive or negative information exists about the asset. This approach prevents the dealer from tilting the quote in a specific direction when being contacted. For example, a dealer may ask a higher price for an RFQ to buy the asset than a bid for an RFQ to sell the asset. As a dealer commits to trading the asset at the submitted quotes, the dealer's response gives the investor an idea of how large the dealer's profit margin is.

However, asserting that the complete difference between the bid and the ask goes into the dealer's profit would be unfair. The dealer suffers from an *adverse selection problem*. If the trader wants to buy the asset, the trader is likely to have positive information about the asset, in which case the asset's fair price should be adjusted upward. The opposite is true when the trader wants to sell the asset. For this reason, the *ask price* (the price at which a dealer is willing to sell the asset to a trader) is naturally higher than the *bid price* (the price at which a dealer is willing to buy the asset from a trader) even if the dealer's profit margins, ignoring so-called markups.

Whereas traders in the OTC market always trade with one dealer (i.e., there is no single place where all the demand and supply of the traders meet), dealers have a centralized interdealer market. Platforms used by dealers usually feature a CLOB, making the interdealer market often an exchange market, like large stock exchanges to which retail traders also have access. A *central limit order book* is a transparent system matching customer orders on a price-time priority basis.

In those markets with a CLOB, market participants usually have the choice between two basic order types: market orders and limit orders. In a *limit order* to buy (sell) an asset, a trader specifies the quantity the trader is willing to buy (sell) at a specific price, similar to a dealer's response to an RFQ. If another limit order submitted to sell (buy) the asset at a lower (higher) price by another trader already exists, those orders are matched. Any quantity not matched stays in the CLOB. A trader can also directly submit a *market order* that will immediately be matched against the limit orders in the CLOB. Retail traders route those orders through their online broker, who may request a commission to perform this act.

At first sight, a CLOB may seem like the most evolved market structure. OTC markets only exist once sufficiently evolved until a CLOB is established. The situation here is more complicated. For instance, some assets, like bonds, used to be traded on exchanges in the early 1900s (Biais & Green, 2019) but are now only traded OTC. Relatedly, exchange markets have become more fragmented after the introduction of Reg NMS. *Regulation NMS* is a set of rules that aims to improve US exchanges through fairness in price execution.

Features of Online Trading

Computer and internet use affected the trading process on various levels. Key areas are trading costs, information, automation, and liquidity.

When online brokers emerged, they usually offered more competitive pricing than their traditional counterparts, charging lower commissions. This trend has continued, with online brokers gradually offering ever cheaper access to the markets and thus offering market access to a wider range of traders. However, commissions are only one part of trading costs. Another part relates to the execution price of orders. Online brokers' incentives may not always align with their client's interests, which illustrates a recent debate about "payment for order flow," to be discussed later in this chapter.

In the OTC market, electronic trading also led to lower trading costs. Hau et al. (2021) show that traders using electronic trading platforms obtain lower markups from dealers. This finding suggests dealers lost some bargaining power with new electronic trading protocols. Although lower markups hurt dealer profits, they benefit traders. Consequently, many traders may find entering an OTC market worthwhile, involving interest rate swaps or currency forwards. Previously, traders found prices too unattractive and did not trade. Dealers need electronic trading platforms to commit to lower markups to attract traders with high search costs. Some traders may find looking for a quote costly because it takes time, and a trader must trade an asset quickly. The cost is paid once a trader exerts effort to contact the dealer. Therefore, the dealer needs an incentive to offer a low quote to attract a trader. On the contrary, the dealer wants to extract the trader's maximum willingness to pay for an asset, as the trader does not continue to search because of the "search costs." Anticipating this behavior of the dealer, the trader may not initially search for a quote.

Electronic trading also facilitates information flow between brokers and dealers on the one side and their clients on the other. This informational role of electronic trading is most exemplified in the early days of the NASDAQ market, a system to keep dealers and brokers informed about quotes from other dealers and brokers. All market participants can obtain real-time prices from the major stock exchanges today. Even in OTC markets, participants are better informed through electronic trading platforms. Besides connecting dealers through CLOBs, trading platforms enable customers to subscribe to streaming quotes to see at which price dealers are prepared to trade.

Computers and online trading enable a high degree of automation. Today, many online brokers offer APIs that allow customers to connect a program written in Python or another popular language to their trading software to manage orders, monitor positions, and obtain market data.

Using computers may also improve market liquidity. The automation made possible by electronic trading enabled the so-called high-frequency traders (HFT) to take over as liquidity providers in CLOBs, who submit limit orders so that traders who demand immediacy can trade against those orders. Hendershott et al. (2011) show that HFT improves bid-ask spreads. A *bid-ask spread* is an amount by which the ask price exceeds the bid price for an asset in the market. As discussed previously, electronic trading improves traders' bargaining power, making entering the market and starting to search for a quote more worthwhile. Benos et al. (2017) contend that using electronic trading platforms increases trading volume in the interest rate swap market.

Order Types With Online Brokers

Electronic trading led to a vast innovation in order types. The online broker Interactive Brokers alone describes over 100 different order types and algorithms available for its clients. Here are the most common order types.

- *Market.* A market order specifies the quantity and direction of the trade. Once submitted, the market order matches existing limit orders, starting with the most favorable price. For example, when there is an order to buy 100 shares of XY stock, 50 shares are offered at $10, and 100 shares are offered at $12, 50 shares will be bought for $10, and 50 shares will be bought for $12.
- *Limit.* A limit order specifies the quantity, direction, and limit price. For a buy limit order, the limit price specifies the maximum price the trader will pay for the asset.
- *Stop.* A stop order specifies the traded quantity and stop price. Once the stop price or a less favorable price is reached, the stop order turns into a market order. This order type is typically used for momentum traders who want to "stop into" a certain position. Investors use stop-loss orders to protect against sharp adverse price movements.
- *Take-profit.* This order specifies the traded quantity and take-profit price. Once this take-profit or more favorable price is reached, the order turns into a market order to close an existing position. As the name suggests, investors use this order type to realize a profit. It is like a limit order, but with a preexisting position in the opposite direction.
- *Market on close.* Many exchanges offer an auction at the close. At the NYSE, a market-on-close order is guaranteed to receive execution.
- *Limit on close.* Similar to the market-on-close order, this order is meant to be executed at the closing auction, but only if the price exceeds the specified limit price.
- *Iceberg.* Submitting orders provides information to other market participants. A large order may cause a price impact that can influence future price movements. To prevent other market participants from reacting to this large order, a trader may want to hide the total quantity or the order, which can be done through an iceberg order. This type of limit order shows only a fraction of the total quantity.
- *Other algorithms.* Although smaller traders usually can submit market orders without having a substantial price impact, avoiding a price impact is an important concern for traders submitting larger orders. Iceberg orders are meant to mitigate information revelation through order size. However, they have some disadvantages for active traders. For example, limit orders are not guaranteed to be executed. Moreover, how the hidden quantity gets revealed is mechanical. To address these shortcomings, brokers offer more complex algorithms to trade larger orders, considering the trader's urgency to trade the asset.

Charting Tools

Although technical analysis precedes computers, computers facilitate using technical indicators and visualizing them in the chart. Price data can be shown as a line or in so-called candle sticks. A *candlestick chart* is a type of financial chart used to describe a security's price movements. It displays a security's high, low, open, and closing prices for a specific period.

The interactive user interfaces of online brokers provide various graphical tools to help investors perform technical analysis. Often, one can see a volume chart below the price chart, indicating how much has been traded in each interval. Furthermore, one can plot lines directly on top of the price. A typical example would be to plot moving averages with different lookback periods and interpret a crossing of the shorter moving average over the longer moving average as a bullish signal and vice versa.

Indicators used for technical analysis are a transformation of the price data, usually the closing prices of the chosen interval for the candlesticks. Those indicators can be used to classify certain situations as "overbought" or "oversold" and to find positive or negative momentum. Below are a few popular examples.

- *Moving average (MA).* A *moving average* computes the average price over a certain period. A slight modification is to weight different periods exponentially to decrease the exponential moving average (EMA). If only a single exponential average is used, technical analysts interpret a crossing of the close of the most recent candle over this indicator as a bullish signal. Traders can combine multiple MAs or EMAs. Technical analysts often interpret a situation where the indicators based on shorter lookback periods (faster exponential decay) are below those with a longer lookback (slower exponential decay) as bullish. Analogous reasoning is then applied for bearish signals.
- *Moving average convergence/divergence (MACD).* The MACD is calculated by subtracting a short EMA from a long EMA. Besides this measure, one can compute a *signal line* representing a moving MACD average. The MACD and signal line crossing can also be used as a trading signal. A crossing of the MACD above the signal line can indicate that a negative MACD will start to revert toward 0, which is a bullish signal. Crossing the MACD below the signal line could be bearish.
- *Bollinger bands.* Besides the moving average of the price, one can plot the range of a multiple of the standard deviation of the close prices. Like the scientific confidence interval of 5%, which is two standard deviations around the estimated value of a normal distribution, a popular practice is to use a two standard deviation band around the moving average. It is considered an overbought signal if the price is above the upper band and oversold if it is below the lower band.
- *Fibonacci retracement.* This indicator compares different extreme points in a chart, like the most recent high and low, which can be found by visually inspecting a chart. Once the trader indicates those local extrema, the levels of the Fibonacci retracement indicator can be used as price targets or levels for take-profit orders.

Account Types

Online brokers offer two account types: cash and margin accounts. With a cash account, the client can buy stocks or bonds for money that the client has in the account. A client cannot trade derivatives that could cause a negative balance in the account, such as the sale of options. The second account type, the margin account, enables clients to borrow money from the broker and use leverage. Moreover, trading of derivatives is possible. A margin account can have different forms. The common Regulation T (Reg T) margin account enables a customer to borrow up to 50% of the transaction's value for stocks. It also enables trading derivatives. For the latter, different margin requirements exist for each type of security. Another distinction is between the initial and variation margin, where the variation margin is often lower than the initial margin. The initial margin determines the customer's equity in the account to purchase a given security. Variation margin determines the amount of equity a client needs to have as a fraction of the portfolio value before a margin call occurs. Certain investors can qualify for different margin policies and obtain a portfolio margin account. For example, many brokers allow traders with a large enough account value to have a portfolio margin account. The margin requirements in this account depend to some extent on the riskiness of the securities the customer holds.

Advantages and Disadvantages of Online Trading

Using computers brought trading costs down in many financial markets, online trading also brought market access to more investors. Broader market access allows retail investors to think more about how to save for retirement or have an income through invested savings. This situation also increases the pressure on professional investment advisors who must add real value to keep clients. As the rise in passive exchange-traded funds (ETFs) shows, many investors prefer to take some responsibility away from professional investment advisors and fund managers. Thus, automation enables investors to harness market risk premia at a low cost. Automated trading also brought some benefits to the market. Although some contend that HFT made markets more susceptible to sudden crashes, evidence suggests that HFT increased liquidity. Automated trading algorithms are also well-suited to handle small arbitrage opportunities, making the market more efficient.

Yet, easy market access and automation also have potential disadvantages. As previously mentioned, the rise of HFTs is associated with flash crashes. A *flash crash* is a sudden and severe drop in the price of a financial asset or market, often followed by a quick recovery (WallStreetMojo Team, 2023). The apparent liquidity improvement in electronic financial markets is somewhat illusionary because HFT often cancels limit orders, which is seemingly when a market order arrives. This behavior is called "spoofing" and is considered market manipulation.

On the side of retail traders, easier market access comes with the benefit of frequently rebalancing a personal investment portfolio and the temptation to trade more than necessary. Barber and Odean (2000) show that more frequent trading is not associated with better performance. This situation is not a problem of the technology but concerns how the technology should be used. Unfortunately, the incentives of brokers and investors are not completely aligned. Although brokers usually earn revenue from every trade a client makes and prefer frequent trading, most clients are better off trading less often.

Whether the more centralized market structures promoted by electronic trading are always desirable remains an open issue. A centralized market, like a stock exchange with a CLOB, is the most advanced structure. Yet, some financial markets developed from a centralized structure result in a fragmented OTC market. A classic example is the market for bonds. In the United States, bonds were traded on exchange markets at the beginning of the 20th century. Today, bonds trade on an OTC market, even though electronic trading platforms have begun to centralize this market. However, an RFQ protocol, which allows one client to contact many dealers ("one-to-many"), does not allow for the same level of centralization as a CLOB, where all traders are connected to all other traders ("all-to-all"). The following sections discuss controversial topics around flash crashes in more detail.

High-Frequency Trading

Using computers enables trading decisions to be made in milliseconds. For long-term investments, this trading speed is unnecessary. However, liquidity providers are incentivized to acquire the fastest technology to incorporate added information into their bid and ask prices to avoid not being noticed as a "stale" quote, thus reducing adverse selection. Adverse selection arises because the liquidity provider may not have all the information the trader submitting a market order has. Information can be related to news (fundamental information) or trades made by other market participants (order-flow information).

Even if the fundamental information has not changed, market makers should know if some market participants make large trades in a specific direction. For instance, if a trader submits a large buy order for a specific security to hedge some risk due to other portfolio holdings, market makers must provide the security to this trader. Since market makers do not like to have a specific (long or short) exposure on their books, they subsequently try to acquire the asset again from other traders by raising bids. A different market maker can also raise the bid when a large order arrives on an exchange. This rational incentive to raise (lower) quotes on some exchanges when a large buy (sell) order exists on another exchange is the basis behind the "spoofing" strategy, which many consider manipulation.

In a market structure with many exchanges, a high-frequency trader can observe a large order on one exchange, and conjecture orders will arrive on other exchanges if the trader is splitting the order, which is a common practice. HFT requires investments in ever-faster technology. For example, a high-frequency trader can rent servers at exchanges called "colocation" or use microwaves to transmit data instead of normal internet cables. Arguably, making trading decisions at the speed of milliseconds does not benefit most investors. This situation has sparked a debate about whether slowing markets down might benefit investors by avoiding the negative consequences of HFT. Budish et al. (2015) advocates frequent batch auctions as an alternative to almost continuous trading.

Kirilenko et al. (2017) contend that HFT may exacerbate crashes, even if they may not cause them. The classic example of a flash crash is May 6, 2010, in which the NASDAQ index declined about 9%, only to recover within 36 minutes. Similar sudden declines with subsequent recoveries have occurred in other markets. On May 2, 2022, the NASDAQ OMX index in Sweden experienced a temporary decline of 8% but was only 1.9% lower for the day. A trading error at Citi seemed to cause this sharp decline (Meredith, 2022). HFT does not seem to be responsible but could have amplified it.

Regulation of Financial Markets

The regulation of financial markets evolved with technological advances. The Regulation National Market System (Reg NMS) affected how exchanges operate in the United States. Reg NMS aims to strengthen the US market system through several initiatives.

An important part of Reg NMS is the requirement for brokers of "best execution." The latter is determined by the National Best Bid and Offer (NBBO), a quote that reports the highest bid price and lowest ask (offered) price in a security, sourced from all available exchanges or trading venues. Trading at prices inferior to the NBBO is called a "trade-through" and should be avoided. Although this rule aimed to promote competition among trading venues, it has led to more fragmentation. Orders must be routed to any exchange that has available quotes. Such routing is one reason some view Reg NMS as leading to market fragmentation. Whether this fragmentation is beneficial is questionable. Different fee structures, like rebates to the market maker, are used to attract market participants, providing limit orders added further to the market structure's complexity. Generally, matching supply and demand in one place seems to save the costs of operating exchanges.

Payment for Order Flow

A controversial topic related to online trading is the practice of *payment for order flow (PFOF)*, where a broker receives compensation for routing client orders to a particular market maker. Hypothetically, a client could benefit from this practice if the market maker passes the compensation for the order flow through to the client (CFA Institute, 2016). The practice has gained much attention with the rise of low-cost brokerages like Robinhood. Those brokerages often charge no commission and receive revenue from sources like PFOF. Although this practice is currently allowed under the FINRA rules, the broker's decisions to route orders to market makers may not be in a customer's best interests. The broker benefits from the compensation received from the market maker but may not pass on part of this amount to the customer.

Centralization Versus Decentralization

This section provides some general considerations on how modern technology should be used to transform financial markets. Electronic trading offers an enormous potential to centralize financial markets and bring trading activity from interactions with individual brokers or dealers to one electronic limit order book. However, many markets evolve in different directions. For example, the bond market has moved from a centralized structure to a decentralized one. As previously discussed, some contend that equity markets have become more decentralized in recent decades with many new exchanges arising and trading activity often automatically split over different places by brokers. This situation begs the question of whether centralization is necessarily a good thing.

Biais and Green (2019) maintain that the bond market became less central due to the importance of institutional investors who wanted to trade large blocks of bonds and negotiate with dealers directly. Also, dealers may prefer an OTC market over an exchange. In the latter, dealers must compete directly against each other as market makers. By contrast, in an OTC market, they can charge substantial markups (Hau et al., 2021). However, too much decentralization may not be preferable for dealers if it prevents customers from entering the market. If so, dealers may prefer a more competitive market featuring trading platforms in which customers can have dealers compete through RFQs. A trading platform can thus be a commitment device to charge markups that are low enough to attract customers and have them enter the market.

This rationale may explain why trading platforms are common in bond markets while they slowly gain traction for more complex derivatives, like credit default swaps (CDS). Arguably, more customers are interested in trading bonds, some of whom find entering the market costly. Electronic trading platforms are useful for dealers to have customers participate in the market. However, for more complex derivatives, potential customers are mostly sophisticated hedge funds that would enter the market in any case, so offering trading platforms would only hurt profits. Some alleged that dealers colluded to keep competition from electronic trading platforms out of the market in a class action lawsuit that ended with a $1.87 billion settlement in 2015 (Stafford, 2015).

Markets may evolve endogenously depending on the preferences of customers, dealers, or market makers. Determining if room exists for regulation requires looking further at the implications for market efficiency. A common assumption in market design is that a trade is mutually beneficial (i.e., the customer does not intentionally trade with a negative value in expectation). Other frictions aside, the market structure that maximizes trading volume is the most efficient. In the above example with the OTC market that may or may not feature trading platforms, a market with trading platforms is preferable if it leads to more trading volume. As discussed above, this is supported by empirical evidence (Benos et al., 2017).

However, financial markets have two other important frictions: search costs and asymmetric information. *Search costs* refer to anything that takes effort to obtain a tradeable quote. A trader not participating in the market can mean setting up a relationship with a broker or dealer. For a trader needing to trade an asset quickly, it can mean the cost of waiting. *Asymmetric information* refers to a situation in which one party knows something about the asset that the other party does not know. In markets where dealers have to give two-sided quotes (i.e., a bid and an ask), the situation in which the customer knows more usually receives more attention: the possibility that the trader knows more than the dealer or market maker is one reason a bid-ask spread is needed for a dealer or market maker not to lose on a trade.

Considering search costs, fragmentation may need improvement. For the OTC market, a trader may need to look for a quote at various places, resulting in a *deadweight loss* (i.e., a trader's search effort is a cost without a benefit to anyone else in the market).

However, if asymmetric information exists, fragmentation may be good. Lee and Wang (2018) show that the presence of an OTC market may increase efficiency in an equilibrium in which informed traders trade on exchanges and uninformed traders trade off the exchange. Glode and Opp (2016) show that intermediation chains in which similarly informed market participants trade with each other may enable trade where it would otherwise not occur due to strong information asymmetries. In both papers, the advantage of OTC markets lies in handling information asymmetries. A key feature is that OTC markets are not anonymous. The dealer knows the customer and can offer customized prices. Although this situation can be abused by charging excessive markups, it protects against asymmetric information and allows for otherwise impossible trades.

Additional work is needed to determine how to organize electronic financial markets best. Centralized and decentralized market structures have merits.

Summary and Conclusion

Online trading and using computers have lowered trading costs and brought market access to many investors. What started as a tool to facilitate trading between brokers and dealers came to the masses with the rise of the internet overall. This chapter discussed the different market structures in which electronic trading is used and the different trading protocols and order types available on electronic trading platforms or with an online broker. It explained how electronic trading allows for greater centralization even in markets that are not organized as exchanges. This chapter also described how the fragmentation of exchange markets accompanied the rise of online trading. Regulation of electronic markets is still evolving; centralized and decentralized market structures have their merits.

Discussion Questions

- Discuss two types of financial markets.
- Discuss how online trading affects the investment process.
- Describe a popular trading protocol on electronic trading platforms in OTC markets.
- Define the NBBO and describe how it affects the brokers' routing of client orders.
- Define PFOF and discuss why it is controversial.
- Discuss some advantages of centralized and decentralized markets.

References

Barber, B. M., & Odean, T. (2000). Trading is Hazardous to your wealth. *The Journal of Finance*, *55*(2), 773–806.

Benos, E., Payne, R., & Vasios, M. (2017). *Centralized trading, transparency and interest rate swap market liquidity: Evidence from implementing the dodd-Frank act*. Bank of England Working Paper No. 580.

Biais, B., & Green, R. (2019). The microstructure of the bond market in the 20th century. *Review of Economic Dynamics*, *33*, 250–271.

Budish, E., Cramton, P., & Shim, J. (2015). The high-frequency trading arms race: Frequent batch auctions as a market design response. *Quarterly Journal of Economics*, *130*(4), 1547–1621.

CFA Institute. (2016). *Payment for order flow*. Policy Brief.

Glode, V., & Opp, C. (2016). Asymmetric information and intermediation chains. *The American Economic Review*, *6*(9), 2699–2721.

Hau, H., Hoffmann, P., Langfield, S., & Timmer, Y. (2021). Discriminatory pricing of over-the-counter derivatives. *Management Science*, *67*(11), 6660−6677.

Hendershott, T., Jones, C. M., & Mendveld, A. J. (2011). Does algorithmic trading improve liquidity? *The Journal of Finance*, *66*(1), 1–33.

Ingebretsen, M. (2002). *NASDAQ: A history of the market that changed the world*. Prima Publishing.

Kirilenko, A. A., Kyle, A. S., Samadi, M., & Tuzun, T. (2017). The flash crash: High-frequency trading in an electronic market. *The Journal of Finance*, *72*(3), 967–998.

Lee, T., & Wang, C. (2018). *Why trade over-the-counter? When investors want price Discrimination*. Paris December 2018 finance meeting EUROFIDAI – AFFI. https://papers.ssrn.com/sol3/papers.cfm?abstract_id=3192484

Marsh, A., & Detrixhe, J. (2016, April 16). *Fixed-income investors have 99 ways to trade and one big problem*. Bloomberg. https://www.bloomberg.com/news/articles/2016-04-14/fixed-income-investors-have-99-ways-to-trade-and-one-big-problem#xj4y7vzkg

Meredith, S. (2022, May 3). Citi says a trader error caused Europe's 'flash cash.' Here's how it unfolded. *CNBC.com*. https://www.cnbc.com/2022/05/03/flash-crash-europes-stock-market-fall-triggered-by-citi-trader-error.html

MTS. (2023). *MTS company timeline*. https://www.mtsmarkets.com/about-us/company-timeline

Stafford, P. (2015, December 5). Europe drops antitrust probe into banks' CDS market activities. *The Financial Times*. https://www.ft.com/content/30135458-9a84-11e5-be4f-0abd1978acaa

Stoll, H. R. (2006). Electronic trading in stock markets. *The Journal of Economic Perspectives*, *10*(1), 153–174.

WallStreetMojo Team. (2023). Flash crash. *Wallstreetmojo.com*. https://www.wallstreetmojo.com/flash-crash/

Chapter 12

Online Trading: Part II

Abdiel Martinez[a]*, Kerem Proulx*[b] *and Andrew C. Spieler*[c]

[a]Independent Financial Consultant, Georgia
[b]Independent Financial Consultant, USA
[c]Hofstra University, USA

Abstract

The history of online trading began in the 1960s with the emergence of electronic communication networks, which allowed the electronic execution of trades outside traditional exchanges. The internet revolution led to the development of online brokerage platforms such as E*Trade and Schwab, enabling non-institutional investors to participate in the digital trading revolution. These platforms have evolved to serve the retail investor market, eventually adapting to mobile-first and commission-free models, significantly lowering the barriers to entry for financial markets. Platforms like Robinhood and other fintech firms have rapidly gained market share by offering services and products previously unavailable, such as commission-free trades, mobile trading, and novel products such as fractional shares and cryptocurrency investing. This chapter provides an overview of the history of online trading. It also introduces several new developments in fintech and the online trading industry and discusses various controversies and future implications of new technologies.

Keywords: Fintech; online trading; Robinhood; high-frequency trading; trading application programming interfaces (APIs); machine learning (ML); artificial intelligence (AI)

Introduction

The development of online trading has fundamentally changed the investment industry since the creation of the first digital portfolio management and trading tools in the late 1980s through the internet revolution. Online and mobile-based trading platforms, such as Robinhood, have democratized access to financial

The Emerald Handbook of Fintech, 221–234

Published under exclusive licence by Emerald Publishing Limited
doi:10.1108/978-1-83753-608-520241026

markets and welcomed a new generation of young investors and traders. Although advances in trading software and lower barriers to entry have increased market accessibility for non-institutional investors, the increasingly gamified nature of modern trading platforms has garnered its fair share of scrutiny among regulators. Controversies such as the "meme-stock" trading frenzies have sparked debates between regulators and investors concerning the effects that ever-evolving brokerage business models have on investors on both ends of the institutional spectrum. This chapter explores modern advancements in online trading, including its development, benefits, drawbacks, and related controversies. It also examines the impact of modern online trading platforms such as Robinhood and the future implications for investors.

Online Trading's Development

The security trading industry has experienced rapid development through its relatively short history, catalyzed by the early days of the internet revolution and even more so by recent advancements in computing and networking infrastructure and technology. The advent of online access has evolved primarily through the technological disruption of the discount brokerage industry (Wu et al., 1999). In the late 1980s, Charles Schwab released the industry's first disk operating system, or DOS-based, portfolio management and trading tool (Schwab, 2023). It subsequently released TeleBroker, a telephone trading application using the phone's keypad as an interface.

In the late 1960s, developments in networking infrastructure gave rise to electronic communication networks (ECNs) that facilitated trading financial products outside of traditional exchanges. As more broadly defined by the Securities Exchange Commission (SEC), ECNs are "any electronic system that is widely disseminated to third parties, ordered entered therein by an exchange or over-the-counter (OTC) market maker, and permits such order to be executed in whole or in part" (Securities and Exchange Commission, 2005, p. 289). ECN adoption was supported broadly by changes in regulation set forth by the SEC in the 1975 Securities Act Amendments, which sought to increase the interconnectedness of all markets through "communication and data processing facilities" (Loomis, 1975).

The National Association of Securities Dealers (NASD), now known as the Financial Industry Regulatory Authority (FINRA), founded the Nasdaq Market (National Association of Securities Dealers Automated Quotations Market) in 1971 following the advent of ECNs. Its purpose was to automate the processing of orders and provide brokers with the latest competitively priced quotes electronically following a 1969 American Stock Exchange study examining the cost of processing handwritten orders and the related errors to brokers (Committee on Banking and Currency, 1969).

Globex was the first electronic trading platform to reach the market in 1992. E*Trade soon also launched a similar platform aimed at the consumer. It soon became the de facto platform for online trading because it pioneered a push into the retail market. Thus, the exponential adoption of discount online trading platforms had begun. As of 2022, Robinhood, a modern, mobile-first brokerage platform founded in 2013, had an estimated 13 million monthly active users (Robinhood, 2022). Subsequent sections discuss the advent of modern technologies and their impact on the trading industry. They also explore the future of consumer electronic trading, including the rise of mobile-first brokers such as Robinhood.

Online Trading's Benefits

The trading industry's increasing electronification has brought about an unprecedented era of openness and accessibility to financial markets, especially for consumer and retail investors, through decreased frictions (e.g., zero-commission trades can be completed through intuitive mobile applications) and increased transparency of financial markets knowledge previously accessible only by those on institutional and professional trading desks. Consumers can now access markets and trade at prices similar to large institutional investors and access essentially the same information, excluding institutions' private information and datasets.

Greater pricing transparency and increased liquidity are similar improvements to financial markets that are direct results of electronic trading and the development of platforms such as Robinhood. BNY Mellon Wealth Management (2021) estimates that upwards of 25% of equity market volume is attributable to retail investors. This volume is partly due to mobile-first brokerages developing applications that optimize for ease of use and smooth user experience. This phenomenon also benefits sophisticated, professional trading firms as increased liquidity, frequent trading activity, and more predictable behavior of retail investors (e.g., retail investors typically trade in even lot sizes of 100 shares due to using graphical interfaces) allow for sufficient exit and entry liquidity for these professional traders' strategies.

Trading costs have dramatically decreased as discount brokers have adopted the zero-commission fee structure. Slippage costs, the cost of price impact, have likewise generally decreased as markets become increasingly liquid, particularly in large exchange-traded fund (ETF) markets that track broad indices, which have become popular among young retail investors (Singh, 2022).

Additionally, fintech firms such as Affirm have developed novel financial products that provide consumers with even greater spending flexibility by offering a "Buy-Now-Pay-Later" option at the point of sale, allowing customers to (almost) instantly be approved for financing of their online purchases. Such innovations would likely be impossible without the technological developments made in the financial and trading industries.

Online Trading's Drawbacks

The electronification of trading has brought several advantages to institutional and retail investors. Yet, the development of advanced trading systems, especially those using artificial intelligence (AI) and machine learning (ML) methods, combined with the processing of customer order flow information purchased by large trading firms through agreements with retail discount brokerages, has led to a murky history of predatory trading practices. The SEC has now outlawed some of these practices. For instance, front-running was a popular strategy employed by many high-frequency trading firms (Hens et al., 2017). *Front-running* involves exploiting advantages in network latency to bid up a security's price when a trader notices high demand by slower traders in the market. The faster trader would then sell the shares purchased ahead of time to the slower traders for a practically risk-free profit. Such trades occur in milliseconds after a market order has been placed. This situation increased trading costs for lower frequency investors, such as mutual funds and pension funds that trade in large lot sizes. As a result, several brokerages that serviced these large funds began to provide sophisticated execution services. They would break down a large order into smaller lot sizes and trade over a specified time window to reduce the likelihood of front-running and target a time-weighted average price.

With the development of highly advanced trading systems and the processing of large, unstructured datasets generated by electronic trading systems, trading firms began to rely heavily on increasingly complex trading models that many criticized as "black boxes." Little intuition existed about why the model made a trading decision. This practice could lead to large market selloffs, including the Flash Crash of 2010, wherein the Dow Jones Industrial Average (DJIA) witnessed a rapid 1,000-point drop in minutes and subsequent reversal to prior levels within 36 minutes (Kirilenko et al., 2017). Such high-velocity events directly resulted from the advancements in trading technology, allowing algorithms and trading systems to trade large quantities at increasingly rapid speeds.

Robinhood and Beyond

Modern online trading platforms such as Robinhood have revolutionized the online trading industry since their founding in 2013. These platforms provide a mobile application experience featuring an accessible user interface, enabling investors to trade securities at potentially zero-commission rates more easily. Although these platforms have democratized access to financial markets and attracted younger generations of investors, they have been at the center of several public debates and controversies. These disagreements, including the "meme-stock" trading frenzies, have affected stocks such as GameStop and drawn scrutiny of online trading platforms and communities by regulators and institutional investors.

Despite these controversies, knowledgeable individuals expect the online trading industry to continue to shape financial markets, especially as new technologies like AI advancements emerge. Investors will have better access to financial markets and data than previously, helping to level the playing field between retail and institutional investors.

High-Frequency Trading

High-frequency trading (HFT) emerged in the early 2000s as the electronification of markets enabled investment firms to take advantage of the developments in high-speed data transfer and low-latency systems (Avellaneda & Stoikov, 2008). Such systems enable building trading strategies wherein security positions are rapidly bought and sold to capture short-term profit opportunities in financial markets. These strategies include order front-running (Xu & Cheng, 2022), quote-stuffing (Egginton et al., 2016), and other algorithmic strategies that take advantage of ultra-low latency data transfer between an exchange and the HFT firm's systems. *Co-location* places their physical servers close to those of the exchange, among other optimizations.

Today, many original strategies developed by HFT firms have been deemed predatory (i.e., deployed to the detriment of other market participants) and outlawed by the SEC (Security Exchange Commission, 2014). However, modern HFT firms have adapted to the ever-evolving regulatory and technological landscape and have built lucrative market-making businesses, providing liquidity for major exchanges. Market makers hold an inventory of securities and employ various methods of matching buyers of securities to sellers. The profit is captured as a *spread* – the difference between the price at which investors can purchase a security (ask) and the price at which investors may sell a security (bid). Besides the bid-ask spread, market makers may collect a commission fee for their liquidity provision services. Not surprisingly, these commissions are more attractive in markets with high volatility and individual security volatility.

Market making can be a lucrative business and, depending on risk management practices, a relatively market-neutral source of income since market makers generally do not take directional bets on securities. The firms employing these strategies rely on an informational edge to ensure adequate positioning to capture a sufficient bid-ask spread, even during heightened volatility. As such, many market-making firms have entered into contracts with online security brokerage firms to purchase clients' order flow to gain an informational advantage. The next section describes the rise of online and mobile-first brokerage firms and how selling order flow has led to a new paradigm of commission-free trading and ushered in a new generation of retail investors.

Trading APIs

Trading application programming interfaces (APIs) have become increasingly popular among retail investors since the early 2010s. These APIs allow individual investors to access real-time market data and execute trades directly from their software or applications by connecting to a real-time market data stream or accessing historic data for strategy development, research, and backtesting.

One major advantage of a trading API is the speed at which trades can be executed. As APIs allow the investor to bypass the traditional graphical trading interface, the speed at which trades can be placed is only limited by the efficiency of a trader's system and network speed. This circumstance is particularly useful in fast-moving markets where every second or fraction is important and in automating an investor's trading strategies. For instance, an investor may follow strict trading rules, using specific timescales, such as monthly portfolio rebalances based on market conditions. Instead of manually inputting these trades, an investor can use public trading APIs to retrieve the necessary data, perform the analysis, and submit the required trades to rebalance the portfolio, all through a customized automated system. This increased level of control and customization can be especially useful for investors utilizing complex strategies that take advantage of market inefficiencies that would be otherwise difficult, if not impossible, to execute manually.

Trading APIs also allow investors to access various markets and financial instruments. Many APIs access multiple exchanges and asset classes, including stocks, bonds, currencies, and derivatives. This access allows investors to diversify their portfolios and exploit opportunities in different markets worldwide. Such access further democratized access to financial market data that may have been much more costly or difficult to obtain, especially for investors lacking institutional resources. However, trading APIs come with risks and challenges. Investors need to be familiar with the API specifications, the platform they are using, and the underlying assets and markets. Carefully considering the costs associated with using a trading API, including any fees or commissions that may be charged for access to live and historical trading data, is prudent.

Trading APIs offer a powerful tool for retail investors looking to execute trades quickly and efficiently and customize and automate their trading strategies. These systems have enabled a new generation of algorithmic retail investors that, combined with innovations in the cloud computing industry, can build advanced trading strategies that take advantage of market inefficiencies and opportunities that traditional retail investors cannot. Provisioning cloud computing resources to build advanced trading systems using public and paid APIs for data has become increasingly commonplace and accessible among savvier retail investors. Services such as Amazon Web Services (AWS), Microsoft Azure, and Google Cloud Platform enable those with the proper technical skills to rent and deploy large clusters of computer resources to build data analysis and processing and trade execution pipelines at a reasonable cost. Cloud computing capabilities continue to increase (McCurdy, 2022). Examples are the rise of high-performance computing and parallelized computing methods using large clusters of highly efficient hardware such as graphics processing units (GPUs) for scientific computing. Thus, small investors' ability to build trading systems that resemble professional, sophisticated trading firms will rapidly increase.

Alternative Data

Alternative data are non-traditional data sources that can supplement traditional financial data in financial market analysis and decision-making. The data can be derived from various sources, such as satellite imagery, social media, web scraping, and wearable devices. Using alternative data has become increasingly popular in recent years as financial firms and investors look for any competitive edge in a constantly evolving and increasingly complex financial landscape. By providing additional insights and context, alternative data can help financial market participants make more informed and potentially more accurate decisions about investments and trading strategies. For instance, several fintech firms scrape the web to mine insights on various companies that they subsequently sell to their clients to provide increasingly granular and timely data compared to relying entirely on public company filings.

One common use of alternative data in financial markets is to identify trends and patterns that may not be immediately apparent from traditional financial data, like stock price and volume. For example, satellite imagery can be used to monitor the activity level at a particular factory or shipping port, providing insight into the production and distribution of goods. Social media data can gauge consumer sentiment about a particular product or brand, providing insight into potential demand and sales. Web scraping can collect data on online pricing and availability of goods and services, providing insight into competitors and pricing trends.

Using alternative data in financial markets can provide valuable additional context and insights, helping financial market participants make better-informed and potentially more profitable decisions. However, carefully considering the data's quality and reliability and any potential biases or limitations is important. Additionally, using alternative data may be subject to various legal and regulatory considerations, such as data privacy and protection laws.

As markets trend toward increasing price efficiency and the lifetime of a trader's edge – also called *alpha decay* (Di Mascio et al., 2022) – shortens, using alternative data and advanced predictive and data analysis methods, like ML, to extract informational content from large unstructured alternative datasets will become a powerful and necessary tool in the professional and retail investor's toolkit. However, as data privacy and protection regulations continue to tighten, especially in a post-General Data Protection Regulation (GDPR) Europe (Prasad, 2020), using such datasets may carry unintended risks that traders should be cautious about before integrating such data into their trading systems.

Machine Learning and Artificial Intelligence

ML and AI refer to a class of models that use computational methods to reach optimal predictive performance on a data set by learning from that data. These methods aim to generate a model that can perform a predictive task without explicit instruction or programming. They are similar to traditional statistical modeling methods, such as linear regression, in that the models are trained on input data using some numerical/computational optimization method, like ordinary least squares (OLS), to make predictions based on these data. At a fundamental level, ML uses algorithms and mathematical functions that receive input data, analyze these data, and output predictions. These models are then fed new data, and the parameters of these algorithms and functions are adjusted based on their predictions' accuracy. ML methods are generally deployed to model nonlinear and highly complex relations in data. They trade off interpretability for predictive performance and perform a defined task. For instance, companies like Netflix use ML models to build effective recommendation systems (Steck et al., 2021). OpenAI uses ML models to create near-human-level chatbots and language models that can follow arbitrary instructions (Ouyang et al., 2022).

ML models involving financial markets and electronic trading have been deployed since the early 2010s. They are used to build advanced trading strategies (Lopez de Prado, 2018) primarily by institutional investors such as hedge funds. Consumer and commercial banks use ML models to develop highly effective fraud detection systems (Priya & Saradha, 2021) to ensure the safety of customer funds.

The electronification of financial markets has led to exponential growth in the data generated, gathered, and mined by retail investors and institutional market participants. *Big data* technologies are designed to "economically extract value from large volumes of a wide variety of data by enabling high-velocity capture, discovery, and/or analysis" (Gantz & Reinsel, 2012, p. 9). Large datasets can be used to make better-informed business and financial decisions across the business landscape. According to the NYSE's data on daily option contract volume, the first half of 2022 saw daily volume grow to 38.8 million contracts, nearly 40 million data points a day, for one class of financial instruments (New York Stock Exchange, 2023).

ML methods can use large, unstructured datasets produced by trading APIs and alternative data sources. These models extract informative insights from the highly complex nature of these data sources and can perform tasks that previously required expert-level humans. For instance, a language model can detect the sentiment of web-scraped tweets associated with a certain company or stock to inform a portfolio manager of potentially deteriorating consumer sentiment toward a portfolio company.

ML and AI methods are commonly used in risk management applications that govern various trading strategies rather than directly attempting to predict the future price of a given security. For example, high-frequency market makers use ML models to predict the probability of adverse selection to determine when to adjust their positions (Easley et al., 2011). ML solutions have been applied to portfolio construction/optimization to model complex, hierarchical relations between securities in a portfolio and generate an optimal allocation scheme to minimize portfolio variance. Another application involves outlier detection, wherein an ML model can outperform traditional statistical methods on large, unstructured datasets to detect regime changes in financial data.

Although applying ML and AI methods across the entire trading process (stack), from price prediction to risk management, may seem attractive, these models are prone to *overfitting*, a model's tendency to bias too much toward training data, losing their ability to predict new data points out of sample. Such models also exhibit other risks generally present in predictive modeling methods. Therefore, traders employing these methods should ensure adequate controls are in place to mitigate the financial impact of these risks. With the advent of advanced ML models, especially in language modeling, many financial institutions and investment managers will likely explore applying them to other parts of their business besides making trading decisions. Advanced large language models (LLMs) such as ChatGPT may be deployed as a layer between institutional traders and their counterparties, perhaps even replacing portions of or entirely the sales trader's role. Such models are *few-shot learners* and can be fine-tuned to perform arbitrary tasks with high fidelity (Brown et al., 2020). Perhaps in a not-so-distant future, many OTC products could likewise be traded with advanced chatbots that are augmented with various data feeds and client-specific information to provide a layer of automation to high-touch traded products or possibly augment the skills of the sales traders that manage such trading desks.

The continued democratization of such advanced ML/AI models by organizations such as OpenAI, HuggingFace, and StabilityAI has enabled individual researchers and developers to train and deploy sufficiently advanced AI models. This technology will eventually find its way into the hands of retail investors. Open data-science competitions and tournaments already leverage the expertise of hundreds of distributed data engineers and computer scientists to generate trading strategies and models that trade in the open market, rewarding participants for their contributions (Craib et al., 2017).

Cryptocurrency and Automated Market Makers

A *cryptocurrency* is a digital or virtual currency that uses cryptography for security and is not backed by any government or central authority. Crypto allows for peer-to-peer (P2P) transactions and operates on a decentralized network (i.e., not subject to traditional financial intermediaries like banks). A main attraction of cryptocurrencies is the ability to trade 24/7 on various online exchanges. These exchanges facilitate the buying and selling of cryptocurrencies and are often open for trading around the clock, allowing traders to take advantage of market movements at any time. However, the 24/7 nature of cryptocurrency markets also makes them highly volatile, with prices fluctuating rapidly based on various factors such as news events, regulatory developments, and investor sentiment. This volatility can make executing trades at the best possible price difficult, especially when the market is moving quickly. This situation is where automated market makers (AMMs) enter. An *automated market maker* is a computer program that automatically uses algorithms to buy and sell cryptocurrencies on exchanges, typically to provide liquidity to the market. These market makers can operate 24/7, making them an attractive option for traders looking to take advantage of market movements anytime.

Besides providing liquidity, AMMs can also help to reduce the spread between the bid and ask prices on an exchange, facilitating trading at a fair price. This feature is especially important in P2P markets, where there may be fewer participants and lower liquidity than in traditional exchanges. P2P markets are decentralized platforms allowing individuals to buy and sell cryptocurrencies directly with each other without needing a centralized exchange. These markets can offer greater privacy and security for traders but also come with risks, such as the potential for fraud. AMMs can help mitigate these risks by providing a level of liquidity to the market and helping to ensure that trades are executed at fair prices.

Thus, AMMs play an important role in the cryptocurrency market by providing liquidity and helping to ensure that trades are executed at fair prices. Although not without risks, AMMs offer several benefits to traders looking to take advantage of the 24/7 nature of cryptocurrency markets.

Robinhood and Mobile-First Brokerages

Advances in electronic trading infrastructure have given rise to a cohort of brokerage firms dedicated to mobile-first and web-application-based retail trading interfaces. Investors of all backgrounds, from the novice to the experienced, can now open a mobile or web application on their smartphone and have similar access to markets as most institutional investors. One platform that has gained considerable notoriety is Robinhood, a mobile stock trading platform credited with revolutionizing the retail trading business.

Founded in 2013, Robinhood has disrupted the traditional brokerage model by allowing users to trade stocks, ETFs, options, and, more recently, cryptocurrencies under a commission-free trading model through their simple mobile interface. This approach departs markedly from the traditional business model where brokerage firms charge a fee on a per-trade basis and make trades over the phone or through a complex online interface. Although Robinhood is not meant to replace highly sophisticated trading software used by institutional professionals, its simplicity, ease of use, no account minimums, and zero-commission model have catalyzed its exponential adoption among young, less-experienced investors.

However, this focus on simplicity and accessibility has led to several notable controversies. Critics contend that the platform's lack of educational resources and emphasis on quick, short-term trading, further popularized by online communities on sites such as Reddit (White & Irrera, 2021), encourages highly risky behavior and perpetuates a casino-like approach to investing.

There has been public outcry and investigation into Robinhood's sale of customer order flow to large market makers to fund its zero-commission revenue model (Duggan, 2022). Order flow sales are common in today's electronic trading landscape. These sales are the primary revenue source for zero-commission brokerages. They transfer customer order data, such as buy and sell actions undertaken through the mobile platform, bundled as a data stream to large market-making firms that execute the orders and use this order flow information to inform their trading decisions. This process benefits market makers as they are less likely to face adverse selection (Hoffman, 2013) by small retail orders versus large institutional orders. Similarly, retail investors benefit from more attractive execution, such as faster execution and lower costs in the form of low slippage or price impact, as market makers indirectly compete with each other for this order flow. However, retail investors may trade at disadvantaged prices or wider bid-ask spreads compared to larger institutional clients who may place orders through prime brokerage desks at large investment banks to offset additional costs associated with zero-commission trades.

However, this relationship between brokers and market makers has many critics. They believe misaligned incentives exist between the two parties. Some have even accused brokers such as Robinhood of colluding with large market makers such as Citadel Securities during events wherein trading certain stocks had been halted during the meme-stock trading frenzies (Lyons, 2021) to prevent adverse trading environments for their largest market-making partners.

Despite these concerns, Robinhood and mobile-first brokers have helped to democratize stock market investing, even in complex instruments such as options, by increasing accessibility to investment markets for those who may not have had the means to participate historically. Still, the future may give way to a different retail trading landscape as the SEC continues to propose major policy changes that directly affect the methods by which brokerages such as Robinhood generate revenue and provide commission-free order execution. In June 2022, SEC Chair Gary Gensler directed staff to research methods of increasing market efficiency for small retail investors and public companies (Gensler, 2022). This inquiry includes the potential for requiring brokerages to route orders to auctions wherein market makers would compete for execution, fundamentally changing the business model of market makers. They typically generate greater revenues from the direct routing of order flow rather than competing openly against other potentially sophisticated traders – thus increasing the probability of adverse selection.

Current debate exists about whether this approach would harm or benefit retail order execution. Market makers claim that "order-by-order competition" may have unintended consequences that increase trading expenses by removing the brokers' operational leverage over market makers and wholesalers to demand the best execution for their customers and threaten to bring their business elsewhere if they cannot provide attractive execution. Therefore, this open competition model may lead to less efficient order execution as market makers may decide participating in such a market is too costly.

Mobile-first brokers such as Robinhood have solidified their market position with the younger generations of investors, enabling an unprecedented era of democratization of stock market investing and broader financial market participation. Although regulatory uncertainty about the future of retail investing still exists, emerging technologies and a growing tech-conscious population will continue to shape the investing landscape toward a more open, efficient, and data-centric marketplace.

Summary and Conclusions

Financial markets are ultimately shaped and influenced by the technology supporting them. From the earliest days of computer networking to the internet revolution, the securities trading industry has transitioned from a market exclusive to large institutional investors to a diverse and democratized landscape where investors of all sizes and resources participate. Although the playing field is not necessarily level, online trading has opened the financial markets to diverse investors, due partly to platforms such as Robinhood, which provides accessible mobile interfaces at no cost to users. Yet, this accessibility has brought several controversies. It has also generated public debate and scrutiny from regulators as the business models currently employed to sustain such low barriers to entry have led to events including the "meme-stock" trading frenzy. Despite these controversies, the online trading industry will continue to evolve and adapt to new technologies as brokerages and trading venues compete to bring innovative products to their clients. Technologies such as AI and ML will continue to reduce the marginal cost of intelligence and intelligent systems, paving the way for platforms such as Robinhood to provide even more bespoke and powerful products to their clients with major effects on the evolution of modern financial markets.

Discussion Questions

- Explain online trading's benefits and drawbacks.
- Discuss the advantages and disadvantages of selling customer order flow.
- Discuss how market participants use AI and ML to accomplish their trading strategies.
- Explain how Robinhood revolutionized the retail trading business.
- Describe how retail traders may use APIs to develop trading strategies.
- Describe how alternative and traditional data sources differ.

References

Avellaneda, M., & Stoikov, S. (2008). High-frequency trading in a limit order book. *Quantitative Finance*, *8*(3), 217–224. https://doi.org/10.1080/14697680701381228

BNY Mellon Wealth Management. (2021). *The rise of retail traders*. https://www.bnymellonwealth.com/insights/the-rise-of-retail-traders.html#:~:text=Retail%20investors'%20share%20of%20total,%2D15%25%20the%20preceding%20decade

Brown, T., Mann, B., Ryder, N., Subbiah, M., Kaplan, J., Dhariwal, P., Neelakantan, A., Shyam, P., Sastry, G., Askell, A., Agarwal, S., Herbert-Voss, A., Krueger, G., Henighan, T., Child, R., Ramesh, A., Ziegler, D. M., Wu, J., Winter, C., … Amodei, D. (2020, April). Language models are few-shot learners. *Arxiv – Computation and Language*. https://doi.org/10.48550/arXiv.2005.14165

Committee on Banking and Currency. (1969, April). Problems in the security industry. Hearings Before the Subcommittee on Securities.

Craib, R., Bradway, G., Dunn, X., & Krug, J. (2017, February). Numeraire: A cryptographic token for coordinating machine intelligence and preventing overfitting. https://numer.ai/whitepaper.pdf

Di Mascio, R., Lines, A., & Naik, N. (2022). Alpha decay and institutional trading. https://papers.ssrn.com/sol3/papers.cfm?abstract_id=2580551

Duggan, W. (2022, August 22). What is payment for order flow? *Forbes Advisor*. Forbes. https://www.forbes.com/advisor/investing/payment-for-order-flow/

Easley, D., del Prado, M. L., & O'Hara, M. (2011). The exchange of flow toxicity. *Journal of Trading 2*(March), 8–13.

Egginton, J. F., Van Ness, B., & Van Ness, R. (2016). Quote stuffing. *Financial Management*, *45*(3), 583–608. https://doi.org/10.1111/fima.12126

Gantz, J., & Reinsel, D. (2012, December). The digital universe in 2020: Big data, bigger digital shadows, and biggest growth in the far east. *IDC*.

Gensler, G. (2022, June 8). Market structure and the retail investor: Remarks before the Piper Sandler global exchange conference. https://www.sec.gov/news/speech/gensler-remarks-piper-sandler-global-exchange-conference-060822

Hens, T., Lensberg, T., & Schenk-Hoppé, K. R. (2017). Front-running and market quality: An evolutionary perspective on high frequency trading. *International Review of Finance*, *4*(October), 727–741. https://doi.org/10.1111/irfi.12159

Hoffman, P. (2013, March). *Adverse selection, market access and inter-market competition*. European Central Bank Working Paper Series. https://www.ecb.europa.eu/pub/pdf/scpwps/ecbwp1519.pdf

Kirilenko, A., Kyle, A. S., Samadi, M., & Tuzun, T. (2017). The flash crash: The impact of high frequency trading on an electronic market. *The Journal of Finance*, *72*(3), 967–998. https://doi.org/10.1111/jofi.12498

Loomis, P. (1975, November). *The Securities Acts Amendments of 1975, Self-Regulation and the National Market System*. Securities Exchange Commission.

Lopez de Prado, M. (2018). *Advances in financial machine learning*. John Wiley & Sons, Inc.

Lyons, K. (2021, January 22). GameStop stock halts trading after Reddit Drama. *Verge*. https://www.theverge.com/2021/1/22/22244900/game-stop-stock-halted-trading-volatility

McCurdy, W. (2022, May 9). AWS is spending billions on five new data centers. TechRadar. https://www.techradar.com/news/aws-is-spending-billions-on-five-new-data-centers

New York Stock Exchange. (2023). Trading & data – NYSE. https://www.nyse.com/trading-data

Ouyang, L., Wu, J., Jiang, X., Almeida, D., Wainwright, C. L., Mishkin, P., Zhang, C., Agarwal, S., Slama, K., Ray, A., Schulman, J., Jacob, H., Fraser, K., Miller, L., Simens, M., Askell, A., Welinder, P., Paul, C., Jan, L., & Lowe, R. (2022, March 4). Training language models to follow instructions with human feedback. *ArXiv – Computation and Language*. https://arxiv.org/abs/2203.02155

Prasad, A. (2020, September 2). *Two years later: A look at the unintended consequences of GDPR*. Regulatory Studies Center, George Washington University. https://regulatorystudies.columbian.gwu.edu/unintended-consequences-gdpr

Priya, G. J., & Saradha, S. (2021). *Fraud detection and prevention using machine learning algorithms: A review*. 7th International Conference on Electrical Energy

Systems (ICEES), Chennai, India, 564–568. https://ieeexplore.ieee.org/document/9383631/authors#authors

Robinhood. (2022). Robinhood Markets, Inc. Reports August 2022 operating data. https://investors.robinhood.com/news/news-details/2022/Robinhood-Markets-Inc.-Reports-August-2022-Operating-Data/default.aspx

Schwab. (2023). Company history | About Schwab. https://www.aboutschwab.com/history

Securities and Exchange Commission. (2005, August). *Final rule: Regulation NMS.*

Securities and Exchange Commission. (2014, August 16). *SEC charges New York-based high frequency trading firm with fraudulent trading to manipulate closing prices.*

Singh, M. (2022, December 16). Retail investors turn to ETFs as recession fears knock down meme stocks. *Reuters.* https://www.reuters.com/markets/retail-investors-turn-etfs-recession-fears-knock-down-meme-stocks-2022-12-16/

Steck, H., Baltrunas, L., Elahi, E., Liang, D., Raimond, Y., & Basilico, J. (2021). Deep learning for recommender systems: A Netflix case study. *AI Magazine, 42*, 7–18. https://doi.org/10.1609/aaai.12013

White, L., & Irrera, A. (2021, February 9). Reddit-fueled retail trading frenzy spreads to Europe. *Reuters.* https://www.reuters.com/article/us-retail-trading-europe/reddit-fuelled-retail-trading-frenzy-spreads-to-europe-idUSKBN2A9284

Wu, J., Siegel, M., & Manion, J. (1999). Online trading: An internet revolution. Massachusetts Institute of Technology.

Xu, Z., & Cheng, X. (2022, November). "Are front-running HFTs harmful?" *Arxiv. Org – Trading and market Microstructure.* https://doi.org/10.48550/arXiv.2211.06046

Chapter 13

Personal Finance Applications of Fintech

Sumit Agarwal and Tan Chek Ann

National University of Singapore, Singapore

Abstract

Fintech has revolutionized personal finance, introducing innovative tools that offer unprecedented access, efficiency, and security in managing finances. This chapter explains fintech's personal finance applications, from intuitive budgeting apps and advanced robo-advisors to peer-to-peer payment platforms. It articulates how these tools have shifted the control and management of finances into the hands of consumers, providing real-time financial data, customized investment strategies, improved credit scores, and streamlined transactions that eliminate the need for traditional intermediaries. Furthermore, this chapter features a select list of FinTech50 firms and highlights how individuals can leverage their services. This comprehensive guide is invaluable for individuals seeking to leverage fintech for personal finance optimization and for professionals keen on understanding and navigating the rapidly evolving fintech landscape.

Keywords: Fintech; peer-to-peer (P2P) lending; mobile payments; personal banking; FinTech50

Introduction

Financial technology (fintech) has emerged as an influential game-changer in the evolving financial landscape. *Fintech,* coined by Citicorp in 1993, is a financial industry that applies technology to improve its financial activities (Schueffel, 2017). This technology enabled firms to specialize and offer products and services tailored to customer preferences (Thakor, 1999) across different arenas such as internet banking, mobile payments, peer-to-peer (P2P) lending, robo-advisory, cryptocurrency, security, identification, and other forms of innovation (Lagna & Ravishankar, 2022).

The Emerald Handbook of Fintech, 235–248

doi:10.1108/978-1-83753-608-520241029

Fintech advancements transformed many people's lives (Agarwal & Chua, 2020). Personal finance was once a complex and time-consuming process. Individuals had to manually track their spending, save for retirement, and invest their money. Banking activities had to be done physically at a bank branch. Today, fintech companies reduce these financial contracting frictions (Philippon, 2015), giving individuals real-time control over their finances (Brainard, 2016) and making these tasks much easier and more efficient. For instance, introducing debit cards, a product many take for granted, reduced the median travel distance to banking branches by 73% from 2.98 to 0.81 miles. This greater convenience led to a huge reduction in travel costs, and households needing to forgo daily activities fell from 84% to just 25% (Bachas et al., 2018).

Fintech has made these tasks much easier and more efficient by revolutionizing every aspect of personal finance. It offers individuals many innovative tools and platforms to manage their financial lives more productively. From online banking and transparent budgeting to comprehensive credit score understanding, enhanced security, and efficient debt consolidation, fintech provides various solutions to enhance financial management. This chapter delves into how people can harness fintech's power to streamline their financial lives.

A Brief History of Fintech in Personal Finance

The history of fintech in personal finance is a story of innovation and disruption, accelerating at a breakneck speed in response to changing global economic circumstances, technology advancements, and evolving consumer needs. Fintech has fundamentally transformed how individuals manage their finances, ushering in an era of democratized access to financial services and greater financial inclusion. This chapter briefly traces fintech's development from its embryonic stages to its current expansive reach in personal finance.

Fintech's modern roots can be traced back to the inception of the financial services sector with the introduction of credit cards in the 1950s and the advent of automated teller machines (ATMs) in the 1960s. ATMs were the first major disruptor, automating the process of cash withdrawals and reducing reliance on human bank tellers. The next significant leap occurred with the advent of electronic trading and the mainstream adoption of personal computers in the 1980s and 1990s. These developments allowed individuals to take charge of their investments, paving the way for online brokerages like E*TRADE. During this era, financial data also became digitized, with companies like Bloomberg providing electronic delivery of financial information.

The *global financial crisis* (GFC) was a period of extreme stress in global financial markets and banking systems between mid-2007 and early 2009. It marked a turning point for fintech in personal finance. Dissatisfaction with traditional banks combined with advancements in mobile technology and internet penetration provided the catalyst for fintech companies to flourish. Pioneers like PayPal, Square, and Mint began offering innovative digital solutions in money transfers, payment processing, and personal finance management. P2P lending platforms such as Lending Club and Prosper also emerged, providing alternatives to traditional bank loans. The past years saw huge growth in the market share of fintech lenders. In the United States, lending increased from $34 billion to $161 billion, and market share from 2% to 8% (Buchak et al., 2018; Fuster et al., 2019). Robo-advisors like Betterment and Wealthfront surfaced, offering low-cost, automated investment management services, possibly outperforming that of traditional advisory services (French, 2008; Gennaioli et al., 2015; Jensen, 1968; Rossi & Utkus, 2021)

The ubiquitous adoption of smartphones and mobile internet significantly amplified fintech's reach and impact. Mobile banking apps from traditional banks and fintech start-ups enabled consumers to manage their finances, execute transactions, and access financial services from anywhere at any time. This innovation was a game-changer, enhancing the user experience and enabling the proliferation of app-based personal finance management tools. Simultaneously, developing nations with large unbanked populations leapfrogged traditional banking infrastructures and embraced mobile money solutions like M-Pesa in Kenya. These mobile-driven financial services expedited financial inclusion (Demirguc-Kunt et al., 2020). They laid the groundwork for a comprehensive ecosystem of fintech solutions through the positive externalities that fintech brings about (Higgins, 2022).

Nakamoto (2008) published the Bitcoin white paper in 2008, and bitcoin's first trades occurred in 2009. These events and the underlying blockchain technology marked another transformative moment in fintech's history. Bitcoin and subsequent cryptocurrencies offered a decentralized, digital alternative to traditional fiat currencies. Although their adoption in personal finance has been tumultuous, they have provoked important dialogues around monetary policy, value storage, and the nature of money itself. Blockchain technology has also had significant implications for personal finance, particularly in remittances, which promises to reduce costs and increase speed. Similarly, "smart contracts" built on blockchain platforms like Ethereum have potential applications in automating insurance claims, thus impacting personal insurance management. A *smart contract* is a digital contract stored on a blockchain that automatically executes after meeting predetermined terms and conditions (IBM, n.d.).

Fintech's evolution in personal finance has been an intricate interplay of technology, regulation, and changing consumer needs. Over time, fintech has reshaped the financial landscape, democratizing access to financial services, enhancing financial literacy, and promoting financial inclusion. The ongoing advances in artificial intelligence (AI), machine learning (ML), and blockchain, coupled with increasing global internet penetration, promise even more transformative changes in personal finance. The intersection of these technologies with the regulatory and economic trends will undoubtedly continue to shape fintech's future trajectory in personal finance.

Personal Banking With Fintech

The proliferation of smartphones and high-speed internet has precipitated the widespread adoption of mobile banking, allowing customers to access banking services conveniently. Mobile banking apps provided by traditional banks and fintech start-ups have become a fundamental tool for individuals seeking to expedite their banking processes. Through mobile banking, customers can swiftly check balances, review transactions, transfer funds, pay bills, and even deposit checks using their device's camera. Advanced security measures like encryption, biometric authentication, and multi-factor authentication (MFA) are often incorporated to protect users' data and transactions.

Fintech has also revolutionized person-to-person money transfers. Platforms like Venmo, Zelle, and Square Cash facilitate instantaneous transactions, bypassing the delays inherent in traditional bank transfers or check-based payments. These P2P payment platforms integrate seamlessly with users' bank accounts, providing a more convenient and quicker way to transfer money to peers. Digital wallets such as Apple Pay, Google Pay, and Samsung Pay have dramatically reduced the time spent completing transactions. By storing card details securely on devices, these services enable customers to make contactless payments, bypassing the need for physical cards or cash. The introduction of quick response (QR) code payment solutions also quickly gained prominence, accelerating point-of-sale transactions and leading to strong mobile payment adoption. These effects are stronger among smaller merchants who see a larger increase in sales vis-à-vis their larger counterparts (Agarwal et al., 2022). These digital payment solutions enhance transaction speed and convenience, significantly improving the banking experience.

Fintech's integration into banking has undeniably accelerated and streamlined banking processes. From basic banking functions such as balance checking and fund transfers to more complex tasks like investment management and financial planning, Fintech solutions have enabled a swifter, more efficient banking experience. As the fintech landscape evolves, the blend of technology, regulation, and changing consumer needs will undoubtedly herald even more advancements in fast banking. Consequently, consumers, institutions, and policymakers must stay abreast of these developments and leverage them for an enhanced banking experience.

Making Better Budgets

Among the various aspects of personal finance, budgeting is a major beneficiary of fintech innovation. This section explores how individuals can harness fintech tools for rapid and transparent budget creation and management.

Budgeting is a critical aspect of sound financial management, necessitating a clear understanding of income, expenses, savings, and investments. Fintech applications can aid in creating, tracking, and managing budgets effectively, offering features like the automatic categorization of expenses, real-time budget tracking, and personalized saving suggestions. These fintech tools can enable individuals to create budgets swiftly and gain a transparent view of their financial health in real time (Brainard, 2016).

Budgeting apps constitute a prominent subset of fintech, offering tools to streamline the budgeting process. Renowned apps like Mint, You Need a Budget (YNAB), and PocketGuard enable users to connect their bank accounts, credit cards, loans, and investments, automatically importing and categorizing transactions in real time. These apps offer a comprehensive picture of an individual's financial landscape, allowing for the quick creation of personalized budgets. By automatically tracking and categorizing expenses, these apps bring transparency to spending habits, illuminating areas where the budget can be adjusted or optimized.

Integrating AI and ML into fintech has further elevated the capabilities of budgeting tools. AI-powered personal finance assistants can analyze spending patterns, predict future expenses, and offer personalized budgeting advice. For example, platforms like Cleo and Olivia use AI to interact with users, provide insights into spending habits, and suggest custom budgets based on their financial goals.

Fintech has revolutionized goal-based budgeting, allowing users to set financial targets and allow real-time tracking of their progress. Apps like Qapital and Acorns facilitate micro-saving by rounding up the change on purchases and investing the difference. These apps make saving and budgeting transparent and accessible, helping individuals work toward their financial goals more effectively.

Many fintech tools provide real-time alerts and notifications on spending, bill due dates, low balances, or suspicious account activity. These alerts can help users stay within their budgets, avoid late fees, and protect against potential fraud. This level of instant communication is a hallmark of fintech's contribution to making budgeting faster and more transparent.

Using budgeting apps, AI-powered personal finance assistants, goal-based budgeting tools, open banking, and real-time alerts, fintech provides individuals with a fast, transparent, and integrated approach to budgeting. These tools democratize access to financial management services and promote financial literacy, enabling individuals to gain control over their financial health. As fintech continues to evolve, it promises to bring even more innovative tools and strategies to streamline the budgeting process further.

Understand, Manage, and Improve Credit Scores for Better Loans

Credit scores are numerical representations of an individual's creditworthiness based on that person's credit history. Traditional financial institutions rely heavily on these scores to make lending decisions, affecting individuals' access to credit and the terms of any loans for which they are approved. Therefore, maintaining a good credit score is vital for financial well-being. However, understanding and managing credit scores can be complex, creating a barrier for many individuals.

Fintech's most immediate contribution to credit scores is increased accessibility. Traditional credit reports can be difficult to obtain and understand. However, numerous fintech companies offer easy and often free access to credit scores. Platforms such as Credit Karma and Credit Sesame allow users to monitor their credit scores and reports regularly, increasing awareness of credit standing and encouraging proactive management of credit health.

Another advantage of fintech platforms is their ability to provide users with educational resources and personalized insights. Many platforms offer detailed breakdowns of the factors affecting credit scores, guidance on improving them, and personalized suggestions based on the user's specific credit situation. This interactive and personalized approach to credit education helps individuals to understand what actions they can take to improve their credit scores. Fintech has also pioneered unique solutions to help individuals with low or no credit scores build their credit. Some fintech companies offer secured credit cards or credit-builder loans designed specifically for those aiming to establish or repair their credit. An example is Self (formerly Self Lender), which offers a credit-builder account that allows customers to build credit while saving money.

Additionally, certain fintech companies are exploring alternative data to assess creditworthiness. One example includes *mobile footprints*, which refer to individuals' online behavior or call logs captured from mobile phones. These footprints allow fintech firms to proxy for aspects of behavior that are hard to quantify or observe. Leveraging such alternative metrics outperforms traditional credit bureau scores in predicting loan approvals and defaults (Agarwal et al., 2021; Berg et al., 2020). It allows lenders to make more informed lending decisions, opening lending opportunities to those lacking credit access and improving financial inclusion (Berg et al., 2020).

By increasing accessibility to credit information, providing personalized insights and education, offering innovative credit-building solutions, and facilitating real-time credit monitoring, fintech companies empower individuals to control their credit health. As fintech continues to evolve, many expect it to democratize access to financial services further and promote financial literacy. The intersection of technology, big data, and ML holds enormous potential for refining credit scoring models and offering more personalized credit management solutions. As the industry navigates this promising landscape, the continued exploration and adoption of fintech solutions for credit score management is paramount.

Security in Personal Banking

The digitization of personal banking has made financial management more accessible and introduced a new set of security concerns. Cybersecurity breaches, identity theft, and online fraud pose significant risks in an increasingly interconnected financial ecosystem. As such, fintech's role in bolstering personal banking security is critical.

Fintech enhances banking security by implementing advanced user authentication mechanisms. Traditional username-password combinations are increasingly supplanted by biometric authentication methods such as fingerprint scanning, facial recognition, and voice recognition. These biometric modalities offer a higher level of security as they are unique to each individual and much more difficult for a malicious actor to replicate.

Additionally, MFA, combining two or more independent credentials, is becoming standard across fintech applications. A typical MFA process might involve something the user knows (password or PIN), something the user has (mobile device or hardware token), and something the user is (biometric information). MFA considerably heightens the security barrier, making unauthorized access exceedingly challenging.

AI and ML are instrumental in fintech's drive toward improving banking security. AI/ML algorithms can analyze patterns in transaction data, learn a user's typical behavior, and flag anomalous transactions that deviate from the norm. By identifying potential fraud in real time, these systems provide an additional layer of security that surpasses traditional fraud detection methods. For instance, if an unusually large transaction is made or multiple transactions occur rapidly in a foreign location, AI/ML systems can detect this abnormal behavior and immediately alert the user and the bank, often preventing fraudulent transactions before they are completed.

Blockchain technology has broader applications in securing personal banking. The distributed ledger technology (DLT) inherent in blockchain creates a decentralized, immutable record of transactions. Each transaction is cryptographically linked to the previous one, making altering past transaction data nearly impossible without detection. Applying blockchain technology to banking processes can enhance security by preventing unauthorized alterations to transaction data. Furthermore, *smart contracts* – self-executing contracts with the terms of the agreement directly written into code – can automate and secure various banking transactions.

Fintech companies heavily employ data encryption to safeguard personal and transaction information. Encryption involves converting information into an unreadable format, decipherable only with the correct decryption key. Advanced encryption algorithms ensure that even if data are intercepted during transmission, they remain unintelligible to unauthorized individuals.

As the realm of personal banking continues its trajectory toward complete digital integration, fintech's role in enhancing banking security becomes increasingly significant. Through advanced authentication mechanisms, AI-powered fraud detection, blockchain technology, and data encryption, fintech is fortifying the defenses of the digital banking landscape.

Leveraging Fintech to Minimize Financial Mistakes and Maximize Savings

Through innovative digital solutions, fintech provides tools to help individuals avoid common financial mistakes and enhance their savings. This section explores how fintech can aid in reducing financial errors and promoting efficient money-saving strategies.

One of fintech's beneficial applications lies in automating financial management. Manual management of finances can lead to errors due to oversight, lack of knowledge, or complexity. Fintech applications can automate many aspects of financial management, including bill payments, budget tracking, and investments. Automatic bill payments, facilitated by most digital banking and budgeting apps, ensure timely payments, thus avoiding late fees and potential damage to credit scores. Automated budgeting tools categorize expenses and monitor spending against budget limits, helping users avoid overspending. Furthermore, robo-advisors can automate investments based on user-defined goals and risk tolerance, mitigating the risk of investment errors due to emotional decision-making or lack of expertise.

A lack of financial literacy often leads to costly financial mistakes. Fintech can help bridge this knowledge gap through educational resources and personalized advice. Many fintech platforms offer interactive learning tools, educational articles, and personalized financial coaching. By increasing financial literacy, these tools empower individuals to make informed financial decisions and avoid common pitfalls.

Real-time monitoring is another significant feature offered by fintech tools. These tools provide up-to-the-minute information on account balances, transactions, and budget status. Consequently, they help users stay on top of their finances and avoid costly errors like overdrafts or exceeding credit limits. Moreover, many fintech apps offer real-time alerts for unusual account activity, potential fraud, or deviations from set budgets. These alerts allow users to take swift corrective action, reducing the risk of financial mistakes.

Aside from minimizing financial errors, fintech provides innovative tools to bolster savings. For example, automatic savings apps like Digit and Qapital analyze users' income and spending patterns to determine an affordable amount to save regularly. Some apps also offer micro-savings features, rounding up the change from purchases and depositing it into a savings account.

Investment apps like Acorns and Robinhood lower the entry barrier for investing, allowing users to grow their savings. These apps provide a straightforward way for individuals to start investing small amounts of money, making saving and investing more accessible.

Effective debt management is another aspect of personal finance where fintech can have a significant impact. Fintech apps like Tally and Payoff are designed to help users manage and pay down debt more efficiently. These platforms offer features such as debt consolidation, personalized payoff plans, and lower interest rates, helping users save money on interest and avoid the common mistake of making minimum-only payments.

Financial Goals With Fintech

Fintech has enhanced an individual's ability to set, track, and achieve personal finance goals by providing various tools and resources. This section explores how fintech can aid individuals in reaching their financial objectives.

Setting personal finance goals is the first step toward achieving financial wellness. Fintech platforms provide user-friendly interfaces and tools to help individuals establish clear and achievable financial goals. For example, apps like Mint and YNAB offer features that enable users to input their financial goals, such as saving for a down payment on a house or paying off student loans.

A critical aspect of personal finance management is budgeting and tracking expenses, another area where fintech shines. Many fintech apps offer budgeting tools that categorize expenses, track spending patterns, and provide real-time updates on budget utilization. For instance, YNAB uses a unique budgeting approach where every dollar is assigned a specific job, helping users control their spending and save more effectively. Conversely, Mint provides a comprehensive view of a user's financial status, including bank accounts, credit cards, bills, and investments, enabling individuals to understand their financial standing and manage their money accordingly.

Lastly, fintech can play a role in improving financial literacy, a key to achieving personal finance goals. Platforms like Khan Academy and NerdWallet offer resources and guides on various personal finance topics, empowering individuals to make informed financial decisions.

Fintech provides many tools and resources to aid individuals in setting, tracking, and achieving their personal finance goals. Through effective budgeting, saving, investing, and financial education, individuals can leverage fintech to navigate their financial journey more effectively.

Fintech 50 Companies and Their Impact on Personal Finance

The FinTech50's annual curated list highlights the most innovative and powerful companies using technology to disrupt and transform the global financial services industry. These companies, characterized by innovative technology, strong market presence, and impactful financial solutions, provide individuals with many tools to manage their finances. This chapter examines some pioneering companies and explores how individuals can leverage their offerings for improved financial management.

Personal Finance Management

The following are different platforms for personal financial management:

- *Mint* is a financial management platform that allows users to aggregate their financial information, including bank accounts, credit cards, loans, and investments. With features like real-time expense tracking, budget creation, and financial goal setting, individuals can gain comprehensive oversight of their financial landscape.
- *Personal Capital* is another robust personal finance platform emphasizing investment tracking and retirement planning. Its retirement planner can

simulate various financial scenarios, allowing users to strategize effectively for their retirement.
- *Zeta* is a fintech company that specializes in helping couples manage their finances. Their app provides tools for tracking individual and joint expenses, creating budgets, and setting financial goals as a couple.

Budgeting and Saving

The following are apps focusing on budgeting and saving:

- *You Need a Budget (YNAB)* takes a proactive approach to budgeting. It is based on giving every dollar a job, thus promoting conscious spending and saving.
- *Digit* is a savings app that uses AI to analyze spending patterns and automatically transfer surplus funds to a savings account. This app helps individuals save without significant lifestyle changes.
- *Qapital* is an app that takes a behavioral approach to personal finance. Users can set up rules for saving, such as rounding up every purchase to the nearest dollar and saving the difference or saving a certain amount whenever they indulge in a guilty pleasure.

Investment and Trading

Many fintech companies offer services involving investment and trading. Here are a few of them.

- *Betterment* and *Wealthfront* are leaders in the robo-advisory market, offering automated, personalized investment management services. Users can set their financial goals, risk tolerance, and timelines, and the platforms create tailored investment portfolios.
- *Robinhood* democratizes stock trading by offering commission-free trades. Its user-friendly interface encourages individuals to invest and become shareholders in their preferred companies.
- *Stash* is an investment platform that allows users to start investing with as little as $5. It provides educational content to help novice investors understand the basics and its features, like fractional shares, making investing more accessible.
- *eToro* is a social trading platform enabling users to follow and copy the trades of successful investors. This feature, called *copy trading*, can be an effective way for novice investors to learn from experienced ones.

Peer-to-Peer Lending and Crowdfunding

P2P lending enables individuals to obtain loans directly from others, cutting out the financial institution as the intermediary. *Crowdfunding* is funding a project or new business venture using small amounts of money from many individuals. The following fintech platforms offer P2P and crowdfunding.

- *LendingClub* and *Prosper* are renowned P2P lending platforms. Individuals can invest by lending money to borrowers for potentially higher returns than traditional savings accounts or borrowing money at competitive interest rates.
- *Kickstarter* and *GoFundMe* are popular crowdfunding platforms. Individuals can raise money for personal projects and causes or support others' initiatives.
- *Funding Circle* is a P2P lending platform focused on small business loans. It enables individuals to invest in small businesses, potentially earning higher returns than traditional savings or investment products.
- *Indiegogo* is a crowdfunding platform that allows individuals to raise funds for innovative products, creative projects, or community causes. It also allows them to contribute to these initiatives.

Cryptocurrencies and Blockchain

Digital currencies and blockchain technology are among the more important innovations in fintech. *Digital currency* exists only in digital or electronic form, operating independently of a central bank. *Blockchain technology* is a distributed database or shared, immutable ledger that facilitates recording transactions and tracking assets. Here are several leaders in this domain.

- *Coinbase* is a prominent cryptocurrency exchange, providing an accessible platform for individuals to buy, sell, and store cryptocurrencies like bitcoin (BTC) and ether (ETH). It also offers educational resources to understand these digital assets.
- *Ripple* provides blockchain-based remittance services. By leveraging the power of blockchain, it allows individuals to send and receive international payments quickly and inexpensively.
- *Binance* is one of the world's largest cryptocurrency exchanges. It offers a wide variety of cryptocurrencies for trading, advanced features for experienced traders, and educational content for those new to crypto.

Insurtech

Insurtech is the innovative use of technology in insurance and a subset of fintech. Examples include the following.

- *Lemonade* is a pioneer in insurtech, providing digitized insurance services, including homeowners' and renters' insurance. It simplifies purchasing insurance, making it more accessible for individuals.
- *Metromile* offers pay-per-mile car insurance, a potentially cost-saving solution for low-mileage drivers. The company uses telematics technology to track mileage and determine premiums.

Digital Banking

Digital banking enables customers to access banking products and services via an electronic/online platform – a website or mobile app. The following are examples of digital banks.

- *Revolut* and *Monzo* are leading the charge in digital banking. These mobile-first banks offer features like instant spending notifications, budgeting tools, and fee-free international spending, offering individuals a new way to bank.
- *N26* is a digital bank offering various financial products, including checking accounts, savings accounts, and personal loans. Real-time notifications, savings goals, and spending statistics give users detailed insight into their finances.
- *Starling Bank* is another digital bank that offers a range of features, including real-time notifications, spending insights, savings goals, and easy international money transfers.

Payment Processing

Payment processing is the series of actions that occur when a business initiates digital payment transactions. These actions include processing credit or debit card transactions, opening secure gateways, and communicating with issuing banks and consumer accounts.

- *Square* offers financial services, including payment processing, point-of-sale software, and business financing. For individuals running small businesses or freelancing, Square can simplify payments and provide valuable business insights.
- *Stripe* provides online payment processing solutions suitable for businesses of all sizes. For individuals running online businesses, Stripe can simplify the process of accepting payments from customers worldwide.

The diversity and innovation of fintech companies are rapidly reshaping the personal finance landscape, democratizing access to financial tools and services previously limited to financial institutions. The FinTech50 companies represent the cutting edge of financial technology, providing innovative solutions for personal finance management. They embody democratizing finance, giving individuals the tools to save, invest, borrow, and manage their finances with newfound efficiency and transparency. Although the previous discussion does not include all FinTech50 companies, it provides a glimpse into the diverse ways in which fintech is transforming personal finance.

Summary and Conclusion

The flourishing fintech sector has brought a profound transformation to personal finance, enabling individuals to gain greater control over their financial lives. Through simplified transactions, personalized investment platforms, P2P lending, and budgeting tools, fintech democratizes access to financial services. It is paving the way for a future where financial wellness and literacy are within everyone's reach, breaking down traditional barriers and reducing inequality. The disruption caused by fintech is nothing short of a financial revolution, making personal finance more accessible, understandable, and tailored to individual needs. As this revolution continues to evolve, one can look forward to witnessing the emergence of even more innovative solutions that further empower individuals to manage their financial futures effectively.

Discussion Questions

- Define fintech.
- Identify advantages of fintech.
- Suggest how fintech can serve the underbanked and raise financial inclusion.
- Identify how fintech may help reduce personal financial mistakes.
- Explain multi-factor authentication (MFA) and how it raises security in personal banking.

References

Agarwal, S., Alok, S., Ghosh, P., & Gupta, S. (2021). *Financial inclusion and alternate cedit scoring for the millennials: Role of big data and machine learning in fintech.* Indian School of Business. https://papers.ssrn.com/sol3/papers.cfm?abstract_id=3507827

Agarwal, S., & Chua, Y. H. (2020). FinTech and household finance: A review of the empirical literature. *China Finance Review International*, *10*(4), 361–376.

Agarwal, S., Qian, W., Ren, Y., Tsai, H.-T., & Yeung, B. Y. (2022). The real impact of FinTech: Evidence from mobile payment technology. https://papers.ssrn.com/sol3/papers.cfm?abstract_id=3556340

Bachas, P., Gertler, P., Higgins, S., & Seira, E. (2018). Digital financial services go a long way: Transaction costs and financial inclusion. *American Economic Association Papers and Proceedings*, *108*, 444–448.

Berg, T., Burg, V., Gombovic, A., & Puri, M. (2020). On the rise of the FinTechs: Credit scoring using digital footprints. *Review of Financial Studies*, *33*(7), 2845–2897.

Brainard, L. (2016). *Conference on financial innovation at the Board of Governors of the Federal Reserve System*. The Opportunities and Challenges of Fintech.

Buchak, G., Matvos, G., Piskorski, T., & Seru, A. (2018). Fintech, regulatory arbitrage, and the rise of shadow banks. *Journal of Financial Economics*, *130*(3), 453–483.

Demirguc-Kunt, A., Klapper, L., Singer, D., Ansar, S., & Hess, J. (2020). The global findex database 2017: Measuring financial inclusion and opportunities to expand access to and use of financial services. *The World Bank Economic Review*, *4*(Suppl. 1), S2–S8.

French, K. R. (2008). Presidential address: The cost of active investing. *The Journal of Finance*, *63*(4), 1537–1573.

Fuster, A., Plosser, M., Schnabl, P., & Vickery, J. (2019). The role of technology in mortgage lending. *Review of Financial Studies*, *32*(5), 1854–1899.

Gennaioli, N., Shleifer, A., & Vishny, R. (2015). Money doctors. *The Journal of Finance*, *70*(1), 91–114.

Higgins, S. (2022). *Financial technology adoption: Network externalities of cashless payments in Mexico*. Northwestern University.

IBM. (n.d.). What are smart contracts on blockchain. https://www.ibm.com/topics/smart-contracts

Jensen, M. C. (1968). The performance of mutual funds in the period 1945–1964. *The Journal of Finance*, *23*(2), 389–416.

Lagna, A., & Ravishankar, M. N. (2022). Making the world a better place with fintech research. *Information Systems Journal*, *32*(1), 61–102.

Nakamoto, S. (2008). Bitcoin: A peer-to-peer electronic cash system. https://bitcoin.org/bitcoin.pdf

Philippon, T. (2015). Has the US finance industry become less efficient? On the theory and measurement of financial intermediation. *The American Economic Review*, *105*(4), 1408–1438.

Rossi, A. G., & Utkus, S. P. (2021). Who benefits from robo-advising? *Evidence from Machine Learning*. https://papers.ssrn.com/sol3/papers.cfm?abstract_id=3552671

Schueffel, P. (2017). Taming the beast: A scientific definition of fintech. *Journal of Innovation Management*, *4*(4), 32–54.

Thakor, A. V. (1999). Information technology and financial services consolidation. *Journal of Banking & Finance*, *23*(2–4), 697–700.

Section V

Emerging Innovations: Blockchain and Cryptocurrencies

Chapter 14

Blockchain in Fintech: A Catalyst for Disrupting the Financial World*

Halil Kiymaz[a] *and Carlos Humberto Munoz Valdez*[b]

[a]Rollins College, USA
[b]IPADE Business School, Mexico

Abstract

Blockchain technology and its applications have recently received the attention of practitioners and academics. Visualizing the full impact these technologies will have on the world is challenging since their adoption is still in the early stages. This chapter explores how blockchain can disrupt the general business and financial world. Blockchain offers information transparency, live data synchronization, and immutable records that prevent fraud. Digital contracts and digital asset management may heavily depend on the development of blockchain and the adoption of smart contracts. Smart contracts can execute financial transactions automatically and enforce all parties' obligations without needing an intermediary and its cost. They can increase speed and simplify processes, reducing licensing ticketing costs and overhead charges. Blockchain also offers technology adoption solutions, like fair payment, cloud storage, smart contracts for financial assets, and international transactions with bilateral double taxation. It has further facilitated the creation of decentralized finance.

Keywords: Fintech; blockchain; smart contracts; technology adoption; immutable records

Introduction

Cryptocurrencies and blockchain technology have been among the most interesting developments in recent years. Major accounting firms, the Big 4

This chapter was developed in parallel, used material from, and cited in Valdez and Humberto (2023).

The Emerald Handbook of Fintech, 251–265

Published under exclusive licence by Emerald Publishing Limited
doi:10.1108/978-1-83753-608-520241032

(Deloitte, Ernst & Young [EY], PricewaterhouseCoopers [PwC], and Klynveld Peat Marwick Goerdeler [KPMG]), are working and developing applications using blockchain technology and promoting its acceptance (Atik & Kelten, 2021). Visualizing the full impact these technologies will bring on the world is difficult since their adoption is still in the early stages. That is why there is increasing interest from practitioners and academics to understand better the possibilities and applications of these technologies. Central banks, technology, and financial companies are in the vanguard of researching the advantages and disadvantages of applying blockchain technology and its potential (Kapadia, 2020).

Cryptocurrencies rely on blockchain to keep track of all transactions and ownership to preserve the system's integrity. This technology has promising applications beyond cryptocurrencies and is also the driver behind web 3.0. In Web3, "...data are interoperable, decentralized, and controlled by individual users rather than centralized companies..." (Harvey et al., 2022, p. 6). Although blockchain might be an appealing technology for businesses, companies are still working to figure out how to take advantage of it and address security risks to protect the information stored in a blockchain. Companies must address these two challenges before massive adoption of blockchain technology occurs.

The rest of the chapter has the following structure. The next section defines blockchain technology, followed by a discussion on how blockchain works. The following section explains how blockchain applications can disrupt business, including a debate about smart contracts, financial sector applications, triple-entry accounting, real estate, and supply chain applications. The next section discusses blockchain's disadvantages and risks, followed by blockchain adoption. The chapter concludes with a discussion of R3 Corda and a summary.

What Is Blockchain?

Kapadia (2020) defines blockchain as an incorruptible digital ledger of economic transactions that can be programmed to record financial transactions and virtually everything of value. A blockchain is a secure distributed database that preserves ordered lists of records, known as *blocks*, which cannot be changed. Among blockchain's characteristics are security, a shared database, and records kept in chronological order registered in linked blocks, creating a data chain. Blockchain also offers information transparency, live data synchronization, and immutable records that prevent fraud. The blockchain design does not allow retroactively altered records, so it is an immutable system and temper resistance technology (Chong et al., 2019). Blockchain is also known as the next-generation internet. Trivedi et al. (2021) claim blockchain will impact the economy and individual interactions. The World Economic Forum (WEF) estimates that by 2025, 10% of the world's gross domestic product (GDP) will be associated with blockchain platforms (Chong et al., 2019). Blockchain offers transparency, verifiability, and immutability to commercial transactions. It also provides security and resilience, individual data protection, and promotes cooperation among participants.

As a developing technology, blockchain may revolutionize how digital operations are registered, retrieved, and shared. It operates as a decentralized peer-to-peer (P2P) transaction ledger without third-party intermediaries. It is considered an anonymous, secure, transparent, efficient, and traceable system. *Anonymity* refers to how the sending and receiving parties are unidentifiable, and *transparency* denotes the possibility for anyone to track all transactions stored in the blocks. Some describe blockchain as a "trustless" technology because it replaces trust in a particular party with trust in the consensus algorithms and the system's code (Kostić & Sedej, 2022).

Blockchain is a distributed ledger without a third party that verifies and registers information in that ledger. As Chong et al. (2019, p. 1309) note, "Blockchain resembles a fully distributed, decentralized system that captures and stores an immutable chronological log of every transaction among actors on its peer-to-peer network." Blockchain is coded to promote the active participation of actors to add computational power to the verification and recording of information. This process guarantees the integrity of the transactional data in an immutable and transparent manner.

Blockchain is a technology used by distributed ledger technologies (DLT). Storing records of transactions and activities has been a common need since the origins of human history, but how individuals and institutions do it has dramatically changed recently. There are three categories of blockchains based on control and access permissions: public, private, and consortium. All members have access, share information, and control the blockchain publicly. In a private blockchain, a third-party grants permission and has some degree of centralization. Parties participating in the consensus algorithms govern consortium cases (Atik & Kelten, 2021). In the case of private and consortium, both blockchains require some degree of trust (Kostić & Sedej, 2022). For example, bitcoin, the first cryptocurrency, relies on blockchain technology, an open distributed ledger that records transactions. Blockchain solves the double spending problem without an authority or third-party intervening. It also provides increased record capacity, higher security, and improved processing time for settlement (Creed & Northard, 2021).

Several studies (Allayannis & Fernstrom, 2017; Meiklejohn & Cary, 2018) report the blockchain's advantages over legacy technologies as follows.

- *Consistent.* All users keep the same copy of information across the ledger.
- *Democratic.* All participants agree on the rules to manage the network.
- *Resilient.* Information is still accessible, even when many peers go offline.
- *Secure and accurate.* Digital keys and signatures relying on cryptography protect information integrity. They are easy to set and almost impossible to undo.
- *Segmented and private.* Users can customize the access levels within the network.

- *Permanent and tamper resistant.* Historical records cannot be changed without the complete agreement of all network members.
- *Quickly updated.* New transactions are recorded on the network almost in real time.
- *Intelligent.* Users can program event-triggered transactions with smart contracts.
- *Verifiable.* Anyone can review if transactions comply with the system rules.

How Blockchain Works

Blockchains have a genesis block that has no previous link to another block. Once a block is full, it connects to a new block using a hash value that identifies the connection and sequence among different blocks (Atik & Kelten, 2021). Users who want to connect to a specific blockchain use nodes or connected computing devices. Every new block must be approved or rejected by other nodes. Users are regulated by *consensus algorithms*, agreements that state the rights of the blockchain users. As examples of consensus algorithms include proof of work, proof of stake, delegated proof of stake, proof of elapsed time, practical Byzantine fault tolerance, delegated Byzantine fault tolerance, proof of weight, proof of burn, proof of capacity, proof of importance, proof of activity, and directed acyclic graphs (Atik & Kelten, 2021). Each algorithm has different levels of security, decentralization, difficulty, and participation, requiring different energy levels.

Proof of work (POW) is a consensus mechanism used for bitcoin and is the earliest verification method. It depends on computer power to confirm a transaction and add it to the most recent "block" of data in the "chain" (Folkinshteyn & Lennon, 2016). Computer power solves mathematical problems involving a hash of the operations waiting to be included in the blockchain and an additional number called a "nonce," connecting with the previous block's hash. It is an iterative process in which computers try to find the right number. This process is designed to consume time, hence the proof of work definition. This time-consuming process is a barrier to modifying and rewriting historical records, not only because of the time required to do it but also because of the complexity of correctly connecting with the hash of the previous work. A corrupt participant in the system must control at least 51% of its computing power to surpass the remaining nodes' processing capacity and modify historical information. This situation is a *51% attack*, also known as a *majority attack* (Coyne & McMickle, 2017). The set of transactions that will have the highest probability of solving the mathematical puzzle first is the one that attracts more computer power to work on it.

Ethereum uses *proof of stake* (POS), another common consensus mechanism. Instead of computer power, POS requires confirming stake positions in the blockchain (number of Ether for Ethereum). The position's size is directly proportional to the voting power to validate transactions (Folkinshteyn & Lennon, 2016). This characteristic makes POS less resource-demanding than POW. Some criticize its computer power use due to its environmental side effects. The higher a participant's stake in the system, the higher the participant's incentive to preserve the data's integrity. Participants registering invalid transactions might receive a fine against their position (Coyne & McMickle, 2017).

Mining is part of creating new blocks. It is resource-intensive, and its complexity makes fraudulent transactions difficult to execute. Once a new block is accepted, the information is shared among all nodes to include the latest block in the current chain. Every new accepted block contains a *hash*, a unique digital fingerprint, of the preceding block (Creed & Northard, 2021).

How Blockchain Disrupts the Financial World

Many industries use blockchain technology beyond cryptocurrencies and financial activities. Its P2P technology has improved internet security (Creed & Northard, 2021). For example, as Atik and Kelten (2021, p. 499) note, it can be used in "supply chain management, voting in elections, healthcare records management, identity management systems, access control systems, decentralized notary and tourism organizations." Integrating blockchain technology in supply chain processes can provide accurate and complete information for sustainable reports. Other services take advantage of the blockchain's permanent nature to not erase documents, issue and transfer licenses or digital art, enable faster post-trade settlement of securities, and provide secure communications and verify website certifications (Meiklejohn & Cary, 2018).

Blockchain can also verify pharmaceutical supply chains and the authenticity of drugs and facilitate and monitor the exchange of medical records among physicians and hospitals. In finance, blockchain can support transactions requiring security, trust, and consensus. Different uses include storing medical insurance information, healthcare data like medical records, diagnosis certificates, and patient-owned medical apps (Liang et al., 2021). Other studies report different blockchain applications. For example, Yang and Hwang (2020, p. 2) offer the following examples: "*e*-government, food supply information security, energy systems, sharing economy, health care, education, online education, intellectual property management, banking, personal identity, asset ownership, supply chains, and the prevention of unethical business transaction." Pestunov (2020) examines how governments use blockchain technology to create national currencies.

Smart Contracts

Buterin (2014) published a White paper representing a milestone in the practical use of cryptocurrencies. Referring to Nakamoto (2008)'s grand experiment, this paper highlights the concept of a proof-of-work-based blockchain, facilitating consensus on the chronological order of transactions. It also proposed one of the most important characteristics of Ethereum, the ability to create smart contracts using programming, contracts that automatically reallocate digital assets depending on pre-specified parameters (Buterin, 2014).

Blockchain allows independent parties to create, manage, synchronize, and update common share records. It also supports decentralized data management and enforcement using algorithms with a smart contract. A *smart contract* is

> a means by which obligations can be recorded, triggering other obligations that can be set up to operate in an automated way. Benefits stemming from Blockchain's distributed data management, consensus mechanisms, and automated execution through smart contracts are viable primarily for transactions that can be handled exclusively through blockchain, but also for highly standardized, verifiable, and codifiable transactions.
>
> Kostić and Sedej (2022, p. 125)

Smart contracts are a set of covenants programmed into a blockchain's code. They trigger executing these covenants when predefined conditions are met. This execution is automatic and deterministic, always leading to the same result. Blockchain's immutability feature safeguards a contract's terms against manipulation or alteration. A smart contract can also store a digital asset before the exchange, for example, withhold payment to a vendor after the customer has confirmed full reception and under the agreed conditions. In this case, shipment is not released until the blockchain's customer first transfers the funds. The future of digital contracts and digital asset management may heavily depend on blockchain development and smart contracts adoption (Coyne & McMickle, 2017). Smart contracts technology is safe and transparent. Additionally, cryptography protects information, and coded processes run automatically (Rijanto, 2021).

Smart contracts are one of the most promising uses of blockchain technology. They can execute financial transactions automatically. Smart contracts enforce all parties' obligations without an intermediary and its cost. They can increase speed and simplify processes, reducing licensing ticketing costs and overhead charges. At the same time, data integrity during transmission is protected, and transactions are only executed after meeting programmed conditions. All parties involved in the transaction can access recorded information, dramatically reducing the possibility of error (Kapadia, 2020). A fascinating application would be supply chain finance where smart contracts could decrease manual operational risks. When the parties share contractual information on a distributed, not centralized, ledger, and with access to the bank, customer, and supplier, payments can be processed with specific times and conditions programmed in smart contracts.

Several organizations are considering the application of smart contracts. For example, an individual can create a smart contract to manage a will imprinted in the blockchain's code. The contract automatically transfers all the testator's money and assets to the beneficiary when the person dies. Additionally, the testator can include limits or conditions like triggering the contract when the beneficiary reaches a certain age (Trivedi et al., 2021).

Financial Sector

Blockchain offers meaningful financial solutions, like fair payment, cloud storage, smart contracts for financial assets, and international transactions with bilateral double taxation (Liang et al., 2021). Table 14.1 compares legacy banking and internet finance systems, showing blockchain banking offers advantages.

Table 14.1. A Comparison of Legacy Versus Blockchain-Based Banking.

Legacy Banking	**Parameter**	**Blockchain-Based Banking**
Undifferentiated and limited	Customer experience	Personalized and superior
Sluggish, complex clearing protocols with multiple processes	Efficiency	Direct transmission, distributed ledger, and a streamlined process
High, with several manual tasks and participants	Cost	Low, automated, and a disintermediated process
Poor, centralized data (one point of attack), and data leaking potential	Security	Higher level, immutable records, asymmetric encryption, and user's data are more difficult to hack

Source: Inspired by Guo and Chen (2016).

Note: This table compares legacy banking with blockchain-based banking concerning customer experience, efficiency, cost, and security.

Blockchain has facilitated the creation of decentralized finance (DeFi). Trust, visibility, digital operation, multi-user platforms, and others are blockchain characteristics supporting DeFi's development. Blockchain reduces the risk of a central point vulnerability when relying on a third party for validation is unnecessary. Also, a one-direction hashing technique protects the information sent on the platform, and relevant stakeholders scrutinize all transactions (Trivedi et al., 2021).

Another advantage of blockchain for financial institutions is fraud reduction. Compared to more hackable and vulnerable centralized databases, there is no chance of an individual point of failure in blockchain due to its distributed nature. Using cryptography enables protecting and saving transactions. Also, using private keys and smart cards help to prevent fraud. Regarding knowing your customer (KYC) policies, blockchain automates opening new accounts and sharing documents with all parties using a single source identification. These advantages eliminate the cost and protect the privacy of customers' information. Blockchain can record policies free of errors and link them with claims in the insurance field. It can also reduce fraud by tracing asset ownership like real estate and vehicles.

Additionally, blockchain can improve risk modeling, validating information across sources (Kapadia, 2020). Insurance companies are investing in improving their understanding of blockchain's uses in their sector. Blockchain could improve several operations like detecting fraud, acquiring new clients, and expanding to different fields (Trivedi et al., 2021).

Correct blockchain implementation in the financial system will eliminate manually processed tasks and the need for a third party to verify transactions. Blockchain automatically enforces covenants embedded in a smart contract code, like debt amortization and tax payments, in real time and error-free (Lee et al., 2019).

An exciting example of blockchain implementation in the banking system is occurring in India. The Reserve Bank of India, State Bank of India, and Axis Bank are analyzing blockchain technology's deployment to serve their customers faster, with higher transparency and stronger protection protocols (Poonam et al., 2021). Blockchain implementation will also support compliance responsibilities like KYC and prevent financing illicit activities and money laundering. Blockchain is useful for tracking transactions and identifying users for effective audits, protecting the confidentiality and integrity of information at lower processing costs.

Credit information in current databases is inefficient, limited, and offers low-quality data to define a customer's real credit capacity. Privacy restrictions may complicate sharing this information with other financial institutions, and blockchain is a promising solution. Another advantage of blockchain technology is information privacy. However, trust is challenging because users trust financial institutions much more than distributed ledgers (Kapadia, 2020). Using private keys as part of cryptography is another reason for adopting blockchain technology, a characteristic that improves security.

Triple-Entry Accounting

Applying blockchain has the potential to disrupt the role of accountants and auditors alike, with a shared accounting record that could transform the use of accounting, with a system that does not require trust and that not only records information but also dynamically settles and orders it (Pascual Pedreño et al., 2021). Triple-entry accounting works as follows. When a transaction happens, users sign it digitally; transactions are visible to all users in the operation. The system seals this operation, known as the third entry. This last seal is the *proof of transaction*, the proof given by the network of nodes to a direct connection between the two users involved. This process eliminates the need for reconciliation because all parties update their records in real time. The revolutionary characteristic of blockchain applied to accounting is that the authenticity of transactions no longer depends on the control of the parties involved or external auditors but on the network itself.

Atik and Kelten (2021) contend that blockchain technology will highly affect accounting. Operations like billing, documenting, treating, registering, bookkeeping, budgeting, and reconciliation might be done automatically by this technology. The Institute of Chartered Accountants in England and Wales (ICAEW) views blockchain as an accounting technology focusing on asset ownership transfer and keeping an accurate record of information in ledgers (Kostić & Sedej, 2022).

Blockchain has emerged as a technology to replace traditional ledgers. Some authors call it the future of accounting and information storage (Coyne & McMickle, 2017). Open systems like Bitcoin and Ethereum have the disadvantage that anyone can access the information in the network, an idea that most companies are reluctant to accept. But developing private blockchains with additional controls is more attractive than accounting ledgers. Private blockchains add privacy and permissioned access. *Privacy* refers to the fact that a private blockchain is limited to the agents involved in the operation. *Permissioned access* concerns how much information a user can get, a need-to-know basis filter, and the network's system administrators manage this access.

The current accounting system is time-consuming, expensive, and exposed to human error. It offers accuracy and verifiability but also depends on auditors to serve this purpose. Blockchain integrates the verification process of information recording, saving time and re-work efforts when the traditional system detects a mistake (Woodside et al., 2017).

Triple-entry accounting can improve audit processes and lower costs because of the speed and reduced cost of keeping and reconciling ledgers. Blockchain technology can act as a "neutral intermediary" to deliver more reliable financial statements (Kostić & Sedej, 2022). Keeping transactions in an independent and verifiable system can help companies keep validated journal entries in a triple-entry system (Atik & Kelten, 2021). Also, managers can use smart controls or smart contracts to control the program's business processes, programming rules, and conditions. This new approach may replace the double-entry system; software like Request Network, Balanc3, Ledgerium, and Pacio are examples of systems based on triple-entry accounting. The Big 4 auditing companies are actively developing their blockchain platform; Deloitte launched Rubix, EY has its project Libra, PWC is focusing on the energy sector to launch its blockchain solution, and KPMG is offering a joint solution with Microsoft for its clients (Pascual Pedreño et al., 2021). Blockchain DLT offers records immutability and traceability and delivers a consensus view of all the parties involved. It will improve the reliability and quality of financial statements, transforming financial reporting activities from a business-centric to an exchange-centric scheme.

Real Estate

Commercial real estate could have several advantages of tokenization. A *token* is a "blockchain-based digital representation of an asset" (Smith et al., 2019, p. 7). A common approach is to tokenize portions of shares in a trust or special purpose vehicle (SPV) that owns a real estate asset on its books. Tokenization improves transparency, and transactions can be programmed to be executed in real time, like payments or voting. From an investment portfolio perspective, investors can diversify their investments in real estate and customize them depending on their risk appetite and preferences by acquiring property-specific tokens.

Another solution that blockchain offers to commercial real estate is liquidity. Property is an illiquid asset by nature, and the dollar amount for acquisitions is out of reach for many retail investors. Tokenization fragments the initial investment for this asset. It allows the creation of a secondary market of tokens that will open new investment opportunities to retail investors (Smith et al., 2019). Tokenization will also facilitate due diligence processes and prevent information asymmetry between sellers and buyers since all asset information, like maintenance, taxes, and occupancy rates can be registered.

Supply Chain

Maritime shipping documentation is burdensome and provided by participants from various countries and under different legal obligations. This situation makes delivering products from the origin to the destination slow and complex. It has become an incentive for companies in this industry to look for solutions to improve the information and documentation process with the challenge of keeping it cost-effective. Blockchain has the potential to solve this problem by digitalizing records, providing real-time tracking of shipments, optimizing customs clearance time, and increasing visibility while reducing risks and costs (Yang, 2019).

Smart contracts are important in linking and confirming transactions to authorize payments. For example, once proof of delivery is issued, this can trigger a settlement between the banks of each party. Currently, intermediaries must match registers of buyers and sellers and confirm that all parties are satisfied with the terms and delivery specifications to transfer resources to settle the payment. Although blockchain can accelerate this process, only large trade groups supported by financial institutions and authorities can access this solution (Rijanto, 2021).

Blockchain Disadvantages

As an emerging technology, blockchain has some areas of opportunity: storage and execution costs, its intensive use of electricity, and the side effect of global warming, security issues, and cybercrime. Blockchain technology is still expensive, and its hardware requires large amounts of energy (Atik & Kelten, 2021). From an operational perspective, the speed of blockchain is growing, creating increased traffic. Access to blockchain platforms is becoming more congested as adoption accelerates. Addressing the need to develop more capacity is critical (Kapadia, 2020).

One particularly sensitive issue is the carbon footprint that blockchain technology adds to the environment. When countries struggle to agree on what to do with the global warming problem, blockchain has a long way to go to participate in a greener economy. Solving this problem is critical for the technology's massive adoption (Kapadia, 2020).

Another challenge for blockchain is the regulatory framework. In most countries, how to handle conflict, fraud, terrorism financing, and cybercrime involving blockchain is unclear (Atik & Kelten, 2021). Although blockchain technology is promising for the banking industry, its vulnerabilities could limit its application, especially in more sophisticated markets like Western Europe and the United States. Blockchain requires proper monitoring of international standards (Kapadia, 2020). All efforts in this direction will accelerate the adoption of blockchain technology.

The current configuration of blockchain platforms makes them inefficient compared to other payment systems like Visa or Mastercard. The time needed to validate a transaction represents an important disadvantage for massive adoption. Eventually, the information's size and technology's storage capacity will critically limit its expansion. For example, a single network node requires more than 170 gigabytes of capacity (Liang et al., 2021). Some other challenges that blockchain technology faces are hard forks, compatibility among different chains, and security issues like a 51% attack. A *hard fork* branches a cryptocurrency's blockchain, splitting a single cryptocurrency into two (CFI Team, 2023).

Regardless of the potential benefits of blockchain technology implementation, it still faces many hurdles for massive adoption. In accounting, for example, public blockchains are against the need for confidentiality of information, the limitation to alter historical data, and restricted transaction verification. According to some authors, these characteristics make blockchain undesirable for business accounting (Coyne & McMickle, 2017). Other challenges are cost, efficiency, regulation, security, and system scalability. As a reference, using Ethereum costs twice as much as available cloud services supported by Amazon Simple Workflow Service (Amazon SWF) (Poonam et al., 2021).

In sectors like supply chains, blockchain is in an early stage, where implementation costs and technical complexity are major barriers to its expansion. Problems like integration with information technology (IT) legacy systems, scalability, regulation, and a major investment in the required computer power prevent blockchain from gaining momentum (Rijanto, 2021). Few start-ups implement blockchain on a sizable scale. Despite the interest in applying blockchain to fix market inefficiencies and reduce costs and delays, the technology's early stage implies a long way to go before blockchain becomes a standard in the business world. Blockchain continues its experimentation and improvement phase to explode its full potential eventually (Yang, 2019).

Blockchain Adoption

Blockchain technology is so different from the financial system's current infrastructure that even complying with regulatory obligations represents a limitation to its implementation. Blockchain adoption is like "... the development of transmission control protocol/Internet protocol (TCP/IP), which revolutionized computer networking, but took many years since its initial introduction in 1972 to gain widespread acceptance" (Lee et al., 2019, p. 3).

As an emerging technology, blockchain must mature before massive user adoption occurs. It also requires building access, operation, and performance capacity to support more business processes. Managers can visualize blockchain technology's potential but are cautiously adopting it until they understand if it makes sense for their business model (Liang et al., 2021). Blockchain is a groundbreaking technology but lacks widespread use. It also requires a substantial investment, representing a risk, like every investment in new technology. Few experts are in the field, and limited companies have absorbed blockchain in their daily operations (Liang et al., 2021). A common issue in adopting new technologies like blockchain is security, and the possibility of a cyberattack or any other unknown threat is a limitation for further implementation (Trivedi et al., 2021).

Although blockchain continues in an experimental phase, it shows some signs of a relatively mature technology. Allowing independent parties that do not necessarily trust each other to do business with transparency and reliable records with additional supervision is one of the most distinctive qualities of adopting blockchain technology (Kostić & Sedej, 2022). However, this interest does not exempt companies from uncertainties from financial, technical, and operational perspectives.

Despite the trustless attribution of blockchains, relying on consensus rules and the system's underlying code demands a certain level of trust. Additionally, permissioned blockchains require trust in a "gatekeeper" who manages the platform and the rest of the system's participants. According to Kostić and Sedej (2022, p. 127), "... some level of familiarity and ex-ante trust needs to be established between partners." Also, collaboration among parties becomes critical for successfully adopting blockchain technology since it is a multi-party system that creates interdependence and follows a sequence of user interactions. Finally, once users adopt blockchain technology, it will dramatically affect how companies organize information and activities to exploit the technology's characteristics fully.

Blockchain has evolved through three different stages. The first generation was bitcoin as a cryptocurrency, and the second generation evolved beyond monetary transactions to smart contracts and blockchain-supported services. The world is beginning the third generation of adopting blockchain as a universal platform for research, healthcare, entertainment, government, and bookkeeping. Blockchain adoption may have huge implications for sensitive topics like democracy. Blockchain could be used to vote, save the results, and make the information more visible to the public (Trivedi et al., 2021).

Business Case: R3 Corda

Various cases of companies working to capitalize on the advantages of blockchain technology are available. One example is the system Corda designed by the company R3. R3 brought together a group of companies from the financial and technological sectors to develop a blockchain solution considering the regulatory burden that applies to the financial sector. Corda's goal is to improve the operating infrastructure of banks that is costly and with processes that require a higher level of automation, leading to billions of dollars of savings (Woodside et al., 2017). In 2018, the Corda system successfully supported a letter of credit operation for exporting soybeans to Malaysia from Argentina (Rijanto, 2021).

According to R3, Corda is a distributed ledger software intended to enforce agreements coded in smart contracts and to store transaction data with legally binding obligations in a permissioned network. The system brings together agents that trust each other to do business but not enough to let counterparties keep all recorded information (Brown, 2018). In 2016, R3 decided to make Corda an open-source software to facilitate a higher level of adoption through convenience and flexibility.

Summary and Conclusion

Cryptocurrencies and blockchain technology have been among the fascinating developments in recent years. Many businesses are working to develop applications using blockchain technology and promoting its acceptance across many industries. Visualizing the full impact these technologies will bring on the world is difficult because their adoption is still in the early stages. That is why practitioners and academics show increasing interest in improving their understanding of these technologies' possibilities and applications.

This chapter explores how blockchain can disrupt the general business and financial world. Among blockchain's characteristics are security, a shared database, keeping records in chronological order registered in linked blocks, and creating a data chain. Blockchain also offers information transparency, live synchronization of data, and immutable records that prevent fraud. Blockchain provides transparency, verifiability, and immutability to commercial transactions. It also offers security and resilience, individual data protection, and promotes cooperation among participants. Blockchain technology applies to cryptocurrencies and financial activities. For example, smart contracts and decentralized application platforms represent a milestone in the practical use of cryptocurrencies. The future of digital contracts and digital asset management may heavily depend on blockchain development and smart contracts adoption. Smart contracts can execute financial transactions automatically. They enforce all parties' obligations without needing an intermediary. Smart contracts can increase speed and simplify processes, reducing licensing ticketing costs and overhead charges.

Blockchain also offers such finance solutions as fair payment, cloud storage, smart contracts for financial assets, and international transactions with bilateral double taxation. It has facilitated the creation of DeFi. Trust, visibility, digital operation, and multi-user platforms are blockchain characteristics supporting DeFi. Blockchain reduces the risk of central point vulnerability when no third-party validation is required.

Adopting blockchain technology in the business and financial world is in its early stage. Yet, indications show that it can provide immense benefits in improving the efficiency and security of financial transactions.

Discussion Questions

- Define blockchain.
- Identify some blockchain advantages.
- List some blockchain applications in the business world.
- Identify major obstacles to the widespread adoption of blockchain technology.

References

Allayannis, G., & Fernstrom, A. (2017, October 3). *An introduction to blockchain*. Darden Business Publishing. Technical Note F-1810.

Atik, A., & Kelten, G. S. (2021). Blockchain technology and its potential effects on accounting: A systematic literature review. *Istanbul Business Research*, *50*(2), 495–515.

Brown, R. G. (2018, May). *The Corda platform: An introduction*. White paper.

Buterin, V. (2014). *Ethereum: A next-generation smart contract and decentralized application platform*. White paper.

CFI Team. (2023). *Hard forks*. Computer Finance Institute. https://corporatefinanceinstitute.com/resources/cryptocurrency/hard-fork/

Chong, A. Y. L., Lim, E. T. K., Hua, X., Zheng, S., & Tan, C.-W. (2019). Business on chain: A comparative case study of five blockchain-inspired business models. *Journal of the Association for Information Systems*, *20*(9), 1308–1337.

Coyne, J. G., & McMickle, P. L. (2017). Can blockchains serve an accounting purpose? *Journal of Emerging Technologies in Accounting*, *14*(2), 101–111.

Creed, R. R., & Northard, A. (2021). The role of blockchain technology in cryptocurrencies. *Journal of New Business Ideas & Trends*, *19*(3), 8–13.

Folkinshteyn, D., & Lennon, M. (2016). Braving bitcoin: A technology acceptance model (TAM) analysis. *Journal of Information Technology Case and Application Research*, *18*(4), 220–249.

Guo, Ye, & Chen, L. (2016). Blockchain application and outlook in the banking industry. *Financial Innovation*, *2*(24), 1–12.

Harvey, C. R., Abou Zeid, T., Draaisma, T., Luk, M., Henry, N., Rzym, A., & van Hemert, O. (2022). An investor's guide to crypto. http://doi.org/10.2139/ssrn.4124576

Kapadia, J. M. (2020). Blockchain technology: Application in the financial industry. *Scholedge International Journal of Management & Development*, *7*(8), 130–135.

Kostić, N., & Sedej, T. (2022). Blockchain technology, inter-organizational relationships, and management accounting: A synthesis and a research agenda. *Accounting Horizons*, *36*(2), 123–141.

Lee, C. C., Kriscenski, J. C., & Lim, H. S. (2019). An empirical study of behavioral intention to use blockchain technology. *Journal of International Business Disciplines*, *14*(1), 1–21.

Liang, T.-P., Kohli, R., Huang, H.-C., & Li, Z.-L. (2021). What drives the adoption of the blockchain technology? A fit-viability perspective. *Journal of Management Information Systems*, *38*(2), 314–337.

Meiklejohn, S., & Cary, N. (2018). Introduction. In W. Bob & C. Nicholas (Eds.), *The future is decentralized* (pp. 4–8). United Nations Development.

Nakamoto, S. (2008). *Bitcoin: A peer-to-peer electronic cash system*. White paper. https://bitcoin.org/bitcoin.pdf

Pascual Pedreño, E., Vera, G., & Pascual Nebreda, L. (2021). Blockchain and its application to accounting. *Intangible Capital*, *17*(1), 1–16.

Pestunov, A. I. (2020). Cryptocurrencies and blockchain: Potential applications in government and business. *Problems of Economic Transition*, *62*(4–6), 286–297.

Poonam, G., Gupta, B., Chauhan, A. K., Sivarajah, U., Gupta, S., & Modgil, S. (2021). Measuring the perceived benefits of implementing blockchain technology in the banking sector. *Technological Forecasting and Social Change*, *163*(February), 120407.

Rijanto, A. (2021). Blockchain technology adoption in supply chain finance. *Journal of Theoretical and Applied Electronic Commerce Research*, *16*(7), 3078–3098.

Smith, J., Vora, M., Benedetti, H., Yoshida, K., & Vogel, Z. (2019). *Tokenized securities & commercial real estate* (Vol. 46). MIT Digital Currency Initiative.

Trivedi, S., Mehta, K., & Sharma, R. (2021). Systematic literature review on application of blockchain technology in E-finance and financial services. *Journal of Technology Management and Innovation*, *16*(3), 88–100.

Valdez, M., & Humberto, C. (2023). *Blockchain adoption and the volatility of Bitcoin and Ethereum* (Vol. 50). Dissertations from the Executive Doctorate in Business Administration Program. https://scholarship.rollins.edu/dba_dissertations/50.

Woodside, J. M., Augustine, F. K., Jr., & Giberson, W. (2017). Blockchain technology adoption status and strategies. *Journal of International Technology & Information Management*, *26*(2), 65–93.

Yang, C.-S. (2019). Maritime shipping digitalization: Blockchain-based technology applications, future improvements, and intention to use. *Transportation Research Part E: Logistics and Transportation Review*, *131*(November), 108–117.

Yang, Y.-J., & Hwang, J.-C. (2020). Recent development trend of blockchain technologies: A patent analysis. *International Journal of Electronic Commerce Studies*, *11*(1), 1–12.

Chapter 15

Cryptoassets and Fintech

Hugo Benedetti[a] *and Sean Stein Smith*[b]

[a]Universidad de Los Andes, Chile
[b]City University of New York, USA

Abstract

Cryptoassets are a diverse category of digital assets that rely on blockchain technology. They encompass various categories, such as cryptocurrencies, utility tokens, security tokens, tokenized assets and securities, and stablecoins. Cryptocurrencies are decentralized digital units of value that enable secure and transparent transactions. Utility tokens provide access to specific services or products within a blockchain network. Security tokens offer rights and entitlements similar to traditional securities, representing ownership in real-world assets or participation in investment opportunities. Tokenized assets and securities are digital representations of tangible or intangible assets, allowing for fractional ownership and enhanced liquidity. Stablecoins are blockchain-based digital assets designed to maintain a stable value, often pegged to fiat currencies or physical assets. This chapter examines each category's characteristics, benefits, and risks; explores their implementations and current applications in the fintech ecosystem; and discusses relevant regulations and future development opportunities.

Keywords: Cryptoassets; fintech; cryptocurrencies; utility tokens; security tokens; tokenized assets; stablecoins; non-fungible tokens

Introduction

Financial technologies, commonly known as fintechs, have emerged as a catalyst for revolutionizing and reshaping various aspects of the financial industry. These innovative technological applications introduce novel approaches to financial processes, business models, services, and products. Fintech's impact can range from incremental improvements, enhancing efficiency and accessibility, and introducing new features to a more radical and disruptive transformation. By

The Emerald Handbook of Fintech, 267–281

doi:10.1108/978-1-83753-608-520241034

leveraging advanced technologies and digital platforms, fintechs have the power to create entirely new financial products and services that were previously unimaginable. This disruptive nature changes the traditional financial landscape, paving the way for more inclusive and dynamic financial systems. As a result, individuals, businesses, and even underserved populations can benefit from the advancements and conveniences offered by these cutting-edge technologies, propelling the evolution of financial markets into a more interconnected and innovative era.

Blockchain is one of these cutting-edge technologies. It is an innovative and transformative concept that has revolutionized how information is stored, processed, and verified. At its core, *blockchain* is a decentralized and distributed digital ledger that operates across a network of computers. This network ensures that data are securely and transparently recorded, reducing the risk of corruption or manipulation. Each transaction or piece of information, referred to as a *block*, is time-stamped and linked to the previous block, forming a chronological chain. This interconnected structure ensures that any attempt to alter a block would require modifying subsequent blocks, making the technology highly secure and resistant to fraud. The decentralized nature of blockchain technology ensures that no single entity controls the entire network. Instead, consensus algorithms and cryptographic techniques are employed to validate transactions and maintain the ledger's integrity. This distributed nature enhances security, transparency, and reliability, making blockchain an ideal solution for issuing, storing, transferring, and managing digital assets.

Digital assets based on blockchain technology are called *cryptoassets*. Given the wide range of programable features available through blockchain technology, cryptoassets can be tailored to specific use cases, commonly classified as cryptocurrencies, utility tokens, security tokens, tokenized assets and securities, and stablecoins. *Cryptocurrencies* are decentralized digital units of value that serve as mediums of exchange, stores of value, and units of account, allowing secure and transparent transactions without intermediaries. *Utility tokens* are digital assets designed to access specific services or products within a blockchain network. *Security tokens* are digital assets that provide rights and entitlements, such as dividends or profit-sharing, similar to traditional securities. *Tokenized assets* are digital representations of tangible or intangible assets on a blockchain, allowing for fractional ownership and easier transferability. *Stablecoins* are blockchain-based digital assets designed to maintain a stable value, often pegged to a fiat currency or a physical asset such as gold.

Additionally, blockchain enables decentralized and automatic program execution through smart contracts. *Smart contracts* are self-executing agreements with predefined conditions and rules encoded within the blockchain. Once these conditions are met, the contract is automatically executed, eliminating the need for intermediaries and reducing the potential for human error or manipulation. These smart contracts allow the creation of additional financial products and services such as decentralized marketplaces, financial derivatives (e.g., call and put options, synthetic contracts, futures, and forwards contracts, among many others), and financial services (e.g., trading pools, liquidity pools, or decentralized investment funds).

The cryptoasset and fintech sectors continue to develop, innovate, and grow at an accelerating rate. This growth has continued even in the face of an increasingly stringent and antagonistic regulatory environment. For example, several nation-states, such as El Salvador and the Central African Republic, have adopted bitcoin with varying adoption rates as legal tender. Adopting a financial instrument created in 2008 as a viable medium of exchange by any country is worthy of further analysis. The crypto space has continued to develop quickly, attracting billions of dollars and other currencies in capital from some of the world's largest and most significant investment funds and venture capitalists. Alongside this meteoric rise in capital raised and media attention dedicated to the space, there has been a corresponding increase in the attention paid to the sector by regulators and policymakers worldwide.

Cryptoassets have created new opportunities and challenges for adopters, developers, investors, and users. After the crypto exchange FTX collapse in 2022 and its ripple effects throughout the blockchain and cryptoasset space, increasingly pointed questions are being asked about the wide array of cryptoassets entering the market. Even seemingly simple and stable assets such as stablecoins have come under scrutiny and are experiencing a regulatory crackdown. In contrast, more speculative cryptoassets have suffered dramatic valuation and trading volume drops. This situation also means that fintech firms and organizations have rapidly grown in scope, assets under management (AUM), and influence over the global financial sector.

The core of the idea is not a radically new concept. Fintech organizations seek to integrate technology and its applications more comprehensively into the current US payment system on a wholesale and retail basis. However, operationalizing this idea is complicated because many organizations are neither chartered as banking institutions by the Office of the Comptroller of the Currency (OCC) nor fall under the purview of state banking regulations.

From a consumer perspective, the appeal of fintech firms is clear on multiple fronts. Due to the lack of legacy costs – both physical and digital – the operating cost and structure of these firms tend to be much lower than traditional operators. These lower costs allow (1) a higher level of investment in technology and automation to accelerate transactions, (2) a more sustained and consistent flow of investments in these spaces, and (3) the ability to pass these savings on to users and customers. Fintechs can pass savings to customers through free services, lower service fees, and higher deposit rates to end users. From a regulatory perspective, however, multiple issues can emerge as obstacles to the wider integration of fintech operators into the mainstream financial and economic system.

This chapter has four sections. The first section explains blockchain technology, followed by a section describing the main characteristics, benefits, risks, and current applications of the different cryptoasset categories: cryptocurrencies, utility tokens, security tokens, tokenized securities, and stablecoins. The third section discusses regulatory challenges. The final section summarizes and concludes the chapter.

Background on Blockchain Technology

Blockchain technology is a revolutionary concept encompassing a decentralized digital ledger that securely records information across numerous computers, ensuring the data are tamper-resistant and verifiable. Blockchain originates from the distinctive manner of storing information. It draws inspiration from Lamport (1978), a proposal of an ordered, time-stamped, and distributed record system. Since its inception, blockchain technology has emerged as the foundational technology underpinning various distributed financial applications, prominently including cryptoassets.

At blockchain's core lies the concept of a distributed ledger. In a blockchain, data are not stored in a centralized database but distributed across multiple computers, often called *nodes*, within a network. Each node in the network maintains a copy of the complete ledger, ensuring redundancy and resilience. This decentralized nature eliminates the reliance on a single point of control or failure, enhancing the system's security and robustness.

Blockchain's fundamental feature is its ability to ensure the integrity and immutability of data. Information is organized into blocks, which are chronologically linked using *cryptographic hashes*. These hashes serve as unique digital signatures that summarize the data contained within each block. Any alteration of, or tampering with, the data within a block would necessitate modifying subsequent blocks, leading to a detectable inconsistency within the blockchain. This feature makes blockchain highly resistant to tampering, forging a *trustless environment* for the participants. In a trustless environment, transactions can occur anonymously without knowing or trusting the counterparty.

Blockchain technology has gained significant recognition due to its transformative impact on finance and beyond. Cryptocurrencies, including bitcoin and others, have emerged as tangible blockchain applications, offering decentralized digital currencies that enable secure and efficient transactions. The transparent and auditable nature of blockchain fosters trust among users, reducing the need for intermediaries in financial transactions.

Moreover, blockchain technology has the potential to extend beyond currencies. It enables the development of smart contracts. *Smart contracts* are self-executing contracts with predefined rules encoded on the blockchain. Introduced by Szabo (1996), smart contracts revolutionize how agreements are verified and enforced by eliminating the necessity for intermediaries like lawyers, trustees, or banks. These contracts contain all the essential information and instructions within the program, outlining the processes that must be carried out. By embedding the terms, conditions, and actions directly into the code, smart contracts automate the execution of agreements, ensuring reliable and transparent enforcement without reliance on third parties.

Cryptoassets

This section describes cryptocurrencies, utility tokens, security tokens, tokenized securities, and stablecoins. For each cryptoasset category, the key characteristics, benefits, risks, and current applications are presented.

Cryptocurrencies

A *cryptocurrency* is a blockchain-based digital unit of value that serves as a medium of exchange, store of value, and unit of account, allowing secure and transparent transactions without intermediaries. These digital currencies are secured through cryptography on a distributed or decentralized ledger that is the foundation for storing and settling transactions. This decentralized nature reduces the potential for interference or manipulation by centralized or state institutions.

Since Nakamoto (2008) published the bitcoin "white paper," cryptocurrencies have witnessed a consistent growth trajectory, evident in bitcoin's price development and the increasing number of individuals embracing cryptocurrencies. Cryptocurrencies have become a significant investment asset for individual and professional investors. Cryptocurrency markets are still relatively less regulated than traditional financial markets. These markets exhibit characteristics ranging from providing high returns to potential total losses and instances of fraud (Benedetti & Nikbakht, 2021; Le Pennec et al., 2021; Momtaz, 2021).

Cryptocurrencies have advantages, disadvantages, and risks. One notable advantage is the ability to transfer value directly without intermediaries like banks or payment processors. The security aspect is handled through public and private key encryption and economic and technical incentive systems. This approach eliminates the traditional role of intermediaries in ensuring security. Users can engage in transactions directly over the internet, resulting in relatively low transaction costs depending on the specific cryptocurrency. Additionally, the transparency of the cryptocurrency network allows for clear visibility into the currency's total supply and, depending on the network's privacy features, information regarding its location and transfers.

The level of transparency or pseudo-anonymity associated with cryptocurrencies can be considered a potential disadvantage and a risk. Cryptocurrencies offer varying degrees of privacy and, in some cases, complete anonymity, which can be comparable to cash transactions. This aspect makes cryptocurrencies appealing to individuals and entities seeking to safeguard their privacy. Cryptocurrencies provide a convenient means to send values privately over the internet, which criminals could exploit for purposes such as tax evasion or money laundering.

Traditional cryptocurrencies like bitcoin or litecoin have a transparent architecture that limits their suitability for extensive involvement in illicit activities. In these examples, every transaction is openly accessible, enabling law enforcement agencies to perform real-time network-wide monitoring and forensic analysis of any previous transaction. This level of transparency does not extend to privacy-centric cryptocurrencies like Monero or Zcash, prioritizing maximum anonymity for their users.

Utility Tokens

Unlike cryptocurrencies, which serve as digital currencies for users who freely and willingly accept them as payment, utility tokens are digital assets designed to provide access to specific services or products within a blockchain network. They function as cryptocurrencies and grant users consumptive rights to services and products via a blockchain-based platform (Lambert et al., 2021).

The consumptive rights associated with a utility token can vary depending on the specific business models implemented by blockchain projects. Different approaches are observed in determining the number of tokens required for a particular service. For instance, some projects grant users and providers the flexibility to determine the number of tokens needed for a specific service, such as the number of tokens necessary for storing a gigabyte of data on a decentralized network for a month. In contrast, others have a fixed amount of tokens assigned to a service or employ a combination of a predetermined baseline and an additional variable cost.

A prime example is Ethereum, a blockchain network that Buterin (2013) introduced. The native utility token of the Ethereum blockchain is known as ether. When using Ethereum's smart contracts, users are required to pay ether. Smart contracts enable various functionalities such as creating new tokens, receiving funds, conducting book building for sales, executing the sale process, distributing tokens, and implementing restrictions or conditions on token transfers.

Utility tokens play a crucial role in the operation of a blockchain ecosystem. Issuers of utility tokens typically operate within the framework of network economics, where the value obtained by participants in the network increases with the growing number of network participants (Benedetti & Nikbakht, 2021). The presence of network economics offers issuers the opportunity to leverage token issuance and distribution as a mechanism to enhance the network effects within the ecosystem.

Utility tokens facilitate various use cases, functions, and organizational models. Examples include Filecoin, a decentralized storage network that uses its native token (filecoin) to reward storage providers and charge users for data storage. Another example is Mana, the internal currency used within the Decentraland metaverse, a virtual world platform.

Given their smart contract infrastructure and blockchain-based nature, utility tokens can evolve and adapt in response to the evolving needs of the ecosystem. For example, ether was originally intended to be the exclusive payment method for transaction processing on the Ethereum blockchain. As the Ethereum blockchain gained widespread adoption and numerous applications were built upon it, ether gained recognition as a widely used cryptocurrency, requiring modifications to cope with the increasing user demand. These modifications included implementing a priority fee to expedite transaction processing and a *burning rate* that reduces the overall token supply by destroying a portion of the transaction fee. Additionally, advancements involve the introduction of a new mining mechanism based on ether reserves, diverging from the current computationally intensive approach.

Regulating utility tokens has posed challenges, as issuers often take precautions to avoid distributing tokens to parties in jurisdictions without clear rules and regulations. The classification of utility tokens can vary across different jurisdictions, as they can serve as cryptocurrencies and grant users certain decision-making power within the issuer's business. Some jurisdictions may consider utility tokens as securities, while others view them as digital currencies or utility tokens. Regulations often describe utility tokens by exclusion, meaning they are defined as tokens that do not fall under the definition of other token types or digital financial instruments. The regulatory landscape for utility tokens continues to evolve as governments and regulatory bodies navigate the complexities of this emerging asset class.

Security Tokens

Security tokens are blockchain-native tokens that exist within the blockchain ecosystem (Smith et al., 2019). Security tokens, sometimes called "native digital securities," are uniquely programmable, allowing customized functions and properties. Each security token can possess distinct characteristics and ownership rights, making it highly flexible and adaptable to specific requirements.

Due to their classification as financial securities, security tokens are subject to stringent regulatory compliance and approval processes. They must comply with the relevant federal securities laws in the jurisdictions where they are issued and traded. This compliance ensures that security token issuance, transaction, and processing adhere to the established legal frameworks and provide investors with the necessary protections.

The programmability and compliance requirements of security tokens distinguish them from other tokens. These tokens enable the synthetic representation of ownership rights and various financial instruments, such as equities, bonds, or investment funds, on the blockchain without requiring an underlying financial instrument. By leveraging blockchain technology, security tokens offer enhanced transparency, efficiency, and liquidity compared to traditional securities. Their digital nature enables fractional ownership and facilitates streamlined and automated processes, benefiting issuers and investors.

As the regulatory landscape evolves, the issuance and trading of security tokens continue to undergo advancements and refinements. Market participants and regulators work together to establish frameworks that ensure investor protection, market integrity, and the growth of this innovative segment of the blockchain ecosystem.

Tokenized Assets

Tokenization is a process or system for issuing, registering, storing, and transferring tokens representing ownership rights over digital or physical assets or rights over the provision of activities. Each tokenized asset possesses a special programming code and operates within an applicable legal framework governing its usage and associated rights. Tokens adhere to coding and consensus protocols agreed upon by the participating parties, ensuring their proper functioning within the blockchain network. In some instances, tokens incorporate a governance system in their code, allowing predefined rules and automated decision-making processes. This feature makes tokens predictable, scalable, automatic, and adaptable to changes within their environment, fostering a dynamic ecosystem.

Although "tokenized securities" and "security tokens" are often used interchangeably, significant distinctions exist between the two. Tokenized securities and security tokens are digital assets that bring advantages compared to traditional securities. However, the distinction lies in the underlying asset. *Tokenized securities or assets* refer to digital representations of real-world assets or securities embedded within a blockchain. These tokenized assets mirror and represent ownership or rights to physical assets, financial instruments, or securities. In essence, tokenized securities leverage the benefits of blockchain technology to enhance the efficiency, accessibility, and liquidity of traditional assets.

On the other hand, security tokens are not tied to preexisting real-world assets or securities. Instead, security tokens are newly created digital securities designed to comply with regulatory frameworks governing traditional securities (Lambert et al., 2021; Smith et al., 2019). These tokens are issued and traded as digital representations of investment contracts, equities, bonds, or other financial instruments.

When compared to centralized registries, tokens offer numerous advantages. They can generate higher efficiencies by reducing reliance on intermediaries and streamlining processes. Tokens also have the potential to improve liquidity by enabling fractional ownership and facilitating peer-to-peer (P2P) transactions. Tokens enhance trust and traceability through transparent information sources and leveraging blockchain technologies' inherent transparency and security.

Stablecoins

Stablecoins are digital assets built on blockchain technology, designed to maintain a stable price by pegging their value to traditional currencies like the US dollar or commodities such as gold. By combining the advantages of blockchain technology, such as fast transactions, transparency, and global accessibility, with the stability of fiat currencies, stablecoins offer a hybrid instrument for the crypto industry. These stablecoins enable access to lower volatility assets, providing stability and confidence to users in the highly fluctuating cryptocurrency market.

Stablecoins adopt three primary strategies to uphold their peg to a benchmark asset: (1) maintaining a reserve of the benchmark asset (referred to as "fiat-based collateral"), (2) holding blockchain-enabled assets as a reserve (known as "crypto-based collateral"), and (3) using algorithms to manage the stablecoin's market supply and demand in response to price fluctuations ("algorithmic"). Each approach carries distinct features and challenges without a definitive trajectory for its future development (Briola et al., 2023; Catalini et al., 2022).

Fiat-backed stablecoins are the dominant category among stablecoins. In this framework, a central authority or entity holds the benchmark asset, such as US dollars or similar equivalents (i.e., US-denominated financial instruments such as bonds or bills), as collateral. Subsequently, they issue a corresponding amount of a blockchain-based digital asset. Many projects aim for a fully collateralized reserve system, striving for a one-to-one alignment with the benchmark asset's price.

Fiat-backed stablecoins have demonstrated reduced volatility when the collateral is deemed secure and reliable. However, since the collateral is not native to the blockchain, its management adheres to conventional financial procedures. As a result, the administration of the collateral reserves is controlled by centralized entities, potentially introducing vulnerabilities as single points of failure (Grobys et al., 2021). At times, concerns have arisen surrounding the transparency and adequacy of these reserves, leading to potential impacts on the stablecoin's price parity and consequentially affecting the broader crypto market (Griffin & Amin, 2020).

The second approach for maintaining price pegging involves using cryptoasset reserves. In this framework, stablecoin issuers accept tokens as collateral and issue a benchmark-denominated token, such as a token pegged to the value of the US dollar. Under this model, the token represents a loan secured by cryptoasset reserves. Most projects adopt an over-collateralization system, where the initial reserves exceed 150% of the loan value. When the market value of the cryptoasset reserves falls below a specific threshold, typically around 120% of the loan value, the reserves are liquidated to cover the loan and associated liquidation costs. A central authority can implement this mechanism or through a decentralized protocol.

The third mechanism for price pegging relies on algorithmic rebalancing, which involves dynamically adjusting the issuance and destruction of stablecoin tokens. This approach aims to maintain the target price by adapting the relative supply of tokens in response to price fluctuations. When the market price rises above the peg, the supply of tokens increases; when the price falls below the peg, the supply decreases. This mechanism is commonly implemented through a dual token system, where one token represents governance rights, and another token functions as the stablecoin. Projects following this approach issue and sell the governance token to build reserves, while a predetermined amount of stablecoin tokens is distributed to governance token holders. Projects often maintain a *fractional reserve*, meaning the value of the reserves is lower than the total value of stablecoin issuance. Some algorithmic stablecoins, such as Terra USD and its governance token Luna, have failed to maintain their desired peg to the US dollar.

Stablecoins offer numerous advantages that make them particularly beneficial for transactional purposes. With their low transaction costs, stability in value, and near-instant transaction settlements, stablecoins provide a reliable and efficient means of transferring funds within and across borders. The immutability of transactions recorded on the blockchain ensures transparency and security. Additionally, stablecoins operate on decentralized networks, enabling seamless transactions at any time, regardless of geographical boundaries or time zones. These characteristics make stablecoins attractive for individuals and businesses seeking cost-effective, fast, and accessible value transfers, revolutionizing the traditional payments industry.

Use Cases and Examples

Use cases for cryptoassets vary and often differ depending on the specific cryptoasset being examined. Use cases for cryptocurrencies generally include (1) use as a medium of exchange, (2) nonfinancial tokens used as part of larger software applications, and (3) a store of value. This chapter discusses bitcoin separately from other cryptoassets due to its size and influence over the crypto market and sentiment.

Bitcoin merits additional analysis because it possesses multiple traits in the crypto space. Several nations use bitcoin as the bedrock for a parallel and blockchain-based financial system. However, this use case has not yet achieved mass adoption. In 2023, the first-ever bitcoin non-fungible tokens (NFTs), ordinal NFTs, were issued into the marketplace (Nelson, 2023). By integrating bitcoin into the NFT space, developers and users seek to combine the scale and bitcoin utilization with the varied use cases that NFTs can fulfill.

Stablecoins are a unique subset of the cryptoasset space since these instruments have been specifically designed to mitigate some issues (namely volatility) that continue to cause issues for bitcoin advocates for use as a medium of exchange. Even as regulatory actions increasingly target the stablecoin space, the total market capitalization of stablecoins continues to increase as the crypto market matures and develops (Morris, 2023).

Stablecoins play important roles as a medium of exchange for individuals and institutions seeking to use crypto on a transactional basis and as a foundational layer for decentralized finance (DeFi). While looking to integrate crypto into mainstream organizations, payroll operators and organizations often use stablecoins as an on-ramp for accepting payments from customers and vendors and how best to do so while minimizing tax liabilities that often accompany such integration.

Applications on the Fintech Ecosystem

Fintech start-ups and organizations might have begun the organizational journey as disruptors intending to upend the existing financial system. However, that situation has rapidly changed and evolved, alongside the growing importance involving the scope of operations and AUM. Besides these firms' disruptive ability, two other primary applications should concern users and investors moving forward.

One application involves fintech's integration within existing financial institutions. Fintech growth and the ability to attract large amounts of capital have also led to the attractiveness of these firms from an acquisition perspective. This integration and combining of fintech firms and existing financial institutions also highlights the importance of fintech firms for international payments, low-cost payments, and the ability to expand their customer base. These are also benefits commonly associated with cryptoassets, ranging from bitcoin to stablecoins.

Other use cases and applications connected to the rise of fintech operators relate to the influence on the traditional financial sector. Beyond the regulatory implications and allegations being leveled against fintech operators, firms bring several applications and implications to the marketplace.

First, firms' ability to deliver personalized, customized, and on-demand services has expanded, with virtually every major financial firm deploying chatbots, app-based services, and customizable products for customers and investors. Although these innovations have not been universally successful or always worked as intended, they have delivered competitive pressure to the marketplace. Even for fintech firms that do not use cryptoassets or other non-fiat currencies, the ability to deliver and provide P2P payments, lending, and borrowing services is changing the financial ecosystem.

Regulatory Challenges

The regulation and regulatory outlook for cryptoassets and fintech operators has been ambiguous. Although some countries have actively moved to embrace aspects of the crypto landscape, with several, including El Salvador, adopting bitcoin as legal tender or issuing a central bank digital currency (CBDC), other countries have taken a more confrontational approach. The most powerful regulator in the United States is the Securities and Exchange Commission (SEC). It filed dozens of enforcement actions in 2023, leading to a degradation in market sentiment and a less hospitable environment for capital deployment. Specific cases brought by the SEC against operators in the space include actions taken against Kraken, Ripple, Coinbase, and dozens of other crypto firms (Securities and Exchange Commission, 2023) and fines that exceeded $2.6 billion between 2018 and 2022 (Nagarajan, 2023). Although cases and enforcement actions vary, several underlying issues and questions recur and cause frustration for firms and investors seeking to operate in the space.

Accounting Classification

Since bitcoin entered the mainstream financial markets conversation in 2016, a topic of interest has been how to classify these instruments from an accounting and financial reporting perspective. Accounting standard setters have begun this process with a multi-month public comment window allowing firms and practitioners to provide feedback to the Financial Accounting Standards Board (FASB) (Lugo, 2023). Although bitcoin and other cryptoassets possess some characteristics of multiple existing financial instruments, crypto does not appear to fall into a single existing category. Cryptoassets have been included with other intangible assets under current generally accepted accounting principles (GAAP) in the United States. This approach means that cryptoassets have been held at historical cost, less impairment losses recorded due to annual impairment testing. Such an arrangement and the economic distortions that arise from it are a driving force behind efforts at the FASB to create and publish crypto-specific accounting standards. Despite SEC chair Gary Gensler's opinion that all cryptos are securities except bitcoin, this view represents an ongoing challenge, drawing bipartisan scrutiny. Even as the cryptoasset marketplace has continued to develop and evolve, the lack of consistent regulatory classification has remained an obstacle to further adoption. As detailed below, regulatory questions and open items also exist for other cryptoassets, even if those assets are less volatile than bitcoin from a price perspective. This situation includes stablecoins, which aim to develop cryptoassets with low to minimal volatility, and instruments as nascent as governance tokens, NFTs, and DeFi applications.

Institutional Challenges

Beyond the regulatory challenges facing individual cryptoassets, firms and institutions attempting to operate in the sector as start-up entities or modify existing operations to include crypto functionality face multiple regulatory issues. Besides the actions taken by the SEC, both the Federal Reserve (Fed) and the OCC began to issue more stringent regulatory opinions and interpretations in 2023. The gist of these publications was that financial institutions wanting to offer cryto-adjacent products and services would face increasing difficulty.

Highlighting this antagonistic turn in the regulatory landscape is the denial of Custodia to gain access to the Fed banking system. For years, Custodia attempted to dialogue with the Fed and work with state regulators in Wyoming to establish a special purpose depository institution (SPDI) and gain public support from politicians and market participants. The Fed continually denied its request to gain full access to US banking rules and regulations, stifling crypto banking innovation.

In March 2023, the uncertainty and doubts regarding the crypto space burst into the mainstream and front-page news. Within days, the three largest banks and financial institutions that offered services to the crypto community collapsed. Regulators shuttered Silvergate Bank, Silicon Valley Bank, and Signature Bank after a series of bank runs left these organizations unable to meet the liquidity demands, with billions being withdrawn in a few days. Although the crypto market did not entirely drive the causes of these collapses, a few core factors and drivers contributed to these rapid and devastating collapses (Stein Smith, 2023).

First, after years of near-zero interest rates, the rapid rate hikes deployed by the Fed placed pressure on the balance sheets of these institutions. With low rates across the board, depositors and customers of financial institutions were content to leave those funds on deposit at the banks. As interest rates increased, more options became available that would allow investors to earn almost 5% via risk-free options. Customers noticed this, and from an institutional perspective, they began withdrawing funds from these institutions.

Second, the sell-off in the crypto sector placed pressure on the assets and valuations on the balance sheets of these major financial institutions. Declining prices and increased withdrawal requests led to forced selling and liquidating of portfolio assets. As liquidations occurred and news associated with these losses became more public knowledge, pressure to sell these investments increased. With withdrawal requests totaling tens of billions of dollars in a single day, the equivalent of a modern-day bank run, these institutions had to look for financiers and buyers to offset these losses.

Closing these financial institutions will cause significant pressure on this sector, including limiting the ability of firms to integrate cryptoassets successfully into operations. Stablecoins, the traditional on-ramp that allowed firms to onboard crypto and fintech operations into mainstream operations, have also been swept up in this regulatory and policy whirlwind affecting every aspect of the crypto and existing financial markets.

An offshoot resulting from this volatility and market destruction has been revitalizing the conversation around state-issued or state-supported stablecoins and the opportunity for crypto-specific banking institutions to enter the marketplace and assume a leadership position.

Specifically, one such instance of the possible regulatory shift is the conversation around Custodia Bank. During the fourth quarter of 2022, the Fed denied access to a Federal Reserve Master Account, which is necessary for any banking institution to gain access to the US banking system. The collapse of multiple financial institutions increased instability, causing concern about the strength and viability of the global banking system and placing fractional reserve banking under more scrutiny.

The primary upshot of Custodia Bank concerns the premise that this institution, a form of SPDI, was approved, legalized, and authorized by the banking regulator in Wyoming. Such a banking model would be 100% reserved, a radical departure from the fractional reserve model employed by virtually all financial institutions. This model is not a cure-all for financial pressures and the limitations placed on banking institutions by higher inflation and rapidly increasing interest rates. However, a 100% reserve model would make a run on the bank virtually impossible, like those that ultimately brought down Silicon Valley Bank (SVB) and Signature Bank. The rationale is that because every loan or asset created by the institution would be fully reserved, customers and depositors could access their funds anytime.

Summary and Conclusion

Cryptocurrencies and fintech have brought about significant changes in the financial industry, introducing innovative technologies, products, and services. Fintech companies leverage advanced technologies to reshape traditional financial processes and offer novel solutions. Blockchain technology plays a crucial role in this transformation, providing secure and transparent information storage and enabling the issuance and management of cryptoassets. Cryptoassets encompass various categories, such as cryptocurrencies, utility tokens, security tokens, tokenized assets, and stablecoins, each serving different purposes within the fintech ecosystem.

However, the rapid growth of the cryptoasset and fintech sectors has attracted attention from regulators worldwide. Although these technologies offer opportunities, they also pose challenges and require careful consideration of their impact on financial systems. Recent events, such as the collapse of certain exchanges and increased regulatory scrutiny, have sparked discussions and calls for closer examination of cryptoassets. Fintech firms have grown in influence and assets, providing consumers with technological advancements and cost-efficient services. Still, regulatory complexities and obstacles hinder integrating cryptoassets and fintech into the traditional financial system.

The continued evolution of the cryptoasset and fintech sectors requires striking a balance between innovation and regulation to foster a sustainable and inclusive financial ecosystem. The specifics of how cryptoassets and fintech firms will be combined and fully integrated within the existing payment systems and regulatory frameworks remain somewhat ambiguous. This uncertainty stems from the current regulatory, legal, and economic issues affecting the cryptoasset and fintech worlds as well as traditional financial markets.

Discussion Questions

- Discuss the difference between cryptocurrencies and utility tokens.
- Explain the difference between security tokens and tokenized securities.
- Identify three features of stablecoins applicable to traditional finance.
- List three regulatory issues facing cryptoassets.
- Describe the current and proposed accounting treatment and rules for cryptoassets under US GAAP.

References

Benedetti, H., & Nikbakht, E. (2021). Returns and network growth of digital tokens after cross-listings. *Journal of Corporate Finance*, *66*(C), 101853.

Briola, A., Vidal-Tomás, D., Wang, Y., & Aste, T. (2023). Anatomy of a Stablecoin's failure: The Terra-Luna case. *Finance Research Letters*, *51*(2), 103358.

Buterin, V. (2013). *Ethereum white paper – A next-generation smart contract and decentralized application platform*. Blockchain Lab. http://blockchainlab.com/pdf/Ethereum_white_paper_next_generation_smart_contract_and_decentralized_application_platform-vitalik-buterin.pdf

Catalini, C., de Gortari, A., & Shah, N. (2022). Some simple economics of stablecoins. *Annual Review of Financial Economics*, *14*, 117–135.

Griffin, J. M., & Amin, S. (2020). Is bitcoin really untethered? *The Journal of Finance*, *75*(4), 1913–1964.

Grobys, K., Junttila, J., Kolari, J. W., & Sapkota, N. (2021). On the stability of stablecoins. *Journal of Empirical Finance*, *64*(December), 207–223.

Lambert, T., Liebau, D., & Roosenboom, P. (2021). Security token offerings. *Small Business Economics*, *59*(1), 299–325.

Lamport, L. (1978). Time, clocks, and the ordering of events in a distributed system. *Communications of the ACM*, *21*(7), 558–565.

Le Pennec, G., Fiedler, I., & Ante, L. (2021). Wash trading at cryptocurrency exchanges. *Finance Research Letters*, *43*(November), 101982.

Lugo, D. (2023). *FASB proposes accounting rules for measuring, presenting and disclosing crypto assets*. Thomson Reuters. https://tax.thomsonreuters.com/news/fasb-proposes-accounting-rules-for-measuring-presenting-and-disclosing-crypto-assets/

Momtaz, P. P. (2021). The pricing and performance of cryptocurrency. *The European Journal of Finance*, *27*(4–5), 367–380.

Morris, D. (2023). The big issues of stablecoin issuance. *CoinDesk*. https://www.coindesk.com/consensus-magazine/2023/04/19/the-big-issues-of-stablecoin-issuance/

Nagarajan, S. (2023). SEC crypto-related fines hit $2.6B through 2022. *Blockworks*. https://blockworks.co/news/sec-crypto-related-fines-hit-2-6b-through-2022

Nakamoto, S. (2008). Bitcoin: A peer-to-peer electronic cash system. https://bitcoin.org/bitcoin.pdf

Nelson, J. (2023). What are ordinals? A beginner's guide to bitcoin NFTs. *Decrypt*. https://decrypt.co/resources/what-are-ordinals-a-beginners-guide-to-bitcoin-nfts

Securities and Exchange Commission. (2023). Crypto assets and cyber enforcement actions. https://www.sec.gov/spotlight/cybersecurity-enforcement-actions

Smith, J., Vora, M., Benedetti, H., Yoshida, K., & Vogel, Z. (2019). Tokenized securities and commercial real estate. https://papers.ssrn.com/sol3/papers.cfm?abstract_id=3438286

Stein Smith, S. (2023). Crypto takeaways from recent bank failures. *Forbes*. https://www.forbes.com/sites/digital-assets/2023/03/20/crypto-takeaways-from-recent-bank-failures/?sh=3d1e4d0b2ea0

Szabo, N. (1996). Smart contracts: Building blocks for digital markets. *Extropy: The Journal of Transhumanist Thought*, *16*(18.2), 28.

Section VI

Harnessing Data With Artificial Intelligence and Machine Learning

Chapter 16

Big Data's Role in Fintech

John W. Bagby

The Pennsylvania State University, USA

Abstract

Financial technologies form the heart of considerable disruptive innovation. Fintech is the emerging financial infrastructure for modern business. Big data are the feedstock for artificial intelligence (AI) that drives many fintech sectors – start-up finance, commodities and investment instrumentation, payment systems, currencies, exchange markets/trading platforms, market-failure response forensics, underwriting, syndication, risk assessment, advisory services, banking, financial intermediaries, transaction settlement, corporate disclosure, and decentralized finance. This chapter demonstrates how analyzing big data, largely processed through cloud computing, drives fintech innovations, scholarship, forensics, and public policy. Despite their apparent virtues, some fintech mechanisms can externalize various social costs: flawed designs, opacity/obscurity, social media (SM) influences, cyber(in)security, and other malfunctions. Fintech suffers regulatory lag, the delay following the introduction of novel fintechs and later assessment, development, and deployment of reliable regulatory mechanisms. Big data can improve fintech practices by balancing three key influences: (1) fintech incentives, (2) market failure forensics, and (3) developing balanced public policy resolutions to fintech challenges.

Keywords: Fintech; big data; artificial intelligence; regulatory lag; financial infrastructure; cloud computing

Introduction

Big data serve as the primary feedstock to artificial intelligence (AI). Financial technological innovations (fintech) adjust, and sometimes replace, legacy financial service practices as fintechs accrue to financial services. Finance and banking are essential *critical infrastructures*:

The Emerald Handbook of Fintech, 285–301

Published under exclusive licence by Emerald Publishing Limited
doi:10.1108/978-1-83753-608-520241036

> systems and assets, whether physical or virtual, so vital to the United States that the incapacity or destruction of such systems and assets would have a debilitating impact on security, national economic security, national public health or safety, or any combination of those matters. Critical Infrastructures Protection Act of 2001 (2001)

The long history of finance illustrates that big data innovations in data collection and archival, information technology, communications, and various security regimes are combined to incentivize fintech innovations. Fintech increasingly relies on big data to spark innovation, reduce costs, and speed up transaction processing (Cao, 2021). Many AI algorithms rely on the adaptability of machine learning (ML). This chapter uses a past, present, and future perspective to demonstrate the persistence of fintech's evolution, how fintech under current practice increasingly requires access to big data, and how this perspective should enable predicting fintech's future – most all will be based on big data.

Big Data

Scholars and practitioners continue to debate the definition of big data. Some seek to reserve "big data" exploration for the challenges of novel research projects. Others recognize how the burgeoning scale of new floods of data requires novel treatment. This chapter uses this later perspective that big data pose great challenges to legacy analytical techniques. Furthermore, information and communications technologies (ICTs) play catch-up as big data processing capacity stretches thin. Many legacy statistical techniques are eventually scaled up to accommodate emerging big data collections. Most developing data sources can be initially explored using big data techniques of clustering, association, precedence, and hypothetical causation to spark insights that trigger useful analysis and predictions (Balazka & Rodighiero, 2020). Many big data accumulations are unstructured, challenging processing efficiency using traditional statistical and data analytical tools that depend on reliable formatting, placement, and organization.

Furthermore, there is an explosion of data from various sensors, transactions, and sources, relating directly and inferentially to decision-making in financial services. This phenomenon makes big data analytics increasingly attractive, particularly when prospecting for evidentiary leads and initial hypotheses as human analysts explore massive or unstructured numerical data. This challenge is magnified when natural language data accumulations are part of big data. Big data, increasingly archived in the cloud, requires an architectural approach to interpreting the information supply chain.

Fintech's Big Data History: Past, Present, and Future

Financial history teaches that innovation occurs with changes in data availability, communication, and the volume and velocity of transactions, producing even more data to archive. This change enables new analytical methods (Arner et al., 2015). There are four major historical eras of fintech: (1) ancient to medieval times – the preindustrial period, (2) industrial capitalism, (3) computerization, and (4) ICT. These eras are bounded by technical watersheds that increase big data and incentivize fintech – the Industrial Revolution, analog telecommunications, computerization, and AI (Bagby & Reitter, 2019). Here, a historical fintech ontology envisions nearly a dozen general clusters of financial service innovations relevant to this histography: enforceability of obligation under a contract, development of money (coin and currency), payment systems and financial instrumentation, specialized financial institutions providing intermediation and syndication, exchange markets (platforms), debt legitimation, financial regulation and disclosure, algorithmic analytics, financial intellectual property, and regulatory technologies (RegTech).

Preindustrial: Ancient to Medieval Times

The preindustrial period extended from ancient through medieval times. It was largely centered in ancient Greece and Rome as globalism began. Their economic influence grew rapidly during the Crusades and the mercantilism that connected the West, the Mideast, and the East. Fintechs of this era have endured as information proliferated to enhance contract enforcement of binding obligations, the emergence of money as a storehouse of value and standardized medium of exchange, agency and service providers functioning as specialized intermediaries, centralization developed in markets for goods, services, and financial transactions. Debt was eventually legitimized, thus overcoming religious and cultural taboos in many parts of the world. These institutions have endured obviating much of the spot market and inefficiently disorganized barter transactions, assured reliable payments and asynchronous (serial, nonparallel) full performances, and induced trust in government infrastructure by sponsoring standardized transaction methods and means. Financial intermediaries and other agents eventually developed, arguably adding value by facilitating trust and increasing transaction process resilience. For example, consider how the Knights Templar provided security for Western Europeans' physical pilgrimages to the Holy Land during the Crusades. The Templars developed payment orders by deploying negotiable instrumentation and intermediary bankers. Order payments became much more reliable because they resisted rampant highwaymen theft. These advancements were fintechs of their time, and data enabled these innovations, resulting in transaction variety and efficiency. This change resulted in more useful data that enabled future fintech innovation in all later eras.

Similar and culturally distinctive historical traditions also developed in the Middle East and East Asia. For example, Roman promissory notes, Chinese feitsyan (8th century), and Indian third-party orders were also ancient forms of negotiable instrumentation. By contrast, debt was legitimized much more slowly. Debt was historically considered illegitimate as a form of usury based on religious principles in many societies. Debt generally received moral condemnation by at least three major world religious traditions – Judaism, Christianity, and Islam. Legitimizing debt in Western societies expanded credit markets to strangers and distant borrowers, a major fintech advancement. Still, even today, Islamic finance prohibits interest (riba) under Sharia-compliant financing (El-Gamal, 2006). This convention has likely inspired some novel fintechs, such as renaming interest as capital gain, a return of capital, or sale-leaseback.

Industrialization

The Industrial Revolution quickly outmoded most independent crafts and custom services, except in high-cost, nonstandard, extravagant situations. Standardized production severely narrowed the range of products and services, enabling efficient quality control. This disruption rendered legacy craftwork much less efficient. When combined with near instant, analog electronic communications, faster transportation, and more mobile markets, increased economic activity and efficiency gains boosted living standards, raising gross economic product worldwide. Centralized exchanges and markets eventually hosted feverish trading in standardized instruments (e.g., stocks, bonds, derivatives, currencies, and commodities). This change produced a flood of transaction information, some remaining anonymized. In contrast, other transaction information flows may identify counterparties, subject matter, prices, volumes, delivery timing, and performance locations, all revolutionizing 19th-century markets. Today, big data still provide immediate visibility to opaque supply and demand. The heavily segmented legacy of regional and decentralized markets transitioned into more permanent, centralized, and interdependent regional markets. As data grew, financial services were democratized, broadening access to capital in a national market system. Democratization and financial inclusion remain enduring fintech goals and depend on big data forms.

Consider how the Union and Confederacy experimented with fintech before and during the Civil War. New instruments like cotton bonds might have succeeded if the Confederacy had better access to quality engraving services. Syndication of the Union/North's civil war debt created the infrastructure that eventually built Wall Street, enabling financial capitalism based on expanding data. Huge new swaths of transaction recordkeeping by brokers, dealers, specialists, and market makers informed more accurate predictability of supply and demand. Telegraphy, at first, then telephony enabled electronic funds transfers (EFT), which was eventually a major line of business for Western Union by the 1870s. Credit markets broadened and deepened to serve geographically and demographically dispersed market segments. State and federal regulation of financial services eventually developed an enduring example of RegLag. The emergence of negative externalities in capital markets constituted side effects widely considered ripe for regulation. For example, Kansas enacted the first "blue sky" state regulation.

The Stock Market Crash of 1929 and the Great Depression followed more than a decade of the Roaring Twenties, evidencing perhaps the most convincing

RegLag in all financial economics. Comprehensive regulation eventually arrived with the creation of the Securities and Exchange Commission (SEC). Banking regulation was erratically deployed throughout the 19th and 20th centuries. Intermediary service providers became ubiquitous as financial services, such as consulting, auditing and attesting, investment advisory, and the accumulation, transmission, and archiving of securities and commodities trading information. This era witnessed a significant upsurge in data generation, archival, transmission, and accessibility, informing the analytics. All these were fintechs, although some appeared in the form of RegTech from the regulatory perspective (Bagby & Packin, 2021)

Computerization

Much like the status of AI today, computerization in financial services has profoundly impacted fintech. From the 1970s into the new millennium, computerization enabled high-speed and accurately archived transaction processing (e.g., order matching and settlement between parties by financial intermediaries). Computerization spawns greater transaction velocity and increases transaction turnover. Computer services require comprehensive and accurate collection, archival, processing, and accessibility of giant troves of transaction records derived from burgeoning big data inputs. Big data have been the feedstock required to enable transformative effects during the computerization and AI eras.

Big data enhance payments. The once dominant localized general credit business of store credit has been largely replaced by electronic processing and the ubiquity of payment cards (credit and debit cards). Largely undocumented movement of currencies with serial numbers is declining as electronic payment systems are secured and proliferate when reliant on data. Bank checks and drafts clearance using automated clearing house (ACH) networks have developed in the private sector. Automated processing of checks (e.g., reading, archiving, transmission, receipt, and payment execution) is enabled by electronic scanning using magnetic ink character recognition (MICR) technologies requiring standardized fonts under the International Standards Organization (ISO) requirements. There are now big data-driven payment card operations: proximity (tap), magnetic (swipe), and chip-enablement at automated teller machines (ATM) and retail points of sale (PoS). These payment methods predominate in the developing world and have the largest share of payments in the developed world. All are based on archival and currently generated big data.

Financial markets now have a much better approach to the efficiency ideal arguably produced by perfectly competitive markets as information becomes more symmetrical among counterparties. For most of history, asymmetric information influenced enough transactions to render many markets inefficient. With the enhanced availability of transactional, financial, and production data, most risk classes are susceptible to big data analysis to reduce uncertainty. Disclosure is a key financial infrastructure, once suffering RegLag, that has enabled the growth of the accounting profession and financial analysis. All these financial market institutions improve symmetrical information that informs investor transaction decision-making.

Consider how academic research in financial economics expanded with the introduction of robust computer archives of securities trading based on computer records, such as the big data collections accessible from the University of Chicago, Booth School's Center for Research in Securities Prices (CRSP "tapes"). Proprietary databases such as Compustat, Bloomberg, and Value Line now abound for analysis by academics, institutional investors, and investment advisors. Government and self-regulatory organizations (SROs) have introduced computerized information sources like the SEC's Electronic Data, Gathering, Analysis, and Retrieval (EDGAR) and other facilities (rogue-broker hotlines) of the Financial Industry Regulatory Authority (FINRA).

The beginnings of AI-era "smart contracts" were developed in the 1970s, initially as electronic data interchange (EDI). *EDI* is a standardized business-to-business (B2B) wholesale supply chain management system of electronic transaction ordering, confirmation, and commercial documentation. Furthermore, EDI can include actual electronic delivery of the contract's subject matter for intangibles such as intellectual property (IP), software as a service (SaaS), data sales, and making required payments. These big data-intensive innovations were fintechs of this era, and they set the stage for the modern ICT era of big data-induced fintechs.

The Era of ICT and AI

Today, big data are the feedstock of most fintechs in the new millennium. AI cannot function as touted without big data. Fintech sectors inspire most of the other chapters in this handbook. Almost all require a big data conducive architecture composed of connectivity, reliable and ubiquitous ICT communications, robust availability of dependable cloud computing, reliable interoperability standards and fintech incentives derived from IP, first mover advantage, replete competitive environment of competent service providers throughout the fintech, and information supply chain's architectures.

Several big data-inspired fintechs will receive considerable attention in the present and future. Cryptocurrencies based on blockchain (distributed ledger) technologies use big data in at least two ways. First, *crypto mining*, the initial creation of crypto tokens or coins, is a computationally intensive method to limit the volume of new crypto creation. As a backlash to the arguably unlimited and inflationary government creation of fiat currencies (printed notes, bank lending under relaxed reserve requirements, and base metal coin), crypto mining requires a huge diversion of electric-powered computing capacity into crypto mining. This reality limits a cryptocurrency's total capitalization size, total float, and available supply such that money-supply expansion-induced inflation may be controlled. Second, considerable big data are needed for any large-scale, decentralized, and geographically distributed ledger across the network. Dispersed recordkeeping may enhance security and resilience, which is sometimes elusive for centralized databases. Multiple recordkeeping locations cede (somewhat costly) redundancy for resilience. Central databases risk the single point of failure vulnerability compared to payment records stored in multiple redundant repositories; the latter increasingly promised to achieve resilience at the cost of maintaining very large data accumulations.

The geographic dispersion of blockchain servers was once hailed as the essence of internet exceptionalism. *Internet exceptionalism* is the forensic difficulty in isolating a particular online activity to apply the laws of any jurisdiction because the internet appears to have no inherent geographic location. Allegedly, many fintech proponents have primarily sought opacity in their transactions, and geographic dispersion complicates accurate forensics for regulatory monitoring or private lawsuits. Some contend that opacity is an enduring, initial, and primary rationale for attracting cryptocurrency participation. Predictably, crypto advocates now complain that "over-regulation" will drive crypto offshore, further deepening the risks for domestic crypto users and speculators. However, experience is growing that exceptionalism opacity can be overcome with successful regulatory enforcement by various authorities: (1) the SEC designates cryptocurrencies as regulable securities, (2) the Commodity Futures Trading Commission (CFTC) may designate some crypto schemes as commodities, and (3) the Treasury Department can classify crypto as money and transactions as regulable money transfers (Bagby et al., 2019). Despite fierce opposition to crypto regulation, there are mounting crypto failures, widespread customer losses, platform insolvencies, and outright thefts. Such predictable developments appear to be ending crypto's RegLag. Some more onerous legislative proposals could drive some crypto schemes to offshore havens. However, crypto's nearly decade-long RegLag may engender a more vibrant domestic crypto industry. For example, fintech developments in stablecoins and central bank digital currencies (CBDC), particularly if standardized under proposed federal law, perhaps co-regulated by states, may significantly diminish many demonstrated crypto risks.

Numerous electronic payment systems flourish, all dependent on big data. PayPal and other nonbank payment systems (Venmo) avoid at least some traditional banking regulation by using the platform as a service (PaaS) and SaaS technologies. Electronic toll collection was initially based on radio frequency identification (RFID) proximity-read toll tags. This approach was expanded to include additional fintechs like license plate photographic recognition. Many of these electronic payment system architectures, like PayPal and toll tags, will continue to depend, at least partially, on the back end of automated credit card payments or other bank interactions. The physical movement of bank checks is now replaced with the Federal Reserve's Check 21 system of networked transmittal, presentment, recordkeeping and payment using digital photographic facsimiles based largely on big data.

Tracing cash payments remains a costly perennial challenge yet continues to be the holy grail of anti-money laundering (AML) regulation. For example, like RegTech, fintech may use big data when currency is sensed from RFID embedded in banknotes or optically sensed from MICR magnetic paper currency traces. AML enforcement is particularly important in investigating tax evasion, terror financing, and crime concealment. Most of the financial services industry is required to deploy AML techniques, which generally results in big data. AI pattern recognition of such transactions often produces useful investigatory leads. AML mines huge online databases of disguised and fictitious transactions to discover the layered subterfuge of facially legitimate but illegal and unethical transactions. AML is regulated by FINRA and the Financial Crimes Enforcement Network (FinCEN).

Fintech's Future Promise

When funneled through fintech, big data-fed AI promises additional efficiencies, new products, and customer services. Several areas seem ripe for fintech innovation: payments, investment advice, loan qualification, and peer-to-peer (P2P) financing. These services offer disintermediation that bypasses traditional financial service providers using network linkages developed with big data. For example, automated electronic investment advice conceptually deploys robo-advisors to computerize analysis of client needs and preferences with various available markets, all based on big data and algorithms. Client cash flow needs and risk tolerances are accommodated by algorithmic analysis using complex models embodied in algorithms. The transition to robo-advice will likely combine human assessment and oversight of big data-fed and AI-generated recommendations derived from securities performances and industry prospects. These may be frequently adapted using ML to capture changing market conditions and evolving client preferences. However, things may change as robo-advisories transition from a consulting information tool that only informs human advisors to more direct, immediate, and un-curated implementation. For example, robo-advisors may use smart contracts to connect directly to market clearance mechanisms and automatically execute portfolio trades. This "black box" problem already challenges AI governance. Without an audit trail of AI decision-making, evident in some AI systems, public policy will demand accurate transparency, also called explainable AI, to accurately reveal how all AI-induced transaction execution decisions were made (Houser & Bagby, 2023).

P2P and crowdfunding models promise lower transaction costs and better matching using computers to connect clients with service providers or lenders. All such proposals rely on big data as feedstock to AI. Each seeks to bypass traditional business models while democratizing fundraising. Many P2P loans are unsecured by collateral, may involve higher default risk, and their P2P intermediary clearing houses may be short-lived. However, the default risk problem may also have a decentralized finance (DeFi) solution with the development of reliable, automated credit scoring (Packin & Lev Aretz, 2023). Traditional credit scoring is a risk prediction based largely on credit histories that reveal outstanding loan balances, cash flow capacity, and payment promptness history (FICO scoring). Fintech credit scoring may potentially use mountains of "alternative data" such as telecom histories, social media activities, and many nonfinancial-related online profiles.

Alternative data are also useful to other fintechs. Alternative data inform robo-advice and socially responsible investing using many environmental, social, and governance (ESG) information sources. Data about the side effects of business operations, decision-making, and supply chain-partner performance increasingly use various screening techniques. Although the SEC's standardization of ESG financial reporting has weakened, users are nevertheless developing alternative ESG forensics methods. Furthermore, the number of privately held and publicly traded firms actively deploying ESG is increasing. ESG delivery devices include financial disclosures, advertisements, podcasts, and third-party analytics in an expanding competition to attract capital, employees, service providers, downstream wholesale, and retail distribution networks (Bagby, 2023).

Fintech Technical Architecture: An Information Supply Chain

Fintech innovation is generally achieved when novel collections of elements are assembled. Often fintechs are composed of a selection and arrangement from many existing, off-the-shelf components in the information supply chain. Key elements in recurring fintechs include high-speed telecommunications network connections, cloud computing services, high-speed algorithm processing, connections fed by existing sensors, and developing and deploying novel sensors. Big data are the information flowing through and enlightening such architectures. Of course, some fintechs may include other, perhaps unforeseen, even critically novel, and inventive elements. All this implicates a growing role for IP in big data and fintech innovation and fintech operations, as well as a generalized big data architecture. IP-protected innovations in big data flows and AI require close attention because IP often defines at least part of the information supply chain's architecture. IP may become part of the blueprint for future fintech innovations.

Intellectual Property Defines Fintech Architectures

Most inventors aspire to protect and exploit their inventions under intellectual property regimes because IP lengthens their monopolistic advantages, offers opportunities to monetize research and development (R&D) investments, and IP rights suppress direct competition. IP law affects big data and AI. Patents, trademarks, copyrights, and trade secrets are all conceivably involved. Acquisition, use, and resale of big data in the United States primarily implicate trade secrecy and contract law. In some other nations, like those of the European Union (EU), databases are more clearly and directly protected under "sui generis" (special purpose) database protection laws (Bagby, 2003). AI is likely to exploit goodwill accumulation based on trademark protections. Some big data methods and some forms of AI may become patentable subject matter in the United States. AI could create copyright-protected works by itself, but it cannot be the inventor under US patent law interpretation. Software is largely protected under copyright and trade secrecy. A trademark protects the goodwill of software, platforms, and many fintech innovations.

Patents

Patents may be the strongest protection among all rights in the IP world. Although copyrights and some trade secrets have enjoyed much longer useful lives (e.g., the Coke formula), a patent is a strong IP for its 20-year patent term. Improvement patents can further extend an invention's profitable life. However, at least three barriers exist to the widespread deployment of patent protection on big data-fed AI in most application domains/fields of endeavor, including fintech. First, copyright and patent laws do not protect databases very well. Second, AI is considered software. Software was once widely patentable in the United States; most business method patents were fintechs during the couple of furious decades they persisted. Patent law generally recognizes that combinations of components can include sequences or steps in a process, physical and raw materials, or mechanical components that comprise a useful, nonobvious invention.

Today, software, standing alone, particularly business methods embedded in software, is generally not "patentable (patent-eligible) subject matter" under the 2014 US Supreme Court's decision in *Alice v. CLS Bank Int'l* (Alice Corp v. CLS Bank International, 2014). Abstract ideas and algorithms are not patentable, and embedding software into a general-use computer is insufficient for patentability. *Alice* requires that patent-eligible software not be directed to laws of nature, natural phenomena, or abstract ideas and must be embodied in a process, machine, manufacture, or composition of matter.

Most software involves processes, but patentable software may also be embedded in a machine or manufacturer. Software, as the essential control of physical elements, may become patentable by implementing some technical method to perform a task. This change likely requires the patent developer and consulting patent experts (e.g., an advisor, lawyer, agent, and practitioner) to conduct significant patentability homework to discover the prior art. *Prior art* is all that existing, publicly available knowledge found in publications, issued (nonsecret) patents, and oral disclosures (speeches, lectures). Curiously, the prior art is itself big data that are constantly growing and must be regularly consulted in preparing patent applications and prosecution (patent application process). Prior art big data are also essential to all subsequent patent rights vindication (infringement and validity litigation). Prior art is big data that will likely become susceptible to AI analytics in determining if an invention surpasses what is already known in the public domain when the invention is screened as novel and nonobvious. This scenario is the test of true innovation for inventions that differ sufficiently from knowledge of a field evident in the prior art as interpreted by a person of ordinary skill in the art. Subjective factors are also relevant, such as inventions that solve some long-felt but unsolved need or inventions that advance beyond the failure of other prior inventors. Patentable fintechs must pass these tests based on prior art big data.

The depth and breadth of patent data are massive. They are largely couched in technical natural language, although supplementary numerical databases often appear as patent specifications. Patent-prior art is frequently technically complex – knowledge resides at every domain's cutting edge. All these database size and complexity factors suggest future deployment of AI in patent-prior art interpretation. Prior art search, retrieval, and application have always been the work of human experts in every patentable field.

Nevertheless, emerging AI validating patentability may soon supplement a patent search. Fintech inventors are far more likely to secure fintech patents if they comprehensively understand the prior art. Big data and AI may be organized, processed, and implemented to improve an invention's patentability prospects. This potential could add extrinsic incentives (monetizing) to the intrinsic incentives (e.g., intellectual satisfaction and inventor's pride) already motivating AI developers.

Trade Secrecy

Copyright protection of databases is mostly ineffective without originality. Thus, when the data are sourced from various databases and accessible to others, these data become ineligible for copyright protection. This situation makes trade secrecy the primary IP form available in the United States to protect the big data feedstock from fintech innovations. Still, obtaining and maintaining trade secrecy can be challenging once the key secrets underlying the innovation become evident to users, clients, competitors, or others. Reverse engineering (disassembly and dissection) often reveals most trade secrets but can be constrained with adequate controls (Friedman, 2021). Trade secrecy is best protected with reasonable measures that establish and enforce administrative, physical, and cybersecurity controls and contractual restrictions. Noncompetition clauses, nondisclosure/confidentiality agreements (NDAs), data licensing, and other contracts (e.g., employment or supply chain service agreements) are generally the most effective legal devices in trade secrecy. Controls must be designed to prevent users with data access from appropriating or mimicking the key secret invention element(s). AI algorithms, big databases, and resulting fintech innovations can be protected under trade secrecy laws. Effective licensing of databases, or the derivative insights and recommendations from AI outputs, generally limits the buyer/user of data or AI recommendations to particular times, durations, and fields of use.

Trademarks

Trademarks are commercial symbols most useful to distinguish the "mark" holder's business model, products or service quality, and functionality from the confusion of generic or competing products in a crowded market. Many online services, such as social media, search, and communications, depend heavily on their trademarked logos and other commercial symbols to enhance brand image, increase distributional efficiencies, and reduce search costs by easily attracting eyeball attention. Trademarks generally imply service quality, familiar functionality, and user interfaces, fulfilling users' expectations for product and service satisfaction. Domain names system (DNS) and URL structures manifest this form of online goodwill as a separate trademark asset where distinctive and neither solely functional nor generic. Special DNS dispute regimes have reduced some litigation costs of trademarks, such as the private sector's Uniform Domain-Name Dispute Resolution Procedure (UDRP) and the US federal law Anti-Cybersquatting Consumer Protection Act (ACPA) (Bagby & Ruhnka, 2004).

Trademarks can be registered with the US Patent and Trademark Office (PTO) to provide stronger protection when compared with the parallel but weaker state or common law trademark protections. Trademarks can be deployed to distinguish software, apps, data brokerages, data management methods, platforms, and various service providers, such as those selling IaaS, PaaS, and SaaS. A trademark appears appropriate for big data and AI service providers. It may appear in their company names, trade dress (look and feel, visual design elements, packaging, and premises design), lines of business, and special, memorable features such as jingles or catchphrases. As with the mandatory search of prior art for patent eligibility, trademark search involves exploring big data. It can be expected to utilize AI as it becomes available to determine trademark protection eligibility in infringement litigation. Fintech products seem particularly well-suited to big data-enhanced trademark protection of brand image.

Big Data Architectures in the Information Supply Chain

Understanding big data architecture is essential for analyzing AI systems because the latter depends on big data. Architectural analysis is also essential to responsible but eventual RegTech regulation of fintech innovations when they externalize social costs. All these phenomena require an understanding of architecture schematically. *Big data architecture* is the accurate mapping of all data infrastructure elements and the complex arrangement of these elements that comprehensively comprise the sequences, the functions, and the hierarchal order of data flows. The architectural analysis identifies all control mechanisms and reveals how results are developed and delivered through the system to ultimate users. Information supply chain models vary over time and complexity and may be redesigned as competition, regulatory control, or quality control problems are encountered and resolved. Thus, only a simplified model is described here.

In the developing and complex environment of big data and AI services that enable fintech innovations, additional elements must be identified beyond this generic model. The starting point for fintech big data analysis requires identification and details about how data are captured, transmitted between elements, repeatedly archived, processed, revised, and passed onward to users. This process is most successful under some value-added business model that promises to produce a return on investment to the fintech entrepreneur that subsidizes suppliers and operators and provides value to investors.

Phenomena and Occurrences Feed Data Acquisition

Many activities and phenomena occur. That is, much "stuff happens". Activities trigger (mostly electronic) sensors to perceive, detect, and capture. Data capture creates data in (still quite often) analog form, but data capture increasingly involves digital form. Analog data must be digitized for timely and efficient transmission, multiple archivals, and big data processing. Data about individual humans, or data from which activities about subject individuals can be inferred, often become the subject of privacy protections in many US states, the EU, and various other nations. Privacy laws may regulate or be deployed to prevent collecting personally identifiable information (PII). Privacy restricting data collection throttles the information supply chain at its inception. Restrictions can occur throughout the information supply chain by limiting data processing, archival, retention, and use throughout the system. However, unless the data capture is somehow intrusive, several constitutional rights permit the use of human perception. This process amounts to the right to learn. The First Amendment to the US Constitution encourages free speech and press primarily to enhance every individual human's direct observation. The First Amendment is far less for the self-actualization of the press despite the ubiquity of that general impression. Free speech and press contribute to a vibrant "marketplace of ideas" that informs political and commercial choices by individuals who exercise their right to learn.

Archival Data

After data are acquired by sensors or perceived as direct observation by humans, those data are recorded and archived. Archival data storage usually happens along the information supply chain. Analog writing and recording device inscription create data records. Increasingly, analog records must be digitized almost immediately to enable future search and retrieval. Real-time digital conversion of analog records can be costly, resulting in delays and may make the data less reliable.

Besides the direct content captured by sensors, another information class may be deliberately added. However, the default setting often creates it automatically, unbeknownst to some users. *Metadata* (i.e., data about/describing other data) are increasingly important, particularly in forensics. Metadata are analogous to "covers" of mailed correspondence that appear on the outside (cover) of otherwise confidential communications. Metadata can include the source, destination, names, addresses, postmark times, and dates. In the wiretapping world and the unlawful interception of communications, the metadata may also include time, duration, date, phone numbers, the existence of and filenames of attachments, and static landline address or in-transit cell device location-based data during the call or the composition or reception of text messages and email. Cookies and web bugs are generally also considered metadata. Metadata are not the content; metadata are data about the content. This relation also means that metadata is not the telephonic voice, written word, or images transmitted as content. Some communications include metadata in a subject line. When accurate, this may reveal or implicate some summary of the content. Many big data-fed AI projects successfully use metadata for various purposes, particularly in national security and cybersecurity applications. Successful functional cybersecurity is a key element of many fintech innovations.

Data are initially archived, then again stored over and over many times. Data are temporarily stored during transmission and archived by data brokers, warehouses, or other data providers (government agencies) until supplied to users. Users also frequently archive data when bought, licensed, and used for analysis by the user or the user's service provider. Thus, the same data may be stored dozens of times in transit and probed at many user locales. As big data business models increase and some of these data become more valuable, fintech based on such high-quality data will likely cause frequent access to the same data. Data are exposed to frequent intermediation, intermediate storage, enhancement, or destruction. Data are exposed to archiving long-term data, causing many separate data storage episodes. These storage locations are increasingly in the cloud, making cloud computing a near-essential element in AI and fintech. The outsourcing and offshoring phenomena suggest that the physical location of cloud data repositories may frequently change with fluid cloud pricing and reliability. The physical location of user data in the cloud in foreign jurisdictions triggers many additional legal and practical difficulties.

As discussed in the IP section above, when data acquire IP status, this usually implicates licensing restrictions. Licenses arguably impact every participant in the information supply chain by enabling or limiting each participant's rights to use, pass onward (sell, lease, license, and barter), or limit the data's use for only particular purposes (fields of use). Fintech itself can often be manifest as a service subject to license and similar contract restrictions.

Data Processing and Data Analysis

Big data are mostly useless without context and interpretation, necessitating data processing that provides valuable information for AI algorithms, users, and customers. Fintech is no exception because big data are used to develop recommendations, directly execute smart contracts, trade in securities, commodities, derivatives, and currencies, or participate in some novel investment scheme. Statistical methods are deployed where feasible. Big data analytics are deployed using evolving data organization methods, structuring, filtering, aggregation, association, causation linkage, cluster analytics, and analysis. Querying large databases was traditionally known as data mining.

Data are frequently riddled with errors, making error correction an ongoing challenge for the success of fintech innovations. For example, in data arrays, some data points become misplaced; they seem to jump between predetermined columns or expected variable locations. Such problems suggest that two validating fixes are needed: one type is ex ante, and another is ex post. Increasingly, both are used. First, the standardization of data structures is an ex ante preventative measure. Second, data cleansing is an ex post curative measure. Many data-standardized formats are becoming useful, including extensible markup language (XML) and the regulatory-mandated extensible business reporting language (xBRL) format. xBRL is particularly important to many fintech innovations because registered, publicly traded companies must assemble, format, audit, and deliver annual and quarterly financial reporting (SEC, FDIC, FASB, and International Financial Reporting Standards [IFRS]) in quantitative (numerical) and qualitative (natural language) formats. Application programming interfaces (APIs) are standardized data interchange methods that can also perform data cleansing.

Data processing methods, factors, and formulae, embedded in algorithms and then modified as computing machines learn, can produce biased results or contain bias in their initial or developing modeling. Such biases change decision-making, affecting the rights and property interests of users, clients, and prospective counterparties. AI is frequently criticized when it operates in secret. Indeed, AI is considered an opaque "black box" when it uses proprietary, closed systems that fail to provide faithful audit trails. The problem is exacerbated when AI directly makes life-changing decisions with scant opportunity for human intervention (smart contracts). For example, creditworthiness decisions are becoming a major sector of fintech innovation. Generally, credit scoring is initially based on traditional payment histories but is increasingly proposed to be enhanced by alternative data, some AI developed. Although black box AI may permit visibility to inputs and outputs, developers may seek to obscure its static and dynamic algorithms to protect their IP by closing their systems to real-time visibility or ex post forensics. This situation is the AI "black box" problem that many policy commentators increasingly advocate should expose AI to greater regulation. Opening AI to audit transparency could address this black box problem. However, transparency is very likely to impact fintech innovation incentives.

Use of Knowledge

When mining and interpreting big data in AI and operating many fintech innovations, all must have some ultimate purpose. Fintech big data produce and then use recommendations in decision-making. The use of information monetizes the big data and investment in the design of fintech algorithmic processing. Fintech enables the dynamic discovery of underlying phenomena using big data-fed ML. Without a value proposition underlying a fintech business model, there are scant incentives to invent. Therefore, using big data-fed AI likely must result in value to clients, allowing such services to attain profitability for the platform deploying big data usage. A fintech innovation might conceivably use the big data-derived knowledge in-house and sell it to external constituencies.

Summary and Conclusions

Fintech's history illustrates that financial innovation is (1) incremental, sparked by the introduction of new ICT and big data accumulations, (2) built on and generally integrated with existing financial services, practices, and products, and (3) created novel regulatory methods, despite recurring RegLag. Like most start-ups, many novel fintechs rely on venture capital (VC) funding. Fintechs are mostly network industries that must accumulate critical mass to self-sustain. Fintechs likely depend on unique business models, address unmet emerging demand, are temporarily advantaged by suppressed potential competition, may use unique IP, and most have an industrial organization architecture, a nexus of contracts pervasively deploying licensing contracts among various outsourced service providers.

This chapter's industrial organization lens focuses on information supply chain architectures underlying fintechs. Big data have been essential to fintech over most of history. Fintechs generally orchestrate elements from independent vendors because employees, in-house departments, or captive subsidiaries cannot easily or quickly supply such support. Most Fintech enterprises are not initially vertically integrated, making them mostly flat organizations reliant on outsourcing to geographically dispersed, independent, decentralized service providers. Decentralization initially delivers jurisdictional obscurity that fosters RegLag. RegLag provisionally offers internet exceptionalism – an early environment conducive to attaining critical mass. This environment likely shields fintech innovation from legal or regulatory scrutiny. However, opacity eventually erodes as externalities trigger RegTech innovations that develop in RegLag to fintech.

Fintech firms will likely continue to require wide ranges of highly specialized expertise. These are all prodigious barriers to entry into all the necessary and specialized fields servicing fintechs. Big data require frequent intermediate and penultimate cloud computing storage. This insatiable data appetite is unlikely to decline. Fintechs are contemporary examples of bundles of contracts nexus that require considerable outsourcing (Jensen & Meckling, 1976). Long delays and prodigious entry barriers exist to acquiring physical facilities, developing reliable expertise, and scaling indispensable ICT, making fintechs into decentralized, flat organizations. Small to medium-sized fintech firms are unlikely to integrate vertically initially. However, with some sustained success, some fintechs will predictably achieve vertical integration as they achieve critical mass in reliability, ubiquity, and value addition for expanding user/customer bases.

All this suggests a standard fintech architectural model based on the big data supply chain. Successful fintech innovations will require continuous process improvement in data processing. Big data-fed AI is most likely to generate high-quality value addition. Many fintechs will enjoy initial RegLag providing shelter during start-up and critical mass development. RegTech will eventually respond to public policy pressures to eliminate whatever perceived harmful externalities are linked to fintech.

Discussion Questions

- Discuss how big data have inspired innovation in the major contemporary tranche of modern financial services.
- Exemplify several emerging big data accumulations, then link them to a modern developing fintech practice, analytical method, or financial service.
- Explain how many legacy financial services were developed using big data and ICT innovations.

- Compare and contrast numerical big data search and retrieval from natural language analysis.

References

Alice Corp v. CLS Bank International, 573 U.S. 208. (2014).

Arner, D. W., Barberis, J., & Buckley, R. P. (2015). The evolution of fintech: A new post-crisis paradigm. *Georgetown Journal of International Law*, *47*(4), 1271–1319.

Bagby, J. W. (2003). Outlook: Who owns the data? *Research Penn State*. https://www.psu.edu/news/research/story/who-owns-data/

Bagby, J. W. (2023, April 14). ESG big data science: AI closes the forensics gap between corporate strategic opacity and corporate performance. *2023 Data Law & AI Ethics Research Colloquium*. Penn State University.

Bagby, J. W., & Packin, N. G. (2021). RegTech and predictive lawmaking: Closing the RegLag between prospective regulated activity and regulation. *Michigan Telecommunications and Technology Law Review*, *10*(2), 127–177.

Bagby, J. W., & Reitter, D. (2019). Anticipatory FinTech regulation: On deploying big data analytics to predict the direction. *Impact and Control of Financial Technology*. https://papers.ssrn.com/sol3/papers.cfm?abstract_id=3456844

Bagby, J. W., Reitter, D., & Chwistek, P. (2019). *An emerging political economy of the BlockChain: Enhancing regulatory opportunities* (Vol. 88, pp. 419–474). University of Missouri-Kansas City Law Review.

Bagby, J. W., & Ruhnka, J. C. (2004). Protecting domain name assets. *CPA Journal*, *74*(4), 64–69.

Balazka, D., & Rodighiero, D. (2020). Big data and the little big bang: An epistemological (R)evolution. *Frontiers in Big Data*, *3*, 1–13. https://doi.org/10.3389/fdata.2020.00031

Cao, L. (2021). *The next big thing: The age of fintech, AI, and big data*. The CFA Institute. https://blogs.cfainstitute.org/investor/2021/10/20/the-next-big-thing-the-age-of-fintech-ai-and-big-data/

Critical Infrastructures Protection Act of 2001. (2001). *42 U.S. Code §5195c, S.1[40]7, 107th Congress*.

El-Gamal, M. A. (2006). *Islamic finance: Law, economics, and practice*. Cambridge University Press.

Friedman, R. (2021, November 4). You can learn anything through reverse engineering. *Harvard Business Review*. https://hbr.org/2021/11/you-can-learn-anything-through-reverse-engineering

Houser, K., & Bagby, J. W. (2023). Next-generation data governance. *Duke Law & Technology Review*, *22*, 61. https://dltr.law.duke.edu/2024/02/17/next-generation-data-governance/

Jensen, M. C., & Meckling, W. H. (1976). Theory of the firm: Managerial behavior, agency costs and ownership structure. *Journal of Financial Economics*, *3*(4), 305–360.

Packin, N. G., & Lev Aretz, Y. (2023). Decentralized credit scoring: Black box 3.0. http://doi.org/10.2139/ssrn.4375920

Chapter 17

How Alternative Data Are Changing Finance

Douglas J. Cumming and Zachary Glatzer

Florida Atlantic University, USA

Abstract

This chapter focuses on how alternative data can change the nature of financial forecasting through improved short-term forecasting techniques and decreased informativeness from longer term sources. Increased use of social media data leads the charge in transforming this transition. Alternative data are data not from standard financial statements or formal reports. This chapter looks at alternative data from new sources (e.g., social media, Internet of Things [IoT], and digital footprints) and alternative data from new collection methods like web scraping for textual analysis, image analysis, and vocal analysis). It first discusses standard data in financial forecasting. Next, this chapter examines alternative data in financial forecasting. Finally, it discusses alternative data used in studying finance more broadly.

Keywords: Fintech; alternative data; web scraping; Internet of Things (IoT); digital footprints

Introduction

This chapter examines the alternative data used in finance, emphasizing financial forecasting. Alternative data are not from standard financial statements or formal reports (Cong et al., 2021). New technologies, such as blockchain technology, using text mining in machine learning (ML), and cloud computing that has reduced the cost of storing big data, have driven the rise in these alternative data. This dramatic rise and corresponding impact motivates the discussion in this chapter. Academics and practitioners can exploit these new forms of data to improve financial forecasting and gain new insights into burgeoning areas of finance more broadly. Alternative data reduce the cost of gathering information

The Emerald Handbook of Fintech, 303–314

doi:10.1108/978-1-83753-608-520241040

(Goldfarb & Tucker, 2019), lowering the costs of analyzing financial subjects. Academics and practitioners should understand this opportunity to improve financial forecasting and discover new insights concerning finance more broadly.

This chapter discusses the sources and applications of some common alternative data. The remainder of this chapter has four sections. The first section discusses traditional data used in finance. It is followed by a survey of the most prominent alternative data sources used in financial forestating. The third section discusses alternative data being used in areas of finance outside of forecasting. The chapter ends with a summary and conclusion.

Standard Financial Data

In general, institutions formally produce and report traditional data. This section breaks down the discussion of traditional finance data into those regarding public institutions and private institutions.

Public Data

This subsection discusses traditional finance data on public institutions. These data include but are not limited to publicly traded companies, central banks, and subjects of public finance. Some empirical forecasting is cited for reference when discussing the data.

Historically, some of the most widely used stock market data come from the Center for Research in Security Prices LLC (CRSP). CRSP maintains a robust collection of security data from several stock markets worldwide. In 1977, the starting point of the CRSP data collection was updated to begin on January 30, 1926. Some of the many variables reported are security prices, returns, trading volume, stock indices, and debt instruments. Many seminal finance works use these data (Fama & Kenneth, 1992, 1993, 2006).

Researchers have also used data on the firm's leadership, board members, and key personnel in forecasting models (Chee et al., 2023; Cohen et al., 2010; Custódio & Metzger, 2014). A widely used source for these data is BoardEx (2023). BoardEx has data on the current and past employment, education, and other activities of the C-suite, board members, committee members, and other key decision-makers. Moreover, BoardEx has a proprietary relationship mapping algorithm that identifies business connections by leveraging publicly available data.

Researchers and analysts often incorporate macroeconomic variables, inflation, labor income, unemployment rate, and consumption, in financial forecasting (Asgharian et al., 2013). These data can be gathered from several sources. S&P statistical services offer historical macroeconomic and financial data across time and countries (Qi & Zhang, 2001). The Federal Reserve Economic Data (FRED) of the St Louis Federal Reserve has offered economic data since 1991 and tracks several US and international time series. FRED aggregates data from banks, exchanges, companies, and individuals (Shammre et al., 2023). The US Census

Bureau also contains a historical account of public sector finance, employment, pensions, and tax data (Lunsford, 2015).

Private Data

This subsection discusses traditional finance data from private institutions. These data include but are not limited to data on private firms and financial intermediaries. Some empirical forecasting is cited for reference when discussing the data.

Researchers and practitioners have used data on private firms in financial forecasting. Some of the variables include projected cash flows, analyst reports, and survey data (Akbas et al., 2018; Amoroso et al., 2021; Cumming et al., 2021; Gompers et al., 2016; Kapinos et al., 2016; Kruglikov et al., 2020). These data come from PitchBook, Thomson Reuters, and Crunchbase sources. These sources gather the data from reports, regulatory filings, websites, and interviews and organize the data before making the data available to be communicated.

Data on intermediaries have been used in financial forecasting. Some intermediary data contains industry-level indices, returns, qualitative reports, credit ratings, and metrics of intermediary performance (Buvzynski et al., 2021; Dethier, 2009; Dettling et al., 2015; Ghysels et al., 2013; Gogas et al., 2014). These data come from Eurekahedge, Lipper Tass, the World Bank, and the Survey of Consumer Finance.

Alternative Data in Financial Forecasting

This section discusses alternative data from either new sources or new collection methods used in work on financial forecasting. Some empirical forecasting using the data is cited for reference.

Web Scraping for Textual Data

Web scraping collects data from web pages (Śpiewanowski et al., 2022). Manually scraping the web and collecting the data is now antiquated, given computer programs that can automate data extraction from websites. ML and textual analysis can be applied to the data obtained from web scraping to identify sentiments, connections, and broader patterns.

A few websites scraped for financial forecasting are social and professional networks, financial news, and report repository websites. Social network websites, like Reddit, Twitter/X, and Facebook, are often scraped to extract relevant determinants of a particular research question, such as product data, timestamp of news, and trends, and to gauge consumer, political, or cultural sentiment (Rani et al., 2019; Sidhu et al., 2022, pp. 747–753). Professional network websites, like Monster, LinkedIn, and Yelp, have also been scraped for data. Specifically, LinkedIn has been scraped to build a credit-scoring model that gathers data on an individual's analytical skills, professional influence, and authenticity (Ramadhani et al., 2022). Financial news articles from *The Wall Street Journal* or *Financial*

Times can convey firm-specific information, market trends, and information about corporate network structures. Maurice (2022) scraped *The New York Times* text to forecast economic indicators.

Researchers also use formal report repositories to web scrape 10-Ks, analyst reports, and financial statements. Web scraping includes simulating user interaction with a website to extract the data. For example, they simulate clicking links on a website to access reports from a repository. For example, Li et al. (2023) web-scraped formal analyst reports and applied generative AI (ChatGPT and Google's PaLM) to analyze the data and extract culture, tone, and other relationships. All the above sources can be scraped and used in the same analysis. Sidhu et al. (2022, pp. 747–753) scrape a combination of sources, like Reddit, Twitter, and Yahoo Finance, to conduct their sentiment analysis.

Web Scraping for Other Sensory Data

The most common data collected from web scraping are textual. This subsection discusses the less common but arguably more useful sensory data collected from web scraping, like images and sounds.

Researchers have scraped and analyzed images to improve forecasting models. One example includes satellite imagery of commercial or economic activity, where hedge funds use the number of cars in parking lots of major retailers to forecast sales (Brei et al., 2023; Counts, 2019). Researchers have used other types of images. For example, He et al. (2019) document that facial width to height ratio (fWHR) of Chinese male sell-side analysts is associated with higher forecast accuracy.

Researchers have scraped and analyzed sounds and voices to improve forecasting models. Mayew and Venkatachalam (2012) measure managerial emotion during earnings conference calls by analyzing audio files using vocal emotion analysis software. They find that the emotional response from scrutiny by analysts during conference calls can be used to forecast a firm's financial future. Additionally, Gorodnichenko et al. (2021) investigate emotions embedded in the voice of the Federal Reserve Board of Governors during press conferences. This line of research has shown that vocal cues contain useful information about market and firm fundamentals.

The Internet of Things

Cloud computing has fostered the communication between devices. The *Internet of Things (IoT)* is a network of devices capable of exchanging data (Hazar & Yilmaz, 2019). Technology embedded with sensors and monitoring devices makes up the IoT. Examples include patient implants that adjust to physiological data, agricultural devices that respond to the soil, and disaster warning systems that respond to flammable gases.

IoT data can be categorized into three classes (Ahmed et al., 2017; Linthicum, 2016; Pelaez, 2021; Snowflake, 2023; Zhou et al., 2021).

- *Status/passive/equipment data.* Data that communicate the condition of a device or system.
- *Location/active/environment data.* Data that communicate the external information of the device or system, such as location, air quality, and movement.
- *Automation/dynamic/submeter data.* Data created by devices and systems, like smart thermostats and automated lighting.

These types of data have affected several industries. IoT has impacted the insurance sector, with sensors on automobiles and neighborhoods that can help predict and measure damages and potential losses. The banking sector uses IoT for wealth management personalization, improved payment security, transaction automation, improved transparency, optimized capacity management, and voice assistants (Digiteum, 2019). IoT can affect daily business operations, including inventory management, billing services, auditing, and budgeting. By looking at data from central banks and small and medium enterprises (SMEs), the IoT can be leveraged to communicate early warning signs of financial distress (Koyuncugil & Ozgulbas, 2012). Stock price forecasting using data from the IoT seems to be still in its infancy (Li et al., 2020).

Digital Footprints and Microdata

The World Bank defines microdata as unit-level data that contain information about individuals, households, and firms. The rise in the volume of transactions and commerce that occurs online has generated vast amounts of data of this sort. Microdata exists at the transaction level and takes the form of digital footprints, such as log files, cookies, geolocation, web traffic, and other data created from online browsing.

One example of digital footprints used in forecasting models is the proprietary customer transaction data from JPMorgan Chase. These data contain information about payment channels, merchants, stores, and products, among other pieces of information. They have been used to forecast the impact changes in customer traffic will have on retailers (Relihan, 2022). Another example is the data on an insured client. Insurance companies retain microdata on residential or business insurance policy characteristics. These characteristics include the time between the initiation of a contract and the first claim, the number of past claims, income level, and policy characteristics. These data are useful in forecasting property insurance claims and detecting fraud (Severino & Peng, 2021).

Regulatory Data

Various data sources on regulatory sanctions are available from the US Securities and Exchange (SEC) webpage and other SEC filings. These SEC filings include but are not limited to equity crowdfunding offerings in the United States (Cumming & Reardon, 2023).

Other regulatory data include surveillance data from NASDAQ (Akter et al., 2023). Surveillance information comprises data on trading misconduct detected by computer algorithms for various forms of improper trading. These include, for example, *wash trading* (the same client reference on both sides of the trade), *spoofing* (entering an order and deleting it as it is about to execute, with no bona fide interest in trading), *frontrunning* (trading ahead of a client's order knowing the client's order will move the price), *layering* (placing three or more orders on one side of the market designed to move the price followed by an order and trade on the opposite side to benefit from the price change (Financial Conduct Authority, 2015), *marking the close*, *marking the open*, *corners*, *squeezes*, among other forms of manipulation.

Alternative Data Applications in Other Areas of Finance

This section discusses alternative data from new sources or new collection methods used in studying finance. Some empirical forecasting is cited for reference.

Cryptoasset Data

Cryptoassets are a novel asset class that brings new characteristics into the fold that has not been thoroughly investigated. For example, cryptocurrencies have protocol rules that govern their blockchain. Cumming, Glatzer, et al. (2023) look at how the capacity protocol for Bitcoin can be gauged and evaluated to determine when the network is most vulnerable to money laundering before exiting the network. This area is still burgeoning, and data availability on different blockchains continues to grow.

Data on cryptoassets can be gathered from several sources. For cryptoassets that have an underlying public blockchain, the data are publicly available by downloading them from a specific blockchain's software, such as the bitcoin core software for the bitcoin blockchain, and directly querying the blockchain can generate data that describes blockchain dynamics, such as the mempool or miner fees for bitcoin. Additionally, whitepapers that discuss a cryptocurrency in technical detail are common. These whitepapers typically precede a blockchain's genesis block, like Nakamoto (2008). Data were gathered by scraping published whitepapers for variables capturing the technical details in the text. For example, these whitepapers have been scraped to forecast the development of central banks' digital currencies (Corbet et al., 2023).

Moreover, several databases have been generated from hand-collecting data on cryptocurrency characteristics of coins and tokens from primary and secondary sources. Examples include Fahlenbrach and Frattaroli (2020) and the Token Offerings Research database. A subset of the cryptocurrencies that go through an initial coin offering (ICO) is used to generate funding for an entrepreneurial endeavor. The databases previously mentioned aggregate data on these ICO startups from primary sources, such as ICO whitepapers, ICO's Medium,

Twitter/X, Telegram, LinkedIn and other verified accounts, GitHub, and blockchain data, and secondary sources, like ICObench, ICOmarks, icorating.com, smithandcrown.com, icowatchlist.com, Blockchain.com, and coinschedule.com. Characteristics of cryptocurrencies aside, the data on the return performance of cryptoassets (including prices, market capitalization, trading volumes, indices, and benchmarks) can be found in tracking institutions like CoinMarketCap.com, Crunchbase, and Crypto Fund Research.

Other Data

Developments in technology have affected financial markets that practitioners and academics desire to investigate. The dynamics and transformation of previously traditional data can be leveraged to investigate these impacts. High-frequency trading (HFT) has raised concerns that some may leverage electronic and algorithmic trading technology to manipulate and extract wealth from financial markets. The HFT that occurs in the electronic markets has manifested, in part, in higher *order-to-trade ratios*, the number of order enter/amend/cancel messages divided by the number of trades (Aitken et al., 2015; Khomyn & Putniņš, 2021).

The work on HFT has been a data problem for many academics worldwide. The issue is identifying when HFT and algorithmic trading (AT) started (Aitken et al., 2023). Following the approach of Aitken et al. (2015), Boehmer et al. (2021) used colocation dates when exchanges started renting out space to traders to store equipment within the exchange to reduce distance and improve trading speed.

A recent approach of many academics has been to combine different datasets. Combinations of datasets that have never before been combined enable new topic areas for empirical inquiry. Also, it enables a temporary monopoly on the topic, particularly if it takes a long time to bring about the merger. Some examples from published work using fintech or regtech data include merging data on market surveillance (trading misconduct) with data on patents (Cumming, Ji, Peter, & Tarsalewska, 2020) and M&As (Cumming, Ji, Johan, & Tarsalewska, 2020). Further examples from recent working papers include merging data on market surveillance with corporate venture capital (CVC) (Cumming, Li, et al., 2023) and corporate culture (Akter et al., 2022). The idea behind this work has been to integrate work on regtech in microstructure more closely with topics in corporate finance. These fields have normally been considered quite separate without much overlap. Combining datasets reveals strong links between these two disciplines. In particular, trading misconduct has numerous spillovers for traditional topics in corporate finance. Regtech data combined with corporate finance data reveals that trading misconduct negatively affects innovation, innovation culture, and mergers and acquisitions. Also, trading misconduct has consequences for CVC programs. Despite significantly reducing trading misconduct around establishing a CVC program, some misconduct remains. That misconduct increases the difficulty for the CVC to exit its portfolio companies through an initial public offering (IPO). The hazard rate to an IPO is around 0.5% among CVCs in firms that face trading misconduct. These findings are just an early look at things that can be learned from combining datasets. Numerous other angles can be explored with these types of data merges and from merging other datasets.

Summary and Conclusion

Alternative data are important to understand as they are used more broadly to improve the informativeness of financial forecasts and finance. New technologies have been the driver of the rise in these alternative data. The field of finance has seen practitioners and academics leverage these alternative data to understand better traditional financial markets and burgeoning areas of financial technology. Leveraging these alternative data has had real impacts.

One notable impact is on the significance of traditional data, such as in financial forecasting. The relevance of financial documents to investors tends to deteriorate over time. The hypothesis is that alternative data capture relevant information not found on traditional financial statements, such as corporate network structures, competitor moves, regulatory changes, and brand development. This evidence may affect the accounting profession and the skill set demanded by analyst firms, institutional investors, and financial managers.

Discussion Questions

- Define alternative data and contrast them with traditional data used in financial forecasting.
- Identify and discuss the sensory alternative data in the academic literature.
- Discuss how and what technology has given rise to alternative data.
- Discuss the sources of cryptoasset data.

References

Ahmed, E., Yaqoob, I., Hashem, I. A. T., Khan, I., Ahmed, A. I. A., Imran, M., & Vasilakos, A. V. (2017). The role of big data analytics in Internet of things. *Computer Networks*, *129*(December), 459–471.

Aitken, M., Cumming, D. J., & Zhan, F. (2015). High frequency trading and end-of-day price dislocation. *Journal of Banking & Finance*, *59*(October), 330–349.

Aitken, M., Cumming, D. J., & Zhan, F. (2023). Algorithmic trading and market quality: International evidence of the impact of errors in colocation dates. *Journal of Banking & Finance*, *151*, 106843.

Akbas, F., Markov, S., Subasi, M., & Weisbrod, E. (2018). Determinants and consequences of information processing delay: Evidence from the Thomson Reuters Institutional Brokers' Estimate System. *Journal of Financial Economics*, *127*(2), 366–388.

Akter, M., Cumming, D. J., Ji, S., & Verdoliva, V. (2022). *Market manipulation and corporate culture*. https://ssrn.com/abstract=4080428; http://doi.org/10.2139/ssrn.4080428

Akter, M., Douglas, C., & Ji, S. (2023). Natural disasters and market manipulation. *Journal of Banking & Finance, 153*, 106883.

Amoroso, N., Bellantuono, L., Monaco, A., De Nicolò, F., Somma, E., & Bellotti, R. (2021, March 19). Economic interplay forecasting business success. *Complexity*. e8861267. https://www.hindawi.com/journals/complexity/2021/8861267/

Asgharian, H., Hou, Ai J., & Javed, F. (2013). The importance of the macroeconomic variables in forecasting stock return variance: A GARCH-MIDAS approach. *Journal of Forecasting, 32*(7), 600–612.

BoardEx. (2023). About us. https://boardex.com/about-boardex

Boehmer, E., Fong, K., & Wu, J. (2021). Algorithmic trading and market quality: International evidence. *Journal of Financial and Quantitative Analysis, 56*(8), 2659–2688.

Brei, V. A., Rech, N., Bozkaya, B., Balcisoy, S., Paul Pentland, A., & Netto, C. F. S. (2023). Satellite imagery and machine learning for channel member selection. *International Journal of Retail & Distribution Management*, forthcoming. https://doi.org/10.1108/IJRDM-02-2023-0073

Buvzynski, W., Cuzzolin, F., & Sahakian, B. (2021). A review of machine learning experiments in equity investment decision-making: Why most published research findings do not live up to their promise in real life. *International Journal of Data Science and Analytics, 11*, 221–242.

Chee, S., Matsunaga, S., & Wang, S. (2023). Effective board monitoring over earnings reports and forecasts: Evidence from CFO outside director appointments – ScienceDirect. *Journal of Accounting and Public Policy, 41*(5), 106981.

Cohen, L., Frazzini, A., & Malloy, C. (2010). Sell-side school ties. *The Journal of Finance, 65*(4), 1409−1437.

Cong, L. W., Li, B., & Zhang, Q. T. (2021). Alternative data in fintech and business intelligence. In M. Pompella & R. Matousek (Eds.), *The Palgrave handbook of FinTech and blockchain* (pp. 217–242). Palgrave Macmillan.

Corbet, S., Cumming, D. J., Glatzer, Z., & Johan, S. (2023). Monetary doping? Understanding the rapid development of CBDC in emerging economies. https://scholar.google.com/citations?view_op=view_citation&hl=en&user=FcbZY3sAAAAJ&citation_for_view=FcbZY3sAAAAJ:u-x6o8ySG0sC

Counts, L. (2019). How hedge funds use satellite images to beat Wall Street—And Main Street. *Berkeley Haas*. https://newsroom.haas.berkeley.edu/how-hedge-funds-use-satellite-images-to-beat-wall-street-and-main-street/

Cumming, D. J., Glatzer, Z., Hendrickson, J. R., & Luther, W. J. (2023). Bitcoin Blocksize, custodial security, and price. https://papers.ssrn.com/sol3/papers.cfm?abstract_id=4242246

Cumming, D. J., Ji, S., Johan, S., & Tarsalewska, M. (2020). End-of-day price manipulation and M&As. *British Journal of Management, 31*(1), 184–205.

Cumming, D., Ji, S., Peter, R., & Tarsalewska, M. (2020). Market manipulation and innovation. *Journal of Banking & Finance, 120*, 105957.

Cumming, D. J., Johan, S. A., & Reardon, R. S. (2021). *Governance and success in US equity crowdfunding*. CFS Working Paper Series, No. 668.

Cumming, D. J., Li, Y., & Yu, Y. (2023). *Stock market manipulation and corporate venture capital investments*. https://ssrn.com/abstract=4427743

Cumming, D. J., & Reardon, R. S. (2023). COVID-19 and entrepreneurial processes in US equity crowdfunding. *Journal of Small Business Management*, *61*(5), 2326–2349.

Custódio, C., & Metzger, D. (2014). Financial expert CEOs: CEO's work experience and firm's financial policies. *Journal of Financial Economics*, *114*(1), 125–154.

Dethier, J.-J. (2009). *World Bank policy research: A historical Overview*. Policy research working papers: The World Bank. https://doi.org/10.1596/1813-9450-5000

Dettling, L., Devlin-Foltz, S., Jacob, K., Pack, S., & Thompson, J. (2015, October). Comparing Micro and Macro sources for household accounts in the United States: Evidence from the survey of consumer finances. *Finance and Economics Discussion Series*, *1*, 1–69. https://doi.org/10.17016/FEDS.2015.086

Digiteum. (2019, June 6). How IoT is changing financial services and banking. https://www.digiteum.com/internet-of-things-banking-finances/

Fahlenbrach and Frattaroli. (2020). *Initial coin offering database*. Zenodo. https://zenodo.org/records/4034258

Fama, E. F., & French, K. R. (1992). The cross-section of expected stock returns. *The Journal of Finance*, *47*(2), 427–465.

Fama, E. F., & French, K. R. (1993). Common risk factors in the returns on stocks and bonds. *Journal of Financial Economics*, *33*(1), 3–56.

Fama, E. F., & French, K. R. (2006). The value premium and the CAPM. *The Journal of Finance*, *61*(5), 2163–2185.

Financial Conduct Authority. (2015). The Financial Conduct Authority v. Da Vinci Invest Ltd. England and Wales High Court (Chancery Division). https://www.casemine.com/judgement/uk/5a8ff7bd60d03e7f57eb1afe

Ghysels, E., Plazzi, A., Valkanov, R., & Torous, W. (2013). Forecasting real estate prices. In G. Elliott & A. Timmermann (Eds.), *Handbook of economic forecasting* (Vol. 2(A), pp. 509–580). Princeton University Press.

Gogas, P., Papadimitriou, T., & Agrapetidou, A. (2014). Forecasting bank credit ratings. *The Journal of Risk Finance*, *15*(2), 195–209.

Goldfarb, A., & Catherine, T. (2019). Digital economics. *Journal of Economic Literature*, *57*(1), 3–43.

Gompers, P., Kaplan, S. N., & Mukharlyamov, V. (2016). What do private equity firms say they do? *Journal of Financial Economics*, *121*(3), 449–476.

Gorodnichenko, Y., Pham, T., & Talavera, O. (2021). *The voice of monetary policy*. Working Paper. Working Paper Series: National Bureau of Economic Research. https://doi.org/10.3386/w28592

Hazar, H. B., & Yilmaz, N. K. (2019). The rise of Internet of Things (IoT) and its applications in finance and accounting. *Pressacademia*, *10*(10), 32–35.

He, X., Yin, H., Zeng, Y., Zhang, H., & Zhao, H. (2019). Facial structure and achievement drive: Evidence from financial analysts. *Journal of Accounting Research*, *57*(4), 1013–1057.

Kapinos, P., Gurley-Calvez, T., & Kapinos, K. (2016). (Un)expected housing price changes: Identifying the drivers of small business finance. *Journal of Economics and Business*, *84*(March/April), 79–94.

Khomyn, M., & Putniņš, T. J. (2021). Algos gone wild: What drives the extreme order cancellation rates in modern markets? *Journal of Banking & Finance*, *129*(August), 106170.

Koyuncugil, A. S., & Ozgulbas, N. (2012). Financial early warning system model and data mining application for risk detection. *Expert Systems with Applications*, *39*(6), 6238–6253.

Kruglikov, N., Forthun, A., & Otneim, H. (2020). *Predicting private equity fund performance with machine learning*. Master's thesis. https://openaccess.nhh.no/nhh-xmlui/handle/11250/3055171

Li, H., Hua, J., Li, J., & Li, G. (2020, June 20). Stock forecasting model FS-LSTM based on the 5G Internet of Things. *Wireless Communications and Mobile Computing*. https://doi.org/10.1155/2020/7681209

Li, K., Mai, F., Shen, R., Yang, C., & Zhang, T. (2023). Dissecting corporate culture using generative AI – Insights from. *Analyst Reports*. https://doi.org/10.2139/ssrn.4558295

Linthicum, D. (2016, March 29). Three types of IoT data sources. *RTInsights (blog)*. https://www.rtinsights.com/three-types-of-iot-data-sources/

Lunsford, K. G. (2015). Forecasting residential investment in the United States. *International Journal of Forecasting*, *31*(2), 276–285.

Maurice, C. (2022). *Operationalizing the New York Times to forecast economic indicators*. PhD dissertation. The University of Chicago.

Mayew, W. J., & Venkatachalam, M. (2012). The power of voice: Managerial affective states and future firm performance. *The Journal of Finance*, *67*(1), 1–43.

Nakamoto, S. (2008). A peer-to-peer electronic cash system. https://papers.ssrn.com/sol3/papers.cfm?abstract_id=3440802

Pelaez, A. (2021, December). *Here's how IoT data collection works [complete guide]* (Vol. 30). Ubidots Blog. https://ubidots.com/blog/iot-data-collection/

Qi, M., & Zhang, G. P. (2001). An investigation of model selection criteria for neural network time series forecasting. *European Journal of Operational Research*, *132*(3), 660–680.

Ramadhani, D. P., Wijaya, P. M., & Alamsyah, A. (2022). Credit scoring model construction based on LinkedIn social media data. In *Proceedings of the international conference on industrial engineering and operations management* (pp. 1890–1900). IEOM Society International. https://doi.org/10.46254/EU05.20220379

Rani, N., Akshay, A., & Shakir, M. B. (2019). Social media and sentiment analysis of Nifty 50 Index. *Journal of Prediction Markets*, *13*(1), 50–56.

Relihan, L. (2022). Is online retail killing coffee shops? Estimating the winners and losers of online retail using customer transaction microdata. https://doi.org/10.2139/ssrn.4065950

Severino, M. K., & Peng, Y. (2021). Machine learning algorithms for fraud prediction in property insurance: Empirical evidence using real-world microdata. *Machine Learning with Applications*, *5*(September 15), 100074.

Shammre, A., Sultan, A., & Chidmi, B. (2023). Oil price forecasting using FRED data: A comparison between some alternative models. *Energies*, *16*(11), 4451.

Sidhu, A. S., Misra, N., Kaushik, V., Shankar, A., Joshi, K., & Singh, R. (2022). Analysis of global finance using web scraping and topic modeling. In *3rd International Conference on Intelligent Engineering and Management (ICIEM)*. IEEE. https://doi.org/10.1109/ICIEM54221.2022.9853165

Snowflake. (2023). *Internet of Things (IoT)*. https://www.snowflake.com/guides/what-iot

Śpiewanowski, P., Talavera, O., & Vi, L. (2022). Applications of web scraping in economics and finance. In *Oxford research encyclopedia of economics and finance*. https://doi.org/10.1093/acrefore/9780190625979.013.652

Zhou, J. X., Shen, G. Q., Sun, Ho Y., & Jin, X. (2021). Customization of on-site assembly services by integrating the Internet of Things and BIM technologies in modular integrated construction. *Automation in Construction*, *126*(June), 103663. https://doi.org/10.1016/j.autcon.2021.103663

Chapter 18

Artificial Intelligence and Machine Learning in Finance: Key Concepts, Applications, and Regulatory Considerations

Alessio Azzutti

University of Glasgow, UK

Abstract

This chapter explores the role of artificial intelligence (AI), particularly its subfield of machine learning (ML) methods, as a core technology of the fintech revolution in the financial services industry. It simplifies some of the complex concepts related to AI by introducing the main ML paradigms and related techno-methodic aspects. This chapter uses real-world examples to illustrate how next-generation AI powered by ML is transforming the financial services industry. Next, in illustrating the risks associated with AI adoption, this chapter discusses the need for regulation to address the essential facets of AI governance, including transparency, accountability, ethics, and responsible use. Lastly, it looks at emerging regulatory approaches across leading global jurisdictions. The primary goal is to give readers an initial understanding of AI's profound impact on the financial sector.

Keywords: Artificial intelligence; machine learning; fintech; AI governance; AI regulation

Introduction

The financial sector has historically been at the forefront of adopting innovative technologies. The recent surge of artificial intelligence (AI), particularly its

The Emerald Handbook of Fintech, 315–339

Published under exclusive licence by Emerald Publishing Limited
doi:10.1108/978-1-83753-608-520241042

subfield of machine learning (ML), has solidified the position of financial services as one of the most innovation-driven sectors of the economy.

The massive investments in AI-related technology within the financial sector underscore its potentially revolutionary role, as evidenced by the Organization for Economic Cooperation and Development (OECD) report (2021b) indicating global spending exceeding $50 billion in 2020 alone. This financial and strategic commitment has corresponded with a significant upswing in scientific publications and a burgeoning demand for AI-related professional roles worldwide. Similarly, the recent (McKinsey Global, 2022) report indicates a marked increase in integrating AI across several industries, especially in the financial sector. The multifaceted benefits of AI have gained attention, evidenced by the high percentage of organizations attesting to its potential for enhancing customer experiences, as highlighted by NVIDIA (2023). Major players in AI in the fintech space are big tech companies such as Microsoft, Google, and Amazon and technology companies like IBM Corporation, Intel Corporation, and NVIDIA. The AI's size in the fintech market is expected to grow at a compound annual rate of about 30% until 2028 (The Business Research Company, 2023).

Although AI deployment has gained considerable momentum, industry perceptions reflect a prevailing sentiment that the technology is still nascent. Deloitte (2022) reveals substantial incorporation of AI solutions within financial institutions (FIs), but the industry acknowledges that AI's full potential has yet to be tapped. Most recently, the emergence of generative AI models has further bolstered expectations, with projections (Deloitte, 2023) suggesting a substantial productivity upsurge for FIs in the future.

Amid this optimistic outlook, however, the growing complexity introduced by AI has ushered in a range of uncertainties and potential risks, prompting a pressing need for appropriate governance and regulation (Boukherouaa et al., 2021; FSB, 2017; OECD, 2021a). Considering these developments, this chapter is (i) a high-level introduction to AI, particularly its subfield of ML methods, (ii) its application within the financial services domain, and (iii) the related regulatory considerations to ensure effective AI governance.

AI and ML: A Primer

This section discusses the role of AI-based technologies in reshaping the financial service industry. It begins with a brief yet tentative chronicle of technology development through three "AI generations." Next, this section delves into the core "ML paradigms" underpinning state-of-the-art AI applications in finance. Lastly, it discusses the relevance of the "AI lifecycle" concept.

AI Generations

AI denotes the theory and practice of computer systems capable of executing tasks that traditionally require human cognitive abilities. The OECD (2023b, p. 7) defines the term *AI system* as "a machine-based system that, for explicit or implicit objectives, infers, from the input it receives, how to generate outputs such as predictions, content, recommendations, or decisions that can influence physical or virtual environments."

The field of AI can be traced back to the mid-20th century when a group of visionary scientists aimed to replicate human intelligence in machines (McCarthy et al., 2006). This early phase of AI research laid the foundational principles that would influence subsequent advances in various application domains. The history of AI applications has gone through a continuous, albeit nonlinear, evolutionary path, ideally characterized by three distinct generations, each marking significant strides in developing intelligent systems. The following discussion concisely explores the three main "AI generations."

Early AI Systems

The first AI generation is the so-called era of "symbolic AI." *Early AI systems* relied on human knowledge encoded into formal rules, like in "expert systems" or "rule-based systems." These systems tackle complex problem-solving tasks using predefined rules, often structured as "if-then" commands. Although succeeding in automating tasks traditionally performed by human experts, early AI systems application has been limited due to inherent limitations. Their reliance on explicitly encoded human domain knowledge within rigid rule-based frameworks often restricts their ability to effectively handle uncertain and ambiguous situations. These systems cannot adapt to novel scenarios or learn from new data, impeding their scalability and real-world applicability (Buchanan, 2019). Despite early AI systems' fundamental role in subsequent developments in the field, their limitations have underscored the need for more dynamic and adaptable approaches to knowledge representation and problem-solving.

Evolution to ML

The second generation of AI applications marks a shift toward adopting *ML methods*. Although the terms AI and ML are often, and improperly, used interchangeably, ML represents a more recent subfield of AI research. In essence, ML encompasses data-driven computational methods aimed at acquiring knowledge and skills through systematic analysis of empirical data, with minimal or no human intervention. The proliferation of ML applications can be attributed to the simultaneous progress in computer processing power and data storage capacities, coupled with the growing availability of data, algorithms, and associated products and services (FSB, 2017). The advent of ML applications laid the groundwork for data-driven approaches, which form the core of the latest developments in AI.

Latest ML Advances

The third generation, the era of increasingly sophisticated and powerful AI systems, is based on the *latest ML advances*. These systems may combine several innovative ML methods, including but not limited to "deep learning," "adversarial learning," and "transfer/meta-learning" (Koshiyama et al., 2020). These advanced ML methods have led to several transformative breakthroughs in many application domains. These include, for instance, image recognition, natural language processing (NLP), and predictive analytics in many fields, such as finance. Cao (2022, pp. 2–3) effectively coined the term "smart fintech" to describe the growing set of innovative methods, tools, and applications related to AI in finance.

Main ML Paradigms

ML encompasses a broad spectrum of algorithms and methods to model information based on empirical data. This section introduces the main ML paradigms, including (1) "supervised learning" (SL), (2) "unsupervised learning" (UL), (3) "reinforcement learning" (RL), and (4) "deep learning" (DL). Next, it examines the fundamental distinctions between traditional AI and generative AI models, offering an initial insight into their different roles and functionalities.

Supervised Learning

In SL, computer algorithms are trained with data prelabeled by human experts, meaning that the input data are paired with the corresponding desired output. The goal is to enable the algorithm to learn a function mapping from inputs to outputs by inferring the underlying patterns and relationships within the data. An SL model gradually adjusts its parameters through training to minimize errors between the predicted output and the target. Thus, the model learns to make accurate predictions or classifications on new, previously unseen data at this stage. SL methods find application in various tasks, including (1) "regression" for predicting continuous numerical values and (2) "classification" of discrete categorical labels. These methods form the basis of many practical applications, such as NLP, image recognition, and predictive analytics (Russell & Norvig, 2021).

Unsupervised Learning

In UL, computer algorithms are trained with unlabeled datasets, where the input data are not paired with corresponding outputs. Unlike SL methods, UL algorithms focus on identifying patterns, structures, and relationships within the data without explicit guidance from labeled examples and other human feedback. Through tasks such as "clustering" and "dimensionality reduction," UL models can autonomously discover hidden patterns and group similar data points, facilitating the extraction of valuable insights and knowledge from complex datasets. Thus, UL methods are valuable for exploratory data analysis and feature extraction. These methods are commonly used, for example, in customer segmentation, anomaly detection, and pattern recognition applications, where the objective is to uncover structures and relationships within the data without predefined target variables (Russell & Norvig, 2021).

Reinforcement Learning

RL is the foundational ML paradigm that enables the development of artificial agents (e.g., robots and software agents). RL-based agents can self-learn from experience within a given environment to pursue a predefined goal. Unlike SL and UL, RL operates on the principle of trial and error, where the agent receives feedback in the form of "reinforcements" (i.e., rewards and penalties) based on its actions. Through a process of "exploration" and "exploitation," the agent aims to maximize cumulative rewards by learning optimal decision-making policies (Sutton & Barto, 2018). RL is commonly employed in sequential decision-making tasks, such as game playing, robotics control, and autonomous systems, where the agent dynamically adapts its behavior to achieve long-term goals in complex and uncertain environments (Mnih et al., 2015).

Deep Learning

As a more recent subfield in ML, *DL* focuses on modeling high-level abstractions in data through complex architectures known as "artificial neural networks" (ANNs). By comprising multiple layers of interconnected nodes, these networks mimic the structure and functioning of the human cortex, enabling the automated extraction of features and patterns from input data (Deng & Dong, 2014). ANNs' design can follow diverse approaches influenced by the chosen network architecture, which can entail various levels of abstraction and "hidden layers" (Olorunnimbe & Viktor, 2023). Fig. 18.1 shows a representation of ANN architecture comprising a single hidden layer.

In ANN models, the training objective involves optimizing network parameters by minimizing the error between predicted and actual output values in a given dataset. This process entails iterative parameter tuning using labeled training data to minimize a so-called "loss function." The ultimate goal is to learn a generalized function that performs well with unseen data.

By leveraging hierarchical representations and a vast amount of labeled and unlabeled data, DL models can autonomously learn to recognize and interpret nonlinear relationships and latent patterns in data. This class of ML methods facilitates performing complex tasks such as image and speech recognition, NLP, and decision-making in various application domains, including finance (Ozbayoglu et al., 2020). Although DL methods can be integrated with the previously mentioned ML paradigms to achieve powerful applications, their deployment in risky domains raises concerns about trustworthiness. The so-called "black box" problem is a major source of this risk.

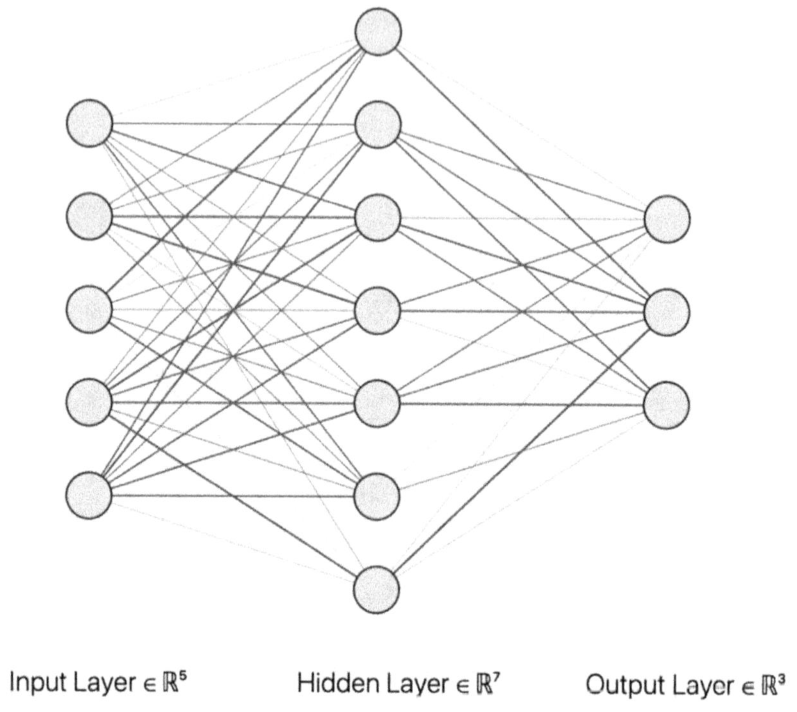

Fig. 18.1. Representation of an ANN Architecture With a Single Hidden Layer. *Note:* The figure represents an ANN architecture with a single hidden layer between the input and output layers. ANNs consist of interconnected "nodes" or artificial neurons. These neurons transmit and receive "signals" — real-number values — that capture nonlinear relationships between the sum of the inputs for a given artificial neuron. The connections between nodes, known as "edges," possess adjustable weights that modify the signal strength. Each layer may perform distinct input transformations, with signals passing through layers from input to output. ANNs with multiple hidden layers constitute "deep neural networks." The figure was generated using the NN-SVG online tool (https://alexlenail.me/NN-SVG).

Traditional AI Versus Generative AI

Another key concept in AI research entails distinguishing between *traditional* AI and *generative AI*. Traditional AI, including the ML models seen above, predict or label a data point in regression or classification tasks. These methods, mainly employed in SL settings, enable the automation and optimization of various tasks. Their performance can be ascertained via somewhat well-defined performance bars and metrics.

Conversely, *generative AI* models, popularized by the emergence of "large language models" such as ChatGPT, are designed to output new data points, such as text, images, or video. Unlike traditional ML models, developed to address a narrow task, (some) generative AI models have broader capabilities and can be adapted to different and more specific tasks (cf. "foundational models") (Toner, 2023). From a user perspective, these methods are generally implemented in so-called "human-in-the-loop" settings, which involve cooperative human–machine interactions (i.e., typically in a dialogue). As generative AI models provide probabilistic outcomes, evaluating their performance proves less straightforward as commonly accepted metrics or standards are yet to be established. Despite their increasing adoption, a comprehensive understanding of the functioning and capabilities of various applications, including their capabilities and methodic limitations, remains relatively limited (Bommasani et al., 2022).

The AI Lifecycle of an ML Project

The "AI lifecycle" concept provides an engineering perspective to better understand AI systems and their operation. De Silva and Alahakoon (2022) provide an excellent conceptualization of the AI lifecycle. In their view, the operationalization of any ML-based project occurs through the three main phases of (1) "design," (2) "development," and (3) "deployment." Each phase requires the joint work of human experts from various technical fields such as data science, computer science, computer engineering, and other relevant fields like ethics, law, and regulation, as well as specific domain knowledge relevant to the task. In turn, these three main phases encompass several distinct yet interconnected stages at the base of the AI lifecycle. Without purporting to be exhaustive, the following discussion focuses on the stages of (1) problem formulation, (2) data acquisition and preprocessing, (3) training and optimization, (4) model testing, (5) model interpretability, and (6) postdeployment monitoring.

Problem Formulation

Problem formulation constitutes the initial and fundamental step of any ML-based project. This stage requires a comprehensive understanding of the underlying problem, including its objectives, the available data, and the specific constraints or requirements to inform the selection of the appropriate ML approach – such as determining the relevant variables or "features" to consider – and evaluation metrics. A well-defined problem formulation lays the foundation for addressing the specific challenges and objectives of the task performed by a given AI system.

Data Acquisition and Preprocessing

Data acquisition and *preprocessing* involve collecting, organizing, and refining the "training data." The training data, which act as the basis for ML models to recognize patterns and associations within input data to make predictions or decisions, may consist of "structured" (i.e., standardized and quantitative) and "unstructured data" (i.e., data in their native form, such as text, audio, and video). ML methods enable innovative data analytics applications leveraging big data and "alternative data," or AltData, to inform financial decision-making.

Data acquisition involves defining, identifying, and sourcing relevant datasets from various reliable and diverse sources, ensuring the data are comprehensive and statistically representative to deal with the problem. Subsequently, the *pre-processing* stage deals with data cleaning, transformation, validation, and feature engineering (e.g., "feature extraction" and "feature selection") to enhance data quality and adapt it to an appropriate format before model training. According to the so-called "garbage-in-garbage-out" principle, the performance of ML methods is highly dependent on large amounts of quality data. When empirical data are limited, "data augmentation" techniques may be employed to supplement them. However, this process requires human experts to make assumptions about the statistical properties of the generated "synthetic data" and verify its appropriateness for its intended use (Assefa et al., 2020).

Model Training and Optimization

Model training entails initiating the development of an ML model by applying learning algorithms to the training dataset. The "training data" represent a collection of examples, encompassing pairs of inputs and outputs, used to fit the model's "parameters." Following initial training, *model optimization* involves iteratively tuning the model's "hyperparameters" and evaluating model performance on the "validation data," which must be distinct from training data, to minimize the disparity between predicted and actual outcomes. The ultimate goal of these two stages is to optimize model performance to achieve the desired accuracy and generalization capability by applying various learning algorithms and optimization techniques.

Model Testing

The model learned from the previous stages requires rigorous testing before actual deployment to ensure trustworthiness in its real-world application. *Model testing* allows a model's performance and generalization ability to be evaluated on previously unseen data, measuring its predictive accuracy and robustness in making predictions or other decisions. This stage enables an unbiased final evaluation of how an ML model would perform in a live environment when encountering new observations. The "testing data" are distinct from training and validation data but must possess the same statistical properties (i.e., probability distribution). Techniques like "hold-out validation," "cross-validation," and "bootstrapping" enable testing ML models on separate datasets, offering insights into their accuracy as well as potential shortcomings beyond the scope of training. However, "model validation" and "model testing" may often overlap, and the two terms are sometimes used interchangeably in practice.

Model Interpretability

Model interpretability relates to the ability to comprehend the reasoning behind the predictions or decisions made by a trained ML model. The term is often confused with "model explainability," which refers to the ability to explain the decision-making process followed by an AI system in human-comprehensible terms (Rudin, 2019). Model interpretability is crucial for understanding how a given ML model arrives at specific outcomes and identifying the key factors influencing its decision-making process. Techniques such as "feature importance analysis" and "interpretability algorithms" contribute to a clearer understanding of an ML model's inner workings, identifying critical risk factors and assuring the model's reliability and accuracy. Ensuring adequate levels of model transparency is vital for building confidence in the AI decision-making process and fostering trust among various stakeholders (e.g., developers, providers, users, regulators, and consumers).

Postdeployment Monitoring

Postdeployment monitoring involves tracking and analyzing a deployed model's performance and behavior in real-world applications. The ongoing evaluation of the model's predictive accuracy, generalization capabilities, and adherence to predefined performance metrics enables practitioners to identify potential issues (such as "model drift," "data degradation," or "model decay" over time). This oversight also facilitates timely interventions and updates to maintain the model's sustained effectiveness against changing market environments and alignment with evolving business needs (Vela et al., 2022).

The AI Lifecycle in Finance

The "AI lifecycle" concept holds paramount importance to ensure trustworthy applications. From an engineering perspective, it offers a holistic framework that assists FIs through the various stages of an AI project. Adopting an engineering approach ensures that AI initiatives align with strategic business objectives and fosters an environment of innovation, responsibility, and expertise within the organization. Thus, within the financial sector, this approach may help promote trust and transparency to various stakeholders, including regulatory bodies and consumers. Despite industry participants deploying increasingly sophisticated ML systems, however, recent research shows a relatively low understanding of the AI lifecycle by FIs. Haakman et al. (2021) find important shortcomings in the documentation and reporting activities of the various stages of AI projects.

AI Applications in Finance

This section discusses the transformative role of AI in finance. It begins by providing an overview of the benefits and opportunities AI applications can offer markets, financial organizations, and their clients. Subsequently, the section considers some prominent AI use cases in the financial services sector.

Benefits and Opportunities

AI adoption is proposed to revolutionize how financial services have traditionally been delivered, with many benefits and opportunities for organizations and their clients. For FIs, a notable advantage is AI's positive impact on operational efficiency through process automation and optimization. According to industry reports, over one-third of financial firms have reduced annual costs by at least 10% in 2022 alone (NVIDIA, 2023). By automating routine tasks and workflows, AI allows organizations to allocate resources strategically and prioritize growth-focused initiatives. In addition, firms can streamline complex business processes and reduce the likelihood of human errors or bias. These adjustments can ensure more accurate data processing to make informed decisions amid evolving market dynamics and changing consumer needs and preferences. In short, AI enhances operational efficiency and fosters innovation and growth within the financial sector (FSB, 2017; OECD, 2021a).

For consumers, business adoption of AI can also result in various benefits, including lower costs for financial services, improved customer experiences, and personalized offerings. For example, by harnessing advanced analytics and predictive capabilities, FIs can offer increasingly tailored financial services, including personalized product recommendations and customized investment strategies. AI adoption enables more customer-centric business approaches, fostering stronger engagement, loyalty, and overall satisfaction. Furthermore, AI adoption has fueled a culture of innovation within the sector, boosting the development of novel financial products and services that cater to consumers' ever-evolving needs and expectations (FSB, 2017; IOSCO, 2021; OECD, 2021a).

Integrating AI into business activities has brought about a paradigm shift in the financial sector, paving the way for a new era of efficiency, innovation, and financial inclusion. As these technologies evolve and mature, the potential for further advancements and opportunities remains vast, promising a future characterized by enhanced accessibility, productivity, and sustainable growth.

Use Cases

This subsection provides a snapshot of better-known use cases, illustrating AI's practical implementation in various financial contexts. AI adoption spans the entire value chain, involving back-office and front-office operations (FSB, 2017). The following is illustrative, as AI use cases often increase. The focus is on key AI application areas, such as (1) risk management – e.g., credit scoring, (2) chatbots – e.g., robo-advisors, (3) financial trading and asset management, (4) cybersecurity and fraud detection, (5) regulatory technology, or regtech, (6) supervisory technology, or suptech.

Risk Management and Credit Scoring

For FIs, identifying, measuring, and mitigating various forms of financial risk are vital to running the business. Because of ML, AI-based risk management tools can assist organizations in solving optimization problems in financial *risk management*, including credit, market, operational, legal, and compliance risks (Aziz & Dowling, 2019).

Consider, for instance, *credit scoring*, a crucial activity for banks to assess the creditworthiness of potential borrowers. Due to ML, lending institutions can analyze vast amounts of historical data for analysis, assessments, and even predictions. By automating the evaluation of multiple factors such as credit history, income levels, existing debts, employment status, and other relevant personal information, AI-powered credit scoring models support human experts in determining the likelihood of borrower default, ensuring accurate and consistent evaluations of credit applications. Thanks to automation, firms can streamline the lending process and optimize exposure to financial risk. At the same time, AI-based credit scoring may foster financial inclusion by allowing individuals with limited or no credit history to access vital financial services, thus contributing to a more equitable and accessible financial system (Tok & Heng, 2022).

Chatbots and Robo-Advisors

A *chatbot* is a computer program designed to simulate conversation with human users, usually over the internet. Chatbot applications improve tasks such as consumer-facing financial service and support. One prominent example of chatbots in finance is a *robo-advisor*, a digital investment advice tool that matches consumers to certain financial investments based on their needs and preferences (Ringe & Ruof, 2021).

Like human professionals, these "conversational AI" agents are programmed to interact with customers, providing personalized assistance and offering relevant information on financial products and services. By integrating NLP and ML algorithms, chatbots can understand and respond to natural language queries, enabling clients to access real-time assistance for various financial inquiries, including account information, transaction history, investment options, and financial advice. Implementing chatbots thus facilitates round-the-clock customer service and promotes an improved user experience, fostering customer engagement and satisfaction.

Lastly, the emergence of generative AI models offers further exciting prospects for innovative and successful applications, which may have fundamental implications for the future development of the financial sector (Capgemini Research Institute, 2023).

Financial Trading and Asset Management

AI has led to a paradigm shift in how investment decisions are made and executed. AI generally allows for identifying market trends and patterns, enabling data-driven financial decisions and anticipating market shifts more effectively.

In *financial trading*, AI systems allow the processing of vast amounts of financial data (e.g., historical market data and real-time market indicators) and AltData to identify, manage, and execute profitable trading opportunities. ML methods allow FIs and individual investors to analyze market trends, predict asset prices, and optimize trading strategies. By employing sophisticated predictive models and algorithmic trading strategies, AI enables traders to automate trading processes, minimize risk, and capitalize on market fluctuations with greater efficiency and accuracy (Azzutti et al., 2021).

In *asset management*, AI affects how investment portfolios are constructed, monitored, and optimized. As a result of ML, AI systems can identify potential investment opportunities, assess risks, and construct diversified portfolios tailored to specific investment objectives and risk preferences. AI-powered asset management also permits continuous portfolio monitoring and real-time risk assessment, allowing for timely portfolio adjustments and rebalancing to maximize returns in a more informed and dynamic manner (IOSCO, 2021).

Cybersecurity and Fraud Detection

AI applications enable FIs to bolster their defensive and reactive capabilities in a context of increasingly sophisticated and evolving cyber threats and fraudulent activities. By monitoring network activities, user behavior, and transactional data, AI-powered *cybersecurity* systems can detect and respond to suspicious activities, enabling proactive threat mitigation and safeguarding sensitive financial information. Moreover, ML-based *fraud detection* mechanisms can enhance the accuracy and efficiency of fraud identification by spotting irregular transaction patterns, unusual account behavior, and potentially fraudulent activities in real time (Raghavan & El Gayar, 2019).

Overall, integrating AI in cybersecurity and fraud detection can reinforce FIs' organizational and operational resilience, thus contributing to the integrity and safety of the financial system and fostering trust in digital finance among various stakeholders.

Regulatory Technology (Regtech)

Regtech refers to using cutting-edge technologies, such as AI and ML, to assist FIs in meeting compliance requirements more efficiently and effectively (Arner et al., 2016).

Owing to AI, organizations can automate and streamline compliance processes, enhance transparency, and ensure adherence to complex and evolving regulatory frameworks. Regtech solutions aim to optimize resource allocation, minimize costs, and enhance accuracy while mitigating risks of human error and other threats. These innovative tools not only automate time-consuming compliance tasks but also enable proactive risk management, fraud detection, and the implementation of robust security protocols to safeguard sensitive financial data and the integrity of information and communication technologies (ICTs) networks and infrastructures (Miglionico, 2020).

The strategic adoption of regtech allows FIs to embrace a proactive approach to compliance, ensuring alignment with industry standards and best practices while fostering a resilient and adaptable regulatory environment.

Supervisory Technology (Suptech)

Suptech refers to using advanced technologies, including AI and ML, to enhance the regulatory oversight capabilities of financial supervisors (Menon, 2017). AI tools allow supervisors to analyze enormous volumes of regulatory and other data to detect anomalies, suspicious patterns, or potential fraudulent activities. With enhanced cognitive capability, competent authorities can perform real-time monitoring and gain comprehensive insights into market trends, firm-specific and systemic risks, and other potential areas of vulnerability. This knowledge is then helpful to guide regulatory decision-making, policy formulation, supervisory activities, and the implementation of measures to mitigate risks.

For example, in banking supervision, AI can assist competent authorities in various tasks, such as risk and suitability assessments (Azzutti et al., 2023). Suptech can also play a critical role in market conduct supervision by facilitating the identification of illicit practices and their effects on markets. In addition, ML methods can extend to auditing algorithmic systems (e.g., behavioral testing) employed by market participants, supporting greater transparency and integrity in automated financial activities (Azzutti, 2023).

In sum, suptech is poised to become an indispensable component of financial supervisors' arsenal to promote consumer protection, market integrity, and financial stability.

Risks and Regulatory Considerations

Although AI can offer numerous advantages for FIs and their clients, some fundamental risks and limitations are associated with its adoption. Concerns are rising about the possible negative impact of AI adoption in finance on consumer protection, competition, market integrity, and financial stability (Boukherouaa et al., 2021; FSB, 2017; OECD, 2021a).

AI, particularly ML methods, gives rise to substantial legal and regulatory concerns. These concerns are primarily due to the potential for inaccurate and biased outcomes and the inherent difficulties of comprehending the inner workings of AI systems and their decision-making process – commonly known as the "black box" problem. But before delving into regulatory considerations, this section introduces the key techno-methodic specificities of AI that, due to ML, can negatively affect the trustworthiness of applications.

The Techno-Methodic Specificities of ML Systems

Due to ML, examining the distinctive attributes of AI systems is necessary to address the risks associated with their adoption and related regulatory aspects. This subsection addresses six techno-methodic specificities of ML-based systems: (1) "data dependency," (2) "correlation focus," (3) "complexity," (4) "autonomy," (5) "opacity" or the "black box" problem, and (6) "vulnerability."

Data Dependency and Bias

ML heavily depends on the availability of high-quality *data* to achieve accurate decision-making and predictive capabilities. The trustworthiness of ML-generated outcomes can be impaired by several factors, including inherent *biases* within the data or those introduced by humans along the AI lifecycle. Additionally, the requirement for substantial and diverse datasets to achieve optimal performance can pose challenges, mainly when such data are scarce or costly. Thus, ensuring the integrity and quality of training, validation, and testing data is crucial to mitigate the risks associated with biased or flawed datasets (Mehrabi et al., 2021).

All these considerations highlight the importance of robust data governance measures to safeguard against potentially detrimental outcomes, thus ensuring trustworthy AI applications.

Correlation Focus

The notion of *correlation focus* in ML underscores the potential risk of mistaking "correlation" for "causation" in analyzing complex datasets. Although ML-based systems can help identify latent patterns and relationships within data, they emphasize correlations without necessarily capturing causal relationships. Consequently, blind reliance on correlations alone can lead to erroneous assumptions and misguided conclusions, potentially impacting decision-making processes. This limitation is particularly critical when dealing with complex financial data (e.g., nonstationary and noisy), which may require establishing causal relationships to ensure accurate risk assessment and well-informed decisions (Lommers et al., 2021).

Because of this feature, human experts must take preventive measures, such as employing robust validation and testing techniques, to ensure trustworthy AI applications. A challenging task is effectively discerning causal links from mere correlations requires solid domain knowledge and skills as basic prerequisites.

Complexity

ML-based systems are characterized by high technical *complexity* that manifests in various dimensions. First, complexity arises from AI systems' intricate technical design and operational functioning. Second, complexity can be amplified by integrating sophisticated architectures, diverse components, and intricate methods within AI systems. These systems can be conceptualized as complex networks of algorithms in which multiple software and hardware components interact to achieve specific business objectives. Third, engineering advanced AI systems demands a confluence of expertise from various highly specialized fields. As a result, assembling a team of experts with diverse skill sets is crucial to ensure trustworthy AI adoption (Rodríguez de Las Heras Ballell, 2019).

As the complexity of AI systems increases due to ML, so does the challenge of controlling and predicting their operations. This complexity contributes to the potential risks of unforeseen behavior and operational failures, even in the presence of diligent user oversight. Complexity, thus, raises critical ethical and legal concerns about human accountability and liability. All these risks underpin the necessity to understand the various sources of system complexity and implement adequate measures (e.g., validation, testing, and monitoring) to mitigate potential failure points.

Autonomy

Integrating AI into business operations enables greater automation in decision-making processes. The *autonomy* of ML-based systems denotes their capacity to make decisions and take actions with limited or no human intervention due to predefined physical-digital infrastructures, algorithms, and datasets. Although this autonomy can enhance decision-making efficiency, it also introduces inherent risks. Complex ML methods may produce difficult-to-understand and challenging results, potentially leading to errors and biased outcomes, raising fundamental issues of human accountability and responsibility (Rodríguez de Las Heras Ballell, 2019).

A lack of adequate human oversight and control over algorithmic decision-making compounds these risks. Moreover, the "automation bias" phenomenon, whereby AI users tend to accept recommendations or decisions made by automated systems as valid, further exacerbates these challenges (Skitka et al., 2000).

Given the diverse spectrum of system autonomy, from limited decision-support functions to highly autonomous actions, robust governance frameworks are essential to ensure trustworthy AI adoption. This framework is especially true in critical domains such as finance, where an AI system's decisions or outcomes can have far-reaching implications for the entire financial sector.

Opacity

Many challenges human experts face in understanding AI systems' inner workings and decision-making processes are due to *opacity* issues. Although ML models can lead to highly accurate predictions and insights, they may lack transparency and interpretability. This opacity can stem from various practical factors. First, it may result from a deliberate choice by private organizations aiming to protect their competitive advantage. Alternatively, opacity may result from a lack of specialized expertise within organizations in handling complex AI systems. Lastly, specific ML models' complex, nonlinear nature (e.g., because of DL) may inevitably contribute to opacity (Burrell, 2016).

Despite the source, opacity complicates identifying potential biases or errors in a system. This limitation concerns transparency, accountability, and overall trust in AI operations and generated outcomes. In sectors such as finance, where understanding the rationale behind decisions is critical for regulatory compliance and risk management, opacity poses major challenges. To mitigate these risks, for example, efforts are being made to develop "explainable AI" (xAI) techniques and tools that can provide insights into "black box" AI's decision-making process, thus safeguarding transparency and trust in their operations (Adadi & Berrada, 2018; Arrieta et al., 2020).

Vulnerability

The highly technical nature of ML-based systems, reliant on data-driven decision-making, sophisticated algorithms, and complex ICT architectures, renders them susceptible to various *vulnerabilities*. These risks include threats such as cyber-attacks, software glitches, and other malfunctions that can lead to system failure or unintended behavior (Rodríguez de Las Heras Ballell, 2019).

Instances of system breaches by external actors concern so-called "adversarial attacks." A striking example is "data poisoning," which involves exploiting weaknesses within the underlying data used for training and live operations (Yerlikaya & Bahtiyar, 2022). These system breaches can further complicate accountability and liability issues, as uncovering the root cause of malfunctions necessitates substantial technical expertise and investigative efforts.

Given the impossibility of eliminating cybersecurity risks, organizations must foster a culture of vigilance and cyber resilience. This process requires robust cybersecurity policies and measures, including developing, deploying, and maintaining comprehensive security protocols to uphold operational integrity and business continuity.

Challenges for Regulation

With financial firms' widespread adoption of AI, policymakers and regulators must ensure responsible and safe applications within the industry. This subsection discusses key regulatory considerations underpinning the policy quest for effective AI governance. These considerations include (1) transparency and explainability,

(2) fairness and nondiscrimination, (3) data privacy and security, and (4) human control and oversight.

Transparency and Explainability

A lack *of transparency and explainability* in AI systems is a primary concern, especially in risky applications where "black box" models may result in unfair or discriminatory outcomes, ultimately harming consumers and markets. Although regulators are increasingly alert to the risks associated with "black box" AI, several possible approaches are becoming available to achieve greater transparency. For instance, FIs must disclose their use of AI systems in providing financial services to their clients. In addition, FIs should maintain detailed documentation of how their AI systems are developed, including information on datasets used, models, and human intervention. This information should be readily accessible for regulatory review to ensure that AI systems are adopted responsibly and ethically. Moreover, FIs might be mandated to explain to consumers or other stakeholders how decisions were made using AI systems (Bibal et al., 2021).

Fairness and Nondiscrimination

AI systems may be susceptible to bias, impinging on considerations of *fairness* and *nondiscrimination* toward certain groups of people. For example, an ML-powered credit scoring system may inadvertently favor or discriminate against individuals from specific ethnic or socioeconomic backgrounds (Tok & Heng, 2022).

Regulatory authorities may require FIs to monitor their systems regularly for signs of bias and discrimination to counter these risks. This process involves, for instance, reviewing datasets for potential biases or conducting regular audits of AI systems to ensure they are not producing unfair or discriminatory outcomes. Moreover, FIs may be required to undergo "external audits" to ward off issues of fairness and nondiscrimination in their AI systems (Koshiyama et al., 2021).

Data Privacy and Security

With regard to aspects of data confidentiality and integrity, AI applications must adhere to high standards of *data privacy* and *security*. FIs must ensure that any data processed by their AI systems are obtained legally and stored securely. Consumers must also be duly informed about how their data are being used and have the right to access, correct, or delete it.

To ensure compliance, regulators may mandate appropriate safeguards for FIs to protect customer data. These measures include, for instance, implementing encryption protocols, access controls, and regular data backups. Furthermore, FIs may also be required to undergo regular data security assessments to ensure that their AI systems are cyber-secured and do not impose risks to the integrity and confidentiality of personal data (Aggarwal, 2023).

Human Control and Oversight

In balancing automation with *human control* and *oversight*, the "human-in-the-loop" and "human-on-the-loop" represent two key approaches. The former approach denotes active human participation alongside AI systems, involving direct intervention and oversight during decision-making. The latter approach, instead, describes a supervisory role where humans only oversee AI systems from a higher level perspective, providing guidance and adjusting parameters whenever deemed necessary.

In addressing concerns surrounding the autonomous and opaque nature of specific AI applications, the human factor is essential for effective AI governance. To this end, FIs should establish specific roles or committees responsible for overseeing AI systems' design, development, and deployment. FIs may also be required to develop contingency plans to address potential malfunctions or unexpected outcomes. For instance, this requirement has long been seen in the algorithmic trading domain, where firms must equip their systems with "kill-switch" functionality (Buckley et al., 2021).

Emerging Regulatory Trends and Best Practices in AI Governance

If left unregulated, financial markets may lead to market failures and instability. Thus, financial regulation aims to protect consumer protection, market integrity, and financial stability while promoting economic efficiency. In this context, effective AI governance presents a complex challenge for policymakers and regulators, who must balance fostering technological innovation with achieving broader public goals. Hence, this section reviews emerging regulatory approaches in selected jurisdictions to promote effective AI governance. It also introduces the concept of "regulatory sandboxes" as experimental regulatory regimes that facilitate innovation.

Emerging Regulatory Approaches

Diverse regulatory approaches to AI governance have emerged globally, reflecting varied socio-economic contexts and policy priorities across jurisdictions. Although some countries have embraced a proactive stance, others have opted for more permissive models that encourage self-regulation (Wu & Liu, 2023).

China's "state-led" approach emphasizes centralized control to align innovation with strategic national objectives. This regulatory strategy aligns with the government's broader agenda of steering technological development to ensure social stability and advance China's global competitive position (Cheng & Zheng, 2023). Regulations addressing recommender systems, synthetic content, and generative AI represent the most significant initiatives in this area. Although

Chinese FIs rapidly embrace AI, they face challenges such as limitations in the availability of Chinese-language data for AI training and regulatory concerns about data security, bias, and ethical implications. All these uncertainties underlie the need for adequate expertise in the field and may require additional regulations to ensure effective AI governance (Ran and Zhang, 2023).

Jurisdictions like the United States (US), the United Kingdom (UK), and Singapore have embraced a "pro-innovation" approach characterized by minimal regulatory intervention and industry participants' voluntary adoption of best practices. In the US, only nonbinding guidelines are available so far. In late 2022, the US government released its Blueprint for an AI Bill of Rights, a high-level statement on the risks associated with AI adoption (White House Office of Science and Technology Policy, 2022). More recently, the National Institute of Standards and Technology (NIST) issued the AI Risk Management Framework, providing nonbinding guidance to standardize AI risks and promote trustworthy AI adoption across various economic sectors (NIST, 2023). As for the financial sector, only scattered initiatives are reported. For instance, the Securities and Exchange Commission (SEC) has proposed rules for financial firms offering AI-powered investment services designed to prevent conflicts of interest from arising with clients (Securities and Exchange Commission, 2023).

The UK government has implemented a cross-cutting, context-specific, and principle-based regulatory framework. While having a nonbinding nature for FIs, this framework complements existing sector-specific legislation. The objective is to foster innovation while encouraging ethical and responsible AI deployment, ensuring high levels of compliance with existing regulations (UK Department for Science, Innovation and Technology, 2023).

Known for its innovation-friendly ecosystem, Singapore has enacted soft-law instruments to guide FIs toward trustworthy AI adoption. The Monetary Authority of Singapore (MAS) introduced the Fairness, Ethics, Accountability, and Transparency (FEAT) Principles in 2018, marking the world's first regulatory initiative targeting AI and data analytics in finance (MAS, 2018). More recently, the same MAS released Veritas Toolkit 2.0, an open-source toolkit for financial firms that provides a methodology for assessing their compliance with the FEAT principles. This collaborative initiative between MAS and industry participants exemplifies Singapore's holistic and multi-stakeholder approach to AI governance (MAS et al., 2023).

The European Union (EU) AI governance approach somewhat represents a middle ground characterized by a "right-based" perspective. Notably, the recently agreed AI Act aims to regulate AI systems that pose potential threats to individual safety and fundamental rights, employing a risk-based approach. Accordingly, while some excessively hazardous applications are banned, requirements proportional to the associated risks apply to other applications (European Parliament, 2023). Although the AI Act is designed to be universally applicable to all AI systems, regardless of their specific scope, it complements and overlaps with existing sectorial legislation targeting AI applications. Significantly, the AI Act only explicitly addresses AI applications in credit scoring as "high-risk," which are therefore subject to more stringent regulatory requirements. For other financial AI applications, less stringent obligations will likely apply. Nevertheless, some ambiguity remains about applying the AI Act to those AI use cases that do not involve risks to fundamental rights but only risks of a strictly financial nature (Alibrandi et al., 2023).

Overall, the examples above demonstrate that the global landscape of AI governance and regulation is evolving. In acknowledging risks and perils associated with a fragmented regulatory environment, enhanced international cooperation and standardization are becoming imperatives to mitigate potential risks of "forum-shopping" and "regulatory arbitrage." Therefore, a more unified and coordinated global approach to AI governance may soon become desirable (Schmitt, 2022).

Regulatory Sandboxes

Regulators generally lack the necessary expertise to address matters of AI governance. At the same time, placing exclusive reliance on industry-led self-regulation may not always fully align with the public interest (Hadfield & Clark, 2023). In this context, *regulatory sandboxes* have emerged as experimental platforms to address this knowledge asymmetry and, at the same time, facilitate innovation while maintaining essential regulatory standards (e.g., consumer protection and compliance). Regulatory sandboxes are controlled regulatory environments that allow businesses to experiment with new business models under relaxed regulatory requirements. This innovative approach creates a conducive space for businesses and regulators to collaborate and understand how to best approach technology development and regulation (Buckley et al., 2020).

Building upon early experiences within the fintech domain, "AI regulatory sandboxes" could offer numerous advantages. These experimental regulatory frameworks may help address the expertise gap within regulatory bodies by enabling multidisciplinary and multi-stakeholder cooperation. By fostering meaningful dialogue among various stakeholders and regulators, regulatory sandboxes could promote the development of global standards and frameworks for AI governance. In activating such initiatives, however, both policymakers and competent authorities are called upon to think carefully about key aspects governing AI regulatory sandboxes (e.g., concerning their scope and institutional organization), given the potential negative impacts on innovation, competition, and industry governance and regulation (OECD, 2023a).

Summary and Conclusions

This chapter offers a synoptic overview of the transformative role played by AI, particularly its subfield of ML, in driving the ongoing "fintech revolution." It introduced key concepts such as (1) the three "AI generations," (2) the main "ML paradigms," and (3) the notion of the "AI lifecycle." After discussing some of the benefits of integrating AI/ML in financial services, it presents some prominent use cases, including (1) risk management and credit scoring, (2) financial trading and investments, (3) cybersecurity and fraud detection, (4) regtech, and (5) suptech.

In contrast, this chapter highlights the multifaceted risks and regulatory considerations associated with AI adoption. Remarkably, given the techno-methodic specificities of ML-based systems and the resulting uncertainties to achieve trustworthy applications (e.g., in terms of transparency, fairness, safety, human accountability, and liability), this chapter emphasizes the need for (1) robust governance measures and (2) appropriate regulatory frameworks. In light of these imperatives, it then briefly reviews emerging regulatory approaches to AI governance in selected jurisdictions (i.e., China, the US, the UK, Singapore, and the EU). Lastly, it discusses the possible merits of experimental approaches such as "regulatory sandboxes."

Nevertheless, as progress in AI/ML continues to advance and new applications emerge, it will become increasingly important for policymakers and regulators to address the following questions:

- What specific knowledge do policymakers and regulators need to effectively address the challenges of regulating AI in finance?
- What role should regulation play in incentivizing AI innovation while protecting against potential risks?
- How can regulatory frameworks dynamically cope with rapid progress in AI and continue to safeguard the goals of consumer protection, market integrity, and financial stability?

Discussion Questions

- Using credit scoring as an illustrative use case, explain how ML methods differ from early AI methods such as "expert systems."
- Using algorithmic trading as an illustrative case, describe the "AI lifecycle."
- Using regtech as an illustrative use case, identify and discuss two primary risks associated with AI adoption that may impact consumer confidence.
- Identify the main differences among emerging regulatory approaches to AI governance.

References

Adadi, A., & Berrada, M. (2018). Peeking inside the black-box: A survey on explainable artificial intelligence (XAI). *IEEE Access*, *6*, 52138–52160.

Aggarwal, N. (2023). AI, Fintech, and the evolving regulation of consumer financial privacy. In J. B. Bullock, Y-C Chen, J. Himmelreich, V. M. Hudsond, A. Korinek, M. M. Young, & B. Zhang (Eds.), *The oxford handbook of AI governance, C51. S1−C51.N45*. Oxford University Press.

Alibrandi, S., Rabitti, M., & Schneider, G. (2023). The European AI Act's impact on financial markets: From Governance to Co-regulation. European Banking Institute Working Paper Series 2023 – No. 138. https://ssrn.com/abstract=4414559

Arner, D., Barberis, J., & Buckley, R. P. (2016). FinTech, RegTech, and the reconceptualization of financial regulation. *Northwestern Journal of International Law & Business*, *37*(3), 371−413.

Arrieta, A. B., Diaz-Rodriquez, N., DelSer, J., Bennetot, A., Tabik, S., Barbado, A., Garcia, S., Gil-Lopez, S., Molina, D., Benjamins, R., Raja, C., & Herrera, F. (2020). Explainable Artificial Intelligence (XAI): Concepts, taxonomies, opportunities and challenges toward responsible AI. *Information Fusion*, *58*, 82–115.

Assefa, S. A., Dervovic, D., Mahfouz, M., Tillman, R. E., Reddy, P., & Veloso, M. (2020). Generating synthetic data in finance: Opportunities, challenges and pitfalls. In *ICAIF '20: Proceedings of the First ACM International Conference on AI in Finance*. Association for Computing Machinery. Article No. 44.

Aziz, S., & Dowling, M. (2019). Machine learning and ai for risk management. In T. Lynn, J. G. Mooney, P. Rosati, & M. Cummins (Eds.), *Disrupting finance. Palgrave studies in digital business and enabling technologies* (pp. 33–50). Palgrave Macmillan.

Azzutti, A. (2023). The algorithmic future of EU market conduct supervision: A preliminary check. In L. Böffel, & J. Schürger (Eds.), *Digitalisation, sustainability, and the banking and capital markets Union, EBI studies in banking and capital markets Law* (pp. 53–98). Palgrave Macmillan.

Azzutti, A., Ringe, W.-G., & Batista, P. M. (2023). Navigating the legal landscape of AI-enhanced banking supervision: Protecting EU fundamental rights and ensuring good administration. *Columbia Journal of European Law (Forthcoming)*. Working paper version. https://ssrn.com/abstract=4430642

Azzutti, A., Ringe, W.-G., & Siegfried Stiehl, H. (2021). Machine learning, market manipulation and collusion in capital markets: Why the "Black Box" matters. *University of Pennsylvania Journal of International Law*, *43*(1), 79–135.

Bibal, A., Lognoul, M., de Streel, A., & Frénay, B. (2021). Legal requirements on explainability in machine learning. *Artificial Intelligence and Law*, *29*, 149–169.

Bommasani, R., Hudson, D. A., Adeli, E., Altman, R., Arora, S., von Arx, S., Bernstein, M. S., Bohg, J., Bosselut, A., Brunskill, E., Brynjolfsson, E., Buch, S., Card, D., Castellon, R., Chatterji, N., Chen, A., Creel, K., Davis, J. Q., Demszky, D., & Wang, W. (2022). On the Opportunities and Risks of Foundation Models. arXiv preprint. https://arxiv.org/abs/2108.07258

Boukherouaa, B., Shabsigh, G., AlAjmi, K., Deodoro, J., Farias, A., Iskender, E. S., Mirestean, A. T., & Ravikumar, R. (2021). *Powering the digital economy: Opportunities and risks of artificial intelligence in finance*. International Monetary Fund.

Buchanan, B. G. (2019). Artificial intelligence in finance. The Alan Turing Institute.

Buckley, R. P., Arner, D., Veidt, R., & Zetzsche, D. (2020). Building fintech ecosystems: Regulatory sandboxes, innovation hubs and beyond. *Washington University Journal of Law Policy*, *61*(1), 55–98.

Buckley, R. P., Zetzsche, D. A., Arner, D. W., & Tang, B. (2021). Regulating artificial intelligence in finance: Putting the human in the loop. *Sydney Law Review*, *43*(1), 43–81.

Burrell, J. (2016). How the machine 'thinks': Understanding opacity in machine learning algorithms. *Big Data & Society*, *3*(1), 1−12.

Cao, L. (2022). AI in finance: Challenges, techniques, and opportunities. *ACM Computing Surveys*, *55*(3), Article No. 64.

Capgemini Research Institute. (2023). Why consumers love generative AI. https://prod.ucwe.capgemini.com/wp-content/uploads/2023/05/Final-Web-Version-Report-Creative-Gen-AI.pdf

Cheng, J., & Zheng, J. (2023). Shaping AI's future? China in global AI governance. *Journal of Contemporary China*, *32*(143), 794–810.

De Silva, D., & Alahakoon, D. (2022). An artificial intelligence life cycle: From conception to production. *Patterns 3*, Article no. 100489.

Deloitte. (2022). Finance innovation survey 2023: How finance executives in Switzerland see the current state of AI and its potential in finance. https://www2.deloitte.com/content/dam/Deloitte/ch/Documents/strategy-operations/deloitte-ch-finance-innovation-survey-2023.pdf

Deloitte. (2023). The implications of generative AI in finance: A new frontier in artificial intelligence and for finance. https://www2.deloitte.com/us/en/pages/consulting/articles/generative-ai-in-finance.html

Deng, L., & Dong, Y. (2014). Deep learning: Methods and applications. *Foundations and Trends in Signal Processing*, *7*(3–4), 197–387.

European Parliament. (2023). Artificial intelligence act: Deal on comprehensive rules for trustworthy AI. Press releases of December 9. https://www.europarl.europa.eu/news/en/press-room/20231206IPR15699/artificial-intelligence-act-deal-on-comprehensive-rules-for-trustworthy-ai

FSB. (2017). Artificial intelligence and machine learning in financial services: Market developments and financial stability implications. https://www.fsb.org/wp-content/uploads/P011117.pdf

Haakman, M., Cruz, L., Huijgens, H., & van Deursen, A. (2021). AI lifecycle models need to be revised: An exploratory study in fintech. *Empirical Software Engineering*, *26*. Article No. 95.

Hadfield, G. K., & Clark, J. (2023). Regulatory markets: The future of AI governance. arXiv preprint. https://arxiv.org/pdf/2304.04914.pdf

IOSCO. (2021). The use of artificial intelligence and machine learning by market intermediaries and asset managers. Final Report. https://www.iosco.org/library/pubdocs/pdf/IOSCOPD684.pdf

Koshiyama, A., Firoozye, N., & Treleaven, P. (2020). Algorithms in future capital markets: A survey on AI, ML and associated algorithms in capital markets. *ICAIF'20: Proceedings of the First ACM International Conference on AI in Finance*, Article No. 14. Association for Computing Machinery.

Koshiyama, A., Kazim, E., Treleaven, P., Rai, P., Szpruch, L., Giles, P., Ahamat, G., Leutner, F., Goebel, R., Knight, A., Adams, J., Hitrova, C., Barnett, J., Nachev, P., Barber, D., Chamorro-Premuzic, T., Klemmer, K., & Lomas, E. (2021). Towards algorithm auditing: A survey on managing legal, ethical and technological risks of AI, ML, and associated algorithms. Working Paper. https://ssrn.com/abstract=3778998

Lommers, K., El Harzli, O., & Kim, J. (2021). Confronting machine learning with financial research. arXiv preprint. https://arxiv.org/pdf/2103.00366.pdf

MAS. (2018). Principles to promote fairness, ethics, accountability and transparency (FEAT) in the use of artificial intelligence and data analytics in Singapore's financial sector. https://www.mas.gov.sg/publications/monographs-or-information-paper/2018/feat

MAS. (2023). Veritas document 5 – from methodologies to integration. https://www.mas.gov.sg/news/media-releases/2023/toolkit-for-responsible-use-of-ai-in-the-financial-sector#1

McCarthy, J., Minsky, M. L., Rochester, N., & Shannon, C. E. (2006). A proposal for the dartmouth summer research project on artificial intelligence. *AI Magazine*, *27*(4), 12–14.

McKinsey Global. (2022). The state of AI in 2022 — A half decade in review. https://www.mckinsey.com/capabilities/quantumblack/our-insights/the-state-of-ai-in-2022-and-a-half-decade-in-review

Mehrabi, N., Morstatter, F., Sexena, N., Lerman, K., & Galstyan, A. (2021). A survey on bias and fairness in machine learning. *ACM Computing Surveys*, *54*(6). Article No. 115.

Menon, R. (2017). Financial Regulation — The Forward Agenda." Keynote Address at the Australian Securities and Investment Commission (ASIC) Annual Forum 2017 on March 20, 2017. https://www.mas.gov.sg/news/speeches/2017/financial-regulation, 2017

Miglionico, A. (2020). Automated regulation and supervision: The impact of RegTech on banking compliance. *European Business Law Review*, *31*(4), 641–662.

Mnih, V., Kavukcuoglu, K., Silver, D., Rusu, A. A., Veness, J., Bellemare, M. G., Graves, A., Riedmiller, M., Fidjeland, A. K., Ostrovski, G., Petersen, S., Beattie, C., Sadik, A., Antonoglou, I., King, H., Kumaran, D., Wierstra, D., Legg, S., & Hassabis, D. (2015). Human-level control through deep reinforcement learning. *Nature*, *518*, 529–533.

NIST. (2023). Artificial intelligence risk management framework (AI RMF 1.0). https://nvlpubs.nist.gov/nistpubs/ai/nist.ai.100-1.pdf

NVIDIA. (2023). State of AI in financial services: 2023 trends. Survey Report. https://resources.nvidia.com/en-us-state-ai-report

OECD. (2021a). Artificial intelligence, machine learning and big data in finance: Opportunities, challenges, and implications for policy makers. https://www.oecd.org/finance/financial-markets/Artificial-intelligence-machine-learning-big-data-in-finance.htm

OECD. (2021b). OECD business and finance outlook 2021. https://www.oecd.org/finance/oecd-business-and-finance-outlook-26172577.htm

OECD. (2023a). Regulatory sandboxes in artificial intelligence. OECD Digital Economy Papers No. 356. https://www.oecd.org/publications/regulatory-sandboxes-in-artificial-intelligence-8f80a0e6-en.htm

OECD. (2023b). Recommendation of the Council on Artificial Intelligence. OECD/LEGAL/0449.

Olorunnimbe, K., & Viktor, H. (2023). Deep learning in the stock market — A systemic survey of practice, backtesting, and applications. *Artificial Intelligence Review*, *56*(3), 2057–2109.

Ozbayoglu, A. M., Gudelek, M. U., & Sezer, O. B. (2020). Deep learning for financial applications: A survey. *Applied Soft Computing*, *93*. Article No. 106384.

Raghavan, P., & El Gayar, N. (2019). Fraud detection using machine learning and deep learning. In *International conference on computational intelligence and knowledge economy (ICCIKE)* (pp. 334–339). Institute of Electrical and Electronics Engineers.

Ran, L., & Zhang, Y. (2023). Chinese banks jump on AI Bandwagon to cut costs. https://asia.nikkei.com/Spotlight/Caixin/Chinese-banks-jump-on-AI-bandwagon-to-cut-costs

Ringe, W.-G., & Ruof, C. (2021). Robo advice–legal and regulatory challenges. In I. Chiu & G. Deipenbrock (Eds.), *Routledge handbook of financial technology and law* (pp. 193–212). Routledge.

Rodríguez de Las Heras Ballell, Teresa. (2019). Legal challenges of artificial intelligence: Modelling the disruptive features of emerging technologies and assessing their possible legal impact. *Uniform Law Review*, *24*(2), 302−314.

Rudin, C. (2019). Stop explaining black box machine learning models for high stakes decisions and use interpretable models instead. *Nature Machine Intelligence*, *1*, 206–215.

Russell, S., & Norvig, P. (2021). *Artificial intelligence: A modern approach* (4th ed.). Person Higher Education.

Schmitt, L. (2022). Mapping global AI governance: A nascent regime in a fragmented landscape. *AI and Ethics*, *2*, 303−314.

Securities and Exchange Commission. (2023). Conflict of interest associated with the use of predictive data analytics by broker-dealers and investment advisers. Release Nos. 34-07990; IA-6353; File No. S7-12-23.

Skitka, L. J., Mosier, K., & Burdick, M. D. (2000). Accountability and automation bias. *International Journal of Human-Computer Studies*, *52*(4), 701–717.

Sutton, R. S., & Barto, A. (2018). *Reinforcement learning: An introduction*. MIT Press.

The Business Research Company. (2023). AI in FinTech Global Market Report 2023. https://www.thebusinessresearchcompany.com/report/ai-in-fintech-global-market-report#

Tok, W. Y., & Heng, D. (2022). Fintech: Financial inclusion or exclusion? International Monetary Fund Working Paper No. 2022/080. https://www.imf.org/en/Publications/WP/Issues/2022/05/06/Fintech-Financial-Inclusion-or-Exclusion-517619

Toner, H. (2023). What are generative AI, large language models, and foundation models? Center for security and emerging technology. https://cset.georgetown.edu/wp-content/uploads/What-Are-Generative-AI-Large-Language-Models-and-Foundation-Models.pdf

UK Department for Science, Innovation Technology. (2023). A Pro-Innovation Approach to AI Regulation. Policy paper. https://www.gov.uk/government/publications/ai-regulation-a-pro-innovation-approach/white-paper

Vela, D., Sharp, A., Zhang, R., Nguyen, T., Hoang, A., & Pianykh, O. S. (2022). Temporal quality degradation in AI models. *Scientific Reports*, *12*, Article No. 11654.

White House Office of Science and Technology Policy. (2022). Blueprint for an AI bill of rights: Making automated systems work for the american people. https://www.whitehouse.gov/wp-content/uploads/2022/10/Blueprint-for-an-AI-Bill-of-Rights.pdf

Wu, W., & Liu, S. (2023). A comprehensive review and systematic analysis of artificial intelligence regulation policies. arXiv preprint. https://arxiv.org/abs/2307.12218

Yerlikaya, F. A., & Bahtiyar, S. (2022). Data poisoning attacks against machine learning algorithms. *Expert Systems with Applications*, *208*, Article No. 118101.

Section VII

Understanding Other Applications of Fintech

Chapter 19

Insurtech: Disrupting the Insurance Industry

Iván Sosa Gómez

Camilo Jose Cela University, Spain

Abstract

The insurance industry has been slow to adopt digital technologies due to high barriers to entry, product complexity, capital reserves, solvency requirements, and regulatory constraints. This chapter focuses on how insurtech is disrupting the insurance industry, resulting in a transformation from a traditional structure to a dynamic user-centric ecosystem. Next, it highlights the insurtech ecosystem by providing an in-depth analysis of the new paradigm on how insurtech is transitioning from the linear value chain to a more dynamic and interconnected value network. Finally, this chapter defines a perspective of insurtech's impact by identifying three waves of transformation within the insurance industry and understanding the evolution and chronology of insurtech's influence. Thus, this chapter provides insights into the opportunities and challenges of this technological breakthrough, offering a comprehensive view of insurtech's transformative journey within the insurance landscape.

Keywords: Insurtech; insurance industry; disruption; value configuration; ecosystem

Introduction

This chapter explores the disruptive impact of insurtech on the insurance industry. *Insurtech* refers to any innovation boosted by technology that creates value in the insurance sector by delivering data-driven and customer-oriented solutions in a digital landscape.

The emergence of insurtech has caused a disruptive effect in the insurance industry, challenging traditional practices and transforming the way insurers design, distribute, and underwrite products. This transformation has forced

The Emerald Handbook of Fintech, 343–362

doi:10.1108/978-1-83753-608-520241043

traditional insurers to adapt or risk being left behind. Despite the challenges presented by legacy systems, regulatory constraints, and cultural resistance to change, insurtech start-ups are leveraging digital technologies to improve customer experience, reduce costs, and increase efficiency.

The remainder of this chapter is organized as follows. The first section focuses on how insurtech is disrupting the insurance industry by highlighting some critical drivers of this transformation and discussing some challenges that insurers face in adapting to this new environment. Next, this section provides an overview by revealing how insurtech has transformed the insurance sector from the traditional structure, leading to a dynamic user-centric ecosystem.

Moreover, insurtech has created a new ecosystem of collaboration, innovation, and co-creation. This ecosystem is evolving from a traditional linear value chain to a more dynamic and interconnected value network, enabling insurers and insurtechs to collaborate in new ways to create innovative products and services that meet changing customer needs. Insurers who balance maintaining their traditional strengths and investing in new capabilities will be better positioned to succeed in the sector.

The second section explains that the disruptive potential of insurtech has not only transformed the insurance industry's structure but also altered and disrupted the insurance value chain. This section provides an overview and an insightful analysis of how insurtech is shifting from a traditional linear value chain to a value network. It highlights the opportunities and challenges the insurtech ecosystem presents for insurers and customers.

Insurtech is creating waves of disruption in the insurance industry. These waves transform the industry from within, creating new business models, products, and services that meet changing customer needs. Insurers must adapt to this new landscape to stay relevant and competitive. In addition, the emergence of the liquid insurtech ecosystem presents opportunities for insurers to partner with these start-ups to increase their capabilities and enhance their offerings to customers.

The third section concerns how insurtech has created waves of disruption in the insurance industry. This section points out some challenges insurers face in adapting to this new landscape by detailing the waves in the insurance industry's transformation driven by insurtech.

The concluding section provides a valuable resource for academics, researchers, practitioners, and policymakers interested in understanding how insurtech disrupts the insurance industry. Furthermore, it offers an insightful contribution that aims to add value to the ongoing debate on how to harness the potential of insurtech while addressing its risks and challenges.

How Insurtech is Transforming the Insurance Industry

The insurance sector has slowly adopted digital technologies because high entry barriers, product complexity, capital reserves, solvency, and regulatory requirements have traditionally prevented new participants from competing. Consequently, many established insurers have had little reason to transform their business model by adopting new technologies, lagging other sectors in digital maturity, and operating with a business structure over 300 years old (Puschmann, 2017; Yan et al., 2018). Greineder et al. (2020) research on the structure of the insurance sector identifies four extensive generic areas in the traditional insurance sector, which relate to the (1) insurer process, (2) product, (3) distribution, and (4) small external service and support. These four broad generic areas in the traditional insurance sector are illustrated in Fig. 19.1.

However, due to the emergence of technological innovation, the insurance sector is transforming, mainly because of new industry entrants such as insurtechs

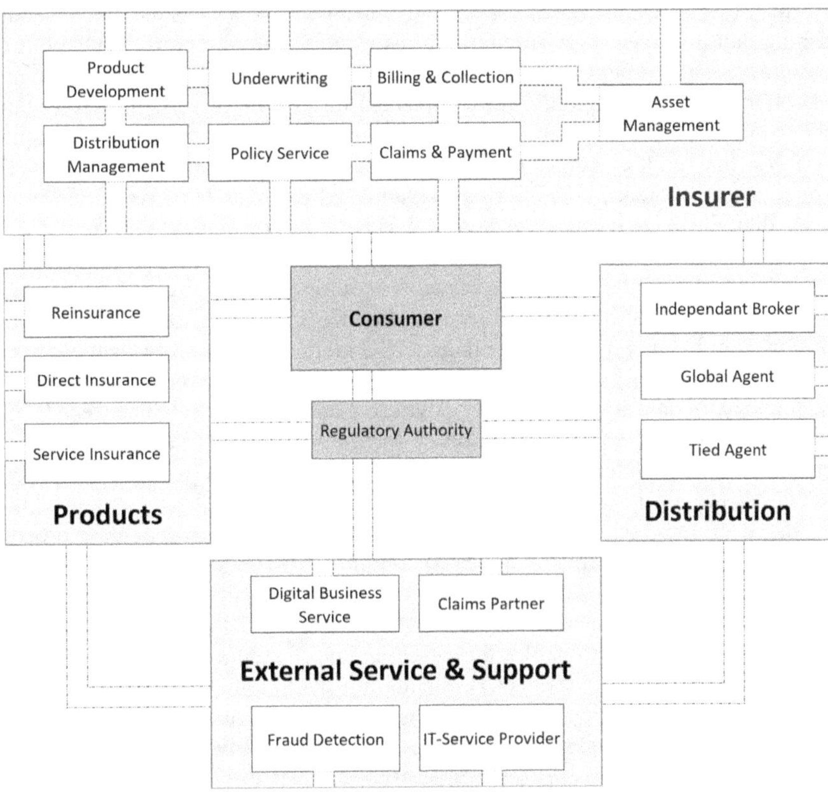

Fig. 19.1. Generic Configuration of the Insurance Sector. *Source:* The author's elaboration is based on Greineder et al. (2020). *Note:* This figure shows the structure of the insurance sector's configuration by pointing out four broad generic areas in the traditional insurance sector, which refer to the insurance (1) process, (2) product, (3) distribution, and (4) small external and support services.

(Greineder et al., 2020). For this reason, insurance companies are hampered by their business architecture and infrastructure, negatively affecting their ability to respond to changing consumer needs agilely (Catlin & Lorenz, 2017; Yan et al., 2018). Therefore, in a fast-moving and technology-driven environment, innovation is essential. Numerous scholars maintain that insurtechs target digital products and services, processes, and innovations in the business model (Lee & Shin, 2018). Because of the previously mentioned changes in customer demands, the entrance of new competitors (insurtechs as start-ups), and the increasing pressure of digitalization, insurers need to reorganize and close the digital gap (Greineder et al., 2020).

This digital gap can be characterized by the existence of 14 transformational capabilities of insurtech for understanding insurance value creation in a digital world (Stoeckli et al., 2018). Specifically, insurtech creates value by (1) establishing digital service provisioning and distribution infrastructure, (2) exploiting data for risk assessment and underwriting, (3) exploiting data for claims handling, (4) offering services digitally, (5) complementing insurance with prevention and recovery services, (6) integrating insurance with related services, (7) developing services that fulfill customer needs, (8) adapting to changes of insured risks, (9) covering of new risks, (10) offering risk-adjusted pricing, (11) distributing insurance digitally, (12) harnessing digital marketing opportunities, (13) acting as a digital broker, and (14) forming strategic partnerships.

In this digital context, all the players in the insurance sector are called to operate in a context where insurtechs are expanding rapidly (Cappiello, 2020). Based on the argument previously introduced, Eling and Lehmann (2018) identify technologies in the insurance sector by referring them into three main areas for categorization: (1) technology for data acquisition and analysis (big data, artificial intelligence [AI], and internet of things [IoT]), (2) technology for data storage (blockchain and cloud computing), and (3) technology for communication and sales (robo-advisor, social networks, mobile devices, apps, video calls, and websites).

Based on these scholars, insurtech provides data resources to achieve a better segmentation of customers (big data), obtaining better data for enabling the insurer to reorganize risk groups, which allows the application of more appropriate risk pricing for risk assessment by reducing information asymmetry. Furthermore, insurtech enables the development of automated responses to service queries through chatbots (AI), facilitating the automated calculation of the value of damages in decision-making, assisting in fraud prevention through data analysis, and providing new possibilities for risk assessment through image or language processing. In this sense, insurtech involves using telematic devices to obtain customer data for risk assessment, connecting, and receiving information through sensors (IoT), which enables the launch of new products focused on prevention or the development of situational insurance tailored to the customer. Furthermore, insurtech has enabled the digital storage of information, allowing customers to access their data anytime and anywhere (cloud computing).

As for blockchain-driven innovations, insurtech has allowed the use of a centralized database and checking legal requirements in automated underwriting processes, facilitating smart contract implementation. Finally, these technology-enhanced innovations for communication and sales have to enable the transformation of customer service by offering a real-time response solution (social networks, chat, video calls, and Messenger), enabling the use of new channels for customer acquisition, automating channels for information and sales (social networks, mobile devices, apps, video calls, and websites), as well as providing information, product announcements and brand reputation management (video platforms).

Therefore, based on the previous arguments detailed in the section, establishing the "innovation and technology" binomial in the insurance sector as the foundation for defining insurtech's impact in this sector is considered necessary. From the preceding, scholars have identified five insurtech driving capabilities that have been instrumental in boosting innovations in the insurance sector by defining them as the technological capabilities for applying innovation in the insurance sector (Sosa & Montes Pineda, 2022). These driving capabilities are:

(1) implementing digital capabilities,
(2) providing data-driven solutions,
(3) integrating services and customer experience,
(4) creating and developing digital insurance offers, and
(5) distributing digital insurance.

The potential of the five driving capabilities in transforming the insurance sector has arisen from combining the innovations themselves, establishing real-time remote connectivity, which is essential to improve data-driven decisions, using technology to hold digital conversations and provide virtual advice to consumers, which supports the automated formulation of new insurance tailored to consumers' needs, facilitating greater penetration of digital insurance distribution.

According to what has driven insurtech, these capabilities suggest 15 innovations transforming the insurance sector, as shown in Fig. 19.2.

(1) Developing configurable modules using cloud-native platforms and solutions.
(2) Providing efficiency through real-time automation of insurance transactions.
(3) Improving the operational workflows and work processes of companies across the entire value chain.
(4) Empowering companies with analytical tools through real-time data modeling.
(5) Allowing them to increase the value of these data by calculating insurance premiums accurately.
(6) Improving substantially risk assessment and prediction results in indifferent value chain areas.
(7) Automating virtual advice in customer service as well as interactive communication with consumers.
(8) Unlocking new service possibilities and integrating them into the value chain.

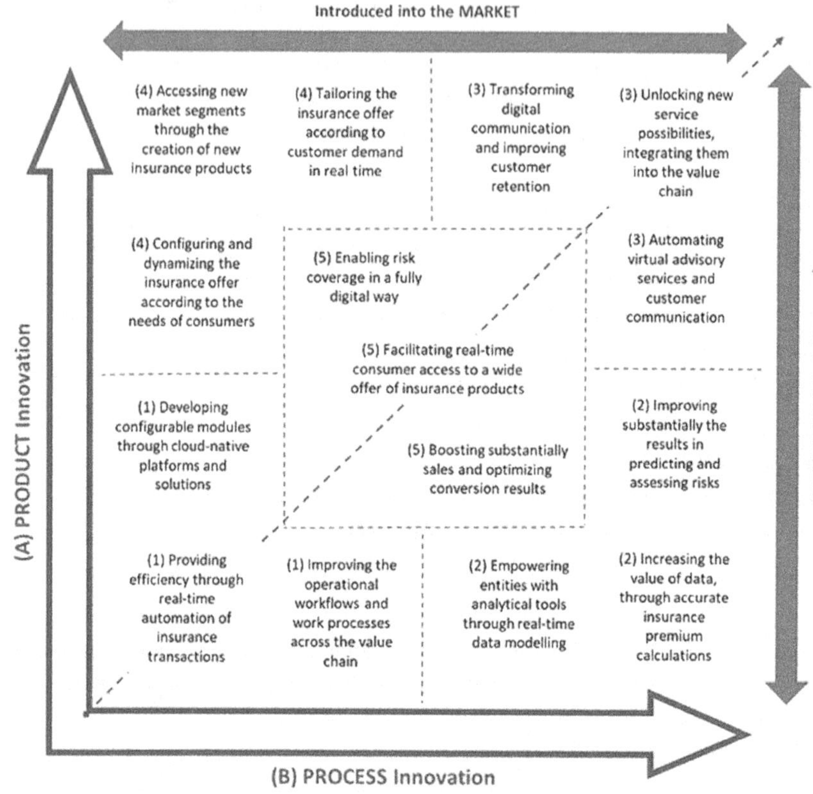

Fig. 19.2. Innovations Transforming the Insurance Sector. *Source:* The author. *Note:* This figure shows 15 innovations that are transforming the insurance industry through an Insurtech matrix in which innovations are classified by type of innovation (product or process) and by origin of innovation (company or market).

(9) Transforming digital communication and improving customer retention.
(10) Tailoring the insurance offers according to the typology of customer demand in real time.
(11) Accessing new risks through creating new insurance products.
(12) Configuring and dynamizing the insurance offers according to the customer's specific needs.
(13) Allowing customers to cover their risks in a fully digital way.
(14) Facilitating them in real time when accessing wide offers of insurance products

(15) Enabling a substantial increase in insurance policy sales and optimizing the conversion results in marketing campaigns.

Thus, insurtech's disruptive potential has emerged from the simultaneous occurrence of innovations and their connections to each other, altering and disrupting the structure of the insurance sector (Sosa & Montes Pineda, 2022). Insurtech supports this fact in the insurance sector since digital insurance distribution is not limited to obtaining quotes online but offers opportunities to find new ways to market and build closer relationships with consumers. This situation is interesting from a digital distribution perspective and those offering insurance services, given that the future potential relies on developing an offer tailored to the target audience, which can be combined simultaneously with data-driven solutions. In this respect, the increasing dissemination of new data on the policyholders, using new data sources via sensors and devices related to IoT technology, could revolutionize product design.

This scenario unlocks many new opportunities in proposing integrated services related to homes, vehicles, and connected healthcare solutions, allowing more accurate identification of insured risks. In addition, advisory services provided in the form of conversations via virtual assistants are increasingly used to formulate recommendations through quotes and insurance offers calculated by algorithms. This sequence of events is possible due to AI technology that minimizes human involvement, facilitating greater penetration of electronic commerce in insurance, reducing operational costs in business processes, and offering the consumer a multichannel experience.

Furthermore, implementing digital capabilities supported by cloud services technology enables faster connectivity across all parties, allowing innovation to automate processes and verification of claims, thereby increasing customer satisfaction. In this sense, it will enable setting up insurance products digitally, giving customers an overview of their policies, automating queries, and modifying their policies. Moreover, the more risk data is available, the greater the possibility of analyzing the available data and extracting new information about the customers. Consequently, big data technology can establish exact customization according to customer profiles and their specific needs to improve or create a new offer adapting the insurance products. Carrying out contracting transactions is possible through digital processes securely employing blockchain technology, which facilitates administering insurance policies through digital storage in cloud services.

Academics agree that the low rates of digitization in the insurance sector and the wave of technological advances in the external environment pose a dilemma for existing insurers, which will have to adapt or face the insurtech threat (Catlin & Lorenz, 2017; Puschmann, 2017; Yan et al., 2018), This dilemma mainly occurs because of an industry influenced by technological innovation, whose logical approach focuses on an increasingly favorable landscape for insurtech (Bussmann, 2017; Lee & Shin, 2018; Puschmann, 2017). Following the research work carried out by Greineder et al. (2020), this landscape is presented, defining the current structure of the insurance sector after the impact of insurtech. Fig. 19.3 shows the configuration of the insurance sector after the impact of insurtech.

Therefore, the actual structure of the insurance sector states that this sector belongs to the network economy and is shaped by complementary network effects (Greineder et al., 2020). Previous research (Sosa & Montes Pineda, 2021) reflects this structure, where their findings reveal how insurtech has transformed the insurance sector from the traditional structure, leading to a dynamic user-centric ecosystem where insurtech activity does not focus exclusively on an isolated part of the insurance value chain but, on the contrary, they target almost all stages of the ecosystem (Braun & Schreiber, 2017).

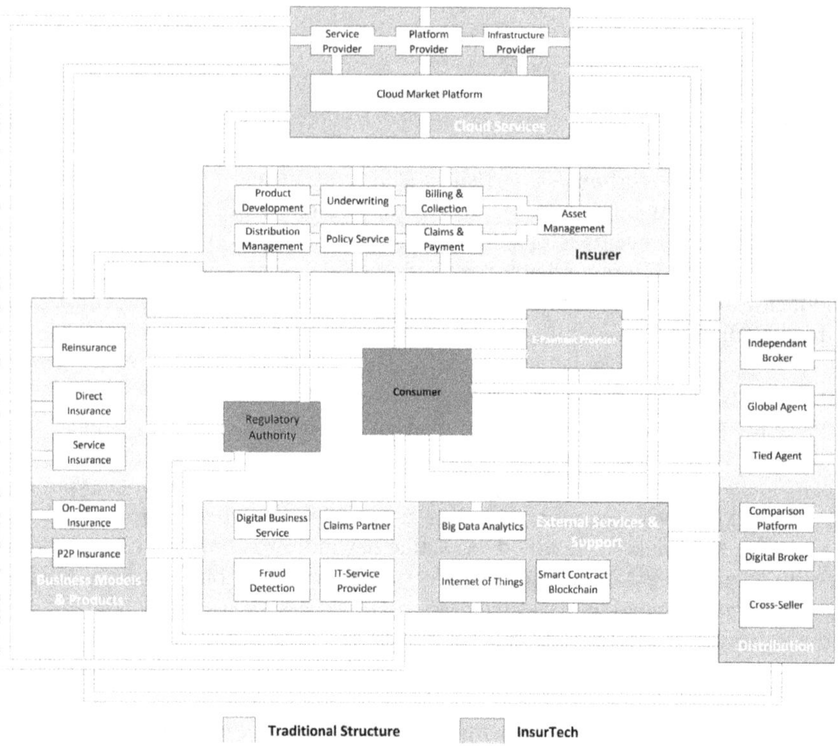

Fig. 19.3. The Shape of the Insurance Industry after the Impact of InsurTech. *Source:* The author's elaboration is based on Greineder et al. (2020). *Note:* This figure highlights insurtech's' impact on the structure of the current configuration of the insurance industry in each of the four major generic areas of the traditional insurance industry.

Insurtech Ecosystem: From Value Chain to Value Network

Insurtech's disruptive potential has emerged from the simultaneous occurrence of innovations. Additionally, their connections with each other have transformed the insurance structure and disrupted the value chain (Sosa & Montes Pineda, 2022).

This context is reflected in insurtech's impact in all areas of the value chain. Notably, innovations in (1) marketing related to insurtechs such as *HazardHub*, which also enables transforming large amounts of data into the actuarial calculation and underwriting processes insurtechs, like *Aventus*, integrated throughout the insurance value chain, offer an insurance experience tailored to customers' needs. The innovations in (2) product development are related to insurtechs such as *Kakau*, which, through its platform, offers seamless insurance from underwriting to claims management, and *FloodFlash*, an insurtech that provides loss payments within a few days after a flood.

Innovations related to (3) sales include insurtechs such as *Novidea*, which also cover all aspects of the insurance business, automating workflows and streamlining every phase of the customer journey. Another insurtech is *Cheche Technology*, which offers risk rating and underwriting services by providing users with direct selling prices from insurance companies. As for innovations in (4) underwriting insurtechs, such as *Omniscience*, improve the processes of actuarial calculation, claims management, capital management, and sales. Likewise, *Praedicat*, an insurtech, uses prospective data to quantify the loss potential in an insurance portfolio probabilistically. Innovations in (5) contract management and customer service insurtechs, like *ManageMy*, offer marketing and sales campaigns to their customers through their digital platforms. Another instance is *IBA*, an insurtech that, through end-to-end insurance, offers a solution covering all end-to-end processes for insurers, including marketing, sales, and claims.

Within the innovations related to (6) claims management, insurtechs such as *SO-SURE* enable exceptional performance in customer retention while working with distribution partners to create integrated insurance solutions. Insurtechs, such as *FRISS*, support complete end-to-end digital processing across underwriting using myriad data source integrations. Finally, the innovations identified in (7) asset and risk management are related to insurtechs, such as *Ecopia*, which helps insurance companies transform their underwriting, risk, and claims operations into a model. Another case is *Betterview*, an insurtech platform that helps property insurers analyze, rate, manage, and monitor property. Thus, technology-driven innovations (insurtechs) have enabled the disruption of the insurance value chain. Insurtech's disruptive potential has arisen from the simultaneous impact of insurtech innovations in each value chain area, altering and disrupting the insurance value chain. This fact is supported by academics who argue that the adoption of insurtech involves using innovative technology to disrupt the insurance value chain (Andrews, 2018; Catlin & Lorenz, 2017).

However, the value chain analysis does not provide any guidance on identifying the source of this market disruption. Instead, the value network perspective naturally places this disruption at the center of the analysis (Fjeldstad & Ketels, 2006). In this sense, Stabell and Fjeldstad (1998) define three main categories of activities in the value network. The activities carried out are represented in layers rather than sequentially, as in the value chain. These activities are (1) network infrastructure operation, (2) service provisioning, and (3) network promotion and contract management. According to scholars, these differences can be captured by different value configurations, as the value chain and value network representations capture different ways in which the activities of firms interact to create value, depending on the underlying value creation logic and economics of the firms and their associated industries. From a general approach, the value chain and the value network representations capture different ways a firm's activities interact to create value, depending on the underlying value creation logic and economics of enterprises and their associated industries (Fjeldstad & Ketels, 2006).

Furthermore, the activities performed in the value network are represented in layers rather than sequentially, as in the value chain (Stabell & Fjeldstad, 1998). According to these academics, Stoeckli et al. (2018) show that the disruptive potential of insurtech emerges through the continuous alignment of (1) infrastructure operations with (2) service delivery, the continuous alignment of (1) infrastructure operations, and (3) network promotion, and the continuous alignment of (3) network promotion and (2) service delivery. Consequently, the insurtech dynamic has transformed the insurance sector by disrupting the value chain and resulted in a new context in the insurance sector.

Insurtech reflects this new context with companies like *Sureify* providing omnichannel sales capabilities (selling) while increasing placement rates through quoting, electronic application, and automated underwriting (risk analysis and pricing). At the same time, it offers customers in force comprehensive self-service portals and native apps (customer service). It uses insights to foster lifelong digital relationships with policyholders through multiple forms of engagement (building the brand).

Insurtechs like *Moonshot Insurance* combine innovative insurance coverage (product development) with a fully digital experience to enrich the customer experience (build the brand) by adapting their product to cover new risks hampered by new uses (product packaging). Moreover, while paying attention to its customer journey design, it meets changing consumer needs with automated solutions (customer service).

Thus, it is understandable that insurtechs like *Zelros* enable insurance industry players to deliver a personalized experience throughout the insurance customer journey (building the brand) by connecting all types of data to insurance-specific predictive models (risk analytics and pricing). It provides real-time recommendations to the advisor and the policyholder (sales). It also automates customer service from underwriting coverage to claim processing (payment to the insured) without compromising fraud detection.

This disruptive potential enables insurtechs like *Slice Labs* to develop and launch cloud-based insurance products (product development). This fact facilitates creating on-demand insurance (product packaging) by offering insurers a deeper insight into data sources (risk analysis/rating).

This context allows insurtechs, such as *Pentation Analytics*, to facilitate modular applications to enable workflows that add value to customer retention and cross-selling processes. Consequently, it increases business relationships throughout the customer lifecycle (building the brand) by helping to address underinsurance through analytics-based interventions (risk analysis and pricing).

Therefore, the disruptive potential of insurtech that has emerged from combining and aligning value network activity categories reveals a new paradigm. As a result of the insurtech dynamic from value chain to value network, a new paradigm suggests the transformation of the value configuration of the insurance industry, revealing that insurtech has altered the way value is created, delivered, and captured. Fig. 19.4 shows the transformation of the insurance sector's value configuration.

This new paradigm of the value configuration in the insurance sector is explained by the fact that, while traditional players focus on specific solutions in the value chain, insurtech focuses on the large insurance sector, approaching the challenge from a holistic perspective. As a result, it digitally connects the insurance ecosystem for the benefit of the whole, digitizing risk, enriching data, and providing a secure environment to connect risk managers, brokers, and insurers. Following this new paradigm, insurtech offers a suite of digital insurance distribution, automated underwriting, and administration solutions for various insurance programs.

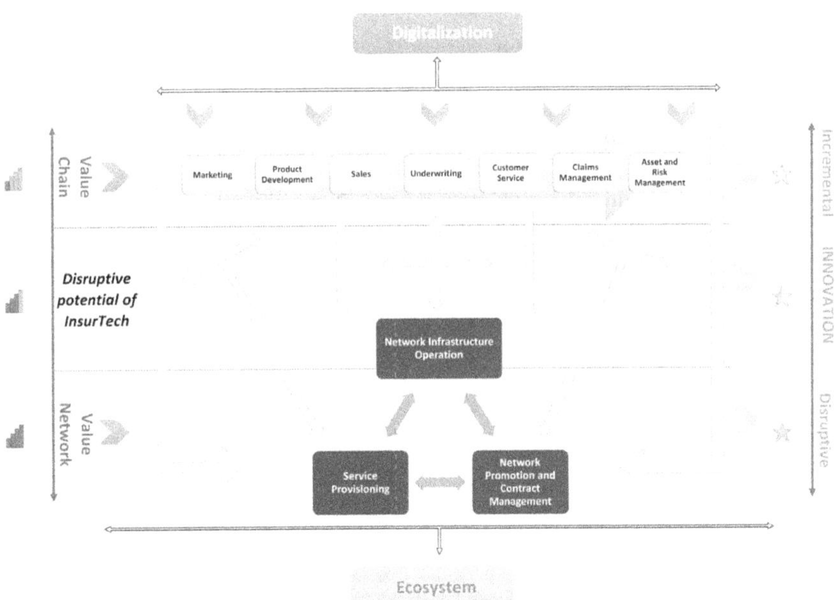

Fig. 19.4. Transformation of the Insurance Sector's Value Configuration. *Source*: The author. *Note:* This figure shows a framework of how the insurtech dynamic has transformed the value configuration of the insurance sector from a value chain to a value network, called an ecosystem.

These programs focus on migrating the workflow of insurance companies from manual, analog, and paper-based processes to a fully automated, digital, product management, and paperless ecosystem. In this regard, insurtech enables an end-to-end claims management platform that connects to a marketplace of third-party suppliers and access to a performance-managed repair network through a modular ecosystem of claims products and solutions for leading insurance businesses, enabling seamless customer experiences.

Thus, insurtech enables the insurance ecosystem to offer a more user-friendly and intuitive user experience for all processes, from onboarding, underwriting, pricing, user identification, policy operations, and claims, providing an end-to-end insurance solution as an integrated white-label platform. A *white-label platform* is software designed to automate the sales and marketing funnel for marketing services providers looking to scale. As a result, insurtech enables the creation of a robust insurance ecosystem to distribute the right products at the right time by offering a set of insurance application programming interfaces (APIs) to the market where insurers can integrate with distribution partners, increasing connectivity and automating all insurance processes. An *API* is a software intermediary that allows two applications to talk to each other. In this regard, insurtech enables the expansion of the managing general agent (MGA) ecosystem to enable distribution for insurance and non-insurance entities, solving insurance market inefficiencies in building insurance programs and infrastructure, using an API-based platform to support the entire insurance distribution workflow.

Furthermore, the open architecture of insurtech allows it to easily integrate with other technology components through a new digital ecosystem to meet the needs of consumers, businesses, and distribution partners. This architecture enables designing and delivering insurance products to the market faster and more cost-effectively than any traditional policy administration platform. Therefore, in this new paradigm, insurtech also appears, acting as a digital orchestrator shaping the insurance ecosystem through the revolutionary combination of disruptive insurance technology and the power of data, new usage-based and data-driven products that merge seamlessly into customers' everyday lives.

This new paradigm suggests transforming the insurance sector's value configuration. This transformation results in the insurtech dynamic from the value chain to a value network, an insurtech ecosystem. Nicoletti (2021) supports this situation and points out that organizations will increasingly move from a linear value chain to a value network called an ecosystem.

Waves in the Insurance Industry's Transformation

An *ecosystem* is an interconnected set of services or products that allows users to satisfy various needs in one seamless experience (Catlin & Lorenz, 2017). According to McKinsey & Company (2019), three archetypes of ecosystem players exist:

(1) Builders plan to construct a new ecosystem business designed to provide diversified products and services that constitute a break with tradition.
(2) Orchestrators help to connect different players in an ecosystem by developing a series of strategic partnerships and alliances using digital technology to make links, provide products and services, and share customers and data with partners.
(3) Participants provide products and services in an ecosystem using partners' resources and capabilities to enhance their business and upgrade products to adapt to ecosystems and meet customers' needs.

Empirically classifying the type of archetype within the insurtech ecosystem is impossible. The reason is mainly because more knowledge of critical external variables, such as market size, growth potential, profitability, and competitive strategy, is needed for their assessment. However, this approach enables showing how insurtech has transformed the insurance sector through the emergence of three waves of innovation (1.0, 2.0, and 3.0) and understanding how insurtech dynamics have transformed the insurance sector from the traditional structure toward a dynamic user-centric ecosystem (Sosa & Montes Pineda, 2021). Fig. 19.5 shows insurtech dynamics in transforming the insurance sector.

In this sense, insurtechs can be categorized into three types depending on their integration level in the insurance sector: (1) distributors, (2) enablers, and (3) full carriers, as set out in the Capgemini Research (2020) classification. This report indicates that the earliest innovations in the insurance sector focused on enhancing distribution, improving the customer experience, and offering potential price savings. Insurtechs acting as distributors of insurance products have been instrumental in transforming the insurance sector. Stoeckli et al. (2018) maintain that the threat of insurers losing direct access to end customers in the personal insurance market may have been a catalyst for enabling innovations that provided software solutions for insurers seeking to enhance their technological capabilities and adapt their business models. This situation highlights the role of insurtech enablers, who provide technical solutions to insurers that allow them to improve their operations and offer more innovative products and services. As the insurtech phenomenon continued to impact all stages of the customer journey and value chain (Cappiello, 2020), the convergence of innovations led to full insurtech carriers that developed and distributed insurance products. This scenario represents a major shift from traditional insurance models and reflects the transformative power of insurtechs in the insurance sector. Examining the waves of innovation can help to understand the landscape of the insurance sector's transformation from a traditional structure to a dynamic user-centric ecosystem.

Insurtech 1.0

Insurtechs are new entrants that set new standards where the first wave's value (Insurtech 1.0.) is the change in customer expectations. Thus, the first wave is characterized by speeding up the digital adaptation of insurance sector players by

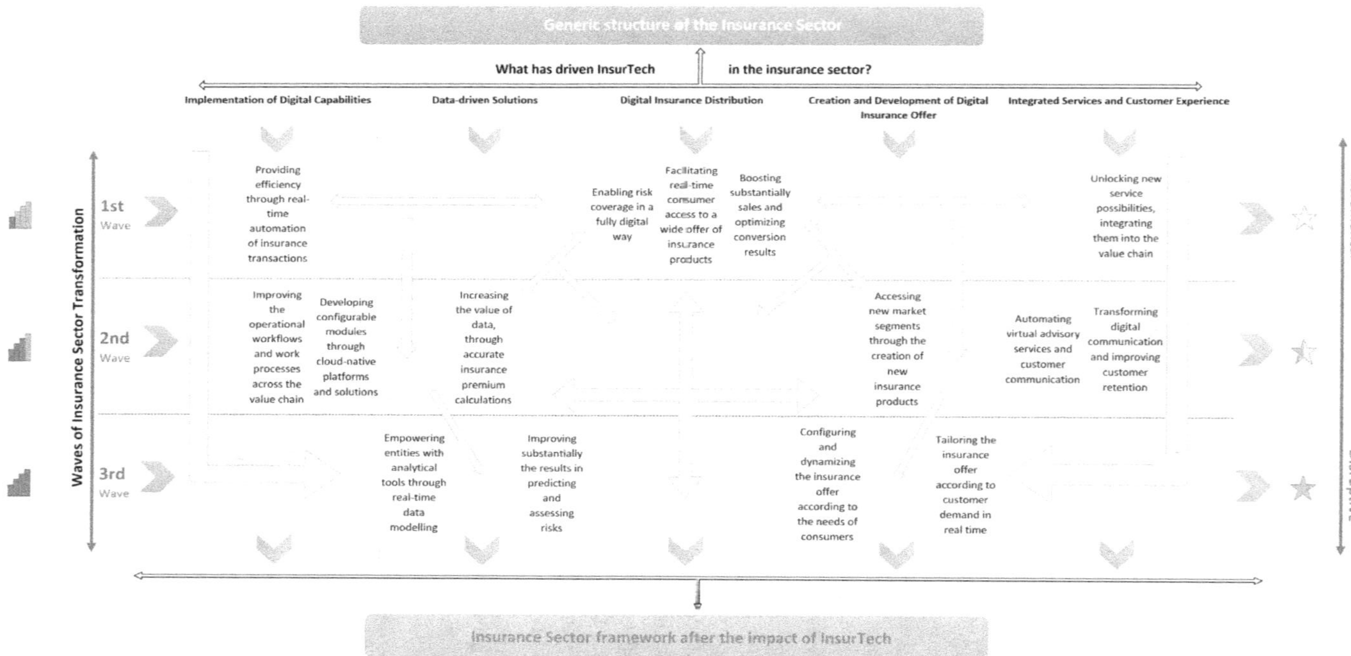

Fig. 19.5. Insurtech Dynamics in the Transformation of the Insurance Industry. *Source:* The author. *Note:* This figure shows how insurtech has transformed the structure of the insurance industry configuration by reflecting the emergence of the three waves through the simultaneity of innovations.

helping companies digitize their business processes and enhancing more innovative insurance distribution (Peverelli & de Feniks, 2019). Not surprisingly, scale is the primary cost driver from the generic value chain (Stabell & Fjeldstad, 1998).

In this sense, this context arises from offering insurance products online, allowing customers to cover their risks entirely digitally, and providing them with easier access to a wide range of insurance products across the insurance value chain. However, given accelerating media and channel fragmentation and evolving new customer expectations, the insurer's omnichannel management has become more complicated. Insurers also have much less control over the customer experience and the customer journey (Lemon & Verhoef, 2016), so insurers need to develop a new base of digital clients by launching and supporting a new direct-to-customer channel, which is shown in the aggregation of intermediaries by insurtechs' roles as comparison platforms or robo-advisors (Greineder et al., 2020).

This scenario enables a substantial increase in insurance policy sales and the optimization of conversion results in marketing campaigns, improving the performance of cross-selling processes. Thus, the impact of technology-driven incremental innovations in the chain configuration begins, reducing costs by automating processes along the value chain and creating value for customers due to the possibility of implementing real-time insurance transactions. This fact is supported by Porter (1985), as the main activities in the value chain configuration are directly involved in creating and delivering value to the customer.

Therefore, some innovations are related to delivering more value to customers, allowing them the opportunity to submit quotes digitally by building and optimizing digital customer journeys. Such innovations unlock new service possibilities by integrating them into the value chain (Sosa & Montes Pineda, 2022).

Insurtech 2.0

Incumbents' sense of urgency fuels the second wave by exploring the potential of new data streams to improve pricing and automate claims. The value of the second wave (Insurtech 2.0) is reflected by the impact of insurtechs on the incumbents' top and bottom lines (Peverelli & de Feniks, 2019). Due to the change in customer demands at the first wave, new competitors, such as insurtechs, and increasing pressure from digitalization are pushing insurers to reorganize and close the digital gap (Greineder et al., 2020).

Thus, the second wave is characterized by enablers, often inspired by new challengers, who focus on helping incumbents improve specific parts of the value chain or even helping them create new ones. This new context provides the opportunity to foster digital relationships with policyholders, facilitating access to the market to understand new risks and avoid preventable losses, creating a full range of protection products, covering new risks with new uses, and creating new insurance products.

The need to identify customers' hidden interest in insurance coverage emerges without an insurance stimulus on the customer side, making it critical for the insurer in this context (Greineder et al., 2020). At that moment, that scenario allows insurance companies to become more agile by affecting operational workflows and business processes throughout the entire value chain, enabling virtual advice in customer service and transforming digital communication with customers and consumers. So, the second wave takes off by developing configurable modules based on cloud-native platforms and solutions, increasing data value by calculating insurance premiums accurately and substantially improving underwriting and pricing processes (Sosa & Montes Pineda, 2022). Furthermore, this environment allows the emergence of cloud-based services using modular cloud infrastructure that enables quick scalability and, therefore, eliminates the boundaries of the traditional insurance administration, products, or services bound to the insurance institution's capacities (Böhm et al., 2010).

Therefore, in an environment of constantly increasing demands coupled with enormous cost pressure, new types of collaboration empowered through cloud-based services and new organizational and working methods encounter different cultures, visions, goals, and strategies (Greineder et al., 2020). This environment reflects that the macro innovation trend is leading to a much more dynamic state in the sector where the boundaries start to disappear by demonstrating the same dynamic in the insurance sector as that which has affected the entire financial service industry (Swiss Re Institute, 2017).

Insurtech 3.0

Insurtech's third wave emerges by embracing different technology companies from adjacent sectors and relevant ecosystems. The third wave's value (Insurtech 3.0) is about increasing relevancy and opening up new business models and revenue streams (Peverelli & de Feniks, 2019). In this scenario, insurance behaves like a massively interconnected network of organizations, technologies, consumers, and products by integrating partners with complementary services in the ecosystem (Greineder et al., 2020).

Hence, the third wave is characterized by ecosystem partners, as companies whose aim is to solve real needs by thinking about services beyond coverage, even beyond the boundaries of the insurance sector. In particular, the third wave's emergence arises from providing companies with analytical tools and a real-time data modeling landscape, which substantially improves risk assessment and predictive outputs in the different areas of the value chain. This situation disrupts, revamps, and accelerates the transformation of the value configuration from the value chain to the value network. The combination and simultaneity of the innovations characterize this wave.

Some innovations are reflected by calculating relative risk in real time, assessing the quality of risk coverage, detecting claims in real time, and settling insured items within a few minutes. Such innovations revamp the customer's claims experience, offering better value to the customer by applying streaming data and neural networks. In addition, natural language processing (NLP) is initiated by turning motion data into contextual insights in this new context.

NLP refers to the branch of computer science related to AI concerned with enabling computers to understand text and spoken words in much the same way human beings can. Doing so enables the configuration and dynamization of the insurance offers according to customers' specific needs. This situation enables the development of hyper-personalized AI products that emerge by tailoring products and services to individual needs (Sosa & Montes Pineda, 2022).

Therefore, in this third wave, linking and thus value creation in the value network is the organization and facilitation of exchange between customers, where one customer is not directly related to another. Instead, a group of customers is linked through a shared pool of funds (Stabell & Fjeldstad, 1998). This situation reflects the core of the value network configuration of the insurance sector, where the value proposition can become the integration of a set of multiple modules belonging to different players in an ecosystem (Nicoletti, 2021).

Summary and Conclusion

Insurtech has emerged as a disruptive global player in the insurance industry, challenging the status quo and transforming traditional practices within the insurance industry. Insurtech start-ups leverage digital technologies to deliver innovative solutions, improve customer experience, reduce costs, and increase efficiency. These changes have led to the disruption that forces traditional insurers to adapt or risk being left behind. However, this transformation is challenging, as insurers face legacy systems, regulatory constraints, and cultural resistance to change. Despite these obstacles, the insurtech phenomenon shows no signs of slowing down, and the insurance industry must continue to embrace innovation to remain relevant in today's rapidly evolving business landscape.

Therefore, this chapter focuses on how Insurtech is transforming the insurance industry. It notes that the insurance industry has been slow to adopt digital technologies due to high barriers to entry, product complexity, capital reserves, solvency requirements, and regulatory constraints. However, insurtech start-ups are challenging this status quo by leveraging technological innovations to improve customer experience, reduce costs, and increase efficiency. This disruptive effect transforms the insurance industry from within.

This chapter also explains how insurtech is changing how insurers design products, distribute them to customers through new channels such as mobile apps or online platforms, and underwrite them using data-driven analytics. This chapter also highlights the driving capabilities of this transformation, such as changing customer demands and the increasing pressure of digitalization. It provides an overview of how insurtech is transforming the insurance industry, highlighting some of the opportunities and challenges presented by this disruption.

This chapter continues focusing on the insurtech ecosystem and how it is evolving from a value chain to a value network. It explains that insurtech's disruptive potential has transformed the insurance industry's structure and altered and disrupted the insurance value chain. In this regard, this chapter describes how insurtech creates a new ecosystem of collaboration, innovation, and co-creation. This ecosystem is shifting from a traditional linear value chain, in which each participant adds value to the product or service before passing it on to the next participant, to a more dynamic and interconnected value network, in which participants collaborate and share resources to create new value propositions for customers. This chapter highlights some critical elements of this new ecosystem, such as digital platforms, data analytics, a customer-centric approach, and open innovation. It explains how these elements enable insurers and insurtechs to collaborate in new ways to create innovative products and services that meet changing customer needs.

Overall, the third section provides an insightful analysis of how insurtech is transforming the insurance industry's value configuration from a traditional value chain to a more dynamic and interconnected value network. It notes some opportunities and challenges this transformation presents for insurers and customers.

The chapter concludes by focusing on the waves of transformation that insurtech has driven in the insurance industry. To this purpose, an ecosystem must be defined as an interconnected set of services or products that enable users to meet diverse needs in a seamless experience. This framework describes how insurtech has created waves of disruption in the insurance industry, each with its challenges and opportunities. In the first wave, insurtech focused on distribution by leveraging digital platforms to reach customers more effectively and efficiently. A second wave dealt primarily with underwriting, with insurtechs using data analytics and machine learning (ML) to improve risk assessment and pricing. The third wave, which is currently underway, mainly concentrates on claims management. Insurtechs use technologies such as AI and blockchain to streamline claims processing and improve the customer experience. These waves have transformed the insurance industry from within, creating new business models, products, and services that meet changing customer needs. Overall, Section 4 provides a detailed analysis of how insurtech has made waves of disruption in the insurance industry's transformation, highlighting some main drivers of this transformation and some challenges insurers face in adapting to this new landscape.

Therefore, insurers face a capability dilemma where insurtech has disrupted the insurance industry. On the one hand, they must maintain their traditional strengths, such as underwriting, claims handling, and risk management. On the other hand, they must invest in new capabilities, such as data analytics, digital channels, and customer experience. Thus, insurers that balance these two opposing forces will be better positioned to succeed in the market. Moreover, in today's insurance industry, data play a crucial role, where insurers must collect, analyze, and leverage data to understand better customer behavior, risks, and insurance sector trends. To do so, they must invest in advanced data analytics tools to better understand their customers and personalize their offerings. In this sense, insurers who master the data game will have a competitive advantage mainly because the Insurtech ecosystem is evolving rapidly and becoming more liquid, with new start-ups constantly emerging. As a result, insurtech start-ups are leveraging cutting-edge technology to disrupt the traditional insurance sector and offer new products and services. Therefore, the emergence of this liquid insurtech ecosystem will create opportunities for insurers to partner with these start-ups to increase their capabilities and enhance their offerings to customers.

Discussion Questions

- Define insurtech.
- Identify the driving capabilities in transforming the insurance sector.
- Discuss how insurtech has transformed the value configuration in the insurance industry by evolving from a value chain to a value network.
- Explain the waves resulting from the insurance industry transformation driven by insurtech's impact.
- Discuss the opportunities in the insurance industry's current landscape.

References

Andrews, D. L. (2018). InsurTech: The next disruptor to the insurance industry. *Predictive Analytics & Futurism News*, *18*, 22–25.

Böhm, M., Koleva, G., Leimeister, S., Riedl, C., & Krcmar, H. (2010). Towards a generic value network for cloud computing. In J. Altmann & O. F. Rana (Eds.), *Economics of grids, clouds, systems, and services* (pp. 129–140). Springer.

Braun, A., & Schreiber, F. (2017). The current InsurTech landscape: Business models and disruptive potential. Institute of Insurance Economics. University of St. Gallen. No.62.

Bussmann, O. (2017). The future of finance: FinTech, tech disruption and orchestrating innovation. In R. Francioni & R. A. Schwartz (Eds.), *Equity markets in transition: The value chain, price discovery, regulation, and beyond* (pp. 473–487). Springer International Publishing Switzerland.

Capgemini Research. (2020). World InsurTech Report. Capgemini Research Institute.

Cappiello, A. (2020). The technological disruption of the insurance industry: A review. *International Journal of Business and Social Science*, *11*(1), 1–11.

Catlin, T., & Lorenz, J. T. (2017). Digital disruption in insurance: Cutting through the noise. *McKinsey*. https://www.mckinsey.com/industries/financial-services/our-insights/time-for-insurance-companies-to-face-digital-reality

Eling, M., & Lehmann, M. (2018). The impact of digitalization on the insurance value chain and the insurability of risks. *The Geneva Papers*, *43*(2), 359–396.

Fjeldstad, Ø. D., & Ketels, C. H. M. (2006). Competitive advantage and the value network configuration. *Long Range Planning*, *39*(2), 109–131.

Greineder, M., Riasanow, T., Bohm, M., & Krcmar, H. (2020). Generic InsurTech ecosystem and its strategic implications for the digital transformation of the insurance industry. Universitat Munchen. Conference: 40th GI EMISA.

Lee, In, & Shin, Y. J. (2018). Ecosystem, business models, investment decisions, and challenges. *Business Horizons*, *61*(1), 35–46.

Lemon, K. N., & Verhoef, P. C. (2016). Understanding customer experience throughout the customer journey. *Journal of Marketing*, *80*(9), 69–96.

McKinsey and Company. (2019). The ecosystem playbook: Winning in a world of ecosystems. Global Banking Practice.

Nicoletti, B. (2021). *Insurance 4.0. Benefits and challenges of digital transformation.* Palgrave Macmillan.

Peverelli, R., & de Feniks, R. (2019). The four waves of insurtech. *The digital insurance agenda community.* https://www.digitalinsuranceagenda.com/thought-leadership/the-four-waves-of-insurtech

Porter, M. E. (1985). The value chain and competitive advantage. *Competitive advantage: Creating and sustaining superior performance.* Free Press.

Puschmann, T. (2017). Fintech. *Business & Information Systems Engineering, 59*(1), 69–76.

Sosa, I., & Montes Pineda, Ó. (2021).The impact of InsurTech on the transformation of the insurance sector. *RESER Conference 2021 – Proceedings.*

Sosa, I., & Montes Pineda, Ó. (2022). Understanding the InsurTech dynamics in the transformation of the insurance sector. *Risk Management and Insurance Review, 26*(2), 125–173.

Stabell, C. B., & Fjeldstad, Ø. D. (1998). Configuring value for competitive advantage: On chains, shops, and networks. *Strategic Management Journal, 19*(5), 413–437.

Stoeckli, E., Dremel, C., & Uebernickel, F. (2018). Exploring characteristics and transformational capabilities of InsurTech innovations to understand insurance value creation in a digital world. *Electron Markets, 28*, 287–305.

Swiss Re Institute. (2017). Technology and insurance: Themes and challenges. https://www.swissre.com/institute/research/topics-and-risk-dialogues/digital-business-model-and-cyber-risk/technology-and-insurance-themes-and-challenges.html

Yan, T. C., Paul, S., & Chen, D. L. K. (2018). InsurTech and Fintech: Banking and insurance enablement. In D. L. K. Chuen & R. H. Deng (eds.) *Handbook of blockchain, digital finance, and Inclusion, Volume 1: Cryptocurrency, FinTech, InsurTech, and regulation* (pp. 249–282). Elsevier. Academic Press.

Chapter 20

Revolutionizing the Real Estate Industry With Fintech

Jeffrey M. Clark

University of Massachusetts, USA

Abstract

The real estate industry has rapidly changed due to technological advances across residential and commercial real estate from the perspective of occupiers, investors, and service providers. Owners and buyers of properties have access to increasing information in the marketplace, including access to residential real estate platforms such as Zillow. Automated appraisals and artificial intelligence (AI) in the mortgage application process speed up home buying. Commercial real estate uses fintech to source deals, perform due diligence, and execute property management requests. This chapter includes a practitioner's view of the current and future information data needs, processes, and point solutions in the evolving technology landscape, including how tools such as ChatGPT apply. It concludes that the real estate fintech revolution has only begun, as data gaps in the real estate market require resolution before yielding better process automation and as the business model of real estate service providers shifts to strategic advisory roles.

Keywords: Fintech; real estate; artificial intelligence (AI); machine learning (ML); ChatGPT

Introduction

Imagine interacting with ChatGPT by simply asking questions and receiving quality advice from the tool regarding the breadth of information and decision-making in real estate. What house is best for my situation, and can I afford it? Where should I locate my eCommerce site to meet my customers while being highly cost-effective based on my corporate cost structure? What is the best

The Emerald Handbook of Fintech, 363–380

doi:10.1108/978-1-83753-608-520241044

strategy, location, size, and optimal financing arrangement to buy a multifamily investment? The potential for such an artificial intelligence (AI) interaction and outcome exists, but the real estate industry and current technology tools are not there yet.

The term *real estate* has many applications across the physical world, the practice of real estate, and those who invest in or occupy real property. A global asset class, physical real estate is heterogeneous (Vanags et al., 2017) regarding quality, characteristics, current or future use, investment potential, and the regulatory environment.

Historically, this heterogeneity has translated into data and information challenges for those investing in, occupying, or lending money on real estate. Among those who practice real estate as service providers, such as brokers and appraisers, a large area of the practice includes having the local market knowledge of real estate prices, transaction processes, valuations, trends, regulations, and the property's highest and best use. As real estate technology, data, process automation, AI, and general fintech have expanded in recent years, the information and knowledge previously exclusive to local real estate service providers have become accessible to everyone.

This chapter discusses the information data needs, processes, and business logic of those who practice in the real estate industry. It also examines the current state of the technological revolution in the real estate industry and discusses future possibilities. This chapter has five sections: (1) physical real estate, (2) practice of real estate, (3) technology, processes, and tools, (4) future technology and limitations, and (5) summary and conclusion.

Physical Real Estate: Global Market Value of Commercial and Residential Properties

Residential real estate is a property where people reside for personal use: homes, apartments, and condominiums (Taylor, 2022). These real estate types also include student housing, vacation, and multifamily properties, regardless of whether the occupier owns or leases the property. According to Savill's research, the value of all global residential real estate was $258.5 trillion as of 2020 (Tostevin, 2021).

Commercial real estate is generally business property, including retail, office, distribution, industrial, manufacturing, data centers, and eCommerce uses. Tostevin (2021) estimates the total global value of commercial real estate in 2020 to be $32.6 trillion, whereas "other" properties, such as agriculture, were valued at $35.4 trillion.

With a total estimated global value of $326.5 trillion for all property types, real estate is the single largest store of wealth in society, far exceeding equities. One valuable and insightful view is to divide the perspective into occupiers or investors for those individuals and entities involved in these properties' direct ownership or use. An *occupier* of real estate in a residential or a commercial setting can be an owner or a tenant who lives in (residential) or uses the real estate for business operations (commercial). An *investor* in real estate will have a different decision-making model than an occupier. Investors are primarily interested in current and future cash flows from real estate ownership and the asset's capital appreciation.

From an occupier and investor perspective, using leverage via debt or a mortgage when owning real estate is extremely common (Katz, 2014). Residential occupiers often need to decide whether to rent or own their residence. They typically base such a decision on an analysis of monthly payment comparison of the options, along with taxation and capital appreciation factors. In the United States, the basic "how much of a house can I afford" question is usually answered by the size of the monthly mortgage payment on the prospective home. As such, interest rates and the amount of debt one can obtain for the home purchase, described as loan-to-value (LTV), drive the decision.

As an investor, leverage is also crucial to the investment decision model. Although many investment valuation models and methods are available, real estate is often valued based on cap rates, as shown in Eq. (19.1).

$$\text{Value} = \text{NOI}/\text{Cap rate} \tag{19.1}$$

where net operating income (NOI) is the gross rental income received from the occupier minus any costs to operate the property (operating expenses). Considering investment risk, cap rates are usually 150–200 basis points higher than mortgage rates for the same property. Therefore, investors can boost the yield on their equity investment by adding such leverage at a lower cost than the cap rate. Here is an example further exploring this concept of leverage, yield, and cap rates.

Table 20.1 (Part A and B) is an example of calculations that combine mortgage rates, cap rates, and value using a fictional income-generating investment property. In the current lending environment, an investor may expect to achieve an 8% cap rate on an investment, assuming a 200 basis points spread over a 6% mortgage rate. Consider a hypothetical property that generates $1,000,000 of "top line" annual potential gross revenue, which, under typical market assumptions of property operating costs, would yield about $617,500 of NOI. With the investment yielding $617,500 of NOI the first year, an investor requiring the stated 8% cap rate would be willing to pay $7,718,750 for this NOI.

The decision, as shown in Table 20.1 (Part A and B), becomes whether using mortgage funds (leverage) is beneficial: the investor will need less cash equity to buy the investment property using mortgage funds. However, this decision will decrease the investor's before-tax cash flow (BTCF) due to having to make debt service payments required to pay the mortgage lender their monthly mortgage principal and interest. Table 20.1 (PART A and B) shows that by using leverage at a lower cost than the cap rate, the investor can boost the yield from the unlevered "pay cash" option at an 8% cap rate to about 11%.

Practice of Real Estate: Scale and Areas of Specialization

Real estate is a massive asset class with varying local laws regulating the use, lending, transaction process, management, rights, and taxation. Real estate practice involves complicated investment decision-making for occupiers and investors, which gives

Table 20.1. Cap Rate and Leverage Example.

Part A: This Table Demonstrates How to Determine Value Based on a Cap Rate and the Impact of Leverage

Lending Assumptions		**Property Assumptions**	
Mortgage term (years)	30	Potential annual gross revenue	$1,000,000
Loan-to-value (LTV)	80%	−Vacancy (5%)	(50,000)
Mortgage interest rate	6%	Effective gross revenue	950,000
Cap rate spread	2%	−Operating expenses (35%)	(332,500)
Cap rate target	**8%**	Net operating income (NOI)	**$617,500**

Part B: The Investment Decision Looks Like the Following

	Unlevered (Cash)	**Levered**
Purchase price	$7,718,750	$7,718,750
Equity needed	7,718,750	1,543,750
Loan amount (80% LTV)		6,175,000
Net operating income	617,500	617,500
−Debt service payments		(444,267)
Before-tax cash flow	617,500	173,233
Return on equity	**8%**	**11%**

Property value = NOI/Cap rate = $7,718,750.

rise to using service providers to support this decision-making. Additionally, the lack of easy access to information and data and the disaggregation of all the component activities of investing in or occupying real estate have given rise to very specialized service providers in the information area and the management of properties.

Considering just the transactional portion of the business conducted in global real estate supported by real estate service providers across leasing, buying, and selling, Research and Markets (2023) estimates this value to be $3.69 trillion in 2021. In the United States alone, annual sales of single-family homes as a subset of this massive market generate about $70 billion in commissions paid to real estate sales agents (Leanprop, 2022).

In a general sense, the life cycle of real estate and its practice is equally applicable to occupiers, investors, and residential and commercial properties, with some variations. Table 20.2 describes the typical decision gates (life cycle) of the real estate process in a commercial real estate environment, with the various service provider roles and responsibilities noted. The data needed for each stage are critical to the occupier or investor making a go/no go decision to proceed.

Real Estate service providers create value for their clients in these specialized practice areas, allowing investors to focus on the investment strategy rather than the property's operation. Additionally, real estate service providers possess specialized knowledge, process management, and market data that many occupiers and investors lack. As technology has grown, data are now becoming more accessible to all engaged in real estate, although it still often varies in quality and completeness.

Technology, Processes, and Tools

The following examines some use cases of differing technology applications, addresses these issues of specialized data and process management, and considers business logic. It also defines some terms of technology. This chapter further separates data from process management and business logic methods to demonstrate the evolution of real estate technologies.

A few key terms regarding data, process management, and business logic are relevant to the use case discussion. Different definitions exist in the tech industry regarding systems and applications, starting with business logic. For this chapter, *business logic* includes the processing of data to make business decisions. A simple

Table 20.2. Life Cycle of a Typical Commercial Real Estate Process.

Stage	Service Providers	Process / Data Needs / Decisions
Strategy	Brokers and advisors	Where do you occupy or invest, and why? Cap rates, rent, and tax rates
Transaction	Brokers, lenders, legal, appraisers	Transaction process, valuation, and optimization of leverage
Project/ Construction	Contractors, project managers, designers, and architects	Development process, costs, and use regulations
Operate + manage	Property, lease, and facility managers	Rent, maintenance, repair, bill payment, and lease management
Dispose	Asset managers and brokers	Optimize investment return, taxation, and updated strategy

Note: This table shows the life cycle of a typical commercial real estate occupier's real estate process, the service providers' role, and the required data and decisions to be made.

business logic description would be the processing of calculations executed upon a business's data for decision-making. Expanding on this description, consider again Table 20.1 (Part A and B), where an investor first obtains data about mortgage terms and an investment's income and makes calculations (the business logic) to optimize the investment decision about using leverage.

Also, consider a common definition of AI. Krohn et al. (2019, p. 86) define *AI* as a "machine that inputs data from the real world, processes it, and makes specific decisions as a result to achieve a goal," and note that *machine learning (ML)* "focuses on developing software, mostly algorithms that can learn to accomplish tasks by themselves without a developer explicitly telling it how to."

AI's potential becomes the ability to disrupt the current real estate industry across real estate's life cycle, particularly the roles, interactions, and functions of the occupiers, investors, and service providers. AI can be envisioned to gather the required real estate data, manage all the life cycle processes, apply required business logic, and perhaps finally make the actual business decisions. The following use cases consider how far technology has progressed toward AI's full potential.

Use Case Data: Residential Multiple Listing Services

A *multiple listing service* (MLS) is a data aggregation technology. In the United States, brokers are licensed by each state and operate as agents of buyers and sellers. The concept of the MLS developed as a trade group operation that would allow different brokers to showcase and share properties they had listed for sale in one database location. In the past, this task was done via a physical book. Due to the nature of the state licensing and the evolution of multiple chapters of the trade group in each state, many MLS operations have emerged across the country. Such a system allowed buyers and sellers, but only via their broker or agent, to access most properties offered for sale, yet only in the geography of that specific MLS.

The National Association of Realtors (Realtors) is the trade group that arranged these MLS operations. As website technology evolved during the 1990s, the website Realtor.com replaced the physical books that were exclusive to brokers and agents. This change was important because the full national website was accessible to the public. As such, all buyers and sellers now had instant information in the marketplace of what was for sale and what had been previously sold. Historical price information was now accessible outside of visiting a physical county records office. The National Association of Realtors also managed Realtor.com, making all this real estate data available to consumers nationally rather than just for that specific MLS trade area.

The limitation of Realtor.com was that, as an MLS, it would only include those properties for sale from paying members of the local MLS, which was also limited to licensed brokers. Thus, the MLS excluded properties for sale by the owner (FSBO) or for sale by nonmember brokers. As data became more prevalent in the general marketplace for these excluded properties, aggregator sites emerged, including Zillow.com. Zillow includes both MLS listings and many

FSBO listings, thus breaking down yet more data gaps in the marketplace. Further, with deep and broad data available, Zillow began to add more business logic tools to the consumers: how much of a home can someone afford? The next use case explores this affordability question.

Use Case – Data, Process, and Business Logic: Residential Mortgage Approval

Lenders underwrite residential mortgages using various criteria, including income, job history, credit history, down payment, property value, and qualifying ratios. Each criterion requires solid data and business logic to decide whether to lend to the borrower applicant. Historically, users obtained and processed much of the data manually. Now, services such as Rocketmortgage.com use data and business logic via their technology platforms to automate what was once a cumbersome process.

Exploring this cumbersome process, consider that the source of funds for mortgage lenders often comes from the secondary mortgage market, whose requirements often drive residential real estate mortgage lending terms. A major player in the secondary mortgage market is the Federal National Mortgage Association (FNMA or Fannie Mae), a government-sponsored entity with established underwriting guidelines (Fannie Mae, 2023). Investors in residential mortgages in the secondary mortgage market are the source of funds for mortgage lenders, and these investors seek standardized borrower and property underwriting across the previously mentioned residential mortgage criteria. Standardized underwriting becomes part of the business logic analysis when qualifying a borrower and a property for the loan. Today, technology has created efficiency, sped up this process, and provided greater accuracy.

Income, Job, and Credit History

Lenders of residential mortgage monies and secondary mortgage market investors seek borrowers with a documented work history to forecast the likelihood of stable future income to make the required monthly mortgage payments. In addition to whether the borrower has the necessary income, understanding a borrower's history of debt repayment from other lenders creates comfort in forecasting future payments for a new mortgage loan. The most straightforward way to obtain data for this underwriting is through electronic credit reporting, a FICO score including employment history, and US federal tax forms. FICO is the acronym for Fair Isaac Corporation and the name for its credit scoring model. Using electronically signed authorizations for an employer to release employment verification is also a common practice.

Down Payment

Using the example of a Fannie Mae conforming loan, the typical down payment required versus the property value would be 20%, resulting in an LTV of 80%.

New electronic tools are useful in determining whether the borrower has the 20% down payment, how long these funds have been in the borrower's savings account, and the source of money having been earned rather than borrowed.

Property Value

Understanding the borrower's LTV ratio includes the borrower's down payment (the numerator) and the property's value (the denominator). Value in residential markets is simply what the market is willing to pay. As real estate is a heterogeneous market, finding a property's specific market value requires strong data and business logic. In the United States, a *residential appraiser*, a third-party independent service provider, is paramount for establishing such an impartial valuation. The appraiser first obtains data on historical comparable sales for the subject property being appraised. But what makes a property comparable? Is it location, size, amenities, features, date when sold, age of property, condition, and certain "curb appeal"? The answer is yes to all these factors. An appraiser would apply a process to review, adjust for variations in factors, and apply judgment in the final appraisal report – in short, business logic that follows from clean and robust data.

Fig. 20.1 outlines the Uniform Standards of Professional Appraisal Practice (USPAP) steps that an appraiser uses to establish a property's value, per the AppraisalFoundation.org. Throughout this process, the appraiser needs data, applies business logic, and makes a business decision (valuation report).

This table shows an appraiser's steps to determine a residential property's value.

A proper and full appraisal is a formal report that follows this defined process. Companies such as Walker & Dunlop (W&D) have created specific automated appraisal tools, including W&D's Apprise tool (Apprise.us). Often, a consumer may seek an "opinion of value" rather than a full appraisal, and Zillow uses its

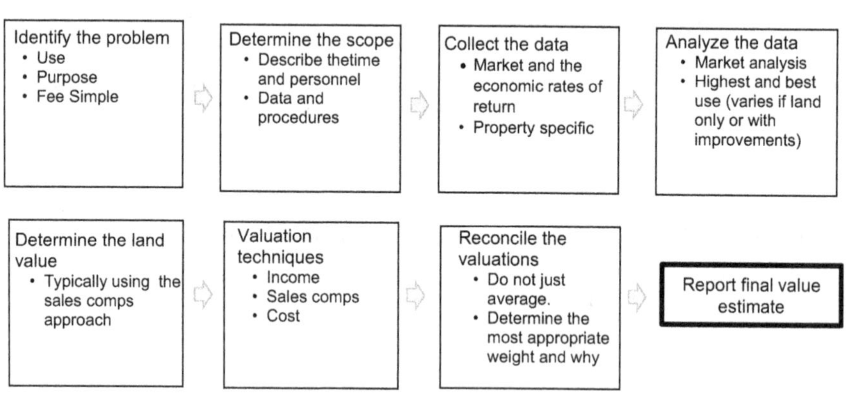

Fig. 20.1. The Appraisal Process.

extensive database to create such estimates of value called a "Zestimate." Based on standards similar to an appraisal, a Zestimate is not a substitute for a formal appraisal. Zillow (2023) states,

> The nationwide median error rate for the Zestimate for on-market homes is 2.4%, while the Zestimate for off-market homes has a median error rate of 7.49%. The Zestimate's accuracy depends on data availability in a home's area. Some areas have more detailed home information available – such as square footage and number of bedrooms or bathrooms – and others do not. The more data available, the more accurate the Zestimate value will be.

The data becomes the limiting factor in estimating value or producing a proper appraisal report rather than the business logic.

Qualifying Ratios

Once a borrower's income has been verified via an online application tool, which may take only seconds instead of weeks, in the low-tech past, the specific loan amount and terms must be compared to the borrower's ability to repay the loan. In this analysis, business logic is applied using the data obtained in the prior steps of the process. Considering the Fannie Mae guidelines as an example, one would need to apply business logic as follows.

(1) The loan amount is determined based on the property's value, less the down payment.

(2) Principal and interest (PI) payment. A monthly PI payment is determined based on the loan amount and the specific terms, like the amortizing term and interest rate.

(3) Taxes and insurance (TI) payment. Property taxes and property insurance costs are data points easily obtained: municipal taxing authorities publicly publish tax rates and property valuation electronically, and visibility of property insurance costs has benefited from the technology revolution and online quotations ubiquitous in the marketplace.

(4) Can the borrower afford the monthly principal, interest, taxes, and insurance (PITI)? A typical Fannie Mae loan would calculate this affordability using two ratios, typically 28% and 36% (Fannie Mae, 2023).

- Is the PITI monthly payment equal to or less than 28% of the borrower's income?
- Is PITI plus all other long-term debt (LTD), such as credit cards, student loans, and car loans, monthly payments equal to or are less than 36% of the borrower's income?

Table 20.3 (Part A and B) considers a hypothetical home with a purchase price of $500,000 and a monthly TI of $1,000. The mortgage market conditions in this example include annual interest rates of 6% amortized over 30 years, based on an 80% LTV. Further, assume a borrower with other LTD payments of $1,500 per month. The question then becomes, how much income does the borrower need to qualify for the mortgage?

The calculations in Table 20.3 (Part A and B) convert the stated mortgage annual interest rate to a monthly rate and the 30-year mortgage term to its corresponding number of months: 0.50% monthly interest and 360 months of amortization. Following the process and steps of the business logic of the loan qualification above:

Table 20.3. Loan Qualification.

Part A: This Table Provides an Example of Qualifying a Borrower's Income Using Fannie Mae Guidelines

Mortgage Assumptions		Property and Borrower Assumptions	
Annual interest rate	6%	Purchase price	$500,000
Term (years)	30	Monthly taxes and insurance	$1,000
LTV	80%	Monthly LTD payments	$1,500

1. Determine the loan amount
   $500,000 purchase price × 80% LTV = $400,000

2. Monthly PI payments
   Excel: PMT (0.50% monthly interest rate, 360 months term, $400,000 loan) = $2,398

3. Determine the total monthly PITI
   $2,398 PI + $1,000 TI = $3,398

4. Monthly income needed

Part B

	PITI	PITI + LTD
Fannie Mae ratio	28%	36%
PITI	$3,398	$3,398
LTD		$1,500
Monthly income needed (use higher amount)	$12,136	**$13,606**

- Using an 80% LTV on the $500,000 purchase price (value), the lender is willing to lend $400,000 against the home.
- By applying the monthly interest rate and the mortgage term to the $400,000 loan, the PI required to amortize the loan is $2,398 monthly.
- Business logic. The lender now adds the TI to this monthly cost to determine the full PITI as $3,398.
- The lender makes the two required calculations of how much monthly income the borrower needs to afford the PITI of $3,398 per month. PITI cannot exceed 28% of the borrower's income, but one must also calculate that PITI plus LTD monthly cannot exceed 36% of the borrower's income.

For example, a borrower would require $13,606 of monthly income, or $163,273 annually, to qualify for the mortgage.

The revolution in residential real estate has evidenced itself by nearly complete market data and information to all buyers and sellers, breaking down the prior information gatekeepers of specialized service providers. Further, the ease and speed at which consumers can obtain mortgage financing through business logic technologies can arguably increase market demand, thus fueling economic growth.

Use Case – Data: Commercial Real Estate

Commercial real estate as a practice and asset class differs from residential real estate concerning complexity and data gaps. Regarding complexity, consider the prior discussion on the real estate life cycle. Recall that the stages included strategy, transaction, project/construction, operating + managing, and disposal. Consider the complexity in just one of the phases and perhaps the most difficult regarding data needs, namely, strategy.

Table 20.4 documents a partial list of data needs required for the strategy stage of the real estate life cycle, which varies based on an occupier's or investor's perspective. Many questions need to be answered in the strategy stage, using business logic, assuming the needed data are accessible and accurate.

Commercial strategy is much more complex than residential in many aspects. An occupier of commercial real estate may be concerned with customers, competition, access to transportation, labor availability and cost, energy costs, local regulations, and the business operation's timeframe. As an investor in commercial real estate, recall the cap rate discussion of a real estate investment's value. The demand for real estate from occupiers and their decisions affect the local market rent and NOI, which drives an investor's investment decision and strategy. Suppose a local market is attractive to an investor. In that case, other competing investors are likely interested in this market and may be building real estate that affects long-term prices, rent, and NOI. This complexity in commercial real estate requires more data and more profound business logic than a residential real estate decision.

Table 20.4. Data and Processes to Support Commercial Real Estate Decision-Making.

Data Need	Occupier Concerns	Investor Concerns
Customers	Where are customers located, and what are their needs? Example: If Amazon creates space to deliver to consumers directly, their buying habits + demands drive proximity (size of packages, frequency of delivery, speed.)	What are the tenant base, credit, space demand, and long-term plans? Example: Where is Amazon expanding, why, and what type of asset? How long a lease is desirable?
Competition	Is the market saturated, or is there an opportunity to meet a demand?	Do any vacancies exist in the market? How much space is already planned for future development based on building permits? Is over-supply a concern over time, as tenant leases expire?
Lending market	Is it better to own or lease based on cap rates and the lending environment? Is there a future trend on which to structure that decision?	Is there enough cap rate spread over lending terms to add leverage? If mortgage rates may increase, does that affect the decision on the note's term?
Transportation	How close is transportation to my customers regarding the total time to meet their needs?	What do customers need?
Labor	What is the total cost to train, retain, and compensate employees in this market?	Is sufficient labor available, and what is the cost to develop the property?
Energy	How do energy costs and availability affect the total cost to operate the facility?	What do customers need?
Regulations	How difficult and costly will it be to operate in this location? Will future regulatory trends, such as green energy, impact operational costs? What are the risks?	What can the regulatory environment build, and how long will it affect the budget and schedule?

Note: This table shows a partial list of the data and processes needed to decide the strategy stage of a commercial real estate life cycle.

Yet, commercial real estate often has less data than residential real estate. For example, no equivalent of a commercial MLS is available formally today. Companies such as CoStar.com and its subsidiary Loopnet.com have attempted to become data aggregators with some success. Aggregating historical sales data for commercial real estate and data on what is for sale or lease is more feasible than the data regarding historical lease rates. Why are actual lease rates important in commercial data? The value of properties using the cap rate formula drives what tenants pay. As previously demonstrated, such information is not public. Unlike real estate ownership records maintained as public records by law, a lease between two private parties is not typically publicly recorded. One way CoStar has dealt with this issue is to provide lease administration for occupiers and investors, giving it access to nonpublic information regarding actual lease rates.

Further adding to the complexity of commercial real estate in recent years has been the massive change in demand for differing asset types. The rise of eCommerce has increased demand for distribution and warehouse properties while decreasing demand for certain retail properties. On the office side, the post-COVID-19 world has driven remote work, thus reducing demand for certain office types and the size of leases. Understanding, accessing, and obtaining these data in a macro sense and then specific to a local market is challenging.

Yet, more complexity in commercial real estate involves determining what can be built on a site, creating a design, driving sustainability goals, managing complex buildings and leases, and then making the own versus lease decision. All these complexities involve data, process management, and business logic, and the technology market has responded with many tools.

Table 20.5 is a selected list of current technologies in the complex commercial real estate market, characterized by their use in obtaining data, creating processes, and performing business logic.

Future Technology and Limitations: Data Access and Storage

Categorizing technology, AI, and ML use cases in the real estate industry into data, process automation, and business logic involves a mutual dependency among these categories. Process automation depends on strong and clean data, and business logic depends more on solid data.

Real estate technologies have become focused on obtaining clean and reliable data rather than analyzing and using process automation or business logic. Categorizing the evolution of data can be described from low to high quality and the ability to access:

1. Unstructured local data. Data that reside on paper notes, Word documents, and images.
2. Structured local data. Data stored in spreadsheets and other tools.
3. Semantic local data. Data that include computer-based project management applications and tools.

4. Semantic cloud data apps. Data that include Salesforce and modern Enterprise Resource Planning (ERP), Software as a Service (SaaS) project management tools.
5. Cloud backends. Databases that cloud data apps connect to for analytics potentially exist in a single cloud infra stack combining computing and storage, such as in Amazon Web Services (AWS).
6. Cloud warehouse/lake house. Unified cloud data that stores separate "compute" from storage, such as through a Platform as a Service (PaaS) provider such as Databricks.

Table 20.5. Commercial Real Estate Technologies.

Technology	Focus	Function	Data	Process	Business Logic
Deepblocks	Zoning and development	Select, investigate, and analyze any parcel of land for potential projects within a city.	X	X	X
MRI Contract intelligence	Contracts	Automate the data extraction and contract review process.	X	X	
Tango analytics	Life cycle	Engage in real estate lifecycle management and integrated workforce management.	X	X	X
Tririga	Space planning	Create visibility into space and facility utilization, tenant experience, capital projects, lease administration, and accounting.	X	X	
Hyro AI	AI data	Scrape data via conversational AI.	X		
CoStar, Visual Lease, VTA, RDM	Lease administration	Pay bills and administer lease portfolios.	X	X	
CoStar	Market data	Analyze real estate marketplaces and information.	X	X	

Table 20.5. *(Continued)*

Technology	Focus	Function	Data	Process	Business Logic
Cherre, CompStak, Reonomy, RCA, Moody's, and others	Market data	Source, collect, aggregate, and add value to real estate data.	X		
Recognizer	Sustainability	Reduce commercial properties' energy consumption using AI.	X	X	X
GeoPhy	Site selection	Understand the attractiveness, health, and risk of a property, its tenants, and its surrounding area.	X	X	X
Apprise	Appraisal	Deliver USPAP/ FIRREA-compliant multifamily appraisals.	X	X	X
Cape analytics	Conditions insights	Provide instant property intelligence for buildings via deep learning and geospatial imagery.	X		
R8 Tech	Energy	Achieve ESG goals by increasing the performance of HVAC via cloud-based and AI-driven software.	X	X	X
Dabble	Sustainability	Automate buildings via an AI-autonomous system.	X	X	X

Continued

Table 20.5. *(Continued)*

Technology	Focus	Function	Data	Process	Business Logic
Restb.AI	Image recognition	Discover data hidden within property photos to solve real estate's most challenging problems.	X		
C3AI	Appraisal	Engage in automated appraisal using AI.	X	X	X
Measurabl	Sustainability	Achieve ESG data management.	X		
Asana, Smartsheet, Salesforce, Monday, and Basecamp	Project management	Streamline workflow and processes.	X	X	
Real AR	Design	Conduct a walkthrough of new building plans.	X	X	
ChatGPT	AI	Engage in natural language processing	X	X	X
Procore	Project management	Construction management.	X	X	
Building Connected	Project management	Engage in bid management.	X	X	
IMS, Juniper square, Dealpath	Investment management	Achieve investor-facing reporting and compliance.	X	X	
MRI, Buildium, Yardi, and others	Property management	Engage in tenant requests, lease management, and OpEx.	X	X	

Note: This table shows a partial list of commercial real estate technology applications categorized by function. It also indicates primary use across data, process automation, or business logic.

Although specific to each function, use, or point solution of real estate technology, real estate technologies appear somewhere in stages 4 or 5, as listed previously. Data gaps across such broad types and categories of real estate data potentially limit the development of new tools to continue to capitalize on the efficiency, speed, and ability to obtain a strategic focus via good process automation and business logic tools.

Summary and Conclusion

The revolution in real estate technology has only started, considering the vast potential for the entire industry. Consumers engaging in residential real estate have substantially benefited from the technology revolution. For example, market data, process knowledge, and speed of financing a home are now simple, quick, and accessible.

Commercial real estate has also improved as a practice with the development of technology, AI, and automation, yet complete data to drive better outcomes remains an issue. The need for commercial real estate data is broad and deep due to a globally heterogeneous regulatory environment, legal issues, complexity of agreements, market data, and decision-making criteria by commercial occupiers and investors like customers, labor, transportation, and other business needs. Although data are now more available and accessible in an electronic format, the semantics of the data, translating the disparate data into consistent formats, and creating complete information remain limited.

The technology revolution will continue. Tools such as ChatGPT and related interfaces will help guide the planning and strategy of resolving these data needs while concurrently developing more process automation and better business logic tools. This growth will continue to shift the role of certain real estate service providers from information gatekeepers to true strategic advisors and partners for occupiers and investors in residential and commercial real estate.

Discussion Questions

- Describe the underwriting of a borrower requesting a residential mortgage loan and how technology increases the speed and accuracy of the process.
- Describe the process of appraising a residential home value for a mortgage loan, including sources of data and business logic technology tools.
- Explain how an income property is valued using cap rates and what areas of automation can assist investor decision-making.
- Discuss the complexity of commercial real estate data needs, gaps, and how business logic depends on clean data.

References

Fannie Mae. (2023, August). Selling guide, Fannie Mae single family. https://selling-guide.fanniemae.com/Selling-Guide/Origination-thru-Closing/Subpart-B3-Underwriting-Borrowers/Chapter-B3-6-Liability-Assessment/1064501811/What-is-the-maximum-DTI-ratio-allowed.htm

Katz, L. (2014, July 15). Share of homes bought with all cash hits 30% for first time since 2014. *Redfin News.* https://www.redfin.com/news/all-cash-home-purchases-2021/

Krohn, J., Beyleveld, G., & Bassen, A. (2019). *Deep learning illustrated: A visual, interactive guide to artificial intelligence.* Addison-Wesley.

Leanprop. (2022). *Residential real estate market size and trends.* leanprop.com/posts/residential-real-estate-market-size-and-trends

Research and Markets. (2023). https://www.globenewswire.com/en/news-release/2023/05/29/2677723/28124/en/Global-Real-Estate-Market-Report-2023-A-6-13-Trillion-Market-by-2030-Size-Share-Growth-Analysis-Competitive-Analysis-Industry-Forecasts.html

Taylor, M. (2022, October 22). *What is residential real estate?* Bankrate. https://www.bankrate.com/residential-real-estate-definition/

Tostevin, P. (2021, September). The total value of global real estate. *Savills.* https://www.savills.com/impacts/market-trends/the-total-value-of-global-real-estate.html

Vanags, J., Geipele, I., Sarkans, A., & Usenieks, D. (2017). Housing heterogeneity dimensions and their elements: A systemic approach. *Baltic Journal of Real Estate Economics and Construction Management*, *5*(1), 23–37.

Zillow. (2023). What is a zestimate? https://www.zillow.com/z/zestimate/

Chapter 21

Fintech in Capital Markets

Christian Rauch

Umm Al Quwain University UAE

Abstract

In recent years, new and technologically innovative financial products and services, generally subsumed under the fintech umbrella, have permeated all areas of capital markets at an exponential rate. Primarily driven by developments in Web3 and advancements in artificial intelligence (AI), fintech solutions offer valuable benefits to all existing markets and participants and are the basis for introducing wholly new segments to classic capital market ecosystems. However, this increasing fintech adaptation does not come without challenges. Due to the technologies' nascent nature and often unregulated status, many products are susceptible to manipulation and fraud. The result can be sizable investor losses and excessive regulatory and public scrutiny. This chapter highlights the most essential and prominent fintech solutions used in capital markets today, along with their features, value additiveness, and degree of adaptation.

Keywords: Fintech; capital markets; artificial intelligence; Web3; trading

Introduction

The finance industry has always quickly adopted cutting-edge technology in capital markets. This development has seen substantial growth in recent years, predominantly driven by advancements in internet and communication technologies paired with the contemporaneous exponential growth in computing power.

Despite no fixed definition of the term and its exact origins, the industry now known as fintech, particularly those fintech products and services used in modern capital markets, resulted from two major developments: (1) the internet and its evolution from Web1 to the ongoing creation of Web3 since the inception of bitcoin and blockchain technology and (2) the rise of machine learning (ML) processes and artificial intelligence (AI), fostered by ever-increasing data availability.

The Emerald Handbook of Fintech, 381–396

doi:10.1108/978-1-83753-608-520241045

Fintech first started its rise to prominence in capital markets in the 1990s with the onset of the Web1 version of the internet. At the time of dial-up internet connectivity and static websites, simple web-based tools started to arise. The main purpose was to facilitate capital market access, particularly for retail traders, and to create transparency by making market-relevant information more widely available. Some popular examples are introducing the Securities and Exchange Commission's (SEC) Electronic Data Gathering, Analysis, and Retrieval (EDGAR) system as a website or, starting with Charles Schwab, the first online brokerages.

As the internet morphed into its Web2 phase by becoming more social and interactive, so did fintech solutions for capital markets. An early example from the late 2000s is the Israeli-based online broker eToro, which allows traders to connect to discuss trading strategies. A more recent example that received widespread attention was the combined use of online forums and brokerage apps to facilitate retail investors' speculative stock trades during the early stages of the COVID-19 pandemic in the spring and summer of 2020, involving the Robinhood trading app and Reddit online forums. The Reddit Wall Street Bets forum is the most prominent example.

More importantly, however, the 2010s saw the inception of online peer-to-peer (P2P) markets for capital. The first iterations were lending marketplaces such as Prosper or LendingClub, in which individuals could solicit debt-type investments into their commercial or noncommercial endeavors. By starting what would later become highly professionalized crowdfunding platforms facilitating millions of investments across thousands of companies, these marketplaces marked an important milestone in how fintech affected capital markets. For the first time, seekers and providers of capital could match without any financial intermediary's involvement.

The most recent evolution of capital market-related fintech products and services can be attributed to the emergence of blockchain technology and the advent of cryptocurrencies like bitcoin as part of the transition to Web3. These technologies have provided the foundation for developing decentralized finance (DeFi) solutions, which have since found widespread use across capital markets. Blockchain technology has revolutionized many areas in capital markets, particularly through its ability to perform classic administrative back-office tasks, such as making securities settlement and clearing faster, more cost-efficient, and with fewer errors. Additionally, and in a revolutionary step, Web3 introduced a new form of securities for firms seeking capital as coins or tokens, thereby creating a new market for securities that can function without intermediaries or market makers.

The second critical development driving technological innovation and adaptation in capital markets has been twofold: (1) advancements in ML and AI and (2) increased availability of or possibility to collect new and unique datasets with market-relevant information. ML-based processes can analyze vast amounts of structured and unstructured data with unprecedented speed and minimal human supervision. Through this rapid analysis of data and the use of so-called *high-frequency trading (HFT) systems*, market participants can execute well-informed trades faster, which has led to substantial gains in market efficiency.

Market participants – particularly hedge funds – have also started using previously unavailable data to gain further insight into markets or anticipate market-relevant news announcements through real-time analysis of the underlying data. Frequently labeled *big data*, these datasets can contain a plethora of information ranging from satellite imagery, corporate jet flights, or GPS-based movement tracking. Analyzing these data in real time can, for example, foreshadow gross domestic product (GDP) or consumer spending by displaying port activity and the percentage of occupied parking spaces outside supermarkets. It also allows for anticipating corporate news announcements by tracking chief executive officer (CEO) movements in their corporate jets.

A prominent example is Bridgewater Associates, the largest global hedge fund by assets under management (AUM). It partnered with big data analytics firm Palantir to use its Metropolis software, an AI-based capital market data analysis tool. Although still in their infancy, these technologies can potentially revolutionize how capital market participants trade securities and make investment decisions and how efficiently information is included in securities prices.

Today, fintech products and solutions are applied in all areas of capital markets. They offer various advantages to all market participants, including cost savings in market access, use, administration, and more efficient and fair securities and asset pricing.

On a grander scheme, the one development where fintech products and services have been especially supportive is the so-called *democratization of finance*, particularly regarding capital market access and use. Before fintech's onset, capital markets could only be accessed through a limited number of gatekeepers such as banks or brokerage firms. Securities trading was only possible through regulated exchanges or – often bilateral or unregulated – over-the-counter (OTC) markets. Although those gatekeepers created value by acting as intermediaries between seekers and providers of capital or facilitators of secondary market trading, they also imposed barriers to entry, resulting in low competition for legacy players and more limited and expensive access to markets, particularly for noninstitutional players.

The fintech industry has disrupted this model by developing various products and services that allow for more cost-effective and straightforward access to capital markets and by creating wholly new capital markets that bypass the need for traditional intermediaries or market makers altogether. A positive byproduct of this disruption and the increasing competition is that all legacy gatekeepers have been forced to embrace the fintech industry by collaborating with up-and-coming players in the field or by developing fintech products, leading to further democratization of capital markets.

However, despite these advantages and the resulting increase in welfare creation, adapting fintech solutions in capital markets has not always been smooth. Various challenges and risks have emerged when adapting every nascent technology. For example, the largely unregulated nature of many fintech products has opened the door for fraud from which retail investors have suffered greatly. Additionally, regulatory frameworks and compliance requirements have struggled to keep pace with fintech's rapid evolution, creating uncertainty and potential obstacles for market participants.

This chapter helps to explain fintech in modern capital markets. It aims to deepen the knowledge of market participants, regulators, supervisors, and interested third parties by discussing the most important technological innovations and the resulting products and solutions used in today's capital markets. The chapter highlights the value-added and the challenges of each fintech innovation to exhibit how capital markets can benefit from those innovations. It also identifies what work is needed to solve existing problems and help advance the successful implementation of future market innovation.

Fintech and Securities Trading

The fintech industry has developed various products and services that assist retail and institutional traders in securities trading. These tools facilitate all aspects of trading, including trade execution, portfolio management, and investment decision-making. The most significant and value-creating tools for retail traders are trading apps with built-in robo-advisers. For institutional investors and traders, the most important technological advancements in securities trading have been twofold: (1) advancements in trading technology, particularly the speed, velocity, and frequency at which trades can be executed and (2) the availability of new data sets and their exploitation through smart analytical processes typically involving ML and AI.

Retail Solutions: Brokerage Apps and Robo-Advice

A major technological breakthrough in retail-based capital market solutions was developing online brokerage tools, allowing retail investors to manage their trades and portfolios. Pioneered by Charles Schwab in the mid-1990s, every major bank offered early iterations of those tools to their customers through simple web-based platforms that contained, besides the portfolio itself, the tools to execute trades, market news, technical chart analysis tools, or stock analyst recommendations. Recently, these tools have become mainly app-based and are offered by more providers than just the major banks. A driving force was the development of so-called *challenger banks*, a movement in which independent start-up companies offered selected and simple retail banking services in cheap and customer-friendly ways, thereby challenging the legacy banks for their retail customers. Besides checking- and savings-depositing services, the most widely offered tools have involved trading and portfolio management.

One app in particular, US-based Robinhood, reached prominence during the early days of the COVID-19 pandemic in 2020. Welch (2022) provides an overview and explanation of those events. During lockdowns and in the absence of other pastimes, new and inexperienced retail investors started speculating on stocks heavily (Barber et al., 2022). The unique part of this surge in retail trading was its social aspect. Traders flocked to online forums to discuss trading strategies and individual stocks, most prominently the Wall Street Bets forum on Reddit. Albeit only for short periods and non-blue chip stocks, the combination of social interaction, concerted trading efforts, and the ease of conducting trades allowed amateur retail traders to move the prices of individual stocks. This pairing of one of the earliest and most widely used Web2 tools in Reddit and a newly developed challenger brokerage app is a great example of how fintech can impact modern capital markets. Also, it is a testament to the democratization of capital markets.

Another relevant technological development in the retail trading space, particularly in equity markets, builds on the initial brokerage technology and is nowadays frequently embedded in trading or brokerage apps: so-called *robo-advisors*. These software tools provide automated investment advice and portfolio management services tailored to users' investment needs and risk-return preferences. These fully automated platforms can perform numerous services. Upon onboarding, built-in chatbots discuss the investment strategy with users and subsequently construct and (re-)balance the resulting portfolios. Robo-advisors can also take a more active approach by suggesting individual securities or feeding a user's account with relevant news and interpreting it in light of the trading strategy or portfolio composition. In line with a classic wealth management scope, many advisors also offer medium- or longer-term savings products such as investment funds and assist users in achieving specific savings goals.

Robo-advisors have proven valuable for providers and users. Providers offer a cost-efficient and highly scalable way to offer customized advice for different retail clients that would typically only be available for premium customers. For users, robo-advisors' main advantage is their ability to assist in professionalizing their portfolios, particularly by achieving optimal diversification levels and by assisting in overcoming the most common behavioral trading biases, such as trend-chasing and disposition or rank effects (D'Acunto et al., 2019).

Although robo-advisors have proven more effective in this regard than any other form of financial advice, their biggest problem is adoption. If offered, only the most sophisticated investors least needing unbiased financial advice tend to use it most. However, less sophisticated investors either do not use robo-advisors, decide not to follow their advice, or only engage in minimal interaction with the advisor (Bhattacharya et al., 2012). As robo-advisors can only maximize their potential if users engage with them frequently (Capponi et al., 2022), the resulting quality of advice diminishes for infrequent users. The result can be a downward spiral of poor advice triggering less use, which, in turn, leads to worse advice and even less use.

However, despite these challenges, capital markets have benefited from the increasingly widespread usage of robo-advisors. Their ease of access and helpful advice have attracted a new group of people to capital markets that, without the support through those tools, would have never participated in capital markets (Barber et al., 2022). Besides furthering the democratization of capital markets, these users contribute liquidity and information to every security they trade, thereby benefiting the quality and efficiency of capital markets.

Institutional Solutions: Trade Algorithms and HFT Technology

Institutional investors have experienced two major advancements in securities trading due to technological innovation in capital markets. The first advancement is the speed, velocity, and frequency at which trades can be executed. The second advancement is the development of automated software-based trading algorithms that can self-execute trades based on rapid input data analysis in a few milliseconds.

Regarding pure trading speed improvements, two factors are crucial. The first is the time a trader needs to obtain and analyze the information upon which the trade is based. The second is the time required for the trader to place the desired trade with the respective securities market. The internet and modern communication channels have made capital market-relevant information available almost instantaneously. However, institutional traders do not rely on regular online information channels despite the ready availability of data and information. Instead, to gain an informational edge over other market participants, they use so-called *ultra-low latency systems*, trading software applications specifically designed for speedy data updates directly connected to major data service providers. Thomson Reuters, for example, provides a Binary Multicast Feed for its foreign exchange Matching platform. It lowers data update speeds to as little as 25 milliseconds or offers services to update data on certain economic indicators up to 1 second before their availability via regular channels such as public website updates. The servers running the ultralow latency systems are placed in *co-location* (i.e., close physical proximity) to the servers at the securities exchange to avoid losing time executing a trade based on these input data. As measured from information input to trade placement, these processing times are unachievable with a human trader. All ultrafast trading software tools rely on *trading algorithms*, preprogrammed software tools that self-execute trades in milliseconds following a specific data input.

Traders who rely on trading algorithms and ultrafast timings are so-called *high-frequency traders*. Besides relying on ultralow latency trading systems and fast data input feeds, HFT firms employ trading strategies that benefit from their unique ability to analyze data and execute trades within milliseconds. A crucial tool in these strategies is *market pattern recognition*. These strategies include monitoring order flows to determine buy/sell imbalances and liquidity pockets or forecast the short-term trading direction.

The evidence of HFT's impact on capital markets is still mixed and inconclusive. High-frequency traders can incorporate new information accurately and quickly into asset prices (Carrion, 2013; Chakrabarty et al., 2022). Therefore, they contribute to an increase in price discovery and pricing efficiency in individual securities (Brogaard et al., 2014). Heightened HFT activity also benefits market-wide quality measures by boosting overall liquidity, increasing order book depth, decreasing spreads, and lowering short-term volatility (Bongaerts & Achter, 2021; Hasbrouck & Saar, 2013).

On the other hand, HFT can also impact markets negatively. High-speed algorithms can diminish the returns of other institutional traders based on costly information acquisition, especially when using strategies based on order flow analytics. It can lower the incentives for other traders to acquire costly information, resulting in less informed prices (Weller, 2018). The close and instantaneous monitoring of order flows can also facilitate the front- or back-running of trades. Lastly, some allege that HFT can contribute to unanticipated, sudden, and steep falls in security prices, so-called *flash crashes*, because many high-frequency algorithms trade directionally, meaning investors buy (sell) when buying (selling) behavior in the market is high. Additionally, many high-frequency traders provide market liquidity, which typically retracts in falling or volatile markets. Jointly, these features can create a feedback loop in which high-frequency algorithms exacerbate market-wide sales pressure while simultaneously retracting liquidity.

Institutional Solutions: Alternative and Big Data as a Basis for Investment Decisions

In the last few years, technology has significantly facilitated access to capital markets and market-relevant data and increased the speed and accuracy it reaches markets with. A prominent example is the SEC's introduction of its online EDGAR tool during the early days of Web1 and how it has been used to communicate corporate information to market participants. Before its implementation between 1993 and 1996, public companies only provided paper-based filings to the SEC, making them available for viewing and copying in several public reference rooms in major US cities. Due to EDGAR's introduction, investors, especially individual retail traders, made faster and more informed investment decisions, and equity analysts' stock evaluations improved (Gao & Huang, 2020). Due to EDGAR and other technological advancements in information dissemination, managers even changed the way they disclosed corporate news to markets (Ni et al., 2021), for example, by hoarding bad information prior to release. Web search engines further improved the benefits of web-based information dissemination in the 1990s, as looking up information enhanced investors' ability to process information into more informed investment decisions (Drake et al., 2012; Xu et al., 2021).

Besides more readily available information for all investors from primary sources, technological advancements in recent years have seen a surge in secondary or alternative data. Generally, analysts and investors use these sources to track developments in markets, the economy, or corporations, frequently in real time, to anticipate official announcements. One example is tracking corporate jet flight patterns to predict corporate events, such as good or bad news announcements (Yermack, 2014) or fundraising activities (Bushee et al., 2018). Another example is using satellite data to predict economic strength indicators. This approach has proven effective in substantially lowering markets' surprise at macro data announcements by government entities. As satellites review economic movement in real time, investors can instantaneously price the information instead of waiting for the government to announce it ex post (Mukherjee et al., 2021).

Another, arguably more revolutionary, development in capital market data has been the more widespread use of so-called *big data* (Goldstein et al., 2021). Big versus small datasets are commonly defined through the three Vs – volume, velocity, and variety/variability. Volume and velocity define the mass of data included in big datasets and the speed at which it is collected, respectively. An example is option market microstructure data, which, if collected, would result in over one terabyte of new raw data in one single trading day. Big data's variety/variability refers to its contents and structure. Big datasets are typically unstructured and contain many variables relative to the number of observations. Due to this size and structure, recent advancements in ML processes have substantially aided the analysis and interpretation of big data, as off-the-shelf data analysis software and average computing or data storage tools cannot handle them.

A prominent example of how big data sets can be compiled is the so-called *web scraping* methodology, in which large amounts of text data are collected from websites, primarily social media. Other examples are using credit card data or mobile phone-based geolocation data. Jointly, these datasets can reveal information about customer behavior to forecast economic growth or, more specifically, reveal information about brand perceptions or shopping habits. More sophisticated big data tools involve applying ML-based classification algorithms to predict market microstructure features (Easley et al., 2021) or using natural language processing (NLP) models to interpret corporations' earnings calls (Li et al., 2021).

Hedge funds have been the earliest adopters of big data-based investment processes, most prominently Ray Dalio's Bridgewater Associates and its use of Palantir's *Metropolis software*, a capital market (big-) data tool built on pattern analytics originally developed for governmental agencies in the defense sector. Recent years have seen a rapidly increasing adoption of big data tools across the whole spectrum of institutional investors. The perception among capital market participants is that to generate sustained returns, investors must acquire, analyze, and understand the ever-growing data universe. Moreover, capital markets also benefit. By lowering price acquisition costs, the availability and use of big data have informed securities' prices and contributed to capital market efficiency (Zhu, 2019).

Back-Office Solutions: Securities Clearing and Settlement

Through the development of Web3-based technologies, fintech tools have become increasingly material in revolutionizing the back-office administrative part of securities trading in capital markets, particularly the administrative process that ensures the correct payment for the security as well as the successful transfer of its ownership from one transaction party to the other. This process involves multiple consecutive steps, including trade confirmation, reporting, clearing, and settlement. The exact process varies across security types, takes anywhere from 1 to 2 days in regulated exchanges to 30 days in bilateral OTC trades, and involves various institutions such as clearing houses, custodian banks, and securities exchanges.

The first major evolution in trade execution and the more complicated clearing and settlement processes started in the late 1970s when software systems replaced paper-based processes. The transition, however, was gradual, slow, and not without issues. For example, the London Stock Exchange (LSE) had to replace its initial electronic settlement system, TALISMAN, twice over ten-plus years throughout the 1980s and 1990s, with entirely new software (TAURUS and CREST) due to continued faults within the systems. Despite these early problems, the software-based clearing and settlement processes allowed capital markets' back offices to operate faster, cheaper, and less error-prone.

These efficiency gains proved highly valuable for capital markets, and modern-day trading in regulated exchanges or OTC markets would not be possible without them. However, changing the original paper-based process of executing, clearing, and settling trades into electronic formats did not change the clearing and settlement process. The computer-based systems still involve the same subsequent steps and rely on the same institutions in brokers, exchanges, clearing houses, and custodian banks as the paper-based processes did.

The innovation believed to have the potential of genuinely revolutionizing all back-office work in capital markets is the blockchain or so-called *distributed ledger technology* (DLT). Born out of Satoshi Nakamoto's invention of Bitcoin in 2008 (Nakamoto, 2008), blockchains are distributed digital ledgers consisting of blocks created and linked through cryptographic hashes by decentralized online P2P networks. Blockchains lend themselves to efficient and secure recordkeeping through various features, particularly in capital markets. Any information, such as securities' ownership, can be stored on blocks, and ownership transfer from one party to another is recorded in a secure and immutable way. In contrast to legacy database systems in which one central party manages all administrative duties – as in the traditional clearing and settlement process described above – distributed ledger data are managed and administered jointly by all peers participating in the network.

The specific degree to which blockchains can impact capital markets depends on the degree of adoption. Blockchains could bypass all intermediaries previously mentioned and directly connect security buyers and sellers. The fact that the blockchain hosts and updates ownership and transfers data in a decentralized and public way means that specialized intermediaries or any other third-party infrastructure becomes obsolete. Security buyers and sellers could interact directly, and the automated ownership transfer could rule out many risks associated with clearing and settlement. This efficiency improvement could lead to various gains in capital markets. For example, US corporate debt market research shows that blockchain-based settlement processes could lower settlement cycles from 1 or 2 days to less than half an hour, leading to gains of 1–4 basis points per trade (Chiu & Koeppl, 2019). Additionally, the risks emanating from having one central counterparty in clearing would be eradicated, something that has proven risky in the past in case multiple buyers and sellers default on their obligations and the central clearing house has to take the brunt of the losses.

However, despite these benefits, challenges are associated with introducing DLT into capital markets. First, each market would have to agree on one blockchain technology, and the blockchain itself would have to be provided by a specific entity/model, introducing new idiosyncratic risks to capital markets. Which party, for example, would be in charge of changing the blockchain's protocol (i.e., the code) if needed, and would all participants have the same rights in the blockchain? A related problem is that the consensus algorithms and cryptographic verification methodologies needed to run a blockchain can cause latency and limit the number of transfers processed concurrently. For capital markets where transactional speed is important, this issue can be a cause for concern. The storage capacity of many layers of transactional history may add to these latency issues.

Second, specific securities markets would still need intermediaries without whose services the markets could not function. For example, brokerages maintain margin accounts in noncash futures markets to secure open positions against uncovered losses. Pure P2P markets would also require these services, so completely eradicating all intermediary services is unlikely, at least in specific markets.

Lastly, and on a broader level, the existing question concerns the degree to which P2P networks desire a truly and fully decentralized network. In its earliest Bitcoin-based form, blockchains use so-called *proof-of-work* (PoW) mechanisms. Any network party can introduce new blocks to the chain by exerting sufficient computational power (work) to solve cryptographic puzzles faster than other network parties. However, more recent blockchain applications have been switching to so-called *proof-of-stake* (PoS) methods due to various issues associated with the PoW technique, such as environmental concerns due to heavy energy consumption involving the exerted computational power. In the PoS system, the blockchain selects individual network participants to validate transactions and adds new blocks to the chain. These individuals are typically large players in the network and earn their rights through their economic stake in the blockchain. A prominent example of a switch from PoW to PoS is the Ethereum blockchain, which performed the switch in 2022.

Why are the features of different blockchain mechanisms relevant to capital market applications of blockchain-based solutions? The largest blockchain participants maintain and update the chain in a PoS concept. Based on PoS in a capital market setting, most de facto 'administrators' would likely be money centers and bulge-bracket banks. A *bulge-bracket bank* is a multinational, brand-name bank that regularly handles large transactions and employs many people in financial centers worldwide. Therefore, today's major facilitators and intermediaries in capital markets are the same entities. Although the underlying technology would change toward a decentralized network, capital markets would still rely on singular entities to manage the market. In this case, the technological switch might be less efficient or desirable than otherwise estimated.

ICOs, Crowdfunding & CO: Fintech and Creating New Capital Markets

A major contribution that technological innovations have brought to global finance in the past 10–20 years is creating entirely new capital markets. Before the democratization of capital markets through fintech, capital markets only existed on regulated exchanges or OTC between institutional investors. As discussed, fintech solutions have greatly facilitated access to these markets. However, and arguably in a more crucial step, fintech solutions have created new markets with low entry barriers and cheap access for all retail and institutional investors.

Generally, two main developments led to the creation of these new capital markets. The first development was the beginning of social interaction on the internet during the transition from Web1 to Web2 in the early 2000s. The first web-based P2P lending platforms emerged during this time. These primary debt markets allowed participants to seek capital from or provide debt capital to their fellow platform users without any financial intermediaries in the classic sense. An early example is US-based Prosper, which allowed individual users to invest fractionally or fully in loans sought by individual borrowers. The loans could be for any purpose, personal or commercial, and borrowers would advertise them through an individual Facebook-like profile in which they provided information about the loan and themselves. Although initially focusing on loan origination only, these P2P lending platforms also introduced secondary markets for the originated loans in which investors could sell their stakes in loans or acquire new loans they did not originate. Although on a small scale and often not highly professionalized, these markets were fully P2P. They were the first of their kind to connect individual capital market participants without involving any financial intermediaries. In doing so, they paved the way for introducing the larger and highly professional, both equity- and debt-based, crowdfunding markets that exist today.

The second and more striking milestone was the development of blockchain technology and cryptocurrencies, which allow for a new fundraising methodology to serve as an alternative to classic initial public offerings (IPOs) or debt issuances. In so-called *initial coin offerings* (ICOs), a company seeking to raise funds creates and sells coins or tokens to outside investors in exchange for fiat money or cryptocurrency. The coins generally sold are utility and security coins. The former mainly grants buyers and holders the right to use a product or service the issuer offers, while the latter grants cash flow and voting rights. Although security coins resemble regular equity or debt securities more closely, companies can sell both for fundraising purposes.

In many ways, the ICO process and subsequent coin trading resemble IPOs or, depending on the contractual features of the coin, bond issuance, and secondary trading. For example, ICOs are advertised through *white papers* containing information about the coins, the offering, and the issuer, like an IPO prospectus containing information about the share issuer and issue.

The benefits of using cryptographically secured tokens or coins over classic equity funding via an IPO are not yet fully established, as coins offer some advantages but also come with various challenges. Arguably, the most noteworthy advantage is an ICO's cost. Although comparing IPO and ICO costs is not straightforward due to the differing structures, ICOs are generally substantially cheaper than IPOs. They do not require legal expenses to ensure compliance with securities laws or the extensive documentation that an IPO necessitates. The same situation applies to marketing-related expenses with IPO road shows or steep underwriter discounts at the IPO itself.

Besides the costs, a coin offering can bring other advantages. Companies using the issued coins as a payment means on their platform or to drive business to their product or service in other ways (e.g., through utilities embedded in the coins) can benefit from the cash flow rights embedded in the tokens. Cash flow participation drives coin demand, which benefits the issuer's product or service's cash creation potential, drives the coins' value, and spurs demand (Cong et al., 2021; Gryglewicz et al., 2021). A regular equity issuance would not offer these benefits to the issuer.

The other side of that dynamic can result in severe underinvestment problems, which are detrimental to the issuer and the investor. Suppose coins, as the primary funding source, are issued to finance corporate growth, and these investments prove unsuccessful. In that case, coin owners abandon both the coins and the platform, leaving the issuer with the prospect of potentially abandoning the business or raising costly external financing. The result is a strong incentive to underinvest the raised proceeds (Cong et al., 2022). On a broader level, an argument can be made that security coin issuance, particularly if paired with utility features, creates welfare on an economy- and capital-market-wide basis. Investors in security coins with utility features derive financial and consumption benefits from their investment. Therefore, more projects and businesses are likely to receive funding via coins than they would via regular funding tools, which do not receive consumption benefits (Lee & Parlour, 2022).

Given these benefits, will capital markets see a stronger shift toward coin financing and away from traditional equity and debt funding sources in the future? Although ICOs have been on a growth trajectory, certain impediments threaten to limit their future potential for widespread adoption and, ultimately, of becoming a more mainstream funding tool across a wide range of companies, at least unless certain core features are changed.

One impediment to future ICO growth is their limited potential to raise sufficient funds (Chod et al., 2022). The average ICO fundraising volume is $22 million (Howell et al., 2020), whereas IPOs raise, on average, 10–15 times this amount, according to data by Ritter (2023). A second impediment concerns ICOs' agency implications, especially when compared to equity. Although some agency problems are solved through coins, such as lack of entrepreneurial effort (Chod & Lyandres, 2021), new problems, such as moral hazard-induced quality (mis-) signaling, might arise (Momtaz, 2021).

A third impediment is that as smaller start-up-like businesses often sell coins that do not get listed on a major and well-known centralized exchange, they might be more difficult to advertise. Thus, issuers frequently resort to expensive marketing campaigns featuring, for example, celebrity endorsements. Although these campaigns promise access to a broader audience, the associated costs can use a substantial portion of the savings achieved by issuing coins instead of equity through IPOs.

Fourth, following the initial sale, coins are more difficult to trade for investors. Because only roughly half of all coins are listed on centralized exchanges, this lack of secondary market liquidity can make them unattractive to investors (Howell et al., 2020). Additionally, those exchanges that decide to list coins often charge exorbitant listing fees substantially higher than those of traditional exchanges such as the National Association of Securities Dealers Automated Quotations (NASDAQ), further adding to the cost of ICOs (Bloomberg, 2018).

Lastly, and perhaps most importantly, coins have severe regulatory concerns. Coins should be structured to resemble classic equity issued in IPOs to appeal to the largest number of possible investors. However, structuring coins like common shares makes them likely to match the criteria outlined in the so-called *Howey Test* for what constitutes a securities contract under the Securities Acts of 1933 and 1934. Following this test, securities must be registered with and regulated by the SEC if they are sold to investors (1) by a common enterprise, (2) in exchange for money, (3) with the reasonable expectation of profits that are (4) derived from the efforts of others in the future. Although much debate has occurred as to which degree tokens, coins, and cryptocurrencies meet those criteria, a recent landmark ruling by a US district court in Manhattan has strongly backed the SEC's case that tokens and cryptocurrencies are securities and should fall under SEC regulation. In March 2020, the court sided with the SEC in a case against US-based messaging service Telegram, prohibiting the company from selling its digital coins (called Grams) because these constitute unregistered securities, and their sale would violate federal securities laws. Due to the ruling, Telegram agreed on a settlement with the SEC to resolve the charges, returned more than $1.2 billion to the original investors in the coins, and paid $18.5 million in fines.

The SEC plans to pursue other similar cases to regulate token and coin sales on the grounds of the ruling. Investors would benefit from this development as it would eradicate the many fraudulent cases an unregulated market brings. Yet, it would also make coin and token sales more complicated, expensive, and less attractive as a fundraising tool than equity sales in IPOs.

Summary and Conclusions

Capital markets have benefited from adopting various technological advancements, which are generally subsumed under the term fintech nowadays. These technological tools have enhanced the welfare of all market participants by (1) lowering information asymmetries and making capital markets more efficient; (2) lowering participation costs and barriers to entry, making capital markets more accessible and democratic; and (3) allowing the development of new financial products, fine-tuned to the specific needs of market participants and covering all relevant areas such as investment decision-making, portfolio administration, or back-office management.

The result is a more attractive and value-enhancing environment for capital flows in public and private markets.

Despite its many benefits, fintech in capital markets faces challenges before it can reach widespread adoption. For example, can the fintech industry adapt to the increasing regulatory pressure? Will a more stringent regulation adversely affect the current competitive edge fintech products and services have over legacy systems? Should the industry embrace more regulation to tackle the many fraud-related scandals and investor losses it has suffered?

Further problems lie in the development stages of the technology itself. In blockchain-based solutions, for example, a consensus has yet to be reached on the optimality of PoW versus PoS methodologies in running and building chains. Another example is teething problems in, for example, HFT algorithms and their roles in market-wide flash crashes, which are not fully understood. As long as technologies are in those nascent stages and appear not fully developed and lacking reliability, their mainstream adoption in capital markets seems unlikely.

However, the rapid speed of technological advancement will likely produce swift solutions to all technical issues. Hence, the substantial economic benefits fintech solutions can bring to capital markets will create urgency for regulators and market participants to reach agreements on all regulatory frameworks. Overall, fintech's prospects in capital markets are highly promising.

Discussion Questions

(1) Explain why fintech is often credited with democratizing capital markets.
(2) Discuss so-called HFT algorithms, and how their increasingly widespread use affects capital markets.
(3) Explain how ML-based data analysis has affected capital markets, particularly when applied to big data.
(4) Discuss capital markets' challenges in adopting blockchain technology in securities clearing and settlement processes.
(5) Explain why ICOs have faced regulatory backlash.

References

Barber, B. M., Huang, X., Odean, T., & Schwarz, C. (2022). Attention-induced trading and returns: Evidence from robinhood users. *The Journal of Finance*, *77*(6), 3141–3190.

Bhattacharya, U., Hackethal, A., Kaesler, S., Loos, B., & Meyer, S. (2012). Is unbiased financial advice to retail investors sufficient? Answers from a large field study. *Review of Financial Studies*, *25*(4), 975–1032.

Bloomberg. (2018). Crypto exchanges charge millions to list tokens. https://www.bloomberg.com/news/articles/2018-04-03/crypto-exchanges-charge-millions-to-list-tokens-autonomous-says#xj4y7vzkg

Bongaerts, D., & Van Achter, M. (2021). Competition among liquidity providers with access to high-frequency trading technology. *Journal of Financial Economics*, *140*(1), 220–249.

Brogaard, J., Hendershott, T., & Riordan, R. (2014). High-frequency trading and price discovery. *Review of Financial Studies*, *27*(8), 2267–2306.

Bushee, B. J., Gerakos, J., & Lee, L. F. (2018). Corporate jets and private meetings with investors. *Journal of Accounting and Economics*, *65*(2), 358–379.

Capponi, A., Olafsson, S., & Zariphopoulou, T. (2022). Personalized robo-advising: Enhancing investment through client interaction. *Management Science*, *68*(4), 2485–2512.

Carrion, A. (2013). Very fast money: High-frequency trading on the NASDAQ. *Journal of Financial Markets*, *16*(4), 680–711.

Chakrabarty, B., Moulton, P. C., & Wang, X. F. (2022). Attention: How high-frequency trading improves price efficiency following earnings announcements. *Journal of Financial Markets*, *57*(C), 100690.

Chiu, J., & Koeppl, T. V. (2019). Blockchain-based settlement for asset trading. *Review of Financial Studies*, *32*(5), 1716–1753.

Chod, J., & Lyandres, E. (2021). A theory of ICOs: Diversification, agency, and information asymmetry. *Management Science*, *67*(10), 5969–5989.

Chod, J., Trichakis, N., & Alex Yang, S. (2022). Platform tokenization: Financing, governance, and moral hazard. *Management Science*, *68*(9), 6411–6433.

Cong, L. W., Li, Y., & Wang, N. (2022). Token-based platform finance. *Journal of Financial Economics*, *144*(3), 972–991.

Cong, L. W., Li, Y., & Wang, N. (2021). Tokenomics: Dynamic adoption and valuation. *Review of Financial Studies*, *34*(3), 1105–1155.

D'Acunto, F., Prabhala, N., & Rossi, A. G. (2019). The promises and pitfalls of robo-advising. *Review of Financial Studies*, *32*(5), 1983–2020.

Drake, M. S., Roulstone, D. T., & Thronock, J. R. (2012). Investor information demand: Evidence from google searches around earnings announcements. *Journal of Accounting Research*, *50*(4), 1001–1040.

Easley, D., Lopez de Prado, M., O'Hara, M., & Zhang, Z. (2021). Microstructure in the machine age. *Review of Financial Studies*, *34*(7), 3316–3363.

Gao, M., & Huang, J. (2020). Informing the market: The effect of modern information technologies on information production. *Review of Financial Studies*, *33*(4), 1367–1411.

Goldstein, I., Spatt, C. S., & Ye, M. (2021). Big data in finance. *Review of Financial Studies*, *34*(7), 3213–3225.

Gryglewicz, S., Mayer, S., & Morellec, E. (2021). Optimal financing with tokens. *Journal of Financial Economics*, *142*(3), 1038–1067.

Hasbrouck, J., & Saar, G. (2013). Low-latency trading. *Journal of Financial Markets*, *16*(4), 646–679.

Howell, S. T., Niessner, M., & Yermack, D. (2020). Initial coin offerings: Financing growth with cryptocurrency token sales. *Review of Financial Studies*, *33*(9), 3925–3974.

Lee, J., & Parlour, C. A. (2022). Consumers as financiers: Consumer surplus, crowdfunding, and initial coin offerings. *Review of Financial Studies*, *35*(3), 1105–1140.

Li, K., Mai, F., Shen, R., & Yan, X. (2021). Measuring corporate culture using machine learning. *Review of Financial Studies*, *34*(7), 3265–3315.

Momtaz, P. P. (2021). Entrepreneurial finance and moral hazard: Evidence from token offerings. *Journal of Business Venturing*, *36*(5), 106001.

Mukherjee, A., George, P., & Shon, J. (2021). Eye in the sky: Private satellites and government macro data. *Journal of Financial Economics*, *141*(1), 234–254.

Nakamoto, S., (2008). Bitcoin: A Peer-to-peer Electronic Cash System. White Paper.

Ni, X., Wang, Y., & Yin, D. (2021). Does modern information technology attenuate managerial information hoarding? Evidence from the EDGAR implementation. *Journal of Corporate Finance*, *71*(C), 1–19.

Ritter, J. (2023). Initial Public Offerings: Updated Statistics. https://site.warrington.ufl.edu/ritter/files/IPO-Statistics.pdf

Welch, I. (2022). The wisdom of the robinhood crowd. *The Journal of Finance*, *77*(3), 1489–1527.

Weller, B. M. (2018). Does algorithmic trading reduce information acquisition? *Review of Financial Studies*, *31*(6), 2184–2226.

Xu, Y., Xuan, Y., & Zheng, G. (2021). Internet searching and stock price crash risk: Evidence from a quasi-natural experiment. *Journal of Financial Economics*, *141*(1), 255–275.

Yermack, D. (2014). Tailspotting: Identifying and profiting from CEO vacation trips. *Journal of Financial Economics*, *113*(2), 252–269.

Zhu, C. (2019). Big data as a governance mechanism. *Review of Financial Studies*, *32*(5), 2021–2061.

Section VIII

Shaping the Future of Fintech: What Lies Ahead?

Chapter 22

Technologies and Emerging Trends Shaping Fintech

Omer Unsal[a] *and Bora Ozkan*[b]

[a]Merrimack College, USA
[b]Temple University, USA

Abstract

This chapter examines the patterns influencing the trajectory of fintech enterprises. With the looming challenge of climate change, the financial realm's responsibility in mitigating climate risks has surged into focus. This chapter investigates fintech enterprises' response to climate-related corporate social responsibility in six main domains: (1) climate risk assessment tools, (2) green bonds and sustainable investment tools, (3) ESG integration, (4) carbon trading and carbon credits, (5) sustainable banking, and (6) DeFi and climate initiatives. It also investigates how fintech firms recognize the impact of climate change within their official declarations and efforts to amplify consciousness about climate-related concerns. This chapter assesses climate-linked terminology and expressions using quantitative and qualitative approaches, illuminating these firms' dedication to assimilating climate risk within their operational blueprints.

Keywords: Fintech; fintech enterprises; climate risk; sustainable investment; corporate social responsibility; green bonds; ESG; sustainable banking

Introduction

Disruptive digital technological innovation can alter the corporate landscape (Choi & Ozkan, 2019). The world is experiencing an unprecedented environmental crisis known as climate change, and no industry, including the financial sector, is exempt from it. With the rise of climate risk, financial technology (fintech) firms started becoming important players in creating innovative solutions and transforming the industry. This chapter investigates the essential technologies

The Emerald Handbook of Fintech, 399–418

doi:10.1108/978-1-83753-608-520241046

and applications affecting fintech, focusing on climate change, climate risk, and global warming.

Financial institutions started using advanced data analytics, artificial intelligence (AI), and machine learning (ML) to evaluate climate risks associated with their and their clients' investments. These tools analyze large datasets such as satellite imagery of deforestation and predictions of rising sea levels, enabling institutions to determine the potential financial consequences of environmental events on their assets and loans.

Green bonds, designed to finance environmentally conscious projects, have recently increased in popularity. Fintech platforms now offer specialized services that connect investors with sustainable investment opportunities, allowing capital to be directed toward initiatives that address climate change. Investors increasingly view integrating environmental, social, and governance (ESG) metrics as a critical factor in their investment decisions. AI using fintech platforms now provides insights into companies' ESG performance, facilitating data-driven and sustainable investment choices.

Carbon trading platforms increasingly use blockchain and distributed ledger technology (DLT), allowing them more transparency and traceability in carbon credit transactions. These platforms enable businesses to buy and sell emission allowances, driving a market-based approach to reduce carbon footprints.

Digital banks, or 'neo-banks,' lead the way with sustainable characteristics. They offer paperless operations and fund green projects, using the latest fintech solutions to appeal to eco-conscious consumers. Decentralized finance (DeFi) platforms provide ways to support climate action. These decentralized platforms offer funds for green initiatives, reward carbon sequestration, or back climate-friendly projects without the traditional banking intermediaries.

Reviewing the implications of fintech firms mentioning climate risk-associated terminology in their official filings is worthwhile. Such terminology indicates a growing awareness of the interconnection between finance and environmental well-being by fintech firms. By acknowledging climate risk, these firms understand the evolving environment in which climate-related issues influence business conduct, investment decisions, and customer preferences.

In conclusion, fintech is important in the global fight against climate change. Redirecting available funds, optimizing risk assessments, and fostering transparency reshapes the financial landscape and drives momentum toward a more sustainable and robust global economy. As the threat of climate change increases, the association between fintech and sustainability becomes even more critical, allowing a future where finance and technology collectively address one of humanity's most pressing challenges.

Climate Risk Assessment Tools

Various financial institutions worldwide have started leveraging advanced data analytics and ML to assess climate-related risks associated with their investments.

BlackRock (2023) develops tools like Aladdin Climate to help investors understand and act on climate risk and investment opportunities.

UBS, a global financial services company, has worked on integrating sustainability metrics into its investment decisions and has used various tools, including AI, to evaluate the impact of climate risks on its portfolios. Its 2022 sustainability report states, "We want to be the financial provider of choice for clients who wish to mobilize capital toward the achievement of the 17 Sustainable Development Goals and the orderly transition to a low-carbon economy" (UBS 2022, p. 1). The report highlights that sustainable investing assets under management (AUM) reached $268 billion, representing a 6.5% increase in 2022.

HSBC's Centre of Sustainable Finance fully supports the shift to a net zero economy. The firm is working with academic, industry, and government experts to encourage emissions outcome-based decisions. HSBC also launched a new HSBC Sustainability Tracker, a simple tool for businesses relatively new to their sustainability journey. This tool offers tailored suggestions and tangible actions to help clients create a more sustainable business across their operations, energy use, and products (HSBC, 2023).

In 2019, Moody's, a credit rating agency, acquired a major stake in climate risk firm Four Twenty Seven, Inc., a leading data, intelligence, and analytics provider. According to Moody's (2020), this acquisition allows Moody's to use advanced analytics to integrate climate risk metrics into its credit risk assessments. Adding Four Twenty Seven enhances Moody's growing portfolio of risk assessment capabilities and emphasizes its work to advance global standards for assessing environmental and climate risk factors.

The Task Force on Climate-related Financial Disclosures (TCFD), formed by the Financial Stability Board, is an initiative created to develop recommendations for voluntary and consistent climate-related financial risk disclosures in official filings. The TCFD framework guides companies to report on their climate risks in a standardized manner, encouraging more institutions to adopt advanced analytics to make sense of these data (Moody's, 2020). As time progresses, more financial institutions will likely adopt these advanced methods to evaluate climate risks, given the increasing importance of climate change in investment and risk management considerations.

Green Bonds and Sustainable Investment Tools

Demand for green bonds has been increasing in recent years. These bonds are designed to finance environmentally focused projects, such as renewable energy, energy efficiency, and sustainable agriculture. Fintech platforms have also emerged to offer specialized services that connect investors with green and sustainable investment opportunities. These specialized services ensure capital flows toward projects and initiatives addressing climate change and promoting sustainable development. Sustainability-focused investment opportunities allow investors to affect the environment and earn a positive return.

What Are Green Bonds?

Green bonds work like regular bonds, but the money raised from investors is used exclusively to finance projects with a positive environmental impact, such as renewable energy, pollution prevention, sustainable agriculture, and green buildings. Corporations, municipalities, sovereign countries, and financial institutions typically issue green bonds. According to an agenda article by Henry (2021) published on the World Economic Forum website, the European Investment Bank issued the first green bond in 2007, followed by the World Bank in 2008. Since then, many governments and corporations have used green bonds to finance environmentally friendly projects.

Fintech's Role in the Green Bond Market

Fintech and green bonds represent a meeting of dynamic technology and sustainable finance. Traditionally, large institutional investors dominated the global bond market. Through their digital platforms, fintech companies can make the green bond market more accessible to individual investors. Since fintechs can manage data more efficiently, they can help their clients make faster and more informed decisions about the sustainability and impact of potential projects on the environment. They also help connect investors with suitable green projects based on risk tolerance, return expectations, and specific environmental interests. Several fintech firms also aim to educate their investors and increase financial literacy. These educational initiatives offer the potential for fintech firms to raise awareness about the importance of sustainable investment and educate investors about the green bond market.

ESG Integration

Sustainable finance is the practice of considering ESG factors when making investment decisions. According to Gayle and Lacina (2021), investment funds that use ESG have more than $50 trillion in capital. ESG factors have emerged as a key consideration for investors and companies, reshaping investment ideas and corporate strategy. Bergman et al. (2020) maintain that the three ESG categories are increasingly integrated into investment analysis, processes, and decision-making.

(1) *Environmental.* Environmental aspects capture the company's impact on nature. This category includes energy efficiencies, carbon footprints, greenhouse gas emissions, deforestation, biodiversity, climate change and pollution mitigation, waste management, and water usage.
(2) *Social.* Social aspects pertain to a company's handling of its interactions with employees, suppliers, customers, and the local communities in which it functions. This category encompasses labor regulations, compensation and benefits, workforce and board inclusivity, racial fairness, salary parity, human rights, and other factors tied to human resources and social equity concerns.

(3) *Governance.* Corporate governance deals with a company's leadership, executive pay, board composition and structure, audits, internal controls, shareholder rights, political contributions, and transparency.

Investors increasingly value ESG criteria in their investment choices, understanding that firms with robust ESG metrics might be more adept at navigating risks and seizing opportunities. Businesses also acknowledge the significance of ESG elements, implementing measures like carbon reduction, championing diversity and inclusion, and refining their governance approaches.

ESG integration refers to the deliberate and comprehensive incorporation of ESG elements into financial assessments and investment strategies. Through this lens, investors and stakeholders gain a thorough insight into a company's long-term viability and ethical integrity.

Importance of ESG Integration

ESG integration incorporates ESG factors into investment decisions and corporate strategies. Through ESG integration, investors can pinpoint and navigate risks tied to ESG challenges, such as extreme climatic events, limited water resources, and carbon emissions that present environmental threats. By embracing ESG integration, investors can evaluate these hazards and make enlightened investment choices.

Companies with strong ESG performance may be better positioned to manage risks and capitalize on opportunities. According to Whelan et al. (2021), ESG investing provides downside protection, especially during social or economic crises. ESG integration can support the analysis of corporate decisions that affect operational efficiency and future direction, as well as increased risk-adjusted returns and long-term viability. A successful ESG program can help companies access vast pools of capital from investors looking for ESG-friendly investments. A growing demand exists for financially sound and ethically aligned investments, especially among millennials. Governments and regulatory bodies worldwide started to require ESG disclosures for publicly traded companies, mandating them to integrate and report on ESG factors. ESG integration is important because it can help investors make informed decisions, improve corporate performance, provide access to capital, and enhance reputation and brand value.

Challenges to ESG Integration

Integrating ESG factors into business and investment decisions can present various challenges. Key challenges include lack of standardization, limited data availability, the subjective nature of ESG assessments, and keeping up with regulatory changes.

With increased awareness around pressing global issues such as climate change, social inequalities, and corporate governance, ESG integration is poised to take an even more important role in the financial sector. Advancements in fintech simplify the process of gathering, processing, and weaving ESG data into investment strategies. At its core, ESG integration reflects a general trend toward accepting that sustainable business success is more than mere financial success. It implies a move toward a more sustainable, ethical, and comprehensive perspective on business and investment in today's age.

Carbon Trading and Carbon Credits

Carbon trading is a market-based buying and selling of permits that allow a company to emit a certain amount of carbon dioxide or other greenhouse gases. One credit permits the emission of one ton of carbon dioxide or the equivalent of other greenhouse gases. By paying someone else to reduce their emissions or capture their carbon, companies can compensate for their environmental footprint and even use carbon credits to get to carbon-neutral status in the most ambitious cases. Carbon trading and carbon credits have emerged as innovative tools in the global arsenal to combat climate change. By leveraging market mechanisms, they incentivize businesses to reduce their carbon emissions.

The Need for Transparency and Traceability

Given the financial stakes and the environmental goals of carbon trading, the system demands the utmost integrity. Transparency and traceability are essential for the effective functioning of carbon trading and carbon credits. The digitalization of carbon credits is revolutionizing how carbon markets operate and manage carbon emissions. As digital platforms replace traditional systems, tracing and verifying carbon credits has become more efficient and transparent. However, challenges require attention. The absence of an interoperable global marketplace restricts liquidity and limits the opportunities for market participants to trade carbon credits on a larger scale. The lack of liquidity constrains the development of a robust and transparent price discovery mechanism, which is pivotal for ensuring fair and efficient trading.

Blockchain and Distributed Ledger Technology in Carbon Trading

Blockchain and DLT can play a significant role in carbon trading and credits. According to Cointelegraph (2022), blockchain technology can be implemented in many ways to make climate change-related initiatives more efficient. DLT offers several advantages for carbon market infrastructure, especially given the global nature of those markets, the need for immutable records, and the ability to program smart contracts. Like other markets using DLT, such as equity derivatives, DLT, and blockchain applications can enhance the functioning of voluntary carbon markets.

Adopting these technologies creates an opportunity to observe DLT's impact on carbon markets and reflect on how regulators may support their development. DLT can help increase the integrity of carbon markets, make offset markets more efficient, facilitate increased access and demand, unlock supply, and clarify the relationship between voluntary and compliant carbon markets.

Several startups and established firms have integrated blockchain into carbon trading. Norway's Empower uses blockchain technology to trace the collection and recycling of plastic waste, converting these data into verifiable carbon credits. IBM's Carbon Credit Management platform leverages blockchain technology to manage carbon allowances and credits, ensuring transparency and traceability.

Although blockchain technology promises transformative change for carbon trading, some challenges cannot be ignored. Current blockchain platforms might face challenges processing large volumes of carbon trades. A global consensus on carbon trading standards on blockchain platforms is also needed. Existing carbon markets and systems must be integrated with new blockchain-based platforms.

Blockchains and DLT have the potential to rejuvenate and solidify the carbon trading system by ensuring transparency and traceability. As the world grapples with the pressing need to reduce carbon emissions, integrating modern technologies into environmental solutions can pave the way for a sustainable future.

Sustainable Banking

The world is increasingly recognizing the urgency of sustainability, not just as an environmental necessity but as a critical business requirement. In the financial sector, this shift is obvious, with the emergence of digital-first, sustainability-focused banks. Often referred to as 'neo-banks,' these institutions marry fintech innovations with environmental stewardship.

What Is Sustainable Banking?

Sustainable banking refers to financial institutions prioritizing ESG factors in their banking operations, investments, and decision-making. It involves assessing the impact of banking activities on the environment and society while endorsing sustainable development through responsible lending and investment practices. Sustainable banking aims to secure financial goals and align them with the duty of further sustainable development and society's well-being. It is not merely about mitigating risks but actively contributing to a more sustainable and inclusive economy. Achieving sustainable banking status involves minimizing the environmental footprint of banking operations, such as using renewable energy for data centers or going paperless. It also involves prioritizing loans to projects and businesses that align with sustainable principles, like renewable energy installations or organic farms. Finally, ensuring that bank practices are ethically sound and corruption-free and that stakeholders are informed is important.

Neo-Banks and Their Sustainable Characteristics

A *neo-bank* is a digital-only bank that operates without physical branches and offers services through online and mobile platforms. Neo-banks with sustainable characteristics aim to balance their financial goals with their responsibility to contribute to sustainable development and society's well-being. They often offer products and services that support sustainable practices, such as green loans for environmentally friendly projects and investments in renewable energy. By prioritizing sustainability, these neo-banks help to drive positive change and promote a more sustainable future.

Several neo-banks have a strong focus on sustainability and ethical practices. For example, Aspiration, a US-based neo-bank, offers socially responsible and sustainable banking and investment products. The bank donates 10% of its earnings to charities that support economic opportunity and environmental conservation. German neo-bank Tomorrow offers sustainable banking products, including a current account and debit card made from sustainable products. Dutch neo-bank Tridos Bank focuses on sustainable banking and only lends to and invests in organizations that positively impact society and the environment. Several more examples of neo-banks with sustainable characteristics are available.

Challenges and the Road Ahead

Neo-banks have emerged as digital disruptors with a promise of a seamless and innovative banking experience. Unfortunately, several neo-banks have failed in this competitive environment. Sustainable banking encounters numerous challenges, such as balancing financial goals with social and environmental responsibilities, the absence of standardized methods for measuring and reporting sustainability performance, and the need to integrate sustainability priorities into decision-making processes. Despite these challenges, the future of sustainable banking looks promising. More traditional and neo-banks acknowledge the significance of sustainable practices and incorporate ESG factors into their operations and decision-making. This incorporation extends to launching new products and services that promote sustainable practices like green loans and renewable energy investments. By prioritizing sustainability, banks have the potential to catalyze transformative change and promote a sustainable future.

Defi and Climate Initiatives

A *blockchain* is a decentralized ledger that securely and transparently records transactions and enables secure information sharing across a network. DeFi is still a niche market with a relatively low volume that is growing rapidly. Schar (2021) shows that the value of funds in DeFi-related smart contracts crossed the $10 billion threshold in 2020. Although various industries use this technology, its potential applications in fighting climate change are promising. DeFi could become a game-changer in climate initiatives and green finance by introducing new ways to support sustainable projects.

DeFi Platforms Supporting Climate Action

Several DeFi platforms are emerging, explicitly designed to support environmental causes.

- *Green bonds on DeFi.* Traditionally issued to raise capital for climate and environmental projects, green bonds can now be issued on DeFi platforms.
- *Carbon credit marketplaces.* Decentralized platforms are being developed where individuals and companies can buy and sell tokenized carbon credits.
- *Eco-friendly staking.* Certain platforms offer staking rewards for supporting eco-friendly projects, where users can "stake" their cryptocurrency and earn returns from green initiatives.
- *Crowdfunding climate projects.* DeFi platforms enable decentralized crowdfunding, where global participants can financially back promising climate-friendly projects.

According to Schloesser and Schulz (2022), DeFi can democratize the financial sector by bypassing intermediaries and equalizing access to high-return financial products. It can also enable access to climate finance and insurance for the unbanked. Several DeFi platforms support climate action by providing new ways to find and incentivize sustainable projects. For example, Poseidon, a Singapore-based DeFi platform, uses blockchain technology to create, trade, and retire carbon credits. The platform allows individuals and organizations to offset their carbon emissions by purchasing credits from projects that reduce or remove greenhouse gases from the atmosphere. Another example is Nori, a Seattle-based DeFi platform that uses blockchain technology to create a transparent and traceable market for carbon removal. The platform allows individuals and organizations to purchase carbon removal certificates from farmers and other land managers using regenerative practices to remove carbon from the atmosphere.

Challenges in DeFi's Support for Climate Initiatives

DeFi, despite its vast potential, is not without its challenges. Several challenges need addressing to harness its power for climate initiatives. Some of these challenges include the absence of industry regulation and standardization, issues with scalability, and a lack of awareness and understanding. DeFi struggles with the lack of regulation and standardization in the industry. The absence of regulation can hinder DeFi's capacity to support climate initiatives since no clear guidelines or standards are available for their operation. Scalability, a common issue for blockchain-driven initiatives, might constrain DeFi's effectiveness in supporting climate projects. Schar (2022) contends that decentralized block creation may cause severe transaction costs. Additionally, given that many remain unaware of or are misinformed about DeFi, attracting the necessary support and funding for climate-focused projects can be challenging. In summary, although DeFi offers a promising path for supporting climate actions, several challenges must be addressed for it to grow in this domain.

One path forward in DeFi climate finance could be to direct a percentage of a fund's profits over its lifetime toward climate-focused foundations and projects or to a non-profit that mitigates climate risk. MOVE Capital, a NEAR-based seed grant fund, is sharing its profits according to Medium (2021).

Another way DeFi can support climate initiatives is by adapting existing tools to carbon credits and other climate-related assets. For example, smart contracts could automatically retire carbon credits to match when CO_2 exhaust is created, and DeFi mechanisms could directly plug in. Investors can hedge carbon offsetting obligations, speculate on price movements, and earn a yield on pre-financing carbon offsetting measures.

Defi's alignment with climate initiatives promises to reshape the finance-climate connection. By creating a transparent, global, and democratized financial system, DeFi can offer unprecedented support to eco-friendly projects. Tapping into this potential requires a collaborative effort involving DeFi developers, regulators, environmental advocates, and the public. Together, they can transform a decentralized financial landscape into a revolutionary financial force and a strong partner in fighting climate change.

Fintechs Addressing Climate Risk Awareness

This section addresses how fintechs address climate risk awareness within their official statements. It also investigates whether these mentions are genuine commitments or superficial claims.

Data

This section provides an overview of the datasets employed in our study. The primary dataset, the "Firm Data," is the key information about fintech firms. It also outlines the criteria used to screen and select these firms for analysis in the "10-K Statements Section," which examines official documents to gather information about climate awareness by the fintech companies within the sample. The "Violation Data" segment describes corporate misconduct observed within the sample, allowing exploration of whether fintech firms uphold their societal responsibilities as professed.

Firm Data

Several datasets examine how fintech firms raise climate risk awareness issues. The S&P Capital IQ Universe was used to find fintech firms using the following criteria.

- *Industry classifications.* Software and Services (Primary) OR Financial Software (Primary) OR Financial Consolidation and Reporting Software (Primary) OR General Ledger and Accounting Software (Primary) OR Financial Services Software (Primary) OR Research and Consulting Services (Primary).

- *Business description: Keyword.* "Financial Institutions" OR "Banking" OR "Financial Services" OR "e-Banking" OR "Wealth Management" OR "Finance" OR "Credit" OR "Financial Crime."

These criteria identified 173 fintech firms in the sample between 2000 and 2020. All firms are publicly traded and headquartered in the United States.

10-K Statements and Other Corporate Filings

After creating the main sample of 173 fintech firms, the Capital IQ universe is revisited, and the screening section is used to access their annual filings, such as 10-K, 10-Q, or DEF 14A statements. Within those statements, the following words are searched: "climate risk," "climate change," "global warming," and "environmental actions."

Violations Data

Data on regulatory breaches is collected to determine whether fintech firms comply with relevant environmental regulations and corporate governance standards. The Capital IQ Screening tab is used to access Corporate News announcements. Those announcements include news related to lawsuits and legal issues. Between 2000 and 2021, 323 corporate misconduct incidents were identified. Out of 323 wrongdoings, 157 instances of misconduct were identified as related to financial or environmental offenses, where a fintech firm is directly or indirectly involved, and 166 misconduct incidents were related to wage and employment offenses, where a fintech firm is directly or indirectly involved.

Methodology

The sample consists of firm-year observations where how many times fintech firms mention climate-related words each year are identified. The total number of mentions at the firm level and the yearly trends are counted. In addition, the number of corporate violations fintech firms commit each year is counted. Labor-related offenses from financial and environmental-related offenses are separated to distinguish each trend.

Main Findings

The discovery of climate risk-associated terminology within the official declarations of fintech firms carries noteworthy implications for the sector's trajectory and wider societal resonance. This presence underscores a burgeoning cognizance within the fintech domain concerning the intricate interlinkage of finance with environmental well-being. By acknowledging climate risk (Matsumura et al., 2022), these entities understand the evolving milieu wherein climate-induced predicaments sway business conduct, investment choices, and client predilections (Doran & Quinn, 2008).

This section discusses the study's major findings. Fig. 22.1 presents examples of how fintech firms raise awareness by mentioning climate risk in their statements.

The Securities and Exchange Commission's (SEC's) EDGAR filing database scans mentioned words in major filings between 2000 and 2020. Mentioning climate risk is important because climate change substantially threatens and affects long-term corporate value. It is not only limited to physical impact (e.g., extreme

Visa, Inc. 10-K filing for 2015

"The perception of our brands and our business could be harmed if our transaction processing systems are disrupted or compromised.

Processing or other technology malfunctions, fires, natural disasters, power losses, disruptions in long-distance or local telecommunications access, fraud, military or political conflicts, terrorism, effects of climate change or other catastrophic events may disrupt or compromise our transaction processing systems."

PayPal, Inc. DEF 14A for 2021

Environmental Suitability, or How We Responsibly Advance Sustainable Business Practices

"This category includes addressing climate change, promoting renewable energy use, mobilizing on environmental action and driving environmental innovation across our products, services and value chain."

Splunk, Inc. 10-Q for 2020

"Natural disasters and other events beyond our control could harm our business.
Natural disasters or other catastrophic events may cause damage or disruption to our operations, international commerce and the global economy, and thus could have a negative effect on us. Our business operations are subject to interruption by natural disasters, flooding, fire, power shortages, pandemics such as the COVID-19 pandemic, terrorism, political unrest, telecommunications failure, vandalism, cyber-attacks, geopolitical instability, war, the effects of climate change (such as drought, wildfires, increased storm severity and sea level rise) and other events beyond our control."

Zscaler, Inc. 10-K for 2021

"Our data centers are vulnerable to damage or interruption from a variety of sources, including earthquakes, floods, fires, power loss, system failures, computer viruses, physical or electronic break-ins, human error or interference (including by disgruntled employees, former employees or contractors), and other catastrophic events, including those exacerbated by the effects of climate change."

Fig. 22.1. Mentioning Climate Risk in Official Filings. *Note:* This chart illustrates how fintech firms mention climate risk in their statements. The following are examples of 10-K filings and how these firms mention climate issues in official documents. *Source:* Securities and Exchange Commission (SEC) EDGAR Filings Search. https://www.sec.gov/edgar/search/#

weather events) but also includes regulatory actions (e.g., government policies) resulting from climate change.

By acknowledging climate risk, fintech firms may signal an understanding of the potential risks and take actions to mitigate them. Those actions may include taking environmentally friendly projects, supporting green financing options (e.g., green bonds), and raising awareness about climate change among companies. From investors' perspective, all stakeholders, including investors, demand more actions regarding climate risk. Some states have introduced laws for mandatory reporting and actions targeting climate change. Hence, by disclosing the climate risk, fintech firms may show their commitment to socially responsible behaviors to meet the expectations of all stakeholders.

Furthermore, fintech firms' cognizance of climate risk can mold the industry's future in many ways. Basu et al. (2022) suggest that it showcases a proactive stance toward tackling ecological apprehensions, nurturing a more conscientious and principled image for these establishments. This transformation can pave the way for heightened credibility, augmented investor faith, and a closer unity with the sensibilities of environmentally aware patrons.

Fig. 22.2 presents how many fintech firms mentioned climate risk in their official statements between 2000 and 2020. In early 2000, only a few fintechs

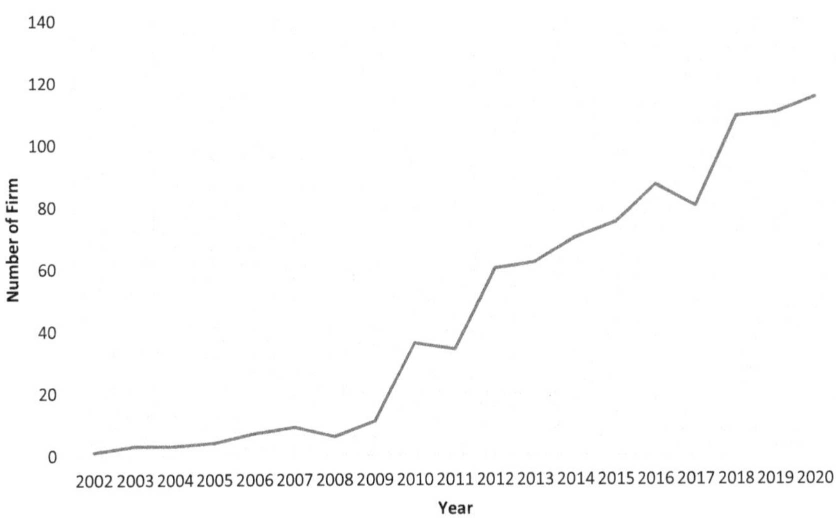

Fig. 22.2. The Number of Fintech Firms Mentioning Climate Risk in Their Statements. *Note:* This figure illustrates the number of fintech firms mentioning climate risk in their filings between 2000 and 2020, based on a search of the following words: "climate risk," "climate change," "global warming," and "environmental actions" in all filing types. *Source:* The author's calculations.

mentioned climate change in their filings. After 2008, a sharp increase occurred in companies raising awareness about climate issues.

Fig. 22.3 shows the total number of climate-risk words mentioned in filings documented during the sample period. By the beginning of 2000, filings mentioned climate risk less than 10 times. By the end of 2019, this number exceeds 230.

Fig. 22.3 also shows that fintech firms rapidly increased the climate risk in their statements after the 2010s. Mentioning climate risk could be due to several reasons. First, growing awareness about climate change made firms realize its potential financial and social costs. Second, stakeholders started to pressure companies to address the climate issues in their governance. Third, environmental regulations enforced by federal and state governments pushed firms to act regarding the climate risk. Finally, companies realized that sustainable practices in the market give them a competitive advantage over those who fail to embrace the new practices. Table 22.1 documents the raw data used in the figures. Column (2) shows the total number of firms mentioning climate risk, whereas column (3) reveals the total number of climate words mentioned by fintech firms in the sample between 2000 and 2020.

Identifying climate risk-related terminology within fintech firms' official statements holds relevant implications for the industry's trajectory and broader societal impact. This presence underscores a growing awareness within the fintech

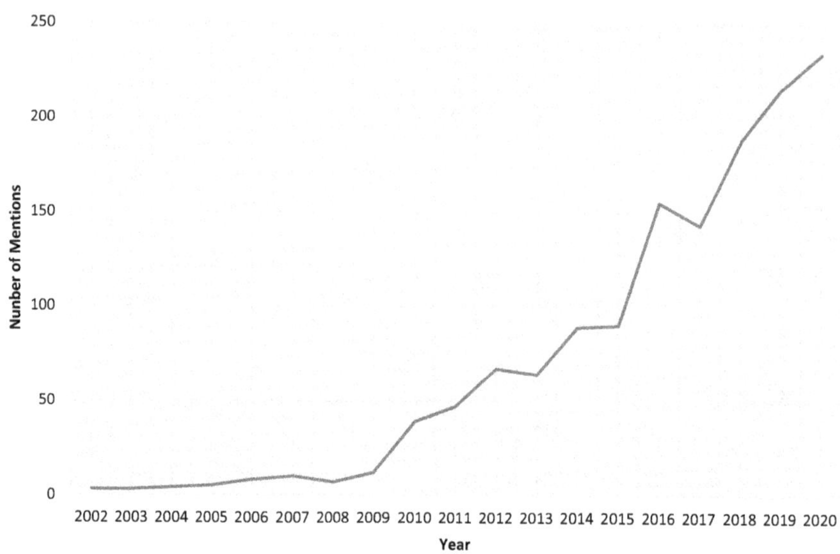

Fig. 22.3. The Number of Climate-Risk Mentions in Statements. *Note:* This figure illustrates the number of climate-risk-related words mentioned in fintech firms' filings between 2000 and 2020. Those words include "climate risk," "climate change," "global warming," and "environmental actions" in all filing types. *Source:* The author's calculations.

Table 22.1. Raising Climate Change Awareness.

Year	Number of Firms	Number of Mentions
2002	1	3
2003	3	3
2004	3	4
2005	4	5
2006	7	8
2007	9	10
2008	6	7
2009	11	12
2010	36	39
2011	34	47
2012	60	67
2013	62	64
2014	70	89
2015	75	90
2016	87	155
2017	80	143
2018	109	188
2019	110	215
2020	115	234
Total	882	1,383

Source: The authors' calculations.

Note: This table shows the number of fintech firms mentioning climate risk in their statements. Column (2) shows the total number of unique firms mentioning climate risk in the statements. Column (3) shows the number of times words are mentioned in the statements. The sample includes all publicly traded fintech firms between 2000 and 2020.

sector about the interplay between finance and environmental sustainability. By acknowledging climate risk, these firms recognize the evolving landscape, where climate-related challenges can influence business operations, investment decisions, and customer preferences.

Including climate risk-linked phraseology within the official narratives of fintech firms encapsulates a calculated acknowledgment of commercial exigencies and overarching societal duties. This recognition bolsters their resilience in confronting environmental challenges and propels the sector's capacity to assume a pivotal role in nurturing a more sustainable and conscientious global financial paradigm.

Greenwashing or Green Talking

Although companies mention climate risk in their statements, their actions sometimes contradict them. This process is called *greenwashing*, where companies make false claims about their environmental practices or make products to appeal to environmentally conscious customers. Pimonenko et al. (2020) suggest that greenwashing reveals guilty firms' characteristics. Szabo and Webster (2021) posit that greenwashing creates ethical harm to firms that hurts their reputation.

Conversely, *greentalking* refers to clear communication about the company's environmental goals and sustainable practices to all stakeholders. Hence, the motivation of this chapter is to understand whether fintech firms commit greenwashing or are honest about greentalking since they use transparent language about climate risk in their official statements. Exploring the potential occurrence of "greenwashing" within fintech companies, where they may project an appearance of environmental concern without substantive action, is important in sustainable finance and corporate ethics.

To study whether fintech firms are greenwashing or greentalking, corporate misconduct data they committed are collected during the sample period. Fig. 22.4 presents the results.

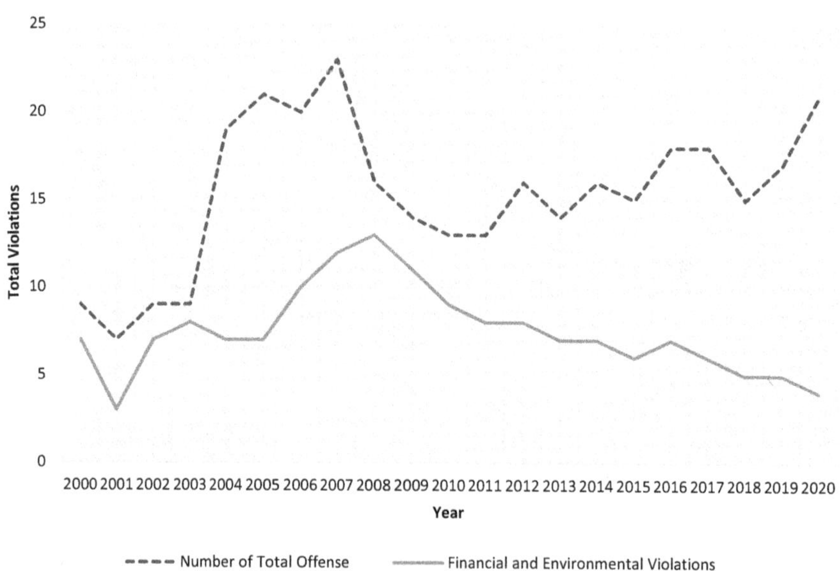

Fig. 22.4. The Number of Corporate Violations. *Note:* This figure illustrates the corporate violations committed by fintech firms in the sample between 2000 and 2020. The dashed line shows all violations by firms. The solid line represents the financial or environmental misconduct by fintech firms either directly or indirectly. *Source:* The author's calculations.

Fig. 22.4 represents the corporate violations for the sample firms. The evidence shows that total offenses (dashed line) increased over time. It also shows the first peak before the 2008 banking crisis and another increase over time before the 2020s. However, these include all violations, including labor and employment (e.g., discrimination and wrongful termination). After excluding labor-related violations, the results show the financial and environmental misconducts fintech firms commit (solid line). The results show that, after 2009, fintech firms committed fewer violations than in previous years. Table 22.2 presents the raw data number.

These findings are important, given that the number of climate-risk mentions increased since 2009. Similarly, financial and environmental misconduct involving

Table 22.2. Corporate Misconducts.

Year	Number of Offenses	Financial and Environmental Violations
2000	9	7
2001	7	3
2002	9	7
2003	9	8
2004	19	7
2005	21	7
2006	20	10
2007	23	12
2008	16	13
2009	14	11
2010	13	9
2011	13	8
2012	16	8
2013	14	7
2014	16	7
2015	15	6
2016	18	7
2017	18	6
2018	15	5
2019	17	5
2020	21	4
Total	323	157

Source: The authors' calculations.

Note: This table shows the number of corporate misconducts and violations committed by fintech firms in the sample. Column (2) represents all offenses by fintech firms. Column (3) represents financial and environmental misconduct (labor and employment excluded) by fintech firms.

fintech firms decreased after 2009, which may signal greentalking more than greenwashing. However, a total increase in violations should be taken seriously. Because the total number includes labor issues, it involves employee treatment, hiring practices, wage and labor issues, and discriminatory practices. Hence, fintech firms should pay equal attention to employee treatment as much as they address climate risk. Because employees are one of a firm's most important assets, their well-being is directly linked to operating performance (Unsal, 2019).

Summary and Conclusion

Given the recent interest in the intersection of fintech firms and climate risk, illuminating how these firms are taking proactive steps to address such risks and elevate awareness about climate change is imperative. Fintech's ascendancy in academic discourse is evident, and this chapter introduces a novel perspective. As researchers delve deeper into the implications of fintech firms advocating for climate consciousness, exploring the following questions is essential as novel practices emerge.

- What underpins the motivations and driving forces compelling fintech firms to prioritize climate-friendly finance, and how harmoniously does this commitment resonate with their business objectives?
- In what ways do fintech firms deploy inventive strategies, technologies, and communication channels to amplify awareness about climate change among their clientele, investors, and the broader public?
- How pivotal is the infusion of climate-friendly principles and practices into financial services for ensuring fintech firms' enduring stability and resilience and the overarching financial landscape?

This chapter encompasses sustainable finance methodologies, emerging trends in environmentally conscious finance, and the influence of climate change on conventional financial paradigms. It also provides insights into how investors should approach financial instruments within the context of climate risk. Subsequent sections undertake analyses of green bonds, ESG metrics, sustainable banking, and DeFi vis-à-vis climate initiatives.

Lastly, an examination of a sample of US fintech firms reveals that they incorporate an increasing number of climate-risk-related terms in their official statements each year. They also exhibit fewer infractions in finance and the environment than other corporate transgressions. Thus, comprehending the current trajectories among fintech firms is crucial for environmentally conscious investors seeking enhanced insights into their journey toward more sustainable practices.

Discussion Questions

- Define the term green bonds.
- Identify and discuss ESG integration.
- Identify and discuss carbon trading and carbon credits.
- Discuss neo-banks and their sustainable characteristics.

References

Basu, S., Shared, B., Bhattacharya, M., & Pathak, J. (2022). Climate-related discussions in firms' 10-K: Who does it and what is its impact? *Economics Letters*, *220*, 110855.

Bergman, M. S., Deckelbaum, A. J., & Karp, B. S. (2020). Introduction to ESG. *Harvard Law School Forum on Corporate Governance*.

BlackRock. (2023). What is Aladdin climate? https://www.blackrock.com/aladdin/products/aladdin-climate

Choi, J. J., & Ozkan, B. (2019). Innovation and disruption: Industry practices and conceptual bases. In J. J. Choi & B. Ozkan (Eds.), *Disruptive innovation in business and finance in the digital world*. Emerald Publishing Limited. (International Finance Review, 20, pp. 3−13).

Cointelegraph. (2022). Decentralized solutions for climate change are key as COP disappoints. https://cointelegraph.com/news/decentralized-solutions-for-climate-change-are-key-as-cop-disappoints

Doran, K. L., & Quinn, E. L. (2008). Climate change risk disclosure: A sector by sector analysis of SEC 10-K filings from 1995−2008. *North Carolina Journal of International Law*, *34*(3), 721–745.

Gayle, M., & Lacina, L. (2021). How will we fund the shift to a more sustainable future? 4 experts explain. *World Economic Forum*. https://www.weforum.org/agenda/2021/09/how-will-we-fund-the-shift-to-a-more-sustainable-future-4-experts-explain/

Henry, P. (2021). What are green bonds and why is this market growing so fast? *World Economic Forum Agenda Articles*. https://www.weforum.org/agenda/2021/10/what-are-green-bonds-climate-change/

HSBC. (2023). Centre of sustainable finance. https://www.business.hsbc.com/en-gb/campaigns/sustainability/centre-of-sustainable-finance

Matsumura, E. M., Prakash, R., & Vera-Muñoz, S. C. (2022). Climate-risk materiality and firm risk. *Review of Accounting Studies*, 1–42.

Medium. (2021). How DeFi on NEAR is helping combat climate change. https://medium.com/nearprotocol/how-defi-is-helping-combat-climate-change-be627f4441b5

Moody's. (2020). *Task force on climate-related financial disclosures (TCFD) report*. https://www.moodys.com/sites/products/ProductAttachments/CSR/Moodys_2020_TCFD_Report.pdf

Pimonenko, T., Bilan, Y., Horak, J., Starchenko, L., & Gajda, W. (2020). Green brand of companies and greenwashing under sustainable development goals. *Sustainability*, *12*(4), 1679.

Schar, F. (2021). Decentralized finance: On blockchain- and smart contract-based financial markets. *Federal Reserve Bank of St. Louis Review*, *103*(2), 153–174.

Schar, F. (2022). *DeFi's promise and pitfalls*. International Monetary Fund Publications. https://www.imf.org/en/Publications/fandd/issues/2022/09/Defi-promise-and-pitfalls-Fabian-Schar

Schloesser, T., & Schulz, K. (2022). Distributed ledger technology and climate finance. In F. Taghizadeh-Hesary & S. Hyun (Eds.), *Green digital finance and sustainable development goals* (pp. 265−286). *Economics, law, and institutions in Asia Pacific*. Springer.

Szabo, S., & Webster, J. (2021). Perceived greenwashing: The effects of green marketing on environmental and product perceptions. *Journal of Business Ethics*, *171*, 719–739.

UBS. (2022). *Sustainability report 2022*. https://secure.ubs.com/minisites/group-functions/investor-relations/sustainability-report/2022/sustainability-report-2022/SR22-digital/SR22-digital/index.html#book_1

Unsal, O. (2019). Employee relations and firm risk: Evidence from court rooms. *Research in International Business and Finance*, *48*(C), 1–16.

Whelan, T., Ulrich, A., Van Holt, T., & Casey, C. (2021). ESG and financial performance: Uncovering the relationship by aggregating evidence from 1,000 plus studies published between 2015-2020. NYU Stern Center for Sustainable Business Report. https://www.stern.nyu.edu/sites/default/files/assets/documents/NYU-RAM_ESG-Paper_2021%20Rev_0.pdf

Chapter 23

The Future of Fintech: Challenges and Opportunities

Dianna Preece

University of Louisville, USA

Abstract

This chapter explores the vast array of fintech opportunities. The industry commanded approximately $250 billion in revenue in 2022, which is predicted to grow to $1.5 trillion by 2030. Fintech firms are involved in everything from digital currencies to payment systems, lending platforms, and embedded finance. Firms use artificial intelligence (AI) and machine learning (ML) to create personalized financial products. One of the most important benefits to society is that fintech makes finance more inclusive to the traditionally underserved. However, fintech has its challenges. Regulations evolve, making compliance a challenge. Also, the industry is vulnerable to cyberattacks and money laundering. Companies hold large amounts of sensitive data, making them obvious targets for bad actors. As with many industries, governance, compliance, and transparency are essential for fintechs as they transform the financial services landscape.

Keywords: Fintech; artificial intelligence (AI); regulation; money laundering; embedded finance

Introduction

This chapter explores the ever-evolving world of financial technology, or fintech, focusing on the industry's opportunities and challenges. Fintech aims to improve and automate financial services via new technologies. The goal is to make managing their financial operations more straightforward and efficient for businesses, governments, and consumers. People look to fintech for ease of use, speed, and convenience. COVID-19 brought a mass adoption of fintech to users worldwide, but still, according to the World Bank, 1.4 billion people remain unbanked. The

The Emerald Handbook of Fintech, 419–435

doi:10.1108/978-1-83753-608-520241048

opportunities are astounding in the field, but firms also face severe challenges as cyberattacks become more insidious. Governments and global regulatory bodies must regulate the industry.

The global financial services industry earns approximately $12.5 trillion in revenue; fintech claims about 2% of that revenue. By 2030, that share is expected to increase sixfold, from roughly $250 billion to $1.5 trillion, according to a recent report by Boston Consulting Group (BCG) (Boston Consulting Group, 2023). Interestingly, people think of fintech arriving on the scene in the last decade or two, perhaps emerging during the global financial crisis (GFC) of 2007–2008 or with the first online banking platforms, rudimentary forms of which first appeared in Wells Fargo's account services in 1995.

However, fintech's origin started long before the ability to transfer money using smartphones. The first transatlantic cable connected the United States to Europe in 1858. In 1918, the Federal Reserve developed Fedwire, which allowed for the electronic transfer of funds to member banks. Diners Club offered the first credit card in the 1950s. These examples illustrate that fintech has been a long time in the making as entrepreneurial minds have continued to innovate in the financial space for more than 150 years.

Fintech services include digital banking, digital lending, payment technologies, equity financing, wealthtech, insurtech, regtech, and banking as a service (BaaS). The field is ever-evolving. Traditional financial firms such as banks and insurance companies are buying fintech companies and developing applications. As technology advances, so does fintech. Key opportunities available to fintech firms and others on the periphery include embedding finance in nonfinancial company products, making finance more inclusive, using artificial intelligence (AI) and machine learning (ML) to personalize financial products and services, and digital currencies and blockchain technology. However, new challenges emerge each year, and firms that plan to succeed must be ready to meet these challenges. Complying with evolving regulatory changes is one of the most daunting hurdles. Like many things, larger firms may be better equipped to survive than start-ups and smaller firms. Opportunities for fintechs are described in the next sections, followed by a discussion of the challenges faced by the industry. The chapter concludes with a summary and conclusion.

Opportunities for Fintech

Many of the most promising and lucrative opportunities for fintech are the "boring" ones. That means payment processing services, regulatory compliance, taxes, fraud prevention and cybersecurity, and infrastructure. Although not the most exciting new and innovative financial technology solutions, they are the services that the industry must get correct to survive. For example, in compliance, something that is not regulated today may become a future target of regulation. Firms must be ready for the rapid changes continuously transforming the industry (Thomas, 2022).

COVID-19 was hugely detrimental to many industries, including hotels and restaurants. It did, however, mark the beginning of mass adoption of fintech solutions globally. The World Bank reports that as of 2021, 76% of people globally have an account at a bank, another financial institution, or a mobile financial provider, up from 51% in 2011 (World Bank, 2022b). However, the World Bank is clear that much work remains to be done by governments and the private sector. Fintech is an excellent tool for governments, allowing state and federal governments to improve efficiency and make financial services more accessible to those historically underserved. But the private sector must work with governments to make this a reality. One way that companies are reaching more customers is through embedded finance.

Embedded Finance

Embedded finance includes financial solutions into product offerings that are not financial. It has existed since people started selling capital goods such as furniture and appliances. For example, furniture stores offered credit to customers. A store might offer free financing for a year before charging interest on the remaining balance. An automobile repair shop might offer credit and payment plans to customers getting car repairs.

Although financing was part of the package for large, expensive purchases in the past, embedded finance is now commonplace for small purchases. Embedded finance has hit e-commerce, and customers can now pay over time, often interest-free, for purchases much smaller than refrigerators, couches, and carburetors. It is now possible to "buy now and pay over time" for anything from a 10-pack box of noodles to arts and crafts supplies. Embedded finance increases revenue for sellers, attracting customers who might be unable to pay for the product or service directly or to charge the entire purchase on a credit card. Zero-interest, point-of-sale loans may make a reluctant customer say yes. Brand rewards are also appealing to consumers. Andreessen Horowitz, a venture capital (VC) firm backing entrepreneurs who use technology to build the future, believes embedded finance will increase revenue two to five times per customer in the coming years (Trificana, 2022). Firms providing these embedded finance products and services to businesses have growth potential because, as Trificana asserts, people should expect to see it everywhere. And in terms of opportunity, it is still in its infancy.

Digital Currencies and Decentralized Finance

The world of digital currencies and decentralized finance (DeFi) is complex. Those involved, from digital platforms to "investors," may feel like they are riding a rollercoaster. For example, the industry might be in a freefall, and then it is the future. Yet, despite these challenges of regulatory scrutiny, outright failures such as FTX, a cryptocurrency exchange, and government lawsuits such as the one filed in June 2023 against the most prominent crypto asset trading platform

Binance, the future is still bright for digital currencies and the technologies and infrastructure surrounding them.

Digital ledger technology (DLT) is the umbrella under which blockchain sits. It is a decentralized database system. Participants share a synchronized ledger. The ledger includes transactions that any party may update without an intermediary. Changes and updates to the ledger show up in real time in the ledger copies held by each party. Cryptographic principles can ensure security, transparency, and immutability. Blockchain is the most well-known implementation of DLT. Blockchain technology verifies and records cryptocurrency transactions. But DLT has broader implications. It has applications in healthcare, supply chain management, voting systems, and financial services. Fintechs have opportunities to engage DLT in cryptocurrency and more general financial services domains.

The popularity of Bitcoin and other digital currencies has paved the way for companies to provide products and services that leverage blockchain technology. According to Shousany (2023), a digital transformation expert, fintech companies are racing to develop the best blockchain platforms. However, he maintains that traditional financial institutions still have a place worldwide. First, some people are uncomfortable with digital currencies. Currency values are often volatile. If someone wants a safe place to store cash, a traditional bank with a stable currency in any country is likely better than a digital currency such as Bitcoin. Banks also provide, at least at this point, a better way to safeguard one's money from theft and fraud.

But Shousany (2023) notes that blockchain technology will allow even traditional financial institutions to cut costs. Because blockchain is programmed to accept information from any source without human intervention, it can speed up processes like applying for licenses to do business. Additionally, users can manage their data without intermediaries.

Because parties cannot erase blockchain records, the blockchain is potentially more transparent than transactions using intermediaries. For example, the Securities and Exchange Commission (SEC) can easily trace trades, getting to the roots of insider trading, which is more difficult, time-consuming, and costly for traditional institutions. According to Jung (2019), "When its properties of decentralization, immutability, transparency, and security are combined, a notion of 'trustlessness' is created. The trust typically expected of vendors to sell their services is no longer required thanks to blockchain." This idea of trustlessness, used as a "good thing" in Jung's quote, is curious. Many are generally highly distrustful of digital currencies, but this suggests that it is the opposite. Blockchain technology implies that people do not need to trust a financial institution as the technology handles this concern. As such, blockchain will potentially democratize finance and result in the decentralization of traditional financial institutions.

Fintechs are at the forefront and will continue to push these technologies forward. Fintechs that develop the most innovative solutions using blockchain in payments, lending, and security will likely be the big winners. According to several sources, and despite the 2022 hiccup in the digital currencies sector, this situation may be the most promising opportunity for fintechs.

AI and ML

AI and ML gained popularity, especially in the financial services industry. Banks, insurance companies, stock and bond traders, and fintech firms are all looking to AI to speed up cost-cutting and make personalized financial solutions for individuals and firms a reality. These cutting-edge technologies offer great opportunities but also risks. The financial services industry and many others have been labeled a "volatility, uncertainty, complexity, and ambiguity" (VUCA) industry. Fintech is about disruptive innovation, changing financial services to eliminate intermediaries, save costs, and make finance more inclusive to the traditionally underserved. Millar et al., 2018, p. 6) state, "VUCA is both an outcome of disruptive innovation and a driver of it." Fintechs must harness technologies like AI and ML to manage VUCA for customers.

AI thrives as the cloud has created almost unlimited data processing and storage (Ashta & Herrmann, 2021). In addition, data have become a critical asset, more important even than oil. Financial institutions have a wealth of data to exploit for good or ill. Firms can use data-driven insights to make decisions, assign credit scores to customers, and assess risks.

For example, many contend that some firms use data in such a way that it harms, financially speaking, those who can least afford it. For example, fintechs and other financial firms make loan decisions based on insights gleaned from big data. *Big data* refers to data that contains greater variety, arriving in increasing volumes and with more velocity. Firms often use the social contacts of customers as part of the metrics used to assign credit scores. Companies use data from a person's smartphone (e.g., from whom and when a person receives and makes calls, location information, and the phone's apps) to understand who they are, both to target "good" potential customers and limit exposure to the "bad." Even the way a person fills out an application for a loan, including from what device and from what location the person accesses the phone, is being used in lending decisions, according to British firm P.I., a company challenging the exploitation of people by governments and companies using technology (PI, 2017). But while these examples are shocking to some, they illustrate the potential of the data available to fintech companies. The PI examples were from 2017; the data available in 2023 and beyond dwarf that available to firms in 2017. The entrepreneurial spirit continues to identify and exploit possibilities that did not exist in the past.

But despite whether one views AI, ML, and big data as positive or negative, opportunities are available for fintechs beyond credit scoring and customer risk assessment. AI allows firms to develop chatbots that can reduce the cost of customer service. AI is highly valuable in helping companies identify fraud and money laundering. Firms are using AI to automate investment decision-making and portfolio management services. Some customers and probably employees whose jobs are now at risk are unhappy with recent developments. For example, in the summer of 2023, Hollywood writers had an ongoing strike. One of the critical areas of contention was the potential for AI and ML (e.g., ChatGPT) to make the writers obsolete. The concern was that AI would write television shows and movies, reducing the need for writers and their associated costs.

In general, AI can help fintechs and other companies be more customer-centric. For fintechs and traditional financial institutions, AI and ML enable the development of personalized financial products and solutions rather than relying on a one-size-fits-all approach.

Follow the Money

One way to examine opportunities for fintech entrepreneurs is to consider where the funding goes. What are venture capitalists interested in financing? Funding in fintech soared from $49 billion in 2020 to $131.5 billion in 2021 (Finnovating, 2022). Additionally, 2020 saw 27 fintech unicorns. The number increased more than fivefold to 157 in 2021. A *unicorn* is a privately owned business worth $1 billion or more. Several areas of focus from investors will persist in the next few years, according to Finnovating. This AI service platform matches corporations with tech start-ups so that they can do business.

At the 2023 Money20/20 Europe, the premiere European financial technology event, Browne, Kharpal, and Sigalos, reporting for CNBC, found the key topics' representatives from the industry were discussing embedded finance, open banking, and BaaS (Browne et al., 2023). A primary area of opportunity that continues to fuel growth in the fintech industry is integrating other businesses' products into fintech platforms. But the industry, according to the authors, seems to have moved on from technologies and solutions aimed at individuals. At the conference, business-to-business (B2B) opportunities took center stage. Airwallex, Payoneer, and Clearbank (i.e., B2B companies) dominated, while consumer apps such as Revolut and Starling were absent. Richard Davies, CEO of Allica Bank, said he thought fintechs realized that the unit economics on consumer apps were insufficient. *Unit economics* in financial services relates the customer's lifetime value to the cost of acquiring the customer. Making the numbers work regarding profitability is more challenging when targeting individual customers than business customers.

Open Banking

Open banking is a more recent trend that involves financial firms securely sharing customer data with third parties who have developed applications that can be useful to customers. Open banking encourages competition. For example, a credit card company may categorize a customer's spending into travel, grocery, restaurants, and home improvement. Another firm may develop an app that uses these data to help customers track spending and create a budget. Before opening banking, a person manually inputs the information into a budgeting app; with open banking, data load automatically, saving time and the potential for mistakes. Open banking may have the added social benefit of improving financial literacy and financial responsibility, helping individuals and businesses make better financial decisions (Grinberg, 2023).

According to Grinberg (2023), open banking has many benefits, including:

- *Transparency*. Makes financial activities and transactions less ambiguous.
- *Aggregation*. Compiles financial information into fewer places, helping people better manage and understand their financial situation.
- *Personalization*. Encourages developing and using personalized financial products and services. Companies are developing personal financial management (PFM) tools to assist in this endeavor. AI and ML can also improve personalization.
- *Competition*. Creates opportunities for companies to innovate and generates competition among fintechs, improving customers' options for managing their individual and business finances.

Many fintechs from different countries are in the open banking space. Companies such as Plaid, Mint, and Cleo (the United States), Tink (Sweden), Yapily (the United Kingdom), and Figo (Germany) offer services from account aggregation and budgeting tools to lending platforms and more. This area is ripe for continued investment and innovation.

Insurtech

Another sector attracting VC funding is insurtech. *Insurtech* refers to technological solutions for the insurance industry. Insurance companies, like banks, are moving toward reaching customers via apps. New streams of data from internet-based devices are now available to companies. These companies use data for many insurance-related fintech opportunities.

Many VC firms believe the insurance industry is ripe for disruption and see opportunities in the space. One area that is not part of the mainstream insurance business is ultra-customizable insurance contracts. These contracts, like commercial loans, are specific to the individual customer regarding features and pricing. Banks have become more focused on customization as they target diverse customers for different interest rates for loans and deposits. But insurance companies are just beginning to tap the customization market. Dynamic pricing of insurance products is another area of opportunity. Using data from internet devices, insurance companies can target discounted pricing for some customers and premium pricing for others based on factors such as health and lifestyle. Personalized pricing will likely generate higher company revenues and attract investor funds.

Regtech

The fintech sector is not regulated in the strict manner that banks are regulated. However, they must adhere to some rules. As a result, fintechs are devising ways to comply with regulations. Firms must determine how to comply with regulations for mass adoption to continue. Investors are funding these initiatives, given that regulatory hurdles will increase depending on the types of products and their impact on customers' financial well-being.

The industry is seeking solutions to improve regulatory compliance. Data from Appinventiv suggest a compound annual growth rate in investment in this sector of 20.8% between 2021 and 2026, from $7.6 billion in 2021 to $19.5 billion in 2026 (Finnovating, 2022). Investors are willing to extend capital to fund compliance. Areas of investment include knowing your customer (KYC), anti-money laundering (AML), data management, tax management, and regulatory change management.

Online Payment Processing

Some prominent fintech firms, like Adyen, Stripe, and Klarna, are in payment processing and money transfers. Adyen is a payments specialist, partnering with companies like eBay, Uber, and Facebook to solve payment processing issues. Stripe builds economic infrastructure for the internet, partnering with companies to accept payments and help manage online businesses. Google Workspace, Zara, and Lotus are just a few companies partnering with Stripe. Klarna provides a shopping app that allows consumers to pay over time for purchases. Although these firms generate multi-billions of U.S. dollars in revenue, problems still need to be solved in the payment processing space. Investors continue to fund start-ups in this area.

Making Finance More Inclusive

One of fintech's greatest strengths and opportunities is making finance more accessible and inclusive. Finding digital solutions to help the traditionally underserved is a noble pursuit. According to Trificana (2022), minorities cite banking fees as a barrier to traditional banking at a rate higher than nonminorities. Trificana reports that a 2021 Plaid survey reports that 31% of Hispanics, 20% of Blacks, and 15% of whites cited fees as one of their biggest financial challenges. Plaid's stated mission is to democratize finance services through technology.

Some fintech companies provide online banking services with little or no fees. Peer-to-peer (P2P) lending platforms make low or no-fee loans possible for individuals and small businesses. Black, indigenous, and people of color (BIPOC) may rely on fintech to overcome financial hurdles that may have stopped them from starting and expanding businesses. For example, a digital lending platform, Dollarito, assists the Hispanic population with no credit history or low credit scores to access fair credit at a reasonable interest rate. Kaoshi, a P2P platform, allows immigrants to send money to family members and other beneficiaries in countries like Nigeria and Ghana. They leverage open finance application programming interfaces (APIs), eliminate the go-between, and can support these money transfers with low fees and low rates. These solutions are invaluable to people seeking a foothold in a complex financial world. They are practical and provide solutions for people with less access and fewer resources.

COVID-19 caused harm and hindered growth in many areas as it spread across the globe beginning in early 2020. However, it increased the adoption of fintech. The World Bank estimates 1.4 billion unbanked citizens worldwide (World Bank, 2022a). These people are difficult to reach and are generally poorer, less educated, women, and people who live in more rural parts of the world. Lower barriers to access are critical to reaching these citizens. Technology is the obvious solution but firms in the financial services industry, specifically fintechs, and governments, must work together. Fundamental barriers such as internet access impede progress. Also, according to the World Bank (2022b), significant investment is needed in trusted and accessible identification systems. For example, a lack of identity documents remains a barrier to citizens living in Sub-Saharan Africa, preventing them from opening mobile financial accounts. Historically, a lack of trust exists in governments and the financial sector. Thus, in terms of opportunity, these underserved populations in Africa and other places offer an important untapped market, yet difficult to tap.

Challenges for Fintech

Although opportunities abound for fintech companies, the industry also faces many challenges. The sector is vulnerable because many companies rely on similar inputs, from VC funding to open-source technologies, to the same cloud services. Complying with ever-changing regulations is also a challenge. Another challenge is avoiding bad actors who want access to data and may harm individuals and the environment. Firms need capital, and many rely on VC firms, sometimes to their detriment.

Reliance on Venture Capital Funding

Finding investors and securing funding is a crucial challenge for many fintech firms. Fintechs rely heavily on VC funding. VC funds were happy to fund fintechs as the rapid adoption of financial technologies during the COVID-19 shutdowns highlighted industry growth prospects. In 2021, about 20% of the $681 billion of VC funding went to fintechs (Teare, 2023). Funding went to fintechs of all types, from cryptocurrency to neobanks (also called challenger banks, which are tech companies that provide online banking services through a partnership with a commercial bank), wealth management firms, and insurance brokers. Two companies that received VC funding, Robinhood and Nubank, went public. However, most VC-funded firms are still private and exist in more challenging markets with higher interest rates and inflation. VCs and other private equity firms funded seed and early-stage companies in 2021. Early-stage fintechs could not generally raise capital. Bankingly (2022) notes that investors initially provided capital, not expecting an immediate return. However, they are becoming impatient and are now expecting returns. Valuations are dropping, and capital has been more difficult to access.

Teare (2023), using data gathered by Crunchbase, a data collection and analysis firm, expects to see significant decreases in funding for the fintechs. Funding fell each quarter of 2022 and dipped more than overall VC funding. Fintech decreased by 40%, while overall funding was down 35%. Less capital flowing to fintechs is concerning as it is another of the sector's vulnerabilities. Sometimes, VC money flows freely, and at other times it dries up. Beginning in 2022, VC firms became more discerning about which firms should and should not receive funding. Yet, company needs do not necessarily follow the same pattern. To manage this reliance on VC firms, some suggest that fintechs should tap debt markets instead to postpone raising equity funding until more favorable market conditions emerge. That, however, may be more difficult and painful in an environment with a high interest rate. Others suggest that founders raise money before they need it rather than waiting for the perfect moment. Still, others propose that founders tighten their belts and lengthen the runway to postpone fundraising as long as possible. Long-term growth in the industry is vital. VC capital will be available to some but not as abundant for all. However, relying heavily on VC funding for survival is challenging.

Data Privacy and Security

Data privacy and security are hurdles for companies in most industries. For example, consumers routinely receive notices of data breaches from companies where they purchase products and services. Although disconcerting to customers, such notices can feel less invasive if provided by a financial institution. The volume, sensitivity, and personal nature of data held by financial companies make them particularly vulnerable to security issues. Consumer confidence in the safety of personal data and trust in the companies handling the data is tenuous at best. Any data breach, real or perceived, can shatter that confidence. Fintechs must build trust by being transparent about data privacy practices and sharing the processes used to secure customer data.

Governments and regulators are also concerned about personal and financial data privacy and security. Many of the regulations fintechs must comply with are related to security. Thus, a key challenge fintechs must manage is regulatory compliance. Countries and states have different expectations about what firms must do to ensure privacy and safety. It is a monumental hurdle facing the industry. As part of the regulatory oversight, fintechs must invest in security infrastructure, from secure data storage to data encryption systems. The pressure to secure data will increase as the "bad actors" get more sophisticated in hacking into company systems.

Money Laundering: AML Policies

Money laundering is the process of making ill-gained funds appear legitimate by disguising the actual source of the funds. Fintech firms handle high volumes of financial data and transactions, making them a target for money laundering.

As with data privacy and security, regulatory compliance with KYC and AML requirements will be an immense challenge. Fintechs must monitor transactions. They must also develop customer monitoring processes and improve customer due diligence (CDD) to spot suspicious activities and report them to government regulators and other relevant officials. Fintechs using AI and ML are more successful in identifying and mitigating malicious activities, including money laundering. As such, firms must invest in these advanced technologies to enhance monitoring activities. As with data privacy and security, this situation requires customer trust. Therefore, fintechs must diligently mitigate the risks associated with money laundering.

Cyberattacks

Fintechs use cutting-edge technologies to produce and sell products and services. They are also deeply involved in their customers' finances via payment systems, lending, deposits, and other financial solutions. They process sensitive financial information. As data are valuable, firms are incentivized to store as much data as possible. For many firms, these data are like those held by banks. Information includes account numbers, balances, transaction histories, and contact information. As such, these firms are prime targets for cyberattacks.

Some fintechs are in direct competition with traditional banks and are handling many of the same assets on behalf of customers – from customer funds to customer data. IBM (2022) conducts an annual study on data breaches. They list several threats to firms, including:

- phishing
- compromised email
- vulnerability of third-party software
- stolen or compromised credentials
- malicious insider(s)
- cloud misconfiguration
- social engineering
- physical security compromises
- accidental data loss or lost device
- system errors
- ransomware.

For example, ransomware increased by 41% from 2021 to 2022, taking 45 days longer to identify and contain than the average system breach. Less in the public eye, but perhaps even more critical, are threats associated with intellectual property theft, data destruction, espionage, crippling critical infrastructure such as power grids, and other systemic threats.

According to the IBM (2022) study, detecting and containing a breach in 2022 took an average of 277 days or about nine months. Earlier detection lowers a breach's cost. Also, firms using AI and automation detect breaches earlier, with a

74-day shorter breach cycle and substantial average savings. According to the study, the average data breach cost was $9.44 million in the United States, more than double the global cost of $4.35 million. Although healthcare was hit the hardest in terms of cost (i.e., the cost rose 40% between 2020 and 2022), the financial services industry is a close second.

When a bank suffers a breach, it must bear direct and indirect costs. The media tend to focus on the direct costs associated with the breached data because that affects individuals and businesses (e.g., personal health and financial data). A breach is costly. A 2016 Deloitte report notes that while high direct costs are associated with breaches, hidden threats, and below-surface costs may be overlooked or ignored (Powers et al., 2016). According to the report, at least seven "above the surface," or well-known, direct costs are associated with cyberattacks. They include the following:

- Technical investigation to determine what happened and who is responsible.
- Costs associated with notifying customers of the breach.
- The protection provided to customers.
- Regulatory compliance, including fines and fees.
- Expenses related to litigation and attorney fees.
- Direct expenses associated with post-breach technical improvements to monitoring, security, and infrastructure.
- Public relations costs associated with managing the fallout and the resulting communications and brand monitoring associated with the breach.

However, seven largely hidden cyberattack costs may prove costlier than direct costs (Don & Mossburg, 2016). They include the following.

- Higher insurance premiums.
- Higher cost of debt.
- Costs associated with the disruption to the company's operation.
- Costs related to losing customer trust (i.e., reputational costs).
- Lost contract revenue as customers leave.
- Impaired brand and devaluation of trademarks associated with the firm.
- Loss of intellectual property.

Fintech companies should be proactive and create an incident response plan. However, developing a plan is insufficient. Fintechs must test response plans. Crowdstrike, a company that provides incident response services, defines *incident response (IR)* as the steps a company takes to prepare for, identify, contain, and recover from a cyberattack (Crowdstrike, 2023). The firm maintains that the IR plan created to describe a company's intended response to a potential cyberattack continues to be useful after the attack, guiding the litigation phase, providing documentation for auditors, and offering historical knowledge to aid the risk management process.

As with most large companies today, one of the biggest challenges fintechs face is cyberattacks. In a shocking report by Gartner, a leading research and advisory company in the information technology (IT) space, the company paints a bleak picture of the future (Moore, 2021). Gartner argues that by 2025 cyberattackers will have weaponized operational technology environments to harm or kill humans or the environment. Gartner suggests that various companies need to worry less about the theft of information and more about real-world hazards to humans and the environment. The company recommends improving security controls on operational technologies. Although this warning may be more prescient for manufacturing and transportation companies than for financial firms, the world of cyberattacks is changing so rapidly that it probably should be heeded by all.

Open-Source Applications

Fintech firms move fast. Firms race each other to launch the newest and best products on the market. One issue inherent in this mode of operation is the reliance on open-source technologies. *Open source* refers to software for which the original code is available and accessible to the public. Users can modify and redistribute the code to fit their own needs. Cloud applications also integrate open-source libraries and services. Open source is helpful in fintech as it allows companies to leverage work that others have done, speeding up the time needed to update or launch products and services. However, using open-source libraries and packages allows attackers to breach networks, making firms more vulnerable to cyberattacks (Synk Limited, n.d.).

Regulation

Fintech disrupts traditional banking and financial services. One of the criticisms of fintech levied by the banking industry is the heavy regulation of banks and the lesser regulation of fintechs, despite the similar products, services, and customers. Fintech has many of the same risks to customers and society as banking but much less oversight. The laws are not comprehensive enough or have not kept up with the fast-evolving sector. Online lenders, digital wallets, and others are neither subject to the same strict rules as banks, nor do they have the same safety nets. Fintech can threaten individuals, nations' financial stability, and even the global financial system. Oversight is thus critical. Regulators worldwide continue to grapple with how to take traditional laws and regulations and adapt them to this new digital world. Uncertainty around regulations is challenging for fintechs as the regulatory landscape continually changes.

However, the focus on risks changes as regulators face concerns ranging from data privacy to cyberattacks. Laws and regulations differ from country to country. The goals of regulators are similar, however. Regulators seek to ensure that transactions are safe, secure, and smooth. One challenge for regulators is understanding the complexities and nuances of these ever-evolving technologies.

It pressures regulators to create the right balance of regulations that protect consumers and not inhibit growth and innovation. Regulators must also fully understand complex technologies such as blockchain and AI.

Money laundering is of great concern, and most countries and jurisdictions require fintech firms to be licensed and comply with AML and KYC requirements. Market participants, whether individuals or businesses, need to feel comfortable and safe with new technologies, especially relating to their financial lives and well-being. Consumer interest in using fintech will wane if consumers feel at risk. Regulation can help mitigate user fears (Bankingly, 2022).

One of the factors that makes fintech vulnerable as an industry is that many of the firms, technologies, and platforms use similar technology stacks. A *technology stack* is the set of technologies used to create the product (e.g., databases, frameworks, and programming languages). Companies often rely on a few large cloud service providers, such as Amazon's Amazon Web Services (AWS) and mobile platforms (i.e., iOS and Android). Additionally, 90% of fintechs rely on Visa and Mastercard.

Bankingly (2022) states that fintechs fall under the Consumer Financial Protection Bureau (CFPB) if operating in the United States. Other regulatory bodies have some authority over fintech companies. They include the following:

- The Office of the Comptroller of Currency (OCC), a national bank charter regulator, ensures that transactions fall under the appropriate financial rules and regulations.
- The Federal Deposit Insurance Corporation (FDIC) regulates online banks and mobile-only banks.
- The Financial Crimes Enforcement Network (FinCEN) gathers transaction information to thwart or mitigate financial crimes.
- The Commodity Futures Trading Commission (CFTC) has a role in how fintech will progress. It launched LabCFTC in 2017 to foster innovation in the space and encourage competition, transparency, openness, and soundness.
- The SEC supervises trading platforms.

Several laws have been enacted over the last decade that impact those offering financial services, both traditional and technologically driven. Regulatory compliance has become a considerable expense for fintechs, putting pressure on smaller firms to survive. Pressure on smaller financial organizations trying to comply with new regulations is like the banking industry after the passage of Dodd-Frank. Smaller banks had difficulty investing in compliance, resulting in mergers and acquisitions with other banks.

Retaining Top Talent

Although attracting, training, and retaining talent is a challenge in many industries, one advantage fintech has is a more entrepreneurial environment than a traditional financial institution (Shevlin, 2023). Top talent at fintechs has generally attracted higher salaries than employees in conventional banks. That is good news for fintechs. However, the competition for top talent is not just other fintechs but also banks. Banks are buying fintech start-ups and are developing digital applications, making it difficult for fintechs as banks have higher name/brand recognition and resources than many fintech firms. Furthermore, fintechs are looking for talent with both technological and financial skills, reducing the potential talent pool.

Although fintech and other big tech companies such as Amazon and Meta have laid off people in 2023, traditional banks have often hired the available talent to assist in their endeavors to move into the digital world (Shevlin, 2023). This situation increased competition for talent from traditional finance, increasing the difficulty for fintech to hire and keep talent. Fintech requires not only a unique skill set of technological and financial expertise but also adaptable talent. Their skill set must evolve and keep up with the trends in a fast-moving industry.

Customer Acquisition

Customer acquisition is as essential to fintech firms as to companies like Netflix or Meta. A firm cannot generally increase profitability without new products or new customers. Several factors may increase the difficulty for fintechs to acquire new customers in the coming decade. First, COVID-19 resulted in the mass adoption of fintech, to some degree saturating the market. Second, customers, especially tech-savvy customers, are adaptable and may switch to the "latest and greatest" new technologies. As such, fintechs must continue to innovate to hold onto their customer base. Companies must educate customers on why they need new products and services. The challenges discussed in previous sections – regulation, customer trust, and security issues – also challenge fintechs. The long-term viability of fintech depends on companies' abilities to attract and retain new talent and new customers.

Summary and Conclusion

Benefits to consumers are at the heart of opportunity. The fintech industry faces many challenges, many of which are connected to consumers. From democratizing financial services, addressing inequities, protecting customers against breaches and fraud, and providing more personalized services, fintechs answer the call directly.

As fintechs take advantage of them, they must also rise to the challenges introduced by increased regulation, threats from bad actors, and the need to attract and retain talent and customers. AI and ML can help firms, providing opportunities to personalize financial services. AI can also help firms detect fraud and security breaches. New companies face challenges, especially as the costs of complying with regulations make competing with larger, established firms with solid footholds in the industry more difficult. Yet, untapped markets and customers are available. Customers still need the services and products fintechs provide. Whether the industry will consolidate, like the banking industry, or if the innovation and entrepreneurial spirit of the smaller companies can withstand the competition remains to be seen. Consumers and society are the likely beneficiaries either way.

Discussion Questions

- Discuss the impact of the COVID-19 pandemic on fintechs.
- Explain why artificial intelligence (AI) and machine learning (ML) are essential to fintechs.
- Identify the main opportunities available to fintechs.
- Identify the main challenges facing fintechs.

References

Ashta, A., & Herrmann, H. (2021). Artificial intelligence and fintech: An overview of opportunities and risks for banking, investments and microfinance. *Strategic Change*, *30*(3), 211–222.

Bankingly. (2022, December 12). What are the risks and opportunities of the fintech industry. https://www.bankingly.com/news/what-are-the-risks-and-opportunities-for-the-fintech-industry/

Boston Consulting Group. (2023, May 3). Fintech projected to become a $1.5 trillion industry by 2030. https://www.bcg.com/press/3may2023-fintech-1-5-trillion-industry-by-2030

Browne, R., Kharpal, A., & MacKenzie, S. (2023, June 10). Here's what's hot – And what's not – In fintech right now. https://www.cnbc.com/2023/06/10/money-20/20-2023-whats-hot-and-whats-not-in-fintech.html

Crowdstrike. (2023, April 17). Incident response (IR) plan & process. https://www.crowdstrike.com/cybersecurity-101/incident-response/#:~:text=What%20is%20an%20Incident%20Response,supports%20the%20organization's%20broader%20mission.her

Don, J. G., & Mossburg, E. (2016). Seven hidden costs of a cyberattack. https://www2.deloitte.com/us/en/pages/finance/articles/cfo-insights-seven-hidden-costs-cyberattack.htl

Finnovating. (2022, February 7). Most popular FinTech sectors for startup funding. https://finnovating.com/news/popular-fintech-sector-startup-funding/

Grinberg, D. (2023, March 3). Revolutionising banking: The best open banking apps of 2023. https://www.techmagic.co/blog/top-12-open-banking-apps-to-watch/

IBM. (2022). Cost of a data breach 2022: A million dollar race to detect and respond. https://www.ibm.com/reports/data-breach

Jung, T. J. (2019, April 15). How transparency through blockchain helps the cybersecurity community. https://www.ibm.com/blog/how-transparency-through-blockchain-helps-the-cybersecurity-community/

Millar, C., Groth, O., & Mahon, J. (2018). Management innovation in a VUCA world: Challenges and recommendations. *California Management Review*, *61*(1), 5–14. https://doi.org/10.1177/0008125618805111

Moore, S. (2021). *Gartner predicts by 2025 cyber attackers will have weaponized operational technology environments to harm or kill humans.* https://www.gartner.com/en/newsroom/press-releases/2021-07-21-gartner-predicts-by-2025-cyber-attackers-will-have-we

PI. (2017, August 30). Case study: Fintech and the financial exploitation of customer data. https://privacyinternational.org/case-studies/757/case-study-fintech-and-financial-exploitation-customer-data#:~:text=Increasingly%2C%20financial%20services%20such%20as,and%20most%20excluded%20in%20societies

Powers, E. W., Fancher, D., & Justin, S. (2016). Beneath the surface of cyberattacks: A deeper look at business impacts. https://www2.deloitte.com/us/en/pages/risk/articles/hidden-business-impact-of-cyberattack.html

Shevlin, R. (2023, January 12). How to attract and retain talent with big tech and fintechs lay off staff. *Forbes.* https://www.forbes.com/sites/ronshevlin/2023/01/12/how-to-attract-and-retain-talent-when-big-techs-and-fintechs-layoff-staff/?sh=96064c56e07d

Shousany, R. (2023, January 31). How fintech and blockchain are evolving and disrupting financial institutions. *Forbes.* https://www.forbes.com/sites/forbestechcouncil/2023/01/31/how-fintech-and-blockchain-are-evolving-and-disrupting-financial-institutions/?sh=42cb6ed7483a

Synk Limited. (n.d.). Fintech cybersecurity: How to build securely with open source. https://snyk.io/learn/fintech-cybersecurity/

Teare, G. (2023, April 14). The fintech funding crunch in four charts. https://news.crunchbase.com/fintech-ecommerce/fintech-industry-funding-charts-hood-nu/#:~:text=Some%2020%25%20of%20the%20total,to%20the%20fintech%20sector%20alone

Thomas, C. (2022, June 17). Fintech compliance and brief review of US fintech regulations in 2022. https://www.360factors.com/blog/fintech-compliance-regulations-updates-2022/

Trificana, J. (2022, October 3). What is the future of fintech? Six industry shaping trends. https://plaid.com/resources/fintech/future-of-fintech/

World Bank. (2022a). Covid-19 boosted the adoption of digital financial services. https://www.worldbank.org/en/news/feature/2022/07/21/covid-19-boosted-the-adoption-of-digital-financial-services#:~:text=Globally%2C%20some%201.4%20billion%20adults,go%2C%20much%20more%20is%20needed

World Bank. (2022b). Covid-19 drives global surge in use of digital payments. https://www.worldbank.org/en/news/press-release/2022/06/29/covid-19-drives-global-surge-in-use-of-digital-payments

Discussion Questions and Answers: Chapters 2–23

Chapter 2: The Fintech Landscape: A Bibliometric Analysis

(1) Explain the contribution of bibliometrics in understanding the fintech research landscape.

Bibliometrics provides a systematic and quantitative analysis of scholarly publications, citations, and collaboration networks in fintech. It enables assessing the research landscape by identifying publication trends, citation patterns, influential publications, prolific authors, and research institutions. By analyzing thematic clusters and distribution of research output, bibliometrics helps identify emerging trends and provides insights into the prominence of different research themes within fintech.

(2) Discuss how integrating diverse disciplines contributes to an understanding of fintech.

The study highlights the need for methodological advancements and the integration of diverse disciplines to foster an understanding of fintech's multifaceted nature. By drawing insights from various disciplines such as finance, technology, economics, and social science, researchers can gain a holistic view of fintech innovations' complex interactions and implications, enabling a more informed analysis and decision-making.

(3) Explain the prominent themes and trends within fintech identified through the bibliometric analysis.

The bibliometric analysis identified 23 themes within the fintech literature, covering a broad spectrum of topics. These topics include technological advancements, financial inclusion, regulatory compliance, innovation, data analytics, alternative finance, sustainability, global factors, business strategies, infrastructure, governance, consumer behavior, and more. These themes provide insights into the key areas of inquiry and emerging trends within fintech.

(4) Provide examples of how the study's findings can be leveraged to drive innovation and advancements in the financial industry.

The study provides valuable insights for industry practitioners to understand and leverage fintech developments. Industry professionals can stay informed about the forefront of fintech research by identifying influential publications, prolific authors, and their affiliations. Additionally, the distribution of research output across themes offers guidance for industry players to align their strategies and investments with the emerging trends in fintech.

(5) Identify potential research directions and areas for further exploration within fintech.

The study's analysis reveals research gaps and areas with limited scholarly attention within fintech. These gaps present opportunities for future research endeavors and interdisciplinary collaborations. Researchers can explore emerging health and pandemic implications, cultural factors, regulation and legislation, risk and security, international finance, financial centers, efficiency and productivity, and decentralized finance. By addressing these research gaps, scholars can contribute to advancing knowledge in fintech and drive innovation.

Chapter 3: Use Cases in Fintech

(1) List fintech's main use cases that enhance financial services and promote financial inclusion.

Fintech's main use cases relative to enhancing financial services and promoting financial inclusion are (1) digital payments and transfers, (2) digital lending, (3) digital wealth management, and (4) digital insurance.

(2) List the areas where fintech applications can support and bolster financial institutions' management.

Fintech applications for supporting financial institutions' management include (1) risk assessment and management, (2) know your customers, (3) brand and reputation management, and (4) fraud detection.

(3) Discuss fintech's role in supporting financial inclusion and sustainable growth.

Fintech, particularly digital finance, is pivotal in driving global financial inclusion by extending access to banking services to billions of previously unbanked or underbanked individuals. These individuals now have the opportunity to engage in fundamental financial activities, such as savings and borrowing, often through the convenience of their mobile devices. Moreover, digital lending and wealth management offer a fresh avenue for micro, small, and medium-sized enterprises (MSMEs) and startups to secure funding and efficiently manage their wealth. MSMEs account for 90% of businesses, 60%–70% of employment, and 50% of global gross domestic product. Sustained support for these enterprises can lead to more stable and sustainable economic growth. The ease of digital payments has also facilitated expanding healthcare services to remote and underserved areas, reaching a broader population and contributing to sustainable development. Within healthcare, digital insurance or insurtech has revolutionized how insurance coverage is provided, making it more accessible and efficient for customers.

(4) Describe how regtech can benefit legal supervision.

Regtech offers benefits to legal supervision from two distinct perspectives. First, from the government's perspective, regtech can be integrated into its internal control systems to enhance daily management. For instance, the Electronic Data Gathering, Analysis, and Retrieval (EDGAR) system used by the US Securities and Exchange Commission (SEC) is a prime example of regtech's application in government operations. Second, from the standpoint of companies and organizations, developing and adopting regtech solutions can substantially aid the private sector in improving risk management for regulatory compliance and achieving more efficient compliance with government regulations.

(5) Explain the relationship between blockchain technology and cryptocurrencies.

Although widely applicable in various sectors such as smart contracts, financial services, supply chain management, manufacturing, healthcare, energy, and smart cities, blockchain technology originated as the underlying technology for cryptocurrencies like bitcoin. In its initial stages, blockchain technology's first generation primarily served to establish cryptocurrencies as a store of value. Subsequent generations of blockchain systems have evolved to offer more complex functionalities, enabling cryptocurrencies to function as in-system currencies or tokens to identify nodes (users) and initiate a sequence of verifications. These advancements have facilitated decentralized fundraising efforts that raise funds through cryptocurrencies, thereby giving cryptocurrencies purchasing power within blockchain-based ecosystems.

Chapter 4: Regtech Frontiers: Innovations, Trends, and Insights Redefining Compliance

(1) Define regtech in the context of financial services.

Regtech refers to a wide range of data-led technological solutions aiming at helping financial institutions comply with ad hoc regulatory requirements. It involves data, technology, and regulation. Regtech is a new breed of regulation and technology that aims to provide a novel suite of regulatory services, signaling a dynamic shift from manual to digital and smart compliance.

(2) Identify regtech's benefits and challenges.

Regtech's benefits include:

- *Automation and efficiency* by automating repetitive and manual tasks, saving time and costs, and reducing paperwork.
- *Enhanced compliance* by helping organizations navigate complex regulatory requirements and providing real-time monitoring and alerts.

- *Risk assessment accuracy* by using advanced analytics and machine learning algorithms.
- *Improved data security* by reducing unauthorized access to sensitive regulatory data.
- *Enhanced reporting transparency* by providing stakeholders, auditors, and regulators easy access to all relevant information.

  Regtech's challenges include:
- *Implementation and data quality* relating to integration, resource intensiveness, and data quality.
- *Data privacy* regarding potential data breaches and the need for robust data governance schemes.
- *Regulatory complexity* involves vast frameworks, heterogeneity of jurisdictions, and frequent changes.
- *Customization* pertains to potentially limited and costly capacity for tailored-made solutions to specific organizational needs, risk indicators, and typologies.
- *Technology dependency and vendor "lock-in"* involve outsourcing prudential risk, regtech implementation to service providers, and over-reliance on technology.
- *Regulatory lag* involves the pace of technological innovation relevant to regulatory innovation.
- *Workforce displacements and skills gaps* concern the need to reskill employees, a loss of jobs, and the potential lack of specialized technical skills.

(3) List regtech's applications (use cases) in the financial industry and the broader business world.

Regtech's applications in the financial industry and the broader business world concern:

- *Compliance management, monitoring, and reporting solutions* support financial institutions to comply with regulatory requirements by providing monitoring, reporting, and auditing tools.
- *Regulatory intelligence, reporting, and documentation solutions* to help financial institutions automate the process of submitting regulatory reports to regulatory authorities.
- *Risk management and assessment solutions* allow financial institutions to identify, manage, and assess various risks associated with regulatory compliance provisions.
- *Identity and fraud management solutions* provide financial institutions with tools to verify the identity of customers, employees, and other relevant stakeholders and to associate and triangulate the identity with potentially fraudulent transactions and illicit activities.

(4) Identify the most promising dimensions that will determine regtech's future.

Promising dimensions that will determine regtech's future include:

- *Generative artificial intelligence* combines human and machine intelligence for compliance.
- *Digital and cryptographic asset tokenization* position and integrate "decentralized" and "disintermediated" digital and cryptographic assets within extant and new legal frameworks.
- *Detection of fraud, AML/CTF, and sanctions compliance* identify patterns, anomalies, or associations indicative of financial crime phenomena.
- *Decentralized compliance* powers regtech solutions for monitoring and compliance across centralized and decentralized value exchange environments.
- *Quantum computing* can develop post-quantum-resistant cryptographic techniques (PQC) to avoid redundant data encryption systems while ensuring financial data security, value, and integrity.
- *Environmental, social, and governance (ESG) sustainability and humanitarian regulation* integrate ESG considerations within broader, interconnected, and interrelated risk management approaches strategically and organizationally aligned to ad hoc business models and value creation mechanisms.

Chapter 5: Fintech's Impact on the Banking Industry and Financial Services

(1) Define financial intermediation and its core functions and explain what makes it an information business.

Financial intermediation is an ever-evolving concept, adapting to changing economic landscapes. Financial intermediation has evolved substantially. Its theoretical basis has transformed from idealized market conditions to the practical realities of the financial world. Financial intermediation would have no role in a theoretically perfect market with complete information and negligible transaction costs. However, this idealized concept sharply contrasts with the historical and practical significance of financial intermediation throughout human history. Intermediation theory emerges as an attempt to explain the existence and importance of financial intermediaries in the presence of market imperfections, like transaction costs and asymmetric information. These imperfections are key factors in justifying the economic need for financial intermediaries.

However, the traditional view of intermediation alone cannot explain why improvements in market imperfections have not led to reduced intermediation levels. Financial intermediation is summed up by two fundamental functions: asset transformation and brokerage services. Asset transformation involves the process where financial intermediaries convert funds from savers or investors into different assets to meet the needs of borrowers, spenders, or other market participants. This transformation encompasses altering asset attributes such as duration, liquidity, credit risk, divisibility, and currency identity. The brokerage function of financial intermediaries encompasses fee-based activities that connect market participants with complementary needs, such as those needing capital and those with surplus capital or companies requiring intermediation for payment services. Through this role, financial intermediaries serve as crucial liquidity providers in the financial system. In both functions, information plays a crucial and strategic role. Better access to information regarding the quality and quantity of data can make financial intermediaries develop and maintain a competitive edge.

(2) Discuss how technology has shaped the financial services industry.

The financial services industry has a long history of investing in technology, dating back to the mid-19th century with the advent of the telegraph, which revolutionized communication in financial markets. Technological milestones include the pantelegraph and ticker tape for signature verification and financial information dissemination in the late 1800s. In the 1950s, mainframe computers automated financial processes, while electronic trading platforms began replacing open outcry systems in stock exchanges. The 1967 introduction of automated teller machines (ATMs) and the Quotron system providing real-time financial data marked new technological waves. The 1980s saw electronic communication networks (ECNs) enabling direct market access, leading to fully electronic trading on stock exchanges. The 1990s brought online trading and the rise of internet-based brokerages, democratizing access to financial markets. High-frequency trading (HFT) emerged in the early 2000s, transforming market dynamics with rapid trade execution. Despite these technological advancements, traditional financial institutions largely concentrated on expanding their product portfolios and operational efficiency, often leading to silos of information. Recent digitization efforts aim to streamline operations and reduce costs but do not fundamentally reevaluate value chains or align products with the digital age.

(3) Identify the domains that fintech has affected and discuss this impact.

Fintech has profoundly affected several domains within the financial services industry, with notable consequences for traditional financial intermediation. Particularly, lending and payments domains have experienced major disruptions due to the emergence of fintech and big tech firms. Several factors drive the disruption in the lending space. Stricter regulatory requirements for traditional financial institutions have created opportunities for fintech firms. Regulatory arbitrage and the lack of traditional financial infrastructure in some regions have facilitated a trend toward disintermediation. Fintech and big tech companies directly connect borrowers and lenders through online platforms, bypassing traditional financial institutions. Peer-to-peer (P2P) lending platforms, such as LendingClub and Prosper, and e-commerce giants like Amazon and Alibaba, providing loans to small businesses, exemplify this trend. Big tech firms can leverage their access to detailed data acquired through trading records or payment information to evaluate creditworthiness, partly replacing the brokerage function of traditional financial intermediaries.

Fintech and big tech companies have made substantial inroads in the payments domain, challenging traditional financial institutions. Tech giants like Google, Apple, and Alibaba, along with PayPal, offer comprehensive payment solutions and have become preferred interfaces for customers. They bundle various services, transforming them into "super platforms" that provide various products and services previously offered by traditional financial institutions. This approach leverages their online platforms and mobile applications to create one-stop-shop solutions. Tencent's WeChat is a good example of this trend, offering a wide range of financial services, from payments to wealth management and showcasing the potential of super platforms.

DeFi is another disruptive force, providing services through blockchain technology and smart contracts, potentially reducing the reliance on traditional intermediaries. Open banking initiatives like PSD2 in the European Union enable fintech companies to access customer data, fostering competition and enabling new services. Robo-advisors have disrupted wealth management, offering automated investment advice and portfolio management. The insurance sector has also seen innovation through data analytics and artificial intelligence, enabling personalized policies and usage-based insurance models. Finally, challenger banks and neobanks have affected asset transformation, a core function of traditional banks.

(4) Explain how traditional financial intermediaries are responding to the fintech challenge.

Traditional financial intermediaries are actively evolving their strategies and operations to thrive in the digital age and remain relevant in a competitive landscape characterized by rapid technological advancements and new entrants. Specifically, they are adapting to the challenges posed by fintech and the digital era, recognizing the need to embrace technology and innovation to remain competitive. Their responses to this transformation include:

- *Collaboration and investment.* Many traditional financial intermediaries choose to collaborate with or invest in fintech startups. This strategy allows them to leverage the innovation and agility of fintech

firms while benefiting from the established customer base and regulatory compliance of traditional banks. For instance, the six largest banks in the United Kingdom have invested heavily in fintech firms engaged in payments, banking, and financial management solutions, representing 42% of the total funds allocated.
- *Digital service expansion.* Many financial intermediaries are expanding their online and mobile service offerings to compete with fintech firms. They introduce features like robo-advisors for automated investment management, digital payment wallets, and peer-to-peer (P2P) lending platforms, enhancing customer engagement and satisfaction.
- *Customer-centric approaches.* Recognizing the importance of a positive customer experience in retaining and attracting clients, some incumbent banks are shifting toward more customer-centric approaches. They emphasize personalization, offer financial advice, and improve customer service.
- *Digital transformation.* Traditional financial intermediaries are undergoing digital transformation, continuously improving their properties using information, computing, communication, and connectivity technologies. This transformation is evident in reducing physical branches in certain countries, signaling a gradual shift from the traditional brick-and-mortar business model to a digital one.

Traditional financial intermediaries must recognize that they now compete with a broader range of firms, including fintech and big tech companies, neobanks, challenger banks, telecommunications companies, and retail firms, within various domains of the financial services industry. To navigate this changing landscape effectively, traditional financial intermediaries should:

- *Understand new competitors.* Financial intermediaries should gain a deep understanding of their new competitors' business models and processes, including fintech and big tech firms, to identify areas of collaboration or competition.
- *Leverage their centrality.* Traditional financial intermediaries, especially incumbent banks, can capitalize on their role as focal points for customer identification and reference data. This process includes verifying and protecting customer identities in online transactions, emphasizing the importance of identity in the digital age.
- *Embrace innovation.* Financial intermediaries must experiment with business models aligning with their strategic objectives, leveraging novel authentication protocols and communication standards as they adapt to the evolving financial services ecosystem.

(5) Discuss the future of the banking and financial services industry.

The future of banking revolves around technological innovation, customer-centric experiences, data-driven decision-making, sustainability, and responsible banking practices. Financial intermediaries are poised to undergo a major transformation in the digital age, redefining their role in the financial services ecosystem. Specifically, the digital transformation of traditional financial intermediaries should occur by adopting platform-based business models. These models will leverage open banking and finance, allowing financial intermediaries to act as platform providers connecting buyers and sellers using digital technologies, particularly open APIs. This transformation will significantly expand their traditional brokerage capabilities. As platform providers, financial intermediaries can offer customer identification and verification services, account provision, and payment processing. This approach fosters a mutually beneficial ecosystem known as "fintegration," serving as a role model for banks to enter other industries, connect with various applications and platforms, and access new data, ultimately realizing the concept of banking anywhere and anytime.

Under platform-based models, financial intermediaries will effectively transition from money brokers to services brokers, with data as a central asset. They will harness data analytics, including predictive analytics and AI, to enhance customer service, predict customer needs more accurately, and address legacy challenges. This transition enables financial intermediaries to be more agile and embrace innovation in a rapidly evolving industry. To succeed, financial intermediaries must become "digitally ambidextrous," balancing core capabilities with exploring new opportunities, experimenting, and remaining ambitious. In the future, financial intermediaries should shift from fixed product and service propositions to more tailored and dynamic offerings based on customer needs and data-driven insights. Financial services will evolve toward providing experiences rather than products. Digital interfaces, including chatbots, holograms, and augmented reality, will enhance and personalize customer service and convenience. Additionally, AI will play a pivotal role in banking, particularly for financial intermediaries with access to well-structured data. At the same time, privacy and trust will be paramount, making financial intermediaries trustworthy allies in safeguarding customer data.

Emerging technologies like quantum computing will expedite processes and enhance data-driven models. Central bank digital currencies (CBDCs) may also draw attention, offering faster and more secure payments, improved financial inclusion, and enhanced monetary policy implementation. Moreover, financial intermediaries should focus on sustainability and ethical banking practices, supporting environmental causes and encouraging green investing. They can leverage digital channels to communicate sustainability initiatives and incorporate eco-friendly practices into their products, such as recommending green investment opportunities based on carbon emissions data.

Chapter 6: Mobile Payments and Digital Banking Services

(1) Describe the digitalization of the payments system.

Digitalization of the payment system uses electronic means of paying for goods via transferring funds from the buying party to the selling party or similar transactions to move funds from one entity to another.

(2) Identify the two countries with the most market share of digital consumer commerce transactions and discuss the future growth outlook.

China and the United States have the greatest market share of transactions at 42% and 27% in 2022, respectively. The growth in total digital payments is about 12.1%, compounded annually.

(3) Define mobile payment and identify the leaders in mobile payments in the United States.

Mobile payment is paying on the go, typically using a contactless POS (point of sale) payment system. Most are completed using Bluetooth Low Energy (BLE) or Near Field Communication (NFC) devices. The majority of these transactions worldwide are done using a smartphone. In the United States, companies such as Apple (via Apple Pay), Alphabet (via Google Pay), Venmo, and Zelle are some of the leaders in mobile payment transactions.

(4) Discuss the long-term growth trend in mobile payments and how it relates to all digital payments.

The trend in mobile POS payments has been increasing. In 2022, US mobile digital payments were about 31% of digital payments, China was over 44%, and Sweden was almost 37.5%. These payments are expected to grow to 36.4%, 48.8%, and 44.9%, respectively, by 2027. If China and Sweden follow a long-term trend, mobile payments will exceed 50% of all digital payments.

(5) Explain the recent impact of cash and check usage and discuss the most predominant methods.

Business-to-business (B2B) transactions still rely on cash and check payments. In contrast, usage has dropped to nine points to 33% in North America (31% worldwide). ACH credits have increased to 39% and debits to 7%. Wires make up 13% of business transactions.

(6) Discuss how Swish changed the payment landscape in Sweden.

Sweden has about 7% of all transactions reported as completed via cash and other paper-based payments. Card payments comprised about 58% of transactions, as reported by the central bank in 2019. Swish is a contactless payment app managed by Getswish in cooperation with six major banks. Most daily transactions can be completed using the Swish app on a smartphone. Although the average value is small, it indicates widespread use for all levels of transaction values.

Chapter 7: Marketplace Lending Platforms for Borrowers and Investors

(1) Define the term marketplace lending.

Marketplace lending (MPL), often called peer-to-peer (P2P) or platform lending, is a relatively new type of lending that uses online platforms to connect consumers or businesses who seek to borrow money with investors willing to buy or invest in the loan. The MPL model started with the promise that individuals could borrow from often unsophisticated lenders directly and P2P, but now more institutional investors fund MPL activity. An online platform matches borrowers and lenders without a traditional bank as an intermediary. Today, the terms "peer-to-peer lending" and "crowdlending" have largely replaced the term "marketplace lending."

(2) Discuss how market risk factors affect borrowers in MPL.

Marketplace borrowers are often independent of market risk. An idiosyncratic factor describes the correlation of each borrower to market risk. A high idiosyncratic factor means that a borrower is largely independent of market risk factors. Modeling risk in MPL to stress portfolios assumes high idiosyncratic risk factors and a high correlation between borrowers.

(3) Explain why risk assessment is difficult in portfolios of marketplace loans.

In MPL portfolios, a high degree of fuzzy and hidden information prevails, which leads some investors to view MPL as less safe than bank loans. For instance, how borrowers are correlated is largely unclear, which might lead to higher risk than initially perceived.

(4) Identify which techniques can efficiently simulate risk in MPL portfolios.

MPL platforms and lenders should use stochastic (random) processes like Monte Carlo simulation and machine learning (ML) techniques. Deterministic processes, such as scenarios, often fail to capture tail risk appropriately because of bias and hidden information. Stochastic processes like Monte Carlo analysis can simulate all possible scenarios despite fuzzy and missing information. However, Monte Carlo analysis is CPU-heavy and introduces a computation bottleneck when investors have to model portfolios with many loans. Therefore, better alternatives include machine learning approaches, such as Chebychev Tensors (CTs) or Deep Neural Networks (DNNs). These techniques create proxies for cases of tail risk that approximate those in Monte Carlo analysis while using much less CPU power.

(5) Discuss how MPL can improve sustainability and become a viable alternative to bank lending.

All credit loans have risk, including bank credit loan portfolios. When market conditions change quickly and unexpectedly, they may generate lower returns than the cost of their short-term liabilities because they contain mainly fixed long-term loans. This situation led to the collapse of Silicon Valley Bank in 2023. Because marketplace loans typically have a shorter duration, portfolios of such loans can be rebalanced quicker to react to changing market conditions. For this reason, MPL can be a sustainable alternative to bank lending, but only if investors understand the risks involved. Modeling their risks is complex and requires specific expertise and techniques. They often contain fuzzy and hidden information, and the ratings of counterparties change in changing market conditions.

Chapter 8: Risk Management in Fintech

(1) Identify the primary technological innovations reshaping the fintech landscape.

Several technological innovations are reshaping the fintech landscape, including robo-advisors offering personalized investment solutions, blockchain enabling transparent transactions, AI algorithms optimizing credit scoring and fraud detection, and digitization facilitating real-time transactions and data-driven decision-making.

(2) Discuss how technology risks impact the sustainability of fintech ventures.

Technology risks, such as cyberattacks, data breaches, and biases in AI models, can severely impact the sustainability of fintech ventures. These risks can lead to financial losses, erode customer trust, hinder further growth and innovation, and even result in regulatory non-compliance, all of which threaten the viability and stability of fintech companies.

(3) Explain how fintech contributes to financial inclusion and identify the challenges that could hinder this progress.

Fintech contributes to financial inclusion by offering services like mobile money platforms and AI-driven credit scoring that enable access to financial services for underserved communities. However, challenges such as the digital divide, lack of trust, language barriers, and data privacy concerns hinder the full realization of financial inclusion through fintech.

(4) Discuss how collaboration among fintech companies, regulators, and policymakers can responsibly shape the future of digital finance.

Collaboration among fintech companies, regulators, and policymakers is crucial for fostering a responsible and inclusive digital financial future. It can lead to establishing robust regulatory frameworks, open dialogues to address emerging challenges, sharing best practices, and investing in research and development to ensure fintech's ethical and sustainable growth.

(5) Discuss why robust technology risk management is imperative for the long-term success of fintech ventures.

Robust technology risk management is vital for the long-term success of fintech ventures because it safeguards viability, protects customer data, fosters trust, and ensures compliance. Failure to manage technology risks can lead to dire consequences like cyberattacks, reputational damage, and financial instability, hindering growth and innovation while jeopardizing the future of fintech companies.

Chapter 9: Capital Formation and Crowdfunding

(1) Discuss a company's developmental stage and valuation level before it is eligible for funding by an angel or a VC firm.

Angel investors typically invest in a company's seed round, while venture capital firms often come in later rounds, such as the A, B, and C rounds of funding. Companies in the seed stage of funding are often valued at $5 million to $15 million, while later rounds typically have valuations exceeding $15 million. As a result, companies with a valuation below $5 million often have difficulty obtaining funding from angels or VC investors.

(2) Describe the qualifications for accredited investors and the exemptions from regulation that status provides.

Accredited investors can qualify to invest in private placements through educational or wealth-related attributes. PE, VC, and hedge funds have raised the largest capital from accredited investors and institutional investors. Accredited investors can qualify by earning a sustainable individual income of $200,000 annually or $300,000 as a married couple. To qualify by wealth, accredited investors need to have a net worth exceeding $1 million, excluding the value of their primary residence. Recent amendments to the accredited investor standards allow financial professionals to qualify by education, such as by passing specific FINRA regulatory exams or being designated as a knowledgeable employee of a private placement issuer, such as a PE fund.

(3) Explain Regulation Crowdfunding and how the regulation facilitated capital formation by small businesses.

Before the JOBS Act, private companies could only access equity capital through angels or VC funds. Companies with valuations below $5 million had difficulty raising capital from these large and institutional investors. Regulation Crowdfunding allowed retail investors to purchase equity interests in small firms, with companies limited to raising $1 million in any 12-month period. Regulation Crowdfunding allowed more investors and companies to be directly involved in equity investments in small private companies.

(4) Name the three parts of the Howey Test to determine when the SEC requires that a fundraising offering be registered as a security.

According to Howey, the three tests for determining whether fundraising is a securities offering are (1) an investment of money, (2) in a common enterprise, and (3) a reasonable expectation of profits to be derived from the efforts of others.

(5) Name and explain four different types of crowdfunding.

The four types of crowdfunding are donations, rewards/preorders, debt, and equity. Donation crowdfunding, such as GoFundMe, uses the power of the crowd and social media to raise funds for a worthy cause, such as for a community after a natural disaster. Rewards or preorder crowdfunding provides funders of business access to an event or an item produced by the entity using the funds raised. Debt crowdfunding provides capital to a business, with the funders repaying the principal and interest on their original investment. Equity crowdfunding gives investors an equity stake in the entity receiving the invested capital.

Chapter 10: Demystifying Robo-Advisors: Benefits and Limitations

(1) List the main benefits of robo-advisors compared to human financial advisors.

Below are the main benefits of robo-advisors (robos) relative to human financial advisors.

- Robos may be more cost-efficient for clients but may lack transparency.
- Robos may save costs for asset managers.
- Access is possible 24/7 from everywhere with a mobile device.
- Robos use a quantitative investment approach, which may be more rational investors than humans.

(2) List the potential limitations of automated investment advice.

Automated investment advice may have the following limitations.

- Risk profiling may be insufficient.
- A lack of empathy may be an issue during crises.
- Robos are not free from conflicts of interest.
- Investors may be technology-skeptics and lack trust in robo-advisors.

(3) Discuss if robo-advisory is a long-term disruptive force or a short-term fad.

Arguments support both perspectives. Since robo-platforms increase efficiency for asset management companies, they will probably shift new and less profitable clients to their robo-advisors, which causes a long-term disruptive trend for a certain segment of investment clients. Also, since younger people are open to technology, the trend toward robo-advisory may strengthen as young clients gain more wealth to invest. Robo-advisory quality may improve with technological advancements, making it a dominant investment advisor.

Yet, a risk exists regarding the long-term disruptive potential, which could downgrade robo-advisory to a short-term fad. As with crypto-currencies, scandals like heists and hacks could lead to mistrust in robo-advisors. A major stock market crash could cause a loss in wealth and hence reduce investment volumes in robo-advisory. If robo-advisors strongly underperform in a market crash, this could result in a permanent mistrust of the technology.

(4) Explain whether investing with robo-advisors involves ethical dilemmas.

An important ethical question is who takes responsibility for automated investment decisions: the algorithm, the developer, or the investor? Overconfidence in technology could cause unintended consequences and risks to financial market instability. Robo-advisory depends on personal data, making data protection and cybersecurity essential since the exposition of sensible information would also constitute an ethical dilemma. Automated investment decisions may also be a "black hole" regarding ESG stock screening. Although many robo-advisors offer sustainable portfolios, they might not always meet investors' ethical preferences. Finally, the potential integration of AI is also a source of ethical predicaments (e.g., if the reference data are biased and cause unintended discrimination).

(5) Identify the essential factors that individual investors should know when choosing a robo-advisory vendor.

When choosing a robo-advisor, individual investors should know the vendor's:

- Fees and costs.
- Track record regarding past returns and risks.
- Location.
- Quality of recommendations involving personalization or customization.
- Investment strategy.
- Reputation and user experience.

Chapter 11: Online Trading: Part I

(1) Discuss two types of financial markets.

There are exchange and OTC markets. An exchange market is characterized by a central limit order book (CLOB) where supply and demand cross. OTC market is any other type of market where buyers and sellers meet. The most basic financial OTC market is a bilateral market in which one buyer or seller contacts a dealer to request a quote. Computers allow for more complex trading protocols, including RFQ or RFM, where buyers and sellers can ask for available quotes from multiple dealers. Unlike exchange markets, OTC markets are characterized by bilateral transactions, where a trader can pick up quotes on exchanges from multiple other market participants.

(2) Discuss how online trading affects the investment process.

Online trading increases competition among brokers to offer better prices to their clients. It also facilitates dispersing information across market participants, like current market prices. Online trading has great potential for automation and can improve liquidity.

(3) Describe a popular trading protocol on an electronic trading platform in the OTC markets.

A popular trading protocol is RFQ, where a trader specifies an asset's quantity and the trade's desired direction. The contacted dealers can then respond with a quote they are willing to trade. This situation is a first-price auction that a trader can hold among several dealers. The advantage of this protocol is increased competition. However, the trader also gives information about intended trades to many dealers. The RFM protocol, in which two-sided quotes are requested, aims to reduce this concern by not revealing the trade's intended direction. Moreover, two-sided quotes indicate the markup the dealer is charging.

(4) Define the NBBO and describe how it affects the brokers' routing of client orders.

The NBBO is the best price offered on the available exchanges for a security. A broker should consider the client's best interests and avoid trade-throughs at prices worse than the NBBO.

(5) Define PFOF and discuss why it is controversial.

PFOF is a practice in which a market maker pays a broker to execute the trades of the broker's clients. A controversy centers around whether this practice incentivizes the broker to act in the client's best interests, as the compensation may not get passed through to the client.

(6) Discuss some advantages of centralized over decentralized markets.

Exchange markets have market makers compete directly, potentially leading to more competitive prices for liquidity takers. Search costs are lower in a centralized structure. However, research suggests that decentralized markets could better cope with problems related to asymmetric information.

Chapter 12: Online Trading: Part II

(1) Explain online trading's benefits and drawbacks.

The benefits of online trading include greater price transparency, increased liquidity, decreased trading costs, and decreased slippage costs. A drawback of online trading is front-running conducted by high-frequency trading firms based on the availability of customer order flow information. Moreover, developing highly advanced trading systems may lead to sudden and unexpected market sell-offs due to the large quantities and rapid speeds at which these systems operate.

(2) Discuss the advantages and disadvantages of selling customer order flow.

The sale of customer order flow allows market makers to earn substantial revenue and simultaneously offer zero-commission trading. Additionally, market makers are less likely to face adverse selection since they do not have to differentiate between small retail orders and large institutional orders. A disadvantage is that selling customer order flow has led to front-running by high-frequency trading firms, thus leading to increased regulatory scrutiny. Retail investors benefit from more attractive execution but experience potentially wider bid-ask spreads when compared to larger institutional clients. Moreover, retail investors are less likely to be subject to adverse selection.

(3) Discuss how market participants use AI and ML to accomplish their trading strategies.

AI and ML refer to models using computational methods to reach optimal predictive performance on a data set by learning from that data. The goal is to generate a model that can perform a predictive task without explicit instruction or programming. Rather than directly attempting to predict future security prices, the models are more commonly used in risk management applications that govern various trading strategies. They are also used to model non-linear and highly complex data relations that require a large dataset.

(4) Explain how Robinhood revolutionized the retail trading business.

Robinhood has disrupted the traditional brokerage model by allowing users to trade stocks, ETFs, options, and, more recently, cryptocurrencies under a commission-free trading model through a simple mobile interface. The mobile interface's ease of use and Robinhood's no-account minimums and zero-commission model have democratized stock market investing for young and less experienced investors. As the first broker to offer commission-free trading, Robinhood catalyzed the entire industry's transition toward commission-free trading.

(5) Describe how retail traders may use APIs to develop trading strategies.

In the trading strategy development process, retail traders may use APIs for overall strategy development, research, back-testing, and execution. This process is accomplished by accessing historical and real-time market data, allowing the execution of trades from their software. As a result, retail investors may now engage in more sophisticated trading strategies that can be automized, customized, and better controlled.

(6) Describe how alternative and traditional data sources differ.

Alternative and traditional data sources differ because alternative data are derived from various sources and are used to supplement or predict traditional data sources. Alternative data sources include satellite imagery, social media, web scraping, and wearable devices. By contrast, traditional data sources include more conventional data points such as financial statements, stock prices, daily volume, and earnings calls.

Chapter 13: Personal Finance Applications of Fintech

(1) Define fintech.

Fintech, a contraction of "financial technology," refers to applying cutting-edge technology to optimize and automate the delivery and utilization of financial services. It is a swiftly expanding sector that employs novel technological solutions to modernize traditionally manual financial tasks, increasing efficiency, user-friendliness, and reach.

Fintech encompasses various applications, from mobile banking and peer-to-peer payments to wealth management, crowdfunding, insurance, and blockchain transactions. The rise of fintech companies has transformed the financial services landscape, offering new opportunities for startups and challenging established financial institutions to innovate and adapt. This evolution has significant implications for consumers, who now have access to more digital financial tools and services than ever.

(2) Identify advantages of fintech.

Fintech offers the following advantages.

- *Efficiency and convenience.* Fintech solutions, such as digital payments, mobile banking, and automated investment platforms, enable users to manage their financial affairs conveniently from anywhere, at any time.
- *Accessibility.* Fintech can provide financial services to unbanked or underbanked populations, offering access to banking, loans, and other services that might be unavailable in their locality or for which they might not qualify traditionally.
- *Personalized services.* Many fintech companies use artificial intelligence and machine learning to analyze user data and provide personalized financial advice, tailored products, or risk assessments.
- *Lower costs.* Fintech companies often operate with less overhead and regulatory constraints than traditional banks, resulting in lower fees for services such as money transfers, personal loans, and asset management.

- *Innovation.* Fintech companies are at the forefront of financial innovation, developing new products and services, such as robo-advisors for investment management and blockchain-based solutions for secure, transparent transactions.
- *Improved financial literacy.* Many fintech applications provide financial education resources, helping consumers make more informed financial decisions.

(3) Suggest how fintech can serve the underbanked and raise financial inclusion.

Fintech can serve the underbanked and raise financial inclusion in several ways.

- *Digital banking services.* Fintech can bring banking services to remote and underprivileged areas where traditional banks might not have branches. Mobile banking allows users to make deposits, transfers, and payments using a smartphone, reducing the need for physical bank visits.
- *Peer-to-peer lending.* Through fintech platforms, individuals and small businesses that might not qualify for traditional bank loans can access microloans or connect with P2P lenders.
- *Financial literacy tools.* Fintech can offer educational tools and resources to improve financial literacy among the underbanked, helping them understand how to manage money, use financial services, and plan for the future.

(4) Identify how fintech may help reduce personal financial mistakes.

Fintech provides several ways to help reduce personal financial mistakes.

- *Automated budgeting and saving.* Fintech applications like budgeting tools can automatically track income and spending, categorize expenses, set spending limits, and even automate savings. These apps can help individuals avoid overspending and ensure they are saving consistently.
- *Investment guidance.* Robo-advisors and other automated investment platforms can help users avoid common mistakes, such as poorly diversified portfolios or panic selling. These tools use algorithms to create and manage a diversified portfolio based on the user's risk tolerance and investment goals.
- *Alerts and reminders.* Fintech applications can send alerts when users are nearing their budget limit, when bills are due, or when unusual account activity is detected. These notifications can prevent missed payments, overdraft fees, and potential fraud.
- *Debt management.* Fintech solutions can help users manage and reduce their debt. Some tools consolidate loans or negotiate lower interest rates on the user's behalf, while others provide strategies to pay off debt more efficiently.

- *Real-time data access.* Fintech tools provide real-time access to financial data, giving users an accurate and up-to-date picture of their financial situation. This instant feedback can help users avoid making decisions based on outdated information.

(5) Explain multifactor authentication (MFA) and how it raises security in personal banking.

Fintech applications often implement MFA to add an extra layer of security. Besides a username and password (what the user knows), users are required to provide an additional form of verification (what the user has), such as a one-time password (OTP) sent to their registered mobile device or biometric authentication such as fingerprint or facial recognition. MFA mitigates the risk of unauthorized access even if passwords are compromised. This dual verification ensures a high level of security. Thus, MFA may be difficult to replicate and ensures only authorized individuals can access their personal banking accounts or perform transactions.

Chapter 14: Blockchain in Fintech: A Catalyst for Disrupting the Financial World

(1) Define blockchain.

Blockchain is a distributed ledger technology (DLT), which is a decentralized and encrypted digital storage system of information to protect data and manipulation. Information is recorded in blocks linked to a previous block of data to keep the order of records and track any historical transaction. New data are only included after a governing body of nodes reaches consensus, more commonly through proof of work (PoW) or proof of stake (PoS). Although blockchain awareness is due to its use in cryptocurrencies, some companies are developing blockchain solutions specific to companies.

(2) Identify some blockchain advantages.

Some advantages associated with blockchain follow.

- *Consistent.* All users keep the same copy of information across the ledger.
- *Democratic.* All participants agree on the rules to manage the network.
- *Resilient.* Information is accessible, even when many peers are offline.
- *Secure and accurate.* Digital keys and signatures protect information integrity. Keys are easy to set and almost impossible to undo.
- *Segmented and private.* Access levels within the network can be customized.
- *Permanent and tamper-resistant.* Historical records cannot be changed without the complete agreement of all network members.

- *Quickly updated.* Networks record new transactions almost in real time.
- *Intelligent.* Users can program event-triggered transactions using smart contracts.
- *Verifiable.* Anyone can review if transactions comply with the system rules.

(3) List some blockchain applications in the business world.

The following are blockchain applications in business:

- Compensation processes among banks.
- Supply chain documentation and product tracking.
- Smart contracts.
- Healthcare records.
- Identity management systems.
- Notarized services.
- Regulatory processes like Know Your Customer (KYC) and fraud prevention.
- Tokenization of real estate.
- Decentralized finance (DeFi).
- Fair payment.
- Triple-entry accounting.

(4) Identify the major obstacles to the widespread adoption of blockchain technology.

Below are some main obstacles to the widespread adoption of blockchain technology.

- Lack of knowledge and expertise in the technology.
- Integration with legacy systems.
- Investment cost.
- Environmental impact of consensus mechanisms like proof of work (PoW).
- Limited regulatory framework.
- Scalability.
- Process efficiency compared to current payment systems like VISA or Mastercard.

Chapter 15: Cryptoassets and Fintech

(1) Discuss the difference between cryptocurrencies and utility tokens.

Cryptocurrencies function as a medium of exchange, a unit of account, and a store of value. By contrast, utility tokens offer users consumptive rights to access services and products within a blockchain-based platform. Although utility tokens can be used as cryptocurrencies beyond the issuer's platform, their main purpose is facilitating and promoting value creation within a specific ecosystem.

(2) Explain the difference between security tokens and tokenized securities.

Security tokens are designed as newly created securities native to the blockchain. They are created and exist solely within the blockchain environment without a physical or traditional equivalent. In contrast, asset-backed tokens or tokenized securities serve as digital representations of pre-existing assets or securities. Therefore, the key distinction lies in the origin and nature of these tokens. Security tokens are born within the blockchain and do not have an external presence beyond it. By contrast, tokenized securities represent existing assets or securities while maintaining their off-chain existence.

(3) Identify three features of stablecoins applicable to traditional finance.

Stablecoins have several distinctive features.

- They offer low costs, stable value, and fast settlements, making them reliable for fund transfers.
- Blockchain-based transaction records ensure transparency and security.
- Decentralized networks enable seamless transactions across borders and time zones.

(4) List three regulatory issues facing cryptoassets.

Cryptoassets face multiple regulatory issues and questions, especially in the United States.

- No consensus exists among regulators and policymakers about which agency has the purview to regulate cryptoassets, creating a murky and litigious operating environment.
- Because cryptoassets represent such a varied and fast-developing asset class, seeking to develop and implement regulations for the entire space creates inconsistencies that can create legal issues for crypto organizations.
- Having many cryptoassets and crypto organizations headquartered outside of the United States makes enforcing US reporting, disclosure, and investor protection standards more difficult, leading to uninsured investor losses.

(5) Describe the current and proposed accounting treatment and rules for cryptoassets under US generally accepted accounting principles (GAAP).

Under current US GAAP, cryptoassets are accounted for as indefinite-lived intangible assets. With this accounting treatment, cryptoassets are held at cost on an organization's balance sheet. The only changes allowed are losses in value as measured by an impairment test, but none of these losses can be recovered. Under the proposed accounting standard update, set to become effective by the end of 2023, cryptoassets such as bitcoin and ether will be reported and held at fair market value, with any unrealized gains and losses shown in the financial statements.

Chapter 16: Big Data's Role in Fintech

(1) Discuss how big data has inspired innovation in the major contemporary tranche of modern financial services.

Notable fintech innovations affect at least four major tranches of modern financial services. First, cryptocurrencies use and create large data accumulations. Redundancies in recordkeeping in most blockchain systems used in crypto assure data availability from numerous sources. Smart contracts using blockchain also produce comprehensive big data records. Geographic decentralization avoids the single point of failure in centralized data structures. Second, big data lie at the heart of P2P systems, such as disintermediation using big data-enabled search and identification of dispersed investors (lenders), resulting in matching with dispersed borrowers. Third, AI-informed robo-advisory services use big data-fed AI to discover and incorporate alternative data sources that promise better identification of appropriate investment choices. Fourth, automated credit scoring involves big data-fed AI.

(2) Exemplify several emerging big data accumulations, then link them to a modern developing fintech practice, analytical method, or financial service.

Big data in modern fintech are sourced from existing public databases, proprietary databases, government databases, and newly installed or discovered sensors. Much data acquisition is an outsourced activity requiring contractual permission to use, retain, or resell data in license transactions. Data are a mix of numerical arrays in financial reporting using standardized formatting, such as XML. Increasingly, natural language data provides context, detail, and depth but requires AI for organization, selection, and interpretation.

(3) Explain how many legacy financial services were developed using big data and ICT innovations.

Most major financial services used and developed additional big data throughout the four fintech eras. From pre-industrial to medieval times, big data was created as payments moved from currency or coins to orders in negotiable instruments. Legitimizing debt permitted other instrumentation evidencing debt and enabled data informing credit scoring. In the industrial capitalism era, standardized instrumentation spawned centralized markets, deepening liquidity and making for an expanding price discovery system that improves valuation estimation. Electronic communications of that era sped up transactions by enabling electronic funds transfers, deepening markets, and contributing to geographically standardized transactions. In the computerization era, big data enabled specialized financial intermediaries, reduced human intervention in electronic payment systems, and enabled EDI as the precursor to smart contracts. Finally, the ICT and AI era uses big data derived from all the financial service practices of prior eras. The development of crypto, AI-powered financial analysis, and disintermediated matching of counter-parties then produces big data. All these structures persist today: standardized instrumentation, centralized markets, electronic transactions communications, and the development of fintech's next generation of fintech.

(4) Compare and contrast numerical big data search and retrieval from natural language analysis.

Traditional data were numerical, requiring the intervention of human interpretation to provide useful computation and results beneficial to decision-making. Accounting professionals improved the standardization of data structures in formatting financial performance and condition data. Later formatting and data sharing standards like APIs, XML, and xBRL reduced errors and improved numerical data reliability. Natural language analysis remains a developing and difficult problem, given the nuance of meaning and its traditional requirement for human interpretation. AI holds promise to automate natural language processing. For example, ESG claims, interpretations, and refutations are difficult to process without using AI. Future fintech based on integrating numerical and natural language evidence remains in its infancy but holds great future promise.

Chapter 17: How Alternative Data Are Changing Finance

(1) Define alternative data and contrast them with traditional data used in financial forecasting.

Alternative data are not from standard financial statements or formal reports that have been traditionally done. Instead, they come from new sources and collection methods. The rise and ubiquity of technology have fostered the growth of social media, the Internet of Things (IoT), the tracking of digital footprints, and new textual, visual, and audio data methods. Respectively, these are the new sources and methods that help to generate and leverage alternative data. Traditional data in finance have typically come from formally produced information that institutions report. These alternative data and their use in financial forecasting have affected the prevalence of traditional data. This change is partly due to alternative data that capture relevant information that is not captured, or not captured as timely, in financial statements and reports. This information includes but is not limited to corporate network structures, competitor moves, regulatory changes, and brand development. The production and regulatory costs associated with traditional data seem especially large compared to alternative data. If companies seek to leverage alternative data, there may be consequences for practitioners. These consequences would most likely concern increased emphasis on timeliness and new skill sets.

(2) Identify and discuss the sensory alternative data in the academic literature.

Although web scraping is still a burgeoning data collection method, the most common application of this method has been on text. Less common applications have involved other sensory data, such as image or audio data that can be scraped, organized, and analyzed. Various images have been scraped, analyzed, and incorporated into forecasting models. In particular, satellite imagery of commercial or economic activity has been used. For example, hedge funds use the number of cars in parking lots of major retailers to forecast sales.

Others have used photographs of analysts to assess how the facial width-to-height ratio of Chinese male sell-side analysts is associated with forecast accuracy. Various sounds and voices have been scraped, analyzed, and incorporated into forecasting models. Scraping audio files using vocal emotion analysis software during earnings conference calls has captured managerial emotion. The emotional response of firm representatives to analyst questions during conference calls can be used to forecast the firm's financial future. Similarly, the emotions embedded in the voice of the Federal Reserve Board of Governors during press conferences can be scraped and analyzed. These methods and other research have shown that vocal cues contain useful information about a market and firm fundamentals.

Monitoring the significance of the variables that are generated by monitoring individuals, such as executives or board members, will be interesting. If these individuals find out they are being monitored, they may manipulate markets more consciously using tone, word choice, and cadence. It would also be interesting to consider what data remains untapped. Biomarker and biometric data may be too invasive to consider, but new blockchain applications and the ubiquity of smart technology creating a deeper IoT seem plausibly on the horizon.

(3) Discuss how and what technology has given rise to alternative data.

Manually scraping the web and collecting the data has become antiquated due to computer programs that can automate data extraction from websites. Moreover, machine learning and textual analysis can be applied to the data from web scraping to identify sentiments, connections, and broader patterns. The physical storage of traditional data, the local storage of digital data, and the centralized storage of data have helped create an environment that fostered alternative data. Cloud computing has made storing data cheaper and easier to centralize – these technological gains foster communication between devices. The IoT is a network of devices that is capable of exchanging data with each other. Technology embedded with sensors and monitoring devices makes up the IoT. Examples include patient implants that adjust to physiological data, agricultural devices that respond to the soil, and disaster warning systems that respond to flammable gases. Data from the IoT can be categorized into three classes: (1) status data that communicate the condition of a device or system; (2) environment data that communicate the external information of the device or system; and (3) dynamic data created by the interaction between devices and systems.

(4) Discuss the sources of cryptoasset data.

Data on cryptoassets come from several sources. Some cryptoassets have an underlying public blockchain, as opposed to private. The data on public blockchains can be downloaded from the software of a specific blockchain, for example. The Bitcoin core software stores the data for the Bitcoin blockchain. Directly querying the blockchain can generate data describing various dynamics of the blockchain, such as the mem-pool size or fees miners charge to gain priority in the queue. The permissions make the data on private blockchains more difficult to obtain. Still, as application developers' choices for chain infrastructure become more robust, the quantity and insight gleaned from these data will rise. For example, Depository Trust and Clearing Corp are testing a private blockchain to see whether the technology can be used to help improve the efficiency of clearing and settling transactions. If the impacts of less costly clearing are large, then larger-scale adoption of the technology would be more encouraged. Cryptocurrencies also often publish a whitepaper, have a GitHub page, and post information on social media outlining the specific details of a particular cryptocurrency. This text can be scraped to extract data. Also, data are available from secondary sources such as crypto research institutions ICObench, ICOmarks, icorating.com, smithandcrown.com, icowatchlist.com, Blockchain.com, and coinschedule.com and crypto performance tracking institutions, such as CoinMarketCap.com, Crunchbase, Crypto Fund Research.

Chapter 18: Artificial Intelligence and Machine Learning in Finance: Key Concepts, Applications, and Regulatory Considerations

(1) Using credit scoring as an illustrative use case, explain how ML methods differ from early AI methods such as "expert systems."

Credit scoring is an area where ML has significantly outperformed earlier AI methods, such as "expert systems." In the latter's case, the AI decision-making process relies on explicit rules and heuristics provided by human experts. These rules, operating as a set of "if-then" conditions, guide the process of outcome generation by an AI system. However, this approach has limitations, particularly in handling complex and unstructured data such as that found in credit scoring. On the other hand, ML methods can autonomously learn complex patterns and relationships from empirical data, enabling them to make accurate predictions on new and unseen observations. In the context of credit scoring, ML models can process large volumes of historical financial data, identifying hidden correlations that human-designed rules might overlook. Moreover, ML models can continuously learn and adapt from new data, making them more adaptable to changing market dynamics and evolving consumer behaviors than earlier AI methods.

(2) Using algorithmic trading as an illustrative case, describe the "AI lifecycle."

In algorithmic trading, the AI lifecycle begins with identifying specific business objectives and formulating a clear problem statement. This process, for instance, involves defining key aspects, including the desired outcomes, related to the trading strategies to be implemented. Next, the AI lifecycle involves data collection and preparation, where historical market data, financial indicators, and other relevant data are gathered, processed, and refined to create a suitable dataset for training AI models. Following this step, the model development stage entails selecting appropriate ML algorithms and training the models using the prepared datasets. Subsequently, the model deployment phase comes into play, where the trained models are integrated into the trading platform, allowing them to make real-time trading decisions. The AI lifecycle continues with ongoing monitoring and maintenance, continuously evaluating the model's performance, detecting any potential drift or biases, and making necessary adjustments to ensure model effectiveness and regulatory compliance. Eventually, the entire process will discontinue or replace the concerned AI trading system or strategy.

(3) Using regtech as an illustrative use case, identify and discuss two primary risks associated with AI adoption that may impact consumer confidence.

One primary concern involves misusing personal data, where sensitive information could be mishandled or exploited, leading to privacy breaches. For instance, if AI systems are inadequately secured or lack robust data protection measures, consumers' personal and financial information might become vulnerable to unauthorized access or cyberattacks. Whenever this risk occurs, consumer trust in regtech deteriorates.

Another critical risk is associated with the lack of transparency in AI. When consumers cannot understand how AI algorithms arrive at specific decisions or recommendations, this situation can create a sense of uncertainty and apprehension among them. In cases where AI-generated outcomes impact crucial financial decisions or hinder regulatory compliance, the lack of transparency may lead consumers to question the validity and fairness of these outcomes. Inadequate transparency may thus diminish consumer confidence in the reliability and legitimacy of regtech systems.

(4) Identify the main differences among emerging regulatory approaches to AI governance.

AI governance approaches vary substantially, reflecting different balances between policymakers and industry players in regulation. Some jurisdictions favor public regulation by government bodies and public institutions, while others rely more on market self-regulation. The various emerging regulatory approaches have different priorities, from consolidating economic positions to promoting innovation and protecting fundamental rights. For instance, China employs a centralized, state-led strategy, while the United States, the United Kingdom, and Singapore adopt a pro-innovation stance with minimal regulatory intervention. In the European Union, the recently agreed AI Act follows a rights-based perspective, aiming to horizontally regulate all AI systems that may threaten individuals' safety and fundamental rights. Although the optimal approach to AI regulation may not exist, there is a growing consensus that, given the many risks involved, more robust regulation is needed to ensure effective AI governance.

Chapter 19: Insurtech: Disrupting the Insurance Industry

(1) Define insurtech.

Insurtech refers to any innovation boosted by technology that creates value in the insurance sector by delivering data-driven and customer-oriented solutions in a digital landscape.

(2) Identify the driving capabilities in transforming the insurance sector.

The driving capabilities that have been instrumental in boosting innovations in the insurance sector represent the technological capabilities for applying innovation in this sector. The potential of the five driving capabilities in transforming the insurance sector has arisen from the combination of the innovations. These capabilities are:

- *Implementing digital capabilities.* Focused on implementing digital infrastructures through its technological capacity to establish infrastructures (IaaS), software (SaaS), and digital platforms (PaaS).
- *Providing data-driven solutions.* Focused on data-driven operations, applying innovation through its technological capability to extract, analyze, exploit, and evaluate risk-related data.
- *Integrating services and customer experience.* Focused on the complementary proposal of services in the insurance sector, improving interaction and customer experience.

- *Creating and developing a digital insurance offer.* Focused on developing an insurance offer in response to consumer needs and adapting the offer according to specific customer demands.
- *Offering digital insurance distribution.* Focused primarily on distributing insurance through digital delivery systems so customers can research, compare, and purchase insurance online without manual or physical support.

(3) Discuss how insurtech has transformed the value configuration in the insurance industry by evolving from a value chain to a value network.

Insurtech's disruptive potential has transformed the insurance industry's structure and altered and disrupted the insurance value configuration by describing an ecosystem characterized by collaboration, innovation, and co-creation. Specifically, this new value configuration has been evolving from a traditional linear value chain, in which each participant adds value to the product or service before passing it on to the next participant, to a more dynamic and interconnected value network, in which participants collaborate and share resources to create new value propositions for customers. Overall, this new paradigm represents a fundamental transformation in how insurance products are designed, distributed, priced, underwritten, and serviced.

(4) Explain the waves resulting from the insurance industry transformation driven by insurtech's impact.

The insurance industry's transformation has resulted from three waves of change driven by insurtechs. The first wave was characterized by the emergence of insurtech, which disrupted traditional business models by leveraging technology innovations to improve customer experience, reduce costs, and increase efficiency. This wave focused on improving the value chain's operational workflows and work processes. The second wave was characterized by enablers, often inspired by new challengers, who concentrated on helping incumbents improve specific parts of the value chain or even helping them create new ones by creating a full range of protection products, covering new risks with new uses, and creating new insurance products. The third wave is expected to be driven by ecosystem players who leverage their network effects and data-driven capabilities to develop more collaborative and open environments where participants can share information, resources, and capabilities to co-create value for all parties involved.

(5) Discuss the opportunities in the insurance industry's current landscape.

The insurance industry's current landscape presents a capability dilemma due to the disruption caused by insurtech. Furthermore, data analytics has become pivotal, requiring insurers to invest in advanced tools to understand customers and personalize offerings. Balancing traditional strengths with investments in new capabilities is vital for insurers to thrive. Therefore, the insurtech ecosystem offers opportunities for insurers to partner with startups, enhancing their capabilities and meeting customer demands in a rapidly evolving market.

Chapter 20: Revolutionizing the Real Estate Industry With Fintech

(1) Describe the underwriting of a borrower requesting a residential mortgage loan and how technology increases the speed and accuracy of the process.

When considering providing mortgage funds in a residential transaction, lenders underwrite the borrower and the property. The factors of this underwriting process include income and job history, credit history, down payment, property value, and qualifying ratios. The application of technology to each process can add speed and accuracy to data, process automation, and business logic, varying by activity.

- *Income/job history and credit history.* Electronic records make the data collection relatively simple. Data sources include US tax forms, FICO credit scores, and electronically executed employer verification forms.
- *Down payment.* Lenders are concerned with borrowers having sufficient "skin in the game" and money at risk in the real estate transaction. The secondary mortgage market also requires specific loan-to-value (LTV) standards, such as 80% LTV per the Fannie Mae guidelines, thus requiring a borrower to have a 20% down payment. However, to ensure that the 20% down payment is the borrower's saved funds rather than another form of debt in some way, electronic verification from the borrower's savings account can be accessed readily.
- *Property value.* If a lender will lend 80% LTV, the obvious question is – what is the value part of this equation? For lending purposes, value is established using a third-party appraiser who follows a specific, consistent process. Such processes include data collection and business logic that have been automated via tools such as Apprize for a more formal appraisal and Zillow for an estimate, all of which apply business logic driven by good data.
- *Qualifying ratios.* Lenders are concerned with a borrower's ability to repay a mortgage loan based on a monthly payment of principal, interest, taxes, and insurance (PITI). These ratios usually range from 28%/36%, where a borrower can use up to 28% of their monthly income toward PITI or up to 36% of their monthly income toward PITI plus all other long-term debt payments. Technology can easily automate this process and apply business logic if the lender has robust data on the borrower's income and debt.

(2) Describe the process of appraising a residential home value for a mortgage loan, including sources of data and business logic technology tools.

A residential home appraisal follows a specific standard process established by lenders and the secondary mortgage market to create confidence that the value stated is true market value. The steps an appraiser follows include obtaining data, following a process, and applying business logic, which are now being conducted through AI-type technologies such as Apprise and Zillow.

The appraisal process includes:

- Determine the purpose of the appraisal. In this case, the purpose is a residential mortgage loan.
- Determine the scope: How will the appraisal be conducted?
- Collect market data.
- Analyze the data. What is the property's highest and best use (i.e., maximum value)?
- Determine the land value. Use the comparable sales method.
- Apply three valuation techniques: the income, comparable sales, and cost approaches.
- Reconcile the three valuations. Use judgment to weigh the appropriate approaches.
- Report the final value estimate.

(3) Explain how an income property is valued using cap rates and what areas of automation can assist investor decision-making.

Income property is valued using various techniques, all of which are amendable to good technology automation of business logic. The most common value technique is the use of the cap rate formula:

$$\text{Value} = \text{NOI/Cap rate}$$

This formula capitalizes a property's first year's net operating income (NOI) to establish the value. NOI is the amount of cash flow generated by a property each year by taking the property's gross rental income and deducting the costs to operate the building across maintenance, taxes, and insurance, which is called operating expense.

The cap rate is often described as a risk-adjusted rate of return and historically trends with mortgage rates. Cap rates tend to be 150–200 basis points higher than mortgage rates, thus allowing investors to leverage the yield on their equity investment. In short, if one can borrow mortgage debt at 6% and invest it at an 8% cap rate in an investment property, the effective yield on one's remaining equity investment is increased.

Technology plays a role in this process by improving market data availability for the potential rental income and value of investment properties. Companies such as CoStar and Loopnet, while not substitutes for the equivalent multiple list service (MLS) available in the residential world, provide good data on prices, values, market cap rates, and rental income.

(4) Discuss the complexity of commercial real estate data needs, gaps, and how business logic depends on clean data.

Commercial real estate is a complex practice area compared to residential real estate. Commercial real estate involves the business strategy and income of companies who occupy the property. Investors in these same properties base their decisions on the property's NOI, driven by the occupiers' demand and resultant NOI for such real estate. Complexity can be seen in occupier decision-making across location, access to labor, transportation, competition, proximity to customers, and issues of taxes and regulation specific to that property.

These issues have the potential to benefit from strong AI and data tools to resolve data needs, process automation, and business logic in the site selection, pricing, term of occupancy, and the own versus lease decision. Tools such as Tango Analytics are at the edge of bringing together the process part of these needs. Cherre, Deepblocks, and other technology tools seek to obtain, standardize, and resolve data while adding business logic. In the case of Deepblocks, looking at land parcels and considering zoning, setbacks, and building standards, one can answer the question, "What can be built there?"

The data needs are challenging in this environment as the United States does not have national zoning, building codes, and other regulations. Local governments create many regulations and standards and then store and report them differently. Data become the limiting factor in this practice, rather than process automation or business logic, as the semantic consistency of these data points and where the data reside (cloud, server, where?) creates challenges to have clean, strong, usable data.

Chapter 21: Fintech in Capital Markets

(1) Explain why fintech is often credited with democratizing capital markets.

Some credit fintech for its role in democratizing capital markets by increasing capital market accessibility, particularly for retail investors. Innovations such as online brokerages and robo-advisors have dismantled traditional entry barriers by allowing more individuals to trade securities in capital markets easily and cheaply. Users can access professional strategies without extensive financial knowledge by offering automated investment guidance. Additionally, online peer-to-peer markets facilitate direct lending and borrowing, bypassing traditional institutions and promoting financial inclusion. These fintech solutions empower individuals, fostering a more inclusive and accessible financial ecosystem.

(2) Discuss so-called high-frequency trading algorithms and how their increasingly widespread use affects capital markets.

High-frequency trading algorithms are computer-based trading strategies that rely on various features, such as ultra-low latency systems, designed to execute many trades within extremely short timeframes, typically in the range of milliseconds. Their increasingly widespread use has mixed effects on markets. On the positive side, the algorithms' high trading volume increases market liquidity, and their ability to allow traders to include new information in prices instantaneously benefits pricing efficiency. On the negative side, the algorithm's trading style can exacerbate market volatility and potentially contribute to flash crashes.

(3) Explain how ML-based data analysis has affected capital markets, particularly when applied to big data.

ML-based data analysis, particularly involving big data, is important in enhancing capital market pricing efficiency. By using the technology, market participants can identify new patterns or trends in data faster, making more informed investment- and trading decisions. This situation is especially true if the analyzed data were previously unavailable or could not be analyzed manually or with legacy software due to its size, complexity, and lack of structure. One specific example is the real-time analysis of satellite imagery data to forecast economic conditions by, for example, observing activity in major trading hubs such as ports. These real-time capabilities of big data analysis allow markets to instantly incorporate relevant information in securities prices instead of waiting and trading on the release of outdated ex-post information. Therefore, market efficiency is greatly improved.

(4) Discuss capital markets' challenges in adopting blockchain technology in securities clearing and settlement processes.

Despite blockchain's many potential benefits, this technology can only be adopted successfully for back-office tasks in capital markets if some challenges can be overcome. First, users must settle on a single blockchain technology and agree on its governance model. Second, latency and scalability issues that arise from consensus algorithms and cryptographic verification can cause delays, which might impede markets' drive for ever-faster trade execution, clearing, and settlement processes. Third, classic intermediaries will remain necessary for certain market functions, such as margin accounts, meaning that blockchains cannot fully eradicate the need for intermediaries. Fourth, the desired level of decentralization poses questions, as proof-of-stake methods may concentrate power with large entities. Capital markets efficient solutions that consider governance, scalability, and the role of intermediaries.

(5) Explain why initial coin offerings have faced regulatory backlash.

Regulatory concerns pose a major challenge to ICOs, particularly concerning the tokens issued in the ICOs for fundraising purposes. These tokens are typically structured like equity and may be classified as securities under the Howey Test, triggering SEC registration and regulation. A 2020 landmark ruling in a U.S. district court supported the SEC's position, prohibiting Telegram's sale of unregistered tokens and resulting in a substantial settlement. The SEC's intention to pursue similar cases indicates a commitment to regulating token sales. Although this commitment protects investors from fraudulent activities, it also increases complexity and costs, making token sales less attractive than IPOs.

Chapter 22: Technologies and Emerging Trends Shaping Fintech

(1) Define the term green bonds.

A green bond is a type of bond used to fund projects that have a positive environmental impact. Corporations, municipalities, sovereign countries, and financial institutions typically issue green bonds. By investing in green bonds, investors sensitive to environmental issues can support environmentally friendly projects while earning a return on their investment.

(2) Identify and discuss ESG integration.

ESG integration incorporates ESG factors into investment decisions and corporate strategies. Through ESG integration, investors can pinpoint and navigate risks tied to ESG challenges, such as extreme climatic events, limited water resources, and carbon emissions, that present environmental threats. By embracing ESG integration, investors can evaluate these hazards and make enlightened investment choices. Companies with strong ESG performance may be better positioned to manage risks and capitalize on opportunities. A successful ESG program can help companies access vast pools of capital from investors looking for ESG-friendly investments. A growing demand exists for financially sound and ethically aligned investments, especially among millennials.

(3) Identify and discuss carbon trading and carbon credits.

Carbon trading is a market-based buying and selling of permits that allow a company to emit a certain amount of carbon dioxide or other greenhouse gases. Governments and regulatory bodies authorize these carbon credits to reduce overall carbon emissions and mitigate their contribution to climate change. One credit permits the emission of one ton of carbon dioxide or the equivalent of other greenhouse gases. By paying someone else to reduce their emissions or capture their carbon, companies can compensate for their environmental footprint and even use carbon credits to get to carbon-neutral status in the most ambitious cases.

(4) Discuss neobanks and their sustainable characteristics.

Neobanks are exclusively digital financial institutions functioning without brick-and-mortar branches, delivering their services via online and mobile channels. Many neobanks emphasize sustainability and ethical approaches, integrating ESG factors into their strategies and choices. This ESG integration entails assessing how their actions influence the environment and society and advocating for sustainable progress using responsible lending and investment strategies. Neobanks with sustainable characteristics aim to balance their financial goals with their responsibility to contribute to sustainable development and the well-being of society. By prioritizing sustainability, these neobanks are helping to drive positive change and promote a more sustainable future.

Chapter 23: The Future of Fintech: Challenges and Opportunities

(1) Discuss the impact of the COVID-19 pandemic on fintechs.

Because people were shut in and unable to do their everyday business during the COVID-19 pandemic, they were forced to look for alternatives to carry out daily tasks. Consumers can use fintech applications to do many financial tasks online. Many unbanked and underserved people worldwide signed up for accounts during the pandemic, leading to mass adoption of the products and services.

(2) Explain why artificial intelligence (AI) and machine learning (ML) are essential to fintechs.

Fintech firms, banks, and many other companies expect AI and ML to speed up cost savings as they allow firms to accomplish tasks with fewer people and less time. AI and ML also assist firms in detecting fraud, money laundering, and cyberattacks more quickly and at a lower cost than those that do not use these technologies. Firms can also use the technologies to analyze data and offer more personalized financial services to companies.

(3) Identify the main opportunities available to fintechs.

Fintechs have many opportunities available to them, including the following:

- *Incorporating embedded finance.* Embedded finance includes embedding financial solutions into product offerings that are not financial, such as online purchases of everyday items.
- *Using digital currencies, blockchain, and decentralized finance.* Fintechs can develop innovative solutions using blockchain in payments, lending, and security.
- *Adopting AI and ML.* AI and ML will help companies understand their customers better and create personalized financial services targeted at individual customers.

- *Making finance more inclusive by offering services with little or no fees.* Fintechs can more easily reach out to traditionally underserved countries and consumers.
- *Entering new sectors such as regtech (regulatory technology), insurtech (insurance technology, and others).*

(4) Identify the main challenges facing fintechs.

The main challenges facing fintechs are complying with ever-changing regulations, protecting against cyberattacks and money laundering, managing the risks associated with relying too heavily on venture capital and the same technology stacks used by competitors and keeping data secure. Firms must also be able to attract and retain talent and new customers.

Index